QUICK REFERENCE TO OCCUPATIONAL THERAPY

Aspen Series in Occupational Therapy
Rhona Reiss Zukas, MOT, OTR, FAOTA, Series Editor
Assistant Dean
School of Occupational Therapy
Texas Woman's University
Dallas, Texas

Early Occupational Therapy Intervention: Neonates to Three Years
Caryl J. Semmler and Jan G. Hunter

Occupational Therapy and the Older Adult: A Clinical Manual
Jean M. Kiernat, Editor

QUICK REFERENCE TO OCCUPATIONAL THERAPY

Kathlyn L. Reed, PhD, LOTR, MLIS

Education/Information Services Librarian
Houston Academy of Medicine–Texas Medical Center
Houston, Texas

Aspen Series in Occupational Therapy
Rhona Reiss Zukas, Series Editor

AN ASPEN PUBLICATION®
Aspen Publishers, Inc.
Gaithersburg, Maryland
1991

Library of Congress Cataloging-in-Publication Data

Reed, Kathlyn L.
Quick reference to occupational therapy / Kathlyn L. Reed.
p. cm. — (Aspen series in occupational therapy)
Includes bibliographical references and index.
ISBN: 0-8342-0237-9
1. Occupational therapy—Handbooks, manuals, etc. I. Title. II. Series.
[DNLM: 1. Occupational Therapy—handbooks. WB 39 R324q]
RM735.3.R42 1991
615.8'515—dc20
DNLM/DLC
for Library of Congress
91-18038
CIP

The author has made every effort to ensure the accuracy of the information
herein, particularly with regard to techniques and procedures. However,
appropriate information sources should be consulted, especially for new or
unfamiliar techniques or procedures. It is the responsibility of every practitioner
to evaluate the appropriateness of a particular opinion in the context of actual
clinical situations and with due consideration to new developments. Authors,
editors, and the publisher cannot be held responsible for any typographical or
other errors found in this book.

Editorial Services: Lisa Hajjar
Daniel N. da Cruz

Library of Congress Catalog Card Number: 91-18038
ISBN: 0-8342-0237-9

Printed in the United States of America

3 4 5

Table of Contents

Introduction

The purpose of this book is to provide an overview and quick reference to disorders and problems seen by occupational therapists. The majority of the information is based on literature on occupational therapy published from the early 1980s up to the end of 1990. A few classic sources were used to augment current information. Literature by authors who were not occupational therapists was not used unless the articles appeared in an occupational therapy journal. Primary sources included articles appearing in occupational therapy journals; articles in the American Occupational Therapy Association Special Interest Section newsletters; articles either about occupational therapy or written by occupational therapists that appeared in other journals; and articles, chapters, or books written by occupational therapists. All references had to be published materials. Information known by some occupational therapists but not available in printed form was avoided. Articles from newsletters were not included unless the newsletter was available through standard library sources. Assessment instruments and tests were included only if available in published form.

The book is designed as a summary of information about the practice of occupational therapy and specific diseases or disorders. The classification of the diseases or disorders is based on a system used in a medical subject headings list developed by the National Library of Medicine, with the exception of listings related to sensory integrative dysfunction. In general, three or four articles provided enough information to write a section on any one disorder. Among the disorders for which there was insufficient information were pediatric AIDS (acquired immune deficiency syndrome), brachial plexus injuries, Erb's palsy, Hansen's disease (leprosy), Dupuytren's contracture, lupus, phobias, and post-traumatic stress disorders.

Descriptions of disorders in this book usually come from the *Merck Manual,* unless otherwise noted. Information about etiology is generally a combination of information from the *Merck Manual* and statements published in the referenced articles. Assessment lists are based on the types of problems seen in the disorders. The instruments identified are described as published in the occupational therapy literature. The problems listed in each section are based on the references listed at the end of the section. Problems usually associated with a certain disorder are identified with the word "usually." Problems that may occur are identified with the word "may." The treatment/management lists are based on the articles and chapters in books identified in the reference section; at least one author had to be an occupational therapist or the subject matter had to include occupational therapy. Treatment/ management techniques are not covered in detail because such information is beyond the scope of the book; however, references are provided that should permit the practitioner to identify source material. Precautions were drawn from the literature. The prognosis and outcome sections were based on the literature but arranged by the author. Finally, a list of all articles, chapters, and books found on the disorder is provided in the reference sections. Titles of reference journals were written out in full because the author's experience as a librarian indicates that some people do not look up reference resources because they cannot easily translate the journal abbreviation in the correct full title. The appendices contain additional resource materials, including a list of sensorimotor tests and their sources, a list of tests used in descriptive or research articles published during a seven-year period, and lists of articles written by popular theorists.

Part I

Developmental Disorders

Arthrogryposis Multiplex Congenita

DESCRIPTION

Arthrogryposis multiplex congenita (AMC) is a nonprogressive neuromuscular disorder present at birth that is characterized by fibrous ankylosis (contractures) of multiple joints. Muscle development is arrested at some time during the fetal period and fibrous or fatty tissue replaces the muscle, resulting in contractures and abnormal joint surfaces. Types of AMC include neuropathic, myopathic, and mixed.

CAUSE

The cause of AMC is unknown. The disorder is not genetic; individuals have normal chromosomes. Some cases can be traced to neurogenic causes through histologic and electromyographic evidence, or to myopathic causes through studies of muscle fiber. Other causative agents may include prenatal exposure to adverse environmental agents, maternal infection, abnormal connective tissue, chromosomal or genetic defects, and impaired intrauterine fetal movement.

ASSESSMENT

Areas
- range of motion
- muscle strength
- development of gross and fine motor skills
- development of hand skills, grasp, and prehension
- balance and postural control
- self -perception
- family and social support
- daily living skills
- play skills

Instruments

No specific instruments have been developed by occupational therapists to deal with this disorder. The following may be useful:

- developmental assessment
- activities of daily living scale
- play history

PROBLEMS

Motor
- The disorder is usually characterized by rigidity and/or contractures of the joints. Typically, in the upper extremities, the shoulders are adducted and internally rotated, the elbows

are extended but occasionally flexed, the forearms are pronated, the wrists are flexed and ulnarly deviated, the fingers are flexed, and the thumb is in the palm. In the lower extremities, the hips may be dislocated and are usually flexed and externally rotated, the knees are extended but occasionally flexed, and the feet are in equinovarus.

- There is usually severely limited range of motion in all major joints.
- Muscle weakness usually occurs.
- The person may have absence or atrophy of individual muscles or muscle groups.
- The person may have gross abnormalities of the chest and spine (myopathic type).
- Other problems include webbing on the ventral aspects of flexed joints, cleft palate, scoliosis, torticollis, facial palsy, limb deformity, and congenital amputation.
- Achievement of gross and fine motor skills is usually delayed.
- Development of hand functions is usually delayed.

Sensory

Sensory system is intact, but perceptual skills, such as stereognosis, could be delayed due to lack of opportunity.

Cognitive

Cognition is normal and intelligence is average to above average, but learning could be delayed due to lack of opportunity and many surgical procedures.

Intrapersonal

- Parents, especially the mother, may feel guilt about having a handicapped child.
- Child may have tantrums due to frustration.

Interpersonal

Family members may reject the "funny looking" child and leave the parents or mother without support.

Self-Care

Development of self-care skills is usually delayed because the patient's hand functions and fine motor skills are slow to develop.

Productivity

Play skills are usually underdeveloped.

Leisure

See productivity.

TREATMENT/MANAGEMENT

Motor

- Increase and maintain range of motion through activities, such as exercises and stretching.
- Promote achievement of gross and fine motor skills.
- Improve posture and positioning through the use of adapted equipment, such as corner seats, strollers, swivel buckets, or parapodiums.

- Provide splints to maintain gains in range of motion or serial casts to increase range of motion.

Sensory

Provide opportunities to experience sensory input.

Cognitive

- Provide opportunities for learning and encourage child to explore problem-solving methods.
- Provide information to parents about the disorder and encourage parental participation in the therapy program. They should understand the importance of having the child wear splints until bone matures and continuing range of motion activities everyday so the child maintains use of his or her body.
- Provide information about community resources and services.
- Provide information about normal growth and development.
- Provide information about architectural and environmental barriers.

Intrapersonal

- Provide opportunities to develop self-perception through the use of creative activities, such as art, crafts, drama, dance, music, and games.
- Encourage parents to express feelings and concerns about the child's condition and welfare.
- Provide instruction in stress-management techniques.

Interpersonal

- Encourage parent-infant bonding.
- Encourage parents to participate in self-help groups.

Self-Care

- Provide self-help devices to assist in the performance of daily living skills. A lazy susan may be used as a plate. Food can be placed around the edge of the plate.
- Adapted equipment may be necessary for grooming, such as extended handles on combs, brushes, and toothbrushes.
- Clothing adaptations may be needed to account for various deformities, using Velcro and elastic. Providing large rings on zippers or loops to grasp and large buttons is also useful.

Productivity

- Promote development of play skills, especially exploratory and manipulative play.
- Assist teachers in determining what, if any, adapted equipment or devices may be needed to assist child with academic activities. Computers with adapted keyboards may be helpful. The child should be able to attend regular classroom instruction, except for physical education.

Leisure

Usually no special goals or objectives are necessary. The child or an adult will seek those activities that are within the child's functional abilities.

PRECAUTIONS

Bone structure is fragile. Range of motion and stretching exercises should be carefully monitored.

PROGNOSIS AND OUTCOME

- The person has maximum range of motion possible given structural limitations.
- The person achieves gross and fine motor skills, although the development of skills does not progress normally.
- The person has functional hand skills, although the use of the hands may be unorthodox.
- The person has independent mobility with or without powered mobility.
- The person achieves independence in self-care and daily living skills.
- The person develops productive skills.

REFERENCES

Bender, L.H., and C.A. Withrow. 1989. Arthrogryposis multiplex congenita. *Orthopaedic Nursing* 8(5):29-35.

Hodges, J.T. 1989. Arthrogryposis: Team approach can help overcome devastating defect. *Occupational Therapy Forum* 4(34):9-11.

Hunter, J.G. 1990. Orthopedic conditions—Arthrogryposis multiplex congenita. In *Early occupational therapy intervention: Neonates to three years*, ed. C.J. Semmler and J.G. Hunter, 110-4. Gaithersburg, MD: Aspen Publishers, Inc.

Kamil, N.I., and A.M. Correia. 1990. A dynamic elbow flexion splint for an infant with arthrogryposis. *American Journal of Occupational Therapy*, 44(5):460-1.

Attention Deficit Disorders

DESCRIPTION

Attention deficit disorder is a term used to describe children of average or above average intelligence who have developmentally inappropriate degrees of inattention, impulsiveness, and hyperactivity. Boys are more commonly affected than girls. Other terms associated with this disorder are minimal brain dysfunction (MBD), hyperkinesis, hyperkinetic impulse disorder, and hyperactive child syndrome.

CAUSE

The cause of these disorders is unclear. Causative factors may be related to minor impairments of the central nervous system that occur during gestation or the perinatal period. Genetic and psychosocial factors may also be involved. Hyperactivity is thought to be due to a lack of central inhibition of external stimuli.

ASSESSMENT

Areas
- gross motor skills and coordination
- fine motor skills, manipulation, dexterity, and bilateral coordination
- balance and postural control
- motor planning or praxis
- sensory registration
- sensory processing and response to stimuli, especially visual, auditory, tactile, vestibular, and proprioceptive
- level of arousal and alertness
- attention span
- attending behavior
- memory skills
- judgment regarding safety of self and others
- communication skills
- daily living skills
- play development and skills
- leisure skills

Instruments
- Southern California Test of Sensory Integration by A.J. Ayres, Los Angeles: Western Psychological Services, 1980.
- Sensory Integration and Praxis Tests by A.J. Ayres, Los Angeles: Western Psychological Services, 1989.
- Southern California Postrotary Nystagmus Test by A.J. Ayres, Los Angeles: Western Psychological Services, 1975.

Tests used by occupational therapists include:
- Bruininks-Osteretsky Test of Motor Proficiency by R. Bruininks, Circle Pines, MN: American Guidance Services, 1978.
- Davids Hyperkinetic Rating Scale by A. Davids, an objective instrument for assessing hyperkinesis in children, *Journal of Learning Disabilities* 4:499-501, 1971.
- Connors Parent Symptom Questionnaire by C.K. Connors, in *Pharmacotherapy for children*, Washington, DC: Government Printing Office, 1973.
- Neonatal Behavioral Assessment Scale by T.B. Brazelton, Philadelphia: J.B. Lippincott, 1983.
- Connors Teacher Rating Scale by C.K. Connors, a teacher rating scale for use in drug studies with children, *American Journal of Psychiatry* 126:884-8, 1969, and in *Pharmacotherapy for children*, Washington, DC: Government Printing Office, 1983.

PROBLEMS
Frequently, the child has a history of being a "difficult" baby who suffered sleep irregularities; did not like to be cuddled; cried a lot; squirmed when bathed, fed, or diapered; and could not be comforted.

Motor

- The child may be hyperactive or show a high level of activity. He or she often fidgets with hands or feet or squirms when seated and prefers to run rather than walk.
- The child tends to be uncoordinated. Lack of coordination may be related to postural attention righting reactions or to inattention. Differentiate between the two possibilities.
- The child may have poor motor planning skills or praxis, may be clumsy, and seems accident prone. Differentiate between dyspraxia and inattention.
- The child may have delayed or disordered responses to postural attention (righting reactions), especially in antigravity positions. Extension patterns (flight) tend to dominate over flexion patterns (fight). The result is a lack of joint stability and cocontraction, poor protective and equilibrium reactions, and decreased midline stability.
- The child may have shortened duration of postrotary nystagmus.

Sensory

- The child may have increased sensory sensitivity, as illustrated by responses to linear movement, gravitational insecurity, and tactile defensiveness. The result is that the child has difficulty initiating efforts to organize and calm the body systems and shows increased irritability, arching of body, continuous crying, and pushing or turning away from the caregiver.
- The child may have poor or disordered sensory registration (orienting reflex or arrest reaction). The result is lack of coordination between the process of arousal, activation, and effort that leads to difficulty in developing more sophisticated adaptive behaviors. (See cognitive problems below.)
- The child may have unusual patterns of responses in arousal, alerting, and attending that are related to the reticular activating system. The child has difficulty getting to sleep and is restless in bed. In new situations, protective behaviors (fright, withdrawal, and hostility) may be evident.

Cognitive

- The child usually has poor orienting responses, i.e., difficulty in orienting, paying attention, and registering.
- The child usually has a short attention span and poor sustained attention and alertness.
- The child usually has poor selective attention and is easily distracted by extraneous stimuli.
- The child may have memory deficits that lead to losing things necessary for tasks or activities at school or at home.
- The child may have difficulty following through on instructions from others.
- The child may have difficulty learning new approaches or adaptive responses to familiar tasks.
- The child frequently has poor problem-solving skills.
- The child tends to make decisions quickly without considering alternatives.

Intrapersonal

- The child is usually impulsive and lacks self-control, has difficulty waiting for a turn or waiting to be called upon to answer a question, and tends to act before thinking.
- The child may demonstrate emotional lability or mood swings and is easily frustrated.

- The child may have difficulty adapting to new situations or changing behavior in response to old situations.

Interpersonal
- The child may be the class clown or may be withdrawn.
- The child tends to be difficult to discipline and seems unresponsive to punishment.
- The child may become antisocial in adolescence.

Self-Care
- Developmental delay may occur initially; performance thereafter depends on day-to-day problems with neurologic integration.
- The child has difficulty completing chores and often leaves tasks undone or half-done.

Productivity
- Play skills may be delayed. The child may not perform exploratory play well.
- The child often shifts from one uncompleted activity to another.
- The child may have difficulty playing quietly and tends to prefer noisy activities.
- The child may fail in one or more subjects in school.

Leisure
The child may have difficulty participating in leisure groups because of failure to follow the rules and a habit of interrupting, or intruding on others.

TREATMENT/MANAGEMENT
The following treatment and management techniques are drawn primarily from the models of sensory integrative therapy, behavioral management, and cognitive retraining.

Motor
- Decrease hyperactivity through the use of vestibular stimulation.
- Improve bilateral coordination through activities that promote vestibular bilateral integration. (See section on vestibular-bilateral disorder.)
- Provide opportunities to improve motor planning, such as navigating through obstacle courses. (See also section on developmental dyspraxia.)
- Increase postural control and balance. (See also section on gravitational insecurity.)
  1. Increase flexion patterns or decrease reliance on extension patterns.
  2. Increase antigravity extension.
  3. Increase stability and cocontraction in joints and muscles.
  4. Increase use of righting and equilibrium reactions.
- Provide rotational vestibular stimulation. Be sure the child's eyes are closed and his head is in 30 degrees of flexion.

Sensory
- Heighten sensory sensitivity.
  1. Decrease protective patterns and increase discrimination to stimuli through inhibitory input, such as deep pressure, deep massage, slow rhythmic rocking, proximal joint traction and compression, neutral warmth, and low frequency and low intensity vibration.

2. Increase tactile discrimination by applying tactile input to areas of body with highest concentration of tactile receptors, such as the face, mouth, hands, and soles of the feet. (See also section on tactile defensiveness.)

3. Facilitate development of gravity and movement responses. Be sure the head is aligned at 30 degrees of flexion in a vertical or horizontal posture. Movement should be in a straight line.

- Increase sensory registration. Use activities that include input that the child can easily change or control during initial treatment by using tactile, proprioceptive, and vestibular input first and then auditory or visual input.
  1. Increase orienting behavior.
  2. Increase attention to task.
  3. Increase ability to discriminate input.
  4. Decrease protective responses as needed.
  5. Increase the quality and developmental level of adaptive responses.
- Improve arousal.
  1. Use discrimination tasks to assist the child in learning which types of sensory input help him or her organize.
  2. Use antigravity postural responses to assist in self-organization and regulation.
  3. Begin using language to assist in initiating, modulating, and regulating input.

Cognitive
- Increase attending and orienting behavior by using novel variations to familiar activities.
- Improve attention span or attention to tasks by introducing new ways to perform tasks.
- Improve organizational skills.
- Improve memory deficit by suggesting to the child's parents or teacher that they provide reminders at key times of the day.
- Improve problem-solving abilities through rehearsal or questioning techniques.

Intrapersonal
Facilitate self-regulation of behavior. (See #3 under Arousal, above.)

Interpersonal
- Encourage parents to facilitate child's behavior through the techniques described in the sensory and cognitive sections.
- Establish a reward system to encourage the child to try. Avoid punishment. The reward system must be meaningful to the child and be easy for adults to administer. Giving praise and providing opportunities for the child to do things that are fun are best.

Self-Care
Assist child to develop a reminder schedule to complete self-care activities.

Productivity
- Work with the child's teacher to organize the child's classroom environment and schedule of activities. Facilitate performance of desired behavior. Providing rewards in the classroom may be useful.
- Exploratory play may be improved by using problem-solving techniques.

Leisure

Leisure interests may be explored and skills increased as sensory sensitivity decreases, sensory registration improves, and arousal is more self-controlled.

PRECAUTIONS

- Be aware of any drug therapy that may be prescribed. Note changes in behavior and any side effects observed.
- Note whether diet therapy is being used and observe restrictions.
- If a total behavioral management program has been prescribed, observe the schedule of reinforcement.

PROGNOSIS AND OUTCOME

- The child demonstrates improved ability to control his own responses to sensory stimulation and is less dependent on the external environment.
- The child demonstrates improved ability to discriminate between various types of stimuli.
- The child demonstrates improved balance between flexion and extension patterns, such as increased stability and improved righting, rotation, and equilibrium patterns.
- The child is oriented and alert to a variety of stimuli without overresponding (protective responses or unregulated reactions).
- The child is able to attend to a task selectively without responding to distractions.
- The child is able to sustain attention to a task.
- The child is able to attend to and follow verbal commands.
- The child is able to describe alternate approaches to solving a problem.
- The child is able to play quietly with self-control.
- The child is able to play in a group and observe the rules.

REFERENCES

Arnold, L.E., et al. 1985. Vestibular and visual rotational stimulation as treatment for attention deficit and hyperactivity. *American Journal of Occupational Therapy* 39(2):84-91.

Cermak, S.A. 1988. The relationship between attention deficit and sensory integration disorders. Parts 1 and 2. *Sensory Integration Special Interest Section Newsletter* 11(2):1-4 and 11(3):3-4.

Kimball, J.G. 1986. Prediction of methylphenidate (Ritalin) responsiveness through sensory integrative testing. *American Journal of Occupational Therapy* 40(4):241-8.

Oetter, P.L. 1986. A sensory integrative approach to the treatment of attention deficit disorders. *Sensory Integration Special Interest Section Newsletter* 9(2):1-2.

Oetter, P.L. 1986. Assessment: The child with attention deficit disorder. *Sensory Integration Special Interest Section Newsletter* 9(1):6-7.

Ottenbacher, K.J., and H.M. Cooper. 1983. Drug treatment of hyperactivity in children. *Developmental Medicine and Child Neurology* 47:358-66.

Ward, J.D. 1989. Attention deficit disorder/hyperactivity. In *A team approach for therapists: Pediatric rehabilitation*, ed. M.K. Logigian and J.D. Ward, 155-69. Boston: Little, Brown & Co.

Cerebral Palsy—Dystonic/Dyskinetic

DESCRIPTION

The term dystonic or dyskinetic cerebral palsy refers to a group of disorders characterized by abnormal fluctuating muscle tone, involuntary muscle action, and uncoordinated movement patterns. (See also section on cerebral palsy—spastic.)

CAUSE

Lesions in the basal ganglia typically cause fluctuations in muscle tone.

ASSESSMENT

Subtypes
- athetosis/athetoid—characterized by alternating, writhing, or rotary movements that tend to increase in response to emotional tension and decrease as the person relaxes
- ataxic—characterized by uncoordinated movements that adversely affect the performance of fine and gross motor skills, posture, and balance
- rigidity—characterized by high muscle tone that continuously resists slow passive movement; sometimes called lead pipe rigidity (rare)
- tremor—characterized by a rhythmic, alternating muscle contraction and relaxation that is involuntary (rare)
- atonic—characterized by a lack of muscle, leading to the use of term floppy infant (rare)

Areas
- muscle tone, hyper- and hypotonic
- reflex development and maturation
- range of motion, functional
- gross motor skills
- fine motor coordination, manipulation, dexterity
- hand functions
- posture control and balance
- functional mobility
- bilateral integration
- praxis, motor planning
- sensory registration
- sensory processing
- perception skills
- visual disorders, such as strabismus, diplopia, amblyopia, cranial nerve paralysis, retrolental fibrophasia, hemianopia
- attention span and concentration
- memory
- self-perception
- coping skills
- social skills

- communication skills
- daily living skills
- play skills
- leisure skills
- architectural and environmental barriers

Instruments

- Developmental Hand Dysfunction: Theory, Assessment, Treatment by R.P Erhardt, Therapy Skill Builders, 3830 E. Bellevue, P.O. Box 42050-E91, Tucson, AZ 85733, 1982.
- Developmental Vision Assessment revised by R.P Erhardt, Therapy Skill Builders, 3830 E. Bellevue, P.O. Box 42050-E91, Tucson, AZ 85733, 1989.
- Behavioral Assessment Scale of Oral Function in Feeding by M. Stratton, *American Journal of Occupational Therapy* 35(11):719-21, 1981.
- Preschool Play Scale by S. Knox, in *Play as exploratory learning*, ed. M. Reilly, Beverly Hills, CA: Sage, 1974. (See also Harrison, H., and G. Kielhofner. 1986. Examining reliability and validity of the Preschool Play Scale with handicapped children. *American Journal of Occupational Therapy* 40(3):167-73.)
- Klein-Bell Activities of Daily Living Scale by R.M. Klein and B. Bell. (See Law, M., and P. Usher. 1988. Validation of the Klein-Bell Activities of Daily Living Scale for children. *Canadian Journal of Occupational Therapy* 55(2):63-8; see also Klein, R.M., and B. Bell. 1982. Self-care skills: Behavioral measurement with the Klein-Bell ADL Scale. *Archives of Physical Medicine and Rehabilitation* 63:335-8.)
- An Asymmetrical Tonic Neck Reflex Rating Scale by C.L. Parmenter, *American Journal of Occupational Therapy* 37(7):462-5, 1983.

PROBLEMS

Motor

- Muscles exhibit fluctuation of tone from low to normal along with hyperextensor tone.
- The person suffers transient subluxation or dislocation of joints.
- Writhing involuntary movements are usually seen in distal joints. Spasticity may be present in proximal joints.
- It is difficult to stabilize joints.
- The person has difficulty performing gross motor activities.
- The person has difficulty performing fine motor activities.
- The person may have muscle spasms.
- There is a lack of cocontraction of muscles.
- There is a lack of muscle grading.
- The person is unable to hold a segment of the body at various points within the range of motion, such as a forearm.
- There is asymmetry in both posture and movement.
- Moving the head affects trunk and limbs.
- The person has incomplete righting reflexes, equilibrium reactions, and protective responses that lead to problems in balance and equilibrium.
- Primitive reflexes, such as an inability to hold the head in midline because of the ATNR (asymmetrical tonic neck reflex), may dominate motor activity.

Sensory

- The person may have hearing loss or other auditory disorder.
- The person may have hyper- or hyporesponsiveness to vestibular stimulation.
- The person may have hyper- or hyporesponsiveness to tactile stimulation.
- The person may have eye motility problems.
- The person may have visual perceptual disorders.

Cognitive

- The person may have difficulty learning due to mental retardation.
- The person may have learning disorders due to perceptual problems.

Intrapersonal

- The person may be emotionally labile.
- The person may have low frustration tolerance and poor coping skills.
- The person may have a poor self-image and low self-esteem.

Interpersonal

The person may have difficulty developing social relations.

Self-Care

- The person has difficulty performing most activities of daily living.
- The person will need assistance to develop independent living skills.

Productivity

- The person may have poorly developed play skills.
- The person may have difficulty with writing skills.
- The person will need assistance to explore career options.

Leisure

The person may have few leisure interests.

TREATMENT/MANAGEMENT

Motor

- Normalize postural muscle tone by increasing low tone and decreasing high tone.
- Increase symmetric muscle activity.
- Focus activity toward the midline.
- Increase muscle control proximally, then work distally.
- Improve holding posture or motion at various points within the range of motion during active movement.
- Assist person to separate movements of the head from the trunk.
- Promote control of muscle spasms.

Sensory

- Facilitate integration of righting reflexes and the development of equilibrium reactions and protective responses.
- Normalize response to sensory stimulation, if necessary.

Cognitive
- Develop cognitive skills.
- Promote development of perceptual skills.

Intrapersonal
Improve self-image.

Interpersonal
Encourage development of social skills.

Self-Care
Promote development and independence in performing activities of daily living.

Productivity
- Promote development of work habits, work skills, and work tolerance.
- Provide opportunities for career exploration.
- Encourage development of independent living skills.

Leisure
Explore with the patient possible leisure interests and promote the development of leisure skills.

PRECAUTIONS
See precautions listed under Spastic Cerebral Palsy.

PROGNOSIS AND OUTCOME
- The person demonstrates more normal movement patterns.
- The person demonstrates improved postural tone, control, and balance.
- The person demonstrates improved gross motor skills.
- The person demonstrates improved hand skill development and fine motor coordination, manipulation, and dexterity.
- The person demonstrates improved sensory processing skills.
- The person demonstrates improved perceptual skills.
- The person has increased attention span and concentration.
- The person has improved learning skills.
- The person demonstrates improved self-image and self-esteem.
- The person demonstrates improved coping skills.
- The person has increased self-care skills.
- The person has increased or improved play skills.
- The person performs productive skills.
- The person performs leisure skills.

REFERENCES

Carrasco, R.C. 1989. Children with cerebral palsy. In *Occupational therapy for children*, 2nd ed., ed. P.N. Pratt and A.S. Allen, 396-421. St. Louis: C.V. Mosby.

Howison, M.V. 1988. Cerebral palsy. In *Willard and Spackman's occupational therapy*, 7th ed., ed. H.L. Hopkins and H.D. Smith, 675-706. Philadelphia: J.B. Lippincott.

Logigian, M.K. 1989. Cerebral palsy. In *A team approach for therapists: Pediatric rehabilitation*, ed. M.K. Logigian and J.D. Ward, 23-61. Boston: Little, Brown & Co.

Nakaoka, Y., et al. 1984. Relation between head control and locomotor ability in atheotid children. *Physical and Occupational Therapy in Pediatrics* 4(2):29-35.

Trefler, E. 1982. Arm restraints during functional activities. *American Journal of Occupational Therapy* 36(9):599-600.

Treviranus, J., and R. Tannock. 1987. A scanning computer access system for children with severe physical disabilities. *American Journal of Occupational Therapy* 41(11):733-8.

Cerebral Palsy—Spastic

DESCRIPTION

Spastic cerebral palsy is a nonprogressive brain disorder characterized by impairment and abnormalities of voluntary movement and posture. Deficits in intelligence and language may occur also. There are two major subclassifications of cerebral palsy based on the type of movement disorder. Spastic palsy refers to the group of persons who exhibit hyperactive reflexes, exaggerated stretch reflexes, and clonus. Dyskinetic or dystonic palsy refers to the group of persons who exhibit involuntary and uncoordinated movements.

CAUSE

The cause of spastic cerebral palsy is often difficult to determine, but uterine disorders, birth trauma, neonatal asphyxia, and neonatal jaundice are involved. Spastic palsy is associated with premature birth and upper motor neuron involvement. Certain severe systemic diseases, such as meningitis, may also occur during early infancy and cause symptoms of cerebral palsy.

ASSESSMENT

Subtypes

- spastic hemiplegia—involvement of the arm and leg on one side of the body
- spastic diplegia—involvement of all four extremities, but the lower extremities are more involved than the upper extremities
- spastic monoplegia—involvement primarily of one extremity (rare)
- spastic triplegia—involvement of three extremities
- spastic quadriplegia, spastic tetraplegia, or bilateral hemiplegia—involvement of all four extremities

Areas

- reflex development and maturation (note all abnormal and obligatory reflex patterns)
- muscle tone—hyper- and hypotonia
- range of motion—functional

- gross motor skills—rolling, sitting, standing, walking
- fine motor coordination, manipulation, dexterity
- hand functions—grasp, pinch, opposition
- balance, postural tone, midline stability, and postural control in movement
- praxis (motor planning)
- bilateral integration
- sensory registration
- sensory processing (note especially problems in eye motility)
- perception skills
- attention span, concentration
- memory skills
- self-perception
- coping skills
- social skills
- language/communication skills
- self-help skills, especially feeding (oral motor skill), dressing, and grooming
- play skills
- academic skills
- leisure skills
- architectural and environmental barriers

Instruments
- Erhardt Developmental Vision Assessment by R.P. Erhardt, Therapy Skill Builders, 3830 E. Bellevue, P.O. Box 42050-E91, Tucson, AZ 85733, 1986. (See also Erhardt, R.P. 1987. Sequential levels in the visual-motor development of a child with cerebral palsy. *American Journal of Occupational Therapy* 41(1):43-8.)
- Developmental Hand Dysfunction: Theory, Assessment, Treatment by R.P. Erhardt, Therapy Skill Builders, 3830 E. Bellevue, P.O. Box 42050-E91, Tucson, AZ, 85733, 1982.
- Behavioral Assessment Scale of Oral Function in Feeding by M. Stratton, *American Journal of Occupational Therapy* 35(11):719-21, 1981.
- Preschool Play Scale by S. Knox, in *Play as exploratory learning*, ed. M. Reilly, Beverly Hills, CA: Sage, 1974. (See also Harrison, H., and G. Kielhofner. 1986. Examining reliability and validity of the Preschool Play Scale with handicapped children. *American Journal of Occupational Therapy* 40(3):167-73.)
- Klein-Bell Activities of Daily Living Scale by R.M. Klein and B.J. Bell, see Self-care skills: Behavioral measurement with Klein-Bell ADL Scale, *Archives of Physical Medicine and Rehabilitation*, 63:335-8, 1982. (See also Law, M., and R. Usher. 1988. Validation of the Klein-Bell Activities of Daily Living Scale for children. *Canadian Journal of Occupational Therapy* 55(2):63-8.)
- An Asymmetrical Tonic Neck Reflex Rating Scale by C.L. Parmenter, *American Journal of Occupational Therapy* 37(7):462-5, 1983.

Other instruments used by occupational therapists:
- Test of Visual-perceptual Skills by M.F. Gardner, Seattle: Special Child Publications, 1982.
- Tennessee Self-Concept Scale, revised by W.H. Fitts and G.H. Reid, Los Angeles: Western Psychological Services, 1988.

PROBLEMS

Motor

- Hypertonicity appears in certain muscle groups of affected people, while hypotonicity appears in the opposing muscle groups. In the upper extremities, hypertonicity is most common in the flexors, adductors, pronators, and internal rotators. In the lower extremities, hypertonicity is most common in the extensors, adductors, invertors, and internal rotators. High tone appears in extremities, while low tone appears in trunk musculature. Around a specific joint the tone may fluctuate, making movement unreliable. Tone may vary from the right to the left side of the body, making coordinate movements and bilateral integration difficult.
- Primitive reflexes persist, such as the asymmetrical tonic neck reflex (ATNR), symmetrical tonic neck reflex (STNR), tonic labyrinthine reflex (TLR), Moro reflex, and positive supporting reflex.
- The person has incomplete or abnormal development of the postural (equilibrium and righting) reactions.
- There is delayed, incomplete, and abnormal motor development and decreased voluntary motor control, including lack of stability or base of support, mobility or point of movement, weight shift or change of body position, and reaction weight shift or postural adjustment.
- The person has developmental delays (development blocks) that stop the developmental process or lead to compensatory movements. The more common blocks are neck hyperextension, neck asymmetry, scapulohumeral tightness and scapular adduction, anterior pelvic tilt (lordosis), posterior pelvic tilt, pelvic femoral tightness, and hip extension adduction.
- Contractures and joint tightness tend to lead to orthopedic deformities.
- Scissor gait results from the extension, adduction, and internal rotation of the hip muscles.
- Toe walking results from the positive support reflex.
- Extremities are maintained in mid-range of motion.
- The person exhibits stereotypical (patterned) movements that include compensatory movements.
- Associated reactions (overflow) may be present.
- Seizure may occur.

Sensory

- The person may have eye motility problems, including diplopia, strabismus, amblyopia, lack of upward gaze, and hemianopia.
- The person may have visual perception problems, such as impaired visual discrimination or impaired space and form perception.
- The person may neglect or ignore one side of the body in the case of hemiplegic palsy.
- Vestibular responses may be hyper- or hyporeactive, including gravitation insecurity.
- Tactile responses may be hyper- or hyporesponsive, including tactile defensiveness.
- The person may have diminished awareness of pain.
- The person may have auditory hypersensitivity.

Cognitive

- The person may be mentally retarded.

- The person may have learning disabilities related to perceptual disorders.

Intrapersonal
- The person may become depressed and express feelings of hopelessness and helplessness.
- The person may have poor self-image and low self-esteem.
- The person may have inadequate coping skills and become easily frustrated.
- The person may have limited opportunities for self-expression.

Interpersonal
- The person may have dysarthric speech and delayed language development.
- The person may have difficulty making friends and developing social skills.

Self-Care
- The person usually has difficulty performing basic ADLs (activities of daily living), such as feeding, dressing, and grooming.
- The person usually needs assistance to achieve independent living status.

Productivity
- Play skills may be delayed due to lack of exploratory play behavior.
- The person usually needs assistance in exploring career options.
- The person may need assistance in adapting working environment to his or her own abilities.

Leisure
- The person may need assistance in exploring leisure options.
- The person may need assistance in adapting leisure environment to his or her own abilities.

TREATMENT/MANAGEMENT
Treatment models in occupational therapy are based on neurodevelopmental therapy (Bobath), sensorimotor therapy (Rood), sensory integration (Ayres), occupational behavior (Reilly), and human occupation (Kielhofner).

Motor
- Inhibit the person's abnormal reflex patterns and facilitate normal posture and movement patterns by handling (guiding) the head and trunk to help the person feel and learn normal sequences of movement in head control, trunk control, weight shifting, weight bearing, and mobility.
- Facilitate head control by improving the balance of neck flexion and extension, lateral flexion, midline control (cocontraction), midline orientation (alignment of head and body) against gravity, and neck mobility (elongation and chin tuck).
- Increase postural tone in trunk musculature and reduce postural tone throughout the extremities to increase postural stability in the trunk while promoting the opportunity for movement in the extremities.
- Balance postural tone (decrease hypertonicity) between opposing groups of muscles to increase cocontraction and alternate contraction and elongation.

- Increase functional range of motion in the extremities as hypertonicity is reduced.
- Promote postural reflex development and maturation (equilibrium and righting reactions) to permit balance (stability) and encourage voluntary movement (mobility).
- Encourage greater variety and differentiation of movement patterns, including varied positions (flex, extend, rotate), speed, and direction by using key points of control (head, shoulder girdle, trunk, pelvis, calcaneus, knees, and the thenar eminence of the hand).
- Promote use of arms and hands to support, reach, grasp, and hold, and decrease dependence on arms for postural control and stability as trunk stability increases.
- Promote weight bearing with movement designed to increase postural control against gravity.
- Inhibit associated (overflow) reactions by anchoring the opposite limb through weight bearing and such actions as grasping a peg with the hand.
- Encourage the patient to initiate movements and avoid long periods in static postures and positions.
- Work toward muscle elongation, joint mobility, proximal stabilization (cocontraction), and active function of muscles around the joint.
- Consider inhibitive casting of the ankle and foot or hand and wrist to reduce distal muscle tone.
- Consider using hand splints to promote thumb abduction, wrist extension, and functional positioning of the digits.
- Consider powered mobility for persons with poor motor control.

Sensory

- Encourage movement against gravity to facilitate learning how to control movement.
- Facilitate experiencing the sensation of movement (with vestibular, proprioceptive, and kinesthetic input) to promote learning about movement.
- Use vestibular stimulation to promote equilibrium reactions.
- Provide tactile stimulation to promote oral motor and hand functions.
- For visual perceptual problems, developmental apraxia, gravitational insecurity, and tactile defensiveness, see sections on these specific problems.

Cognitive

- Instruct parents, caregivers, and teachers in seating and positioning techniques to (a) decrease abnormal tone, such as extensor tone, and (b) facilitate trunk and lower limb stability while promoting mobility in the upper extremities.
- Increase attending behavior and attention span.
- Instruct person to instruct others regarding need for assistance.
- Instruct person, family, or caregivers on the adapted equipment available and methods of adapting the home to increase mobility while maintaining safety.
- Use of computers may facilitate learning tasks and improve the person's ability to function in the classroom.

Intrapersonal

- Provide a safe environment in which the person can experience movement without fear.
- Provide activities designed to improve self-image and increase self-esteem and a sense of mastery through the use of such creative activities as art, crafts, music, drama, dance, or creative writing. (Note: A computer may be useful for writing and art.)

Interpersonal
- Provide opportunities for socialization.
- Assist in development of functional communication and language skills.
- Encourage person, parents, or caregivers to participate in self-help groups, if available.
- Encourage parents to assist the person in understanding role expectations in the home and community.
- Help the family identify community resources.

Self-Care
- Promote oral motor skills to facilitate feeding.
- Suggest clothing adaptations that may facilitate independent dressing.
- Suggest various positions that promote stability during dressing.
- Suggest adapted equipment that may facilitate activities of daily living, such as bolsters, wedges, standers, side-lyers, adapted chairs, and mobility aids.

Productivity
- Increase opportunities for play development. Adapted toys and computer-aided games and toys may expand the person's play environment.
- Encourage parents, caregivers, or teachers to assign responsibilities and duties for person to perform.
- Develop work habits and work tolerance.
- Explore vocational interests and career options.

Leisure
- Explore leisure interests.
- Develop leisure skills through opportunities to participate in activities.

PRECAUTIONS
- Be alert for signs of sensory overload when using sensory stimulation, especially vestibular.
- Be aware if person has history of seizures and report all seizures to the physician.
- Be alert to signs of illness. Person's performance may deteriorate rapidly during minor illness.
- Be alert to any changes in medication and reactions to medications.

PROGNOSIS AND OUTCOME
- The person demonstrates more normal movement patterns.
- The person demonstrates improved postural tone, control, and balance.
- The person demonstrates improved gross motor skills.
- The person demonstrates improved hand-skill development and fine motor coordination, manipulation, and dexterity.
- The person demonstrates improved sensory processing skills.
- The person demonstrates improved perceptual skills.
- The person has increased attention span and concentration.
- The person has improved learning skills.
- The person demonstrates increased self-esteem.

- The person demonstrates improved coping skills.
- The person has increased self-care skills.
- The person has increased play skills.
- The person demonstrates performance of productive skills.
- The person demonstrates performance of leisure skills.

REFERENCES

Anderson, J., J. Hinojosa, and C. Strauch. 1987. Integrating play in neurodevelopmental treatment. *American Journal of Occupational Therapy* 41(7):421-6.

Barnes, K.J. 1989. Relationship of upper extremity weight bearing to hand skills of boys with cerebral palsy. *Occupational Therapy Journal of Research* 9(3):143-54.

Barnes, K.J. 1989. Direct replication: Relationship of upper extremity weight bearing to hand skills of boys with cerebral palsy. *Occupational Therapy Journal of Research* 9(4):235-42.

Bellefeuille, R.D. 1984. Aid to independence—hand splint for cerebral palsied children. *Canadian Journal of Occupational Therapy* 51(1):37-9.

Berman, B., C.L. Vaughan, and W.J. Peacock. 1990. The effect of rhizotomy on movement in patients with cerebral palsy. *American Journal of Occupational Therapy* 44(6):511-6.

Campbell, P.H., W.F. McInerney, and M.A. Cooper. 1984. Therapeutic programming for students with severe handicaps. *American Journal of Occupational Therapy* 38(9):594-602.

Carrasco, R.C. 1989. Children with cerebral palsy. In *Occupational therapy in children*, 2nd ed., ed. P.N. Pratt and A.S. Allen, 396-421. St. Louis: C.V. Mosby.

Cruickshank, D.A., and D.L. O'Neill. 1990. Upper extremity inhibitive casting in a boy with spastic quadriplegia. *American Journal of Occupational Therapy* 44(6):552-5.

Currey, J., and D. Exner. 1988. Comparison of tactile preferences in children with and without cerebral palsy. *American Journal of Occupational Therapy* 42(6):371-7.

Currie, D.M., and A. Mendiola. 1987. Cortical thumb orthosis for children with spastic hemiplegic cerebral palsy. *Archives of Physical Medicine and Rehabilitation* 68(4):214-6.

Einis, L.P., and D.M. Bailey. 1990. The use of powered leisure and communication devices in a switch training program. *American Journal of Occupational Therapy* 44(10):931-4.

Everson, J.M., and R. Goodwyn. 1987. A comparison of the use of adaptive microswitches by students with cerebral palsy. *American Journal of Occupational Therapy* 41(11):739-44.

Flegle, J.H., and J.M. Leibwitz. 1988. Improvement in grasp skill in children with hemiplegia with the MacKinnon splint. *Research in Developmental Disabilities* 9:145-51.

Flegle, J.H. The effect of the MacKinnon splint on grasp skill in three children with hemiplegia. *Proceedings of the Occupational Therapy for Maternal & Child Health Conference*, vol. 2, *Efficacy, Research, & Related Topics*, 175-189. Rockville, MD: American Occupational Therapy Association.

Gisel, E.G., and J. Patrick. 1988. Identification of children with cerebral palsy unable to maintain a normal nutrition state. *Lancet* 1(Feb. 6):283-6.

Hinojosa, J. and J. Anderson. 1987. Working relationships between therapists and parents of children with cerebral palsy: A survey of attitudes. *Occupational Therapy Journal of Research* 7(2):123-6.

Hinojosa, J., J. Anderson, and G.W. Ranum. 1988. Relationships between therapists and parents of preschool children with cerebral palsy: A survey. *Occupational Therapy Journal of Research* 8(5):285-97.

Howison, M.V. 1988. Cerebral palsy. In *Willard and Spackman's occupational therapy*, 7th ed. H.L. Hopkins and H.D. Smith, 675-706. Philadelphia: J.B. Lippincott.

Hulme, J.B., et al. 1987. Effects of adaptive seating devices on the eating and drinking of children with multiple handicaps. *American Journal of Occupational Therapy* 41(2):81-9.

Iammatteo, P.A., C. Trombly, and L. Luecke. 1990. The effect of mouth closure on drooling and speech. *American Journal of Occupational Therapy* 44(8):686-91.

Inge, K.J. 1987. Atypical motor development and cerebral palsy. In *Educating children with multiple disabilities: A transdisciplinary approach*, ed. F.P. Orelove and D. Sobsey, 43-65. Baltimore: Paul H. Brookes Publishing.

Kibele, A. 1989. Occupational therapy's role in improving the quality of life for persons with cerebral palsy. *American Journal of Occupational Therapy* 43(6):371-7.

Laskas, C.A., S.L. Mullen, and D.L. Nelson, et al. 1985. Enhancement of two motor functions of the lower extremity in a child with spastic quadriplegia. *Physical Therapy* 65(1):11-16.

Lawlor, M.D., and A. Zielinski. 1983. Occupational therapy. In *Comprehensive management of cerebral palsy*, ed. G.H. Thompson, I.L. Rubin, and R.M. Bilender, 181-92. New York: Grune & Stratton.

Leiper, C.I., A. Miller, J. Lang, et al. 1981. Sensory feedback for head control in cerebral palsy. *Physical Therapy* 61(4):512-18.

Logigian, M.K. 1989. Cerebral palsy. In *A team approach for therapists: Pediatric rehabilitation*, ed. M.K. Logigian and J.D. Ward, 23-61. Boston: Little, Brown & Co.

Majill, J., and N. Hurlbut. 1986. The self-esteem of adolescents with cerebral palsy. *American Journal of Occupational Therapy* 40(6):402-7.

McPherson, J.J., et al. 1984. The range of motion of long term knee contractures of four spastic cerebral palsied children: A pilot study. *Physical and Occupational Therapy in Pediatrics* 4(1):17-23.

Menken, C., S.A. Cermak, and A. Fisher. 1987. Evaluating the visual-perceptual skills of children with cerebral palsy. *American Journal of Occupational Therapy* 41(10):646-51.

Naritoku, D., C. Sanbongi, and K. Kuba. 1987. Effectiveness of the MacKinnon splint with cerebral palsy children. *Proceedings of the Occupational Therapy for Maternal & Child Health Conference*, vol. 2, *Efficacy, Research, & Related Topics*, 190-2. Rockville, MD: American Occupational Therapy Association.

Neeman, R.L., H.J. Neeman, and M. Neeman. 1988. Application of orthokinetic orthoses in habilitation of a person with upper extremity incoordination secondary to a spastic quadriplegia due to cerebral palsy. *Canadian Journal of Rehabilitation* 1(3):145-54.

Nelson, C.A. 1985. Cerebral palsy. In *Neurological rehabilitation*, ed. D.A. Umphred, 165-83 and 2nd ed. 1990, 239-58. St. Louis: C.V. Mosby.

O'Brien, M., and K. Tsurumi. 1983. The effect of two body positions on head righting in severely disabled individuals with cerebral palsy. *American Journal of Occupational Therapy* 37(10):673-80.

Parette, H.P., Jr., and J.J. Hourcade. 1984. A review of therapeutic intervention research on gross and fine motor progress in young children with cerebral palsy. *American Journal of Occupational Therapy* 38(7):462-8.

Peganoff, S.A. 1984. The use of aquatics with cerebral palsied adolescents. *American Journal of Occupational Therapy* 38(7):469-73.

Petersen, P., and C.E. Petersen. 1984. Bilateral handskills in children with mild hemiplegia. *Physical and Occupational Therapy in Pediatrics* 4(1):77-87.

Powell, N.J. 1985. Children with cerebral palsy. In *Occupational therapy for children*, ed. P.N. Clark and A.S. Allen. St. Louis: C.V. Mosby.

Ray, S.A., A.C. Bundy, and D.L. Nelson. 1983. Decreasing drooling through techniques to facilitate mouth closure. *American Journal of Occupational Therapy* 37(11):749-53.

Rothman J.F. 1989. Understanding the conservation of substance in youngsters with cerebral palsy. *Physical and Occupational Therapy in Pediatrics* 9(3):119-25.

Stout, J.L. 1987. Hemispheric specialization for motor function and hemiplegic cerebral palsy: Is there a difference in function between children with right and left hemiplegia? *Physical and Occupational Therapy in Pediatrics* 7(3):53-67.

Strecher, W.B., et al. 1988. Comparison of pronator tenotomy and pronator rerouting in children with spastic cerebral palsy. *Journal of Hand Surgery* 13A:540-3.

Talbot, M.L., and J. Junkala. 1981. The effects of auditorally augmented feedback on the eye-hand coordination of students with cerebral palsy. *American Journal of Occupational Therapy* 35(8):535-8.

Taylor, C.L., and S.R. Harris. 1986. Effects of ankle-foot orthoses on functional motor performance in a child with spastic diplegia. *American Journal of Occupational Therapy* 40(7):492-4.

Treviranus, J., and R. Tannock. 1987. A scanning computer access system for children with severe physical disabilities. *American Journal of Occupational Therapy* 41(11):733-8.

Weiss-Lambrou, R., S. Tetreault, and J. Dudley. 1989. The relationship between oral sensation and drooling in persons with cerebral palsy. *American Journal of Occupational Therapy* 43(3):155-61.

Weller, R.B., W.O. Truex, and J.C. Mapes. 1988. A longitudinal case study of gait of a child with cerebral palsy following derotation osteotomy. *Physical and Occupational Therapy in Pediatrics* 8(4):53-74.

Williams, S.E., and D.V. Matesi. 1988. Therapeutic intervention with an adapted toy. *American Journal of Occupational Therapy* 42(10):673-6.

Windsor, M.M. 1986. Incorporating sensory integration principles into treatment of children with cerebral palsy. *Developmental Disabilities Special Interest Section Newsletter* 9(1):3-4.

Witt, P.L., and C.A. Parr. 1988. Effectiveness of Trager psychophysical integration in promoting trunk mobility in a child with cerebral palsy: A case report. *Physical and Occupational Therapy in Pediatrics* 8(4):75-94.

Yasukawa, A. 1990. Upper extremity casting: Adjunct treatment for a child with cerebral palsy hemiplegia. *American Journal of Occupational Therapy* 44(9):840-6.

Child Abuse and Neglect

DESCRIPTION

Child abuse and neglect is defined as physical injury, emotional disturbance, sexual abuse, negligence, or maltreatment of a child under the age of 18 by a person who is responsible for the child's welfare.

CAUSE

- Abuse is the breakdown of impulse control in the parent, guardian, or other caregiver. There are four factors involved:
  1. Personality features—The caregiver experienced lack of affection and support as a child and thus does not know how to provide the same for his or her child, or the caregiver is out of control due to substance abuse or psychotic illness.
  2. The difficult or different child—Examples include hyperactive, handicapped, premature, or sickly children or stepchildren.
  3. Inadequate support—The caregiver feels isolated or abandoned by relatives or friends who could provide guidance and assistance.
  4. Crisis situation—Stress overcomes the caregiver's ability to function.
- Neglect is observed in families with multiple problems and disorganized lifestyles. Depression, desertion, drug or alcohol abuse, and chronic medical conditions may be seen in one or more caregivers.

ASSESSMENT

Areas

- gross motor development and skills
- fine motor skills, manipulation, dexterity, and bilateral coordination
- muscle strength
- reflex development and maturation
- postural control (use of protective and equilibrium reactions)
- muscle tone
- joint stability and mobility
- sensory registration/awareness
- sensory sensitivity/processing
- perceptual skills (visual, auditory, tactile, and kinesthetic)
- attending behavior and concentration
- ability to follow directions/sequencing
- motivation or self-initiated activity
- mood or affect
- self-control
- coping skills
- social conduct skills
- daily living skills

- academic readiness or academic skills
- play skills

Instruments
No comprehensive or specific scale for occupational therapists to use in assessing child abuse was identified. The following assessments may be useful:
- Bayley Scales of Infant Development by N. Bayley, San Antonio, TX: The Psychological Corporation, 1969 (not an occupational therapist).
- Brazelton Neonatal Assessment Scale, 2nd ed. by T. Brazelton, Philadelphia: J.B. Lippincott, 1984 (not an occupational therapist).
- A Play Scale (also called Preschool Play Scale) by S. Knox, in *Play as exploratory learning*, ed. M. Reilly, 247-266. Beverly Hills, CA: Sage, 1974. (See also Bledsoe, N.P., and J.T. Shepherd. 1982. A study of reliability and validity of a preschool play scale. *American Journal of Occupational Therapy* 36(12):783-88.
- Child Abuse Potential Inventory by J.S. Milner and R.C. Wimberly, an inventory for the identification of child abuses, *Journal of Clinical Psychology* 35(1):95-100, 1979 (not an occupational therapist).

PROBLEMS
The problems associated with child abuse can be varied and many. The list of problems should be considered as examples and not as a comprehensive list.

Motor
- Developmental milestones may be delayed, especially gross and fine motor skills.
- Muscle weakness may be present if nerve or brain damage has occurred.
- Paralysis may be present if nerve or brain damage has occurred.
- Contractures may be present if condition has existed for some time.
- Reduction of range of motion may be present, depending on the type of injury.
- Reflex maturation may be incomplete, with primitive reflexes continuing to be present.

Sensory
- Sensory loss may have occurred in vision, hearing, touch proprioception, or kinesthesia, and less commonly in taste or smell.
- Body image may fail to develop or an impaired body image may develop.
- Sensory integrative dysfunction may be present, including developmental dyspraxia and vestibular-bilateral disorder.
- Sensory responses may be hypo- or hyperreactive.

Cognitive
- Learning disabilities may be present, including dyslexia, short attention span, and hyperkinetic behavior.
- The child may have poor problem-solving skills.

Intrapersonal
- The child may have a poor self-image and lack self-confidence.
- The child may feel guilty for "causing so much trouble." (Note: The child is not the cause

but may be made to feel so by repeated statements from one or more adults.)
- The child may have blunted or flat affect.
- The child may lack self-control, such as being negative and aggressive or having a low tolerance for frustration.
- The child may act helpless or be overly compliant or withdrawn.
- Role identity within the family unit may be ill-defined or fluctuating.

Interpersonal
- Parent(s) and child may lack coping skills.
- The child may have delayed development of social interaction and conduct skills.
- The child may be delayed in acquiring speech or vocabulary.
- Bonding between parent and child may be inadequate or lacking.
- The child may lack group interaction skills.

Self-Care
- The child may be delayed in developing activities of daily living, such as dressing, tying shoes, or eating with a fork.
- The child may be unable to perform certain ADLs (activities of daily living) if motor skills are involved.

Productivity
- The child may have developmental delays in acquiring play skills.
- The child may use less imagination in play.
- The child may be unable to organize play activities.
- The child may show little exploratory behavior in play.

Leisure
The child may have few leisure interests beyond watching television or video.

TREATMENT/MANAGEMENT
Models of treatment include sensory integration (Ayres), and neurodevelopmental therapy (Bobath).

Motor
- Promote development of gross and fine motor skills according to developmental level.
- Increase muscle strength through progressive resistive exercises.
- Maintain or increase joint range of motion through passive exercises and active involvement in activities.
- Facilitate integration of primitive reflexes.

Sensory
- If sensory loss has occurred, facilitate development of remaining senses.
- Increase body awareness and position in space.

- If sensory dysfunction is noted, see section on the specific disorder for treatment suggestions.
- Modulate hyper- or hyporesponsiveness to stimuli.

Cognitive
- Improve attending behavior and attention span.
- Improve the child's ability to follow directions and sequences.
- Improve problem-solving skills by assisting the child to think through a situation, asking questions and prompting responses.

Intrapersonal
- Improve self-image and sense of mastery through use of creative activities, such as crafts, games, music, dance, or drama.
- Increase self-control by assisting the child to think of alternative approaches to situations and tasks.

Interpersonal
Provide an opportunity for the child to practice social conduct in a group situation.

Self-Care
- Promote self-feeding skills.
- Decrease oral motor sensitivity.
- Increase skills in daily living.

Productivity
- Teach parents or caregivers the child's level of play skills and how to participate in play activities with the child.
- Promote development of play skills.
- Assist in promoting academic readiness skills.

Leisure
Encourage exploration of interests and development of leisure skills.

PRECAUTIONS
Observe child for signs of any additional abuse or neglect.

PROGNOSIS AND OUTCOME
- Parent or caregiver is able to interact with the child without violent or abusive behavior.
- Parent or caregiver demonstrates knowledge of the child's level of development and adjusts expectations to the child's level of performance.
- Parent or caregiver is able to manage his or her own life situation and stresses without taking anger or frustrations out on the child.

- Child demonstrates improved developmental profile in motor, sensory, language, and self-care skills
- Child demonstrates improvement in play skills.

REFERENCES

Esdaile, S., and A. Sanderson. 1987. Teaching parents toy making: A practical guide to early intervention. *British Journal of Occupational Therapy* 50(8):266-71.

Howard, A.C. 1986. Developmental play ages of physically abused and nonabused children. *American Journal of Occupational Therapy* 40(10):691-5.

Irving, N., A. Carr, G. Gawlinski, and D. McDonnell. 1988. Thurlow House child abuse assessment programme: Residential family evaluation. *British Journal of Occupational Therapy* 51(4):116-9.

Lewis, J.A. 1982. Oral motor assessment and treatment of feeding difficulties. In *Failure to thrive in infancy and early childhood: A multidisciplinary team approach*, ed. P.J. Accardo, 265-95. Baltimore: University Park Press.

Lloyd, C., and D. Watson. 1989. Parenting: A group programme for abusive parents. *Australian Occupational Therapy Journal* 36(1):24-33.

Ramm, P.A. 1988. Child abuse and neglect. In *Willard and Spackman's occupational therapy*, 7th ed., ed. H.L. Hopkins and H.D. Smith, 668-73. Philadelphia: J.B. Lippincott.

Semmler, C.J. 1990. Child abuse and neglect. In *Early occupational therapy intervention: Neonates to three years*, ed. S.J. Semmler and J.G. Hunter, 197-219. Gaithersburg, MD: Aspen Publishers, Inc.

Failure to Thrive

DESCRIPTION

Failure to thrive is a disorder characteristic of infants and young children who do not grow at a rate normal for their age, sex, or race. The term may be applied to those whose height or weight falls below the fifth percentile on standard growth charts, those who have an atypical weight to height ratio in which the weight is less than 90 percent of expected weight for measured height, or those whose growth chart shows a downward trend instead of a parallel line. Subtypes include organic failure to thrive (OFTT) and nonorganic failure to thrive (NOFTT).

CAUSE

The causes may be organic, nonorganic, or a combination of the two. Examples of organic causes include defects in the gastrointestinal system, such as short-bowel syndrome, renal failure, congenital cardiac disease, chronic lung disease, cystic fibrosis, biliary atresia, certain genetic disorders, chromosome abnormalities, and chronic infections. Nonorganic causes are external to the infant or child and include such examples as trauma, neglect, rejection, poor mother-infant relationships, inadequate mothering skills, and family stress due to divorce, unemployment, poverty, and overcrowded living conditions.

ASSESSMENT

Areas
- developmental profile
- reflex maturation and development (especially poor sucking reflex in infants)
- posture (note atypical postures)
- oral motor functions (note also such behaviors as perseveration of sucking, turning head away from food, pushing food away, crying, refusing the nipple, falling asleep during feedings, vomiting, fighting with caregiver, and refusing solid foods)
- gross motor skills and coordination
- fine motor skills, manipulation, dexterity, and bilateral coordination
- sensory registration
- sensory sensitivity (note staring behavior)
- arousal and attending behaviors (note avoidance behaviors)
- mood or affect (note level of irritability, listlessness, or apathy)
- infant-caretaker interaction (note lack of cuddling behavior, inability to be soothed)
- social interaction skills (note interaction with persons other than primary caretaker)
- daily living skills
- play skills (note perseveration of midline play)

Instruments
- Occupational Therapy Protocol for Infants Who Fail to Thrive by R. Denton. *American Journal of Occupational Therapy* 40(5):354, 356, 1986.
- The Gesell Developmental Schedules by A. Gesell, in *Developmental diagnosis*, ed. H. Knoblock and B. Pasamanick, 1974. Hagerstown, MD: Harper & Row, 1984 (not an occupational therapist).
- *Sewell Early Education Developmental Profile* by J. Herst, S. Wolfe, G. Jorgenson, and S. Pallan. Denver, CO: Sewell Rehabilitation Center , 1976 (not an occupational therapist).
- *The Vulpe Assessment Battery* by S. Vulpe, Downsview, ONT: National Institute of Mental Retardation, 1977.

PROBLEMS
The list of problems can vary from child to child because failure to thrive is not a single disorder.

Motor
- The child may have developmental delay in attaining motor milestones.
- The child may have decreased motor activity (hypoactivity) and lack of purposeful movements.
- The child may have infantile posture (note flexed hips and knees, arms flexed at 90 degrees or more at the elbow, or forearms held above the head).
- The child may have increased hand and finger activity.
- The child may have muscle weakness.
- The child may have primitive reflexes that are not integrated.

Sensory
- The child may under- or over-react to stimuli (hyposensitivity or hypersensitivity).
- The child may have developmental delay in sensory awareness and discrimination.

Cognitive
- The child may have poor attending behavior.
- The child may have short attention span.
- The child may have poor or impaired memory.

Intrapersonal
- The child may be hyperalert or disinterested.
- The child may have no facial expression, lack of affect.
- The child may be withdrawn.
- The child may be listless or apathetic.
- The child may be irritable.
- The child may ruminate.

Interpersonal
- The child may lack vocalization or have developmental delays in communication skills, including a decrease or absence of cooing, squealing, babbling, laughing, vocalizing syllables, or saying words.
- The child may cry when approached.
- The child may avoid eye contact, stare, or look disinterested.
- The child may not smile in social situations.

Self-Care
- The child may be anorexic or have a voracious appetite.
- The child may have developmental delay in attaining independence in activities of daily living.

Productivity

The child may have poorly developed or absent play skills.

Leisure

The child may have few, if any, interests in toys, games, or group activities.

TREATMENT/MANAGEMENT

Treatment models are not well defined. Such models as neurodevelopmental and sensory integration should be useful. Treatment should be aimed at decreasing the impact of the root cause. A multidisciplinary approach is frequently used.

Motor

Increase/improve gross and fine motor skills to range of normal development.

Sensory

Increase or decrease response to stimuli to range of normal. See sections on sensory integration for specific examples.

Cognitive
- Increase or improve attention span.
- Increase or improve memory and retention skills.
- Instruct caregiver regarding normal growth and development, selection of toys and games, play activities with infants and young children, and adequate nutrition.

Intrapersonal
Decrease signs of apathy, withdrawal, and irritability by engaging the child in play activities that require physical motor skills that are within the child's developmental level and are fun for the child to do.

Interpersonal
Encourage and promote interaction and communication between child and caregivers by establishing eye contact, talking, singing, or gesturing to the child, and touching or holding the child within the level of the child's tolerance. Avoid overfatigue and overstimulation.

Self-Care
- Develop or improve feeding skills, integrate oral reflexes, reduce oral-tactile hypersensitivity, and promote swallowing pattern.
- Increase independence through improvement in skills in daily living tasks.

Productivity
Develop or improve play skills.

PRECAUTIONS
- Observe the child carefully for any signs of organic pathology that might contribute to the problem of failure to thrive.
- Make sure the child is not overstimulated or fatigued.

PROGNOSIS AND OUTCOME
- The child demonstrates improved reflex maturation such as integration of primitive reflexes.
- The child demonstrates improved postural reflexes.
- The child demonstrates improved oral motor development.
- The child has progressed developmentally in the areas of gross and fine motor skills.
- The child demonstrates improved orienting to sensory stimuli.
- The child demonstrates normalized response to stimuli and less hyper- or hyporesponsiveness
- The child is able to attend to tasks and activities for a longer time.
- The child smiles, coos, or laughs when enjoying an activity.
- The child interacts with caregiver by cuddling or reaching to be picked up.
- The child has improved skills in daily living.
- The child has improved play skills.
- Parents or caregivers demonstrate improved skills in interacting with the child.

REFERENCES

Denton, R. 1986. An occupational therapy protocol for assessing infants and toddlers who fail to thrive. *American Journal of Occupational Therapy* 40(3):352-8.

Hunter, J.G., and G.F. Powell. 1990. Failure to thrive. In *Early occupational therapy intervention: Neonates to three years*, ed. C.J. Semmler and J.G. Hunter, 185-96. Gaithersburg, MD: Aspen Publishers, Inc.

Lewis, J.A. 1982. Oral motor assessment and treatment of feeding difficulties. In *Failure to thrive in infancy and early childhood*, ed. P.J. Accardo, 265-95. Baltimore: University Park Press.

Martin, H.P., and T. Miller. 1976. Treatment of specific delays and deficits. In *The abused child: A multidisciplinary approach to developmental issues and treatment*, ed. H.P. Marin and C.H. Kempe, 179-88. Cambridge, MA: Ballinger Publishing Co.

Powell, G.F., and J. Low. 1983. Behavior in nonorganic failure to thrive. *Journal of Developmental and Behavioral Pediatrics* 4:26-33.

Rowee, G.F., J.F. Low, and M.A. Speers. 1987. Behavior as a diagnostic aid in failure-to-thrive. *Journal of Developmental and Behavioral Pediatrics* 8(1):18-24.

High Risk Infant

DESCRIPTION

Children are at high risk when factors occur before, during, or after birth that predict a greater probability of the child incurring developmental delays, disorders, or deficits. The body systems involved may include the respiratory, cardiovascular, metabolic, nutritional, immunologic, and ophthalmologic.

CAUSE

Causes may be related to hereditary factors, maternal history, labor and delivery problems, gestational weight and age, prematurity, postmaturity, and social or psychological factors.

ASSESSMENT

Areas

- muscle tone—hyper- or hypotonic
- reflex development and maturation
- range of motion (note discrepancies between the two sides of the body)
- gross motor skills and coordination
- hand functions
- praxis, motor planning
- bilateral integration
- sensory registration, acuity
- sensory processing, hyper- or hyporesponsiveness
- attending behavior—alerting, arousal
- focus of attention, attention span, concentration
- ability to calm oneself after stimuli

- response to being picked up or handled
- vocalization and crying
- oral motor skills

Instruments

- Miller Assessment for Preschoolers by L. Miller, San Antonio, TX: Psychological Corporation, 1982.
- Hawaii Early Learning Profile (HELP), rev. ed. by S. Furuno, et al., Palo Alto, CA: VORT Corporation, 1985.
- Early Intervention Developmental Profile and Developmental Screening of Handicapped Infants by D'Eugenio and Rogers, Ann Arbor, MI: University of Michigan Publications Distribution Service, 1975.
- Southern California Postrotary Nystagmus Test by A.J. Ayres, Los Angeles: Western Psychological Services, 1972. (See Dutton, R.E. 1985. Reliability and clinical significance of the Southern California Postrotary Nystagmus Test. *Physical and Occupational Therapy in Pediatrics* 5(2/3):57-67.)
- Movement Assessment of Infants by L. Chandler, M.S. Andrews, and M.S. Swanson, Rolling Bay, WA: Infant Movement Research, 1980.
- Milani-Comparetti Developmental Examination by D. Kliewer et al., Omaha, NE: Meyer Children's Rehabilitation Institute, 1977 (not an occupational therapist).
- Neonatal Oral Motor Assessment Scale (NOMAS) by M.A. Braun and M. Palmer: A pilot study of oral motor dysfunction in "at risk" infants. *Physical and Occupational Therapy in Pediatrics* 5(4):13-25, 1989. (See also Case-Smith, J., P. Cooper, and V. Scala. 1989. Feeding efficiency of premature neonates. *American Journal of Occupational Therapy* 43(4):245-50.)

PROBLEMS

Motor

- delayed motor milestones
- muscle tone—Hypotonicity or hypertonicity
- obligatory response to reflex stimuli, such as ATNR (asymmetrical tonic neck reflex)
- decreased range of motion
- poor coordination between the two sides of the body
- atypical movement patterns—asymmetries, constant jerkiness

Sensory

- The child may fail to respond to sensory input—visual, aural, tactile, touch, temperature, proprioceptive, kinesthetic.
- The child may have hypersensitivity to sensory input.

Cognitive

- Eye contact is lacking.
- The child has an inability to remain alert even for brief periods of time.

Intrapersonal
- No change in facial expression is apparent.
- The child cries all the time and cannot be consoled.

Interpersonal
- The child does not respond to human contact and stiffens or arches back when picked up.
- The child does not make sounds or makes sounds outside of the human speech range (unusual sounds).

TREATMENT/MANAGEMENT
Models of treatment in NDT (neurodevelopmental therapy, Bobath) and sensory integration (Ayres).

Motor
- Improve muscle tone in trunk, shoulder girdle, and hip girdle (axial skeleton) to increase stability, and in arms and legs (appendicular skeleton) to increase movement.
- Increase flexor patterns in premature infants; increase extension patterns in full-term infants.
- Increase the quality of spontaneous patterns of movement through planned positioning.
- Increase orientation to midline through planned positioning.

Sensory
- Improve visual reactions and responses by putting faces or mobiles in the child's line of vision.
- Improve auditory reactions and responses by talking, singing, or exposing the child to sounds and music.
- Improve tactile reactions and responses by stroking, rubbing with lotions or oils, or allowing the child to touch various textures.
- Improve vestibular reactions and responses by gentle rocking or swinging the child in a hammock.
- Improve proprioceptive reactions and responses by placing weight and deep pressure on the soles of the child's feet.
- Facilitate the development of the child's reflex patterns, beginning with head-righting on through primitive reactions to equilibrium reactions.
- Decrease tactile defensiveness, if present, through the use of deep, rhythmical tactile input.

Cognitive
- Instruct parents about normal growth and developmental patterns.
- Instruct parents or caregivers about positioning and handling techniques.
- Instruct parents about methods of increasing alert state through the use of arrhythmic vestibular stimuli, such as bouncing and upright position, or tactile stimuli, such as a light touch to the face and body.

Intrapersonal
Assist the child to calm her- or himself through relaxation techniques designed to reduce stress, including slow, rhythmical rocking, deep proprioceptive input, and tight swaddling.

Interpersonal

Encourage the child to respond to handling, talking, and seeing human faces.

Self-Care

Encourage oral motor skills, including the suck-swallow reflex to permit feeding with a nipple, by using tactile stimulation of the mouth and gums, pressure on the cheeks and non-nutritive sucking.

Productivity

Help the child develop play skills to entertain him- or herself.

Leisure

Help the child discover preferred activities.

PRECAUTIONS

Watch for signs of sensory overload, including gaze aversion, staring, facial hypotonia, alterations in respiration or heart rate, jerkiness, hiccups, spitting, changes in the color of skin to dark or light tones, and mottling.

PROGNOSIS AND OUTCOME

- Infant's quality of muscle tone has improved, as evidenced by such actions as less extensor thrust.
- Infant's rate of gaining developmental milestones and reflex maturation has increased.
- Infant's response to sensory input has improved, as evidenced by tactile awareness.
- Infant has increased attending behavior (eye contact).
- Infant has increased attention span.
- Infant responds to being picked up by flexing (cuddling) or changing facial expression (smiling).
- Infant is able to calm him- or herself.
- Infant has better oral motor skills.

REFERENCES

Anderson, J., and J. Auster-Liebhaber. 1984. Developmental therapy in the neonatal intensive care unit. *Physical and Occupational Therapy in Pediatrics* 4(1):89-105.

At-risk infants. In *Evaluation and management of infants and young children with developmental disabilities*, ed. M.E. Copeland and J.R. Kimmel, 263-87. Baltimore: Paul H. Brookes Publishing.

Blackburn, S.T. 1986. Assessment of risk: Perinatal, family and environmental perspectives. *Physical and Occupational Therapy in Pediatrics* 6(3/4):1-5, 120.

Braun, M.A., and M.M. Palmer. 1985-86. A pilot study of oral-motor dysfunction in "at risk" infants. *Physical and Occupational Therapy in Pediatrics* 5(4):13-25.

Campbell, S.K. 1986. Organizational and educational considerations in creating an environment to promote development of high-risk neonates. *Physical and Occupational Therapy in Pediatrics* 6(3/4):191-204.

Case-Smith, J. 1987. An efficacy study of occupational therapy with high-risk neonates. In *Proceedings of the Occupational Therapy for Maternal & Child Health Conference*, vol. 2, *Efficacy, Research & Related Topics*, 76-89. Rockville, MD: American Occupational Therapy Association.

Coolman, R.B., F.C. Bennett, C.J. Sells, et al. 1985. Neuromotor development of graduates of the neonatal intensive care unit: Patterns encountered in the first two years of life. *Journal of Developmental and Behavioral Pediatrics* 6(6):327-33.

Deitz, J.C., and T.K. Crowe. 1985. Developmental status of children exhibiting postrotatory nystagmus durations of zero second. *Physical and Occupational Therapy in Pediatrics* 5(2/3):69-79.

Fetters, L. 1986. Sensorimotor management of the high-risk neonate. *Physical and Occupational Therapy* 6(3/4):217-29.

Haley, S.M., et al. 1986. Item reliability of the Movement Assessment of Infants. *Physical and Occupational Therapy in Pediatrics* 6(1):21-39.

Harris, M. 1986. Oral-motor management of the high-risk neonate. *Physical and Occupational Therapy in Pediatrics* 6(3/4):231-53.

Harris, S.R., and D.R. Brady. 1986. Infant neuromotor assessment instruments: A review. *Physical and Occupational Therapy in Pediatrics* 6(3/4):121-53.

Kennedy, K.S. 1987. Occupational therapy parent training techniques for high-risk infants and their families. *Proceedings of the Occupational Therapy for Maternal & Child Health Conference*, vol. 2, *Efficacy, Research & Related Topics*, 90-104. Rockville, MD: American Occupational Therapy Association.

Kopp, C.B., and S.R. Kaler. 1989. Risk in infancy: Origins and implications. *American Psychologist* 44(2):224-30.

Leander, D., and G. Pettett. 1986. Parental response to the birth of a high-risk neonate: Dynamics and management. *Physical and Occupational Therapy in Pediatrics* 6(3/4):205-16.

Majnemer, A., B. Rosenblatt, and P. Riley. 1988. Prognostic significance of the auditory brainstem evoked response in high-risk neonates. *Developmental Medicine and Child Neurology* 30:43-52.

Moore, J.C. 1986. Neonatal neuropathology. *Physical and Occupational Therapy in Pediatrics* 6(3/4): 55-90.

Pelletier, J.M., and A. Palmeri. 1985. High-risk infants. In *Occupational therapy for children*, ed. P.N. Clark and A.S. Allen, 361-81, 292-311. St. Louis: C.V. Mosby.

Roberts, B.L., N. Marlow, and R.W.I. Cooke. 1989. Motor problems among children of very low birthweight. *British Journal of Occupational Therapy* 52(3):97-9.

Rowe, J.S., and J. Geggie. 1987. Intervention for a nonoral feeder: Collaboration between an occupational therapist and a dietician. In *Problems with eating: Intervention for children and adults with developmental disabilities,* ed. K.L. Reed, 15-20. Rockville, MD: American Occupational Therapy Association.

Sehnal, J.P., and A. Palmeri. 1989. High-risk infants. In *Occupational therapy for children*, 2nd ed., ed. P.N. Pratt and A.S. Allen, 361-81. St. Louis: C.V. Mosby.

Semmler, C.J., et al. 1987. Efficacy of positioners in preventing position-induced dolichocephaly in a very-low-birth-weight neonate. *Proceedings of the Occupational Therapy for Maternal & Child Health Conference,* vol. 2, *Efficacy, Research & Related Topics,* 105-118. Rockville, MD: Occupational Therapy Association.

Stern, K.M. 1986. Physical and occupational therapy on a newborn intensive care unit. *Rehabilitation Nursing* 11(1):26-7.

VanderLinden, D. 1985. Ability of the Milani-Comparetti Developmental Examination to predict motor outcome. *Physical and Occupational Therapy in Pediatrics* 5(1):27-38.

Vergara, E.R., and J.C. Angley. 1990. Preparing families to take home a high-risk infant. *Occupational Therapy Practice* 2(1):66-83.

Wilson, M. 1986. Nutrition and feeding of the high risk infant. In *Home care for the high risk infant: A holistic guide to using technology*, ed. E. Ahmann. Gaithersburg, MD: Aspen Publishers, Inc.

Learning Disorders

DESCRIPTION

Learning disorders are characterized by an inability to acquire, retain, or generalize specific skills or sets of information because of deficiencies or defects in attention, memory, or reasoning, or deficiencies in producing responses associated with a desired and skilled behavior. Other related terms are learning disability, neurologically impaired, minimal brain dysfunction, perceptual motor dysfunction, perceptual deficit disorder, dyslexia, attention deficit disorder, and hyperkinesis.

CAUSE

No single cause or set of symptoms has been identified. Genetic and neurologic causes may be involved. The ratio of affected males to females is about 5:1. Between 3 percent and 15 percent of school children may be affected.

ASSESSMENT

Areas

- muscle tone
- reflex development
- gross motor development
- coordination—visual motor, bilateral, reciprocal
- fine motor skills, dexterity, and manipulation
- level of activity, hyper or hypo
- motor planning (praxis) and sequencing skills
- postural control—midline stability, joint stability, use of righting, and equilibrium reactions for balance
- bilateral integration and crossing midline
- ocular motor control and nystagmus
- sensory registration (awareness and orienting behavior)
- sensory sensitivity, including (1) tactile: light touch, pressure, temperature, vibration, and two-point discrimination, (2) proprioceptive, (3) vestibular: linear (vertical and horizontal) and angular, (4) visual: acuity, peripheral vision, color vision, and (5) auditory: localization, discrimination, identification
- perceptual skills, including (1) visual: form constancy, position in space, visual closure, figure ground, depth perception, part-whole, (2) auditory, (3) body scheme: laterality, directionality, right/left discrimination, (4) tactile: stereognosis, graphesthesia, and (5) kinesthesia.
- attending skills
- attention or concentration skills
- short- and long-term memory skills
- concept formation and categorization
- learning skills—integration, generalization, synthesis
- problem-solving skills
- self-perception and mastery
- coping skills
- social conduct skills
- communication skills
- self-control
- daily living skills
- play skills
- academic skills
- productive skills
- leisure skills

Instruments

- Southern California Sensory Integration Tests by A.J. Ayres, Los Angeles: Western Psychological Services, 1980.
- Sensory Integration and Praxis Tests by A.J. Ayres, Los Angeles: Western Psychological Corporation, 1989.
- Sensorimotor Integration for Developmentally Disabled Children, 2nd ed., by P. Montgomery and E. Richter, Los Angeles: Western Psychological Corporation, 1990.
- DeGangi-Berk Test of Sensory Integration by G.A. DeGangi and R.A. Berk, Los Angeles: Western Psychological Corporation, 1983.
- Jacobs Prevocational Skills Assessment by K. Jacobs, in *Occupational therapy: Work related programs and assessment*, Boston: Little, Brown & Co., 1985.
- Miller Assessment of Preschoolers by L.J. Miller, Littleton, CO: Foundation for Knowledge in Development, 1981.
- Prone Extension Posture Test by J.L. Gregory-Flock and E.J. Yerxa, *American Journal of Occupational Therapy* 38(3):187-94, 1984.
- Southern California Postrotary Nystagmus Test by A.J. Ayres, Los Angeles: Western Psychological Corporation, 1972. (See also Polatajko, H.J. 1983. The Southern California Postrotary Nystagmus Test: A validity study. *Canadian Journal of Occupational Therapy* 50(4):119-23.)
- A Guide to Testing Clinical Observation in Kindergartners by W. Dunn, Rockville, MD: American Occupational Therapy Association, 1981. (See also Dunn, W. 1986. Developmental and environmental contexts for interpreting clinical observation. *Sensory Integration Special Interest Section Newsletter* 9(2):4-7.
- An Evaluation of Sensory Integrative Dysfunction, adapted from A.J. Ayres, in *A team approach for therapists: Pediatric rehabilitation*, ed. M.K. Logigian and J.D. Ward, 107-110. Boston: Little, Brown & Co.
- Miller Assessment for Preschoolers by L.A. Miller, San Antonio, TX: Psychological Corporation, 1982. (See also DeGangi, G.A. 1983. A critique of the standardization of the Miller Assessment for Preschoolers. *American Journal of Occupational Therapy* 37(5):333-40; and Banus, B.J. 1984. The Miller Assessment for Preschoolers (MAP): An introduction and review. *American Journal of Occupational Therapy* 37(7):452-61.
- Quick Neurological Screening Test by M. Mutti, H.M. Sterling, and N.V. Spalding, Novato, CA: Academic Therapy Pub., 1978 (not occupational therapists).
- Bruininks-Oseretsky Test of Motor Proficiency by R.H. Bruininks, Circle Pines, MN: American Guidance Services, 1978 (not an occupational therapist).

PROBLEMS

Motor
- The person lacks skill in eye-motor coordination, including being labeled clumsy and performing poorly on eye-tracking tasks.
- The person may have delays in developing gross motor skills needed for such functions as smooth gait, running, skipping, jumping, or throwing and catching a ball.
- The person has difficulties in fine motor dexterity and manipulation that lead to such problems as poor control of a pencil and an inability to cut on a line or color within the lines.
- The person has difficulty in motor planning (dyspraxia) and motor sequencing.

- The person may be hyperactive or hypoactive.
- The person may have unusual movements, such as choreiform (jerky, rapid, irregular) movements of the face, arms, or legs.
- The person may have dysdiadochokinesia or an inability to rapidly and smoothly repeat alternating movements, such as supination and pronation of the forearm.
- The person may have ocular motor apraxia, such as an inability to track or scan smoothly due to strabismus (motor imbalance of the eye muscles), amblyopia, diplopia, nystagmus, or paralysis of gaze.
- The person's primitive reflexes may not be fully integrated, such as the ATNR or STNR (asymmetrical or symmetrical tonic neck reflex).
- The person's equilibrium and postural reactions may be poorly developed.

Sensory

- The person may have difficulties in visual perception, especially figure-ground, part-whole relationships and position in space.
- The person may have poor proprioceptive skills.
- The person may have difficulties in auditory perception, especially discrimination.
- The person may have disturbances in body image, especially integration of the two sides of the body.
- The person may be tactilely defensive and lack tactile discrimination.
- The person may be unaware of position of body or body parts in space (laterality and directionality).
- The person may be hyper- or hyporesponsive to vestibular stimulation and may have gravitational insecurity or intolerance to movement.

Cognitive

- The person may have a short attention span and be inattentive or overattentive (fixates on one aspect of a situation or object).
- The person may be easily distracted.
- The person may have short-term memory loss.
- The person may perseverate.
- The person may have difficulty orienting to time, space, or distance.
- The person may have difficulty understanding concepts of size, color, shape, sameness, and difference.

Intrapersonal

- The person has poor self-perception.
- The person may show poor impulse control.
- The person has non goal-directed behavior.

Interpersonal

- The person may be withdrawn or the class clown.
- The person may have mild dysphasia or inability to process language.

Self-Care

The person may have difficulty performing some activities of daily living, such as tying shoelaces.

Productivity
- The person may have poorly developed play skills.
- The person is at least two years behind age level in one or more school areas, such as reading, spelling, or math.

Leisure

The person may have few leisure activities.

TREATMENT/MANAGEMENT

Motor
- Integrate primitive reflexes and improve muscle tone through positions and tasks designed to counter the effects of the reflex.
- Improve gross and fine motor skills.

Sensory
- Increase the frequency, duration, or complexity of adaptive responses to sensory input.
- Improve motor planning skills.

Cognitive
- Improve the person's ability to organize ideas, plan a sequence of action (steps to take), and execute a plan.
- Increase attention span and concentration.
- Increase memory skills.

Intrapersonal
- Increase the person's self-esteem and self-confidence.
- Improve coping skills.

Interpersonal
- Improve social interaction skills.
- Increase communication skills.

Self-Care

Improve performance of daily living skills.

Productivity
- Improve level of play skills.
- Improve level of academic skills.

Leisure

Increase the person's exposure to possible leisure interests.

PRECAUTIONS
- Observe child for signs of sensory overload, such as flushing, blanching, or perspiring.

- Observe child for signs of overinhibition of brain-stem functions, such as depressed respiratory functions.
- Monitor child for potential accidents due to lack of skills or lack of judgment on the part of the child.

PROGNOSIS AND OUTCOME

- The person demonstrates integration of primitive reflexes and correct use of protective and equilibrium reflexes.
- The person demonstrates normal muscle tone.
- The person performs gross and fine motor skills at appropriate age level.
- The person demonstrates dexterity and coordination tasks at appropriate age level.
- The person demonstrates improvement in motor planning and praxis behavior.
- The person demonstrates improved attention span and concentration.
- The person shows improvement in coping skills.
- The person demonstrates improved social skills.
- The person is able to perform activities of daily living at appropriate age level.
- The person demonstrates improvement in play and academic skills.
- The person demonstrates improvement in leisure skills.

REFERENCES

Anderson, J., and J. Hinojosa. 1984. Parents and therapists in a professional partnership. *American Journal of Occupational Therapy* 38(7):452-61.

Bundy, A.C., et al. 1987. Concurrent validity of equilibrium tests in boys with learning disabilities with and without vestibular dysfunction. *American Journal of Occupational Therapy* 41(1):28-34.

Cermak, S.A. 1984. Right-left discrimination in learning disabled and normal control boys. *Physical and Occupational Therapy in Pediatrics* 4(2):63-77.

Cermak, S.A., and A.J. Ayres. 1984. Crossing the body midline in learning-disabled and normal children. *American Journal of Occupational Therapy* 38(1):35-9.

Cermak, S.A., and A. Henderson. 1985. Learning disabilities. In *Neurological rehabilitation*, ed. D.A. Umphred, 207-48, and 2nd ed. 1990, 283-331. St. Louis: C.V. Mosby.

Clark, F., Z. Mailloux, and D. Parham. 1989. Sensory integration and children with learning disabilities. In *Occupational Therapy for Children*, 2nd ed., ed. P.N. Pratt and A.S. Allen, 457-509. St. Louis: C.V. Mosby.

Clyse, S.J., and M.A. Short. 1983. The relationship between dynamic balance and postrotary nystagmus in learning disabled children. *Physical and Occupational Therapy in Pediatrics* 3(3):63-73.

DeGangi, G.A. 1987. Critique of a sensory-motor appraisal. *Physical and Occupational Therapy in Pediatrics* 7(1):71-80.

DeGangi, G.A., and P.A. Berk. 1983. Psychometric analysis of the Test of Sensory Integration. *Physical and Occupational Therapy in Pediatrics* 3(2):43-60.

Fairgrieve, E.M. 1989. Alternative means of assessment: A comparison of standardised tests identifying minimal cerebral dysfunction. *British Journal of Occupational Therapy* 52(3):88-92.

Humphries, T., M. Wright, B. McDougall, et al. 1990. The efficacy of sensory integration therapy for children with learning disability. *Physical and Occupational Therapy in Pediatrics* 10(3):1-17.

Hung, S.S., A.G. Fisher, and S.A. Cermak. 1987. The performance of learning-disabled and normal young men on the Test of Visual-Perceptual Skills. *American Journal of Occupational Therapy* 41(12):790-7.

Ingolia, P., S.A. Cermak, and D. Nelson. 1982. The effect of choreoathetoid movements on the Quick Neurological Screening Test. *American Journal of Occupational Therapy* 36(12):801-7.

Jacobs, K., and M.K. Logigian. 1989. Learning disabilities. In *A team approach for therapists: Pediatric rehabilitation*, ed. M.K. Logigian, 95-153. Boston: Little, Brown & Co.

Kelly, G. 1985. Motivation in learning disabled children. *British Journal of Occupational Therapy* 48(11):340-2.

Kimball, J.G. 1990. Using the Sensory Integration and Praxis Tests to measure change: A pilot study. *American Journal of Occupational Therapy* 44(7):603-8.

Kinnealey, M. 1989. Tactile functions in learning-disabled and normal children: Reliability and validity considerations. *Occupational Therapy Journal of Research* 9(1):3-15.

McKibbin, E., and J. King. 1983. Activity group counseling for learning-disabled children with behavior problems. *American Journal of Occupational Therapy* 37(9):617-23.

Miller, L.J., and T.A. Sprong. 1987. A comparison of the Miller Assessment for Preschoolers and Developmental Indicators for the Assessment of Learning-Revised. *Physical and Occupational Therapy in Pediatrics* 7(1):57-69.

Morrison, D., and J. Sublett. 1983. Reliability of the Southern California Postrotary Nystagmus Test with learning-disabled children. *American Journal of Occupational Therapy* 37(10):694-8.

Murray, E.A., S.A. Cermak, and V. O'Brien. 1990. The relationship between form and space perception, constructional abilities, and clumsiness in children. *American Journal of Occupational Therapy* 44(7):623-8.

O'Brien, V., S.A. Cermak, and E. Murray. 1988. The relationship between visual-perceptual motor abilities and clumsiness in children with and without learning disabilities. *American Journal of Occupational Therapy* 42(6):359-63.

Ottenbacher, K. 1982. Patterns of postrotary nystagmus in three learning-disabled children. *American Journal of Occupational Therapy* 36(10):657-63.

Ottenbacher, K., D. Haley, C. Abbott, et al. 1984. Human figure drawing ability and vestibular processing dysfunction in learning-disabled children. *Journal of Clinical Psychology* 40(4):1084-9.

Palisano, R.J. 1989. Comparison of two methods of service delivery for students with learning disabilities. *Physical and Occupational Therapy in Pediatrics* 9(3):79-100.

Polatajko, H.J. 1985. A critical look at vestibular dysfunction in learning-disabled children. *Developmental Medicine & Child Neurology* 27:283-92.

Riggan, J.S. 1983. A learning abilities program for learning disabled soldiers. *Occupational Therapy in Mental Health* 3(2):49-54.

Royeen, C.B. 1989. Commentary on "Tactile functions in learning-disabled and normal children: Reliability and validity considerations." *Occupational Therapy Journal of Research* 9(1):16-23.

Schaaf, R.C. 1990. Play behavior and occupational therapy. *American Journal of Occupational Therapy* 44(1):68-75.

Schaffer, R. 1984. Sensory integration therapy with learning disabled children: A critical review. *Canadian Journal of Occupational Therapy* 51(2):73-7.

Schaffer, R., et al. 1989. A study of children with learning disabilities and sensorimotor problems or Let's not throw the baby out with the bathwater. *Physical and Occupational Therapy* 9(3):101-17.

Stephenson, E., C. McKay, and R. Chesson. 1990. An investigative study of early developmental factors in children with motor/learning difficulties. *British Journal of Occupational Therapy* 53(1):4-6.

Stilwell, J.M. 1981. Relationship between development of the body-righting reaction and manual midline crossing behavior in the learning disabled. *American Journal of Occupational Therapy* 35(6): 391-8.

Stilwell, J.M., and M.C. Heiniger. 1983. Tilt reactions in sitting in normal and learning disabled children. *Physical and Occupational Therapy in Pediatrics* 3(4):43-58.

Taylor, J. 1985. The sequence and structure of handwriting competence: Where are the breakdown points in mastery of handwriting? *British Journal of Occupational Therapy* 48(4):2-5,7.

Zemke, R., S. Knuth, and J. Chase. 1984. Change in self-concepts of children with learning difficulties during a residential camp experience. *Occupational Therapy in Mental Health* 4(4):1-12.

Ziviani, J., A. Poulsen, and A. O'Brien. 1982. Correlation of the Bruininks-Oseretsky Test of Motor Proficiency with the Southern California Sensory Integration Tests. *American Journal of Occupational Therapy* 36(8):519-23.

Mental Retardation—Adult

DESCRIPTION

A mentally retarded adult is defined as a person who is 18 years old or older, has been previously diagnosed as mentally retarded, and does not function as an independent adult.

CAUSE

The cause of mental retardation in adults is related to the original diagnosis and the failure to achieve the skills necessary to function independently without a guardian in the community.

ASSESSMENT

Areas
- developmental profile
- gross motor skills and coordination
- fine motor skills, manipulation, dexterity, and bilateral coordination
- motor planning/praxis
- sensory registration and level of responsiveness (hypo or hyper)
- perceptual skills, including matching and discrimination
- attention span
- memory—general knowledge, short-term, long-term
- social skills
- daily living skills
- productivity—work, homemaking, and community skills
- work capacity evaluation
- leisure skills and interests

Instruments
- Motor Development Checklist by A. Doudlah, Library and Information Center, Central Wisconsin Center for the Developmentally Disabled, 317 Knutson Dr., Madison, WI 53704. (See also M. Gevelinger, K.J. Ottenbacher, and T. Tiffany. 1988. The reliability of the Motor Development Checklist. *American Journal of Occupational Therapy* 42(2): 81-6.)
- Adult Screening Questionnaire by C. Exner. (See S. Lefkofsky and T.E. Avi-Itzhak. 1989. On the formative stages of the Adult Screening Questionnaire: A managerial approach for screening adult developmentally disabled clients. *Occupational Therapy in Health Care* 6(2/3):107-28.)
- Adult Skills Evaluation Survey for Persons with Mental Retardation (ASES) by J.T. Herrick and H.E. Lowe, 770 North Fair Oaks Ave., Pasadena, CA 91103.
- Sensory Integration Inventory for Adults with Developmental Disabilities: User's Guide by J.E. Reisman and B. Hanschu, Hugo, MN: PDP Press, 1990.
- Tactile-Vestibular Behavioral Checklist by J. Brocklehurst-Woods, *American Journal of Occupational Therapy* 44(6):536, 1990.

PROBLEMS

Motor
- The person may have poor eye-hand coordination and dexterity.
- The person may have poorly developed gross motor skills and difficulty executing purposeful movements.

Sensory

- The person may have poor discrimination skills in vestibular, tactile, proprioceptive, and visual systems.
- The person may have stereotypical behaviors (head banging, rocking, face or eye rubbing) related to poor integration of sensory input, especially tactile, vestibular, and proprioceptive.

Cognitive

- The person is unable to manage time without guidance from others.
- The person has poor attending behavior and short attention span.
- The person usually does not learn from incidental experiences and generally requires structured learning situations.

Intrapersonal

- The person does not exhibit goal-directed and task-oriented behavior.
- The person has poor self-perception.
- The person may have poor impulse control.
- The person has poor coping skills, especially in handling stress.
- The person frequently withdraws.

Interpersonal

- The person has difficulty in relating to authority figures.
- The person has difficulty relating to peers and peer group.
- The person has poor imitation skills.

Self-Care

The person may not perform activities of daily living without guidance from another person.

Productivity

- The person has not mastered basic educational tasks.
- The person has poor or no work habits and skills.
- The person may have poor home-management skills.

Leisure

The person has poor or no leisure interests.

TREATMENT/MANAGEMENT

Motor

- Increase motor development through involvement in gross motor activities and repetitive actions, such as locomotion, ball playing, and balancing.
- Increase eye-hand coordination.

Sensory

- Increase vestibular, tactile, proprioceptive, and visual input to facilitate motor performance and decrease stereotypical behaviors.
- Improve discrimination skills through use of various movements, various textures, various positions, and by having the person match various sizes, colors, and shapes.

Cognitive

- Increase the person's ability to manage and organize time into cycles of self-care, productivity, leisure, rest, and sleep.
- Increase the person's attention span (amount of time spent working on a task).
- Improve the person's ability to follow directions in completing a task.

Intrapersonal

- Provide opportunities for increasing self-esteem and sense of mastery through successful completion of projects with simple, short-term activities.
- Encourage self-confidence and pride in appearance.
- Provide instruction in stress management to increase the person's coping skills.

Interpersonal

- Provide group experiences through group activities.
- Promote and develop the person's language and communication skills.
- Increase the person's social skills, including concepts of socially acceptable behavior, tolerance, and respect for others.

Self-Care

- Increase the person's ability to function independently in all areas of daily living through structured learning situations.
- Provide adaptive equipment and teach the person to use the equipment if it is needed to help the person perform daily living tasks.

Productivity

- Increase the person's home management skills, including meal planning, cooking, housework, washing clothes, home safety, budgeting, shopping, and simple maintenance tasks.
- Increase basic works and skills.

Leisure

Encourage the person to explore and develop leisure activities.

PRECAUTIONS

No specific precautions are provided in the occupational therapy literature.

PROGNOSIS AND OUTCOME

- The person is able to perform self-care skills independently.

- The person is able to perform independent living skills alone or participate in a group living arrangement, including home management, meal planning and preparation, budgeting, and shopping.
- The person has mastered socially acceptable behaviors, including awareness of self, basic conversation skills, and cooperative behavior.
- The person demonstrates knowledge of how to use adaptive equipment, when to use it, and how to maintain it.
- The person is able to apply and interview for a job and demonstrates skills needed to keep a job, such as coming to work on time, performing assigned duties, and interacting with peers.
- The person demonstrates leisure interests and skills.
- The person demonstrates knowledge of community agencies that can assist in promoting individual rights, attaining government services, and providing personal services.

REFERENCES

Allen, S., and N. Willett. 1986. Improving the communication skills of mentally handicapped adults. *British Journal of Occupational Therapy* 49(4):130-2.

Bodenham, J. 1988. Rehabilitation of long-term mentally handicapped in community housing. In *Occupational therapy in mental health: Principles in practice*, ed. D.W. Scott and N. Katz, 62-76. London: Taylor & Francis.

Brocklehurst, W.J. 1990. The use of tactile and vestibular stimulation to reduce stereotypic behaviors in two adults with mental retardation. *American Journal of Occupational Therapy* 44(6):536-41.

Close, W., M. Carpenter, and S. Cibiri. 1986. An evaluation study of sensory motor therapy for profoundly retarded adults. *Canadian Journal of Occupational Therapy* 53(5):259-64.

Herrick, J.T., and H.E. Lowe. 1989. Developmental growth in "Action": A pilot program for the adult retarded. *Occupational Therapy in Health Care* 6(2/3):189-95.

Hong, C.S., and J. Mussell. 1986. Occupational therapy with the mentally handicapped—assessment and treatment methods. *International Journal of Rehabilitation Research* 9(2):174-8.

Huff, D.M., and S.C. Harris. 1987. Using sensorimotor integrative treatment with mentally retarded adults. *American Journal of Occupational Therapy* 41(4):227-31.

Isaac, D. 1988. Adults with a mental handicap: Working with support staff to achieve occupational therapy aims. *British Journal of Occupational Therapy* 51(4):120-2.

Kelin-Parris, C., T. Clermont-Michel, and J. O'Neill. 1986. Effectiveness and efficiency of criterion testing versus interviewing for collecting functional assessment information. *American Journal of Occupational Therapy* 40(7):486-91.

Kielhofner, G., and S. Miyake. 1981. The therapeutic use of games with mentally retarded adults. *American Journal of Occupational Therapy* 35(6):375-82.

Martin, M.J. 1987. Shoulder mobility in the older mentally retarded adult. *Proceedings of the Occupational Therapy for Maternal & Child Health Conference*, vol. 2, *Efficacy, Research & Related Topics*, 119-128. Rockville, MD: American Occupational Therapy Association.

McGown C. 1986. Moving on: An outline of group work with mentally handicapped people preparing to move out of hospital into a group home. *British Journal of Occupational Therapy* 49(4):114-6.

Morse, A. 1987. A cultural intervention model for developmentally disabled adults: An expanded role of occupational therapy. Chaverim, a non-traditional community based program. *Occupational Therapy in Health Care* 4(1):103-14.

Neistadt, M.E. 1987. An occupational therapy program for adults with developmental disabilities. *American Journal of Occupational Therapy* 41(7):433-8.

Neistadt, M.E. 1986. Occupational therapy treatment goals for adults with developmental disabilities. *American Journal of Occupational Therapy* 40(10):672-8.

Nochajski, S.B., and C.Y. Gordon. 1987. The use of Trivial Pursuit in teaching community living skills to adults with developmental disabilities. *American Journal of Occupational Therapy* 41(1):10-5.

Resman, M.H. 1981. Effect of sensory stimulation on eye contact in a profoundly retarded adult. *American Journal of Occupational Therapy* 35(1):31-5.

Rice, M.S., and D.L. Nelson. 1988. Effect of choice making on a self-care activity in mentally retarded adult and adolescent males. *Occupational Therapy Journal of Research* 8(3):17-85.

Schmidt, D. 1987. Occupational therapy and feeding in a large institution for mentally retarded persons. In *Problems with eating: Interventions for children and adults with developmental disabilities*, American Occupational Therapy Association, 115-28. Rockville, MD: American Occupational Therapy Association.

Shalik, L.D., and H. Shalik. 1987. Cluster homes: A community for profoundly and severely retarded persons. *American Journal of Occupational Therapy* 41(4):222-6.

Smith, J. 1983. An activities approach to the treatment of mentally retarded clients in an acute care psychiatric hospital. *Occupational Therapy in Mental Health* 3(1):31-41.

Stephan, R.A. 1987. Audiotape instruction of face-washing skills for an adult with mental retardation. *American Journal of Occupational Therapy* 41(3):184-5.

Warren, L. 1986. Helping the developmentally disabled adult. *American Journal of Occupational Therapy* 40(4):227-9.

Mental Retardation—Child

DESCRIPTION

Mental retardation in children is defined as significantly subaverage general intellectual functioning existing concurrently with deficits in adaptive behavior and manifested during the developmental period (American Association on Mental Deficiency, 1983). See also Down's syndrome.

CAUSE

Ten groups of etiologic factors are recognized by the American Association on Mental Deficiency: (1) infections and intoxications, (2) trauma or physical agents, (3) metabolism or nutrition, (4) gross brain disease (postnatal), (5) unknown prenatal influence, (6) chromosomal anomalies, (7) other conditions originating in the prenatal period, (8) following psychiatric disorder, (9) environmental influences, and (10) other conditions.

ASSESSMENT

Areas

- reflex development and integration
- muscle tone
- range of motion
- hand functions
- balance and postural control
- muscle strength
- gross motor development and coordination
- fine motor coordination, manipulation, dexterity
- bilateral integration
- praxis or motor planning
- sensory awareness
- sensory processing

- attention span
- ability to follow directions
- self-perception
- social roles
- communication skills
- coping skills
- social skills
- daily living skills
- play skills
- productivity history, skills, values, interests
- leisure skills and interests

Instruments

- Denver Developmental Screening Test by W. Frankenburg, J. Dodds, A. Fandal, et al., Denver, CO: Ladoca Project and Publishing Foundation, 1975 (not occupational therapists).
- Milani-Comparetti Motor Developmental Screening Test by J. Trembath, Omaha, NB: Meyer Children's Rehabilitation Institute, 1977 (not an occupational therapist).
- Vulpe Assessment Battery, rev. ed. by S.G. Vulpe, Laurel, MD: RAMSCO Publishing, 1987.
- The Sensorimotor Performance Analysis by E.W. Richter and P.C. Montgomery, Hugo, MN: PDP Press, 1989.
- Georgia Retardation Center Occupational Therapy Service Screening Tool and Georgia Retardation Center Occupational Therapy Department ADL in Food Preparation Skills, in P.N. Pratt and A.S. Allen. 1989. *Occupational therapy for children*, 2nd ed., 433-6. St. Louis: C.V. Mosby.
- Tennessee Self Concept Scale, revised by W. Fitts and G.H. Reid, San Antonio, TX: The Psychological Corporation, 1988 (not occupational therapists).

PROBLEMS

Motor
- The child may have scoliosis, lordosis, or kyphosis.
- The child may have dislocated hips.
- The child may have ankylosing (fusing) of back, elbow, hips, and shoulders.
- The child may have stiff joints.
- The child may have hyperflexible or hyperextensible joints.
- The child may have various hand deformities, such as syndactyly (fusion of fingers), brachydactyly (shortness of fingers), polydactyly (partial extra finger), oligodactyly (missing finger), clinodactyly (short, tapered fingers), or claw hand deformities.
- The child may have lymphedema (puffy swelling on the dorsum of the hand).
- The child may have spastic paralysis of extremities.
- The child may have atrophy of various tissues.
- The child may have athetosis or choreoathetosis.

- The child may be hypokinetic or hyperkinetic.
- The child may have ataxia.
- The child may have hypotonia or hypertonia.
- The child may have tetany.
- The child may have seizures.

Sensory
- The child may have various visual disorders, such as homonymous hemianopsia, cataracts, strabismus, or nystagmus.
- The child may be hypo- or hyperresponsive to touch stimuli.
- The child may be hypo- or hyperresponsive to vestibular stimuli.
- The child may be hypo- or hyperresponsive to proprioceptive stimuli.
- The child may have a hearing loss.
- The child may have insensitivity to pain.
- The child may have impairment of sense of taste or smell.
- The child may engage in self-stimulation behaviors, such as head banging, rocking, or head rolling. (See section on self-injuries and stereotypical behavior.)
- The child may have a poor body scheme.

Cognitive
- The child may have poor attending behavior.
- The child may lack concentration or have a short attention span.
- The child may have poor visual and auditory memory.
- The child usually has poor short-term memory.
- The child usually lacks good problem-solving skills.
- The child usually has difficulty following directions.

Intrapersonal
- The child may have a poor self-image.
- The child may engage in self-mutilation behavior.
- The child may have a poor sense of self-mastery or internal locus of control.
- The child may lack self-control.

Interpersonal
- The child may lack communication skills.
- The child may lack interaction or social skills in one-on-one, small-group, or large-group situations.

Self-Care
The child may have feeding problems such as
- mouth breathing
- cleft lip or palate
- enlarged, thick, or protruding tongue
- dysphagia (see section on deglutition disorders)
- drooling
- diminished gag reflex

Productivity

Play skills may be underdeveloped.

Leisure

The child may have few or no leisure skills or interests.

TREATMENT/MANAGEMENT

Treatment models include a neurodevelopmental approach (Bobath), behavior modification, sensory integration (Ayres), and human occupation (Kielhofner).

Motor

Occupational therapy is usually needed only for special problems in which multiple disabilities are present or a persistent developmental lag has occurred in spite of intervention by teachers and parents.

- Increase the child's reflex integration when primitive reflexes continue to present.
- Improve postural control and balance reactions, especially trunk stability.
- Increase muscle strength, especially trunk muscles.
- Increase range of motion.
- Increase physical endurance.
- Promote hand skills, especially development of reach, grasp, and release.
- Increase gross motor skills and coordination.
- Increase fine motor skills, manipulation, and dexterity.
- Improve bilateral coordination and integration (see section on vestibular-bilateral disorder)
- Improve motor planning skills (see section on developmental dyspraxia).
- Decrease activity level if overactive or increase activity level if underresponsive.

Sensory

Note the use of occupational therapy for specific problems.

- Decrease tactile defensiveness if present (see section on tactile defensiveness).
- Increase gravitational security if present (see section on gravitational insecurity).
- Decrease self-stimulating activities through use of sensory integrative techniques.
- Improve visual fixation, tracking, and scanning if needed (see section on visual perceptual disorders).

Cognitive

Usually occupational therapy is used for specific problems that have not been remediated by teachers and parents.

- Increase attending behaviors.
- Improve ability to follow directions.

Intrapersonal

Improve self-image through the use of creative activities, such as art, crafts, drama, dance, music, and games.

Interpersonal

Increase group interaction skills.

Self-Care

- Assist in development of self-care skills when special problems exist, such as the feeding problems listed above. Note: Occupational therapy is not needed for routine training.
- Promote independence in daily living tasks.

Productivity

- Develop play skills, especially exploratory and manipulation.
- Explore vocational interests through stimulated work activities and career interest batteries.
- Develop work habits and skills through sheltered workshop programs.
- Develop home management skills through simulation techniques.

Leisure

Explore and develop the child's leisure interests.

PRECAUTIONS

- Avoid developing splinter skills (isolated skills) that will not generalize to other situations.
- Be aware of other medical conditions that are often associated with mental retardation, such as seizures, vision disorders, and anatomical variations in the face, hands, and spine.

PROGNOSIS AND OUTCOME

The prognosis varies depending on the severity of the mental retardation and response to intervention. The outcomes listed below are samples and do not necessarily apply to all persons since intervention frequently is highly specific.

- The person has improved specific motor skills.
- The person has improved sensory integrative skills.
- The person has improved attending skills.
- The person is able to function in a group setting, performing an individual task or participating as a group member.
- The person has improved self-care skills, such as feeding.
- The person demonstrates an ability to perform productive activities.
- The person demonstrates an ability to perform leisure activities.

REFERENCES

Copeland, M.E., and J.R. Kimmel. 1989. Mental retardation. In *Evaluation and management of infants and young children with developmental disabilities*, 305-23. Baltimore: Paul H. Brookes Publishing.

Cronin, A. 1987. Incorporating social/behavioral aspects of eating dysfunction into oral-motor programs. In *Problems with eating: Interventions for children and adults with developmental disabilities*, American Occupational Therapy Association, 51-64. Rockville, MD: American Occupational Therapy Association.

Kantner, R.M., B. Kantner, and D.L. Clark. 1982. Vestibular stimulation effect on language development in mentally retarded children. *American Journal of Occupational Therapy* 36(1):36-41.

Lederman, E.F. 1984. *Occupational therapy in mental retardation*. Springfield, IL: Charles C Thomas.

Lederman, E.F. 1987. O.T. with the mentally retarded: Special concerns for a special population. *Occupational Therapy Forum* 2(8):1, 3-5.

Lyons, M., G. Kielhofner, and M. Kavanagh. 1985. Mental retardation. In *A model of human occupation: Theory and application*, ed. G. Kielhofner, 371-401. Baltimore: Williams & Wilkins.

Martin, M.J. 1989. Children with mental retardation. In *Occupational therapy for children*, ed. P.N. Clark and A.S. Allen, 338-48. St. Louis: C.V. Mosby. Revised in P.N. Pratt and A.S. Allen, eds., 2nd ed., 422-41, 1989.

Nagayda, J.M. 1987. Asocial feeding behaviors associated with severe mental impairment. In *Problems with eating: interventions for children and adults with developmental disabilitie*s, American Occupational Therapy Association, 41-49. Rockville, MD: American Occupational Therapy Association.

Nelson, E.C., T.B. Pendleton, and J. Edel. 1981. Lip halter: An aid in drool control. *Physical Therapy* 61(3):361-2.

Oliver, C.E. 1990. A sensorimotor program for improving writing readiness skills in elementary-age children. *American Journal of Occupational Therapy* 44(2):111-6.

Mental Retardation—Down's Syndrome

DESCRIPTION

Down's syndrome is an inherited autosomal aberration in which there is an extra chromosome, 21, in about 95 percent of patients. Other genetic variations include translocations in which chromosome 21 has attached to another chromosome, such as number 14, and mosaics in which the person has two cell lines, one normal and the other with 47 chromosomes. Also called Down syndrome or mongolism (an old term).

CAUSE

Although the cause of Down's syndrome is unknown, it is associated with mothers over the age of 40, in whom the incidence rises to about 1:40 live births as compared with 1:2000 live births in younger women.

ASSESSMENT

Areas
- developmental milestones
- reflex development, maturation, and integration
- muscle tonus
- gross motor skills and coordination
- fine motor skills, manipulation, dexterity
- hand functions
- range of motion
- oral motor skills
- sensory registration
- sensory processing
- perceptual skills
- attending behavior
- span of attention, concentration

- problem-solving and decision-making
- memory
- learning skills
- self-perception
- coping skills
- social interaction skills
- communication skills
- daily living skills
- productivity history, skills, interests, values
- leisure interests

Comparison of Ages and Types of Grasp of a Pencil

Type of grasp	Down's	Normal
Palmar-supinate	13 to 36 months	1 to 2 years
Digital-pronate	2 to 5 years	2 to 3 years
Static tripod	4 to 8 years	3 to 4 years
Dynamic tripod	5 to 12 years	4 to 6 years

Source: Van Dyke, D.C., et al. 1990. Problems in feeding. In *Clinical perspectives in the management of Down syndrome,* ed. D.C. Van Dyke, et al., 99. New York: Springer-Verlag. See Erhardt in reference section for norms.

Instruments

- Movement Assessment of Infants by L.S. Chandler, M.S. Andres, and M.W. Swanson, Rolling Bay, WA: Infant Movement Research, 1980.
- Peabody Developmental Motor Scales by M.R. Folio and R.R. Fewell, Allen, TX: DLM Teaching Resources, 1983 (not occupational therapists).
- Southern California Postrotary Nystagmus Test by A.J. Ayres, Los Angeles: Western Psychological Services, 1972. (Caution: Consider possible effects of hypotonicity or gravitational insecurity.)
- Bayley Scales of Infant Development by N. Bayley, San Antonio, TX: The Psychological Corporation, 1969 (not an occupational therapist).
- Brazelton Neonatal Behavioral Assessment Scale, 2nd ed., by T.B. Brazelton, Philadelphia: J.B. Lippincott, 1984 (not an occupational therapist).
- Gesell Developmental Schedules—Revised. In *Developmental diagnosis*, 3rd ed., ed. H. Knoblock and B. Pasamanick. Hagerstown, MD: Harper & Row, 1974 (not occupational therapists).
- Bruininks-Osteretsky Test of Motor Proficiency by R.H. Bruininks, Circle Pines, MN: American Guidance Services, 1978 (not an occupational therapist).
- Erhardt Developmental Prehension Assessment, in R.P Erhardt. 1982. *Developmental hand dysfunction*, 49-67. Tucson, AZ: Therapy Skill Builders.

PROBLEMS

Motor
- The person may have hypotonicity (flopping infant) in muscle tone and hypermobility of the joint due to laxness of joint ligaments.
- The person usually has delayed milestones in physical development.
- The person may have missed milestones, such as creeping on hands and knees.
- The person may use alternate forms of locomotion, such as scooting on buttocks or creeping on feet (with extended knees) and hands.
- The person's hands tend to be short and broad and interfere with coordination and dexterity.
- Congenital heart disease may limit the person's physical capacity and lower endurance.
- The person may have malalignment of the neck vertebrae (atlantoaxial joint instability at C1 and C2) that exposes the spinal cord to injury.
- The person usually has shortened bones, especially in the arms and legs, increasing the difficulty of performing such tasks as climbing stairs and propping on elbows.
- The person may have muscle weakness, especially in the trunk and flexor muscle groups. Grip strength is reduced.
- The person may have poor bilateral motor coordination and poor midline stability.
- The person may have poor motor planning skills or dyspraxia.
- The person may have delayed reflex development and maturation.

Sensory
- The person may underrespond to sensory input and exhibit
  1. decreased awareness and attention to tactile stimulation that leads to lack of discrimination and stereognosis through tactile senses and failure to manipulate objects
  2. decreased awareness of the position of the body, which is related to decreased kinesthetic feedback
  3. failure to alter force of movements to accomplish different tasks or results, which is related to decreased kinesthetic feedback
  4. decreased sense of balance and equilibrium responses
  5. decreased duration of postrotary nystagmus.
- The person may overrespond to sensory input and exhibit
  1. resistance to handling, including touching and being touched (tactile defensiveness)
  2. avoidance of weight bearing on the arms, legs, hands, and knees (proprioceptive hyperresponsiveness)
  3. fear of heights and unstable or moving surfaces (gravitational insecurity), such as ramps, swings, slides, ladders, or stairs.

Cognitive
- The person's intelligence may be subnormal.
- The person's mental development may be delayed.
- The person may have poor attending behavior.
- The person may have poor concentration and be easily distracted.
- The person's ability to plan ahead may be limited.
- The person's ability to solve problems may be delayed.

Intrapersonal
- The person tends to be passive and appears to lack motivation.
- The person may have low self-esteem.
- The person's affective behavior may be delayed.

Interpersonal
- Quality of speech production may be affected by the person's thick, broad tongue.
- Lack of physical skills may interfere with the person's ability to develop sports skills and other group activities.
- The person may not initiate social contacts for fear of being laughed at or rejected.
- Social development may be delayed.

Self-Care
- The person usually needs assistance to learn activities of daily living.
- Skills for independent living may not be learned.
- The person's tongue tends to be forward in the mouth, which presents as a slight tongue thrust, and development of tongue movements is delayed. The tongue may appear large due to a small oral cavity secondary to midfacial hypoplasia.
- The palate may be short and narrow. Underdevelopment of the maxilla may alter the position of the muscles used for chewing.
- Duration of chewing cycle is longer than normal and chewing is less vigorous. Person may tend to hold food in the mouth without chewing and demonstrate difficulty in moving food from side to side with the tongue.
- The person may be a mouth breather due to decreased size of nasal passages, which interferes with chewing and swallowing.
- The person may have generalized facial and oral hypotonia, which contributes to poor lip closure, poor suck, poor tongue control, and jaw instability.
- The person may experience difficulty drinking from a glass or cup, which is related to problems in sucking and swallowing.

Productivity
The person is usually most successful at jobs that require repetitive, easy to master tasks.

Leisure
- The person may have difficulty developing leisure skills.
- The person may not use leisure skills already developed without assistance.

TREATMENT/MANAGEMENT

Motor
- For an infant, concentrate on handling (holding, lifting, carrying) and positioning (on stomach, back, side, sitting):
  1. Hold and carry the child with his or her head slightly flexed and arms and legs close together; avoid straddling hips.
  2. Support the infant's head when lifting to avoid hyperextension of the neck.
  3. Position the child so he or she can see and reach for toys or objects.

4. Position the legs in knee flexion; avoid "frog leg" position of hip abduction.

5. Always turn the child to your stomach and push into sitting position; never "pull to sit" because of neck instability.

- Increase the person's muscle strength, especially in the neck, shoulder, trunk, and pelvis, to provide stability by pushing away from surfaces and working against gravity.
- Increase range of motion with activities while supporting the person's major joints and working with gravity.
- Encourage gross motor skills (rolling, propping on elbows, crawling, creeping, sitting, knee standing, pull-to-stand) by incorporating skill practice with visual and auditory stimulation, reaching for toys, and simple games.
- Encourage reflex maturation through tilting and bouncing in the air.
- Improve motor planning by encouraging imitation and gestures.
- Improve bilateral integration by placing objects and requiring the person to pick up the object using the opposite hand (across the body midline).

Sensory
- Provide tactile activities, including differentiation of textures, shapes, and surfaces and experience in sand and water, tactile boxes, feely bags, and with art activities.
- Provide proprioceptive input through games of localization and identification of body parts, wearing a weighted vest or ankle or wrist weights, and bouncing on inner tube or in a hammock.
- Provide vestibular input by encouraging climbing, riding, sliding, swinging, spinning, and hanging upside down.
- Provide auditory input, including differentiation of sounds, playing rhythm instruments, and moving to different rhythms.
- Provide practice in balance and equilibrium with balance beams and by having the person step through the rungs of a ladder, over low hurdles, and in and out of hoops placed on the floor.
- Decrease tactile sensitivity through application of firm tactile stimulation to the body.
- Decrease proprioceptive hyporesponsiveness by encouraging the person to bear weight on his or her bare feet.
- Decrease gravitational insecurity by encouraging vestibular activities in linear and circular form.

Cognitive
- Instruct the person's parents in a home program to increase mobility and hand skills or other developmental skills depending on the child's developmental level.
- Encourage attending behavior and concentration, especially in visual and auditory activities.

Intrapersonal
There were no specific objectives or activities mentioned in the literature.

Interpersonal
Encourage parental involvement in a therapy program that carries over into the home.

Self-Care
- Encourage oral motor development toward self-feeding. Decrease the person's sensitivity and increase tongue control and chewing movement.
- Encourage self-dressing and self-grooming.

Productivity
Encourage exploratory and symbolic play activities.

Leisure
There were no specific objectives or activities mentioned in the literature.

PRECAUTIONS
- Be aware of possible instability or subluxation at the occipitoantlantal or atlantoaxial (C-1, C-2) joints. There may be laxity of ligaments, malformations, or absence of the odontoid process. Spinning may be contraindicated. Physical contact sports may be contraindicated, including participation in Special Olympics. (See Committee on sports medicine. 1984. Atlantoaxial instability in Down syndrome, *Pediatrics* 74:152-54.)
- Be aware of possible cardiac pathology, such as congenital heart disease, which may reduce physical endurance.
- Be aware of possible seizure disorders.
- Be aware of possible allergies to food, chemicals, or fabrics. Asthma may be present also.
- Be aware of difficulties with ears (wax buildup, ear infection, blocked tubes) that may affect balance and hearing.
- Be aware of possible visual disorders related to strabismus, astigmatism, or optic nerve hypoplasia.

PROGNOSIS AND OUTCOME
- The person achieves independent mobility.
- The person achieves oral control and self-feeding skills.
- The person is independent in self-care activities.
- The person demonstrates marketable productive skills
- The person demonstrates homemaking skills needed for independent living.
- The person demonstrates leisure skills and interests.

REFERENCES

Dobrofsky, V. 1987. Treatment of oral-motor delay in the child with Down's syndrome: A case study. In *Problems with eating: Interventions for children and adults with developmental disabilities*, American Occupational Therapy Association, 21-6. Rockville, MD: American Occupational Therapy Association.

Edwards, S.J., and H.K. Yuen. 1990. An intervention program for a fraternal twin with Down syndrome. *American Journal of Occupational Therapy* 44(5):454-8.

Esenther, S.E. 1984. Developmental coaching of the Down syndrome infant. *American Journal of Occupational Therapy* 38(7):440-5.

Fine, M., and F. Johnson. 1983. Groups for parents of children with Down's syndrome and multiple handicaps: A pilot project. *Canadian Journal of Occupational Therapy* 50(1):9-14.

Gallagher, R.J. 1986. Affective expression: Implication for the educator, clinician and therapist. *Physical and Occupational Therapy in Pediatrics* 6(1):65-74.

Gisel, E.G., L.J. Lange, and C.W. Niman. 1984. Tongue movements in 4- and 5-year-old Down's syndrome children during eating: A comparison with normal children. *American Journal of Occupational Therapy* 38(10):660-5.

Gisel, E.G., L.J. Lange, and C.W. Niman. 1984. Chewing cycles in 4- and 5-year-old Down's syndrome children: A comparison of eating efficacy with normals. *American Journal of Occupational Therapy* 38(10):666-70.

Harris, S.R. 1983. Comparative performance levels of female and male infants with Down syndrome. *Physical and Occupational Therapy in Pediatrics* 3(2):15-21.

Hoffman, M.N., and R. Zemke. 1990. Developmental assessment. In *Clinical perspectives in the management of Down syndrome*, ed. D.C. Van Dyke, et. al, 126-38. New York: Springer-Verlag.

Hoffman, M.N., L.L. Peterson, and D.C. Van Dyke. 1990. Motor and hand function. In *Clinical perspectives in the management of Down syndrome*, ed. D.C. Van Dyke, et al., 93-101. New York: Springer-Verlag.

Krakow, J.B., and C.B. Kopp. 1982. Sustained attention in young Down syndrome children. *Topics in Early Childhood Special Education* 2(2):32-42.

Krakow, J.B., and C.B. Kopp. 1983. The effects of developmental delay on sustained attention in young children. *Child Development* 54:1143-55.

Kopp, C.B. 1980. The role of theoretical frameworks in the study of at-risk and handicapped young children. In *Intervention with at-risk and handicapped infants: From research to application*, ed. D.D. Bricker, 13-30. Baltimore: University Park Press.

Lydic, J.S. 1982. Motor development in children with Down syndrome. *Physical and Occupational Therapy in Pediatrics* 2(4):53-74 (see bibliography).

Lydic, J.S, M.A. Short, and D.L. Nelson. 1983. Comparison of two scales for assessing motor development of infants with Down's syndrome. *Occupational Therapy Journal of Research* 3(4):213-221.

Lydic, J.S., M.M. Windsor, M.A. Short, et al. 1985. Effects of controlled rotary vestibular stimulation on the motor performance of infants with Down syndrome. *Physical and Occupational Therapy in Pediatrics* 5(2/3):93-118.

Naganuma, G.M. 1987. Early intervention for infants with Down syndrome: Efficacy research. *Physical and Occupational Therapy in Pediatrics* 7(1):81-92 (see bibliography).

Niman-Reed, C., and D.H. Sleight. 1988. Gross motor development in young children with Down syndrome. In *Down syndrome: A resource handbook*, C. Tingey, 95-118. Boston: College-Hill.

Ramm, P.A. 1988. Down syndrome. In *Willard and Spackman's occupational therapy*, 7th ed., ed. H.L. Hopkins and H.D. Smith, 652-61. Philadelphia: J.B. Lippincott.

Schneider, J.W., and E.A. Brannen. 1984. A comparison of two developmental evaluation tools used to assess children with Down's syndrome. *Physical and Occupational Therapy in Pediatrics* 4(4):19-29.

Van Dyke, D.C., L.L. Peterson, and M.N. Hoffman. 1990. Problems in feeding. In *Clinical perspectives in the management of Down syndrome*, ed. D.C. Van Dyke, et al., 102-6. New York: Springer-Verlag.

Williamson, G.G. 1990. Motor control as a resource or adaptive coping. *Zero to Three: Bulletin of National Center for Clinical Infant Programs* 9(1):1-7.

Zee-Chen, E.L., and M.L. Hardman. 1983. Postrotary nystagmus response in children with Down's syndrome. *American Journal of Occupational Therapy* 37(4):260-5.

Premature Infant

DESCRIPTION

A premature infant is any infant born before 37 weeks gestation.

CAUSE

Generally, the cause of premature labor or premature rupture of the membranes followed by premature labor is unknown. Usually, the histories of women having premature deliveries show low socioeconomic status, lack of prenatal care, poor nutrition during pregnancy, little education, and concurrent infection.

ASSESSMENT

Areas
- muscle tone, hyper- or hypotonic
- reflex development and maturation
- range of motion (note discrepancies between two sides of the body)
- gross motor skills and coordination
- hand functions
- sensory registration—awareness and response to touch, sound, and light
- sensory processing, including visual gaze and tracking
- attending behavior—alertness, arousal
- focus of attention, attention span, concentration
- ability to calm oneself after stimuli
- response to being picked up or handled
- vocalization and crying behavior
- oral motor skills

Instruments
- Movement Assessment of Infants: A Manual by L.S. Chandler, M.S. Andrew, and M.W. Swanson, Rolling Bay, WA: Infant Movement Research, 1980.
- DeGangi G.A., R.A. Berk, and J. Valvano. 1983. Test of motor and neurological functions in high-risk infants: Preliminary findings. *Developmental and Behavioral Pediatrics* 4(3):182-89 (instrument must be obtained from authors).
- Bayley Scales of Infant Development by N. Bayley, San Antonio, TX: The Psychological Corporation, 1969 (not an occupational therapist).
- Brazelton Neonatal Behavior Assessment Scale by T. Brazelton, *Clinics in Developmental Medicine* no. 50, Philadelphia: J.B. Lippincott, 1973 (not an occupational therapist).
- The Milani-Comparetti Motor Development Screening Test by D. Kliewer, W. Brucek, and J. Trembath, Omaha, NE: Meyer Children's Rehabilitation Institute, 1977 (not occupational therapists).
- Neonatal Oral Motor Assessment Scale (NOMAS) by M.A. Braun and M. Palmer, A pilot study of oral motor dysfunction in "at risk" infants. *Physical and Occupational Therapy in Pediatrics* 5(4):13-25, 1986. (See also Case-Smith, J., P. Cooper, and V. Scala. 1989. Feeding efficiency of premature neonates. *American Journal of Occupational Therapy* 43(4):245-50.
- Hawaii Early Learning Profile (HELP), rev. ed. by S. Furuno, et al., Palo Alto, CA: VORT Corporation, 1985.

PROBLEMS

Motor
- The infant is small and weighs less than 2.5 kg or 5.5 lb.
- The infant usually has low spontaneous activity.
- The infant usually has low muscle tone (hypotonicity).
- The infant's extremities usually are partially extended rather than flexed.
- The infant may have respiratory distress syndrome due to underproduction of surfactant needed to prevent alveolar collapse and atelectasis.

- The infant is prone to hemorrhage of the periventricular germinal matrix.
- Hypotension, inadequate brain perfusion, and peaks in blood pressure may cause cerebral injury.
- Infants born prior to 34 weeks gestation usually have inadequate sucking and swallowing reflexes.

Sensory
- The infant's sensory registration may be hyper- or hyporesponsive.
- The infant's temperature regulation may be poor.

Cognition
The infant may have difficulty maintaining an alert state for any length of time.

Intrapersonal
The infant may have difficulty calming him- or herself.

Interpersonal
- The infant usually has some difficulty maintaining eye contact initially.
- The infant may not cuddle when held.

Self-Care
The infant may be unable to handle bottle feeding, necessitating nasogastic or gavage feeding.

Productivity
The infant is unable to engage in play behavior or has poorly developed play skills.

TREATMENT/MANAGEMENT

Motor
- When the infant is medically stable, begin promoting flexion of body and limbs to increase muscle tone.
- Promote development and integration of reflex and reactions.
- Promote development of gross motor skills, including rolling, sitting, creeping, crawling, and standing.

Sensory
- Promote sensory awareness and discrimination, including vestibular, tactile, proprioceptive, gustatory, olfactory, visual, auditory.
- If hyper- or hyposensitivity is present, normalize response.

Cognition
- Increase the length of time the infant can maintain an organized, alert state by encouraging sucking, maintaining eye contact, and swaddling or talking to the infant. Initially the infant may be able to tolerate only one input at a time and then gradually tolerate two or more inputs.

- Instruct the parents on holding, moving, or feeding the infant through demonstration and coaching.

Intrapersonal
Help the infant learn calming behavior (coping skills).

Interpersonal
Promote bonding with the parents or caregivers through use of developmental age-appropriate toys, games, and activities.

Self-Care
Increase oral motor skills, including sucking and swallowing.

Productivity
Promote play skills, especially exploration and manipulation.

PRECAUTION
Do not overload the infant with stimuli. Watch for signs, such as gaze aversion, staring, facial hypotonia, alterations in respiration or heart rate, jerkiness in movements, hiccups, spitting, changes in color of skin to dark or light tones, and mottling.

PROGNOSIS AND OUTCOME
- The infant's quality of muscle tone has improved to include increased flexion.
- The infant's rate and level of reflex maturation has increased.
- The infant's response to sensory input has improved.
- The infant has increased attending behavior (eye contact).
- The infant has increased attention span.
- The infant responds to being picked up by flexing (cuddling) or changing facial expression (smiling).
- The infant is able to calm him- or herself.
- The infant has improved oral motor skills.

REFERENCES

Als, H. 1986. A synactive model of neonatal behavioral organization: Framework for the assessment of neurobehavioral development in the premature infant and for support of infants and parents in the neonatal intensive care environment. *Physical and Occupational Therapy in Pediatrics* 6(3/4):3-53.

Anderson, J. 1986. Sensory intervention with the preterm infant in the neonatal intensive care unit. *American Journal of Occupational Therapy* 40(1):19-26.

Anderson, L.J. and J.M. Anderson. 1986. A positioning seat for the neonate and infant with light tone. *American Journal of Occupational Therapy* 40(3):186-90.

Bellefeuille-Reid, D., and S. Jakubek. 1989. Adaptive positioning intervention for premature infants: Issues for paediatric occupational therapy practice. *British Journal of Occupational Therapy* 52(3):93-6.

Bigsby, R. 1983. Reaching and asymmetrical tonic neck reflex in pre-term and full-term infants. *Physical and Occupational Therapy in Pediatrics* 3(4):25-42.

Case, J. 1985. Positioning guidelines for the premature infant. *Developmental Disabilities Special Interest Section Newsletter* 8(3):1-2.

Case-Smith, J., P. Cooper, and V. Scale. 1989. Feeding efficiency of premature neonates. *American Journal of Occupational Therapy* 43(4):245-50.

Cochrane, C.G. 1986. Vestibular-proprioceptive and tactile-kinesthetic intervention for premature infants. *Physical and Occupational Therapy in Pediatrics* 6(2):87-94.

Cohen, E., K. Lidsky, F. Eyler, et al. 1983. Considerations during intervention with premature infants. *Developmental Disabilities Special Interest Section Newsletter* 6(3):1-2.

Crowe, T.K. 1988. Preschool motor skills of children born prematurely and not diagnosed as having cerebral palsy. *Journal of Developmental and Behavioral Pediatrics* 9(4):189-93.

Girolami, G.L. 1983. Improving preterm motor control: The forgotten area of infant stimulation. *Physical and Occupational Therapy in Pediatrics* 3(2):69-79.

Harris, M. 1986. Oral-motor management of the high-risk neonate. *Physical and Occupational Therapy in Pediatrics* 6(3/4):231-53.

Kelly, M.K. 1988. Periventricular leukomalacia. *Physical and Occupational Therapy in Pediatrics* 8(4):95-110.

Kirschbaum, M.J., and P. Winkelman. 1985. General principles of intervention for the preterm infant. *Developmental Disabilities Special Interest Section Newsletter* 8(3):1, 4.

Laegreid, J.M., C.D. Lew, and J.M. Walker. 1988. Neuromotor behavior and cardiorespiratory responses of premature infants with bronchopulmonary dysplasia. *Physical and Occupational Therapy in Pediatrics* 8(1):15-42.

Niparko, N. 1982. The effect of prematurity on performance on the Denver Developmental Screening Test. *Physical and Occupational Therapy in Pediatrics* 2(1):29-50.

Ochenas, S.F. 1985. Premature, chronically ill children as preschoolers. *Developmental Disabilities Special Interest Section Newsletter* 8(4):4, 6, 8.

Palisano, R.J., M.A. Short, and D.L. Nelson. 1985. Chronological vs. adjusted age in assessing motor development of healthy twelve-month-old premature and fullterm infants. *Physical and Occupational Therapy in Pediatrics* 5(1):1-16.

Pelletier, J., and J.S. Lydic. 1986. Neurological assessment of the preterm and full-term newborn infant: An analysis. *Physical and Occupational Therapy in Pediatrics* 6(1):93-104.

Pelletier, J.M., M.A. Short, and D.L. Nelson. 1985. Immediate effects of waterbed flotation on approach and avoidance behaviors of premature infants. *Physical and Occupational Therapy in Pediatrics* 5(2/3):81-91.

Robert, D. 1983. Effect of gestational age on neuromotor development of preterm infants. *Physical and Occupational Therapy in Pediatrics* 3(2):23-42.

Ross, E.F. 1984. Review and critique of research on the use of tactile and kinesthetic stimulation with premature infants. *Physical and Occupational Therapy in Pediatrics* 4(1):35-49.

Stap, L.J., and P.A. Reinhart. 1987. A seat for premature infants. *American Journal of Occupational Therapy* 41(10):667-71.

Stengel, T.J. 1982. Infant behavior, maternal psychological reaction, and motor-infant interactional issues associated with the crises of prematurity: A selected review of the literature. *Physical and Occupational Therapy in Pediatrics* 2(2/3):3-24.

Sweeney, J.K. 1986. Physiologic adaptation of neonates to neurological assessment. *Physical and Occupational Therapy in Pediatrics* 6(3/4):155-69.

Updike, C., et al. 1986. Positional support for premature infants. *American Journal of Occupational Therapy* 40(10):712-5.

Valvano, J., and G.A. GeGangi. 1986. Atypical posture and movement findings in high risk pre-term infants. *Physical and Occupational Therapy in Pediatrics* 6(2):71-81.

Rett Syndrome

DESCRIPTION

Rett syndrome is a neurodegenerative disorder characterized by progressive loss of intellectual function, loss of fine and gross motor skills, and development of stereotypic hand movement. The disorder was named for Dr. Andreas Rett who reported the syndrome in 1966 in Germany. It was recognized in the United States in 1983 when research was reported in English. Rett syndrome is sometimes confused with infantile autism.

CAUSE

While the exact cause is unknown, the disorder may be a hereditary X-linked disorder of females. Onset usually occurs between 6 to 18 months. The course of the disorder alternates between periods of progression and periods of rapid decline. Death occurs usually between ages 20 and 30.

ASSESSMENT

Areas
- hand functions
- fine motor skills, manipulative, dexterity, and bilateral coordination
- praxis and motor planning
- stereotypic movement or motions
- reflex maturation and development
- attending behavior and concentration
- mood and affect
- communication skills
- daily living skills
- play skills

Instruments

We found no instruments developed by occupational therapists in the literature. The following examples may be useful:

- Peabody Developmental Motor Scales by M.R. Folio and R.R. Fewell, Allen, TX: DLM Corporation, 1983.
- Reflex development test.
- Activities of daily living scale.
- Play history.

PROBLEMS

Motor
- Spasticity is usually present in respiratory muscles, in swallowing, and in the leg flexors, which leads to toe walking.

Stages of Rett Syndrome

Stage I: Onset and Stagnation

Onset between 6 months to 1 1/2 years of age

Developmental progress delayed or arrested

Developmental pattern still not significantly abnormal

Possible deterioration of eye contact and decreased communication skills

Diminishing interest in play activities

Duration of stage is weeks to months

Stage II: Rapid Development Regression

Onset between 1 year to 3 or 4 years of age

Loss of acquired skills in communication

Loss of purposeful hand use

Stereotyped hand movements

Severe dementia with autistic features

Apraxic/ataxic gait

Irregular breathing (hyperventilation)

Mental retardation appears

Duration of stage is weeks to months

Stage III: Pseudostationary Period

Onset begins following Stage II

Some communicative skills may return

Ambulation ability remains but there is prominent gait apraxia and truncal ataxia

Autistic features are less prominent

Variable motor dysfunction

Inapparent, slow neuromotor regression

Seizures

Duration of stage may be years or decades

Stage IV: Late Motor Deterioration

Onset begins following Stage III

Loss of ambulation: becomes wheelchair dependent

Severe disability; wasting of body tissues, spasticity, foot deformities, and scoliosis

Growth retardation, cachexia

Seizures may be less problematic

Improved emotional contact

Staring gaze

Duration of stage may be decades

Note: A few children with early severe neuromotor impairment may never learn to stand or walk and thus do not enter stage III, but go directly from stage II to IV.

Source: Based on Hagberg, B.A. 1989. Rett Syndrome: Clinical peculiarities, diagnostic approach, and possible cause. *Pediatric Neurology* 5:75–83.

- Usually there is progressive loss of purposeful, fine motor hand skills.
- Gait ataxia may result in loss of ambulation skills. Early signs include wide-based gait and locking of joints, such as knees in hyperextension and ankles in pronation.
- Ataxia and apraxia of the trunk muscles may lead to loss of gross motor skills.
- Spinal deformity and scoliosis may be present.

- The person may hyperventilate and hold breath.
- The person usually has stereotypical hand wringing, hand washing, hand biting, hand sucking or licking, and stretching and flexing the middle finger joints.
- The person may exhibit bruxism, or grinding of the teeth.
- The person may have seizures.
- Contractures may occur that are related to spasticity, especially in distal joints.

Sensory

The person may have loss of balance and equilibrium reactions.

Cognitive

- The person usually has progressive loss of intellectual functions.
- The person may have decreased awareness of the environment.

Intrapersonal

- The person may be irritable.
- The person may lose contact with the environment, similar to autistic withdrawal.

Interpersonal

The person may have impaired expressive and receptive language.

Self-Care

The person may have progressive loss of the ability to perform activities of daily living that depend on fine motor hand skills, such as feeding.

Productivity

Play skills are lost due to loss of hand skills, trunk balance, and gait skills.

Leisure

The person may be unable to continue leisure interests that depend on mobility, cognitive functioning, or fine motor skills.

TREATMENT/MANAGEMENT

Note: The use of occupational therapy in treating Rett's syndrome is just beginning to appear in the literature. Treatment approaches are not well identified.

Motor

- Assist the person in developing and maintaining ambulation skills by encouraging weight bearing activities in the upper extremities.
- Consider splinting joints to maintain functional position, such as knee splints to reduce hyperextension and hand splints to decrease wrist flexion and hand-to-mouth stereotypical movements. (Note: Stereotypical hand movements are not learned behavior and do not respond to behavior therapy; the problem is neurological.)
- Normalize or decrease hypertonicity (spasticity) through positioning, aquatic therapy, and vibration.

- Promote good positioning in seating (strollers, wheelchairs, regular chairs) to decrease tendency toward scoliosis.

Sensory

Increase or maintain the person's equilibrium and protective reactions through activities that require changing body position, such as the use of vestibular boards.

Cognitive

Increase the level of awareness through use of visual and auditory stimulation, such as bright colored, battery-operated, or musical toys.

Intrapersonal

Relaxation techniques and sensory desensitization may be helpful in reducing irritability.

Interpersonal

- Promote verbal communication.
- Encourage socialization and interaction. (Note: Lack of eye gaze is not intentional aversion but part of the basic neurologic disorder.)
- Act as an empathic listener, source of information, and referral source for the family.

Self-Care

- Increase purposeful hand to mouth activities to help the person feed him- or herself. Behavior modification techniques may be useful to facilitate achieving this objective.
- Promote better swallowing by decreasing tone and improving positioning.
- Increase ability to perform other self-care activities, such as dressing, brushing teeth and hair, and bathing.

Productivity

Promote play skills to support hand skills and encourage interpersonal relationships.

Leisure

Develop the person's leisure interests.

PRECAUTIONS

Do not promise more than can be delivered. Be realistic about the outcome.

PROGNOSIS AND OUTCOME

The prognosis is generally poor, and the outcome is death. Therapy is focused on slowing the decline, maintaining function as long as possible, and providing as much quality of life as possible.

- The child demonstrates increased hand function.
- The child demonstrates decreased stereotypical hand movements or motions.
- The child increases self-care skills, such as feeding.

REFERENCES

Hanks, S.B. 1986. The role of therapy in Rett syndrome. *American Journal of Medical Genetics* 24:247-252.

Naganuma, G.M. 1988. Effect of hand splints on stereotypic hand behavior in three girls with Rett syndrome. *Physical Therapy* 68:664-71.

Sharpe, R.A., and K.J. Ottenbacher. 1990. Use of an elbow restraint to improve finger-feeding skills in a child with Rett syndrome. *American Journal of Occupational Therapy* 44(4):328-32.

Stewart, K.G., et al. 1989. Rett syndrome: A literature review and survey of parents and therapists. *Physical and Occupational Therapy in Pediatrics* 9(3):35-55.

Spina Bifida

DESCRIPTION

Spina bifida is a spinal cord disorder characterized by failure of the vertebral column to close. The neural tube usually is involved in cases seen by occupational therapists. Spina bifida cystica includes three types: a sac protruding from the spinal cord containing meninges (meningocele), a spinal cord protrusion (myelocele), or both (myelomeningocele).

CAUSE

The exact cause of this disorder is unknown. Spina bifida usually occurs in the lumbar, low thoracic, or sacral region of the spine and extends three to six vertebral segments. A shunt (plastic tube) may be inserted in the ventricle(s) of the brain to drain excess fluid to the kidneys, thereby reducing hydrocephalus.

ASSESSMENT

Areas
- physical abnormalities—head size, brain stem, chest, and hips
- muscle strength
- muscle tone
- range of motion
- reflex maturation development—presence of primitive reflexes or abnormal movements
- postural control—protective and equilibrium reactions, midline stability and orientation, and symmetrical and asymmetrical movement
- gross motor development and skills
- coordination—visual motor, bilateral, and reciprocal
- fine motor hand skills—grasp and release, dexterity, and manipulation
- mobility (with and without aids and equipment)
- ocular motor control, including tracking and scanning
- physical endurance and work tolerance

- motor planning (praxis)
- sensory registration (awareness and orientating behavior)
- sensory sensitivity: (1) tactile: level of sensation, light touch, pressure, temperature, vibration, and two-point discrimination; (2) vestibular: linear (vertical and horizontal) and angular; (3) proprioceptive; (4) visual: acuity, peripheral vision, color vision; and (5) auditory: localization, discrimination identification
- perceptual skills: (1) visual: form constancy, position in space, visual closure, figure ground, depth perception, part-whole discrimination, object permanence; (2) auditory; (3) tactile: stereognosis, graphesthesia; (4) kinesthesia; (5) body scheme: laterality, directionality, right-left discrimination
- attending behavior
- attention span or concentration
- memory skills
- self-perception
- social conduct skills
- daily living skills
- academic skills, handwriting
- play skills
- leisure skills

Instruments

No comprehensive or specific tests for spina bifida, written by occupational therapists, were found. Some types of tests that may be useful are listed below.
- manual muscle testing
- goniometry
- developmental testing—Denver Developmental Screening Test, rev. ed. by W. Frankenberg, et al., Denver: Ladoca, 1975.
- reflex testing
- fine motor and hand testing—Jepsen Taylor Hand Function Test by R. Jepsen, N. Taylor, et al., *Archives of Physical Medicine and Rehabilitation* 50:311-9, 1969, and Erhardt Developmental Prehension Assessment by R. Erhardt, *Developmental hand dysfunction: Theory, assessment, treatment*, Laurel, MD: RAMSCO, 1982.
- mobility testing for walker, wheelchair, powered mobility
- ocular motor testing—Functional Vision Inventory for the Multiply and Severely Handicapped by M.B. Langley, Chicago: Stoeling, 1980, or STYCAR by M.D. Sheridan, Berks, England: NFER Publishing, 1973.
- sensory registration testing
- sensory sensibility testing—Southern California Sensory Integration Tests by A.J. Ayres, Los Angeles: Western Psychological Services, 1980.
- perceptual tests—Developmental Test of Visual Perception by M.A. Frostig, et al., Palo Alto: Consulting Psychologists Press, 1966; Motor Free Visual Perception Test by D. Hammill, Austin, TX: ProED, 1972; or Developmental Test of Visual Motor Integration by Beery and Bukternica, Cleveland: Modern Curriculum Press, 1967.
- activities of daily living assessment (See norms for spina bifida in J.C. Sousa, et al. 1983.) Developmental guidelines for children with myelodysplasia. *Physical Therapy* 63(1):21-9.
- play skills assessment
- leisure interest checklist

PROBLEMS

Motor

- At or above the lesion, muscle weakness may be present. The person may have paralysis below the involved level when spinal cord or lumbosacral nerve roots are involved.
- Physical abnormalities include: (1) hydrocephalus that, if unarrested, increases the size of the head and may create problems in milestone development because the child cannot raise his or her head, (2) Arnold-Chiari malformation, a defect in the formation of the brainstem, (3) kyphosis, or posterior rounding of the thorax region, and (4) dislocated hip or hips.
- The person may have low or abnormal muscle tone.
- The person may have limited range of motion in the upper extremities. Limitations in the lower extremities may result from a dislocated hip.
- The person may have delays in attainment of obtainable gross motor skills, such as sitting.
- The person may have primitive reflexes that have not integrated and/or abnormal reflexes.
- The person may have poor postural control in the trunk with poor midline stability.
- The person may have poor coordination of the two sides of the body or of sensorimotor tasks, such as eye-hand coordination.
- The person may have delays in development of fine motor and hand skills, such as primitive grasp patterns and failure to develop hand dominance.
- The person may have low endurance and low physical tolerance.
- Mobility will be limited.
- The person may have poor ocular motor control due to strabismus or paralysis of gaze or fixation. Tracking (following a moving object), scanning (locating objects in the environment), and fixating may be performed poorly, especially at the midline.
- The person may have dyspraxia and poor motor planning skills.

Sensory

- Tactile, touch, pressure, temperature, proprioception, and kinesthetic sensation may be lost or impaired below the level of spinal cord or nerve root involvement.
- Perceptual problems may occur, especially in persons with unarrested or poorly arrested hydrocephalus, such as (1) visual: visual discrimination (color, size, shape, position, same and different), visual closure (part-whole), figure-ground, form constancy, depth perception, visual orientation in space; (2) auditory: localization, discrimination, identification; (3) proprioceptive: body scheme, right-left discrimination, spatial relationships; (4) tactile: stereognosis; and (5) kinesthestic: position in space.
- The person may be hyper- or hyporesponsive to stimuli with such reactions as tactile defensiveness, auditory defensiveness, intolerance of movement, gravitational or postural insecurity, and inadequate bilateral integration.

Cognitive

- If hydrocephalus is arrested early, intelligence and cognitive functions may be normal, but if hydrocephalus is not arrested, mental retardation and other cognitive disorders usually are present. (Note discrepancies between verbal and motor performance.)
- The person may have poor attending behavior.
- The person may have short attention span and be easily distracted.

- The person may have memory deficits in short- and long-term memory.
- The person may have learning disabilities.

Intrapersonal
- The person may have a poorly developed self-concept, including self-mastery.
- The person may have poor social control, including sense of responsibility for actions.
- The person may have poor coping skills.

Interpersonal
- The person may have poor dyadic skills.
- The person may have poor group interaction skills.
- The person may have limited role responsibilities in the family or support group.
- The person may be hyperverbal (continuous talking; also called chatterbox personality or cocktail personality). He or she uses words fluently but has limited fund of knowledge on subject matters. Level of conversation is shallow or superficial. Person changes topics if pressed for details. This may lead some team members to think the person is brighter than the level of measured intelligence indicates. Hyperverbal behavior may be related to auditory defensiveness, i.e., talking to avoid listening to unwanted sounds.

Self-Care
- Bowel and bladder control may be incomplete.
- Performance of some activities of daily living may be limited due to lack of range of motion and instability of the trunk.

Productivity
- The person may have poorly developed play skills.
- The person may be behind in academic skills, including handwriting, spelling, arithmetic, and reading. Timed tests are difficult because of sensorimotor impairments.
- The person may not contribute to independent living and home management within family or living unit.
- As an adolescent or adult, the person may have few, if any, work skills or identified vocational interests.

Leisure
The person may have few leisure interests or skills.

TREATMENT/MANAGEMENT
Treatment models are based on developmental stages, sensory integration (Ayres), and rehabilitation (compensation techniques).

Motor
- Maintain or increase muscle strength in weak or underused muscles, especially in the trunk and shoulder girdle, to increase stability and facilitate transfers.
- Maintain or improve positioning to prevent deformities and reduce incidence of decubetus.
- Promote integration of primitive reflexes and reduce the influence of abnormal reflexes.

- Improve muscle tone.
- Promote development of gross motor skills through opportunities for frequent (high dose) practice.
- Improve postural control.
- Increase coordination skills.
- Encourage development of hand skills through structured, repetitive practice using such activities as putting small objects in containers, stringing beads, pinching clothes pins, buttoning, or use of zipper boards.
- Maintain or improve endurance and physical tolerance through graded activities.
- Assist in increasing mobility through selective use of walkers, wheelchairs, or powered mobility equipment.
- Improve ocular motor skills through the use of toys with bright colors or auditory output in a light-controlled environment: (1) fixation of visual gaze—place any of the following about 10 to 12 inches in front of the eyes: human face, pinwheels, spinning toys, finger puppets with penlight; (2) shifting of gaze—use two toys or two penlights placed to the left and right, up and down, or in a diagonal; (3) tracking—start at midline moving to the left or right, up or down, or diagonally using battery-operated toys, hand or finger puppets, or a small ball in a clear plastic tube; (4) scanning—games of "find it" or Twenty Questions for older children, pointing to items in a row, uncovering items in a sequence, sequence cards, or duplicating a colored bead or block pattern (see Williamson reference, p. 121-27).
- Improve motor planning skills.

Sensory
- Consider sensory integration techniques to improve interaction of sensory systems.
- Provide sensory stimulation to increase sensory awareness and discrimination within each sensory modality.

Cognitive
- Use visual memory devices, such as wall charts or posters, to outline steps of important tasks that need to be performed.
- Use multisensory instruction combining visual, tactile, and auditory elements for reinforcement. Structured learning using cuing and fading of instruction and reinforcement of successive approximations of desired performance may also be useful.
- Instruct the person in concepts of energy conservation and work simplification.
- Instruct the person in time management.

Intrapersonal
- Provide therapeutic activities designed to increase self-confidence and mastery of the environment.
- Provide opportunities to increase the person's coping skills.

Interpersonal
- Encourage development of dyadic skills.

- Provide opportunities to develop group interaction skills.
- Help family or support group expand the individual's role in the structure.

Self-Care
- Provide step-by-step instruction to assist in the development of self-care skills. Use reminder charts and other multisensory learning aids to assist learning and memory.
- Provide adaptive devices to assist with bowel and bladder care.
- Provide adaptive methods and devices to perform other self-care and ADLs (activities of daily living) that the person may be unable to perform without specific aids.

Productivity
- Provide a play situation designed to increase play skills for children.
- Use of computers that provide structured, repetitive learning may be useful in step-by-step instruction and may permit faster responses to academic instruction since the person does not have to write.
- Provide practice situations designed to increase skills in independent living and home management.
- Provide opportunities to develop work skills, work tolerance, work habits, and attitudes in vocational activities.

Leisure
Assist person to explore and develop leisure interests.

PRECAUTIONS
- Watch for signs of a malfunctioning shunt, such as increased head size, or behavioral changes, such as increased irritability or fussiness, increased sleepiness or drowsiness, seizures, vomiting, headaches, or "setting sun" eyes (partially visible iris).
- Always maintain good skin care techniques. Check skin for pressure sores. Change position frequently. Avoid tight-fitting clothing.
- If hip dislocation is present, use proper joint alignment techniques at all times.

PROGNOSIS AND OUTCOME
- The person demonstrates sufficient strength and endurance to perform functional activities.
- The person demonstrates basic sensory-motor skills to facilitate perception and learning.
- The person demonstrates socially acceptable behavior patterns and participates in age-appropriate activities.
- The person demonstrates emotional and psychological skills necessary to cope with living situation.
- The person is performing at his or her maximum level of independence in self-care and daily living management skills.
- When indicated, the person has developed work skills, work habits, and attitudes related to possible vocational choices.

REFERENCES

Clarkson, J.D. 1982. Self-catheterization training of a child with myelomeningocele. *American Journal of Occupational Therapy* 36(2):95-9.

Colby, C. 1987. An occupational therapy protocol for an outpatient spina bifida clinic. *Developmental Disabilities Special Interest Section Newsletter* 10(2):6, 7.

Copeland, M.E., and J.R. Kimmel. 1989. Neural tube defects. In *Evaluation and management of infants and young children with developmental disabilities*, 325-49. Baltimore: Paul H. Brookes Publishing.

Fay, G., D. Shurtleff, H. Shurlett, and L. Wolf. 1986. Approaches to facilitate independent self-care and academic success. In *Myelodysplasias and extrophies: Significance, prevention and treatment*, ed. D. Shurtleff, 373-96. Orlando, FL: Grune & Stratton.

Grimm, R.A. 1976. Hand function and tactile perception in a sample of children with myelomeningocele. *American Journal of Occupational Therapy* 30(4):232-40.

Hebert, E.B. 1987. Comparative study of the effects of three mobility devices used by children with meningomyelocele. *Developmental Disabilities Special Interest Section Newsletter* 10(2):1, 8.

Land, L.C. 1977. A study of the sensory integration of children with myelomeningocele. In *Myelomeningocele*, ed. R. McLauren, 115-40. New York: Grune & Stratton.

Ramm, P.A. 1988. Spina bifida. In *Willard and Spackman's occupational therapy,* 7th ed., ed. H.L. Hopkins and H.D. Smith, 649-52. Philadelphia: J.B. Lippincott.

Reid, D., and B. Sheffield. 1990. A cognitive-developmental analysis of drawing abilities in children with and without myelomeningocele. *Physical and Occupational Therapy* 10(3):33-57.

Sand, P.L., N. Taylor, M. Rawlings, et al. 1973. Performance of children with spina bifida manifested on the Frostig Developmental Test of Visual Perception. *Perceptual and Motor Skills* 51:431-7 (classic article).

Sand, P.L., N. Taylor, M. Hill, et al. 1974. Hand function in children with myelomeningocele. *American Journal of Occupational Therapy* 28(2):87-9 (classic article).

Shaffer, J., L. Wolfe, W. Friedrich, et al. 1986. Developmental expectations: Intelligence and fine motor skills. In *Myelodysplasias and extrophies: Significance, prevention, and treatment*, ed. D. Shurtleff, 359-72. Orlando, FL: Grune & Stratton.

Williamson, G.G. 1987. *Children with Spina Bifida: Early intervention and preschool programming*. Baltimore: Paul H. Brookes Publishing.

Wolf, L. 1987. Occupational therapy participation in a computer-based management system for children with meningomyelocele. *Developmental Disabilities Special Interest Section Newsletter* 10(2):1, 5.

Wolf, L. 1987. Development of a self-care assessment tool for children with meningomyelocele. *Developmental Disabilities Special Interest Section Newsletter* 10(2):4.

Sensory Integrative Dysfunction— Developmental Dyspraxia/Apraxia

DESCRIPTION

A person who is slow or inefficient at planning and carrying out an unfamiliar action is said to have developmental dyspraxia or apraxia. The difficulty these people have in planning movements involves smooth control of movement, postural reactions, patterns of movement that are programmed into the central nervous system, practiced motor skills, and planned motor activities.

CAUSE

The cause is unknown. The person's brain is dysfunctional so that it hinders the organization of tactile, vestibular, and proprioceptive sensation and interferes with the ability to plan motor activities. The problem begins early in life and may continue into adulthood.

ASSESSMENT

Areas

- reflex development and maturation
- constructional praxis (ability to put parts together to form a unified single object, often a three-dimensional model—also called visuomotor ability, perceptuomotor ability, or visuoconstructive ability)
- design copying praxis (ability to reproduce or copy a design—alternate terms are the same as for constructional praxis)
- postural praxis (ability to imitate positions)
- oral praxis (ability to imitate movements and positions of tongue, mouth, and cheek)
- manual expressions or symbolic praxis (ability to pretend to use objects while looking at pictures of the objects—note: not covered in testing or treatment by Ayres)
- sequencing praxis (ability to order a sequence of movements or make transitions from one position to another)
- verbal command praxis (ability to perform learned gestures purely on verbal command)
- vestibular processing (ability to use postrotary nystagmus and postural reflexes)
- tactile processing (ability to use stereognosis and finger localization)
- proprioceptive processing (ability to use postural control)
- visual and auditory processing (ability to use puzzles, figure-ground perception)
- daily living skills
- play skills

Instruments

- Sensory Integration and Praxis Tests by A.J. Ayres, Los Angeles: Western Psychological Services, 1989. Low scores on postural praxis, sequencing praxis, oral praxis, and praxis on verbal command, FI (finger identification), graphesthesia, LTS (localization of tactile stimuli), and MFP (manual form perception) indicate dyspraxia. CML (crossing midline of body) score is better than CMLX (crossing midline of body with the hand.)
- Southern California Postrotary Nystagmus Test by A.J. Ayres, Los Angeles: Western Psychological Services, 1975.
- A Guide to Testing Clinical Observations in Kindergartners by W. Dunn, Rockville, MD: American Occupational Therapy Association, 1981. (See also Dunn, W. 1986. Developmental and environmental contexts for interpreting clinical observations. *Sensory Integration Special Interest Section Newsletter* 9(2):4-7.)
- Miller Assessment for Preschoolers by L.A. Miller, Littleton, CO: Foundation for Knowledge in Development, 1982, available from Psychological Corporation, San Antonio, TX.
- DeGangi-Berk Test of Sensory Integration by R.A. Berk and G.A. DeGangi, Los Angeles: Western Psychological Services, 1983.

- Stereognostic Test for Screening Tactile Sensation by N. Tyler, *American Journal of Occupational Therapy* 31:256-60, 1972.

PROBLEMS

Motor
- The person usually has deficits in praxis skills, including motor planning and execution.
- The person usually is unable to perform tasks at age-appropriate levels.
- The person tends to perform tasks in an inefficient or clumsy manner.
- The person tends to have low muscle tone and seems weak.
- The person tends to have poor gross motor skills. He or she may be unable to run, hop, skip, or jump.
- The person tends to have poor fine motor coordination, manipulation, and dexterity.
- The person may have poor lateral dominance and tends to be ambidextrous.
- The person may become overactive to avoid performing tasks that are difficult for the person to do.

Sensory
- The person usually has deficits in sensory processing from the tactile, proprioceptive, vestibular, auditory, and visual functions. Responses may be hypo- or hyperreactive.
- The person may complain of minor physical injuries. Bruises, bumps, and cuts seem to cause more pain than the injury would indicate.
- Postrotary nystagmus is depressed or prolonged.
- The person may have poor visual and spatial skills. Other perceptual skills may also be deficient.

Cognitive
- The person may have poor ideational or concept formation skills.
- The person may have poor skills in planning ahead, including sequencing and timing.
- The person may have difficulty following verbal instructions, especially when given a series of instructions or when a single instruction requires that a series of tasks be performed.
- The person may have difficulty with problem solving.

Intrapersonal
- The person tends to be accident prone.
- The person may be easily hurt emotionally.
- The person may not tolerate changes in plans and expectations.
- The person tends to be stubborn, inflexible, or uncooperative.
- The person may have poor coping skills.
- The person usually has a poor self-concept and lacks a sense of mastery.
- The person may be emotionally labile.

Interpersonal
- The person may need more protection than other children.
- Reception and understanding of language may be delayed.

Self-Care

The person may have difficulty performing some activities of daily living or be delayed in acquiring such skills as putting on and taking off clothes.

Productivity

- The person tends to have poor manipulatory play skills (often ends up breaking or damaging the toys).
- The person may have difficulty organizing play activities when alone.
- The person cannot do activities or tasks in a group situation without help from adults.

TREATMENT/MANAGEMENT

Therapy for this condition is based on the model of sensory integration. Techniques are aimed at improving ideation and planning. Execution is assumed to follow.

Motor

- Postural dyspraxia—Use whole body motor patterns, such as total flexion, total extension, rotation, and gross diagonal rotary patterns. Activities include going through an obstacle course or tunnel on a scooter board and aiming an object to knock down a tower.
- Sequencing dyspraxia—Use motor activities with differing demands for timing and sequencing of movements and observe child's transition from one position or aspect of a task to another.
- Dyspraxia on verbal command—Speak slowly, use simple phrases (key words) and ask the child to verbalize what is to be done and what was done after the activity.
- Oral dyspraxia—General sensory stimulation may be given with various textured objects placed against the skin, such as cloth and brushes; vibrators, popsicles and honey dippers may be used in the mouth; licking stickers and blowing bubbles may be used for orofacial tasks.
- Constructional dyspraxia—May be combined with postural activities to reset the obstacle course or rebuild the tower.
- Design copying dyspraxis—Practice with tracing, dot to dot, outlining, or coloring hidden figures.

Sensory

- Provide tactile, vestibular, and proprioceptive input selectively and in combination. For sensory dysfunctions, such as gravitational insecurity, tactile defensiveness, and vestibular-bilateral disorder, see specific sections for treatment programs.
- Focus visual direction on the body part by pointing, tapping, or with verbal reminders.

Cognitive

Help the child select and plan activities by modeling or demonstrating, asking questions, offering solutions, or suggesting alternatives (i.e., work toward independent problem solving).

Intrapersonal

Provide tasks that are challenging but can be completed successfully (i.e., support the development of a positive self-image and a sense of mastery).

Interpersonal
- Interact with the child as a helper or assistant, not as an authority figure.
- Interact with the child to observe whether the task is too easy or difficult.
- Reward success but do not punish failure. Examine failure to determine what modifications are needed to provide success.

Self-Care
- Guide parents to expect performance within the child's ability level, starting with simplest activities the child can perform and increasing the level of difficulty.
- Help parents learn to model or demonstrate.

Productivity
- Guide teachers to expect performance within the child's ability level.
- Play activities may need to be modified to include the child.

Leisure
Leisure skills should improve as praxis skills improve. The therapist may need to assist the child in exploring leisure interests.

PRECAUTIONS
- Always monitor tactile and vestibular stimulation carefully for signs of overload.
- Do not attempt to change hand dominance if the child shows a preference for one hand over the other.

PROGNOSIS AND OUTCOME
- The person demonstrates improved praxis (motor planning) skills.
- The person demonstrates improved performance of gross motor skills, such as running, jumping, hopping, and skipping.
- The person demonstrates improved performance of fine motor skills, including manipulation and dexterity.
- The person has established a preference for use of one eye, hand, foot, or side of body and consistently uses that eye, hand, or foot in performing the same or similar tasks.
- The person's processing of sensory information has improved toward normal range.
- The person is able to follow a series of instructions.
- The person is able to tolerate changes in plans or expectations without becoming upset; coping skills are improved.
- The person is able to perform tasks in a group setting without supervision.
- The person is able to perform self-care activities independently.
- The person is able to organize a play situation or leisure activity without assistance.

REFERENCES

Ayres, A.J. 1972. Developmental apraxia. In *Sensory integration and learning disabilities*, 165-89. Los Angeles: Western Psychological Services.

Ayres, A.J. 1979. Developmental dyspraxia: A motor planning problem. In *Sensory integration and the child*, 91-105. Los Angeles: Western Psychological Services.

Ayres, A.J. 1985. *Developmental Dyspraxia and Adult-onset Apraxia*. Torrance, CA: Sensory Integration International.

Ayres, A.J., Z.K. Mailloux, and C.L. Wendler. 1987. Developmental dyspraxia: Is it a unitary function? *Occupational Therapy Journal of Research* 7(2):93-110.

Cermak, S.A. 1984. Construction apraxia. *Sensory Integration Special Interest Section Newsletter* 7(3):1, 3-4.

Cermak, S.A. 1984. Constructional abilities in children. *Sensory Integration Special Interest Section Newsletter* 7(3):2, 4.

Cermak, S.A. 1985. Developmental dyspraxia. In *Neuropsychological studies of apraxia and related disorders*, ed. E.A. Roy, 225-48. Amsterdam: Elseveir.

Conrad, K.E., S.A. Cermak, and C. Drake. 1983. Differentiation of praxis among children. *American Journal of Occupational Therapy* 37(7):466-73.

Goodgold-Edwards, S.A., and S.A. Cermak. 1990. Integrating motor control and motor learning concepts with neuropsychological perspectives on apraxia and developmental dyspraxia. *American Journal of Occupational Therapy* 44(5):431-9.

Haron, M., and A. Henderson. 1985. Active and passive touch in developmentally dyspraxic and normal boys. *Occupational Therapy Journal of Research* 5(2):101-12.

Koomar, J.A. 1984. Development of praxis tests for children. *Sensory Integration Special Interest Section Newsletter* 7(3):1, 4.

Parham, L.D. 1986. Assessment: The preschooler with suspected dyspraxis. *Sensory Integration Special Interest Section Newsletter* 9(1):1-3, 8.

Parham. L.D. 1987. Evaluation of praxis in preschoolers. *Occupational Therapy in Health Care* 4(2):23-36.

Ramm, P.A. 1988. Sensory integrative dysfunction: Developmental dyspraxia. In *Willard and Spackman's occupational therapy*, 7th ed., ed. H.L. Hopkins and H.D. Smith, 665-8. Philadelphia: J.B. Lippincott.

Sensory Integrative Dysfunction— Gravitational Insecurity

DESCRIPTION

Gravitational insecurity is characterized by an abnormal anxiety or distress that arises when the gravity receptors of the vestibular system are stimulated by head position or movement, especially when the child's feet are not on the ground. The child fears a sudden change of head position or of the body's center of gravity, changes in head and body alignment, or the feet suddenly leaving the ground.

CAUSE

The cause is unknown. The brain is unable to inhibit or modulate vestibular impulses by the macular receptors within the otoliths of the inner ear, which respond to linear acceleration.

ASSESSMENT

Areas

- muscle tone
- reflex development

- developmental milestones
- visual and auditory perception
- postrotary nystagmus
- proprioception
- tactile awareness and discrimination
- kinesthesia
- attention span and concentration
- imitation of postures
- memory
- self-perception
- coping skills
- social skills
- language skills
- activities of daily living
- play skills
- academic skills
- leisure skills

Instruments

No specific test of gravitational insecurity is available. Assessment is based on observations made during administration of the following tests:
- Sensory Integration and Praxis Tests by A.J. Ayres, Los Angeles: Western Psychological Services, 1989.
- Southern California Postrotary Nystagmus Test by A.J. Ayres, Los Angeles: Western Psychological Services, 1972.
- A Guide to Testing Clinical Observations in Kindergartners by W. Dunn, Rockville, MD: American Occupational Therapy Association, 1981. (See also Dunn, W., 1986. Developmental and environmental contexts for interpreting clinical observations. *Sensory Integration Special Interest Section Newsletter* 9(2):4-7.)

PROBLEMS

Motor

- The child does not like to have head upside-down, such as in somersaults, hanging from a bar, or tumbling,
- The child does not like to jump from a higher surface to a lower surface, such as jumping from one platform to another.
- The child is slow at performing unusual movements, such as climbing from the front seat to the back, walking up and down an unfamiliar hill, or walking on uneven ground.
- The child may have been slow to learn to walk up and down stairs and may still use the banister.
- The child does not like walking on a raised surface even if the surface is only a few inches off the ground, such as a balance beam, railroad track, or curb.
- The child does not like to be pushed backwards.
- The child does not like sliding and insists on holding on to the sides of the slide.

- The child shows poor ability to plan body movements within space and thus bumps into things, trips and falls over objects, or loses balance.
- The child does not like to climb or ride equipment or toys that require the feet to leave the ground, such as a jungle-gym or merry-go-round.
- Muscle tone may increase rapidly in response to perceived threat of falling, regardless of the actual risk.

Sensory
- The child does not like to ride passively on moving toys or equipment, such as in a wagon or on a merry-go-round.
- The child does not enjoy spinning or turning around repeatedly for fear of losing balance.
- The child's postrotary nystagmus is hyperreactive.
- The child may have poor awareness of body scheme.

Intrapersonal
- The child is fearful about heights and anxious about falling.
- The child is afraid of any sudden change of position, such as when riding in a car that turns a corner rapidly.

Interpersonal
- The child tends to avoid rough-housing with others.
- The child will not participate in games that require climbing, sudden movements, spinning, or rapid changes of balance.
- The child may grasp the therapist tightly or clutch the therapist in response to a perceived threat of falling, regardless of actual risk.

Self-Care
The child may have difficulty performing activities that require antigravity movements, such as standing on a stool to reach a water faucet, climbing the stairs to get ready for bed, sitting in a chair in which the feet do not reach the floor, or leaning the head back to get soap rinsed out of hair.

Productivity
Play skills in cooperative play may be delayed because of fears related to climbing, sudden movements, spinning, or rapid changes of balance.

Leisure
The child may prefer solitary activities in which he or she remains in control of head and body positions.

TREATMENT/MANAGEMENT
Treatment is based on the model of sensory integration therapy.

Motor
Do not require or force the child to assume any position or engage in any movement that makes the child feel uncomfortable, initiates a fear response, or increases anxiety.

Sensory
- Provide vestibular stimulation beginning with activities that permit the person to keep his or her feet on the floor and head in the upright position, such as in a rocking chair. Other techniques include having the therapist hold the child during early activities and providing helmets, mats, and pillows to increase a sense of security. Gradually some of the supports can be withdrawn.
- Activities may include (1) bouncing, jumping from a kneeling position or from standing on an inner tube, partially inflated large ball, trampoline, or spring or shock cord suspended from the ceiling; (2) swinging on a glider or platform swing, hammock, t-swing, bolster swing, or barrel swing.

Intrapersonal
- Reduce fear of movement by encouraging self-initiated linear vestibular stimulation.
- Positions should be nonthreatening, beginning with feet on the floor and slow speeds, small amplitude, and short durations that are tolerable to the child and within the child's control.

Interpersonal
Reassure the child that he or she will not be asked or required to assume any position or engage in any movement that makes the child feel uncomfortable, initiates a fear response, or increases anxiety.

Self-Care
Therapist may suggest to parents alternate ways of performing self-care activities that do not elicit gravitational insecurity, such as permitting the child to wash hands in a bowl of water placed at the child's height, flexing the head over a sink while standing on the floor to have the hair rinsed, or putting a stool under the feet.

Productivity
Therapist may suggest that the child be excused from play situations that require climbing, jumping, bouncing, or swinging until the gravitational insecurity is reduced.

Leisure
No special suggestions are available. The child will not willingly pursue leisure activities that produce feelings of gravitational insecurity. Therefore, unless gravitational insecurity is reduced, activities that might elicit insecurity are of little value.

PRECAUTIONS
- If the child has cerebral palsy or other brain injury:
  1. The child should avoid supine position if it increases extensor spasticity.
  2. Jumping or bouncing on balls of feet should be avoided if the positive support reaction is elicited or there is an increase in extensor spasticity.
  3. The child should avoid positions that increase internal rotation, adduction of the hips, and retraction of the shoulder.
- Never overarouse or overstimulate the child with vestibular stimulation. Stop immediately if the child asks to stop, becomes sick, feels dizzy, flushes, shows pallor, or begins

sweating. In linear acceleration, overarousal or overstimulation is most likely to occur in response to rapid reversal of movement, inversion of the head, or rapid acceleration or deceleration.

- Stimulation should be stopped if the child becomes withdrawn, destructive, anxious, or resistive.
- Intensity should be reduced if the child experiences sleep disturbances, such as nightmares or sleeplessness.
- Equipment must be kept in good working order. Regular checks of suspension units should be made to be sure the devices can withstand the combined weight of the child and the force of the swinging motion.

PROGNOSIS AND OUTCOME

- The person is able to tolerate the inverted position.
- The person is able to tolerate sudden acceleration and deceleration.
- The person is able to tolerate rotational movement.
- The person is not afraid of falling in normal situations.
- The person is able to maintain balance while moving from one surface to another.
- The person is able to perform activities or tasks that require climbing or stepping off the ground or floor, such as climbing on a step stool or climbing a ladder.

REFERENCES

Ayres, A.J. 1972. *Sensory integration and learning disorders*. Los Angeles: Western Psychological Services.

Ayres, A.J. 1979. *Sensory integration and the child*. Los Angeles: Western Psychological Services.

Fisher, A.G., and A.C. Bundy. 1989. Vestibular stimulation in the treatment of postural and related deficits. In *Manual of physical therapy*, ed. O.D. Payton. New York: Churchill Livingstone.

Kelly, G. 1989. Vestibular stimulation as a form of therapy. *Physiotherapy* 75(3):136-40.

Weisberg, A. 1984. The role of psychophysiology in defining gravitational insecurity: A pilot study. *Sensory Integration Special Interest Section* 7(4):1-4.

Sensory Integrative Dysfunction— Tactile Defensiveness/Hypersensitivity

DESCRIPTION

Tactile defensiveness is an adverse reaction to touch, such as a feeling of discomfort and a desire to escape the situation when presented with certain types of tactile stimuli. The response may be excessive emotional reactions, hyperactivity, or other behavior problems.

CAUSE

The cause is unknown, but was assumed originally by Ayres (1972) to be a failure of the protective tactile system and the discriminative tactile system to attain a natural balance, leaving the protective system predominant. Current theory suggests a failure of the inhibitory or modulating system in the brain.

ASSESSMENT

Areas
- two-point discrimination
- locationalization of stimulus
- stereognosis
- graphesthesia
- social skills (especially those where physical contact may occur)
- dressing and undressing
- eating
- grooming
- play skills

Instruments
- Touch Scale by C.B. Royeen, *American Journal of Occupational Therapy* 40(6):414-9, 1986. (See also Royeen, C.B. 1987. Test-retest reliability of a touch scale for tactile defensiveness. *Physical and Occupational Therapy in Pediatrics* 7(3):45-52.)
- TIP—Touch Inventory for Preschoolers by C.B. Royeen, *Physical and Occupational Therapy in Pediatrics* 7(1):29-40, 1987.
- Sensory Integration and Praxis Tests by A.J. Ayres, Los Angeles: Western Psychological Services, 1989 (especially the subtests Graphesthesia [GRA] and Localization of Tactile Stimuli [LTS]).
- Tactile Sensitivity Behavioral Responses Checklist by B.A. Bauer, *American Journal of Occupational Therapy* 31(6):357-61, 1977. (See also Bauer, B.A. 1977. Tactile-sensitive behavior in hyperactive and nonhyperactive children. *American Journal of Occupational Therapy* 31(7):447-53, 1977. Correction 31(9):611.)

PROBLEMS

Motor
- The child may exhibit hyperactivity or an increase in skeletal movements.
- The child may strike out, hit, or fight anyone who accidentally brushes against the child or whom the child accidentally brushes against.
- The child may physically leave, run (take flight) from a situation in which light tactile stimuli occurred.

Sensory
- The child may react by trying to rub or scratch out light tactile stimuli.
- The child may avoid being touched or having physical contact even with people the child likes.
- The child may avoid touching certain textures, such as sand, paste, or finger paints, and certain surfaces, such as blankets, carpets, or toys.

- The child may prefer to keep arms and legs covered with clothing even when warm.
- The child tends to react strongly to stimuli to the face, hands, and feet.

Cognitive
The child may have a short attention span and become easily distracted.

Intrapersonal
- The person may be accused of lacking self-control because of strange behavior when touching some objects or being touched.
- The person may act fearful, angry, or uncomfortable when approached or touched.

Interpersonal
- The person may verbally express feelings of discomfort or a desire to escape.
- The person may be accused of exhibiting antisocial behavior because he or she withdraws or hits people who accidentally touch him or her or even stand too close.

Self-Care
- The person may react strongly to certain grooming activities, such as having the face washed, hair combed or cut, brushing teeth, or cutting nails.
- The person may refuse to wear clothing made of certain fabrics.
- The person may have difficulty getting dressed because of a reaction to clothing against the skin.
- The person may push up pant legs or shirt (blouse) sleeves.
- The person may frequently adjust clothing as though the items did not fit properly, although the items are the correct size.
- The person may refuse to go barefoot or hate to wear shoes.
- The person may refuse to eat certain textured foods.

Productivity
- The person may avoid certain play activities, such as playing in the sand.
- The person may become a behavioral problem in the classroom because of reaction to accidental or intentional physical contact with others.

Leisure
The person may avoid certain leisure interests that require getting dirty or handling items with a variety of textures.

TREATMENT/MANAGEMENT
Treatment is based on the model of sensory integration. (See section on sensory motor activities in resources for additional activities.)

Motor
- Have the person crawl on all fours or belly crawl on various textured surfaces or through an obstacle course.

- Have the person play animal (assume position of the animal) games, such as snake, duck, crab, or dog while traversing various terrains (various textures of carpets, blankets, or mats).

Sensory

- Apply firm touch pressure using cloth materials of various textures ranging from soft, such as fake fur, to rough, such as corduroy. Play hot dog. The person is the hot dog. Add ketchup (put a blanket, large towel, or fake fur over person and press firmly to body). Add mustard (add other layer and press). Add pickles (add another layer and press). Add relish (add another layer and press). Place in a bun (roll up edges of the mat and press). Variations of the game include ham sandwich or deli sandwich.
- Use pairs of texture boards or cards covered with various materials, such as cotton, fur, corduroy, terry cloth, wool, or sandpaper. The person matches like pairs. Start with only two or three pairs of easy to discriminate textures. Add pairs as defensiveness decreases and matching skill improves.
- Use a large plastic tub or washbasin filled with Cheerios, uncooked rice, small beans, small pasta, small plastic beads, uncooked Cream of Wheat, or sand. Person searches for objects, toys, or shapes hidden in the Cheerios (or other substance).
- Use a small cloth bag or box. Place an object, toy, or shape in the "feely bag" or "feely box." The person reaches in the bag or box, feels the item, and tries to guess what it is or match the item from a group of objects on the table.
- Make craft projects from materials that have various textures or shapes, such as a collage or mosaic of cloth, felt, yarn, string, macaroni, beans, or papier-mâché.
- Use books with tactile or "touch me" panels that the person is encouraged to touch and feel.
- Have person rub body parts with various cloth textures, lotion, or powder. Start with the hands (usually the least defensive), then the arms and legs. The face, neck, anterior trunk, and soles of feet are usually the most sensitive. Play the swimming pool game. A mat is the swimming pool. The person "dives" into the pool (onto mat), swims (belly crawls), gets out and dries off with a towel.
- Finger-painting with sand or uncooked Cream of Wheat added for texture provides longer contact as the person becomes less defensive.
- Trace letters, shapes, roadways, or figures marked on sandpaper, feltboard, corrugated cardboard, or other textured surface.

Cognitive

Teach parents or caregiver to use firm pressure when dressing, washing, or assisting the child with an activity or task.

Intrapersonal

Provide instruction in relaxation techniques, such as slow rocking, rolling in a blanket, a lukewarm bath, or deep breathing.

Interpersonal

Alert teachers or group leaders to the defensive/hypersensitive behavior. The person may need to be first or last in line. The person may need a specific seating assignment.

Self-Care

Encourage the person to perform self-care activities independently, such as washing face and hands, and brushing hair and teeth.

Productivity

Alert parents or supervisor to the defensive/hypersensitive behavior and encourage creative solutions. The child can be assigned other chores or use gloves.

Leisure

The person will select leisure activities that are acceptable to him or her. Parents, caregivers, or friends should not push or encourage the child or person to perform a leisure activity that produces discomfort or other defensive/hypersensitive behavior.

PRECAUTIONS

- Usually treatment should begin on areas of the skin that are least defensive, such as the arms or backs of the hands.
- Avoid brushing against the hairs.
- Avoid crossing the midline of the body during early phases of treatment.

PROGNOSIS AND OUTCOMES

- The person demonstrates less defensive behaviors to touching or being touched.
- The person demonstrates improved attention span.
- The person is able to participate in group activities without withdrawing or striking out.
- The person is able to perform self-care activities without discomfort.

REFERENCES

Ayres, A.J. 1964. Tactile functions: Their relation to hyperactive and perceptual motor behavior. *American Journal of Occupational Therapy* 18:6-11 (classic article).

Ayres, A.J. 1972. Tactile defensiveness and related behavioral responses. In *Sensory integration and learning disorders*, 207-20. Los Angeles: Western Psychological Services.

Ayres, A.J. 1979. Tactile defensiveness. In *Sensory integration and the child*, 107-13. Los Angeles: Western Psychological Services.

Ayres, A.J., and L.S. Tickle. 1980. Hyper-responsivity to touch and vestibular stimulation as a predictor of positive responses to sensory integrative procedures by autistic children. *American Journal of Occupational Therapy* 34:375-81.

Dunn, W., and A.G. Fisher. 1983. Sensory registration, autism and tactile defensiveness. *Sensory Integration Special Interest Section Newsletter* 6(2):3-4.

Fisher, A.G., and W. Dunn. 1983. Tactile defensiveness: Historical perspective, new research—A theory grows. *Sensory Integration Special Interest Section Newsletter* 6(2):1-2.

Larson, K.A. 1982. The sensory history of developmentally delayed children with and without tactile defensiveness. *American Journal of Occupational Therapy* 36:590-6.

Royeen, C.B. 1985. Domain specifications of the construct tactile defensiveness. *American Journal of Occupational Therapy* 39(9):596-9.

Sensory Integrative Dysfunction— Vestibular-Bilateral Disorder

DESCRIPTION

Vestibular-bilateral disorder is characterized by shortened duration of postrotary nystagmus, poor integration of the two sides of the body and brain, and difficulty in learning to read or compute. It is also called postural bilateral integration dysfunction or postural-ocular movement disorder.

CAUSE

This disorder is caused by underreactive vestibular responses and inadequate maturation of postural reactions mediated by the brain stem that interfere with interhemispheric integration and result in limited lateralization of function by the cerebral hemispheres. The disorder is usually not apparent until school age.

ASSESSMENT

Areas

- muscle tone (check for hypertonicity, hypotonicity, and cocontraction)
- reflex maturation (check for failure of primitive reflexes to integrate)
- balance and postural control (check equilibrium and postural reactions and standing balance, eyes open and eyes closed)
- gross motor coordination and skills (check rolling, crawling, creeping, walking, running, jumping, and hopping)
- fine motor coordination, manipulation, and dexterity—hand grasp, diadochokinesis
- endurance and physical fitness
- vestibular-bilateral interaction (check crossing the midline and for lateral dominance)
- praxis or motor planning
- sensory registration—touch, vestibular, proprioception, visual, auditory, smell, and taste
- sensory processing—tactile, vestibular, kinesthesia, visual (including eye motility), auditory, olfactory, gustatory
- somatosensory (stereognosis, graphesthesia, localization, body scheme, lateral dominance), visual (form, figure-ground), and auditory perception
- attending behavior
- attention span
- orientation to person, place, and time
- ability to follow instructions
- problem-solving skills
- memory skills
- integration of learning skills
- judgment of safety

- self-perception and self-esteem
- self-control
- language and communication skills
- social skills
- daily living skills
- academic skills
- play skills
- responsibilities at home
- leisure skills and interests

Instruments

- Sensory Integration and Praxis Tests by A.J. Ayres, Los Angeles: Western Psychological Services, 1989 (low scores on standing balance with eyes open or closed and similar scores on motor accuracy, bilateral motor coordination, space visualization contralateral use, and other tests of right vs. left indicate this disorder).
- Southern California Sensory Integration Tests by A.J. Ayres, Los Angeles: Western Psychological Services, 1980.
- Southern California Postrotary Nystagmus Test by A.J. Ayres, Los Angeles: Western Psychological Services, 1975.
- Fisher, A.G., and A.C. Bundy. 1989. Vestibular Stimulation in the Treatment of Postural and Related Deficits. In *Manual of physical therapy*, ed. O.D. Payton, 241-5. New York: Churchill Livingstone.
- A Guide to Testing Clinical Observation in Kindergartners by W. Dunn, Rockville, MD: American Occupational Therapy Association, 1981. (See also Dunn, W. 1986. Developmental and environmental contests for interpreting clinical observations. *Sensory Integration Special Interest Section Newsletter* 9(2):4-7.)
- An Evaluation of Sensory Integrative Dysfunction (adapted from A.J. Ayres), in *A team approach for therapists: Pediatric rehabilitation*, ed. M.K. Logigian and J.D. Ward, 107-110. Boston: Little, Brown & Co.

PROBLEMS

Motor

- The duration of nystagmus following rotation is usually shorter than normal (depressed).
- The child may have poor gross motor skills and may have difficulty throwing and catching a ball.
- The child may be clumsy and may stumble or fall more frequently than others the same age.
- The child may have poor bilateral coordination of hands and feet.
- The child may not be able to hold head steady against resistance due to poor cocontraction.
- In prone position, the child cannot easily hold up his or her head, arms, and legs at the same time against gravity (pivot prone or prone extension position).
- The child tends to have poor oculomotor control. His or her eyes may jerk as they cross their midline.

- The child tends to have hypotonicity of extensor muscles.
- The child may have poor joint stability due to poor cocontraction.
- Equilibrium and postural reactions are usually underresponsive.

Sensory
- The child may not have established lateralization and dominance as indicated by preference in the use of one eye, hand, or ear over the other. The child may be ambidextrous (uses both hands as the preferred hand about equally).
- The child has difficulty with laterality and direction (confuses right and left).

Cognitive
The child may have difficulty following directions due to lack of laterality and/or a sense of direction.

Intrapersonal
- The child may have low stress tolerance.
- The child may have poor self-image due to repeated failure in performing adaptive responses.

Interpersonal
Language and communication skills may be below age level.

Self-Care
The child may have difficulty performing self-care activities that require laterality or directionality.

Productivity
- Reading and mathematics skills are usually below grade level. The child may read words backwards.
- The child may write letters backwards or upside down.

Leisure
The child is not good at sports and may not like them.

TREATMENT/MANAGEMENT
Treatment is based on the model of sensory integration.

Motor
Increase or normalize extensor muscle tone by encouraging jumping and bouncing while the child is sitting, kneeling, or standing on an inner tube or trampoline. Holding onto ropes at the same time increases upper trunk stability.

Sensory

- Provide tactile stimulation by using deep and light pressure and through such activities as rolling the child up in a blanket, rubbing the child with terry cloth towel, having the child walk barefoot over a variety of carpet textures or in a sandbox, and playing in foam packing material.
- Provide the child with vestibular stimulation through such activities as swinging on a bolster swing, spinning in a hammock, balancing on a vestibular board, riding a scooter board in various positions, or rocking in a rocking chair or on a rocking horse.
- Encourage integration of the tonic neck reflex and activation of the neck righting reflex by having the child roll in a blanket or barrel or ride prone on a scooter board.
- Encourage supine flexion and prone extension postures by having the child ride on a scooter board, swing on a bolster swing, or rock in a hammock.
- Encourage the child's development of equilibrium reactions through a sequence of prone, four-legged, sitting, and standing activities using therapy balls, an equilibrium (vestibular) board, a platform swing, obstacle courses, and such games as hopscotch, jump rope, and bean bag relay.

Types of Equipment Useful in Providing Vestibular Input

Standing/kneeling
- large inner tube lying flat on the floor not fully inflated
- trampoline (Note: Do not tighten fully, keep some slack.)
- glider swing
- platform swing

Sitting
- net hammock suspended from a single point (A variant is to place a ball inside the hammock. The child sits astride the ball.)
- inverted T-swing (two bolsters placed perpendicular to each other in the shape of an upside down T—swing is suspended from the leg of the T)
- bolster swing
- standard swing that may be adapted to provide back or side support
- glider and platform swings can be used in the sitting position also

Quadruped (all fours)—glider or platform swings

Prone or supine (lying on stomach or back)
- barrel suspended at both ends
- scooter board
- wheelchair or gurney
- glider, platform swing, net hammock, and bolster can also be used lying down

---

Types of Equipment Useful in Encouraging Equilibrium Reactions

- tilt board
- large therapy ball
- barrel lying on its side
- inflatables

- various sized bolsters
- ramps
- stairs
- balance boards

Cognitive
- Encourage parents to provide a home program to augment the therapy program.
- Specific therapy is not directed at cognitive functions since the assumption of sensory integrative therapy is that cognitive skills will follow improved sensorimotor integration.

Intrapersonal
Permit child to direct his or her own therapy. The therapist assists, clarifies, suggests, and provides instructions as needed, but does not direct or control.

Productivity
Encourage the child to try out different play activities and explore the play environment.

PRECAUTIONS
- Do not overstimulate the child; avoid sensory overload.
- Keep all equipment in good working order. Make sure suspended items are well anchored in the ceiling and can take the combined force of the child's weight plus the force of the swing motion.
- Keep mats or mattresses on the floor to cushion trips and falls.
- If the child has a seizure disorder, confer with a physician before using vestibular stimulation.

PROGNOSIS AND OUTCOME
- The child demonstrates improved motor planning skills when performing unlearned motor tasks.
- The child demonstrates improved sensory processing skills.
- The child demonstrates increased attention span.
- The child demonstrates improved self-control and an improved ability to organize his or her behavior to interact with people and the physical environment.
- The child demonstrates improved performance in daily living tasks.
- The child demonstrates improved academic performance.
- The child demonstrates an increased level of play skill.

REFERENCES

Ayres, A.J. 1972. Disorders in postural and bilateral integration. In *Sensory integration and learning disorders*, 134-64. Los Angeles: Western Psychological Services.

Ayres, A.J. 1975. Sensorimotor foundation of academic ability. In *Perceptual and learning disabilities in children*, vol. 2, ed. W.M. Cruickshank and D.P. Hallahan, 301-58. Syracuse, NY: Syracuse University Press.

Ayres, A.J. 1979. Disorders involving the vestibular system. In *Sensory integration and the child*, 69-89. Los Angeles: Western Psychological Services.

Fisher, A.G., and A.C. Bundy. 1989. Vestibular stimulation in the treatment of postural and related deficits. In *Manual of physical therapy*, ed. O.D. Payton, 239-58. New York: Churchill Livingstone.

Kelly, G. 1989. Vestibular stimulation as a form of therapy. *Physiotherapy* 75(3):136-40.

Part II
Sensory Disorders

Blind or Visually Impaired Child

DESCRIPTION

An infant or child who loses vision early in life before most major stages of development have occurred is either blind or visually impaired. Blindness as a legal term means that corrected vision in the best eye is less than 20/200 or the visual field has a visual angle of 20 degrees or less (tunnel vision). An infant blind at birth is referred to as congenitally blind, but if the blindness occurs after birth, the child is referred to as adventitiously blind.

CAUSE

The most common cause of seeing disorders is prematurity that requires oxygen be used as a life-support measure. About one-third of these infants will suffer retinopathy, especially retrolental fibroplasia. Other causes include congenital cataracts, optic atrophy, cortical blindness, Leber's congenital amaurosis syndrome, severe infectious diseases, and injuries.

ASSESSMENT

Areas
- muscle tone
- gross motor skills and coordination
- fine motor skills, dexterity, manipulation, and bilateral hand coordination
- motor planning or praxis skills
- reflex development and maturation
- sensitivity to sensory stimuli
- sensory awareness and orientation
- perceptual skills
- problem-solving skills
- imitation and learning skills
- interpersonal relations, especially bonding to parents or caregiver
- activities of daily living
- play skills development
- academic skills

Instruments
- Erhardt Developmental Vision Assessment (EDVA) by R.P. Erhardt, Tucson, AZ: Therapy Skill Builders, 1986.
- Functional Vision Inventory for the Multiply and Severely Handicapped by B.M. Langley, Chicago: Stoelting Co., 1980 (not an occupational therapist).
- Denver Developmental Screening Test by W. Frankenburg, J. Dodds, and A. Fandal, Denver, CO: LADOCA Project and Publishing Foundation, 1967, revised 1970, 1973, 1975 (not occupational therapists).
- Clinical Observation of Neuromuscular Development by A.J. Ayres (adapted by M.P. Gilbert), *Sensory Integration Special Interest Section Newsletter* 5(3):4, 1982.

- activities of daily living scale
- play scale

PROBLEMS

Motor
- The child usually does not use hands for exploring environment and does not bring hands to his or her mouth or together at midline; rather he or she tends to hold hands slightly fisted at shoulder height (high guard).
- The child usually does not like the prone position since vision does not act as a motivator to raise head. The prone position also impedes breathing and freedom of motion.
- The child may have delays in elevating to prone, creeping, crawling, rising to sitting, pulling to standing, and walking (mobility skills) that are assumed to be related to lack of visual stimulation, which in turn delays the development of spatial and temporal relationships.
- Fine motor skills requiring manipulation and dexterity may be delayed because of lack of hand use. The use of Braille slows down learning.
- The child may avoid gross motor activities because of fear of movement; thus coordination and bilateral integration are poor and the child is earthbound, unable to jump, hop, or stand on one foot.
- Muscle tone may be poor (hypotonia), especially in prone extension and full flexion, but may be present throughout the body.
- Development of righting and equilibrium reactions may be delayed. Posture and balance may be poor.

Comparison of Developmental Norms between Sighted and Blind Children (mean ages)

Behavior	Sighted (in months)	Blind (in months)
Midline reach in response to sound only	4 to 5	8.0
Elevates self by arms to prone	2.1	8.75
Rolls from back to stomach	6.4	7.25
Crawling on all fours	7.1	13.25
Raises self to sitting position	8.3	11.00
Pulls up to stand	8.6	13.00
Walks with hands held	8.8	10.75
Walking alone across room	12.1	19.25

Source: Adelson, E., and S. Fraiberg. 1975. Gross motor development in infants blind from birth. In *Annual progress in child psychiatry and child development*, ed. S. Chess and A. Thomas, 130–149. New York: Brunner/Mazel Publishers; and Fraiberg, S. 1977. *Insights from the blind: Comparative studies of blind and sighted infants.* New York: Basic Books, Inc.

Sensory

- Other sensory systems may not be spontaneously explored as a means of learning about the environment. Intentional reaching may be delayed.
- The child may be tactilely defensive when picked up, bathed, or having diapers changed.
- The child may develop blindisms (self-stimulatory mannerisms), such as head-rolling, eye-rubbing, pressing or poking, hand-fingering or rubbing, rocking or swaying the body, flicking or waving the hands in front of the eyes, and dropping the chin to the chest.
- The child may have difficulty with spatial or temporal tasks and become easily lost.
- The child may have poor body awareness, lateralization, and directionality.
- The child may be hyper- or hyporesponsive to vestibular stimulation.
- Proprioception may be inadequate. The child may be unable to replace a limb if it is passively moved to another position.
- The child may be fearful of unfamiliar voices or noises.
- The child may have a strong reaction to certain odors or smells.

Cognitive

- The child may have poor attending behavior and awareness of the environment.
- The child may have a tendency to use haptic memory rather than spatial or auditory memory. He or she has no concept of object permanence.

Intrapersonal

- The child may have a tendency to be passive rather than active in his or her environment.
- The child may seem to withdraw from his or her environment.

Interpersonal

- Bonding between parent and child may be delayed because the child does not take the initiative.
- Early nonverbal language is delayed, such as facial expression and smiling.
- Separation anxiety may be more severe and last longer than in other children.
- The child lacks visual feedback about socially approved behavior and nonverbal communication.

Self-Care

- Self-feeding and drinking are delayed because of a lack of hand-to-mouth skills.
- The child may avoid certain foods because of an odor or taste and become a picky or poor eater.
- Self-dressing skills are delayed due to lack of hand skills or to tactile defensiveness.

Productivity

The child has underdeveloped play skills, especially a lack of exploratory and creative play.

Leisure

- The child may have few, if any, interests in toys, games, or group activities.
- The child does not occupy him- or herself with play or vocalizations.

TREATMENT/MANAGEMENT

Models of treatment are based on sensory integration, stages of development, and neurodevelopmental therapy. Suggested techniques organized by age group are listed in Semmler and Hunter, pp. 270–72 (see reference section under Senitz).

Motor
- Encourage physical movement in space, such as rolling, amphibian crawl, creeping, and walking, using auditory sounds. (Note: Research suggests mobility in the blind child is dependent on an ability to localize sound.)
- Promote reflex maturation through modulation of sensory sensitivities and the opportunity to experience various positions.
- Encourage use of hands for exploration and manipulation. Explore faces, foods, clothing, and common objects in the environment.
- Promote development of fine motor skills, beginning with self-feeding and holding a vibrator.
- Decrease fear of movement through a gradual introduction to vestibular and proprioceptive stimuli. (See the next section.)
- Encourage acceptance of the prone position by gradually introducing the position and using it with rocking or swing motion in the parents' arms or on a bolster. Use a flashlight or other colored lights to attract any remaining vision. Slowly increase the length of time the child is in the prone position to facilitate development of extensor tone.

Sensory
- Encourage sensory registration or awareness, starting with rocking and gentle bouncing, massage, singing to the child, or putting bells on the child's booties.
- Promote tactile sensory sensitivity and discrimination through the use of various textures, a feely bag, or by having the child locate objects hidden in sand.
- Decrease tactile defensiveness, if present, through the use of pressure, such as rolling in a blanket or being sandwiched between two mats.
- Promote vestibular sensitivity and discrimination through linear acceleration and deceleration on a bolster swing, platform swing, hammock swing, or net swing or by jumping, hopping, or bouncing on an inner tube or net swing that is hung from a large spring.
- Promote spatial and auditory relationships by having the child explore a room while creeping or walking. Use obstacle courses or mazes to refine his or her skills; these skills are necessary for the child to be able to use a cane.
- Maximize the use of residual vision through exploration of colored light sources from a flashlight, colored panels, or a string of Christmas tree lights. Add a bell to a penlight to encourage auditory and visual localization.
- Promote the child's response to sound and encourage localization of sounds through use of bells on wrists or feet, crib toys that make a sound if rocked, pressed, or shaken in the hand, and music from a radio, cassette tape player, or toys with music disks. Increase the distance of sounds when the child is able to locate (turn to, touch, or grasp) sounds within arm's length.
- Maximize use of tactile perceptual, auditory perceptual, visual perceptual, and kinesthetic senses.

- Discourage blindisms by changing the child's behavior to some purposeful movement or activity, especially those related to vestibular or proprioceptive stimuli.
- Discourage eye pressing and poking, if present. Watch for infants sleeping with knuckles in the eye sockets. Encourage child to keep fingers out of the eyes. Using arm splints to limit elbow flexion may be necessary to decrease this behavior.

Cognitive
- Encourage concept development, including the concepts of object permanence, object recognition, sameness and difference, cause and effect, and conservation of mass.
- Show the child how to imitate to promote early learning.
- Improve spatial and auditory memory through repetitive practice and games.

Intrapersonal
- Encourage the development of a sense of self.
- Promote exploration of and a sense of control (mastery) over the environment by providing toys that can be acted upon by holding, shaking, stacking, taking apart, nesting, pounding, or climbing into or up.

Interpersonal
- Assist parents in promoting bonding with the child by having parents place the child's hands on the parents' faces and encouraging the child to explore the parents' faces.
- Assist parents in learning to play with the child.
- Encourage language development by talking to the child about what is happening in the environment and what he or she is doing. Encourage parents to describe activities at home when the child is involved or present.

Self-Care
- Promote learning and performance of daily living activities.
- Encourage hand-to-mouth skills by permitting the child to finger feed and be messy.

Productivity
Promote development of play skills.

Leisure
Help the child explore and develop interests to build leisure skills.

NOTES
- Adjusting the lighting in the room may enhance the child's visual performance. Lights, especially fluorescent lights, may need to be dimmed and windows shaded to reduce glare.
- Noise may also need to be controlled so the child can concentrate on the desired tasks without interference from other noises in the environment.
- Always talk to the child and explain activities at the child's level of understanding. Use normal vocabulary, including the words "look" and "see."
- Use materials with a strong contrast between foreground and background, such as black and white.

PRECAUTIONS

The child should have a safe place in which to play that is free of physical hazards. Hang electrical cords and eye-catching objects that might be dangerous, such as Christmas lights, out of range of the child's hands.

PROGNOSIS AND OUTCOME

- The child demonstrates use of hands to explore environment.
- The child demonstrates improvement in mobility skills and an increased level of development.
- The child demonstrates improvement in fine motor skills and an increased level of development.
- The child demonstrates increased muscle tone in prone extension.
- The child demonstrates improved righting and equilibrium reactions that lead to improved balance and posture.
- The child is able to localize sounds.
- The child spends less time using blindisms.
- The child tolerates vestibular stimuli and is less fearful of movement.
- The child has bonded to parents or caregiver.
- The child is able to feed himself or herself at least some foods.
- The child is able to participate in dressing or has gained some independent skills.
- The child has improved play skills.

REFERENCES

Campbell, P.H. 1987. Integrated programming for students with multiple handicaps. In Goetz, L., D. Guess, and K. Stremel-Campbell. 1987. *Innovative program design for individuals with dual sensory impairments*, 159–88. Baltimore, MD: Paul H. Brookes Publishing.

Dreier, S. 1980. Principal goals of occupational therapy for visually handicapped infants and toddlers. In *Rehabilitation of the visually disabled and the blind at different ages*, ed. B. Gloor and R. Bruckner, 28–40. Baltimore, MD: University Park Press.

Falconer, J. 1989. Visual disorders. In *A team approach for therapists: Pediatric rehabilitation*, ed. M.K. Logigian and J.D. Ward, 241-50. Boston: Little, Brown & Co.

Gilbert, M.P. 1982. Adapting evaluation procedures for the blind. *Sensory Integration Special Interest Section Newsletter* 5(3):4.

Nobles, L.B. 1982. Early intervention with the visually impaired infant. *Sensory Integration Special Interest Section Newsletter* 5(3):1–2.

Nobles, L.B. 1982. Sensory integration deficits in retrolental fibroplasia. *Sensory Integration Special Interest Section Newsletter* 5(3):1–2.

Ramm, P.A. 1988. Congenitally blind or visually impaired child. In *Willard and Spackman's occupational therapy*, 7th ed., ed. H.L. Hopkins and H.D. Smith, 636–46. Philadelphia: J.B. Lippincott.

Senitz, C., B. McBride, J. Adrian, and C.J. Semmler. 1990. Visually impaired children. In *Early occupational therapy intervention: Neonates to three years*, ed. C.J. Semmler and J.G. Hunter, 262–82. Gaithersburg, MD: Aspen Publishers, Inc.

Snow, B.S. 1985. Children with visual or hearing impairments. In *Occupational therapy for children*, ed. P.N. Clark and A.S. Allen, 430–55. St. Louis: C.V. Mosby. Revised in P.N. Pratt and A.S. Allen, eds., 2d ed., 1989, 535–62.

Watemberg, J., S.A. Cermak, and A. Henderson. 1986. Right-left discrimination in blind and sighted children. *Physical and Occupational Therapy in Pediatrics* 6(1):7–19.

Blindness

DESCRIPTION

Blindness is defined as a loss of vision in both eyes that cannot be corrected to better than 20/200 feet or 6/60 meters. The term blindness also applies to loss of peripheral vision so that the visual field is restricted to less than a 20 degree angle (tunnel vision). People who have had sight but lost it are referred to as adventitiously or newly blinded, whereas people born without sight are said to be congenitally blind.

CAUSE

There are many possible causes of blindness: a detached retina, diabetic retinopathy, puncture wounds to the eyes, multiple sclerosis, conjunctivitis, retinal hemorrhage, retinal fibrosis, enucleation, glaucoma, pressure on the optic nerve, or rubella.

ASSESSMENT

Areas

People with visual impairments frequently have multiple handicaps that need to be assessed and managed to improve coping skills.
* range of motion
* hand functions and skills—grasp, pinch, and release
* muscle strength
* ambulation and mobility
* postural reflexes and balance/equilibrium reactions
* sensory awareness and discrimination
* auditory localization
* perceptual skills, including directionality and laterality
* self-perception
* interpersonal skills
* self-care skills, including oral-motor skills
* communication skills
* productivity interests and skills
* leisure interests and skills

Instruments

* Screening for Physical and Occupational Therapy Referral (SPOTR) by T. Woosely, D.I. Sands, and W. Dunlap. 1987. An instrument to screen sensory impaired persons for referral to physical and occupational therapy. *Journal of Rehabilitation* 53(4):66–69.
* activities of daily living scale
* occupational history
* leisure checklist

PROBLEMS

Motor
- The person loses ease of mobility.
- Hand functions that normally rely on visual input are decreased.

Sensory
- The person has a loss of acuity.
- The person has a loss of color vision.
- The person may have no awareness of the environment.
- The person may have light perception only (awareness of light and dark).
- The person may have travel vision but cannot move safely about the environment independently.

Cognitive
Learning problems may occur for persons previously dependent on sight for gaining most of their information.

Intrapersonal
- The person has feelings of insecurity.
- The person has feelings of helplessness and hopelessness.
- The person has feelings of inadequacy.
- The person may be depressed.
- The person may become introverted.

Interpersonal
- The person may become dependent on others.
- The person may avoid friends and situations previously enjoyed.

Self-Care
The person may have a loss of skills that depend on vision, such as grooming, telling time, or matching socks, skirt, and blouse.

Productivity
The person may be unable to continue a former occupation or need adjustments in the working environment.

Leisure
The person may be unable to continue some leisure interests previously enjoyed or need adjustments to continue them, such as stamp or coin collecting and reading.

TREATMENT/MANAGEMENT

Motor
- Help the person regain mobility.
- Provide practice in using hands in activities.

Sensory
- Increase the person's skills and awareness of other sensory modalities, including hearing, touch, kinesthesia, proprioception, and vestibulum.

Cognitive
Inform the person of learning options available to the blind, including books on tape and computer programs with sound.

Intrapersonal
Improve self-perception through use of creative activities, such as crafts, drama, dance, or music activities.

Interpersonal
- Encourage the person's family to discuss role changes that may occur because of blindness and what roles the person can perform within the family structure.
- Encourage the person to participate in social activities.

Self-Care
Help the person organize objects needed for activities of daily living, such as marking objects for easy identification and making use of Braille-coded objects, such as watches and timers.

Productivity
- Help the person determine whether previous employment or job interests are feasible with limited or no sight.
- Suggest changes that could be made in the work environment to facilitate continued employment for a person with limited sight.
- Help the person explore alternate vocational interests if continuation of present employment is not possible.
- Help the person organize home living environment to facilitate management of it.

Leisure
Help the person explore new or redevelop old interests adapted for blind persons, including materials that can be purchased, such as Braille-marked cards.

PRECAUTIONS
- Safety is a major concern. Always check equipment and the physical environment for possible hazards.
- If blindness is due to diabetic retinopathy, be aware of other problems associated with diabetes, such as poor circulation and loss of tactile sensation.

PROGNOSIS AND OUTCOME
- The person can demonstrate the ability to perform basic activities of daily living independently.
- The person is able to negotiate home and local community without assistance.

- The person is able to engage in productive activities as a worker, student or volunteer.
- The person participates in a variety of leisure activities.

REFERENCES

Baker-Nobles, L., and M.P. Bink. 1979. Sensory integration in the rehabilitation of blind adults. *American Journal of Occupational Therapy* 33:559–64.

Jacobs, P.L., S. VanZandt, and N. Stinnett. 1983. Working towards independence for the elderly visually impaired. *Physical and Occupational Therapy in Geriatrics* 2(3):39–53.

Kern, T.R., and C.E. Shaw. 1985. An interdisciplinary approach to training the adult blind client: Occupational therapy and orientation and mobility collaborate. *Journal of Visual Impairments and Blindness* 79(8):341–46.

McCormick, D.P. 1984. Handicapped skiing: A current review of downhill snow skiing for the disabled. *Physical and Occupational Therapy in Pediatrics* 4(3):27–44.

Wade, A.tS. 1988. Sensory loss: Blindness and deafness. In *Willard and Spackman's occupational therapy*, 7th ed., ed. H.L. Hopkins and H.D. Smith 582–600. Philadelphia: J.B. Lippincott.

Zemlick, M.E. 1982. Case study: J. *Sensory Integration Special Interest Section Newsletter* 5(3):3.

Chronic Pain

DESCRIPTION

Chronic pain is usually defined as pain that has lost its adaptive biologic role. In other words, the pain persists beyond what could be expected for the course of a disease or persists beyond the time expected for an injury to heal, or it recurs at various times for months or years.

CAUSE

The cause of chronic pain is not completely understood, and several theories exist. Pain can be classified into three major types: (1) nociceptive pain that is due to activation of pain-sensitive nerve fibers, either somatic or visceral, and produces an aching or pressure sensation, (2) deafferentation pain that is due to nerve tissue damage that results in interruption of afferent pathways (the pathophysiology is poorly understood; it produces a burning or lancinating sensation), and (3) psychogenic pain that occurs in the absence of a known organic lesion but does include malingering or Munchausen's syndrome. The types of pain sensation are much more varied.

ASSESSMENT

Areas
- range of motion
- endurance and physical fitness
- pain (note location, intensity, and during which motions or activities)
- self-perception
- coping skills
- support skills

- daily living skills
- productivity (note history, skills, interests, and values)
- leisure interests and skills
- other types of assessment may be needed depending on the location and type of pain

Instruments
- Schultz Upper Extremity Pain Assessment by K.S. Schultz. 1984. The Schultz structured interview for assessing upper extremity pain. *Occupational Therapy in Health Care* 1(3):69–82.
- McGill Pain Questionnaire by R. Melzak. 1975. The McGill Pain Questionnaire: Major properties and scoring methods. *Pain* 3:277–299 (not an occupational therapist).

PROBLEMS

Motor
- The person may protect joints to avoid pain that accompanies movement.
- The person may lose range of motion due to failure to move or exercise joints.
- The person may develop contractures due to failure to move or exercise joints.
- The person may have lassitude or lack of energy.

Sensory
- The person may have aching pain.
- The person may experience pressure pain.
- The person may have burning pain.
- The person may have lancinating pain.
- Loss of sense of taste for food may occur.

Cognitive
The person may be unable to concentrate attention because pain interrupts.

Intrapersonal
- Depression is frequent.
- The person usually has blunted affect.
- The person may experience sleep disorders.
- The person may complain of having decreased appetite.
- The person may feel hopelessness or helplessness and a sense of futility.

Interpersonal
- The person may withdraw from social situations.
- The person may have loss of libido.
- The person may be depressed.

Self-Care
The person may avoid performing certain activities of daily living to avoid associated pain.

Productivity

The person may be unable to perform job tasks because pain interferes.

Leisure

• The person may lack energy to perform leisure activities.
• The person may avoid leisure activities to avoid associated pain.

TREATMENT/MANAGEMENT

Motor

To avoid or reduce immobilization, encourage the person to participate in a graded activity program, beginning with the level of activity the person can tolerate before pain becomes a factor.

Sensory

Focus away from sensory registration and processing.

Cognitive

Help the person learn to manage or organize time rather than pain. Take rest breaks not pain breaks. Rest before pain becomes a factor. Make rest the reward, not pain.

Intrapersonal

• To counteract depression, increase the person's level of activity.
• Participation in activity task groups can help the person reestablish a sense of self.
• Individual activities in creative crafts or competitive games can help the person reestablish a sense of mastery.
• Have the person identify enjoyable rewards that can be used when personal goals are obtained. Charting activity is one useful measure the person can use to see progress by engaging in activity rather than responding to pain.
• Provide training in relaxation techniques if pain is related to stressors in the person's life.

Interpersonal

• Participation in group discussion can assist in identifying stressors that lead to pain.
• Help the person's family decrease and finally stop responding to pain behavior. Encourage other kinds of interaction.

Self-Care

Encourage the person to maintain or increase independence in performing activities of daily living.

Productivity

• Provide work hardening, if needed, to assist in return to work.
• Provide opportunities for the person to explore career options, if needed.
• Provide opportunities for the person to practice home management skills.

Leisure

Explore with the person leisure activities, including old and new interests.

PRECAUTIONS

Be aware of changing theories of pain causation and corresponding changes in treatment techniques. Pain causation is still poorly understood.

PROGNOSIS AND OUTCOME

- The person is able to manage and control pain.
- The person demonstrates ability to solve problems and make decisions.
- The person demonstrates ability to follow a time management plan.
- The person demonstrates a positive self-image.
- The person demonstrates internal locus of control.
- The person has a dependable social support system.
- The person is able to perform self-care and daily living activities independently using self-help devices if needed.
- The person demonstrates performance of productive activities.
- The person demonstrates performance of leisure activities.

REFERENCES

Affleck, A., E. Bianchi, M. Cleckley, et al. 1984. Stress management as a component of occupational therapy in acute care settings. *Occupational Therapy in Health Care* 1(3):17–41.

Ament, P. 1982. Concepts in the use of hypnosis for pain relief in cancer. *Journal of Medicine: Clinical, Experimental and Theoretical* 13(3):233–40.

Bettencourt, C.M. 1987. An occupational adjustment group for a pain population. *Work Programs Special Interest Section Newsletter* 1(4):1, 3.

Blakeney, A.B. 1984. Occupational therapy intervention in chronic pain. *Occupational Therapy in Health Care* 1(3):43–54.

Borrelli, E.F., and C.A. Warfield. 1986. Occupational therapy for chronic pain. *Hospital Practice* 36(Aug. 15):36K–36L,36N,36P,36R,37.

Cardenas, D.D., J. Larson, and K.J. Egan. 1986. Hysterical paralysis in the upper extremity of chronic pain patients. *Archives of Physical Medicine and Rehabilitation* 67(3):190–3.

Costanzo, D.M. 1990. A patient's and therapist's experiences with pain treatment by orthokinetic orthoses. *Occupational Therapy Forum* 5(49):6–7,12–13,18.

Cromwell, F.S., ed. 1984. *Occupational therapy and the patient with pain.* New York: Haworth Press. Published also in *Occupational Therapy in Health Care* 1(3):1–135; 1984.

Curry, R.T. 1989. Understanding patients with chronic pain in work hardening programs. *Work Programs Special Interest Section Newsletter* 3(3):1–2.

Flower, A., E. Naxon, R.E. Jones, et al. 1981. An occupational therapy program for chronic back pain. *American Journal of Occupational Therapy* 35(4):243–8.

Giles, G.M., and M.E. Allen. 1986. Occupational therapy in the treatment of the patient with chronic pain. *British Journal of Occupational Therapy* 49(1):4–9.

Groat, B.A. 1983. The role of the occupational therapist. In *Management of patients with chronic pain*, ed. S.F. Brena and S.L. Chapman, 217–23. New York: SP Medical & Scientific Books.

Gusich, R.L. 1984. Occupational therapy for chronic pain: A clinical application of the model of human occupation. *Occupational Therapy Journal of Research* 4(3):59–73.

Heck, S.A. 1988. The effect of purposeful activity on pain tolerance. *American Journal of Occupational Therapy* 42(9):577–81.

Heck, S.A. 1990. Pain management in the acute care setting. *Occupational Therapy Forum* 5(46):6–8.

Johnson, J.A. 1984. Occupational therapy and patient with pain. *Occupational Therapy in Health Care* 1(3):7–15.

McCormack, G.L. 1988. Pain management by occupational therapists. *American Journal of Occupational Therapy* 42(9):582–90.

Moran, C.A., S.R. Saunders, and S.M. Tribuzi. 1990. Myofascial pain in the upper extremity. In *Rehabilitation of the hand*, 3d ed., ed. J.M. Hunter, et al., 731-56. St. Louis: C.V. Mosby.

Neeman, R.L., and M. Neeman. 1986. Treatment of dyskinesis and pain by orthokinetic orthoses in geriatric practice. *Occupational Therapy Forum* 2(15):19–21.

Neeman, R.L., et al. 1987. Rehabilitation of chronic upper extremity pain in post-CVA hemiparesis; tendonitis; and lateral epicondylistis by orthokinesis analgesia. *Canadian Journal of Rehabilitation* 1:17–28.

Potts, H., and S. Baptiste. 1989. An occupational therapy medico-legal programme for chronic pain patients. *Canadian Journal of Occupational Therapy* 56(4):193–7.

Rogers, S.R., J. Shuer, and S. Herig. 1984. The use of biofeedback techniques in occupational therapy for persons with chronic pain. *Occupational Therapy in Health Care* 1(3):103–8.

Strong, J. 1986. Occupational therapy's contribution to pain management in Queensland. *Australian Occupational Therapy Journal* 33(3):108–13.

Tigges, K.N., L.M. Sherman, and F.S. Sherwin. 1984. Perspectives on the pain of the hospice patient: The roles of the occupational therapist and physician. *Occupational Therapy in Health Care* 1(3):55–68.

Zelik, L.L. 1984. The use of assertiveness training with chronic pain patients. *Occupational Therapy in Health Care* 1(3):109–18.

Deaf-Blind

DESCRIPTION

A deaf-blind person has suffered loss of both hearing and sight. The amount of loss varies.

CAUSE

The most common cause is rubella (measles) occurring in the mother during the first trimester of pregnancy. Causes after birth include meningitis or other infectious diseases that cause edema in the brain.

ASSESSMENT

Areas

- muscle tone
- reflex development and maturation
- muscle strength
- gross motor skills and coordination
- fine motor skills, dexterity, and manipulation
- self-stimulation behavior
- sensory registration
- sensory sensitivity
- attending behavior
- attention span and concentration
- concept formation
- memory
- learning

- self-perception
- social conduct
- social control
- communication skills
- daily living skills
- play skills
- academic skills
- leisure interests and skills

Instruments
- Callier Asuza Scale by R.D. Stillman, Dallas, TX: Callier Speech and Hearing Center, 1973.
- Developmental Programming for Infants and Young Children by D.S. Schafer and M.S. Moersch, eds., Ann Arbor, MI: University of Michigan Press, 1977.
- activities of daily living scale
- play scale

PROBLEMS

Motor
- The person usually has delays in attaining developmental milestones.
- The person may be hypoactive due to lack of stimulation through sensory system.
- The person may have multiple handicaps, including heart defects, neurological problems, or other organ malformations.
- The person may have a hyperresponsive sympathetic nervous system and difficulty maintaining homeostasis.

Sensory
- The person usually exhibits self-stimulation behavior, especially in reaction to light (flipping the fingers in front of the eyes).
- Other sensory systems may be affected, especially the vestibular because of its close proximity to the auditory system.
- The person may have delays in recognizing, receiving, discriminating, integrating, and tolerating sensory input.
- The person may be hypersensitive and tactilely defensive when handling things or being handled.
- The person may have visual problems, such as cataracts or strabismus.

Cognitive
- Mental retardation may be present or the person may be labeled retarded when the real problem is multisensory deprivation.
- The person usually has delays in cognitive development, such as imitative behavior.

Intrapersonal
- The person may lack extrinsic motivation necessary for normal development.
- The person may lack curiosity, which is facilitated normally through vision and hearing.

- The person may cry continuously whether handled or left alone.
- The person may have a poor self-image.
- The person may exhibit behavioral problems.

Interpersonal
- Social skills usually are delayed.
- Communication skills usually are delayed.

Self-Care
Development of daily living skills is delayed.

Productivity
Play skills may be underdeveloped.

Leisure
Leisure interests may be few, if any.

TREATMENT/MANAGEMENT
Models of treatment are based on sensory integration, neurodevelopment, and behavior modification.

Motor
Promote development of sequential milestones. Gross motor skills may be facilitated by use of swings, slides, seesaws, tunnels, jungle gyms, scooters, large balls, and sandboxes that permit swinging, climbing, rolling, crawling, stepping over and under, throwing, catching, and turning around.

Sensory
- Increase sensory awareness of tactile, proprioceptive, kinesthetic, vibratory, and vestibular senses through opportunities to use each sense.
- Develop discrimination skills within each sense through experiences with multiple examples of the same sensory experiences—a variety of textures, positions, speeds, smells, and tastes.
- Develop whatever sight and hearing remains; maximize visual contrasts using flashlights or light bulbs placed under a clear plastic or glass surface; use a variety of prerecorded sounds, percussion instruments, or wind chimes.
- Provide opportunities to integrate sensory input.
- Increase tolerance to sensory stimulation and decrease hypersensitivity. Use pressure to reduce tactile defensiveness. Permit person to control movement to reduce gravitational insecurity or intolerance to movement.

Cognitive
- Teach the use of compensatory skills for sight, such as counting steps, visualizing spatial relationships, or listening for vibrations.
- Teach the person to anticipate a sequence of events through repeated experiences, such as games.

- Develop concepts of object recognition and permanence through exploration of the environment, toys, and games.
- Teach the person cause-and-effect relations by letting the person experience the consequence of his or her actions using the discovery approach—turning on fan, opening a box, peeling a banana.

Intrapersonal
- Provide opportunities to experience control over (mastery of) the environment.
- Provide opportunities for reality testing—liquids can spill; objects can break, tear, or be knocked over; the right tool usually does the job better.
- Increase self-perception through the use of creative activities, such as art, crafts, dance, drama, or music.

Interpersonal
- Encourage social interaction and development of social skills.
- Support other team members in setting and enforcing rules of conduct and behavior.
- Help the parents establish a trusting relationship built on feelings of safety, satisfaction, predictability, and dependability.
- Facilitate language development by using consistent signs and symbols, rhythms, motions, and vibrations.

Self-Care
- Assist in development of skills in activities of daily living, such as feeding and dressing.
- Provide opportunities to learn daily living skills, such as the use of money, how to shop, and preparing a meal.

Productivity
- Develop play skills, including cooperative activities.
- Teach basic work habits and work skills by participation in work activities in the home or clinic.
- Encourage the person to participate in home management activities, such as putting away the groceries, hanging up clothes, putting laundry in the washing machine, and raking leaves.
- Assist in assessing possible career choices.

Leisure
Encourage the development of leisure skills, including solitary, group, and community activities.

PROGNOSIS AND OUTCOME
- The person will be able to perform independent basic activities of daily living.
- The person can perform productive tasks.
- The person can perform leisure activities.
- The person demonstrates language skills.
- The person demonstrates social skills in one-to-one and group situations.

REFERENCES

Campbell, P.H. 1987. Integrated programming for students with multiple handicaps. In *Innovative program design for individuals with dual sensory impairments*, ed. L. Goetz, D. Guess, and K. Stremel-Campbell, 159–88. Baltimore, MD: Paul H. Brookes Publishing.

Harris, S.R., and M. Thompson. 1983. Water as a learning environment for facilitating gross motor skills in deaf-blind children. *Physical and Occupational Therapy in Pediatrics* 3(1):75–82.

Moersch, M.S. 1977. Training the deaf-blind child. *American Journal of Occupational Therapy* 31(7):425–31 (classic article).

Snow, B.S. 1985. Children with visual or hearing impairments. In *Occupational therapy for children*, ed. P.N. Clark and A.S. Allen, 430-55. St. Louis: C.V. Mosby. Revised in P.N. Pratt and A.S. Allen, eds., 2d ed., 1989, 535–62.

Wade, A.S. 1988. Sensory loss—Blindness and deafness. In *Willard and Spackman's occupational therapy*, 7th ed., ed. H.L. Hopkins and H.D. Smith, 582–600. Philadelphia: J.B. Lippincott.

Hearing Loss—Child

DESCRIPTION

Hearing loss means difficulty in hearing normal speech or common sounds in the environment. Normal hearing requires the ability to perceive sounds in the speech range of 500 to 2000 hertz or sound waves measured at approximately 60 decibels. Hearing loss occurs when a person loses 16 decibels in the 500 to 2000 hertz range. A person is described as prelingually deaf if he or she did not have or lost hearing prior to the development of speech, and prevocationally deaf if he or she lost hearing ability before reaching age 19. Adult deafness refers to hearing loss occurring after age 19.

CAUSE

Two major causes are (1) a lesion in the external auditory canal or the middle ear (conductive hearing loss) or (2) a lesion in the inner ear or the 8th nerve (sensorineural hearing loss). Onset may occur at any age.

ASSESSMENT

Areas
- gross motor skills
- muscle tone
- fine motor coordination, manipulation, dexterity
- praxis
- bilateral integration
- balance and postural control
- sensory awareness and discrimination in visual, tactile, proprioceptive, kinesthetic, and vestibular systems
- attention span and concentration
- sequential learning
- self-perception

- coping skills
- social skills
- language development
- daily living skills
- play skills
- leisure skills and interests

Instruments
- Southern California Sensory Integration Tests by A.J. Ayres, Los Angeles: Western Psychological Services, 1980. (Note: Language/communication barriers may make the test difficult to administer. Check child's understanding of language and method of communication before administering the test.)
- Sensory Integration Praxis Tests by A.J. Ayres, Los Angeles: Western Psychological Services, 1989.
- Southern California Postrotary Nystagmus Tests by A.J. Ayres, Los Angeles: Western Psychological Services, 1975.
- Test of Motor Impairment by D.H. Stott, F.A. Moyes, and S.E. Henderson, Guelph, Ontario: Brook Educational Publishing, 1972 (not occupational therapists).
- activities of daily living scale
- occupational history and academic history
- leisure checklist

PROBLEMS

Motor
- The child may be clumsy and uncoordinated, especially in bilateral coordination.
- The child may have poor or inadequate muscle tone and cocontraction.
- The child may have difficulty with fine motor skills, which would limit his or her ability to perform the rhythmic sequencing of fingers and hands necessary for signing.
- The child may have difficulty with praxis (motor planning).
- The child may have inadequate postural reflex integration (equilibrium reactions) or antigravity postural control.
- The child may have poor bilateral integration.
- The child may be hyperactive.
- The child may have poor oral motor functions, including control of saliva, sucking, chewing and swallowing, use of tongue for sound production, and absent or hyperactive gag reflex.

Sensory
- The child may have problems with eye motility, such as fixation, scanning, or tracking.
- The child may have visual perceptual problems related to visual spatial perception, form constancy, and visual sequential memory, which could interfere with learning letters, copying letters correctly in sequence, and spelling.
- The child may have prolonged or depressed postrotary nystagmus. (Note: A child with hearing impairment may have superior visual concentration and refocusing ability because

of dependence on visual input. Vestibular testing should include balance tests as well to determine possible vestibular dysfunction.)
- The child may be tactilely defensive, which interferes with wearing a hearing aid.
- The child may have difficulty organizing multisensory input.

Cognitive
- The child may have poor attending behavior due to visual and/or auditory distractibility.
- The child may have difficulty planning ahead.
- The child may have difficulty with problem-solving and decision-making.
- The child may have delays in developing conceptualization and categorization skills.

Intrapersonal
- The child may have poor self-perception and sense of mastery.
- The child may have low self-identity and self-esteem.
- The child may feel isolated and rejected.
- The child may have low motivation due to overprotection at home.
- The child may be impulsive.
- The child may have behavior problems, such as temper tantrums, stubbornness, or inflexibility.

Interpersonal
- The child may fail to develop or have delayed development of language skills.
- The child usually is delayed in development of social skills.
- The child may be overdependent on others.
- The family usually experiences grief or mourning after initial diagnosis.
- The family may respond to guilt by overprotecting the child.
- The family relations may be strained.
- The child often experiences stereotyping and prejudice in the community.

Self-Care
The child may be delayed in developing daily living skills.

Productivity
- The child may have poorly developed play skills.
- The child usually lags behind peers in developing reading and writing skills due to language deficits.
- The child may experience job discrimination and other work-related difficulties as a young adult.
- The child may lack skills in homemaking and home management due to institutional living situation.

Leisure
The child may have few leisure interests.

TREATMENT/MANAGEMENT

Models of treatment are based primarily on sensory integration and secondarily on neurodevelopmental therapy and behavior modification.

Motor

- Assist the child in developing motor milestones, if needed.
- Improve balance of muscle tone between flexion and extension.
- Develop fine motor skills, especially bilateral coordination.
- Improve bilateral integration, if needed. (See section on vestibular-bilateral disorders.)
- Increase postural security and balance, especially in antigravity positions, if needed.
- Improve motor planning skills, if needed. (See section on developmental dyspraxia.)

Sensory

- Improve the child's eye motility skills, if needed.
- Improve visual perceptual skills, especially form constancy and spatial relationships, if needed.
- Decrease tactile defensiveness, if present. (See section on tactile defensiveness.)
- Moderate vestibular response if hyper- or hyporesponsiveness is present. (See section on gravitational insecurity.)

Cognitive

- Increase attending behavior and attention span, if needed.
- Improve problem-solving and decision-making skills by permitting choice.
- Improve sequential relationship skills through the use of activities and games that have steps or a series of tasks to complete.
- Increase time management skills by planning and following a schedule of activities.

Intrapersonal

- Improve self-perception through creative activities, such as arts, crafts, music, drama, and dance.
- Increase coping skills through a stress management program.

Interpersonal

- Assist in developing the child's language skills. (Note: The most common communication technique is American sign language, or ASL, in conjunction with finger spelling and speech reading, which is called total communication.)
- Improve group interaction skills through use of group tasks or activities.

Self-Care

Assist in developing the child's daily living skills, such as reading a newspaper or bus schedule or filling out a form.

Productivity

- Provide work-related experiences to teach work habits, cooperation with peers, following directions, and applying for a job, including filling out an application and interviewing.
- Provide opportunities for practicing skills in homemaking, home management, and

independent living through simulated experiences or actual experiences, such as shopping for groceries.

Leisure
Provide opportunities to explore leisure interests and develop skills.

PRECAUTIONS

- Vestibular dysfunction may be difficult to determine without the assistance of an audiologist or neurologist because of compensatory behavior through the visual system.
- Communication must be established prior to testing or treatment. The therapist may need to learn signing or use alternate communication symbol systems, such as Bliss symbols, in order to communicate with the child.
- Some deaf children are extremely sensitive to rotation. Watch carefully for signs.

PROGNOSIS AND OUTCOME

- The child is able to coordinate the use of two hands to sign.
- The child is able to perform gross motor skills, including jumping, hopping, and skipping.
- The child is able to maintain balance and postural control in static (standing balance) and dynamic situations.
- The child is able to perform motor planning tasks when presented with activities that are unfamiliar.
- The child's response to visual, tactile, proprioceptive, and vestibular stimuli is within normal range.
- The child has attention span within normal range.
- The child demonstrates the ability to plan and complete a task that requires organizing a sequence of steps or tasks.
- The child is able to plan and follow a daily activity schedule.
- The child demonstrates improved self-perception.
- The child demonstrates knowledge of stress management techniques.
- The child has functional communication skills using oral and/or signing techniques.
- The child is able to interact in group situations within his or her age range.
- The child is able to perform activities of daily living independently within his or her age range.
- The child is able to perform productive activities within his or her age range.
- The child is able to perform leisure activities within his or her age range.

REFERENCES

Crowe, T.K., and F.B. Horak. 1988. Motor proficiency associated with vestibular deficits in children with hearing impairments. *Physical Therapy* 68(10):1493–99.

Finocchiaro, A. 1982. Sensory integration: Considerations for programming for deaf school children. *Sensory Integration Special Interest Section Newsletter* 5(2):1–2.

Horak, F.B., A. Shumway-Cook, T.K. Crowe, et al. 1988. Vestibular function and motor proficiency in children with hearing impairments and in learning disabled children with motor impairments. *Developmental Medicine and Child Neurology* 30:64-79.

Jirgal, D. 1982. Sensory integration and the hearing impaired child. *Sensory Integration Special Interest Section Newsletter* 5(2):1–2.

Madill, H.M., and O.C. Gironella. 1982. Occupational therapy services for hearing impaired children. *Sensory Integration Special Interest Section Newsletter* 5(4):1–3.

Schaaf, R.C. 1985. The frequency of vestibular disorders in developmentally delayed preschoolers with otitis media. *American Journal of Occupational Therapy* 39(4):247–52.

Snow, B.S. 1985. Children with visual or hearing impairment. In *Occupational therapy for children*, ed. P.N. Clark and A.S. Allen, 430–55. St. Louis: C.V. Mosby. Revised in P.N. Pratt and A.S. Allen, eds, 2d ed., 1989, 535–62.

Spiegel, S. 1982. Sensory integration programming for hearing impaired children. *Sensory Integration Special Interest Section Newsletter* 5(2):3–4.

Von, T., J.C. Deitz, J. McLaughlin, et al. 1988. The effects of chronic otitis media on motor performance in 5- and 6-year-old children. *American Journal of Occupational Therapy* 42(7):421–6.

Wade, A.S. 1988. Sensory loss: Blindness and deafness. In *Willard and Spackman's occupational therapy* 7th ed., ed. H.L. Hopkins and H.D. Smith, 582–600. Philadelphia: J.B. Lippincott.

Low Vision

DESCRIPTION

Low vision is defined as bilateral subnormal visual acuity or abnormal visual field resulting from a disorder in the visual system that results in decreased visual performance.

CAUSE

There are multiple causes that include reduced light transmission through the cornea, loss of retinal receptors, and changes in the eye membrane. Diseases associated with low vision include macular degeneration, cataracts, glaucoma, diabetic retinopathy, optic atrophy, degenerative myopia, and retinitis pigmentosa.

ASSESSMENT

Areas
- mobility
- sensory registration
- sensory processing
- perceptual skills
- problem-solving skills
- self-perception
- coping skills
- daily living skills
- productivity history, skills, interests, and values
- leisure activities and skills

Instruments

No instruments developed by occupational therapists were identified in the literature. The following types of instruments may be useful.
- activities of daily living scale
- occupational history
- leisure checklist

PROBLEMS

Motor
- The person has decreased ease of mobility.
- The person has increased incidence of fractures, burns, or other injuries.

Sensory
- There is frequent loss of visual discrimination (contrast perception) of detail versus background.
- The person may lose macular vision, which reduces the ability to focus directly on an object or person.
- The person may lose peripheral vision, which reduces the ability to scan the visual field.
- The person may have night blindness—the inability to see in dim or faint light.
- The person may have color vision defects—reduced ability to see the saturation of light necessary to accurately identify colors.
- The person may lose depth perception, which reduces the ability to orient oneself and objects in space and judge the distance between oneself and objects.
- The person may have increased sensitivity to glare—unable to see in certain lighting conditions.

Cognitive
- Cognitive abilities are not directly affected by the disorder.
- Some indirect consequences may be the loss of opportunities to learn or relearn information because visual conditions were not suited to the person's special needs.

Intrapersonal
- The person usually loses self-esteem and self-confidence.
- The person may feel hopeless and helpless.
- The person may feel anxious and demonstrate increased stress reactions.
- The person may become depressed or angry.
- The person may lack motivation and be apathetic.
- The person may become dependent on others.
- The person may experience a sense of loss and may mourn loss of good sight.

Interpersonal
- The person may reduce social interactions because of difficulty participating with others who have better vision.
- The person may relinquish roles or experience a change of roles in the family.

Self-Care
The person may experience a decrease in ability to perform activities of daily living independently.

Productivity
- The person may experience difficulties in performing home management activities.

- The person may retire from work or quit volunteering because of changes in visual acuity or field of vision.

Leisure
The person may discontinue some leisure activities or interests because of loss of visual acuity or changes in field of vision.

TREATMENT/MANAGEMENT

Motor
Help the person identify situations in mobility that are difficult to negotiate safely and suggest solutions, such as small risers on outside stairs that might be difficult to see on a bright sunny day. A cane can be used to determine the depth and the slope of a railing.

Sensory
- Provide the person with opportunities to practice using new visual equipment or optical aids that may be prescribed.
- Provide practice in using other senses to substitute or compensate for low vision, especially tactile and hearing senses.

Examples of Optical and Nonoptical Aids

- magnifiers
- telescopes
- gooseneck lamps that adjust to a variety of positions to increase illumination
- large print clocks and watches
- bold line checks
- acetate filter to increase contrast between background and foreground
- large print books
- large print playing cards
- color-coded marks on stove or range to indicate temperature

---

Cognitive
- Instruct the person in the possibility of using other senses to substitute or compensate for low vision.
- Dispel stereotypic fears of blindness. Few people are completely blind and few are completely helpless; a decrease in visual acuity is not a death sentence.
- Encourage the person to use creative problem-solving skills for his or her life situation that are satisfactory to the person and family members.
- Instruct the person on how to make the living environment safer by using better lighting, providing better contrasts of light and dark surfaces, and removing items that might trip the person, such as throw rugs, power cords, or small footstools.

Intrapersonal
- Provide opportunities for the person to improve self-perception through the use of creative activities, such as art, crafts, drama, music, and dance.
- Encourage the person to express feelings about decreasing vision and talk about what situations or tasks are most difficult to perform.

Interpersonal
- Encourage the person to participate in group situations with other people who have low vision or are blind to learn how others cope and to trade hints for solving problems.
- Help the family sort out roles in the family unit and encourage the person with low vision to adopt an active role.
- Encourage the person and family to seek out resources in the community and use the resources as needed.

Self-Care
- Explore with the person activities of daily living that have become more difficult to perform and suggest approaches that might improve performance, overcome fear of performing, or make the task easier to do.
- Determine if self-help devices and optical or nonoptical aids may be useful to the person and suggest that the person try using the devices.

Productivity
- Explore with the person any home management activities that may have become more difficult to perform and suggest approaches, including the use of optical or nonoptical aids that might improve performance or make the task easier to do.
- Encourage the person to engage in other productive activities, such as volunteering.

Leisure
- Encourage the person to explore old interests that could be renewed and to develop new interests.
- Suggest modifications, such as the use of optical or nonoptical aids, that might make the activities more fun.

PRECAUTIONS
- Always be alert to safety hazards.
- Always be alert for possible changes in or loss of tactile sensitivity.

PROGNOSIS AND OUTCOME
- The person is able to perform activities of daily living independently.
- The person can perform productive activities.
- The person engages in a variety of leisure activities.
- The person is knowledgeable about community and equipment resources available to people with low vision.

REFERENCES

Jacobs, P.L., S. VanZandt, and N. Stinnett. 1983. Working towards independence for the elderly visually impaired. *Physical and Occupational Therapy in Geriatrics* 2(3):39–53.

Reichley, T.L. 1988. Occupational therapy and low vision rehabilitation. *Occupational Therapy in Health Care* 5(2/3):99–109.

Sensory Deprivation

DESCRIPTION

Sensory deprivation is defined as the decreased ability to cope with the environment due to a lack of adequate sensory input and stimulation.

CAUSE

Contributing causes may include age-related sensory changes associated with loss of acuity, pathological disorders such as mental disorders or brain disorders, and institutionalization.

ASSESSMENT

Areas
- range of motion
- gross motor skills and coordination
- fine motor and hand skills, dexterity, and manipulation
- motor planning (praxis) skills
- posture and postural control using protective and equilibrium reactions
- sensory acuity, especially visual and auditory
- sensory registration
- sensory processing
- attention span and concentration
- problem solving
- memory
- affect or mood
- self-perception
- communication skills
- daily living skills
- productivity history and skills
- leisure interests and skills

Instruments
- Geriatric Interpersonal Evaluation Scale (GIES) by R. Plutchik, et al. (See Paire in reference section.)

- Geriatric Rating Scale (GRS) by J. Parachek, Scottsdale, AZ: Greentree Publications, 1976. (See Paire in reference section.)
- Brayman, S.J., T.F. Kirby, A.M. Misenheimer, et al. 1976. Comprehensive occupational therapy evaluation. *American Journal of Occupational Therapy* 30(2):94–100.
- activities of daily living scale
- occupational history
- leisure checklist

PROBLEMS

Motor
- The person may have decreased range of motion.
- The person may have decreased gross motor skills and coordination.
- The person may show decreased level of activity.
- The person may have psychomotor retardation or restlessness (aimless walking).
- The person may have dyspraxia or poor motor planning skills.
- The person may have flexed posture.

Sensory
- The person may have decreased sensory awareness and processing.
- The person may have perceptual deficits.

Cognitive
- The person may be disoriented regarding time.
- The person may have decreased attention span.
- The person may show decreased use of problem solving.

Intrapersonal
The person may show any or all of the following:
- hostility
- apathy
- withdrawal
- hallucinations
- delusions
- anxiety

Interpersonal
- The person may have loss of role identification and performance.
- The person may show increased dependence on others.

Self-Care
The person usually has decreased performance of self-care and daily living activities.

Productivity
The person may have no identifiable productive role.

Leisure
The person may express few interests and perform few or no leisure activities.

TREATMENT/MANAGEMENT
The model for treatment is sensory integration based on the principles of sensory input as an alerting and organizing mechanism, and sensorimotor activity as meaningful information to the brain that leads to cognition.

Motor
- Increase gross motor skills, especially of the upper extremities, through participation in such games as balloon volleyball or group exercises.
- Improve postural control through social dance and bowling.
- Have the person participate in making short-term art or craft projects to increase fine motor skills.

Sensory
- Increase sensory awareness:
  1. olfactory, with perfume (present first to promote arousal) and food
  2. vision, with mirror and colored shapes
  3. auditory, with familiar sounds on a tape and singing familiar songs
  4. tactile, with warm and cool water and a variety of cloth fabrics
  5. vestibular, with bean bags or sponge balls
  6. gustatory, with hot chocolate, cheese, and crackers (present last to provide reinforcement)
- Increase the person's perceptual skills by working puzzles, playing cards, or playing board games.

Cognitive
- Encourage the person to participate in problem-solving and decision-making activities.
- Encourage the person to integrate the past and present through discussion and remembering activities, life review, or reminiscence.
- Increase orientation through such games as Twenty Questions and Name That Tune.

Intrapersonal
Provide opportunities for the person to regain self-control and a sense of mastery.

Interpersonal
Provide group situations where interaction can take place, such as exploring various stimuli or playing guessing games.

Self-Care
Maintain or increase independent performance of self-care skills.

Productivity
Encourage participation in productive activities, if possible.

Leisure

Encourage the person to regain and reengage in old interests and explore new interests if old ones are not feasible.

PROGNOSIS AND OUTCOME

- The person demonstrates increased level of activity.
- The person demonstrates erect or nearly erect posture.
- The person demonstrates increased range of motion of the head, neck, and upper extremities, especially in extension.
- The person demonstrates improved awareness of the environment, such as responding when greeted.
- The person is able to interact with short verbal responses.

REFERENCES

Corcoran, M.A. 1986. Intervention to promote competence in the elderly: An environment framed by sensory integration principles. *Sensory Integration Special Interest Section Newsletter* 9(4):3–4.

Corcoran, M.A., and D. Barrett. 1987. Using sensory integration principles with regressed elderly patients. *Occupational Therapy in Health Care* 4(2):119–28.

Paire, J.A., and R.J. Karney. 1984. The effectiveness of sensory stimulation for geropsychiatric inpatients. *American Journal of Occupational Therapy* 38(8):505–9.

Richman, L. 1969. Sensory training for geriatric patients. *American Journal of Occupational Therapy* 23:254–7 (classic article).

Rogers, J.C., C.L. Marcus, and T.L. Snow. 1987. Maude: A case of sensory deprivation. *American Journal of Occupational Therapy* 41(10):673–6.

Ross, M., and D. Burdick. 1981. *Sensory integration.* Thorofare, NJ: Slack.

Part III

Nervous System Disorders

Amyotrophic Lateral Sclerosis

DESCRIPTION

Amyotrophic lateral sclerosis (ALS) is a motor neuron disease characterized by progressive degeneration of corticospinal tracts and anterior horn cells of bulbar efferent neurons. Upper motor neuron involvement causes muscle spasticity and loss of muscle strength. Lower motor neuron involvement causes flaccidity, paralysis, and muscle atrophy. There are three subtypes of ALS: progressive muscular atrophy, progressive bulbar palsy, and primary lateral sclerosis, which is rare.

CAUSE

Although the cause is unknown, theories about its etiology include a slow-acting virus, toxic reaction, autoimmune disorder, hormone abnormality, and enzyme deficiency. People aged 40 to 70 are affected most frequently. Men are affected two to three times more frequently than women.

ASSESSMENT

Areas
- muscle strength
- range of motion
- muscle tone
- postural control and balance
- physical endurance
- pain
- sensory registration and processing
- problem-solving and decision-making skills
- memory skills
- judgment of safety
- self-perception
- mood or affect
- social skills
- roles
- daily living skills
- productivity history, skills, interests, values
- leisure skills and interests
- architectural and environmental barriers

Instruments
No specific instruments have been developed by occupational therapists, but some useful instruments include:

- functional muscle strength testing by groups of muscles
- range of motion testing
- activities of daily living testing
- occupational history
- leisure checklist

PROBLEMS

Motor
- Muscle weakness and atrophy (progressive muscular atrophy)
  1. intrinsic muscles of the hand
  2. upper arm and shoulder muscles
  3. lower limbs (usually in later stages) limiting mobility
- muscle spasticity and hyperreflexia (progressive muscular atrophy)
- muscle cramps in thigh muscles, which may result in falling
- muscle fasciculations
- brain stem signs (progressive bulbar palsy)
  1. dysarthria (difficulty articulating words when speaking due to tongue atrophy)
  2. dysphagia (difficulties with chewing and swallowing)
  3. dyspnea (difficulty in breathing due to respiratory muscle weakness)
- fatigue—muscles feel tired and heavy
- reduced range of motion

Sensory
Generally sensation is spared except in some hereditary cases.

Cognition
Generally cognition is intact unless an Alzheimer-type dementia is also present.

Intrapersonal
- The person may become depressed.
- The person may express feelings of hopelessness and despair.
- The person may feel helpless.
- The person may express suicidal thoughts.
- The person may lose self-image related to altered body image.

Interpersonal
The person may become socially withdrawn.

Self-Care
The person may be unable to perform activities that require fine motor skills, such as buttoning, zipping, and typing.

Productivity
The person may be unable to continue working because of physical limitations.

Leisure

The person may be unable to continue participating in sports activities, playing an instrument, or enjoying other leisure activities that require muscle strength or fine motor skills.

TREATMENT/MANAGEMENT

Treatment is based on symptoms and is aimed at maintaining an optimal level of function given the progressive, degenerative nature of the disease.

Clinical Stages of ALS

Stage 1: Person is able to perform normal activities of daily living. Minor limitations and some pain may be present. Endurance is less. Use of work-simplification and energy-conservation techniques can increase activity level.

Stage 2: Person demonstrates muscle imbalance, decreased mobility and function, and increased muscle fatigue due to using more energy to perform activities of daily living. Self-help aids may be useful to reduce the energy expended.

Stage 3: Person demonstrates progressive weakness of axial (trunk) muscles and greater loss of mobility and endurance. A wheelchair is essential to travel any distance. Assistance is needed to perform many activities of daily living.

Stage 4: Person is totally dependent in activities of daily living, a respirator may be needed, and swallowing is difficult or lost.

Source: Janiszewski, D.W., J.T. Caroscio, and L.H. Wisham. 1983. Amyotrophic lateral sclerosis: A comprehensive rehabilitation approach. *Archives of Physical Medicine and Rehabilitation* 64(7):304-07.

Motor
- If the person has muscle weakness
    1. Consider splints or slings to maintain functional position, such as a wrist cock-up, or an opponens, soft cervical collar, or ankle-foot orthosis.
    2. Consider the use of self-help devices to maintain functional performance, such as elongated handles, a zipper pull, button hook, universal cuff, cups with two handles, or a plate guard.
- If the person has muscle spasticity and muscle cramps
    1. Teach the person positions that reduce spasticity.
    2. Teach the person to change positions frequently.
    3. Teach the person to avoid situations that tend to increase spasticity, such as cold.
- If the person has brain stem symptoms
    1. Consider alternate communication if dysarthria becomes severe, such as language boards with words, pictures, or letters.

2. Consider recommending soft foods that require less chewing, moist foods to ease swallowing, eating slowly, and eating smaller bites. Increasing the number of meals and decreasing the size of the meals may also be useful.
3. Encourage good posture when resting or sleeping.
- Maintain the person's physical endurance during the early stages through sports such as swimming or bicycling.
- Help the person select a wheelchair. Generally the chair will need a reclining back, headrest, elevating padded legrest, padded armrest, and safety belt. A laptray and mobile arm supports may also be useful.
- An aquatics program may be useful to the person in practicing range of motion, maintaining endurance, and practicing balance activities.

Sensory
Assist the person in pain management (see section on chronic pain).

Cognitive
- Teach the person work-simplification and energy-conservation techniques.
- Teach the person safety considerations and methods of reducing architectural barriers, such as grab bars, reachers, and shower chairs.
- Teach the person and family about ALS and techniques for managing the progression of the disease.

Intrapersonal
Provide opportunities for the person to maintain a positive self-concept through performance of such activities as computer games, crafts, music, or dance.

Interpersonal
- Help the person select and train for the use of communication aids, including different types of telephones, eye-gaze charts, electronic scanners, and computer add-on boards.
- Discuss with the person's family the changing role and responsibilities that may occur, and help the family rearrange roles as the disease progresses.
- Encourage the family to participate in a self-help group if one is available.

Self-Care
- Consider eating aids, grooming aids, and other devices that will increase the person's level of independence.
- Environment-adapted aids that permit remote operation of lights, television, radio, and speakers may be useful as the disease progresses.

Productivity
- Consider possible modifications of the work environment that might permit the person to continue working or volunteering.
- Consider possible alternative work or volunteer situations.

Leisure
- Consider possible modifications of leisure activities, such as assistive equipment or changes in rules, that might permit the person to continue to participate in some activities.

• Explore with the person possible new interests within the physical capacities available.

PRECAUTIONS
• Muscle strengthening through progressive-resistive exercises is usually not part of the treatment program since strengthening will not alter the course of the disease and may cause cramping and fatigue.
• Watch for signs of decreased respiratory function.
• Avoid fatigue.
• Consider the cost, appearance, and acceptability to the person and the family of any assistive device.

PROGNOSIS AND OUTCOME
• The person is maintaining muscle strength within the level of disease.
• The person or family performs daily range-of-motion exercises.
• The person is maintaining physical endurance within the level of disease.
• The person is using proper positioning techniques to prevent deformity and contractures.
• The person is using adapted equipment, including splints or wheelchairs for positioning and self-help devices for self-care, productivity, or leisure, as needed.
• The person demonstrates knowledge of work simplification and energy-conservation techniques.
• The person and family demonstrate knowledge of safety precautions and techniques to decrease architectural barriers.
• The person is able to perform activities and roles that provide self-satisfaction.
• The person demonstrates independence in self-care activities within the level of the disease.
• The person performs productive activities
• The person performs leisure activities.
• The person and family are knowledgeable about community resources.

REFERENCES

Heidkamp, P.C. 1986. Home care of the amyotrophic lateral sclerosis patient. In *Amyotrophic lateral sclerosis: A guide to patient care*, ed. J.T. Caroscio, 247–55. New York: Thieme.
Johnson, C.R. 1988. Aquatic therapy for an ALS patient. *American Journal of Occupational Therapy* 42(2):115–20.
Kortman, B. 1987. Rehabilitation of patients with motor neuron disease: The occupational therapist's role. *Australian Occupational Therapy Journal* 34(3):114–20.
Pedretti, L.W., ed. 1990. *Occupational therapy: Practice skills for physical dysfunction*, 656–9. St. Louis: C.V. Mosby.
Sinaki, M. 1987. Physical therapy and rehabilitation techniques for patients with amyotrophic lateral sclerosis. *Advances in Experimental Medicine and Biology* 209:239–52.
Takai, V. 1982. ADL and adaptive equipment for ALS patients. *AOTA Physical Disabilities Special Interest Section Newsletter* 6:1–2.
Takai, V. 1986. The development of a feeding harness for an ALS patient. *American Journal of Occupational Therapy* 40(5):359–61.
Takai, V. 1986. Selection of assistive devices for amyotrophic lateral sclerosis patients. In *Amyotrophic lateral sclerosis: A guide to patient care*, ed. J.T. Caroscio, 188–217. New York: Thieme.

Cerebrovascular Disorder—Stroke

DESCRIPTION

A cerebrovascular accident (CVA) or stroke is characterized by the sudden or gradual onset of neurological symptoms caused by a diminished supply of blood to the brain. CVAs range from little strokes, called transient ischemic attacks (TIAs), in which the symptoms are reversible to a major stroke in which the symptoms may never completely go away.

CAUSE

The possible causes of a CVA include arteritis, atherosclerosis, cigarette smoking, diabetes mellitus, elevated levels of cholesterol, lipoprotein, or triglyceride in the blood, a family history of stroke, heart disease, high-estrogen oral contraceptives in women, hypertension, polychythemia vera, and a sedentary lifestyle.

ASSESSMENT

Areas
- range of motion
- muscle tone
- muscle strength
- gross motor coordination
- fine motor coordination, manipulation, and dexterity
- hand functions
- balance and postural control
- praxis and motor planning
- bilateral integration
- sensory registration
- sensory processing
- perceptual skills
- pain
- memory
- level of awareness
- orientation
- problem solving
- learning skills
- judgment of safety
- mood and affect
- self-perception
- language and communication
- social and family support
- daily living skills

- productivity history, skills, interests, and values
- leisure history, skills, and interests

Instruments

- *Hemiplegia evaluation* by B. Baum et al., Occupational Therapy Department, Boston: Massachusetts Rehabilitation Hospital, 1979.
- Brunnstrom Recovery Stages by S. Brunnstrom, *Movement therapy in hemiplegia*. New York: Harper & Row, 1970. (See also Shah, S.K. 1984. Reliability of the original Brunnstrom recovery scale following hemiplegia. *Australian Occupational Therapy Journal* 31(4):144–51.)
- BUSTOP (Burke Stroke Time-Oriented Profile) by J. Feigenson et al., *Archives of Physical Medicine and Rehabilitation* 60:508–511, 1981.
- St. Mary's CVA Evaluation by D. Harlow and J. Van Deusen, *American Journal of Occupational Therapy* 38(3):184–186, 1984. (See also Van Deusen, J., and D. Harlowe. 1986. Continued construct validation of the St. Mary's CVA evaluation: Brunnstrom arm and hand stage rating. *American Journal of Occupational Therapy* 40(8):561–3.)
- Bartel Index by F.I. Mahoney and D.W. Bartel, *Maryland State Medical Journal.* 14:61–65, 1965. (See revised guidelines in Shah, S., F. Vanclay, and B. Cooper. 1989. Improving the sensitivity of the Bartel Index for Stroke Rehabilitation. *Journal of Clinical Epidemiology* 42(8):703–9.)
- Nouri, F.M., and N.B. Lincoln. 1987. Extended activities of daily living scale for stroke patients. *Clinical Rehabilitation* 1:301–305.
- Motor Assessment Scale by J.L. Poole and S.L. Whitney, *Archives of Physical Medicine and Rehabilitation* 69(3):195–197, 1988.
- Kenny Self-Care Evaluation. (See Schoening, H.A., and I.A. Iverson. 1968. Numerical scoring of self-care status: A study of the Kenny self-care evaluation. *Archives of Physical Medicine and Rehabilitation* 49:221–229.)
- Jebsen Hand Function Test. (See Spaulding, S.J., et al. 1988. Jebsen Hand Function Tests: Performance of the uninvolved hand in hemiplegia and of right-handed, right and left hemiplegic persons. *Archives of Physical Medicine and Rehabilitation* 69(6):419–422.)
- Turton, A.J., and C.M. Fraser. 1986. A test battery to measure the recovery of voluntary movement control following stroke. *International Rehabilitation Medicine* 8(2):74–78. (Also in *British Journal of Occupational Therapy* 51(1):11–4,1988.)
- Australian ADL Index. (See Specer, C., M. Clark, and D.S. Smith. 1986. A modification of the Northwick Park ADL Index [the Australian ADL Index]. *British Journal of Occupational Therapy* 49(11):350–353.)
- Sensorimotor Integration Test Battery by L.E. Jongbloed, J.B. Collins, and W. Jones, *Occupational Therapy Journal of Research* 6(3):131–50, 1986. (See also Ottenbacker, K.H., and D. Goar. 1986. Commentary: A Sensorimotor Integration Test Battery for CVA clients: Preliminary evidence on reliability and validity. *Occupational Therapy Journal of Research* 6(3):151–6.)
- Functional Test. (See Wilson, D.J. 1984. Assessment of the hemiparetic upper extremity: A functional test. *Occupational Therapy in Health Care* 1(2):63–9.)
- Ritchie Articular Index. (See Bohannon, R.W., and A. LeFort. 1986. Hemiplegic shoulder pain measured with the Ritchie Articular Index. *International Journal of Rehabilitation Research* 9:379–81, 1986.)

PROBLEMS

Motor
- The person usually has hemiplegia and/or hemiparesis.
- The person may have clonus.
- The person may have spasticity.
- The person may have flaccidity.
- The person may have ataxia.
- The person may have motor perseveration or impersistence.
- The person may develop contractures.
- The person may have tendinitis.
- The person may have an impaired sense of equilibrium.

Sensory
- The person may have visual field deficits.
- The person may have diplopia (double vision).
- The person may have loss of visual acuity.
- The person may have homonymous hemianopsis (visual-spatial neglect).
- The person may have disturbance of body image or prosopagnosia (difficulty in recognizing familiar faces).
- The person may have astereognosis (tactile amnesia).
- The person may have visual-perceptual problems, such as difficulty with figure-ground or depth perception and spatial relations.
- The person may experience numbness or decreased tactile sensation.
- The person may have hyporesponsiveness (diminished or absent response to sensory input).
- The person may develop pressure sores.
- The person may develop pain (causalgia), especially in the shoulder.
- The person may develop shoulder-hand syndrome (see section on reflex sympathetic dystrophy syndrome–shoulder-hand syndrome).

Cognitive
- The person may have a decreased level of consciousness.
- The person may have decreased attending behavior.
- The person may be disoriented and confused.
- The person may have loss of memory.
- The person may have difficulty learning new information.
- The person may have poor judgment of safety.

Intrapersonal
- The person may become depressed or express feelings of despair and hopelessness.
- The person may be labile.
- The person may be anxious or fearful about health.
- The person may become hostile or angry.
- The person may have low frustration tolerance.
- The person may be easily irritated.

- The person may be apathetic or show a flat affect.
- The person may have poor self-concept and loss of self-esteem.

Interpersonal
- The person may have communication problems (expressive or receptive aphasia).
- The person may experience changes in social role.
- The person may experience sexual dysfunction.
- The person may have difficulty with social activities.

Self-Care
- The person usually experiences some difficulty in performing daily living skills, especially eating, dressing, grooming, and toileting.
- The person may be incontinent.
- The person may have dysphagia.

Productivity
- Many problems depend on whether the left or right side is involved.
- The person may be unable to use the involved hand.

Comparison of Left and Right Hemiplegia

Right Hemiplegia	*Left Hemiplegia*
Verbal communication difficulties, such as receptive or expressive or global aphasia	Visual, perceptual deficits
	Left visual field deficit
	Distractable
Right visual field deficit	Denial of problem with left side of body
Decreased computation (mathematics) skills	Impulsive behavior
Left/right confusion	Dressing apraxia
Deficits in memory	Difficulty crossing midline of body
Depression	
Motorapraxia	

Source: Based on Masden, J.C. 1985. The localization of lesions affecting the cerebral hemispheres. In *Localization of clinical neurology*, ed. P.W. Brazis, J.C. Masden, and J. Biller, 301–359. Boston: Little, Brown & Co.

TREATMENT/MANAGEMENT

Motor
- If the person has hemiplegia or hemiparesis (see also section on cerebrovascular disorder—hemiplegia)
  1. Provide range-of-motion exercises using facilitation techniques.
  2. Promote healthy positioning and body alignment.

3. Consider providing a splint to maintain the person's wrist and hand in a neutral or slightly extended position to avoid wrist drop.
- If the person has clonus, placing pressure on the heel or standing with heel down will stop the clonus.
- If the person has spasticity, use facilitation techniques designed to decrease the tone in the flexor muscles of the upper extremity and the extensor muscles in the lower extremity.
- If the person has flaccidity, use facilitation techniques designed to increase muscle tone.
- If the person has ataxia, avoid letting him or her walk unassisted on rough or uneven surfaces.
- If the person has motor perseveration, divert or refocus his or her attention.
- If the person has shoulder-hand syndrome, provide massage, compression, elevation, proper positioning, and vigorous exercise (see section on shoulder-hand syndrome).
- If the person has contractures, apply pressure in the direction opposite to the contracture, especially if the contractures resulted from an activity that required repetitive motions.
- If the person has subluxation, apply compression to the joint capsule and use a sling that holds the upper extremity in place.
- If the person has tendinitis, see shoulder-hand syndrome above.

Sensory
- If the person has visual deficits (see also section on perception and vision disorders), such as
  1. hemianopsia, approach the person from unaffected side, address him or her by name, and teach the person to move his or her head to compensate for lack of visual field.
  2. double vision (diplopia), patch one eye or cover one lens of his or her eyeglasses.
  3. diminished visual acuity, encourage the person to wear eyeglasses, if they were worn before the stroke, and provide good lighting.
- If the person has sensory input (touch, pressure, pain, temperature, proprioception) deficits,
  1. touch the person firmly with your whole hand instead of a finger.
  2. teach the person to protect involved side from mechanical and thermal injuries.
  3. teach the person to inspect skin for signs of injury or irritation.
  4. provide opportunity for the person to handle objects of different weights, textures, and size. Stress recognition of differences.
  5. consider providing a sling if shoulder-hand pain persists.
  6. teach the person to check body position visually.
- If the person has perceptual deficits, such as
  1. body scheme disturbance (amnesia or denial of paralyzed extremities),
     a. direct the person's attention to the involved side and provide sensory input.
     b. teach the person to maintain hygiene for the involved side.
  2. disorientation to time, place, or person,
     a. provide a calendar, clock, and pictures of family members to reinforce orientation.
     b. correct any misinformation expressed by the person.
     c. reorient the person as necessary.
     d. talk to the person about the environment.
     e. attempt to limit the amount of changes in the person's schedule.
  3. apraxia (loss of ability to perform purposeful actions),
     a. correct misuse of objects and demonstrate proper use.

b. note incorrect sequence of actions or steps while the person is performing a task, and demonstrate the proper sequence.
4. spatial orientation (deficits in locating objects in space, estimating size, or judging distance),
   a. reduce or remove stimuli that distract the person.
   b. have the person relearn skills by repeated practice.
   c. place necessary items such as tools and equipment where the person will see them.
   d. remind the person where these items are kept when not in use.
5. right-left disorientation,
   a. point to the side of body that should be used at the same time words or directions are spoken.
   b. point to the direction in space as words or directions are spoken.
- If the person has pressure sores or decubitus ulcers,
   1. prevention should be based on having the person avoid long time intervals in one position. Frequent turning or release of pressure every two hours is recommended.
   2. skin surfaces over bony prominences should be inspected frequently.
- If the person has shoulder pain,
   1. prevention should be based on having the person avoid uncontrolled abduction of the shoulder during exercises (see the Kumar article in the reference section). Avoid use of overhead sling or pulley exercises.
   2. support the person's arm during range-of-motion exercises or skateboard exercises.

Cognitive
- If the person has loss of memory,
   1. correct facts or information that are misremembered.
   2. provide facts or information that cannot be remembered.
- If the person has a short attention span and is easily distracted,
   1. remove or eliminate from the environment stimuli that tend to be distracting.
   2. divide activities into simple, short steps.
   3. work on new tasks when the person is rested.
   4. provide motivation and praise the person for accomplishing or finishing a task.
- If the person has poor judgment or reasoning skills,
   1. protect the person from injury (physical and psychological).
   2. set realistic goals for the person to achieve.
   3. give simple explanations or rationale for doing something in a particular way.
- If the person exhibits poor transfer of learning from one situation to another,
   1. repeat instructions. Do not expect person to remember.
   2. explain similarities in situations simply and briefly.
- If the person has inability to calculate,
   1. review basic math skills.
   2. suggest use of small calculator.

Intrapersonal
- If the person has lability,
   1. disregard bursts of emotions.
   2. explain to the person that emotional lability is part of his illness and that the condition will improve with time.

- If the person shows hopelessness and despair,
  1. provide opportunities for success.
  2. provide feedback on improvement by comparing previous performance with current level when positive change has occurred.
- If the person shows reduced tolerance to stress,
  1. control the amount of stress experienced by the person.
  2. keep practice sessions short.
- If the person shows fear, hostility, frustration, and anger,
  1. accept the person's behavior.
  2. be supportive; allow person to verbalize feelings.
- If the person shows confusion,
  1. clarify misconception.
  2. verify time, date, and place.
- If the person exhibits withdrawal and isolation,
  1. provide stimulation and a safe, comfortable environment.
  2. encourage contact with other people, especially family and friends.
- If the person shows depression,
  1. try to involve the person in activities that he or she enjoys.
  2. observe the person carefully for suicidal tendencies.

Interpersonal

If the person has the following communication problems, work with a speech pathologist, if available:

- expressive aphasia (anomia)
  1. Provide alternate methods of communication, such as the alphabet or symbol boards.
  2. Have the person repeat individual sounds of the alphabet.
  3. Have the person identify common objects in the environment.
  4. Be patient as the person tries to speak or gesture.
- receptive aphasia
  1. Speak clearly and in simple terms, using gestures as needed.
  2. Provide for alternate methods of communication.
- global aphasia
  1. Determine what skills are intact.
  2. Speak in very simple sentences.
  3. Practice individual sounds of the alphabet.
  4. Point to common objects, give them a name, and ask the person to repeat the name.
  5. Have the person write simple words and simple sentences.
- dysarthria
  Provide alternative forms of communication, such as the alphabet or picture boards.

Self-Care
- If the person has dysphagia (see also section on deglutition disorders)
  1. assess palatal and pharyngeal reflexes.
  2. elevate the person's head and turn it toward the unaffected side when feeding.
  3. place food on the unaffected side of the mouth if the person is able to manage oral intake.

- If the person has trouble dressing, teach the person to put the garment on the affected side first, then the unaffected side.
- If the person has trouble transferring
  1. teach the person to put unaffected leg under the affected leg and lift it to move the lower part of body or position the affected leg.
  2. teach the person to use his or her unaffected arm to lift and position affected arm.
- A variety of self-help devices may be useful, including button hooks, utensils, reachers, Velcro fasteners, extended handles, and enlarged handles for eating, writing, and grooming.

Productivity
- Evaluate the person's job requirements and determine level of the person's function.
- Look for possible environmental adaptations or modifications of job tasks that might enable the person to function satisfactorily in the job situation.
- Suggest possible alternative job situations if person is unable to function satisfactorily in his or her old job.

Leisure
Determine what leisure activities the person enjoyed before the CVA and whether the person will be able to continue those activities with or without modification of the tasks or environmental adaptations.

PRECAUTIONS
- Watch for signs of reflex sympathetic dystrophy.
- Watch for signs of depression.
- Watch for signs of contractures.
- Avoid abnormal postures and movements.

PROGNOSIS AND OUTCOME
Major recovery of functional abilities occurs within the first six months after the stroke, but some recovery continues from six months to two years afterward. Of primary importance is the person's ability to learn because rehabilitation is a learning process. Also important are the multiple factors involved, including physical, psychological, and social functions that are intertwined and interrelated. The most frequent measure of recovery is the degree of independence the person has achieved in activities of daily living.

- Muscle strength in upper extremity has improved in all muscle groups.
- Range of motion has improved in all joints of the upper extremity.
- Edema has decreased.
- The person demonstrates skill in performing self-ranging exercises to maintain the involved upper extremity.
- Sensation in the upper extremity has improved so that it is functional in avoiding burns or injuries.
- The person is able to compensate for lack of visual field, if needed.

- The person has improved balance and equilibrium reflexes and reactions.
- The person demonstrates knowledge of safety factors and judgment in selection of activities, tasks, or methods to avoid injury to self or others.
- The person has increased physical endurance and fitness.
- The person demonstrates coping skills needed to live with chronic disability.
- The person and his or her family or support group demonstrate understanding of chronic disability and knowledge of resources needed to reduce the degree of handicap.
- The person is able to perform activities of daily living within limitations of residual disability.
- The person is able to use adapted equipment, if needed.
- The person is able to perform the functional skills needed to survive within his or her living situation.
- The person is able to perform productive activities.
- The person is able to perform leisure activities that provide satisfaction and enjoyment.

REFERENCES

Atler, K.E., and J.A. Gliner. 1989. Post stroke activity and psychosocial factors. *Physical and Occupational Therapy in Geriatrics* 7(4):13–27.

Bjorneby, E.R., and I.R. Reinvang. 1985. Acquiring and maintaining self-care skills after stroke: The predictive value of apraxia. *Scandinavian Journal of Rehabilitation Medicine* 17:75–80.

Bohannon, R.W., and A.W. Andres. 1990. Shoulder subluxation and pain in stroke patients. *American Journal of Occupational Therapy* 44(6):507–9.

Bray, G.P., et al. 1981. Sexual functioning in stroke survivors. *Archives of Physical Medicine and Rehabilitation* 62:286–8.

Bukowski, L., et al. 1986. Interdisciplinary roles in stroke care. *Nursing Clinics of North America* 21(2):359–74.

Chiou, I.L., and C.H. Burrett. 1985. Values of activities of daily living: A survey of stroke patients and their home therapists. *Physical Therapy* 65(6):901–6.

Dittmar, C.M., and J.A. Gliner. 1987. Bilateral hand performance with divided attention after a cerebral vascular accident. *American Journal of Occupational Therapy* 41(2):96–101.

Drummond, A.E.R. 1988. Stroke: The impact on the family. *British Journal of Occupational Therapy* 51(6):193–4.

Earls, K., et al. 1984. Stroke: Occupational therapy. In *Current therapy in physiatry: Physical medicine and rehabilitation*, ed. A.S. Ruskin, 17–47. Philadelphia: W.B. Saunders.

Eriksson, S., B. Bernspang, and A.R. Fugl-Meyer. 1988. Perceptual and motor impairment within 2 weeks after a stroke: A multifactorial statistical approach. *Occupational Therapy Journal of Research* 8(2):114–25.

Evans, R.L., et al. 1987. Prestroke family interaction as a predictor of stroke outcome. *Archives of Physical Medicine and Rehabilitation* 68(8):508–12.

Evans, R.L., et al. 1987. Family interaction and treatment adherence after stroke. *Archives of Physical Medicine and Rehabilitation* 68(8):513–7.

Friedland, J., M. McColl. 1989. Social support for stroke survivors: Development and evaluation of an intervention program. *Physical and Occupational Therapy in Geriatrics* 7(3):55–69.

Hertanu, J.S., J.T. Demopoulos, W.C. Yang, et al. 1984. Stroke rehabilitation: Correlation and prognostic value of computerized tomography and sequential functional assessments. *Archives of Physical Medicine and Rehabilitation* 65(9):505–8.

Hopson, S., S. Morris, and D. Brickl. 1983. Occupational therapy. In *Stroke care: An interdisciplinary approach*, ed. G. Lubbock, 201–17. London, England: Faber & Faber.

Jongbloed, L. 1986. Prediction of function after stroke: A critical review. *Stroke* 17(4):765–76.

Kumar, R., E.J. Metter, A.J. Mehta, and T. Chew. 1990. Shoulder pain in hemiplegia. *American Journal of Physical Medicine and Rehabilitation* 69(4):205–8.

Lincoln, N.B., et al. 1988. The provision of an automatic calendar on a stroke ward: An example of single case methodology to evaluate management procedures. *British Journal of Occupational Therapy* 51(6):195–6.

Logigian, M.K., et al. 1983. Clinical exercise trial for stroke patients. *Archives of Physical Medicine and Rehabilitation* 64:364–7.

Morgan, D., L. Jongbloed. 1990. Factors influencing leisure activities following a stroke: An exploratory study. *Canadian Journal of Occupational Therapy* 57(4):223–9.

Novack, T.A., W.T. Satterfield, K. Lyons, et al. 1984. Stroke onset and rehabilitation: Time lag as a factor in treatment outcome. *Archives of Physical Medicine and Rehabilitation* 65(6):316–9.

Pedretti, L.W. 1990. Cerebral vascular accident. In *Occupational therapy: Practice skills for physical dysfunction*, ed. L.W. Pedretti and B. Zoltan, 603–22. St. Louis: C.V. Mosby.

Pelland, M.J. 1986. Occupational therapy and stroke rehabilitation. In *Stroke rehabilitation*, ed. P.E. Kaplan and L.J. Cerullo, 293–320. Boston: Butterworths.

Reding, M.J., and F. McDowell. 1987. Stroke rehabilitation. *Neurologic Clinics* 5(4):601–30.

Ritchie, C., and J. Lough. 1988. Ritchie/Lough charting system. *British Journal of Occupational Therapy* 51(4):133.

Schuchmann, J.A. 1983. Stroke rehabilitation. Minimizing the functional deficits. *Postgraduate Medicine* 74(5):101–11.

Shah, S., F. Vanclay, and B. Cooper. 1989. Predicting discharge status at commence of stroke rehabilitation. *Stroke* 20(6):766–9.

Smith, M.E., D.L. Smith, and J.A. Akhtar. 1982. Therapy impact on functional outcome in a controlled trial of stroke rehabilitation. *Archives of Physical Medicine and Rehabilitation* 63:21–24.

Soderback, I. 1988. A housework-based assessment of intellectual functions in patients with acquired brain damage. Development and evaluation of an occupational therapy method. *Scandinavian Journal of Rehabilitation Medicine* 20(2):57–69.

Soderback, I. 1988. The effectiveness of training intellectual functions in adults with acquired brain damage. An evaluation of occupational therapy methods. *Scandinavian Journal of Rehabilitation Medicine* 20(2):47–56.

Strub, N., and R.E. Levine. 1987. Self-care: A comparison of patients' institutional and home performance. *Occupational Therapy Journal of Research* 7(1):53–6.

Trombly, C.A. 1989. Stroke. In *Occupational therapy for physical dysfunction*, 2d ed., ed. C.A. Trombly, 308–25. Baltimore: Williams & Wilkins, 3d ed., 454–71.

Trombly, C.A., et al. 1986. The effectiveness of therapy in improving finger extension in stroke patients. *American Journal of Occupational Therapy* 40(9):612–7.

Wade, D.T., et al. 1984. Therapy after stroke: Amounts, determinants and effects. *International Rehabilitation Medicine* 6(3):105–10.

Cerebrovascular Disorder—Hemiplegia

DESCRIPTION

Hemiplegia is defined as loss of sensorimotor function of both limbs on one side of the body. The arm is usually affected more severely.

CAUSE

The cause of this disorder is brain injury involving the sensorimotor pathways. The injury may occur before birth, such as in cerebral palsy, or after birth, such as in cerebrovascular disorders or blunt trauma.

ASSESSMENT

Note: The ability to respond to communication varies among persons with hemiplegia. Determine whether the person responds best through words, pantomime, or written instructions.

Areas
- range of motion
- muscle strength
- muscle tone
- fine motor coordination (note speed and precision), manipulation, dexterity
- hand functions
- balance and postural tone
- bilateral integration
- praxis, motor planning
- sensory registration
- sensory processing
- perceptual skills
- ability to follow simple verbal or pantomimed instruction
- memory (ability to remember what is said and taught)
- problem-solving ability
- attention span
- organized and sequenced tasks or steps in a task
- ability to learn new skills
- judgment (relating to safety) in home management skills
- language and communication skills
- daily living skills
- productivity history, skills, interests, and values
- leisure skills and interests

Instruments
- Functional Test by D.J. Wilson, in Assessment of the hemiparetic upper extremity: A Functional Test. *Occupational Therapy in Health Care* 1(2):63–9, 1984. (See also Wilson, D.J., L.L. Baker, and J.A. Craddock. 1984. Functional test for the hemiparetic upper extremity. *American Journal of Occupational Therapy* 38(3):159–64.)
- Brunnstrom Recovery Stages by S. Brunnstrom, *Movement Therapy in Hemiplegia*, New York: Harper & Row, 1970, 34–55. (See Shah, S.K. 1984. Reliability of the original Brunnstrom recovery scale following hemiplegia. *Australian Occupational Therapy Journal* 31(4):144–51. See also Shah, S.K., S.J. Harasymiw, and P.L. Stahl. 1986. Stroke rehabilitation outcome based on Brunnstrom recovery stages. *Occupational Therapy Journal of Research* 6:365–76.)
- Hemiplegia Evaluation by B. Baum et al., Occupational Therapy Dept., Massachusetts Rehabilitation Hospital, Boston, 1979.
- Brunnstrom–Fugl-Meyer Test by A.R. Fugl-Meyer, L. Jaasko, I. Leyman, et al., The post-stroke hemiplegic patient. *Scandinavian Journal of Rehabilitation Medicine* 7:13–31, 1975 (not occupational therapists).
- Evaluation of the Hemiplegic Subject by F. Guarna, H. Gorriveau, J. Chamberland, et al., *Scandinavian Journal of Rehabilitation Medicine* 20:1–16, 1988.
- The Action Research Armtest by R.C. Lyle, A performance test for assessment of upper limb function in physical rehabilitation treatment and research, *International Journal of Rehabilitation Research* 4(4):483–92, 1981 (not an occupational therapist).

PROBLEMS

Motor
- loss of body symmetry and trunk stability
  1. Body posture and position usually become asymmetrical due to lack of sensory motor feedback.
  2. Trunk instability usually occurs during flaccid stage because trunk weight is shifted to affected side. Spastic phase of recovery usually has trunk instability due to shifting of weight to unaffected side to avoid falling.
  3. The head is usually flexed toward the affected side but rotated away from it.
  4. The affected arm is usually held close to the body with the scapula retracted, shoulder adducted, and the elbow, wrist, and fingers flexed.
  5. The pelvis is usually retracted and elevated, hip is internally rotated, adducted, and extended, knee is extended, ankle is plantar flexed and supinated, and toes are flexed.
  6. Shoulder and pelvis usually approach each other due to flexor spasticity.
  7. In standing and walking, the person usually leads with the unaffected side and drags the affected side toward the unaffected. The effect is that the person moves in a diagonal pattern rather than a vertical (straight forward) pattern.
- changes in muscle tone on affected side
  1. Muscle tone usually shows flaccidity in early recovery followed by spasticity.
  2. Muscle tone may change depending on body position.
  3. Typical hypertonus in the upper extremity results in retraction and depression in the shoulder girdle, internal rotation and adduction of the shoulder, elbow flexion, forearm pronation, wrist and finger flexion, and thumb adduction.
- loss of skilled movement patterns on affected side
  1. The person usually has loss of gross motor skills in the shoulder and elbow.
  2. The person usually has loss of fine motor manipulation and dexterity.
  3. The person usually has loss of hand functions, such as grasp and pinch.
- increase in mass movement patterns on affected side
  1. The person may have flexion synergy (shoulder abduction, extension, and external rotation, elbow flexion, forearm supination, and wrist and finger flexion).
  2. The person may have extension synergy (shoulder adduction, flexion, and internal rotation, elbow extension, forearm pronation, and finger and thumb extension) synergy patterns.
  3. The person may have stereotypical movements.
- loss of automatic reflexes or reactions
  1. The person may have persistent primitive reflexes.
  2. The person may have loss of righting and equilibrium reflexes or reactions that impair a sense of balance.
- loss of bilateral integration of the two sides of the body
  1. The person usually has loss of gross motor coordination, such as bilateral skills and reciprocal skills.
  2. The person usually has loss of fine motor coordination of the hands and fingers to perform activities, such as typing with both hands or playing the piano.
- loss of motor planning skills
  1. The person may have difficulty executing a motor act and appears clumsy.

2. The person may have difficulty with sequential movements.
- edema (dependent) and swelling due to vasomotor changes

Sensory
- The person may have loss of two-point discrimination in the finger tips and palms.
- The person may have loss of proprioception (position sense).
- The person may have loss of stereognosis.
- The person may have loss of light touch and deep pressure.
- The person may have loss of temperature sense.
- The person may have loss of position in space.
- The person may have visual neglect of half of the visual field.
- The person may have visual distortion of verticality.
- The person may have homonymous hemianopsia.
- The person may lack proprioceptive or kinesthetic awareness of body parts.
- The person may lack proprioceptive or kinesthetic awareness of the relationship of body parts to one another.
- The person may lack the ability to interpret the relation of body parts in space.
- The person may experience pain in the back and neck related to postural strain.
- The person may experience shoulder pain.

Cognitive
Cognitive disabilities are discussed in the section on cerebrovascular disorders.

Intrapersonal
- The person may deny that the involved side of body exists.
- Other intrapersonal and psychological problems are discussed in the section on cerebrovascular disorders.

Interpersonal
- The person may have loss of receptive or expressive language that interferes with communication process.
- Other interpersonal and social problems are discussed in the section on cerebrovascular disorders.

Self-Care
- The person may have difficulty with hand to mouth activity.
- The person may have difficulty in dressing, grooming, and toileting.

Productivity
- The person may be unable to perform tasks due to problems produced by hemiplegia.
- Other aspects of productivity are discussed in the section on cerebrovascular disorders.

Leisure
- The person may be unable to perform some favorite leisure activities due to problems produced by hemiplegia.
- Other aspects of leisure activities are discussed in the section on cerebrovascular disorders.

TREATMENT/MANAGEMENT

Traditionally models of treatment were based on compensatory or substitutive techniques (using one hand, changing dominance), and biomechanical/orthopedic techniques (muscle strengthening, increasing endurance and range of motion). Current models include neurodevelopmental treatment (Bobath), movement therapy (Brunnstrom), and proprioceptive neuromuscular facilitation (Knott), techniques that focus on correcting, restoring, and normalizing sensorimotor organization and performance, and rehabilitative techniques for regaining functional independence.

Motor
- Improve, maintain, and restore body symmetry and trunk stability.
  1. In bed, the person's head should be on a pillow to prevent lateral flexion. In a side-lying position on the affected side, the person's shoulder should be brought forward, arm extended to a right angle with the body or on a diagonal, the affected hip extended, and the knee flexed. The person may perform simple craft or game activities.
  2. If the person is sitting, use the back and seat of the chair to form a right (90 degree) angle. The person should be positioned at right angle with both hips flexed and feet flat on the floor or foot board. If the chair is too deep, place a firm cushion behind the back. Weight should be evenly divided over hips. Both arms should be kept on the table surface and both hands should be within visual field.
  3. To ensure trunk stability, have the person (a) practice leaning forward with hands clasped and arms extended, (b) practice shifting weight from one hip to the other (shifting from the affected side back to the unaffected is harder) with hands clasped and extended, (c) practice diagonal weight shift using forward right, back left movement and then forward left, back right, with hands clasped and extended, and (d) practice rotating from left to right, right to left, with hands clasped and extended. Craft and game activities should be incorporated into movement patterns, such as block printing (hands clasp a dowel attached to the block print).
- Normalize muscle tone on affected side.
  1. To inhibit the position for spasticity of the upper extremity, bring the scapula forward and upward by holding the person's upper arm in the axilla and rotate inward and upward on the medial border of the scapula. The shoulder is externally rotated, elbow is extended, forearm is supinated, wrist is dorsiflexed, fingers are extended and abducted, and the thumb is abducted. Always feel for tone changes but do not force (stretch) spastic muscle. Tapping the muscle belly of a hypotonus (low tone) muscle, placing weight on the palm of the hand (or heel of the foot), and gently but firmly pushing the distal end of a joint toward the proximal end are useful techniques for reducing the effect of hypertonus.
  2. To promote the inhibiting position, use crafts or games that require gross motor functions. While spasticity is present, fine motor activities generally should be avoided, especially those that require that the activity be performed close to the body.
- Decrease mass movement (synergies or stereotypical) patterns while improving skilled movements.
  1. Position the person in a correct posture and the upper extremity in an inhibiting pattern.
  2. Use gross motor patterns combined with fine motor movements, such as using large pieces for prehension in selected crafts or games. Grade requirements for prehension as mass movement patterns become less dominant.

- Improve the person's postural control, equilibrium, and balance.
  1. In a sitting position on a bench, the person reaches over his or her head, to the front, to the left, and to the right for objects; then he or she reaches to the floor for objects in front, to the left, and to the right. The bench may be lowered at the beginning of the activity to facilitate reaching.
  2. In a standing position, the person performs the same activities and self-care activities, such as dressing and homemaking, that require items be put on a high or low shelf and then removed. For the low shelf, vary the position from bending over to stooping.
- Increase bilateral integration of the two sides of the body.
  1. Activities begin with bilateral movement of both arms and hands doing the same activity. The affected arm or hand may be held by the unaffected hand or tied to a handle or dowel.
  2. The next activities are performed unilaterally with the affected arm or hand. Unilateral activities may begin with holding objects while bearing weight on the palm that the unaffected hand can manipulate; then have the person hold objects using grasp of the affected hand that the unaffected hand can manipulate; and finally have the person manipulate (reach, grasp, and release) objects with the affected hand (with no assistance from the unaffected hand).
  3. The next activities are performed with both hands in parallel (both hands reach, grasp, and release) or in alternate (right-left, right-left) patterns.
- Improve praxis, and motor planning.
  1. Familiar objects that can be taken apart and put back together provide excellent practice for motor planning. Examples include a coffee pot, meat grinder, or vegetable chopper.
  2. Preparing and serving a meal provides a variety of motor planning opportunities.
- Decrease edema and swelling.
  1. Place the person's arm in an elevated position.
  2. Consider using continuous passive motion.
  3. Use resting or positioning splints, if needed.

Sensory
- Increase tactile awareness, discrimination, and stereognosis.
  1. Select a variety of tactile sensations, such as hard, soft, wet, dry, smooth, and rough.
  2. Tactile retraining is best combined with motor activities, especially bilateral integration and self-care activities, such as washing and drying the affected side; but games of Feely Bag or "What's in the box?" may be added.
- Increase proprioceptive and kinesthetic awareness of position of body parts in relation to each other.
  1. Usually no special activities are needed since proprioception and kinesthesia are inherent in most motor activities.
  2. Use hand games, such as "How far is this?" (variations of Ayres kinesthesia subtest).
- Improve eye motility and visual perceptual skills.
  1. Orient the person toward the affected side. Approach the person from the affected side.
  2. Position the person's hand on the affected side within the visual field. The person should position the affected arm or hand while in a sitting position. Do not perform this task for the person.
  3. Activities should be performed bilaterally and the person should focus vision on the hands and the task. Remind the person to watch or pay attention if necessary.

- Improve body schema and awareness of the body in space.
  1. Encourage the person to initiate movement with both sides of the body, such as rolling, coming to a sitting position, and walking.
  2. The person should be encouraged to dress the affected side independently.
- Decrease shoulder pain and suluxation.
  1. Use of a sling may be helpful. (See the reference section for articles on the choice of the sling. Note that research studies suggest that pain is not related to subluxation or to flaccidity but to uncontrolled abduction. See Kumar article in the reference section.)
  2. Avoid using overhead sling or pulley exercises that permit uncontrolled abduction. (See Kumar article, which suggests that shoulder pain is related to problems in muscle tone of the rotators and soft-tissue damage, which are aggravated during abduction activity without support to the shoulder.)

Cognitive
See section on cerebrovascular disorders.

Intrapersonal
See section on cerebrovascular disorders.

Interpersonal
See section on cerebrovascular disorders.

Self-Care
- Self-care activities can be integrated into motor and sensory retraining program as described above. Dressing, bathing, grooming, and feeding all provide motor and sensory tasks.
- Use self-help devices to facilitate function, such as universal cuffs to hold such objects as a spoon while grasp is poor, enlarged handles to promote grasp, and bilateral handles on cups or glasses to encourage use of both hands.

Productivity
- Specific homemaking tasks can be used in the therapy program, such as washing dishes (use nonbreakable ones), putting groceries away, folding laundry, dusting and polishing, setting or clearing the table, and ironing.
- Work tasks that are useful in therapy include sorting and counting, stocking shelves, folding letters and putting them in envelopes, wrapping packages, and pushing a cart.

Leisure
- Many crafts can be adapted to facilitate the therapy program, such as holding paint brushes with both hands, putting handles on block print, or turning a table loom around to use gross movement to beat the weft.
- Games can be adapted by enlarging the size of the pieces of a puzzle, using large diameter dowels as pegs, or using door handles to enlarge grasp surface. Tic-tack-toe and checkers can be easily adapted.

PRECAUTIONS
- Contractures may occur if the flexion synergy pattern persists.
- Avoid abnormal movements. Reposition the person to inhibit or reduce engaging the abnormal movement patterns.

PROGNOSIS AND OUTCOME
- The person demonstrates symmetrical posture in static positions.
- The person's muscle tone has normalized (spasticity has decreased).
- The person is able to perform gross motor movements with the affected side without effects of mass synergies. For example, the person is able to selectively extend the fingers and thumb without simultaneously extending the elbow or engaging mass extensory synergy.
- The person is able to perform hand skills (grasp and prehension) with the affected hand.
- The person is able to maintain static and dynamic balance.
- The person is able to perform bilateral and reciprocal movements using both sides of the body.

Order of Return of Voluntary Movement in the Upper Extremity

- flexion of the shoulder (initially results in flexion of the elbow, wrist, and fingers)
- flexion of the elbow (initially may result in flexion of the shoulder, wrist, and fingers)
- flexion of the wrist
- flexion of the fingers
- supination of the forearm
- extension of the shoulder
- extension of the elbow
- flexion of the shoulder independent of the elbow, wrist, and fingers
- flexion of the elbow independent of the shoulder, wrist, or fingers
- alternate flexion and extension of all fingers together
- selective flexion and extension of the index finger, then the middle
- thumb opposition to lateral side of the index finger (key pinch)
- thumb opposition to the finger tips

Source: Waters, R.L., P.J. Wilson, and C. Gowland, Rehabilitation of the upper extremity after stroke. In *Rehabilitation of the hand*, ed. J.M. Hunter, et al., 956, 3d ed., 1990.

- The person is able to plan and execute motor activities that are unfamiliar.
- Edema and swelling are controlled.
- The person is able to use visual system for fixation, gaze, scanning and tracking throughout the visual field.
- The person is able to perform tasks requiring visual perception.
- The person is able to respond to, discriminate among, and identify tactile input.

- The person is able to accurately respond to changes in position of body parts.
- The person is able to move his or her body through space without bumping into walls or falling over objects.

REFERENCES

Bernspang, B., M. Viitanen, and S. Eriksson. 1989. Impairments of perceptual and motor functions: Their influence on self-care ability 4 to 6 years after a stroke. *Occupational Therapy Journal of Research.* 9(1):27–37.

Bourbonnaie, D., and S. Vanden Noven. 1989. Weakness in patients with hemiparesis. *American Journal of Occupational Therapy* 43(5):313–9.

Bowen, M., and L. Germanos. 1988. Orthotic management of the flaccid upper limb in hemiplegia: Two case studies. *Australian Occupational Therapy Journal* 35(3):130–8.

Boyd, E., and A. Gaylard. 1986. Shoulder supports with stroke patients: A Canadian survey. *Canadian Journal of Occupational Therapy* 53(2):61–8.

Claus, B.S., and K.J. Godfrey. 1985. A distal support sling for the hemiplegic patient. *American Journal of Occupational Therapy* 39(8):536–7.

DePoy, E. 1987. Community-based occupational therapy with a head-injured adult. *American Journal of Occupational Therapy* 41(7):461–4.

Eggers, O. 1983. *Occupational therapy in the treatment of adult hemiplegia.* London, England: William Heinemann Medical Books.

Guidice, M.L. 1990. Effects of continuous passive motion and elevation on hand edema. *American Journal of Occupational Therapy* 44(10):914–21.

Harvey, G., and T. Simard. 1984. Functional reeducation and electromyographic evaluation of left handwriting in right hemiplegic patients: A pilot study. *Canadian Journal of Occupational Therapy* 51(5):225–30.

Kumar, R., E.J. Metter, A.J. Mehta, and T. Chew. 1990. Shoulder pain in hemiplegia. *American Journal of Physical Medicine and Rehabilitation* 69(4):205–8.

Levine, R.E. 1984. The cultural aspects of home care delivery. *American Journal of Occupational Therapy* 38(11):726–33.

Mathiowetz, V., D.J. Bolding, and C.A. Trombly. 1983. Immediate effects of positioning devices on the normal and spastic hand measured by electromyography. *American Journal of Occupational Therapy* 37(4):239–46.

Meredith, J., G. Taft, and P. Kaplan. 1981. Diagnosis and treatment of hemiplegic patient with brachial plexus injury. *American Journal of Occupational Therapy* 35(10):656–60.

Mitcham, M. 1982. Visual perception and its relationship to an activity of daily living. *Occupational Therapy Journal of Research* 2(4):245–6.

Neeman, R.L., et al. 1987. Rehabilitation of chronic upper extremity pain in post-CVA hemiparesis: Tendonitis and lateral epicondylitis by orthokinesis analgesia. *Canadian Journal of Rehabilitation* 1(1):17–28.

Neuhaus, B.E., E.R. Ascher, B.A. Coullon, et al. 1981. A survey of rationales for and against hand splinting in hemiplegia. *American Journal of Occupational Therapy* 35(2):83–90.

Osterhout, B.M., E.S. Wittbrodt, and M.S. Pinzur. 1987. Pre- and postsurgical approaches to the treatment of the adult with hemiplegia. *Occupational Therapy in Health Care* 4(3/4):135–53.

Reid, D., and R. Koheil. 1987. EMG biofeedback training to promote hand function in a cerebral palsied child with hemiplegia. *Occupational Therapy in Health Care* 4(3/4):97–107.

Rocker, J.D. 1988. Promoting occupational therapy by using a simulated hemiplegic arm to demonstrate dressing technique. *American Journal of Occupational Therapy* 42(2):123–6.

Rose, V., and S.A. Shah. 1987. A comparative study on the immediate effects of hand orthoses on reduction of hypertonus. *Australian Occupational Therapy Journal* 34(2):59–64.

Ryerson, S., and K. Levit. 1987. The shoulder in hemiplegia. In *Physical therapy of the shoulder*, ed. R. Donatelli, 105–31. New York: Churchill Livingstone.

Shah, S.K., and B.I. Cooper. 1987. Performance on a fine motor task by dominant hemiplegics. *Occupational Therapy Journal of Research* 7(5):259–72.

Shah, S.K., and J. Cornes. 1980. Volition following hemiplegia. *Archives of Physical Medicine and Rehabilitation* 61:523–7.

Shumway-Cook, A., D. Anson, and S. Haller. 1988. Postural sway biofeedback: Its effect on reestablishing stance stability in hemiplegic patients. *Archives of Physical Medicine and Rehabilitation* 69(6):395–400.

Spaulding, S.J., et al. 1989. Wrist muscle tone and self-care skill in persons with hemiparesis. *American Journal of Occupational Therapy* 43(1):11–6.

Stanton, K.M., M. Pepping, J.A. Brockway, et al. 1983. Wheelchair transfer training for right cerebral dysfunctions: An interdisciplinary approach. *Archives of Physical Medicine and Rehabilitation* 64(6):276–80.

Strub, N., and R.E. Levine. 1987. Self-care: A comparison of patients' institutional and home performance. *Occupational Therapy Journal of Research* 7(1):53–6.

Sullivan, B.E., S.L. Rogers. 1989. Modified Bobath sling with distal support. *American Journal of Occupational Therapy* 43(1):47–9.

Trombly, C.A., and L.A. Quintana. 1983. The effects of exercise on finger extension of CVA patients. *American Journal of Occupational Therapy* 37(3):195–202.

Walker, J. 1983. Modified strapping of roll sling. *American Journal of Occupational Therapy* 37(2):110–1.

Walsh, M. 1987. Half-lapboard for hemiplegic patients. *American Journal of Occupational Therapy* 41(8):533–5.

Warren, M.L. 1984. A comparative study of the presence of the asymmetrical tonic neck reflex in adult hemiplegia. *American Journal of Occupational Therapy* 38(6):386–92.

Waters, R.L., D.J. Wilson, and C. Gowland. 1984. Rehabilitation of the upper extremity after stroke. In *Rehabilitation of the hand*, 2d ed., ed. J.M. Hunter, et al., 705–15. St. Louis: C.V. Mosby. Revised in 3d ed., 1990, 953–63.

Woodson, A.M. 1987. Proposal for splinting an adult hemiplegic hand to promote function. *Occupational Therapy in Health Care* 4(3/4):85–96.

Yarnell, P.R., B.B. Friedman. 1987. Left "hemi" ADL learning and outcome: Limiting factors. *Journal of Neurologic Rehabilitation* 1(3):125–30.

Young, G.C., D. Collins, and M. Hren. 1983. Effect of pairing scanning training with block design training in the remediation of perceptual problems in left hemiplegics. *Journal of Clinical Neuropsychology* 5(3):201–12.

Coma and Stupor

DESCRIPTION

Coma is an unresponsive state of consciousness from which a person cannot be aroused even after vigorous and repeated stimulation. Stupor is an unresponsive state of consciousness from which the person can be aroused only briefly after vigorous and repeated stimulation.

CAUSE

Impaired consciousness can be caused by any of the following: (1) supratentorial mass lesions, (2) subtentorial lesions, (3) diffuse and metabolic cerebral disorders, or (4) psychiatric disorders.

ASSESSMENT

Areas

- reflexes
- muscle tone, especially spasticity
- range of motion
- balance and postural control
- praxis
- sensory registration
- sensory processing
- perceptual skills

- attending behavior
- attention span, concentration
- orientation
- ability to follow direction
- judgment of safety
- problem-solving skills
- daily living skills

Instruments

No specific instruments developed by occupational therapists were identified in the literature. The scales below are used frequently as reference points for persons recovering from comatose states.

- Glasgow Coma Scale by G. Teasdale and B. Jennett, Assessment of coma and impaired consciousness: A practical scale, *Lancet* 2(July, 13):81–3, 1974. (See also Jennett, B., and G. Teasdale. 1981. *Management of head injuries*, 77–84. Philadelphia: F.A. Davis.)
- Rancho Los Amigos Cognitive Functioning Scale by C. Hagen, Language disorders in Head Trauma, in *Language disorders in adults: Recent advances*, A.L. Holland, 245–81, San Diego, CA: College-Hill Press, 1984. (The scale is on pp. 257–8. See also Malkmus, D., B.J. Booth, and C. Kodimer. 1980. *Rehabilitation of the head injured adult: Comprehensive cognitive management*. Downey, CA: Professional Staff Association of Rancho Los Amigos Hospital.)

PROBLEMS

Motor (Based on the Glasgow Coma Scale)

- *Level I* (No response). No change to stimuli occurs, no movement occurs, no change in muscle tone occurs, the eyes do not open, and the face does not twitch.
- *Level II* (Extensor response). The person responds with generalized movement patterns known as decerebrate rigidity or extensor posturing. The head retracts, the trunk extends, the shoulders and hips extend, adduct, and rotate internally, the elbows and knees extend, the forearm pronates, the wrist and fingers flex, and the feet plantarflex and invert. Spinal reflexes and lower brain stem reflexes may be present, such as the tonic labyrinthine reflex and asymmetrical tonic neck reflex.
- *Level III* (Abnormal flexion). The person responds with generalized movement patterns known as decorticate rigidity or flexor posturing. The shoulders are slightly flexed, adducted, and internally rotated, the forearm is pronated, and the wrist and fingers are flexed. No change occurs in the lower extremities. Midbrain reactions, such as neck and body righting reactions, may be elicited.
- *Level IV* (Withdraws). The person's response to stimulation is withdrawal of the entire limb even though only the hand or foot is touched. Spontaneous, nonpurposeful movements may occur without any apparent external stimulation.
- *Level V* (Localizes). The person may brush away painful stimuli, move only the part of the body being stimulated, blink at a light shown in the eyes, turn away from strong light or sound, or follow a beam of light with the head. Cortical equilibrium reactions (protective extension) can be elicited.

- *Level VI* (Obeys). The person is able to respond appropriately to stimuli and only withdraws from noxious or irritating stimuli. Person responds to simple requests and can initiate purposeful activity. Movements include limb abduction and movement away from the midline of the body.

Sensory (Based on Rancho Los Amigos Cognitive Functioning Scale)

- *Level I* (No response). The person is unresponsive to any stimuli.
- *Level II* (Generalized response). The person reacts inconsistently and nonpurposefully to stimuli in a nonspecific manner. The earliest response may be to deep pain.
- *Level III* (Localized response). The person reacts specifically, but inconsistently, to stimuli. Responses are related directly to the type of stimulus presented. The person may turn his or her head toward a sound or focus on an object. The person may withdraw an extremity when presented with painful stimulus.
- *Level IV* (Confused/agitated). The person responds to discomfort by trying to remove restraints or nasogastric tube. The person may respond out of proportion to the stimuli given even after it is removed. The person does not discriminate among persons or objects.
- *Level V* (Confused/inappropriate). The person continues to respond out of proportion to the stimuli presented.
- *Level VI* (Confused/appropriate). The response to stimuli is appropriate. The person is able to tolerate unpleasant stimuli, such as the nasogastric tube when need is explained.

Cognitive (Based on Rancho Los Amigos Cognitive Functioning Scale)

- *Level I* (No response). The person shows no evidence of cognitive response.
- *Level II* (Generalized response). Responses are nonspecific and may include physiological changes, gross body movements, or vocalizations.
- *Level III* (Localized response). The person may follow simple commands, such as, "Close your eyes" or "Squeeze my hand." The person may respond inconsistently, in a delayed manner, and to some people but not to others.
- *Level IV* (Confused/agitated). The person responds primarily to the internal rather than the external environment. Gross attention is very brief, and selective attention is usually nonexistent. The person is unaware of present events, lacks short term recall, and may be reacting to past events.
- *Level V* (Confused/inappropriate/non-agitated). The person appears alert and is able to respond to simple commands fairly consistently but responses to complex commands may be nonpurposeful, random, or fragmented. He or she has gross attention to the environment but is highly distractible and lacks ability to focus attention. Memory is severely impaired. He or she may perform previously learned tasks with structure but is unable to learn new information. Maximum supervision is required to ensure safety.
- *Level VI* (Confused/appropriate). The person follows directions consistently and can perform familiar activities, especially those learned and practiced for many years. New learning is difficult and is not remembered. Attention to tasks is improved for structured tasks but not for unstructured tasks. Past memory is better than recent. The person shows goal-directed behavior but is dependent on the external environment for direction. Moderate supervision is required. The person has vague recognition of some staff members.

- *Level VII* (Automatic/appropriate). The person is oriented and able to function in a structured environment with a dependable routine. Learning new tasks is possible but carryover is poor. Judgment of safety, insight into his or her condition, problem solving, and planning skills are still poor. Minimal supervision is still needed for safety reasons.
- *Level VIII* (Purposeful/appropriate). The person is alert, oriented, can plan ahead, remembers the past, learns new tasks, and functions in an unstructured setting. Return to the community is possible, including working. However, some decrease in quality and rate of processing information may be evident and the ability to reason abstractly may be decreased.

Intrapersonal
- *Level III* (Localized response). The person may have a vague awareness of self and his or her body, such as responding to discomfort by pulling at the nasogastric tube, catheter, or restraints.
- *Level IV* (Confused/agitated). The person is detached from the present and responds primarily to internal agitation, confusion, and a heightened state of activity. Behavior may be bizarre and nonpurposeful to the immediate environment. The person may be euphoric or hostile.
- *Level V* (Confused/inappropriate). The person may become agitated as a result of external stimuli. The person is unable to initiate tasks and may use objects inappropriately. The person responds best to family members.
- *Level VI* (Confused/appropriate). The person is able to be responsible for his or her behavior. He or she has some self-awareness and awareness of basic needs.
- *Level VII* (Automatic/appropriate). The person generally is aware of self, his or her body, family, food, people, and interaction in the environment, but reality testing and reaction to stress are still poor.
- *Level VIII* (Purposeful/appropriate). The person is functional in society but may still show decreased tolerance to stress.

Interpersonal
- *Level IV* (Confused/agitated). Verbalization is frequently incoherent or inappropriate to the environment. Confabulation may be present.
- *Level V* (Confused/inappropriate). With structure, the person may be able to converse on a social, automatic level for short periods of time. Verbalization may continue to be inappropriate at times with confabulation. The person may be able to interact with family members.
- *Level VI* (Confused/appropriate). The person can respond to familiar social situations.
- *Level VII* (Automatic/appropriate). The person can initiate social responses and activities in which the individual has an interest.
- *Level VIII* (Purposeful/appropriate). The person may continue to have difficulty interacting in some social situations.

Self-Care
- *Levels I, II, & III*. The person needs maximum assistance to perform self-care activities.
- *Level IV* (Confused/agitated). The person is able to perform some self-care activities with direct assistance.

- *Level V* (Confused/inappropriate). The person is able to perform self-care activities with assistance and may accomplish feeding with supervision.
- *Level VI* (Confused/appropriate). The person can perform self-care activities with supervision.
- *Level VII* (Automatic/appropriate). The person can perform self-care activities independently but judgment remains impaired.
- *Level VIII* (Purposeful/appropriate). The person is independent in performing all self-care activities.

Productivity
- *Level VI* (Confused/appropriate). The person can perform repetitive work tasks in a structured setting.
- *Level VII* (Automatic/appropriate). The person can participate in work evaluation and explore alternative careers if needed.
- *Level VIII* (Purposeful/appropriate). The person can participate fully in work evaluation and determine productive role.

Leisure
- *Level VI* (Confused/appropriate). The person is able to participate in structured leisure activities.
- *Level VII* (Automatic/appropriate). The person is able to initiate leisure activities in which the person has an interest.
- *Level VIII* (Purposeful/appropriate). The person is able to develop new leisure interests.

TREATMENT/MANAGEMENT
Only levels 1 through 3 of the cognitive levels are addressed here. For higher levels, see section on head injuries. Models of treatment include neurodevelopmental treatment (Bobath), movement therapy (Brunnstrom), proprioceptive neuromuscular facilitation (Knott), and sensory integration (Ayres).

Motor
- *Level I.* Attempt to evoke voluntary motor responses to sensory stimulation. Techniques such as quick stretch, tapping over the muscle belly, joint approximation, and quick icing may be applied.
- *Level II.* Increase variety of voluntary motor responses to sensory stimulation. The person's responses might include turning toward a noise, a change in facial expression to a particular smell, pushing an obnoxious stimuli away, or a change in muscle tone.
- *Level III.* Increase use of gross motor function and muscle tone through use of movement patterns and activities. Encourage the person to respond by verbally requesting the movement with a short command ("Look up," "Reach") and then assisting the person to perform the movement, if needed. Begin with head, neck, and trunk movement and progress from proximal to distal following normal development.

Sensory
Levels I, II, and III
- Apply pressure on the fingernail bed or sternum.

- Use auditory stimulation, such as the actual or recorded voices of family members, familiar musical tapes, or loud noises such as clapping, ringing bells, or calling the person's name. (Note: If startle reflex occurs, stop this approach.)
- Use tactile stimulation, such as rubbing the person's face and body with various textures.
- Use temperature changes, such as warm towels or cold towels to wipe the skin.
- Use vibration with vibrators of various speeds.
- Use vestibular stimulation by changing the person's body position from supine to sitting, rolling, tilting, slow spinning or rocking, and inverting his or her head on a large therapy ball. (Note: This is contraindicated if person has a tracheotomy, increased cranial pressure, or seizures.)
- Use olfactory stimulation by placing noxious or pleasant smells under the nose.
- Use proprioceptive stimulation by moving the person's arms, legs, and body.
- Use visual stimulation by providing brightly colored objects, mobiles over the bed, mirrors, flashlights, photographs, and pictures.

Cognitive
- *Level I.* Attempt to promote awareness through use of various stimuli. Reduce extraneous background, visual, and auditory input as much as possible.
- *Level II.* Increase awareness of environment and promote attending behavior.
- *Level III.* Increase attention span and orientation and promote following directions.

Intrapersonal
See head injury section.

Interpersonal
See head injury section.

Self-Care
- *Levels II and III.* The person needs maximum assistance to perform self-care activities, but encourage the person to assist by providing visual and verbal cues. Facilitate normal oral motor movements. Reduce hypersensitivity and abnormal tone.
- *Level IV.* Help the person perform self-care activities by providing verbal directions.

Productivity
See head injury section.

Leisure
See head injury section.

PRECAUTIONS
- Generally sessions should be kept short, about 15 to 30 minutes. Note increases in posturing or fluctuations in status.
- Remember that responses may be delayed. Wait for a response and repeat the same stimulus before giving a new one.
- Use only one or two different types of stimuli per session to reduce confusion.
- Avoid posturing, such as arching of back and other extensor patterns. Rotate the person's

shoulders opposite the hips, flex hips and knees, generally avoid the supine position, and exert pressure to the back of the head.

- If overstimulation occurs, use pressure to the abdomen, neutral warmth, or reflex inhibiting patterns.

PROGNOSIS AND OUTCOME

The length of coma is indicative of outcome. Comas of more than a few months do not lead to a positive prognosis. Few people recover fully.

- The person is able to control voluntary movements.
- The person is able to respond correctly to sensory stimuli in all senses.
- The person is able to respond correctly to verbal commands and follow simple directions.
- The person is oriented to person, place, and time.
- The person is able to perform basic self-care skills with assistance.

REFERENCES

Dow, P.W. 1989. Traumatic brain injuries. In *Occupational therapy for physical dysfunction*, 3d ed., ed. C.A. Trombly, 484–509. Baltimore, MD: Williams & Wilkins.

Jean, N., and D. Samms. 1985. Ankle-foot positioning splint for comatose patients. *American Journal of Occupational Therapy* 39(10):682–3.

Johnson, D.A., and K. Roethig-Johnston. 1988. Coma stimulation: A challenge to occupational therapy. *British Journal of Occupational Therapy* 51(3):88–90.

Weber, P.L. 1984. Sensorimotor therapy: Its effect on electroencephalograms of acute comatose patients. *Archives of Physical Medicine and Rehabilitation* 65(8):457–62.

Epilepsy

DESCRIPTION

Epilepsy is a recurrent disorder of the brain characterized by sudden, brief attacks of altered consciousness, motor activity, sensory phenomena, or inappropriate behavior.

Site of Brain Pathology	
Focal Manifestation	*Site of Dysfunction*
Localized twitching of muscles	Frontal lobe (motor cortex)
Localized numbness or tingling	Parietal lobe (sensory cortex)
Chewing movements or smacking of lips	Anterior temporal lobe
Olfactory hallucinations	Antero-medial temporal lobe
Visual hallucinations—formed images	Temporal lobe
Visual hallucinations—flashes of light	Occipital lobe
Automatic behaviorisms	Temporal lobe

Source: Berkow, R., ed. 1987. *Merck Manual,* 15th ed., 1368. Rahway, NJ: Merck and Co.

CAUSE

Usually the cause cannot be determined, but it may be related to a microscopic scar or metabolic abnormalities in the brain. Known causes include infectious diseases of the central nervous system, heat stroke, metabolic disturbances, toxic agents, cerebral hypoxia, tumors, brain defects, cerebral edema, cerebral trauma, anaphylaxis, cerebral infarct or hemorrhage, withdrawal symptoms, and occasionally hysteria.

ASSESSMENT

Types of Seizures
- *Partial seizures* (focal or Jacksonian). Symptoms begin in one hand or foot and travel up the extremity, or begin at the corner of the mouth. There is specific motor, sensory, or psychomotor involvement.
- *Partial seizures with complex symptoms.* Symptoms may include impairment of consciousness only, cognitive confusion, affective changes, or a combination. This type is characterized by a variety of patterns of onset. Effects may last from a few minutes to several hours.
- *Partial seizures of the temporal lobe.* Symptoms have been associated with aggressive behavior and schizophreniform or depressive psychoses.
- *Generalized seizures.* Symptoms are bilaterally symmetrical and without local onset; an aura may or may not appear. Types include petit mal, infantile spasms, clonic seizures, tonic seizures, tonic-clonic seizures (grand mal), atonic seizures, and akinetic seizures.
- *Generalized seizures continuous.* Motor, sensory, or psychic seizures follow one another without intervening periods of consciousness (status epilepticus).
- *Other or unclassified.* Unusual forms or cases in which data are incomplete.

Areas
- muscle strength
- range of motion
- fine motor skills, manipulation, dexterity, and bilateral coordination
- sensory registration and processing
- perceptual skills
- motor planning and praxis
- posture control and balance
- attending behavior
- body scheme and image
- decision-making and problem-solving skills
- memory
- time management skills
- coping skills
- self-concept
- social skills
- role performance
- daily living skills
- productive history, skills, interests, and values
- leisure skills and interests

Instruments
- manual muscle test
- goniometry
- dexterity and coordination test, such as the Purdue Pegboard Test
- activities of daily living scale
- occupational history
- NPI Interest Checklist by J. Matsutsuyu, *American Journal of Occupational Therapy*, 23:368–73, 1969. (See also Rogers, J.C., J.M. Weinstein, and J.J. Figone. 1978. The interest check list: An empirical assessment. *American Journal of Occupational Therapy* 32(10):628–30.)
- Occupational and Leisure Assessment for Adults with Epilepsy (OLAAE) by S. Day (1984). (See article in reference section.)

PROBLEMS

Motor
- The person may have uncontrolled muscle twitching during attacks.
- The person may have uncontrolled muscle contractions during attacks.
- The person may have uncontrolled thrashing of extremities during attacks.
- The person may have temporary muscle weakness after an attack.
- The person may have temporary problems of coordination and dexterity after an attack.
- The person may have motor impairments, not related directly to the seizures, that are aggravated by seizure medication, such as cerebral palsy.

Sensory
- The person is usually unable to respond to sensory input during an attack.
- The person may be slow to respond to sensory input after an attack.
- The person may have perceptual disorders, not related directly to the seizures, that are aggravated by seizure medication.

Cognitive
- The person may lose consciousness during a seizure or appear to be conscious but be experiencing attention deficit behavior.
- The person may become confused after a seizure.
- The person may be unable to remember what was happening or what he or she was doing immediately prior to the seizure. He or she may complain of losing track of time.
- The person may forget what was learned just prior to the seizure.
- The person may experience learning disabilities or mental retardation, not related directly to the seizures, that are aggravated by seizure medication.
- The person may experience memory disorders from seizures in the temporal lobe or seizure medication may aggravate memory dysfunction, such as amnesia.

Intrapersonal
- The person may feel inferior because of being different.
- The person may be self-conscious because the attacks draw unwanted attention.
- The person may use attacks (sometimes fake) to draw attention to him- or herself (manipulative behavior).

- The person may view him- or herself as an invalid, a crazy person, or a "retardo."
- The person may have poor coping skills.
- The person may be withdrawn and depressed.
- The person may experience hallucinations, especially olfactory or visual hallucinations, related to seizures.
- The person may have personality or behavior disorders that are unrelated to the seizures or aggravated by seizure medication.

Interpersonal
- The person may fail to tell friends a problem exists.
- The person may avoid social situations to avoid making a scene if a seizure occurs.

Self-Care
- The person may experience temporary problems if confusion follows an attack.
- The person may need to relearn a task learned just before an attack.

Productivity
- The person may have difficulty getting a driver's license if attacks are not controllable.
- Some jobs may be unfeasible or illegal depending on seizure frequency and drug treatment effectiveness.
- The person may have a poor academic record due to frequent absences, frequent seizures, and undetected perceptual or learning problems.

Leisure
Some leisure activities may be risky, depending on the frequency of seizures and the effectiveness of drug treatment.

TREATMENT/MANAGEMENT
Models of treatment are based on occupational behavior and developmental stages.

Motor
- The person should be informed that muscle tone and strength may fluctuate after a seizure.
- If motor deficits exist, refer to section on the specific disorder.

Sensory
The person should be informed if perceptual deficits exist. Treatment suggestions are located in the section on perceptual disorders.

Cognitive
- Instruct the person on safety considerations in daily living activities, homemaking, work activities, and recreation.
- Teach the person to make and keep a schedule of activities, an appointment book for scheduled activities, and a list of assignments or tasks to complete.
- Provide practice in reading and following verbal instructions using crafts or academic lessons. The person should be made aware of possible attention deficits.

- Provide practice in problem solving and decision making through opportunities to choose and make choices.
- Instruct the person in local community resources.

Intrapersonal
- Improve the person's self-concept through creative activities, such as art, crafts, drama, dance, or music.
- Provide instruction in stress management, including relaxation training.
- Improve the person's goal-setting skills and follow-through performance.

Interpersonal
- Improve the person's social skills in one to one relationships and in group situations through structured group activities. Topics for group discussion may include the problem of stigma and how to deal with it, value clarification, and living independently of family.
- Provide the person with opportunities to practice assuming various roles through role playing, task groups, and games or sports.
- Assist the parents to learn how to instruct teachers and friends in seizure management techniques and post-seizure behavior.
- Work with parents or family and the person to plan future goals and objectives.

Self-Care
Increase the person's skills in daily living tasks, such as shopping, meal preparation, budgeting finances, and managing medications.

Productivity
- Increase skills in locating and applying for a job, such as interviewing, filling out an application, and reading want ads.
- Develop work habits through simulated work activities, and volunteering.
- Explore vocational interests and skills.

Leisure
Explore leisure interests and skills.

PRECAUTIONS
- Caution should be used when exploring careers or leisure activities that require climbing (ladders, trees, telephone poles, mountains) or working at heights from which a fall induced by a seizure could cause serious injury or death.
- Some states will not permit a person with a seizure disorder to be licensed to operate certain types of machinery.

PROGNOSIS AND OUTCOME
- The person is able to organize and follow a time schedule of activities and tasks.
- The person is able to manage stressful situations.
- The person demonstrates improved social skills and relationships.
- The person demonstrates improved performance of daily living skills.
- The person demonstrates improved performance of productive activities.

- The person demonstrates improved participation in leisure activities.
- The person is knowledgeable about community agencies and services that may be of assistance.

REFERENCES

Britten, H., N. Britten, and P. Fenwick. 1984. People with epilepsy achieving independence: A study of a rehabilitation hostel. *British Journal of Occupational Therapy* 47(1):7–10.

Clerico, C.M. 1989. Occupational therapy and epilepsy. *Occupational Therapy in Health Care* 6(2/3):41–74.

Day, S. 1982. OT program development within a hospital setting for patients with epilepsy. *Developmental Disabilities Special Interest Section Newsletter* 5(1):1–2.

Day, S. 1984. Occupational therapy assessment and treatment in a hospital setting for patients with epilepsy. *Occupational Therapy in Health Care* 1(2):53–62.

Guillain-Barré Syndrome

DESCRIPTION

Guillain-Barré syndrome is an acute, rapidly progressive form of polyneuritis that causes muscle weakness and distal sensory loss through demyelination of the peripheral nerves. It is also called infectious polyneuritis, infectious neuronitis, polyradiculoneuritis, postinfectious polyneuritis, Landry's syndrome, Landry's ascending paralysis, Landry-Guillain-Barré syndrome, or Landry-Guillain-Barré-Strohl syndrome. The disorder was first described in 1859 by Landry.

CAUSE

While the exact cause is unknown, the disorder may be a response to a virus in which the immunologic system attacks the peripheral nerves causing inflammation and degenerative changes in both posterior (sensory) and anterior (motor) nerve roots. Onset occurs most commonly between the ages of 30 to 50. The disorder has three stages: (1) acute onset, which begins when the first symptoms appear and ends when no further symptoms are noted (usually 1 to 3 weeks), (2) a plateau period when no significant change occurs, which lasts from several days to 2 weeks, and (3) a recovery phase when remyelination and axonal regeneration occur, which may take up to two years.

ASSESSMENT

Areas

- muscle strength (Note: Testing is fatiguing and thus may have to be done over more than one session.)
- range of motion
- physical endurance
- gross motor control
- fine motor coordination, manipulation, and dexterity
- sensory registration or awareness

- sensory processing—discrimination of light touch, stereognosis, pain and temperature, proprioception, and two-point discrimination
- pain
- self-concept
- daily living skills
- productivity history, skills, interests, and values
- leisure interests and skills

Instruments

No comprehensive or specific test for assessing Guillain-Barré syndrome is mentioned in the occupational therapy literature. The following may be useful:

- manual muscle test
- range of motion test
- sensory registration test
- daily living assessment
- occupational history
- interest checklist

PROBLEMS

Motor

- The person usually experiences muscle weakness (flaccid type) that generally begins in the lower extremities and proceeds up the body to the trunk and cranial nerves (VII, IX, X, XI, XII).
- The person usually has loss of range of motion.
- The person may have loss of respiratory control and decreased respiratory volume.
- The person may lose the ability to smile, frown, whistle, or drink with a straw (CVII facial nerves).
- The person may experience difficulty swallowing, coughing, gagging (CIX glossopharyngeal and CX vagus nerves).
- The person may experience deviation or paralysis of the tongue (CXII hypoglossal nerves).
- The person may have hypotonia.
- The person may lose superficial and deep reflexes, such as stretch reflexes, abdominal reflexes, and plantar reflexes.
- The person usually fatigues easily until respiratory sufficiency is fully restored.
- The person may develop contractures from lack of active movement.

Sensory

- The person usually has temporary loss of sensation of touch below the point of the body affected by the disorder. Loss of tactile sensation may include facial muscles if the total body is involved.
- The person may have loss of sensation of proprioception.
- The person may experience increased pain in proximal muscle groups in the thighs, shoulders, and trunk.

- The person may experience pain on passive range of movement.
- The person may experience tenderness when muscles are palpated.

Cognitive
Cognitive faculties are not affected directly by the disorder.

Intrapersonal
- The person may fear becoming dependent.
- The person may express anxiety about the degree of recovery.
- The person may express feelings of frustration at being helpless.

Interpersonal
The person usually has limited endurance for social interaction during early recovery.

Self-Care
The person may be unable to care for him- or herself, depending on the progression of the disorder.

Productivity
The person is usually unable to work or manage a household until the disease has run its course.

Leisure
The person may be unable to engage in preferred leisure activities.

TREATMENT/MANAGEMENT

Motor
- Maintain the person's passive range of motion and encourage active range of motion as motor control returns in descending pattern.
- Increase muscle strength and endurance through gentle, nonresistive activities and games until muscle innervation is normal. Continuous passive motion may be useful when active motion is limited by muscles graded at or below fair. Muscles should be graded fair-plus or better before resistive activities are used.
- Decrease joint stiffness and prevent muscle atrophy or contractures through gentle, nonresistive activities and games.
- Consider splinting to prevent deformity from atrophy and disuse, and maintain functional position during early recovery period.
- Increase coordination and integration of the two sides of the body.
- Increase hand manipulation and dexterity through use of crafts or games that require frequent grasp and release.
- Increase physical tolerance through slowly increasing therapy or work time.

Sensory
- Provide opportunities for sensory stimulation as the person's sensory system function returns.

- Tactile, proprioceptive and vestibular stimulation can be used as the person regains function.

Cognitive
- Assist in instruction about course of disease to decrease the person's anxiety and fear.
- Instruct the person in concepts of energy conservation and work simplification.
- Instruct the person in concepts of joint protection.
- Instruct the person in stress-management techniques.
- Instruct the person in the need to avoid overexertion, which may result in a setback.

Intrapersonal
- Therapists should provide positive encouragement, reassurance, and assistance to decrease the person's fear, anxiety, and feelings of frustration and helplessness.
- Provide training in relaxation techniques.

Interpersonal
Provide opportunities for socialization. Talking to the person about his or her interests will elicit passive range of motion activities.

Self-Care
- Help the person relearn activities of daily living and regain independence.
- Assistive devices, such as arm supports or slings, may be useful for short periods of time to permit earlier function.
- Protective splints may be needed for short periods of time.

Productivity
- Modification of the work environment and some work tasks may permit the person to return to work earlier.
- Temporary modifications of the home environment or homemaking tasks may permit the person to function at home earlier.

Leisure
- Strenuous leisure activities will not be possible until full recovery occurs.
- Explore the person's existing interests that can be incorporated into a total management program.
- Explore new interests that can be developed within the total management program.

PRECAUTIONS
- Watch for redness over bony areas of the body and change the person's position every two hours.
- Watch the person for signs of fatigue. Do not continue activity in presence of signs of fatigue. Also watch for signs of substitution. Use of suspension slings or mobile arm supports may permit hand activities to continue without fatigue to shoulder and upper arms. Alternate resistive and nonresistive activities.
- Have the person maintain good posture and positioning at all times to protect joints while muscles are weak.

• Never range muscles past the point of pain.

PROGNOSIS AND OUTCOME

About 10 to 20% of these persons die from respiratory paralysis. Of the survivors, about 95% recover completely within six months to two years.

• The person has regained muscle strength within good to normal range.
• The person has full or nearly full range of motion in all joints.
• The person is able to walk independently.
• The person is able to perform all basic hand functions.
• The person has normal or near normal sensation in tactile, vestibular, and proprioceptive senses.
• The person is able to perform daily living activities independently.
• The person is able to perform productive activities.
• The person is able to perform leisure activities.

REFERENCES

Drummond, A. 1990. Guillain-Barré Syndrome. Part 1. Background and diagnosis. *British Journal of Occupational Therapy* 53(8):321–2.
Drummond, A. 1990. Guillain-Barré Syndrome. Part 2. Treatment and prognosis. *British Journal of Occupational Therapy* 53(9):360–2.
Mays, M.L. 1990. Case report: Incorporating continuous passive motion in the rehabilitation of a patient with Guillain-Barré syndrome. *American Journal of Occupational Therapy* 44(8):750–4.
McCormack, G.L. 1983. Guillain-Barré syndrome. In *Occupational therapy: Practice skills for physical dysfunction*, 2d ed., ed. L.W. Pedretti, 391–2. St. Louis: C.V. Mosby; 3d ed., 1990, 567–8.
Saul, S.M., and T.L. Baron. 1988. Toileting device for patients with decreased hand function. *Archives of Physical Medicine and Rehabilitation* 69(2):142–3.
Spencer, E.A. 1988. Guillain-Barré syndrome. In *Willard and Spackman's occupational therapy*, 7th ed., ed. H.L. Hopkins and H.D. Smith, 485–6. Philadelphia: J.B. Lippincott.
Van Dam, A. 1987. Guillain-Barré syndrome: A unique perspective. *Occupational Therapy Forum* 2(6):1,3–4. (case report).

Multiple Sclerosis

DESCRIPTION

Multiple sclerosis (MS) is a slowly progressive disease of the central nervous system characterized by demyelination of nerves in scattered areas of the spinal cord and brain that results in multiple and various neurologic signs and symptoms that appear and disappear (exacerbations and remissions).

CAUSE

The specific cause is unknown. Theories of etiology include allergies, decreased blood flow, vitamin deficiency, autoimmune reaction, a slow-acting virus, and trauma. The disease occurs most commonly in people between the ages of 16 and 40.

ASSESSMENT

Note: No two cases of MS are the same. Therefore, the problems listed below are those found in groups of persons. Any given person may experience many or few of the problems. Also, symptoms come (exacerbations) and go (remissions). Thus, some persons experience the same problems repeatedly while others experience a given problem only once or twice.

Areas

- muscle strength
- muscle tone
- fine motor coordination, manipulation, and dexterity
- hand functions and dominance
- hand and grip strength
- static and dynamic balance and postural control
- range of motion
- mobility, with and without aids or assistive devices
- sensory registration, acuity, and awareness
- sensory processing, especially of the upper extremity sensibility—stereognosis, two-point discrimination, and proprioception
- perceptual skills, especially of the visual system
- attending behavior
- concentration
- memory—retention of previous learning
- ability to follow instructions
- problem-solving and decision-making skills
- self-concept
- coping skills
- language and communication skills
- daily living skills—feeding, dressing, bathing, grooming, and toileting
- productivity history, interests, values, and skills
- leisure interests and skills
- architectural and environmental barriers

Instruments

- manual muscle test
- goniometry
- dynamometer and pinch meter (See Mathiowetz, V., N. Kashman, G. Volland, et al. 1985. Grip and pinch strength: Normative data for adults. *Archives of Physical Medicine and Rehabilitation* 66(2):69–74.)
- Nine Hole Peg Test (See Mathiowetz, V., K. Weber, N. Kashman, et al. 1985. Adult norms for the Nine Hole Peg test of finger dexterity. *Occupational Therapy Journal of Research* 5:24–38.)
- Wolf, B. 1981. Occupational Therapy Evaluation: Multiple Sclerosis. In *Interdisciplinary rehabilitation of multiple sclerosis and neuromuscular disorders*, ed. F.P. Maloney, J.S. Burks, and S.P. Ringel, 106–9. Philadelphia: J.B. Lippincott.
- PULSES Profile (See Frankel in the reference section.)
- Barthel Index (See Frankel in the reference section.)

- Minimal Record of Disability (MRD). This scale has been established as the worldwide standard measurement of multiple sclerosis. Therapists should be familiar with the instrument whether or not it is used for each individual therapy. It contains five parts: demographic information, neurological functional systems of Kurtzke, disability status scale of Kurtzke, incapacity status scale, and an environmental scale (obtainable from the National Multiple Sclerosis Society, 205 East 42nd Street, New York, N.Y. 10017).
- Kurtzke Disability Scale (subsection of the MRD) (See Frankel in the reference section.)
- Incapacity Status Scale (subsection of the MRD). (See Mertin, J., L. Jones, R. Trevan, et al. 1984. Critical evaluation of the Incapacity Status Scale. *Acta Neurologica Scandinavica* Suppl. 70(101):68–71.)
- Northwick Park A.D.L. Index. (See J. Benjamin. 1976. The Northwick Park A.D.L. Index. *British Journal of Occupational Therapy* 39(3):1–6.)
- Mini Mental Status Evaluation by M.F. Folstein, S.E. Folstein, and P.R. McHungh, Mini-Mental: A practical method for grading the cognitive state of patients for the clinician, *Journal of Psychiatric Research* 112:189–98, 1975 (not occupational therapists).

PROBLEMS

Motor
- The person usually experiences intermittent muscle weakness.
- The person may experience intermittent paralysis.
- The person usually experiences intermittent ataxia and gait disturbances (tripping or stumbling).
- The person may experience intention tremor.
- The person may have spasticity and/or flaccidity.
- The person may experience incoordination or clumsiness.
- The person usually has low endurance and fatigues easily.
- The person may have contractures.
- The person may have joint stiffness.
- The person may lose range of motion.
- The person may experience cerebellar ataxia.

Sensory
- The person may have partial or total loss of vibratory sense.
- The person may have partial or total loss of temperature sensation.
- The person may have partial or total loss of pain sensation.
- The person may have partial or total loss of the sense of touch.
- The person may have partial or total loss of position sense (proprioception).
- The person may have partial or total loss of joint sensibility (kinesthesia).
- The person may experience vertigo.
- The person may experience paresthesia.
- The person may experience problems of ocular motility such as nystagmus (rapid alternating movements of the eyes) or disconjugate gaze.
- The person may experience episodes of diplopia (double vision).
- The person may have partial or total loss of color vision.
- The person may experience episodes of blurred or dimmed vision or loss of vision.

- The person may experience episodes of acute pain.
- The person may experience Lhermitte's sign (electric-like shocks spreading down the body when the head is flexed forward).

Cognition
- The person may be inattentive at times or have a short attention span.
- The person may show signs of short-term memory loss.
- The person may experience difficulty learning and retrieving new information.
- The person may have difficulty forming new concepts.
- The person may experience reduced capacity to solve problems.

Intrapersonal
- The person may appear apathetic or demonstrate apparent indifference (la belle indifference).
- The person may demonstrate episodes of poor judgment.
- The person may demonstrate emotional lability.

Interpersonal
- At times, the person may experience dysarthria or slurred speech (difficulty pronouncing words correctly because of tongue weakness).
- At times, the person may demonstrate scanning speech (syllables are separated by pauses).
- Family and friends may have difficulty understanding why the person is able to do something one day and not the next. They may think the person is faking illness or disability.

Self-Care
- During exacerbations of muscle weakness, the person may be unable to perform a variety of self-care tasks.
- Visual problems may create problems in performing self-care tasks.
- Loss of touch, pain, or temperature sensation may cause safety concerns in avoiding injury or burns.
- Loss of position sense may lead to falls.
- The person may experience urinary frequency or retention.

Productivity
The person may be forced to give up a job because of inconsistent performance or an inability to perform due to the exacerbations.

Leisure
The person may be unable to participate or unable to participate safely in favorite leisure activities because of periodic motor or sensory dysfunction.

TREATMENT/MANAGEMENT
- Maintain or increase the person's upper extremity strength through progressive resistance exercises within limits of fatigue.

- Maintain or improve coordination and reduce tremor through such techniques as cooling the extensor surface of the upper extremity muscles, rest-and-exercise programs, adding weight to affected limb, and learning or relearning movement strategies.
- Maintain or increase endurance through a rest-and-exercise program that alternates cycles of rest with exercise.
- Prevent contractures through range-of-motion exercises and gentle stretching of tight muscles by using manual and mechanical (splints) methods.

Sensory
- Increase skill of tactile senses to substitute for loss of sight, if needed.
- Teach use of sight inspection to substitute for loss of touch, pain, or position sense in order to reduce the risk of injury to skin or joints, if needed.

Cognition
- Improve cognitive strategies for coping with the disease, such as planning activities in advance, providing for rest cycles, and seeking assistance from others instead of doing it all.
- Increase knowledge of safety to avoid added injuries.
- Provide repeated opportunities to practice new learning to compensate for possible memory and learning deficits.
- Instruct the person in concepts of energy conservation and work simplification.

Intrapersonal
- Provide stress management training to improve emotional control and coping behavior.
- Facilitate emotional adjustment to disability by helping the person establish realistic life goals and take control of a personal rehabilitation program.

Interpersonal
- Suggest participation in group self-help programs to provide opportunity to share problems and solutions with others.
- Encourage the person to involve family in rehabilitation and management program in order to encourage family cooperation and support.

Self-Care
- Provide adaptive equipment and instruction in its use, as needed.
- Instruct the person in the use of a wheelchair, if needed.
- Make recommendations for safety considerations, such as grab bars and nonskid tape in bath or shower, elimination of throw rugs, and use of a railing or banister on stairs.

Productivity
- Make recommendations for modifications of the home or living environment that will facilitate performance of basic homemaking tasks.
- Recommend modification of work environment or task performance if the person is able to continue employment.
- If paid employment is no longer possible, encourage the person to volunteer, take classes, or help with homemaking tasks to maintain participation in productive activities.

Leisure
- Recommend leisure activities based on individual preference and abilities.
- Explore interests to determine possible leisure activities that might replace those that cannot be continued because of disability.

PRECAUTIONS
- There are no known techniques proven to be effective in improving motor control or coordination in persons with cerebellar dysfunction and accompanied spinal motor tract involvement. Each person must be studied to determine which, if any, technique seems to provide some relief from tremor and overall improvement of function.
- Remissions do not mean that the function will suddenly and completely return. The person and therapist should understand that some decrement in function can be expected after each exacerbation.

PROGNOSIS AND OUTCOME
- The person maintains maximum muscle strength within the progressive stage of the disease.
- The person demonstrates use of compensatory techniques for loss of sensory functions (visual and tactile).
- The person demonstrates knowledge and performance of safety factors needed to avoid injuries due to decreased visual and tactile acuity and discrimination.
- The person demonstrates knowledge of good body mechanics and positioning.
- The person demonstrates ability to use adaptive equipment correctly.
- If a wheelchair is used, the person demonstrates mobility techniques and knowledge of routine maintenance of the chair and its parts.
- The person demonstrates knowledge of energy-conservation and work-simplification techniques.
- The person has organized a daily schedule that provides a balance of self-care, productivity, and leisure activities within the person's level of energy.
- The person has identifiable roles within the family or living unit that are satisfying to the individual.
- The person participates in social situations and activities.
- The person is independent in performing self-care activities using adaptive devices, if necessary.
- The person demonstrates the ability to seek assistance when needed and can instruct others regarding the type of care needed.
- The person demonstrates productive work and leisure skills.

REFERENCES

Bahlin-Webb, S.R. 1986. A weighted wrist cuff. *American Journal of Occupational Therapy* 40(5):363–4.

Bhasin, C.A. 1989. Occupational therapy in the management of multiple sclerosis. *Physical Disabilities Special Interest Section Newsletter* 12(4):1–3.

Frankel, D. 1985. Multiple sclerosis. In *Neurological rehabilitation*, ed. D.A. Umphred, 398–415. St Louis: C.V. Mosby; 2d ed., 1990, 531–49.

Goodkin, D.W., D. Hertsgaard, and J. Seminary. 1988. Upper extremity function in multiple sclerosis: Improving assessment sensitivity with box-and-block and nine-hole peg tests. *Archives of Physical Medicine and Rehabilitation* 69(10):850–4.

Kraft, G.H., J.E. Freal, and J.K. Coryell. 1986. Disability, disease duration, and rehabilitation services needs in multiple sclerosis: Patient perspectives. *Archives of Physical Medicine and Rehabilitation* 67(3):164–8.

Linroth, R. 1990. Multiple Sclerosis Achievement Center: A caring environment for a chronic progressive disease. *Occupational Therapy Practice* 2(1):53–9.

Pedretti, L.W., and G.L. McCormack. 1990. Degenerative diseases of the central nervous system—muscle sclerosis. In *Occupational therapy: Practice skills in physical dysfunction*, 3d ed., ed. L.W. Pedretti and B. Zoltan, 648–51, 663–5. St. Louis: C.V. Mosby.

Post, K.M. 1989. Technology for people with multiple sclerosis. *Physical Disabilities Special Interest Section Newsletter* 12(4):3,6.

Schapiro, R.T., et al. 1988. The multiple sclerosis achievement center: A maintenance rehabilitation approach toward a chronic progressive form of the disease. *Journal of Neurologic Rehabilitation* 2:21–3.

Turner A. 1987. Multiple sclerosis. In *The practice of occupational therapy*, 2d ed., ed. A. Turner, 428–39. Edinburgh, Scotland: Churchill Livingstone.

Wolf, B.G. 1985. Occupational therapy for patients with multiple sclerosis. In *Interdisciplinary rehabilitation of multiple sclerosis and neuromuscular disorders*, ed. F.P. Maloney, J.S. Burks, and S.P. Ringel, 103–28. Philadelphia: J.B. Lippincott.

Parkinson's Disease

DESCRIPTION

Parkinson's disease is a slowly progressive, degenerative disorder of the central nervous system.

Stages of Parkinson's Disease

Stage 1: Unilateral involvement only, with no or minimal functional impairment; major symptom usually is resting tremor

Stage 2: Midline or bilateral involvement, without impairment of balance; mild functional impairment related to trunk mobility and postural reflexes, such as difficulty turning in bed and getting in and out of the car

Stage 3: Impairment of balance (postural instability); mild to moderate functional impairment

Stage 4: Increased impairment of balance but still able to walk; functional impairment increases, especially manipulation and dexterity, which interferes with eating, dressing, and washing

Stage 5: Confined to wheelchair or bed

Source: Based on degree of disability stages developed by M.M. Hoehn and M.D. Yahr in Parkinsonism: Onset, progression and mortality. *Neurology* 17(5):427–42, 1967.

CAUSE

The specific cause is unknown, but a slow-acting virus is suspected, such as the one that caused an epidemic of encephalitis lethargica. The disease causes a loss of pigmented neurons in the substantia nigra and other basal ganglia, which results in a loss of the neurotransmitter dopamine. Onset usually occurs after age 40. More men than women are affected. The treatment of choice is dopaminergic or anticholinergic drugs.

ASSESSMENT

Areas
* muscle strength, including grip and pinch strength
* range of motion, active and passive
* muscle tone, especially degree of rigidity
* fine motor control—coordination, manipulation, and dexterity
* gross motor control—rolling, turning, walking, climbing, coming to a sitting or standing position, and transfers
* physical tolerance and endurance
* movement speed, slow, normal
* posture and postural control, especially flexion posture
* balance—equilibrium and protective reactions
* mobility (ease of movement) of the body and face
* ambulation, including gait pattern and speed, especially festinating gait and propulsion
* praxis and motor planning skills
* sensory registration and processing (usually no detailed assessment is needed)
* cognitive skills, especially memory and problem solving
* self-concept
* affect or mood (especially note signs of depression)
* coping skills
* social and family support
* role performance
* daily living skills
* productivity history, skills, interests, and values
* leisure interests and skills
* architectural and environmental barriers

Instruments
No specific or comprehensive instruments developed by occupational therapists could be identified. One instrument that might be explored is illustrated in D.A. Umphred, ed. 1990. *Neurological Rehabilitation*, 2d ed., 564. St. Louis: C.V. Mosby. Other instruments or techniques that appear useful are:

* Unified Rating Scale for Parkinsonism, in *The comprehensive management of Parkinson's disease*, ed. M.B. Stern and H.I. Hurtig, 34–45. New York: PMA Publishing, 1988.
* manual muscle testing, dynamometer, pinch meter
* goniometry
* Purdue Pegboard Test by J. Tiffin, Chicago: Science Research Associates, 1968, and handwriting samples

- timed movements with a stopwatch, such as sitting and standing tolerance and standing balance with eyes open and eyes closed
- observing ability to walk forward and backward and cross one leg over in front of the other (braiding)
- Bradburn Index of Psychological Well-being by N.M. Bradburn, *The structure of psychological well-being*, Chicago: Aldine, 1969.
- Barthel Index by F.I. Mahoney and D.W. Barthel, Function evaluation: The Barthel Index, *Maryland State Medical Journal* 14:61–65, 1965.
- oral sensorimotor battery (See Diamond, S.G., J.S. Schneider, and C.H. Markham. 1986. Oral sensorimotor defects in patients with Parkinson's disease. *Advances in Neurology* 45:335–8.)
- occupational history
- leisure interest checklist

PROBLEMS

Motor
- The person usually has bradykinesia (slow movements).
- The person usually has akinesia and hypokinesis (difficulty and slowness in initiating movement).
- The person usually has resting tremor in forearm and elbow with pill-rolling movements between the fingers and thumb. Later tremor may appear in the legs, trunk, face, lips, tongue, and neck.
- The person usually has rigidity (increased muscle tone) in the muscles of the neck, trunk, and forearm, which may respond to passive stretching with a series of jerky (cogwheel), giving movements or leadpipe movements in which there is slow, smooth resistance.
- The person may have a masklike face (fixed expression).
- The person may have a shuffling gait and acceleration as walking continues.
- The person may have a reduction of motor activity level due to movement difficulties with a corresponding decrease in endurance, physical fitness, and muscle strength from the disuse. Respiratory function is compromised.
- The person may have loss of coordination, manipulation, and dexterity (fine motor coordination).
- The person may lose gross motor skills related to trunk muscle, especially rotation and segmental rolling (difficulty rotating or turning the body, such as rolling over in bed or turning the upper torso while standing).
- The person may have difficulty initiating movements (motor planning).
- The person may have difficulty executing movements with any degree of speed.
- The person may have difficulty with sequences of movement (sequential movement) due to loss of automatic movement sequences.
- The person may have motor restlessness (akathisia) or an inability to lie or sit quietly.
- The person usually has postural instability due to loss of righting reactions, including tilt, or protective reactions and equilibrium reactions.
- The person may have abnormal posture; the neck, if flexed forward of the spine, is fixed and arm swing is lost during walking.

Cognition
- The person may have dementia and memory loss. (Note: The literature is mixed as to whether the dementia is directly related to Parkinson's disease or a coexisting disorder.)
- The person may lose the ability to orient in space (spatial orientation).

Intrapersonal
- The person may have loss of self-esteem.
- The person may express feelings of uselessness and hopelessness.
- The person may become depressed because of increasing disability.
- The person may express suicidal thoughts.

Interpersonal
- The person may have shaky handwriting due to decreased fine motor control and/or micrography (very small handwriting).
- The person may have monotone speech.
- The person may have decreased interest in social activities.

Self-Care
- The person may have increasing difficulty with activities of daily living due to the progression of the disease, especially increasing postural instability.
- Cutting food and chewing may be very slow due to akinesia or bradykinesia.
- The person usually experiences increasing loss of independence related to problems of postural instability.

Productivity
- The person usually has increasing difficulty performing work tasks in the home and on the job.
- The person may have to retire early from work and avoid volunteer positions due to concern about postural stability.

Leisure
The person may have to restrict or curtail favorite leisure activities.

TREATMENT/MANAGEMENT
Treatment models are based on sensory motor activities and sensory integration. The stages listed below may be helpful in organizing the sequence of treatment.

Motor
- Maintain or increase the person's active and passive range of motion, especially extension.
- Prevent contractures by stretching tight muscles.
- Improve speed and flexibility using sports and games.
- Maintain or improve dexterity and coordination through repetitive motions, such as sorting tasks.
- Review gait with emphasis on increasing step length, widening the base of support, increasing the range of hip flexion, enhancing reciprocal arm movements, and improving stops, starts, and turns.

- Maintain mobility through use of rhythm, music, singing, and dancing to initiate movement.
- Improve motor planning and increase speed by adding visual cues, such as looking at others or in a mirror, and adding auditory cues, such as music with a pronounced rhythm, a metronome, verbal suggestions, and reinforcement from the therapist.
- Increase manipulation and dexterity (as measured by speed and accuracy) through use of games, puzzles, writing exercises, and hand crafts, such as mosaics, link belts, felt craft, origami.
- Improve movement patterns through proprioceptive neuromuscular facilitation (PNF) patterns, especially for trunk rotation.
- Enhance awareness of problems in posture and balance and suggest methods to prevent falls, such as removing throw rugs, using banisters when climbing stairs, and wearing flat shoes.
- Provide an opportunity for safe practice of static and dynamic balance activities in a group exercise class. Clients can hold hands to increase stability while standing on one leg, rocking back and forth on heels and then toes, or doing the grapevine step (alternating placing leg in front and then in back while moving to the right or left).
- Consider the use of music or a metronome to provide a beat or rhythm for practicing posture and balance activities.

Cognitive

- Teach concepts of energy conservation and work simplification.
- Teach concepts of home safety, especially those safety considerations that may reduce the possibility of falling, such as non-skid mats, grab bars in the bathroom, and strong railings or banisters.
- Assist in teaching the person and family about Parkinson's disease and about useful treatments.

Intrapersonal

- Promote relaxation by teaching deep breathing and imagery. Include slow rocking, inverted position, and other inhibitory techniques to decrease tone.
- Maintain or increase self-esteem by recognizing special skills or talents and rewarding good effort.

Interpersonal

- Encourage vocalization to increase voice volume through speaking and singing activities.
- Provide support to the family as needed, including instruction for better treatment management.
- Provide practice in writing to increase size and legibility of writing or change to typing or a computer.
- Use a group approach to achieve therapy objectives, especially exercise and teaching groups to improve mood (decrease depression) and increase socialization.
- Encourage the person to discuss roles within the family and living unit. Change only those roles that the person cannot safely do, but maintain as many roles as possible.
- Encourage the family to participate in the treatment program.

Self-Care
- Teach adaptive techniques to reduce effect of tremor, such as using both hands with arms close to the body to lift a glass or cup or using the elbow as a pivot to raise a fork from a plate to the mouth.
- Encourage the person to maintain maximum functional level in all activities of daily living as long as possible. Discourage caregivers from assisting too much.
- Discuss with the caregivers a balance of self-care independence versus energy conservation for productive and leisure activities.

Productivity
- Encourage the person to continue productive activities as long as possible.
- Explore alternate productive activities if previous ones cannot be continued. Consider volunteer, student (classes for older citizens), and homemaking roles.

Leisure
- Maintain and encourage leisure interests that are within the person's physical capacities.
- Encourage and support development of new interests that can substitute or replace interests that cannot be continued safely.

PRECAUTIONS
- The person is prone to loss of balance and may fall on objects. Maintain safety procedures at all times.
- Observe the person for signs of side effects from medication, such as dystonic movements, orthostatic hypotension, mental disturbances, cardiac arrhythmias, or gastrointestinal disturbances.
- Observe the person for signs of severe depression.

PROGNOSIS AND OUTCOME
Parkinson's disease is a progressive disorder. Treatment can slow the degree of disability but not the course of the disease.

- The person is able to perform activities of daily living at the maximum level of independence possible given the current stage of the disease.
- The person demonstrates improvement in ease of movement in trunk muscles.
- The person demonstrates improvement in postural control and balance.
- The person demonstrates improvement in motor planning abilities.
- The person demonstrates improvement in manipulation and dexterity (fine motor coordination).
- The person demonstrates improvement in gross motor coordination.
- The person has the level of endurance needed to perform functional activities.
- The person has increased range of motion to permit performance of functional activities or has learned to use adapted equipment.
- The person demonstrates knowledge of safety considerations.
- The person demonstrates knowledge of energy-conservation and work-simplification techniques.
- The person and family demonstrate knowledge of support services available in the community.

REFERENCES

Caird, F.I. 1986. Non-drug therapy of Parkinson's disease. *Scottish Medical Journal* 31(2):129–32.

Gautheir, L., and S. Gautheir. 1983. Functional rehabilitation of patients with Parkinson's disease. *Physiotherapy Canada* 35:220–3.

Gautheir, L., S. Dalziel, and S. Gautheir. 1987. The benefits of group occupational therapy for patients with Parkinson's disease. *American Journal of Occupational Therapy* 41(6):360–5.

Godwin-Austen, R.B. 1990. Physical treatment. In *Parkinson's disease,* ed. G.M. Stern, 647–62. Baltimore: Johns Hopkins University Press.

Hunt, L. 1988. Continuity of care maximizes autonomy of the elderly. *American Journal of Occupational Therapy* 42(6):391–3 (case study).

Kase, S.E., and C.A. O'Riordan. 1987. Rehabilitation approach. In *Handbook of Parkinson's disease,* ed. W.C. Koller, 455–64. New York: Marcel Dekker.

Manson, L., and F.I. Caird. 1985. Survey of the hobbies and transport of patients with Parkinson's disease. *British Journal of Occupational Therapy* 48(7):199–200.

Turner, A. 1987. Parkinsonism.. In *The practice of occupational therapy,* 2d ed., ed. A. Turner, 486–97. Edinburgh, Scotland: Churchill Livingstone.

Pedretti, L.W., and G.L. McCormack. 1990. Degenerative diseases of the central nervous system—Parkinson's disease. In *Occupational therapy: Practice skills in physical dysfunction,* 3d ed., ed. L.W. Pedretti and B. Zoltan, 651–6. St. Louis: C.V. Mosby.

Weiner, W.J., and C. Singer. 1989. Parkinson's disease and nonpharmacologic treatment programs. *Journal of the American Geriatrics Society* 37(4):359–63.

Post-Polio Syndrome

DESCRIPTION

Post-polio syndrome is a collection of impairments occurring in persons who have had poliomyelitis many years ago and have functioned satisfactorily in the interim time. The condition was first described in 1979 in the *Rehabilitation Gazette*. It may be misdiagnosed as amyotrophic lateral sclerosis.

CAUSE

Persons have a past history of poliomyelitis. The cause of current symptoms is unclear but may be related to chronic mechanical strain of weakened musculature and ligaments and loss (degenerative joint disease or arthralgia) or dropout or dysfunction of axon terminals of reinnervated motor units (muscle overuse, myofascial pain, or compressive neuropathy).

ASSESSMENT

Areas
- muscle strength (Note: Muscles may not be as efficient as their strength suggests and may vary greatly in strength throughout the range of motion.)
- range of motion (functional)
- muscle tone (Note tightness in muscle groups.)
- pain in muscles or joints

- myoclonus
- physical tolerance and endurance
- roles—family, social, work, etc.
- types of self-help devices being used
- daily living activities
- productivity history, skills, interests, and values
- leisure skills and interests
- architectural and environmental barriers

Instruments

No specific tests developed by occupational therapists were identified for this disorder. The following types of tests should be useful:

- manual muscle test
- goniometry
- activities of daily living scale
- occupational history
- leisure checklist

PROBLEMS

Motor
- The person usually has decreased physical tolerance and endurance.
- The person usually has progressive muscle weakness and atrophy in muscles affected and unaffected by polio, called progressive post-polio muscular atrophy (PPMA).
- The person may have fasciculations and myoclonus.
- The person may have respiratory insufficiency.
- The person may have increasing loss of ambulation skills, especially stair climbing.
- The person may awaken with headaches.
- The person may have difficulty swallowing and may choke.
- The person may have transient fatigue, muscle weakness, or pain after exercise, which are early signs of the post-polio syndrome.

Sensory
- The person may have loss of temperature control in the affected limb(s).
- The person may experience muscle pain.
- The person may experience joint pain.
- The person may experience back pain.
- The person may experience increased sensitivity and intolerance to cold.
- The person may have loss of sensation.

Cognitive

The person may experience difficulty in concentration.

Intrapersonal
- The person usually has increased feelings of helplessness.
- The person may become depressed.

- The person may have feelings of anxiety and fear about becoming increasingly disabled.
- The person may express feelings of anger at being unable to perform certain activities.
- The person may refuse to believe that changes in lifestyle may be necessary.

Interpersonal
The person may have decreased participation in social activities due to decreased endurance.

Self-Care
The person may have increased difficulty performing activities of daily living, especially bathing, grooming, and dressing.

Productivity
- The person may experience increased difficulty performing job tasks, such as those requiring walking distances within a building or between buildings.
- The person may experience difficulty performing homemaking tasks.

Leisure
The person may be unable to continue some leisure activities because of decreased muscle strength and increased pain.

TREATMENT/MANAGEMENT
Models of treatment are not well established since this aspect of polio has been documented fairly recently. Models appear to include neurodevelopmental, biomechanical, and orthopedic approaches.

Motor
- Have the person do aerobic exercises to strengthen weakened muscles, such as swimming, or exercises with a group sitting in chairs. (Note: Avoid fatigue and pain.)
- Train the person in the use of a wheelchair or motorized scooter, if indicated, especially in relation to the job and home.
- Assist in training the person to adjust to a new orthosis (a leg brace, for example) if indicated.
- Provide padded gloves or elbow pads to the person with compression injuries resulting from the use of a cane, crutch, or wheelchair.

Sensory
Biofeedback may be helpful in increasing temperature control.

Cognitive
- Teach energy-conservation, pacing, and work-simplification techniques.
- The person may need to learn new eating habits to lose weight and increase his or her energy level.
- Provide the person with an opportunity to solve problem situations that are of greatest concern to the person.

- Teach time management skills to permit cycles of rest and activity.

Intrapersonal
- Encourage the person to speak about his or her feelings. A self-help support group may be useful to encourage the sharing of feelings.
- Teach stress management techniques, including relaxation training.

Interpersonal
- Encourage the person to continue social activities but suggest possible modifications, such as shorter outings.
- Encourage the person to participate in self-help groups and networking among persons with post-polio, such as through the Gazette International Networking Institute.

Self-Care
- Self-help devices should be selected as indicated and training provided.
- Devices that may have been used for many years should be checked to determine if they still function, fit properly, are needed to do a task, and are the best solution for the task.

Productivity
- Discuss and make recommendations for possible changes and adaptations in job tasks or physical work environment.
- Discuss and make recommendations for possible changes and adaptations in living environment to increase safety and accommodate reduced endurance.

Leisure
- Explore existing leisure activities for possible adaptations that might permit continued participation, such as adapted bowling or using a cart for golf.
- Explore interests to determine possible new leisure activities that are within the person's physical limitations.

PRECAUTIONS

Make sure the person avoids the overuse weakness that occurs following strenuous exercise or activities and results in a loss of maximum muscle strength lasting for days or weeks.

PROGNOSIS AND OUTCOME

Prognosis and outcome depend on the degree to which the individual is able to change his or her lifestyle to function within physical limitations instead of overextending the limits. Functional independence using adaptive devices as needed is also a key factor, along with successful management of psychological stress.

- The person has maintained or increased muscle strength.
- The person has maintained or increased range of motion.
- The person has maintained or increased physical tolerance and endurance.
- The person has maintained or increased functional mobility by modification of crutches or use of a wheelchair.

- The person demonstrates knowledge of stress-management techniques.
- The person demonstrates knowledge of energy-conservation, pacing, and work-simplification techniques.
- The person demonstrates knowledge of time-management techniques to balance self-care, productivity, leisure, and rest.
- The person is able to perform self-care activities independently using self-help devices, if needed.
- The person is able to perform productive activities with job modifications, if needed.
- The person is able to perform leisure activities with adaptations, if needed.

REFERENCES

Casper, N.M. 1985. Post polio sequelae: A general overview and a personal encounter. *Occupational Therapy Forum* 1(7):11–12, 1(8):11–13.
Trombly, C.A., and A.D. Scott. 1989. Degenerative disease—post polio syndrome. In *Occupational therapy for physical dysfunction*, 3d ed., ed. C.A. Trombly, 480–2. Baltimore: Williams & Wilkins.
Young, G.R. 1989. Occupational therapy and the postpolio syndrome. *American Journal of Occupational Therapy* 43(2):97–103.

Pseudohypertrophic Muscular Dystrophy (Duchenne)

DESCRIPTION

Pseudohypertrophic muscular dystrophy is a progressive and fatal disorder of the skeletal muscles that begins in early childhood. It is also known as Duchenne's muscular dystrophy and progressive muscular dystrophy.

CAUSE

The cause is a hereditary sex-linked recessive gene carried on the X chromosome. Symptoms usually begin between ages three to seven, predominantly in boys. Pseudohypertrophy is due to fatty and fibrous infiltration of the muscle. Death occurs about age 20-25.

ASSESSMENT

Areas
- gross motor skills
- muscle strength
- functional range of motion
- endurance
- fine motor coordination, manipulation, and dexterity
- balance and postural control
- self-concept

- social roles
- self-care and daily living skills
- productive skills, values, and interests
- play skills development
- leisure interests

Instruments

No instruments developed by occupational therapists were identified in the literature for this disorder. Some useful types of testing instruments include:

- manual muscle test
- developmental test
- activities of daily living scale (For a sample see Occupational therapy assessment in Siegel, pp. 279–81, which is listed in the reference section.)
- play history
- leisure interest survey

PROBLEMS

Motor
- The person usually has weakness in the proximal muscles, starting with the pelvis and then the shoulders.
- The person usually has waddling gait due to an attempt to broaden the base of support.
- The person may be reluctant to run.
- The person may have lordosis due to muscle imbalance.
- The person may have a history of frequent falls.
- The person often stands up by walking his hands up the legs (Gower's sign).
- The person may have difficulty climbing stairs.
- The person may develop flexion contractures.
- The person may develop a scoliosis due to muscle imbalance.
- The person may appear to have enlargement of the calf muscles and sometimes of the forearm and thigh muscles.
- The person may have decreased mobility leading to wheelchair dependence.
- Respiratory muscles usually become progressively weaker, leading to decreased pulmonary function.
- The person may have other deformities that occur as muscles become weaker.
- The person may have a tendency toward obesity, especially as endurance decreases.
- The person may have decreased range of motion.
- The person may have decreased endurance and physical tolerance.

Sensory
Sensory faculties are not usually involved as a direct consequence of the disorder.

Cognitive
The person may have mild mental retardation.

Intrapersonal
- The person may have a poor self-concept, low self-esteem, and a poor sense of mastery.
- The person may lack self-identity and body image.
- The person may have poor coping skills.
- The person may fear dying.
- The person may fear becoming helpless.
- The person may lack motivation.

Interpersonal
- Dependence on others increases as the disability increases.
- The person may become demanding.
- The person may lose role identification in the family as the disability increases.

Self-Care
Loss of self-care and daily living skills increases as the disability increases.

Productivity
- The person may not develop or may lose play skills.
- Productive skills may decrease as the disability increases.

Leisure
Leisure skills may decrease as the disability increases.

TREATMENT/MANAGEMENT

Motor
- Prolong gross motor skills as long as possible.
- Prevent deformities and contractures wherever possible by passive stretching, positioning in prone, and the use of adapted equipment.
- Maintain endurance through activities and games.
- Maintain the person's muscle strength, especially in the hips, through activities and games that require kicking, climbing, pushing, and pulling.
- Maintain muscle tone through walking exercises.
- Maintain grip strength and finger dexterity.
- Maintain upper extremity mobility and range of motion through activities and games requiring throwing, tossing, catching, and reaching. A deltoid aid or overhead slings may be useful when shoulder girdle muscles weaken.
- Consider splinting ankle to maintain dorsiflexion when the person becomes wheelchair dependent.
- Assist the physical therapist in maintaining strength of respiratory muscles through activities and games requiring blowing or taking deep breaths, such as swimming.
- Assist the medical team in selecting powered mobility equipment when walking is no longer feasible.

Stages of Disorder and Treatment

  I. *Diagnostic period* (ages 3 to 4 years). The purpose of treatment is primarily patient and family education to encourage age-appropriate activities.

 II. *Early childhood* (ages 5 to 7 years). The purpose of treatment is to assist the child with early problems in gross motor and upper extremity activities related to play, self-care, and school.

III. *Childhood-ambulatory* (ages 7 to 12 years). The purpose of treatment is to keep the child mainstreamed in school and the community and independent in home activities with self-help aids as needed and lifts, ramps, or other architectural modifications designed primarily to aid mobility.

 IV. *Late childhood-nonambulatory* (ages 13 to 18 years). The purpose of treatment is to maintain range of motion and use of the upper extremities with assistive devices, such as BFO (balanced forearm orthosis), feeding aids, reachers, adaptive clothing, and lap boards. Assist the multidisciplinary team with lower limb stretching and respiratory care.

  V. *Young adulthood* (ages 19 years plus). The purpose of treatment is to maintain as much function as possible and assist with social interaction and educational or vocational planning. Maximum use of adaptive technology is needed.

Source: Based on I.M. Siegel. 1986. Occupational therapy. In *Muscle and its diseases: An outline primer of basic science.* Chicago: Yearbook Medical Publishers, pp. 278–84.

Cognitive
- Instruct the person and family members on concepts of energy conservation and work simplification.
- Assist the dietician or nutritionist in instructing the family about diet and preparation of nutritious, nonfattening meals.
- Discuss with the family and make recommendations regarding modifications of the home that can increase mobility while promoting safety, such as railings, banisters, and grab bars. A later discussion of using a lift or hoist may be useful to avoid back strain in family members.

Intrapersonal
- Encourage the person to express fears or anxieties about his or her changing health status and terminal illness.
- Provide opportunities for creative expression to increase self-concept and self-mastery through crafts, games, music, and computer skills.

Interpersonal
- Facilitate the development and assistance of family support.
- Encourage the family to provide an active role for the person within the family structure.

Self-Care

Provide adapted equipment and instruction on its use if needed to perform activities of daily living. Examples suggested by Siegel (see the reference section) include an easy-lift or raised chair and toilet seat, bathroom grab bars, clothing adaptations, such as Velcro fastenings, large zippers, and oversized buttons, foot boards, over-bed cradles, reachers, hydraulic or electric lifts, deerskin lined shoes, balanced forearm orthosis, button hooks, wrist extension splints, extended and built-up handles for eating utensils, a wheelchair cushion and mattress with alternating pressure, nylon sheets and pajamas, doorknob extensions, wheelchair lap trays, and transfer boards.

Productivity
- Help the family and person identify productive activities that the individual can perform within the family structure.
- Assist teachers in determining positioning and assistive devices to permit the person to participate in educational programs.
- Help the person explore vocational interests and develop occupational skills.

Leisure
- Help the person explore interests and try out new activities.
- Suggest modifications of activities that would permit the person to continue to participate.

PRECAUTIONS
- When possible, avoid exposing persons with Duchenne's muscular dystrophy to others with the common cold or other upper respiratory tract disorders.
- Report signs of respiratory distress (coughing, choking, or difficulty breathing) to the physician and caregivers promptly.

PROGNOSIS AND OUTCOME

Duchenne's muscular dystrophy is a progressive disorder. Death from respiratory failure usually occurs before the person reaches age 25 .

- The person is able to maintain mobility by walking or using a wheelchair.
- The person demonstrates functional range of motion of the upper extremities independently or with the use of mobile arm supports.
- The person has a positive self-concept.
- The person demonstrates stress-management techniques.
- The person is able to perform daily living skills independently or with the use of self-help devices.
- The person demonstrates performance of productive activities.
- The person demonstrates performance of leisure activities.

REFERENCES

Morris, A.G., and P.J. Vignos. 1960. A self-care program for the child with progressive muscular dystrophy. *American Journal of Occupational Therapy* 14:301–5 (classic article).
Schkade, J.K., A. Feibelman, and J.D. Cook. 1987. Occupational potential in a population with Duchenne muscular dystrophy. *Occupational Therapy Journal of Research* 7(5):289–300.
Siegel, I.M. 1986. Occupational therapy. In *Muscle and its diseases: An outline primer of basic science and clinical method*, ed. I.M. Siegel, 278-84. Chicago: Year Book Medical Publishers.
Turner, A. 1987. Paediatrics. In *The practice of occupational therapy*, 2d ed., ed. A. Turner, 465–74. Edinburgh, Scotland: Churchill Livingstone.
Yasuda, Y.L., K. Bowman, and J.D. Hsu. 1986. Mobile arm supports: Criteria for successful use in muscle disease patients. *Archives of Physical Medicine and Rehabilitation* 67(4):253–6.

Reflex Sympathetic Dystrophy Syndrome

DESCRIPTION

Reflex sympathetic dystrophy syndrome (RSDS) is a deafferentation syndrome with autonomic changes that consists of a triad of pain, edema, and sympathetic dysfunction of an extremity following trauma, nerve injury, or central nervous system disorder. Subtypes of the syndrome include shoulder-hand syndrome, causalgia, neurovascular dystrophy, Sudeck's atrophy, idiopathic peripheral autonomic neuropathy, posttraumatic dystrophy, and algodystrophy. RSDS was documented during the Civil War by Silas Weir Mitchell, a neurologist.

CAUSE

The precise cause is unknown, although several theories exist. The syndrome usually occurs secondary to a pre-existing condition, such as a stroke, traumatic injury to the head or spinal cord, major surgery, fracture, pulmonary disease, myocardial infarction, and cervical disk degeneration. Onset usually is identified when the pain, edema, and trophic changes can no longer be attributed to the original cause. Both sexes and all age groups are affected, but the incidence is higher in women and the most common age range is 45 to 65.

ASSESSMENT

Areas
- muscle strength, hand and grip strength
- range of motion
- hand functions
- edema and swelling
- pain
- sensory registration
- sensory processing
- daily living activities

- productivity history, skills, interests, and values
- leisure skills and interests

Instruments

- McGill Pain Questionnaire by R. Melzak, The McGill Pain Questionnaire: Major properties and scoring methods, *Pain*, 3:277–99, 1975 (not an occupational therapist).
- Semmes-Weinstein monofilaments (light touch-deep pressure) (See J.A. Bell-Krotoski. 1990. Light touch-deep pressure testing using Semmes-Weinstein monofilaments. In *Rehabilitation of the hand*, 3d ed., ed. J.M. Hunter, et al., 585–93. St. Louis: C.V. Mosby.)
- Disk-Criminator or Boley Gauge (static two-point discrimination) (See norms in section on median nerve. See also A.D. Callahan. 1990. Sensibility testing: Clinical methods. In *Rehabilitation of the hand*, 3d ed., ed. J.M. Hunter, et al., 605–6. St. Louis: C.V. Mosby.)
- vibrometer or tuning fork 256 cps.
- volumetry (See K. Schultz-Johnson. 1988. *Volumetrics: A literature review.* Santa Monica, CA: Upperextremity Technology, 2210 Santa Monica Blvd., Suite A, Santa Monica, CA 90404. available from Smith & Nephew.)
- goniometry
- Jebsen Test of Hand Function by R.H. Jebsen et al., *Archives of Physical Medicine and Rehabilitation* 50:311–9, 1969.
- activities of daily living scale
- occupational history
- leisure checklist

PROBLEMS

Motor

- reduced range of motion
- swelling
- muscle atrophy
- muscle cramping and spasms
- loss of bone density (osteoporosis)
- trophic changes, such as increased nail curvature, flattening of the cuticle base, loss of pulp bulk, skin and hair changes, and tissue atrophy

Sensory

- pain reported as severe, constant, and burning
- tenderness
- skin and vasomotor changes, including rubor, pallor, and atrophy
- hyperesthesia
- alternating vasodilation and vasoconstriction resulting in alternating sensation of hot and cold

Cognitive

The person may have difficulty with problem-solving tasks because of preoccupation with pain or avoidance of pain.

Intrapersonal
- The person may be emotionally labile.
- The person may be anxious, worried, or apprehensive about the condition.
- The person may exhibit signs of hysteria.
- The person may be defensive or hostile.

Interpersonal
- The person may be dependent on others.
- Conversation tends to be dominated by the subject of pain or disability.

Self-Care
The person may avoid performing some daily living tasks to avoid aggravating pain response.

Productivity
The person may avoid performing productive activities to avoid aggravating pain.

Leisure
The person may stop performing some leisure activities to avoid aggravating pain.

TREATMENT/MANAGEMENT

Motor
- Jobst intermittent compression unit is useful in reducing "pitting" edema.
- Provide range of motion for the person's shoulder and elbow through the use of a skateboard or reciprocal pulleys. A dowel or wand can also provide range of motion exercise for the forearm.
- Increase muscle strength by adding weights to the skateboard, pulleys, dowels, or weight well for progressive resistance exercises for the shoulder, elbow, forearm, wrist, and fingers.
- Splints may be used for positioning. Be alert to swelling. Make the splints adjustable.
- Compression and traction may be used alternately (stress loading). The person scrubs a plywood board while positioned on the floor on all fours. The person is told to scrub by applying as much pressure (compression) as possible using a back and forth motion while leaning on the affected arm. Sessions are three minutes long, three times per day. The person is also told to carry a weighted briefcase or purse in the affected hand (traction), with the arm extended throughout the day. The weight is from 1 to 5 pounds as determined in the initial visit.

Sensory
The use of warm, moist heat is helpful in reducing pain and hypersensitivity.

Cognitive
- Explain the purpose of treatment and the treatment program in easy to understand language, and state what is expected of the person.

- Instruct the person on a home exercise program, providing a specific number of repetitions and the amount of resistance to be used.

Intrapersonal

Use highly structured, purposeful activities, such as link belts, pot holders, or latch rugs, that are highly repetitive and require few problem-solving skills but encourage the use of both hands.

Self-Care

Encourage performance of activities of daily living.

Stages of RSDS

Stage 1
- duration is 1 to 3 months
- severe, burning pain in localized region
- localized edema
- hyperesthesia
- rapid hair and nail growth
- stiffness
- muscle spasm
- loss of joint mobility
- vasospasm affecting color and temperature of skin

Stage 2
- duration is 3 to 6 months
- pain more severe and diffuse
- edema spreads
- hair growth diminishes, nails are cracked, brittle, and grooved
- deossification is apparent on x-ray
- joint thickening
- muscle atrophy

Stage 3
- duration is indefinite and may be permanent
- trophic changes become irreversible
- pain becomes intractable and may spread to include entire limb
- marked muscle atrophy
- severely limited mobility of affected area (joint ankylosing) and pericapsular fibrosis
- flexor tendon contractions and possible subluxations
- marked bone deossification that is more diffuse
- skin has drawn appearance

Source: Based on Malament, I.B., and J.B. Click. 1983. Sudeck's atrophy, the clinical syndrome. *Journal of the American Podiatry Association* 73(7):362–8.

PRECAUTIONS

This syndrome can become a permanently disabling condition if early diagnosis and treatment are not provided. Therapists should be alert to early signs of the syndrome, such as constant complaints about pain, anxious behavior, or complaints about sweating or temperature changes in an extremity, especially the hands or feet.

PROGNOSIS AND OUTCOME

Early therapy is important, although not a guarantee of success. Remissions and exacerbations may occur; however, less than 5% of cases recover spontaneously. Use of TENS (transcutaneous electrical nerve stimulation), nerve blocks, and sympathectomies plus therapy seems to offer the best treatment.

- The person does not complain of pain.
- The person is able to move the affected part normally.
- The person is able to use the affected part to perform daily activities.
- The person does not complain or show continued evidence of temperature changes in the affected part.
- The person demonstrates performance of productive activities.
- The person is able to perform leisure activities.

REFERENCES

Carlson, L.K., and H.K. Watson. 1988. Treatment of reflex sympathetic dystrophy using the stress loading program. *Journal of Hand Therapy* 1(4):149–54.
Clark, V.H. 1988. Reflex sympathetic dystrophy after a fall. *Journal of Hand Therapy* 1(3):127–35.
Watson, H.K., and L. Carlson. 1987. Treatment of reflex sympathetic dystrophy of the hand with an active "stress loading" program. *Journal of Hand Surgery* 12A(5, pt.1):779-85.
Waylett, J. 1984. Therapist's management of reflex sympathetic dystrophy. In *Rehabilitation of the hand*, 2d ed., ed. J.M. Hunter, et al., 533–7. St. Louis: C.V. Mosby. Revised in 3d ed., 1990, 787–92.

Reflex Sympathetic Dystrophy Syndrome—Shoulder-Hand Syndrome

DESCRIPTION

Shoulder-hand syndrome is a reflex neurovascular condition involving the shoulder and hand. At times both upper extremities may be involved or at other times only part of one extremity. Shoulder-hand syndrome is a subcategory of the reflex sympathetic dystrophy syndrome. Other subcategories include Sudeck's atrophy, minor or major causalgia, and minor or major traumatic dystrophy.

CAUSE

The cause is unknown, but the syndrome may be caused by an area of damage to tissue, either peripherally or internally. Afferent stimuli released at this site may enter the spinal cord, spread over several segments to neurons communicating with both lateral sympathetic tracts, and affect motor pathways. The result may be a feedback circuit that aggravates the irritability of already damaged tissue.

ASSESSMENT

Note: shoulder-hand syndrome is a secondary condition arising from a pre-existing condition, such as a fracture, head or spinal cord injury, major surgery, stroke, cervical disk degeneration, or myocardial infarction. Persons should be observed for early signs of shoulder-hand syndrome and such observations reported to the physician immediately to encourage early treatment

---

Stages of Shoulder-Hand Syndrome

Stage 1—Pain, edema, and vasomotor changes, such as hyperhidrosis
Stage 2—The above plus trophic changes in the skin and nails, muscle atrophy, and evidence of osteoporosis on x-rays
Stage 3—Pain and edema are resolved but atrophy and contractures are present, as well as evidence of advanced osteoporosis on x-rays

Source: Based on Chalsen, G.G., et. al. 1987. Shoulder pain in the patient with hemiplegia: A fundamental concept in occupational therapy. *Occupational Therapy in Health Care* 1(3):138.

Areas

- muscle strength
- edema
- pain response to passive movement of the fingers, wrist, and shoulder
- vasomotor changes, such as hyperhidrosis (excessive sweating) and pale, pink or purple skin
- increased skin temperature
- proprioception
- visual neglect
- tactile sensation
- orientation
- memory
- daily living skills

Instruments

- manual muscle test
- volumetry (See K. Schultz-Johnson, *Volumetrics: A literature review*, Santa Monica, CA: Upperextremity Technology, 2210 Santa Monica Blvd., Suite A., Santa Monica, CA 90404. 1988, available from Smith & Nephew.)

- pain—Ritchie Articular Index (See Bohannon, R.W., and A. LeFort. 1986. Hemiplegic shoulder pain measured with the Ritchie Articular Index. *International Journal of Rehabilitation Research* 9:379–81.)
- skin thermometer
- Barthel Index by D. Barthel and F. Mahoney, *Maryland State Medical Journal*, 2:61–5, 1965.
- activities of daily living scale
- occupational history
- leisure checklist

PROBLEMS

Motor
- Motion of the hand or shoulder is restricted by pain.
- Atrophy of muscles may occur in advanced stages.
- Flexion deformities of the finger may occur in advanced stages.
- Stiffness in the hand occurs.
- In the late stages, demineralization of bone and narrowing of joint spaces occur.

Sensory
- pain in the shoulder and hand described as burning, stinging, or constricting, or pressure that is aggravated by motion
- edema in the fingers and hands
- shiny skin with loss of flexor creases and distension of skin folds
- tenderness to touch
- erythema dorsally at the proximal interphalangeal and metacarpophalangeal joints

Cognitive
Cognitive faculties are not affected directly by shoulder-hand syndrome, but pre-existing condition may have resulted in cognitive disorders (stroke) and medication for pain may produce temporary loss of alertness and memory loss.

Intrapersonal
- The syndrome may increase the person's sense of hopelessness and helplessness.
- The syndrome may decrease motivation to work toward rehabilitation and regain independence.
- The syndrome may deepen depression.
- The syndrome may further reduce self-concept.

Interpersonal
- The person may show increased irritability and failure to cooperate.
- The person may guard his shoulder and refuse to permit anyone to touch it.
- Dependence may increase as the person tries to avoid painful activity.
- The person may withdraw from social activities because of the pain.

Self-Care

- Activities of daily living may be ignored because of painful shoulder.
- The person may let others do ADLs (activities of daily living) to avoid the pain.

Productivity

- The person may be unable to perform work-related activities because pain is too great and therefore has to quit work.
- Pain medication may temporarily produce decreased level of alertness, memory loss, or decreased level of judgment.
- The person may be unable to perform home management tasks because of the pain and therefore discontinues performing home management tasks and prefers to rely on others.

Leisure

- The person may be unable to perform some leisure activities because of the pain.
- Pain medication may decrease cognitive skills necessary to perform leisure activities.

TREATMENT/MANAGEMENT

Motor

- To reduce edema and begin increasing range of motion, encourage the person to elevate his or her hand to shoulder height. If the person cannot actively elevate the arm, passive movement can be substituted by using bilateral activities in which the opposite shoulder pulls the weaker shoulder up and then the action is reversed.
- Provide activities that require the hand and shoulder muscles to contract and relax in an elevated position, such as bilateral sanding or using a washrag or polishing rag.
- Light weight-bearing activities can be used to increase hand range of motion, such as pressing clay or dough with the palm.
- Continue to increase range of motion with activities maintained for an increasing length of time at or above the heart.
- Consider splinting to prevent deformities and increase use of hand in the functional position (30° dorsal flexion of the wrist) when the person can tolerate his or her hand being moved.

Sensory

Decrease response to pain through any combination of massage, hot packs, paraffin, ice packs, contrast baths, or TENS (transcutaneous electrical nerve stimulation). Reduction of pain is usually the first step in treatment since the person is not likely to respond to other treatments until the pain is reduced.

Cognitive

- Help the person understand the need to decrease reliance on drugs.
- Provide cognitive (and motor) activities to promote the use of cognitive (and motor) skills and break the cycle of attending to pain.

Intrapersonal

- Use positive reinforcement to overcome resistance to treatment.

- Improve the person's self-image and sense of mastery through use of creative activities, such as crafts, drama, music, or dance.

Interpersonal
- Encourage the person to express anger and frustration caused by the constant pain and discomfort.
- Encourage the person and family to examine what has happened to their roles and responsibilities as a result of the disorder.
- Encourage the person to participate in social activities again.

Self-Care
Provide practice in performing independent activities of daily living.

Productivity
- Help the person reestablish work-related activities. Career exploration may be necessary. Work hardening is likely to be useful. Volunteering may be useful to refocus the person on others' needs.
- Encourage the person to resume home management tasks as rapidly as reduction of pain and increased motion and strength will permit.

Leisure
- Encourage the person to resume leisure activities.
- If the person has discontinued most leisure activities, help the person reexplore old interests and develop new ones.

PRECAUTIONS
Do not treat this syndrome in isolation. Be aware of condition(s) that lead to shoulder-hand syndrome and continue to treat original problem(s) as needed.

PROGNOSIS AND OUTCOME
If treated early, recovery is good, but after six months duration, prognosis is poor.

- The person has functional range of motion.
- The person is able to move hand, arm, and shoulder without complaining of pain.
- Swelling and edema are reduced or have disappeared.
- The person is able to use both upper extremities to perform self-care and daily living activities, using the involved hand as an assist.

REFERENCES

Andersen, L.T. 1985. Shoulder pain in hemiplegia. *American Journal of Occupational Therapy* 39(1):11–9.

Chalsen, G.G., K.A. Fitzpatrick, R.A. Navia, et al. 1987. Prevalence of the shoulder-hand pain syndrome in an inpatient stroke rehabilitation population: A quantitative cross-sectional study. *Journal of Neurologic Rehabilitation* 1(3):137–41.

Gowland, C. 1984. Shoulder pain in the patient with hemiplegia: A fundamental concept in occupational therapy. *Occupational Therapy in Health Care* 1(3):83–91.

Ryerson, S., and K. Levit. 1987. The shoulder in hemiplegia. In *Physical therapy of the shoulder* (Clinics in Physical Therapy, v. 11), ed. R. Donatelli, 105–31. New York: Churchill Livingstone.

Trombly, C.A. 1990. *Occupational therapy for physical dysfunction*, 3d ed. Baltimore: Williams & Wilkins.

Part IV

Cardiopulmonary Disorders

Cardiac Diseases

DESCRIPTION

Cardiac diseases are diseases that affect the blood supply, tissues, and muscles in and around the heart.

Classes of Cardiac Disease

Class I: Patients with cardiac disease but without resulting limitations of physical activity. Ordinary physical activity does not cause undue fatigue, palpitation, dyspnea, or anginal pain.

Class II: Patients with cardiac disease resulting in slight limitation of physical activity. They are comfortable at rest. Ordinary physical activity results in fatigue, palpitation, dyspnea, or anginal pain.

Class III: Patients with cardiac disease resulting in marked limitation of physical activity. They are comfortable at rest. Less than ordinary physical activity causes fatigue, palpitation, dyspnea, or anginal pain.

Class IV: Patients with cardiac disease resulting in inability to carry on any physical activity without discomfort. Symptoms of cardiac insufficiency or of the anginal syndrome may be present even at rest. If any physical activity is undertaken, discomfort is increased.

Source: From the New York Heart Association, Inc.: *Nomenclature and criteria for diagnosis of disease of the heart and great vessels*, 8th ed, Boston: Little, Brown & Co., 1979.

CAUSE

The causes may include blood clots (thrombus or embolus), thickening of the artery walls (arteriosclerosis), bacterial infections (bacterial endocarditis) that result in damage to the valves, high blood pressure, arrhythmias, and other contributing factors, such as diet and nutrition, lack of exercise, high-stress jobs, and poor health habits.

ASSESSMENT

Areas
- blood pressure
- heart rate (pulse rate)
- muscle strength
- physical endurance
- work tolerance

- graded exercise testing, dynamic and static
- time management
- mood or affect
- self-concept
- self-control
- daily living activities
- productivity history, interests, skills, and values
- job analysis, including the amount of dynamic and static work done, energy requirements in terms of metabolic costs, temperature stress, and psychological stress
- leisure interests and skills

Instruments
- Occupational Therapy Initial Assessment by L.O. Niemeyer (see reference section), Section II.
- Daughton, D.M., et al. 1982. Maximum oxygen consumption and the ADAPT Quality-of-Life Scale. *Archives of Physical Medicine and Rehabilitation* 63:620.
- monitor (count) pulse
- measure blood pressure
- observe heart function (electrocardiogram)
- exercise tolerance testing

PROBLEMS

Motor
- poor physical tolerance and endurance
- muscle weakness
- fatigue
- disuse atrophy
- decreased speed and accuracy in fine motor manipulation and dexterity

Sensory
  The person usually has pain upon exertion in the chest or left arm.

Cognition
  Cognitive faculties are usually not affected, but decreased blood supply to the brain may result in ineffective use of cognitive skills.

Intrapersonal
- The person may fear becoming an invalid.
- The person may fear death.
- The person may be depressed.
- The person may be anxious.
- The person may experience loss of self-confidence.
- The person may have feelings of hopelessness and helplessness.
- The person may deny the problem.

Interpersonal
- The person may withdraw from family and friends.
- The person may become demanding.
- The person may become dependent.
- The person may lack a social support system.

Self-Care
- The person may be unable to perform some activities of daily living, especially those that require reaching overhead because of pain or weakness.
- The person may deliberately stop performing daily living activities to avoid straining the heart.
- The person may be overweight and eat a poorly balanced diet.

Productivity
The person may be unable to continue in present occupation because of pain, weakness, or job activities that require exertion beyond safe limits.

Leisure
The person may be unable to continue some leisure activities because of pain, weakness, or activities that require exertion beyond safe limits.

TREATMENT/MANAGEMENT

Motor
- Increase the person's physical and work tolerance within safe limits (such as diastolic blood pressure under 120 mm Hg) through graded activity, such as games and exercises (called GXT for graded exercise testing) performed individually or in groups. Grading is done according to the amount of time, frequency of performance, degree of resistance (weight), or position of the task. Grading may also be accomplished by combinations of static and dynamic activities, such as carrying (holding) a given weight load while walking.
- Help the person avoid loss of muscle strength through participation in graded resistive activity.

Sensory
Analyze activity or task performance to reduce or avoid situations that result in pain and encourage work simplification, energy conservation, or time management.

Cognitive
- Teach concepts of energy conservation, pacing, and work simplification.
- Reinforce concepts of good nutrition through discussion of and practice in the preparation of foods with less salt and saturated fats but more fiber.
- Teach the concept of energy levels required or demanded to perform various tasks using the MET system. One metabolic equivalent table (MET) is the energy consumed at rest equivalent approximately to 3.5 milliliters of oxygen per kilogram of body weight per

minute, i.e., basal metabolic rate (BMR).

- Teach the person to develop a time-management schedule that organizes cycles of rest and activity.
- Assist in teaching the person about his changing lifestyle, including avoiding or reducing risk factors.
- Instruct the person in the use of good body mechanics, such as proper lifting techniques.

Intrapersonal

- Provide instruction and training in stress management, including relaxation techniques.
- Improve self-concept and self-esteem through the use of creative activities, such as art, crafts, drama, music, and games.
- Increase the person's sense of self-control and decrease anxiety and depression through information aimed at increased understanding of the condition, especially the monitoring of activity levels.
- Support the person's role identity within his or her social structure.

Interpersonal

- Encourage the person to express feelings, thoughts, and needs through group discussion sessions.
- Permit the family and the person to discuss their roles and who will assume various roles during the recovery phase.

Self-Care

- Provide instruction in adaptive techniques, such as sitting while grooming instead of standing.
- Provide adapted equipment, such as elongated handles, to reduce the need for raising the arm above the shoulder, and to assist in the performance of activities of daily living, if needed.
- Instruct the person to monitor performance of self-care daily living tasks for signs of cardiac stress.

Productivity

- Explore work interests if the person is unable to continue in present paid employment.
- Help the person maintain or increase home management activities.
- Provide work tolerance or work hardening program to increase the length of time the person can function in a job situation.
- Provide work simulation environment to assist in determining whether the person can return to the same job situation and work setting.
- Suggest possible modifications in the home or work environment, based on ergonomics, that might reduce the cardiac stress.

Leisure

- Help the person modify existing leisure activities to fit within energy expenditure levels permitted.
- Help the person explore new interests that fit within energy guidelines.

PRECAUTIONS

- The symptoms to be avoided are: angina or chest discomfort, dizziness or faintness, dyspnea or difficulty breathing, fatigue, pain, especially in the legs, and palpitations.
- The signs to be avoided are: arrhythmias, ataxic gait, cold sweat, glassy stare, high systolic or diastolic blood pressure, irregular pulse, low blood pressure during exercise, and pallor.
- The symptoms of ischemia or decreased blood flow to the brain include ataxic gait, dizziness, faintness, and glassy stare.
- The signs of pump failure include pallor and lowered blood pressure on exercise.

PROGNOSIS AND OUTCOME

- The person demonstrates knowledge of a safe level of activity during functional activities.
- The person demonstrates knowledge and use of energy-conservation and work-simplification techniques.
- The person demonstrates knowledge of time management and can plan a schedule of activities that conforms with his or her known safe level of activity.
- The person is able to perform activities of daily living at his or her maximum level of independence within medical limitations.
- The person demonstrates the physical fitness, endurance, and psychosocial skills needed to maintain the highest level of functional activities that his or her medical condition will permit.
- The person demonstrates an ability to perform productive activities.
- The person is able to perform leisure activities.

REFERENCES

Bachynski-Cole, M., and G.R. Cumming. 1985. The cardiovascular fitness of disabled patients attending occupational therapy. *Occupational Therapy Journal of Research* 5(4):233–42.

Bird, K., and S. Phelps. 1986. Cardiac rehabilitation: Low energy considerations. *Occupational Therapy in Health Care* 3(1):101–8.

Foderaro, D. 1985. Cardiac dysfunction. In *Occupational therapy: Practice skills for physical dysfunction*, 2d ed., ed. L. Pedretti, 330–58. St. Louis: C.V. Mosby.

Foderaro, D., and S. O'Leary. 1990. Cardiac dysfunction. In *Occupational therapy: Practice skills for physical dysfunction*. 3d ed., ed. L.W. Pedretti and B. Zoltan, 507–31. St. Louis: C.V. Mosby.

Helm, M., and J. Ellson. 1988. Cardiac rehabilitation: occupational therapy enhancement of an existing cardiac outpatient rehabilitation programme. *British Journal of Occupational Therapy* 51(11):385–9.

King, J. 1987. Coronary care. In *The practice of occupational therapy*. 2d ed., ed. A. Turner, 344–56. Edinburgh, Scotland: Churchill Livingstone.

King, J.C., and P.G.F. Nixon. 1988. A system of cardiac rehabilitation: Psychophysiological basis and practice. *British Journal of Occupational Therapy* 51(11):378–84.

Knapp, D., et al. 1986. Returning the patient to work. In *Heart disease and rehabilitation*, 2nd ed., ed. M.L. Pollock and D.H. Schmidt, 647–77. New York: John Wiley & Sons.

Niemeyer, L.O. 1980. *Cardiac rehabilitation: Practice and treatment guidelines for occupational therapists and other health professionals*. Burr Ridge, IL: Fred Sammons, Inc.

Seiser, C.S. 1981. Occupational therapy and cardiac rehabilitation. In *Physical disabilities manual*, ed. B.C. Abreu, 183–99. New York: Raven Press.

Sheldahl, L.M., N.A. Wilke, and F.E. Tristani. 1985. Exercise prescription for return to work. *Journal of Cardiopulmonary Rehabilitation* 5:567–75.

Sheldahl, L.M., N.A. Wilke, F.E. Tristani, et al. 1985. Response to repetitive static-dynamic exercise in patients with coronary artery disease. *Journal of Cardiac Rehabilitation* 5:139–45.

Tomes, H. 1990. Cardiac rehabilitation: An occupational therapist's perspective. *British Journal of Occupational Therapy* 53(7):285–7.

Trombly, C.A. 1983. Cardiac rehabilitation. In *Occupational therapy for physical dysfunction*, 2d ed., ed. C.A. Trombly, 409–27. Baltimore, MD: Williams & Wilkins.

Trombly, C.A. 1989. Cardiopulmonary rehabilitation. In *Occupational therapy for physical dysfunction*, 3d ed., ed. C.A. Trombly, 581–603. Baltimore, MD: Williams & Wilkins.

Wilke, N.A., and L.M. Sheldahl. 1985. Use of simulated work testing in cardiac rehabilitation: A case report. *American Journal of Occupational Therapy* 39(5):327–30.

Cardiac Disease—Myocardial Infarction

DESCRIPTION

Myocardial infarction (MI) is defined as ischemic myocardial necrosis usually resulting from abrupt reduction in coronary blood flow to a segment of the myocardium.

CAUSE

The most common cause of MI is an acute thrombus that occludes an artery previously partially obstructed by an atherosclerotic plaque. Occasionally the cause is an arterial embolism or coronary spasm. MI usually occurs in the left ventricle, but damage may extend into the right ventricle or the atria. The most frequent time of occurrence is during the morning, not during vigorous exercise.

ASSESSMENT

Areas
- blood pressure
- heart rate (pulse rate)
- endurance
- work tolerance
- graded exercise testing, dynamic and static
- self-concept
- mood or affect
- daily living activities
- productivity history, skills, and interests
- job analysis, including the amount of dynamic and static work done, energy requirements in terms of metabolic costs, temperature stress, and psychological stress
- leisure skills and interests

Instruments
- sphygmomanometer (blood pressure cuff)
- stethoscope
- EKG unit with oscilloscope

PROBLEMS

Motor

- The person may have low physical tolerance and endurance.
- The person may develop orthostatic hypotension.
- The person may become inactive in the mistaken belief that overactivity caused the attack.

Sensory

The pain is initially substernal, visceral pain described as an ache or pressure, which may radiate to the back, jaw, or left arm.

Cognitive

Cognitive faculties are not affected directly by the disease.

Intrapersonal

- The person is usually apprehensive and anxious.
- The person may feel distressed and fearful.
- The person may become depressed.
- The person may feel hopeless and helpless.
- The person usually feels a loss of self-esteem.
- The person may be passively dependent and want to be treated rather than participate in the treatment process.
- The person may be obsessive-compulsive and tend to overdo treatment recommendations.
- The person may be irritable when his or her health and career become the focus of concern.
- The person may have a history of stressor factors, such as excessive work and responsibilities, job dissatisfaction, family problems, and life dissatisfaction.
- The person may have poor coping skills and/or a Type A personality that results in a chronic stress response.

Interpersonal

- The person may withdraw from family and friends.
- Family roles may change.
- Family members may become overprotective.
- The person may lack a social support system.

Self-Care

- The person may be unable to perform some daily living skills without undue pain or fatigue.
- The person may deliberately stop performing daily living activities to avoid straining the heart.
- The person may be overweight and eating a poorly balanced diet.

Productivity

- The person may be unable to perform some job tasks because of pain or increased cardiac workload beyond safe limits.
- The person may be unable to return to some jobs because of regulations that prevent a person who has had a heart attack from returning to such employment.

Leisure

The person may be unable to engage in some leisure activities because of pain or increased cardiac workload.

TREATMENT/MANAGEMENT

Motor

Increase the person's work or physical tolerance within safe limits (such as diastolic blood pressure under 120 mm Hg) using graded activities, such as games and exercises (called GXT for graded exercise testing) performed individually or in groups. Grading is done according to the amount of time, frequency of performance, degree of resistance (weight) or position of the task. Grading may also be accomplished by combinations of static and dynamic activities, such as carrying (holding) a given weight load while walking.

Sensory

Help the person learn to function within the limits of his or her pain and monitor heart rate and blood pressure.

Cognitive

Create a time-management plan that provides for cycles of rest and activity and a more balanced lifestyle of self-care, productivity, and leisure.

- Instruct the person on concepts of energy conservation, pacing, and work simplification.
- Instruct the person in the use of good body mechanics, such as proper lifting techniques.
- Assist in instructing the person about the disorder and its prognosis. Focus on risk factors associated with diet, smoking, physical activity, and lifestyle.

Intrapersonal

- Provide stress-management training, including relaxation techniques.
- Provide discussion groups or counseling to promote discussion of subjects related to anxiety and fears, such as lifestyle, sex, diet, coping skills, work, and leisure activities.
- Provide opportunities for improving self-image through the use of creative activities, such as crafts, drama, music, games, or dance.

Interpersonal

- Permit the family and the person to discuss their roles and who will assume various roles during the recovery phase.
- Group activities and discussions with other persons who have cardiac disease can be a support to the family and individual.

Self-Care

- Instruct the person to monitor performance of self-care and daily living tasks for signs of cardiac stress. Selection of activities should be those that the person has noted previously caused pain or discomfort.

- Provide opportunities to practice selecting foods and planning and preparing meals that follow the recommended diet.

Productivity
- If the person must change jobs, help him or her explore career interests and options.
- Provide a work tolerance or work hardening program to increase the length of time the person can function in a job situation.
- Suggest possible modifications in the home or work environment, based on ergonomics, that might reduce the cardiac stress on the home manager or worker.
- Provide a work simulation environment to assist in determining whether the person can return to the same job situation and work setting.

Leisure
- Encourage the person to explore and develop old or new interests that are within safe limits of cardiac capacity.
- Encourage the selection of leisure activities that involve physical and social participation and a balance of leisure activities.

PRECAUTIONS
- Provide activities that keep the person's blood pressure and heart rate within safe limits. Monitor frequently.
- Stop activities if symptoms of anginal pain, dyspnea, fatigue, faintness, dizziness, palpitations, or claudication pain in legs appear. Report symptoms to the physician.
- Stop activities if any of the following signs appear: pallor, excessive sweating, ataxic gait, glassy stare, irregular pulse, pulse above 120 beats per minute, extreme elevation of systolic or diastolic blood pressure, low blood pressure, or electrocardiogram changes, such as arrhythmias, ischemia, or heart blocks. Report signs to the physician.
- The person should be cautioned to avoid the Valsalva maneuver, which involves straining against a closed glottis or holding one's breath and is known to significantly raise blood pressure.

PROGNOSIS AND OUTCOME
- The person demonstrates knowledge of his or her safe activity level during performance of functional activities.
- The person demonstrates the use of energy-conservation and work-simplification techniques in performing daily activities.
- The person demonstrates the ability to monitor activities to stay within safe limits of his or her cardiac status.
- The person is able to perform activities of daily living as independently as possible within safe limits of cardiac status.
- The person demonstrates strength, endurance, and tolerance to perform productive activities within safe limits of his or her cardiac status.
- The person engages in a balance of activities.

REFERENCES

Fitts, H.A., and M.C. Howe. 1987. Use of leisure time by cardiac patients. *American Journal of Occupational Therapy* 41(9):583–9.

Kottke, F.J., W.G. Kubicek, M.E. Olsen, et al. 1962. Five stage test of cardiac performance during occupational therapy. *Archives of Physical Medicine and Rehabilitation* 43(5):228–34 (classic article).

Quiggle, A.B., F.J. Kottke, and J. Magney. 1954. Metabolic requirements of occupational therapy activities. *Archives of Physical Medicine and Rehabilitation* 35(9):567–72 (classic article).

Seiser, C.S. 1981. Occupational therapy and cardiac rehabilitation. In *Physical disabilities manual*, ed. B.C. Abreu, 183–99. New York: Raven Press.

Sheldahl, L.M., N.A. Wilke, F.E. Tristani, et al. 1983. Response of patients after myocardial infarction to carrying a graded series of weight loads. *American Journal of Cardiology* 52:698–703.

Sheldahl, L.M., N.A. Wilke, F.E. Tristani, et al. 1984. Heart rate responses during home activities soon after myocardial infarction. *Journal of Cardiac Rehabilitation* 4:327–33.

Sheldahl, L.M., N.A. Wilke, and F.W. Tristani. 1985. Exercise prescription for return to work. *Journal of Cardiopulmonary Rehabilitation* 5(12):565–75.

Simari, J. 1982. Cardiac rehabilitation. In *Adult rehabilitation: A team approach for therapists*, ed. M.K. Logigian, 169–98. Boston: Little, Brown & Co.

Wilke, N.A., and L.M. Sheldahl. 1985. Use of simulated work testing in cardiac rehabilitation: A case report. *American Journal of Occupational Therapy* 39(5):327–30.

Yates, E. 1988. Coronary rehabilitation. In *Disabling diseases: Physical, environmental and psychosocial management*, ed. A. Frank and P. Maguire, 98–112. Oxford: Heinemann Medical Books.

Chronic Obstructive Pulmonary Disease

DESCRIPTION

Chronic obstructive pulmonary disease (COPD) is defined as obstruction of airways, particularly of small airways such as the bronchioles and alveoli, associated with varying combinations of chronic bronchitis, asthma, emphysema, or restrictive pulmonary disease. Chronic bronchitis involves an inflammation of the bronchi that thickens the lining of the airway and increases the mucous secretions. Asthma involves bronchiospasms that reduce the size of the air passageways. Emphysema decreases the elasticity of the alveoli and the bronchioles leading from the alveoli, which results in a decreased force when blowing out air. Restrictive pulmonary disease prevents a person from getting as much air as needed.

CAUSE

The causes include infections, allergens, skeletal problems, such as scoliosis, obesity, or nervous system diseases that affect the muscles that assist breathing. Any factor that leads to chronic alveolar inflammation, such as smoking, may lead to COPD. Diagnosis is usually made in mid-life but symptoms may have developed much earlier.

ASSESSMENT

Areas

- vital capacity (may include information from pulmonary function tests, auscultation, and blood gas studies)

- range of motion
- muscle strength, especially in the hands and upper extremities
- physical fitness, endurance, and activity tolerance
- postural control and balance
- mobility
- perceptual skills (space, form, depth, praxis, figure-ground, body scheme, part-whole integration)
- cognitive skills (orientation, memory, abstract reasoning, judgment and problem solving, attention span, comprehension, intelligence)
- affect or mood (anxiety, depression, denial, passivity)
- coping skills
- social support
- daily living activities and skills
- productivity history, skills, interests, and values
- leisure activities
- architectural and physical barriers
- environmental safety and adaptability

Instruments
- Subjective ADL Rating Scale for the Pulmonary Rehabilitation Patient by M.A. Phillips, in *Occupational Therapy in Health Care* 3(1):79–88, 1986.
- goniometry
- manual muscle test
- activities of daily living scale
- occupational history
- leisure checklist

PROBLEMS

Motor
- The person usually has decreased physical tolerance and endurance.
- The person usually has shortness of breath upon exertion.
- The person may have decreased range of motion.
- The person may have decreased muscle strength.
- The person may have poor posture.

Sensory
The senses are not directly affected.

Cognition
- The person may have limited knowledge of the disease and its problems.
- The person may have limited knowledge or judgment of safety hazards in the home.

Intrapersonal
- The person may have feelings of hopelessness and helplessness.
- The person may become depressed.

Interpersonal
- The person may withdraw from social activities.
- The person may become dependent on his or her spouse or other caregiver.
- The person may lack a social support system.

Self-Care
- The person may be unable to perform some activities of daily living because of decreased physical tolerance.
- The person may be unable to perform some self-care skills because of architectural or physical barriers, such as inaccessible doorways or shelves that are too high.

Productivity

The person may be unable to continue occupations that expose the person to fumes, gases, or air particles, such as dust or pollen.

Leisure
- The person may be unable to continue leisure activities that require high physical exertion.
- The person may be unable to enjoy outside activities during certain times of year because of particles in the air.

TREATMENT/MANAGEMENT

Motor
- Increase the person's strength and endurance by using gravity resistive exercises, especially for the upper extremities.
- Increase or maintain range of motion through performance of normal activities whenever possible.
- Provide the person with opportunities to practice breathing exercises while performing other activities.

Cognitive
- Teach the person concepts of energy conservation, pacing, and work simplification. Help the person learn problem-solving techniques using the least energy to perform everyday activities, such as sitting instead of standing.
- Teach concepts of good posture and proper body mechanics in lifting, carrying, reaching, pushing and pulling, brushing one's hair, shampooing, and showering.
- Teach recognition of possible hazardous materials that might cause additional breathing problems, such as dust, sprays, cleansers, or polishes.
- Assist in teaching the person about medications, including their effects, side effects, dosages, schedules, and time intervals, so the person can self-medicate.
- Assist in teaching the person to learn about the use and care of various equipment.
- Teach the person concepts of time management and activity scheduling to balance and pace self-care, productivity, and leisure.

Intrapersonal

- Provide training in stress management, including relaxation techniques to control anxiety and panic attacks.
- Encourage a sense of independence and autonomy.

Interpersonal

- Encourage socialization through group activities, such as a self-help group.
- Encourage the person to maintain a role as a responsible, active, and functioning member of the family and household.
- Communicate with the family to inform them of the person's limitations, but promote the person's abilities and assets.

Self-care

- Provide adaptive equipment and training to assist the person in the performance of activities of daily living, if needed.
- Encourage maintenance of activities of daily living through use of task analysis to conserve energy, including pacing of activities and economy of motion.
- Provide information on modifying the home to increase access for self-care activities.

Productivity

- Suggest modifications in the work setting, if needed.
- Assist the person to explore work interests if previous work activities cannot be continued because of health limitations.
- Provide information on modifying the home to permit the person to contribute to home-management activities.

Leisure

- Help the person select leisure activities that are within his or her physical capacities.
- Explore interests to develop new activities if previous leisure activities must be abandoned.

PRECAUTIONS

Avoid the use of activities that may create irritants, such as smoke, solvents, or dust.

PROGNOSIS AND OUTCOME

COPD is a chronic disorder that cannot be totally reversed or corrected. The objective is to maximize function within the limitations of the disorder.

- The person demonstrates physical endurance, strength, and range of motion to perform functional activities.
- The person is able to perform activities of daily living to the maximum level of function consistent with the limitations of the disorder.
- The person demonstrates the ability to breathe properly during performance of activities.
- The person has been provided self-help devices and training in their use to assist in the independent performance of functional activities.

- The person demonstrates knowledge of energy conservation, pacing, and work simplification.
- The person demonstrates knowledge of precautions that avoid further compromising his or her breathing.
- The person is able to reduce reactions to stress through relaxation techniques.
- The person has been provided with information on modifying the home to increase the opportunity to perform self-care and home-management activities.
- The person demonstrates knowledge of community resources.
- If a child, the person is able to perform developmental tasks at an age-appropriate level.

REFERENCES

Bennethum, E., J. Sabari, D. Schanzer, et al. 1984. The role of the occupational therapist in the care of patients with restrictive pulmonary disease. In *Current therapy in physiatry: Physical medicine and rehabilitation,* ed. A.P. Ruskin, 350–1. Philadelphia: W.B. Saunders.

Falconer, J. 1982. Pulmonary rehabilitation. In *Adult rehabilitation: A team approach for therapists*, ed. M.K. Logigian, 199–223. Boston: Little, Brown & Co.

Johnson, N.J., and D. Grindler. 1990. Home rehabilitation for chronic obstructive pulmonary disease: A physical and occupational therapy approach. *Journal of Home Health Care Practice* 2(2):19–43 (includes program descriptions and work sheets).

Pomerantz, P., E.H. Flannery, and P.K. Findling. 1975. Occupational therapy for chronic obstructive lung disease. *American Journal of Occupational Therapy* 29:407–11.

Tiep, B.L., Y. Lewis, N. Branum, et al. 1988. Respiratory management at home. *Physical Medicine and Rehabilitation: State of the Art Reviews* 2(3):385–403.

Walsh, R.L. 1986. Occupational therapy as part of a pulmonary rehabilitation program. *Occupational Therapy in Health Care* 3(1):65–77.

Part V

Injuries

Amputation of an
Upper Extremity—Adult

DESCRIPTION
This condition results from the removal of all or part of an extremity, digit, organ, or projecting part of the body.

CAUSE
The two most common causes are trauma, such as from a cut, tear, freezing, or burning, and surgery performed to remove a diseased or useless part of the body.

ASSESSMENT
Evaluation must be considered in two parts. The first is centered on assessing the person's remaining functional abilities and level of function without the missing part. The second area of evaluation concerns the use of prosthetic devices to replace some of the lost functions.

Areas
• muscle strength in remaining body parts
• range of motion in joints proximal to amputation
• functional gross and fine motor skills available without prosthesis
• pain (phantom sensations)
• hypersensitivity in stump
• self-concept
• attitude or acceptance
• coping skills
• daily living skills
• productivity history, interests, skills, and values
• leisure skills and interests

Instruments
• manual muscle test
• goniometry
• Upper-Extremity Prosthetic Checkout Form by C.A. Trombly, 1989, pp. 614–6 (see reference section).
• Upper-Extremity Preprosthetic Evaluation, Institute of Rehabilitation Medicine, New York University Medical Center, Occupational Therapy Service, in B.C. Abreu, 1981, pp. 278–80 (see reference section).
• Prosthetic Checkout Below-Elbow Prosthesis, Institute of Rehabilitation Medicine, New York University Medical Center, Occupational Therapy Service, in B.C. Abreu, 1981, pp. 280–3 (see Dickey in reference section).

PROBLEMS

Motor
- The person usually has loss of range of motion.
- The person may have loss of muscle strength.
- The person usually has loss of coordination and dexterity associated with the missing part.

Sensory
- The person usually has loss of touch and tactile sensation provided by the missing part.
- The person usually has loss of proprioception and kinesthesia associated with the missing part.
- The person may experience phantom pain (pain from the missing part).

Cognitive
No changes in cognitive ability result directly from the amputation. However, any cognitive limitation present before the amputation may complicate the treatment program, such as difficulty in learning new skills and solving problems.

Intrapersonal
- The person may express frustration at not being able to perform tasks as before.
- The person may suffer from loss of self-worth and self-confidence ("I'm not the person I used to be").
- The person may express feelings of being viewed by others as a freak, a cripple, or a misfit.
- The person may feel anger ("Why me?") or guilt ("If only I had . . .") regarding the amputation.
- The person may experience periods of depression accompanied by feelings of helplessness and hopelessness.

Interpersonal
- The person may avoid social situations in fear of rejection, being stared at, or being seen as different.
- The person may feel awkward (loss of self-confidence) in public situations, especially when tasks demand performance of skills lost because of the amputation, such as writing, handling change, or eating with utensils.

Self-Care
- If the dominant hand is lost, tasks such as writing, handling money, and eating will be affected, as well as two-handed tasks, such as dressing, grooming, and bathing.
- If the nondominant hand is lost, the primary problems involve two-handed activities in which the nondominant hand has been used in parallel (lifting, pushing, or pulling a heavy load or holding a large tool, such as a jack hammer).

Productivity
Problems of productivity are related to the job tasks performed, but some common problems are loss of dominant hand skills and loss of two-handed activities that require

coordination and dexterity. Assess what limitations and assets the individual may face in regaining productive skills.

Leisure
The person may be unable to engage in some favorite leisure activities, or modifications will be required to do so.

TREATMENT/MANAGEMENT
Models of treatment are based on the biomechanical model (Trombly) and orthopedic model.

Motor
• Teach the person to put on and take off the prosthesis.
• Teach the person to use the prosthesis to perform one-handed activities, such as picking up, placing, and releasing objects of various sizes, shapes, textures, and composition.
• Teach the person to use the prosthesis to assist the other hand (or prosthesis, if he or she is a bilateral amputee) in activities that require two hands, such as lifting large objects.

Sensory
• Teach the person limitations of the prosthesis as a sensory-gathering tool.
• Teach the person to substitute the other hand, arm, or other parts of the body to gather such information.

Cognitive
• Teach the person the names of the parts of the prosthesis and what each part does.
• Teach proper care and maintenance of the prosthesis.
• Teach person concepts of work simplification and energy conservation.

Intrapersonal
• The person must learn to adjust to disability by talking about feelings.
• Adjustment includes learning new ways to accomplish tasks that were lost, including the use of a prosthesis.

Interpersonal
• Have the person participate in social activities.
• Have the person participate in a support group for amputees.

Self-Care
• Provide the person with opportunities to practice activities of daily living, including eating, dressing, making change, and signing one's name.
• Have the person practice in social situations, not just in a clinic, room, or home.

Productivity
• Encourage the person to practice skills necessary for the individual to be a productive person, such as driving with hand controls, learning to operate equipment with a prosthesis, and taking lecture notes or recording a lecture.
• Help the person explore possible productive activities.

Leisure
- Explore the person's interests and aptitudes for possible leisure pursuits.
- Provide opportunities for the person to practice various possible choices.
- Consider adaptations of equipment that might facilitate performance of various leisure activities (see examples in the Bradway and Celikyol articles in the reference section).

PRECAUTIONS
- Always check the stump for signs of skin breakdown.
- Always check the prosthesis to be sure it is in good working order.

PROGNOSIS AND OUTCOME
- The person has normal muscle strength in the remaining muscle groups.
- The person demonstrates proficiency in stump care and can perform stump care independently.
- The person demonstrates knowledge of the parts of the prosthesis and the function of each part.
- The person is able to put on and take off the prosthesis independently.
- The person is able to operate the prosthesis to perform a variety of tasks.
- The person demonstrates knowledge and performance of the safe use of the prosthesis to avoid damage to the prosthesis and injury to him- or herself or others.
- The person can perform activities of daily living independently using the prosthesis.
- The person can perform productive activities using the prosthesis.
- The person can perform leisure activities using the prosthesis.

REFERENCES

Atkins, D. 1987. The upper extremity prosthetic prescription: Conventional or electronic components. *Physical Disabilities Special Interest Section Newsletter* 10(1):2,6.

Atkins, D.J. 1989. Postoperative and preprosthetic therapy programs. In *Comprehensive management of the upper-limb amputee*, ed. D.J. Atkins and R.H. Meier, 11–15. London, England: Springer-Verlag.

Atkins, D.J. 1989. Adult upper-limb prosthetic training. In *Comprehensive management of the upper-limb amputee*, ed. D.J. Atkins and R.H. Meier, 39–59. London, England: Springer-Verlag.

Barza, P. 1986. Case report: Occupational therapy with a traumatic bilateral shoulder disarticulation amputee. *American Journal of Occupational Therapy* 40(3):194–8.

Bearfield, K. 1989. OT and lower extremity amputations in geriatrics. *Occupational Therapy Forum* 4(44):1,3.

Bittinger, S. 1987. Voluntary closing: A natural alternative. *Physical Disabilities Special Interest Section Newsletter* 10(1):1,4,5.

Bradway, J.K., J.M. Malone, J. Racy, et al. 1984. Psychological adaptation to amputation: An overview. *Orthotics and Prosthetics* 38(2):46–50.

Celikyol, F. 1984. Prostheses, equipment, adapted performance: Reflections on these choices for the training of the amputee. *Occupational Therapy in Health Care* 1(4):89–115.

Cole, D.P., G.L. Davis, and J.E. Traunero. 1985. The Toledo tenodesis prosthesis: A case history utilizing a new concept in prosthetics for the partial hand amputee. *Orthotics and Prosthetics* 38(4):13–23.

Conder, D. 1987. Amputation. In *The practice of occupational therapy: An introduction to the treatment of physical dysfunction*, 2d ed., ed. A. Turner, 271–94. Edinburgh, Scotland: Churchill Livingstone.

Cummings, V., J. Alexanders, and S.O. Gans. 1984. Management of the amputee. In *Current therapy in physiatry: Physical medician and rehabilitation,* ed. A.P. Ruskin, 212–27. Philadelphia: W.B. Saunders.

Dickey, R.E., and L. Stieritz. 1981. Amputation and impaired independence. In *Physical disabilities manual*, ed. B.C. Abreu, 257–83. New York: Raven Press.

Duncan, S.J. 1986. Knitting device for bilateral upper extremity amputee. *American Journal of Occupational Therapy* 40(9):637–8.

Durance, J.P., and B. O'Shea. 1988. Upper limb amputees: A clinic profile. *International Disabilities Studies* 10:68–72.

Fraser, C. 1984. Does an artificial limb become part of the user? *British Journal of Occupational Therapy* 47(2):43–5.

Fisher, A.G. 1983. Amputation and prosthetics. In *Occupational therapy for physical dysfunction*, 2d ed., ed. C.A. Trombly, 428–48. Baltimore, MD: Williams & Wilkins, 3d ed., 1989, 604–24.

Friedmann, L. 1989. Functional skills in multiple limb anomalies. In *Comprehensive management of the upper-limb amputee*, ed. D.J. Arkins and R.H. Meier, 150–64. London, England: Springer-Verlag.

Livingstone, D.P. 1988. The D-Z stump protector. *American Journal of Occupational Therapy* 42(3):185–7.

Maiorano, L.M., and J.M. Hunter. 1984. Myoelectric prosthesis: Prescription and training. In *Rehabilitation of the hand*, 2d ed., ed. J.M. Hunter, et al., 831–70. St. Louis: C.V. Mosby.

Maiorano, L.M., and P.M. Bryon. 1984. Fabrication of an early-fit prosthesis. In *Rehabilitation of the hand*, 2d ed., ed. J.M. Hunter, et al., 808–12. St. Louis: C.V. Mosby.

Matsushima, D.W. 1986. Crochet aid for the amputee. *American Journal of Occupational Therapy* 40(7):495–6.

Mendelson, R.L., J.G. Burech, E.P. Polack, et al. 1986. The psychological impact of traumatic amputations: A team approach: Physician, therapist and psychologist. *Hand Clinics* 2(3):577–83.

Olivett, B.L. 1984. Management and prosthetic training of the adult amputee. In *Rehabilitation of the hand*, 2d ed., ed. J.M. Hunter, et al., 813–30. St. Louis: C.V. Mosby. Revised in 3d ed., 1990, 1048–56.

Olivett, B.L. 1990. Adult amputee management and conventional prosthetic training. In *Rehabilitation of the hand*, 3d ed., ed. J.M. Hunter, et al., 1057–71. St. Louis: C.V. Mosby.

Patricelli, J., and J. Eckroth. 1982. Adapted knife for partial hand-amputation patients. *American Journal of Occupational Therapy* 36(3):193–4.

Pedretti, L.W. 1985. Amputations and prosthetics. In *Occupational therapy: Practice skills for physical dysfunction*, 2d ed., ed. L.W. Pedretti, 265–78. St. Louis: C.V. Mosby.

Pedretti, L.W., and S. Pasquinelli. 1990. Amputations and prosthetics. In *Occupational therapy: Practice skills for physical dysfunction,* 3d ed., ed. L.W. Pedretti and B. Zoltan, 419–44. St. Louis: C.V. Mosby.

Rose, E.H., et al. 1989. The "cap" technique: Nonmicrosurgical reattachment of fingertip amputations. *Journal of Hand Surgery* 14A:513–8.

Shaperman, J., and Y. Setoguchi. 1989. The CAPP terminal device, size 2: A new alternative for adolescents and adults. *Prosthetics and Orthotics International* 13:25–8.

Spencer, E.A. 1988. Functional restoration: Amputation and prosthetic replacement. In *Willard and Spackman's occupational therapy*, 8th ed., ed. H.L. Hopkins and H.D. Smith, 516–45. Philadelphia: J.B. Lippincott.

Spiegel, S.R. 1989. Adult myoelectric upper-limb prosthetic training. In *Comprehensive management of the upper-limb amputee*, ed. D.J. Atkins and R.H. Meier, 60–71. London, England: Springer-Verlag.

Weiss-Lambrou, R., et al. 1985. Brief or new: Independence for the severe bilateral upper limb amputee. *American Journal of Occupational Therapy* 39(6):397–9.

White, J.G., and B.C. Hilfrank. 1984. Prosthetic and adaptive devices for the partial hand amputee. In *Rehabilitation of the hand*, 2d ed., ed. J.M. Hunter, et al., 795–800. St. Louis: C.V. Mosby.

Wilson, R.L., and M.S. Carter-Wilson. 1983. Rehabilitation after amputations in the hand. *Orthopedic Clinics of North America* 14(4):851–72.

Amputation of an Upper Extremity—Child

DESCRIPTION

This condition is defined as loss of part or all of one or both arms, either through errors of fetal development or surgical removal of the extremity after birth in children ages zero through 12.

CAUSE

The causes of congenital limb deficiencies are thought to include diseases that occur during pregnancy, such as influenza, measles, or rubella; immune reactions, such as Rh (releasing hormone) incompatibility; an endocrine disease, such as diabetes; intrauteral factors, such as an obstructed or twisted umbilical cord or the position of the fetus; toxins; radiation; or nutritional excesses or deficiencies. The causes of noncongenital amputations in young children include traumatic injury, thermal injury, and tumors.

ASSESSMENT

Areas

- muscle strength
- gross motor development and skills
- fine motor skills, dexterity, and coordination
- sensory registration
- learning skills
- coping skills
- daily living skills
- play skills
- prosthetic checkout

Instruments

- Denver Developmental Screening Test revised by W.K. Frankenburg, J.B. Dodds, and A.W. Fandel, Denver, CO: Ladoca Project and Publishing Foundation, 1975 (not occupational therapists)
- Prosthetic Adjustment Scale (PAS) by M. Brooks and J. Shaperman. Infant prosthetic fitting, *American Journal of Occupational Therapy*, 19:329–34, 1965.
- activities of daily living scale
- play history
- prosthetic checkout form

PROBLEMS

Motor

- The child may lack range of motion.
- The child may have decreased muscle strength.
- The child may lack hand skills.
- The child may have developmental delay in gross motor skills.

Sensory

The child lacks tactile sensation from the missing part.

Cognitive

The child may have mental retardation or brain injury depending on the cause of the amputation. Generally, amputees do not differ in levels of intelligence from nonhandicapped children.

Intrapersonal
- The child's parents may react to congenital deficiencies with feelings of guilt, anger, fear, repulsion, shock, or shame.
- The child's parents may act by abandoning the child, isolating him or her or rejecting the child.
- The child's parents may express the wish that the child would die.
- The child will become aware of being different.

Interpersonal
- The child may experience rejection from peers.
- The child may avoid certain activities or situations to escape possible rejection or ridicule.
- The child may become dependent on others to perform certain activities and not attempt to perform the activities for him- or herself.

Self-Care
The child may have difficulty performing some self-care activities, especially if one or both hands are missing or malformed.

Productivity
The child may experience difficulty manipulating and exploring objects in the play environment if one or both hands are missing or malformed.

Leisure
The child may have limitations in the types of leisure interests to pursue if one or both hands are missing or malformed.

TREATMENT/MANAGEMENT
Note 1: If the amputation is unilateral, the partial limb and prosthesis will always be the assisting or holding limb. If the amputation is bilateral, the therapist can assist in determining which limb and prosthesis will be used as the dominant side.

Note 2: A prosthetic unit should always be checked regularly to determine that it is fitted properly, is the correct size, is comfortable, permits performance of the desired actions, is in good mechanical or electrical order, and operates as quietly as possible. Initially the prosthetic checkout will be the therapist's or prosthetist's responsibility. The child can be taught to assist in the checkout and then become responsible for continuing checks of the same prosthesis. A new prosthesis should always to checked out first by the therapist or prosthetist.

Note 3: The trend is toward earlier fitting of the first prosthesis in congenital amputees. In general, sitting balance (in the first six or seven months of the child's life) is considered a prerequisite, but earlier fittings have been reported. Usually the first prosthesis is passive. It can be used to grasp an object by placing the object in the jaw but cannot be opened with shoulder movements because no control line is attached.

Terminology in the Frantz-O'Rahilly Classification System

Major divisions
- *Terminal anomaly.* The distal portion of the limb is missing. The end of the portion that is present may be deformed.
- *Intercalary defect.* The middle portion of the limb is deficient, but the proximal and distal portions are present.
- *Transverse limb deficiency.* The defect extends across the entire width of the limb.
- *Longitudinal limb deficiency.* Only the preaxial or postaxial portion is absent.

Subdivisions
- *Terminal transverse limb deficiencies:*
  1. amelia—absence of a limb
  2. hemimelia—absence of the forearm and hand or the leg and foot
  3. partial hemimelia—part of the forearm or lower limb is present
  4. acheiria or apodia—absence of the hand or foot
  5. compete adactylia—absence of all fingers and thumb or toes, including the metacarpals or metatarsals
  6. complete aphalangia—absence of one or more phalanges from the fingers thumb, or toes
- *Terminal longitudinal limb deficiencies:*
  1. complete paraxial hemimelia—complete absence of one of the bones in the forearm (radius or ulna) or leg (fibula or tibia) and corresponding portion of the hand or foot
  2. incomplete paraxial hemimelia—partial absence of one of the bones in the forearm or leg
  3. partial adactylia—absence of one to four fingers or toes, including their metacarpals or metatarsals
  4. partial aphalangia—absence of one to four phalanges in the fingers or toes
- *Intercalary transverse limb deficiencies:*
  1. complete phocomelia—hand or foot is attached directly to the trunk
  2. proximal phocomelia—hand and forearm or foot and leg attached directly to the trunk
  3. distal phocomelia—hand or foot is attached directly to the arm or thigh
- *Intercalary longitudinal limb deficiencies:*
  1. complete paraxial hemimelia—complete absence of one of the bones in the forearm or leg, but the hand or foot is more or less complete
  2. incomplete paraxial hemimelia—partial absence of one of the bones in the forearm or leg, but the hand or foot is more or less complete
  3. partial adactylia—absence of all or part of a metacarpal or metatarsal from one or more fingers or toes
  4. partial aphalangia—absence of the proximal or middle phalanx or both from one or more fingers or toes

Source: Based on Frantz, C.H., and R. O'Rahilly. 1961. Congenital skeletal limb deficiencies. *Journal of Bone and Joint Surgery* 43A:1202–24.

Motor
- If the child is a below-elbow amputee:
  1. Promote normal growth and development. The child is a person first and an amputee second. Periodic measurement of overall growth and development is important to determine the child's level of performance.
  2. Help the child use compensatory skills to perform tasks or activities for which limb or hand function is not available, such as using the chin and shoulder to hold an object, placing the object between the knees, or pressing the object against the body.
  3. When a control line is added to the child's prosthesis, help the child learn how the terminal device opens, grasps, closes, and releases. The normal age for acquiring these skills is about 15 months for release function but 24 to 30 months for grasp at midline.
  4. Help the child use the prosthesis to perform motor tasks with the terminal device, including picking up and holding large objects as well as manipulating small objects.
- If the child is a shoulder-level amputee:
  1. Promote growth and development. Be aware that developmental patterns will be different from those of children with upper extremities intact. Delays in sitting and walking are common as a result of mechanical differences due to lack of arms to use as props and balancing aids and hands to grasp furniture in pulling to a standing position. The child will scoot on his or her bottom rather than creep. The child will use his or her feet to develop fine motor skills.
  2. No age criteria are suggested for starting the use of a passive prosthesis. Factors to consider include the child's need to use his or her upper extremities, the parents' and child's acceptance, and the child's development level.
  3. Help the child use a passive prosthesis by placing objects in the terminal device. For feeding, a swivel spoon is useful as a substitute for wrist and forearm movements. The elbow unit is unlocked and the child can be taught to use body movements to scoop food onto the spoon. Then the child leans the forearm against the table forcing the elbow to flex and bringing the terminal device and spoon to the mouth.
  4. Help the child use a control cable. Generally, a thigh strap is used because the child can obtain full opening by flexing his or her trunk to open the terminal device and standing upright to close it. As the child gains skill, shoulder elevation motion can be substituted and then a motor unit, if desired. A hook is preferred because of greater visibility.

Sensory
- Provide activities to toughen the skin and reduce pain sensation.
- Assess the prosthesis and stump sock for signs of skin irritation and discomfort due to poor fit, heat, or perspiration.

Cognitive
- Instruct the parents and child on the care and maintenance of the prosthesis.
- Instruct the parents and child on stump hygiene.
- Instruct the parents and child on the steps for putting on and removing the prosthesis.
- Instruct the parents and child on the functional operation of the prosthesis.
- Teach the parents and child the basic concepts of energy conservation and work simplification to account for the increased energy used to operate a prosthesis.

Intrapersonal
- Encourage an older child to discuss his or her anxiety about failure of the appliance to perform or the child's own failure to control the appliance, which may lead to an embarrassing situation such as dropping a glass.

Interpersonal
- Provide information to team members to design or modify the prosthesis so it performs as well as possible to meet the needs of the child.
- Develop a home program for the parents and child to carry out between visits.

Self-Care
Provide instruction, if needed, on how to perform self-care activities with or without the prosthesis. Generally it is useful to know how to perform basic self-care activities without the prosthesis in case the prosthesis is malfunctioning or being repaired.

Productivity
Work with teachers to integrate the child into the classroom. It may be necessary to visit the school to see firsthand the situation in the classroom.

Leisure
Encourage the development of leisure interests within the limitations, if any, of the child's skill level.

PRECAUTIONS
A prosthesis is not the solution for every child amputee. The therapist should understand and support a family's decision not to opt for a prosthesis or to discontinue the use of a prosthesis.

PROGNOSIS AND OUTCOME
- The child is able to operate the prosthesis to perform motions of opening, grasping, holding, and releasing.
- The child and family demonstrate knowledge of how the prosthesis works and how to care for it.
- The child can perform self-care activities with or without the prosthesis at an age-appropriate level.
- The child can perform play and school activities at an age-appropriate level.
- The child can demonstrate leisure activities appropriate to his or her age level.

REFERENCES

Ballance, R., B.N. Wilson, and J.A. Harder. 1989. Factors affecting myoelectric prosthetic use and wearing patterns of the juvenile unilateral below-elbow amputee. *Canadian Journal of Occupational Therapy* 56(3):132–7.

Baron, E., S.D. Clarke, and C. Soloman. 1983. The two stage myoelectric hand for children and young adults. *Orthotics and Prosthetics* 37(2):11–24.

Celikyol, F. 1984. Prostheses, equipment, adapted performance: Reflections on these choices for the training of the amputee. *Occupational Therapy in Health Care* 1(4):89–115.

Celikyol, F. 1988. Comparison of terminal devices and body-powered/myoelectric prosthetics. In *Prehension assessment*, ed. D. Krebs, 33–43. Thorofare, NJ: Slack Inc.

Clarke, S.D. 1986. Outcomes of a problem-solving approach to independence in children with multiple limb deficiencies: A case study of adaptation to the demands of adulthood. *Occupational Therapy in Health Care* 3(1):27–40.

Crone, N. 1986. A comparison of myo-electric and standard prostheses—a case study of a preschool aged congenital amputee. *Canadian Journal of Occupational Therapy* 53(4):217–22.

Friedmann, L.W., and L. Friedmann. 1985. The conservative treatment of the body overgrowth problem in the juvenile amputee. *Inter-Clinic Information Bulletin* 20(2):17–23.

Gregg, G., B. Diurba, and W.T. Green. 1985. Camp workshop for adolescent amputees: An interim report. *Journal of the Association of Children's Prosthetic-Orthotic Clinics* 20(4):49–54,64.

Hart, M.D. 1987. Classroom aids for a child with severe upper limb deficiencies. *American Journal of Occupational Therapy* 41(7):467–9.

Hubbard, S. 1988. Prehension and motor skills testing in the child upper extremities amputee. In *Prehension assessment*, ed. D. Krebs, 25–33. Thorofare, NJ: Slack Inc.

Hubbard, S. 1989. The Toronto experience with pediatric myoelectric training. In *Comprehensive management of the upper-limb amputee*, ed. D.J. Atkins and R.M. Meier, 190–3. London, England: Springer-Verlag.

Maiorano, L.M., and J.E. Sweigart. 1984. Prosthetics for the child amputee. In *Rehabilitation of the hand*, 2d ed., ed. J.M. Hunter, et al., 838–46. St Louis: C.V. Mosby.

Mendez, M.A. 1985. Evaluation of a myoelectric hand prosthesis for children with a below-elbow absence. *Prosthetics and Orthotics International* 9:137–40.

Michael, J. 1990. Pediatric prosthetics and orthotics. *Physical and Occupational Therapy in Pediatrics* 10(2):123–46.

Patton, J.F. 1989. Developmental approach to pediatric prosthetic evaluation and training. In *Comprehensive management of the upper-limb amputee*, ed. D.J. Atkins and R.H. Meier, 137–49. London, England: Springer-Verlag.

Patton, J.F. 1989. Upper-limb prosthetic components for children and teenagers. In *Comprehensive management of the upper-limb amputee*, ed. D.J. Atkins and R.M. Meier, 99–120. London, England: Springer-Verlag.

Watts, H.G., J. Corideo, and M. Dow. 1985. An upper-limb prosthesis for infants. *Journal of the Association of Children's Prosthetic-Orthotic Clinics* 20(4):55–6.

Weaver, S.A., L.R. Lange, and V.M. Vogts. 1988. Comparison of myoelectric and conventional prostheses for adolescent amputees. *American Journal of Occupational Therapy* 42(2):87–91.

Weiss-Lambrou, R. 1981. *A manual for the congenital unilateral below-elbow child amputee.* Rockville, MD: American Occupational Therapy Association.

Athletic Injuries to the Hands

DESCRIPTION

Athletic injuries are defined as injuries to the hand and wrist as a result of participation in sports activities, including training and playing in games.

CAUSE

Injuries occur as a result of high-speed objects or external forces that impact the hand and produce contusions or shearing and repetitive stress.

ASSESSMENT

Areas
- range of motion
- edema

- muscle strength
- grip and hand strength
- hand function (precision grasp and grips)
- light touch and pinprick
- two-point discrimination

Instruments
- goniometry
- volumetry
- manual muscle testing
- dynamometer and pinch meter
- Finkelstein's test—passively abduct and flex the first metacarpal and flex the metacarpophalangeal joint of the thumb to reproduce the pain. Used to evaluate de Quervain's disease.
- Weber two-point discrimination
- Dellon moving two-point discrimination

PROBLEMS

Motor
- The person may incur repetitive stress to a wrist held in extension.
- The person may incur injuries to the wrist from falls on the outstretched hand.
- The person may have wrist (carpal) instability as a result of incompetent ligament support or changes in the joint surface configuration. Radial instability involves the scaphoid, which may collapse, leading to scapholunate dissociation or rotary subluxation of the scaphoid. Ulnar instability includes the lunotriquetrum due to rupture of the lunotriquetral portion of the dorsal radiocarpal ligaments or the palmar radiotriquetral ligament and midcarpal, which in turn is due to abnormal laxity between the proximal and distal row that allows the proximal row to collapse.
- The person may have fractures of carpal bones, especially of the scaphoid or hamatum.
- The person may have Kienbock's disease, which is aseptic necrosis of the lunate that appears to occur secondary to repetitive trauma or undiagnosed fracture of the lunate.
- The person may have fractures of the metacarpophalangeals or phalanges.
- The person may have Bennett's fracture of the thumb in which the abductor pollicis longus muscle pulls the metacarpal proximal while a small bony fragment remains attached to the medial aspect of the volar ligament; or Rolando's fracture, which involves a large dorsal fragment in addition to the fragment on the volar ligament.
- The person may have "gamekeeper's thumb," which is complete or partial rupture of the ulnar collateral ligament at the metacarpophalangeal joint of the thumb due to forced abduction, torsion in combination with abduction and hyperextension, or a combination of stressed abduction and flexion, often resulting from falling on an outstretched hand. Other causes may be ski poles, lacrosse sticks, or hockey sticks.
- The person may have a "jersey finger" injury, which is avulsion of the flexor digitorum profundus and which occurs when an athlete grabs an opponent's jersey and forcibly extends the distal phalanx, usually the ring finger.

- The person may have boutonniere deformity, which is a slit in the dorsal covering of the proximal interphalangeal (PIP) joint that occurs where the central slip of the extensor tendon is avulsed from its insertion on the dorsal base of the middle phalanx, which results in loss of PIP flexion.
- The person may have pseudoboutonniere deformity, which is damage to the proximal membranous portion of the volar plate, usually created by hyperextension or twisting injury to the PIP joint.
- The person may have dorsal displacement of the PIP joint, usually due to hyperextension stress and longitudinal compression.
- The person may have incomplete tears of the ulnar collateral ligament of the PIP joints.
- The person may have mallet finger injury, which occurs when a ball strikes an extended fingertip forcing the distal interphalangeal (DIP) into flexion while the extensor mechanism is actively extended. There are five types of mallet finger injuries: (1) fibers of the extensor mechanism may be stretched but without complete division, (2) the extensory tendon may rupture or avulse from the dorsal base without bony involvement, (3) the tendon avulsion may include a small bony attachment, (4) a true fracture with significant involvement of the articular portion of the collateral ligament of the distal joint, and (5) a fracture dislocation of the epiphyseal plate seen only in children.
- The person may have tendinitis from chronic overstretching or initiation of unaccustomed motion or activity.
- The person may have stenosing tenosynovitis (de Quervain's disease) of the first dorsal compartment of the wrist, which involves the abductor pollicis longus and the extensor pollicis brevis sheaths at the radial styloid process.
- The person may have trigger finger due to repeated trauma to the flexor tendon sheath, which results in an inflammatory reaction with swelling that restricts the normal gliding of the flexor tendon within its sheath.
- The person may have nerve compression injuries to the median or ulnar nerves, such as carpal tunnel syndrome from repeated wrist motion and grasp.

Sensory
- The person may have pain.
- The person may have numbness or loss of feeling.
- The person may have decreased or lost tactile sense, kinesthesis, or proprioception.

Cognitive
Athletic injuries do not directly affect cognitive functioning.

Intrapersonal
The person may experience fear of repeated injuries, disability, or pain.

Interpersonal
The person may experience concern for "letting the team down" during the time the person is unable to participate due to injury and rehabilitation.

Productivity
- The person may be unable to participate in the sport until his or her injury heals.

- The person may be unable to continue participating in the sport because of the severity of the injury.

TREATMENT/MANAGEMENT

Motor

- Control edema using pressure garments or bandaging. Modalities, such as ice, pneumatic compression, paraffin wax, electrical stimulation, low output laser, ultrasound, and heat have been used. Occupational therapists must have special training and permission under state licensure to use such modalities.
- If the person has wrist instability, a cast or splint should be applied to hold the wrist in slight radial deviation and palmar flexion to permit the palm ligaments to relax for four to six weeks. Exercise, joint mobilization, and use of paraffin or a whirlpool may be desirable depending on the specific type of instability.
- If the person has wrist fractures, a short arm-thumb spica cast is used to hold the wrist in slight palmar flexion and the thumb in abduction and opposition for six weeks to four months. If the wrist is unstable, a long arm-thumb spica cast may be used. After the fracture is healed, active exercise and paraffin or a whirlpool should be used to restore mobility to the forearm, wrist, and thumb. Strenuous or resistive exercises should not be permitted for at least two months.
- If the person has Kienbock's disease, acute motion in the digits, elbow, and shoulder should be used to maintain mobility during the time the wrist is immobilized after surgery. After healing, a wrist mobilization program should be initiated. Treatment of Kienbock's disease varies depending on whether ulnar lengthening or radial shortening is used.
- If the person has finger fractures, generally the objectives are to reduce swelling and pain and to avoid abnormalities in motion or permanent deformities.
  1. If the person has metacarpal fractures, immobilization should be maintained between 60 and 70 degrees flexion to prevent extension contractures. An early exercise program should be started to prevent intrinsic tightness by passively extending the metacarpophalangeal joints while flexing the interphalangeal joints. Gentle active motion may be started after three weeks post-injury. Protective splinting should continue until union is established based on radiography.
  2. If the person has interphalangeal fractures, immobilization of minimally displaced fractures should occur for three weeks, after which gentle motion may be initiated. Protective splinting should continue for three more weeks. Fractures requiring open reduction should be immobilized in the extended position for two weeks, followed by gentle exercises. Early motion is recommended to prevent flexor or extensor tendons from adhering to torn periosteum, healing bone, or scarred tendon sheath. Protective splinting should continue for three more weeks.
  3. If the person has thumb metacarpal fractures, gentle exercise should start about three to four weeks post-injury to restore mobility of the thumb and wrist. Protective splinting should continue for six weeks post-injury. After protective splinting is discontinued, exercises should be upgraded and gentle stretching may be needed.
- If the person has gamekeeper's thumb, immobilize it in a thumb spica cast in a slightly adducted position to reduce stress on the ligament for three weeks, and then replace with a volar splint for three additional weeks. At three weeks post-injury, active isolated and composite exercises of the thumb and wrist should be started.

- If the person has jersey finger, use a dorsal splint after surgery to hold the wrist in slight flexion, position metacarpophalangeals at 60 to 70 degrees flexion, and PIPs and DIPs in nearly full extension. The splint is worn for three weeks, after which gentle active exercises through as full range of motion as possible should be initiated to the point of pain tolerance to increase mobility and prevent tendon adherence. When fingers are extended, the wrist should be flexed; when the wrist is extended, the fingers should be flexed. Exercises should be performed several times a day for short time periods (5 to 10 minutes). The splint should be continued through the fifth week. Between five and eight weeks, light functional activities, such as self-care activities, may be done without the splint. Heavy resistive activities should be avoided until the eighth week post-surgery.
- If the person has boutonniere deformity, surgery is usually not necessary. The PIP joint should be splinted in full extension while the DIP is left free to allow active flexion. The splint should be worn for six to eight weeks, after which active exercises may be started. Protective splinting should continue until joint motion is pain free.
- If the person has pseudoboutonniere deformity a safety pin or other splint should be worn at the DIP joint to maintain extension until the contracture has been reduced, and then continued at night to maintain extension. Protective splinting should continue until motion is pain free. Active exercises may be started at six to eight weeks.
- If the person has an unstable dorsal proximal interphalangeal dislocation but no fracture, use a dorsal blocking splint set at minus 30 degrees of extension. The splint should be worn for three to five weeks. Exercises are performed while the splint is worn to isolate the flexor digitorum profundus and flexor digitorum sublimis. After the dorsal blocking splint is removed, exercises should be started to increase extension as well as maintaining flexion. A figure-eight or swan-neck splint may be used to prevent hyperextension by blocking the last 10 to 15 degrees of PIP extension. A dynamic splint may be used six weeks post-injury, if needed.
- If the person has an unstable dorsal proximal interphalangeal dislocation with fractures, immobilize for approximately three weeks. Active and active-resistance flexion exercises may be initiated after three weeks with the digit protected in a dorsal extension blocking splint. Dynamic flexion splints to increase flexion may be used approximately five to seven weeks from the date of surgery, depending on healing.
- If the person has incomplete proximal interphalangeal collateral ligament injuries, splint the joint for comfort. After one week, gentle active motion may be started. Protective splinting should be continued for three to four weeks. Do not use buddy tapes because the protection is not adequate.
- If the person has complete proximal interphalangeal collateral ligament injuries, splints should provide for flexion and extension, but protect against lateral displacement.
- If the person has mallet finger, splint the distal phalanx in extension but not hyperextension. Be sure the splint does not restrict flexion at the PIP joint or irritate the skin. Conservative treatment requires the splint be worn continuously for approximately nine weeks. Skin should be kept dry. When the skin is being cleaned, the distal phalanx should not be permitted to flex. After nine weeks, the splint may be removed to begin active exercises, but it should continue to be worn for three more weeks or until extension of the joint can be maintained.
- If the person has tendinitis, de Quervain's disease, or trigger finger, use a static splint to protect the soft tissues inflamed by overuse. The splint should protect the hand and wrist in a functional position. Modalities such as ice, heat, ultrasound, or transcutaneous

electrical nerve stimulation may be useful if the therapist is trained in the use of the modality. Strengthening using isometric and range-of-motion exercises should be started as soon as the inflammatory reaction is controlled. Isokinetic exercises should not be used during the acute phase because they may aggravate the injury.

- If the person has nerve compression injuries, see the sections on carpal tunnel syndrome, median nerve injuries, ulnar nerve injuries, and radial nerve injuries.

Sensory
- Splints may be used to reduce pain.
- Other modalities may be used to reduce pain, such as ice, heat, TENS, and ultrasound, if the therapist is trained to use such modalities.

Cognitive
Instruct the person in preventive methods, such as the use of gloves, splints, padded handle bars, or other protective devices to prevent injury and reduce repetitive stress.

Self-Care
- Self-care activities are used as gentle exercises following immobilization.
- Self-help devices may be useful during early rehabilitation.

Productivity
Activities based on movements used in the sport may be adapted or used normally when resistive or unrestricted movements are permitted.

PRECAUTIONS
- Splints should be fabricated from material that protects the player but does not cause injury to opposing players.
- Watch for a skin rash under a splint, which may occur from exercise perspiration. A stockinet liner may be needed to absorb perspiration or holes may be made in the splint at random intervals. Be sure the holes do not weaken the splint.
- Examine splints frequently for signs of structural fatigue (cracks or bending) and oxidation.
- Watch for edema or skin redness under and around the splint.
- Always have the person report any pain or numbness associated with the splint.
- Be aware of athletic rules regarding use of protective splints on the playing field. Rules differ for interscholastic, intercollegiate, and professional sports.

PROGNOSIS AND OUTCOME
- The person is free of pain and edema.
- The person has recovered full or near-full range of motion.
- The person has recovered full muscle strength, including grip or hand strength.
- The person has recovered normal gross coordination of the body.
- The person has recovered normal bilateral coordination and dexterity of the hands.
- The person has recovered normal sequence of motions and timing.

• The person uses protective devices during athletic events, if recommended, to prevent additional or recurrent injury.

REFERENCES

Gieck, J.H., and V. Mayer. 1986. Protective splinting of the hand and wrist. *Clinics in Sports Medicine* 5:795–807.
Mayer, V. 1989. Evaluation and rehabilitation of athletic injuries of the hand and wrist. In *Hand and wrist injuries and treatment*, ed. T.R. Malone, 1–28. Baltimore, MD: Williams & Wilkins.
Mayer, V. 1989. Protection of athletic injuries of the hand and wrist. In *Hand and wrist injuries and treatment*, ed. T.R. Malone, 72–90. Baltimore, MD: Williams & Wilkins.
Mayer, V., and J.H. Gieck. 1986. Rehabilitation of hand injuries in athletes. *Clinics in Sports Medicine* 5(4):783–94.
McCue, F.C., V. Mayer, and D.J. Moran. 1988. Diagnosing and treating gamekeeper's thumb. *Journal of Musculoskeletal Medicine* 5:53–63.
McCue, F.C., and V. Mayer. 1989. Rehabilitation of common athletic injuries of the hand and wrist. *Clinics in Sports Medicine* 8(4):731–76.
Moore, J.W., and S.E. Braverman. 1990. Splinting the radial instability of the thumb MCP joint: A case report and description of a splint modification. *Journal of Hand Therapy* 3(4):202–4.

Back Injuries

DESCRIPTION

A back injury is defined as an injury to or diseases of the low lumbar, lumbosacral, or sacroiliac region of the back.

CAUSE

The causes include: (1) acute ligamentous injury (sprain), (2) muscular problems (strain) due to poor posture or poor conditioning and aggravated by mechanical factors, (3) chronic osteoarthritis, (4) ankylosing spondylitis, (5) fibromyalgia, (6) protruding or ruptured intervertebral disk, (7) traumatic ligament rupture, (8) stress fracture of the pars interarticularis, (9) tears of the erectorspinae or multifidus muscles, (10) fracture, infection, or tumor involving the back, pelvis, or retroperitoneum, (11) congenital defects of the low lumbar and upper sacral spine, (12) loss of substance in the pars interarticularis (spondylolisthesis), (13) narrowing of the spinal canal from spinal stenosis, and (14) problems due to adjacent visceral disease.

ASSESSMENT

Areas
• body mechanics used in lifting, carrying, reaching, bending, twisting, and stooping
• posture used in standing, sitting, and walking
• range of motion
• muscle strength
• physical endurance and work tolerance
• repetitive movements, especially those requiring forceful movement

- pain behavior
- vibration experienced during work activity
- mood or affect
- self-concept
- coping skills
- self-care and daily living tasks
- productive activities—home management, work history, interests, and values
- leisure interests and skills

Factors Associated with Lifting

- size of the object being lifted (per square inch, foot, or yard)
- weight of the load being lifted (in pounds or kilograms)
- horizontal distance of the object from the body during the lift (inches from body)
- vertical distance the load is moved during the lift (number of inches object is moved)
- base of support used in lifting (placement of feet and back at the beginning of the lift)
- style of lifting (posture assumed, position of hands and arms)
- speed of the lift (inches or feet per minute)
- frequency of the lift (number of times per minute or hour)
- control of the object being lifted (ability to stop the lift or shift the load)
- environmental factors, such as temperature, lighting, clothing being worn
- anthropometric parameters (safety endpoint based on 50 percent of body weight for women and 60 percent of body weight for men)
- physiologic status of the muscles, joints, ligaments, discs, and bones (psychophysical endpoint determined by pain, aerobic endpoint based on 85% of age-determined maximum heart rate)
- knowledge of the load (center of gravity, stacking arrangement, possible shifting of load during movement)

Source: Adapted from R.C. Sutherland and W.J. Counihan, "Functional Restoration for the Back-Injured Worker: A Sports Medicine Approach," *Occupational Therapy Practice* 1(2):17.

Instruments
- goniometry
- manual muscle test
- Smith Physical Capacities Evaluation. (See Smith, S.L., S. Cunningham, and R. Weinberg. 1986. The predictive validity of the functional capacities evaluation. *American Journal of Occupational Therapy* 40(8):564–7. For a copy of the form, see *Willard and Spackman's occupational therapy*, 7th ed., ed. H. Hopkins and H. Smith, 239–44. Philadelphia: J.B. Lippincott, 1988.)

- Assessment of Body Mechanics in Activities of Daily Living by L.Z. Peterson in *Work Programs Special Interest Section Newsletter* 3(1):7, 1989.
- Job Site Lifting Evaluation Worksheet by K. Schultz-Johnson, Upper extremity factors in the evaluation of lifting, *Journal of Hand Therapy*, 3(2):72–85, 1990.
- *Procedure guidelines for the West Standard Evaluation: Assessment of range of motion under load* by L. Ogden-Niemeyer, Long Beach, CA: Work Evaluation Systems Technology, 1950 Freeman Ave., 1989.
- daily living scale
- occupational history
- leisure checklist

PROBLEMS

Motor
- loss of range of motion
- loss of muscle strength
- decreased ability to lift or carry objects
- decreased physical tolerance and endurance, especially for standing, walking, climbing, stooping, or running
- decreased sense of balance and equilibrium
- decreased postural reactions

Sensory
The person may experience increased pain upon exertion.

Cognitive
Cognitive faculties are not usually affected directly.

Intrapersonal
- The person may have feelings of helplessness.
- The person may be depressed.
- The person may have a lowered self-image and fear becoming an invalid.
- Some persons enjoy secondary gain, thus avoiding responsibility.

Interpersonal
- The person may withdraw from family and social groups.
- The person may become dependent on others.
- The person may order others around.

Self-Care
Activities involving standing, walking, climbing, stooping, or twisting are most likely to be affected.

Productivity
The person may be unable to continue in present occupation due to the severity of injury or lack of job modifications.

Leisure

The person may be unable to continue some leisure activities, such as some sports or other activities requiring long periods of walking, climbing, and running, or frequent changes of posture and position.

TREATMENT/MANAGEMENT

Motor
- Increase muscle strength through progressive-resistive activities.
- Increase range of motion through functional activities.
- Increase endurance and physical tolerance through graded activities.

Sensory

Decrease the person's sensitivity to pain through strengthening and knowledge of lifting techniques.

Cognitive
- Instruct the person in techniques of proper body positioning, lifting, and carrying.
- Instruct the person in safety measures designed to prevent injuries.
- Instruct the person in work simplification, pacing, and energy conservation.
- Instruct the person in concepts of levels of activities and their requirements of body stability, body movements, and energy utilization.

Intrapersonal
- Improve the person's self-concept and mastery through instruction in relaxation designed to reduce muscle strain and tension and increase deep breathing.
- Increase the person's self-identity and sense of self-responsibility.
- Increase the person's coping skills through stress-management techniques, including relaxation training.

Interpersonal

Encourage the person to maintain or increase social and group interactions.

Self-Care
- Help the person perform activities of daily living safely and efficiently.
- Encourage the person to perform all daily living skills independently, if possible. Provide self-help devices if needed.

Productivity
- Recommend modifications in job design and task performance to reduce risk of back injuries.
- If the job cannot be modified satisfactorily, help the person explore vocational interests that might lead to safer job placement.

- Recommend modifications in daily-living and home-management tasks that may reduce the risk of back injuries.

Leisure
- Help the person modify leisure activities to reduce risk of back injuries.
- If previous leisure activities cannot be performed safely, assist the person to explore and develop new leisure interests.

PRECAUTIONS
Monitor the person at all times to ensure the person is performing within safe limits.

PROGNOSIS AND OUTCOME
- The person demonstrates good body position and safe lifting and carrying techniques in all activities, whether at work, in the community, or at home.
- The person performs all self-care and daily living activities at his or her maximum level of independence within physical limitations.
- The person is able to perform most activities without reporting an increase in pain.
- The person demonstrates coping skills necessary to living with the stress of chronic back condition.
- The person is able to perform productive work and leisure activities without reinjuring or aggravating his or her back.

REFERENCES

Bettencourt, C.M., et al. 1986. Using work simulation to treat adults with back injuries. *American Journal of Occupational Therapy* 40(1):12–8.

Carlton, R.S. 1987. The effects of body mechanics instruction on work performance. *American Journal of Occupational Therapy* 41(1):16–20.

Caruso, L.A., and D.E. Chan. 1986. Evaluation and management of the patient with acute back pain. *American Journal of Occupational Therapy* 40(5):347–51.

Caruso, L.A., D.E. Chan, and A. Chan. 1987. The management of work-related back pain. *American Journal of Occupational Therapy* 41(2):112–7.

Flower, A., E. Naxon, R.E. Jones, et al. 1981. An occupational therapy program for chronic back pain. *American Journal of Occupational Therapy* 35(4):243–8.

Hazard, R.G., et al. 1989. Functional restoration with behavioral support: A one-year prospective study of patients with chronic low-back pain. *Spine* 14(2):157–61.

Johnson, C. 1989. Measuring pain and disabilities in patients with low back pain. *Work Programs Special Interest Section Newsletter* 3(3):4.

Kuntavanish, A.A., and P.C. Ostrow. 1985. The outcomes of back conservation education. *Quality Review Bulletin* 6:22–6.

Lewchuk, S. 1980. The occupational therapist in industry: A developing challenge. *Canadian Journal of Occupational Therapy* 47(4):159–64.

Melnik, M.S. 1988. The importance of home movement analysis with the back injury patient. *Work Programs Special Interest Section Newsletter* 2(1):2–3.

Roozee, S.A. 1990. Low back pain. In *Occupational therapy: Practice skills in physical dysfunction*, 3d ed., ed. L.W. Pedretti and B. Zoltan, 532–52. St. Louis: C.V. Mosby.

Sammons, M. 1987. Back pain. In *The practice of occupational therapy: An introduction to the treatment of physical dysfunction,* 2d ed., ed. A. Turner, 295–309. Edinburgh, Scotland: Churchill Livingstone.

Solet, J.M. 1989. Low back pain: An overview. *Occupational Therapy Forum* 4(3):7–8.

Strong, J., T. Cramond, and F. Maas. 1989. The effectiveness of relaxation techniques with patients who have chronic low back pain. *Occupational Therapy Journal of Research* 9(3):184–92.

Sutherland, R.C., and W.J. Counihan. 1990. Functional restoration for the back-injured worker: A sports medicine approach. *Occupational Therapy Practice* 1(2):11–26.

Tyson, R., and J. Strong. 1990. Adaptive equipment: Its effectiveness for people with chronic lower back pain. *Occupational Therapy Journal of Research* 10(2):111–21.

Walsh, N.E., and R.K. Schwartz. 1990. The influence of prophylactic orthoses on abdominal strength and low back injury in the workplace. *American Journal of Physical Medicine and Rehabilitation* 69(5):245–50.

Carpal Tunnel Syndrome

DESCRIPTION

Carpal tunnel syndrome (CTS) is a disorder characterized by disturbances of sensation in the area of the skin supplied by the median nerve affecting the wrist and fingers.

CAUSE

The cause of this syndrome is compression of the median nerve in the volar aspect of the wrist between the longitudinal tendons of the forearm muscles that flex the hand and the transverse superficial carpal ligament. The syndrome is more common in women and in workers with occupations that require repeated forceful wrist flexion. One or both wrists may be affected. Workers with a high incidence of carpal tunnel syndrome include meat and poultry cutters, butchers, mechanics, machinists, carpenters, jack hammer operators, truck drivers, key punch operators, hairdressers, garment factory workers, typists, and piano players. Carpal tunnel syndrome can occur as a posttraumatic condition following a wrist or distal forearm fracture. Other causes include tumors or systemic disease. The age range of those affected is usually 40 to 60, but the syndrome can occur at any age.

ASSESSMENT

Areas
- range of motion
- grip and pinch tests
- muscle strength in the hand, wrist, and forearm
- hand functions
- fine motor coordination, manipulation, dexterity
- physical work tolerance, habits, patterns, and posture
- tactile sensation—light touch or pressure, two-point discrimination
- vibration
- daily living skills
- productivity history, skills, interests, and values
- leisure interests and skills

Instruments

- Moberg pick-up test (See E. Moberg. 1958. Objective methods for determining the functional value of sensibility in the hand. *Journal of Bone and Joint Surgery* 40B:454–66. Modification by A.L. Dellon. 1981. *Evaluation of sensibility and re-education of sensation in the hand*, 100–6. Baltimore, MD: Williams & Wilkins.)
- Phalen's Sign (See American Society for Surgery of the Hand. 1983. *The hand: Examination and diagnosis*, 2d ed., 82–3. Edinburgh, Scotland: Churchill Livingstone.)
- Tinel's sign (See Percussion of the volar aspect of the wrist over the median nerve produces a tingling or prickling sensation. American Society for Surgery of the Hand. 1983. *The hand: Examination and diagnosis*, 2d ed., 81–83. Edinburgh, Scotland: Churchill Livingstone.)
- Semmes-Weinstein Monofilaments (See J.A. Bell. 1984. Light touch-deep pressure testing using Semmes-Weinstein monofilaments. In *Rehabilitation of the hand*, 2d ed., ed. J.M. Hunter, et al., 399–406. St. Louis: C.V. Mosby.)
- tuning forks , 30 cps and 256 cps
- Jebsen Hand Function Test. R.H. Jebsen, et al. 1969. An objective and standardized test of hand function. *Archives of Physical Medicine and Rehabilitation* 50:311–9.
- Nine-Hole Peg Test (See V. Mathiowetz, K. Weber, N. Kashman, et al. 1985. Adult norms for the nine-hole peg test of finger dexterity. *Occupational Therapy Journal of Research* 5(1):24–38.)
- Valpar Work Sample, Valpar Corporation, Tucson, AZ

PROBLEMS

Motor

- The person may experience clumsiness in the use of the affected hand, including dropping things, difficulty in holding small items, and difficulty in writing.
- The person may have edema of the fingers.
- The person may develop weakness or atrophy of the thenar muscles of the thumb.
- The person may have loss of pinch and grip strength.
- The person may have loss of range of motion.

Sensory

- The person may have loss of feeling, numbness, and paresthesia in the palmar aspect of the first three digits, wrist, or distal forearm.
- The person may have pain upon flexion of the wrist, described as tingling or burning. The pain may disrupt sleep (nocturnal pain).

Cognitive

Cognitive faculties are not directly affected by the injury.

Intrapersonal

- The person may fear losing his or her job if unable to continue performing work tasks.
- The person may fear becoming permanently disabled.

Interpersonal
The person may refuse some social events because of the pain.

Self-Care
Activities requiring use of the wrist become more difficult to perform and more painful.

Productivity
The person may be unable to continue his or her job if the tasks are causative factors in the disorder. Examples might include meat cutting, hammering, or using a screw driver.

Leisure
The person may be unable to continue leisure activities that aggravate the disorder. Examples might include digging in a garden, making punch, hooked, or latched rugs, and knitting or other needlework.

TREATMENT/MANAGEMENT

Motor
- Increase the person's hand strength through the use of graded activities.
- Increase hand functions.
- Consider a static volar splint to maintain the wrist in 10 to 20 degrees of extension and prevent motion at the wrist, especially flexion and ulnar deviation.
- Provide dexterity and coordination training.
- Maintain joint mobility through activities (crafts, games, cooking, etc.) that include flexion and extension of the wrist, circumduction of the wrist, opening and closing the hand, extending the thumb, and opposing the thumb and little finger.
- Use tendon-gliding exercises. (See M.A. Wehbe. 1987. Tendon gliding exercises. *American Journal of Occupational Therapy* 41(3):164–7, or refer to Baxter-Petralia in the reference section.)
- Control edema after surgery using elevation and massage.
- Nerve gliding exercises may be needed after surgery. (See Baxter-Petralia in the reference section.)
- Use shoulder exercises to maintain range of motion. (Note: Persons with carpal tunnel syndrome may protect the wrist by not moving the arm, leaving the shoulder subject to inactivity.)
- Prevent adhesions after surgery.

Sensory
- Provide sensory retraining.
- Consider splinting to protect the hand while sensation is returning if surgery is necessary.

Cognitive
- Learn about the disorder and what activities aggravate the condition so that such activities can be avoided or reduced to a minimum, such as avoiding repetitive wrist flexion and extension motions and pinching or gripping objects while the wrist is flexed.

- Learn joint protection concepts, such as lifting a box using the palms of the hands instead of the fingers.

Intrapersonal
- Encourage the person to express his or her feelings.
- Provide an opportunity for improving his or her self-image through creative activities, such as crafts, drama, and music.

Interpersonal
Encourage the person to participate in social activities.

Self-Care
Encourage independence in performing activities of daily living.

Productivity
- Discuss with the person and his or her employer, if possible, job modifications that would reduce or eliminate postures that require frequent wrist flexion and activities that require repetitive wrist movements. Tool redesign may be helpful.
- A change of occupation may be useful or necessary to a job that does not require as much forceful use of the wrist or modification of existing job tasks.
- Provide work-tolerance or work-hardening training.
- Consider recommending the person wear a splint when at work, if the person is returning to the same or a similar job situation.

Leisure
- Explore with the person whether some leisure interests may be contributing factors to CTS and need to be modified or discontinued.
- Encourage the person to explore and develop new interests.

PRECAUTIONS
- If a splint is applied, check to see that the splint maintains the normal hand arches and creases to permit fingers to bend but at the same limits the thumb and wrist, and check for any redness or pressure sores at the wrist or thumb.
- Warn the person that overuse may lead to tenosynovitis.

PROGNOSIS AND OUTCOME
- The person demonstrates normal hand strength considering age, sex, and type of work.
- The person demonstrates hand functions, including pinch and grasp.
- The person demonstrates functional range of motion at the wrist and in fingers and thumb.
- The person demonstrates dexterity and coordination with the involved hand alone or bilaterally.
- The person has sensory awareness and discrimination in the hand.
- The person is able to perform activities of daily living independently.
- The person is able to perform productive activities.
- The person is able to perform leisure activities.

Suggestions for Better Tool Design

- Bend the tool, not the wrist to decrease the need for ulnar deviation.
- Keep the weight of the tool down when possible or provide a strap or harness to reduce the muscle strength needed to hold the tool.
- Keep the center of gravity of the tool aligned with the center of the hand grasp to reduce the unequal pull (contraction) of muscles.
- Adapt the tool to the task rather than requiring the operator to use a general purpose tool that does none of the tasks well.
- Design the tool for use by either hand to reduce the need for the left-handed person to adapt the body and hand to use a tool intended for right handers.
- Handles should be designed for either power or precision grip. Power grip handles should permit the hand to wrap around the handle. Precision or pinch grip should permit the fingers to guide the action.
- Make the grip the proper size and shape. Size should be 1.25 to 1.75 inches and either cylindrical or oval. Flutes, ridges, or other texturing on the handle can improve torque. A t-shaped handle provides the best torque.
- Make the handle long enough, at least 4 inches, to permit the entire hand and all fingers to grip the handle. Short handles may be pressed into the palm to gain leverage and thus press nerves and restrict circulation.
- Adjust the handle span for both men and women. Spans of 2.0 to 2.7 inches are good averages but some individuals may need larger or smaller spans to maintain maximum power.
- Form-fitted or finger-grooved handles should be examined carefully to determine if the handles actually fit the person using the tool or only fit the tool's inventor.
- Spring load pliers and scissors so that the tool opens automatically to reduce the pressure against the hand needed to manually open the tool.
- Make switches large enough to permit two or three fingers to start or stop the tool, thus reducing the pressure on any one finger.
- Handles should be non-porous, non-slip, and non-conductive.

Source: Adapted from *Cumulative trauma disorders: A manual for musculoskeletal diseases of the upper limbs*, ed. Putz-Anderson, V. London: Taylor & Francis, 1988.

REFERENCES

Baxter-Petralia, P.L. 1990. Therapist's management of carpal tunnel syndrome. In *Rehabilitation of the hand*, 3d ed., ed. J.M. Hunter, et al., 640–6. St. Louis: C.V. Mosby.

Bear-Lehman, J., and T. Bielawski. 1988. Primary carpal tunnel syndrome: How are we managing it? *Canadian Journal of Occupational Therapy* 55(5):243–8.

Braun, R.M., K. Davidson, and S. Doehr. 1989. Provocative testing in the diagnosis of dynamic carpal tunnel syndrome. *Journal of Hand Surgery* 14A:195–7.

Dolhanty, D. 1986. Effectiveness of splinting for carpal tunnel syndrome. *Canadian Journal of Occupational Therapy* 53(5):275–80.

Falkenburg, S.A. 1987. Choosing hand splints to aid carpal tunnel syndrome recovery. *Occupational Health & Safety* 56(5):60,63–64.

Gellman, H. 1989. Analysis of pinch and grip strength after carpal tunnel release. *Journal of Hand Surgery* 14A(5):8634.

Groves, E.J., and B.A. Rider. 1989. A comparison of treatment approaches used after carpal tunnel release surgery. *American Journal of Occupational Therapy* 43(6):398–402.

Johnson, S.L. 1990. Ergonomic design of handheld tools to prevent trauma to the hand and upper extremity. *Journal of Hand Therapy* 3(2):86–93.

Cumulative Trauma Disorders

DESCRIPTION

Cumulative trauma disorders are defined as the adverse health effects that arise from chronic exposure to microtrauma, usually in the workplace. Cumulative indicates that the injuries develop gradually over time as a result of repeated stresses on a particular body part and cause bodily injury, physical ailments, and abnormal conditions within the body. Called also "wear and tear" disorders, overuse injuries, osteoarthroses, degenerative joint diseases, repetitive motion injury and repetitive strain injuries. Conditions include tendon disorders, such as tendinitis, tenosynovitis, de Quervain's disease (stenosing tenosynovitis), ganglionic cyst, lateral epicondylitis (tennis elbow), medial epicondylitis (golfer's elbow), and rotator cuff tendinitis. Other conditions include nerve disorders, such as carpal tunnel syndrome, neurovascular disorders, such as thoracic outlet syndrome, and vibration disorders, such as Raynaud's phenomenon.

CAUSE

The major causes include: (1) manual repetitive motion of the hands, wrists, elbows, shoulders, neck, or low back, (2) excessive manual force activities of the upper extremities or lower back, (3) awkward positions, such as static sitting or standing positions with back flexed, which increases intradiscal pressure, or wrist flexion and deviation, which create pressure in the carpal tunnel, (4) vibration that decreases circulation or causes microtrauma to soft tissue, (5) poorly designed work stations that subject a person to potentially injurious positions, put the person at a mechanical disadvantage, or create pressure to get the work done, and (6) low temperature, which causes stiffness in soft tissues, such as tendons and ligaments, and decreases circulation and sensation. Women are affected more often than men.

ASSESSMENT

Have the person list and describe his or her job tasks in detail. Having the person simulate specific job tasks may also be useful in clarifying problem areas.

Considerations in the Physical Demands of a Job

Lifting—weight to be lifted in pounds, size of the load in cubic inches, frequency of lifts per time unit, range through which objects are lifted in inches, use of two-hand (bilateral) lifts versus one-hand (unilateral)

Carrying—weight to be carried in pounds, size of the load in cubic inches, frequency of carrying per time unit, distance through which objects are carried, two-handed versus one-handed carry, position of extremities in relation to the body, hand grasp pattern

Reaching—range of reach in inches from the body horizontally, vertically, and diagonally, arc of reaching range in degrees, and frequency of reach per unit of time

Pushing-pulling—position of body, frequency of push-pull per unit of time, two-handed versus one-handed

Grasping—type of grasp required, repetitions of grasp per unit of time, position of hand in relation to wrist and arm

Source: Based on Bruening, L.A. and D. Beaulieu. 1990. The return to work phase for the patient with cumulative trauma. In *Rehabilitation of the hand*, 3d ed., ed. J.M. Hunter, et al., 1194. St. Louis: C.V. Mosby.

Areas
- range of motion of the upper extremities, active and passive
- muscle strength, grip, and pinch strength
- edema
- fine motor coordination, manipulation, and dexterity
- work positions, posture, and movements
- sensory awareness
- sensory processing using threshold tests, such as the Semmes-Weinstein monofilament, Tinel's sign, and Phalen's sign
- pain
- daily living skills
- productivity history, interests, values, and skills
- leisure interests, values, and skills

Instruments
No specific instruments developed by occupational therapists for this disorder were identified in the literature. Therapists make reference to the following:

- Physical capacity evaluation by P.L. Baxter and P.M. McEntee, in *Rehabilitation of the hand*, 2d ed., ed. J.M. Hunter, et al., 909–18. St. Louis: C.V. Mosby, 1984.
- goniometry—joint motion and method of measuring and recording by the American Academy of Orthopaedic Surgeons. Chicago, IL: The Academy, 1965.
- Jebsen Hand Function Test (See Jebsen, R.H., et al. 1969. An objective and standardized test of hand function. *Archives of Physical Medicine and Rehabilitation* 50:311–9.)

- dynamometer and pinch meter—hand and pinch strength
- manual muscle testing
- Tinel's sign—percussion along the route of a nerve (It is positive when pain or hypersensitivity is elicited.)
- Phalen's sign—wrist is held in maximum flexion for at least one minute (It is positive when pain or paresthesia is elicited.)
- Finklestein's test—person grasps the thumb with the fingers and deviates the wrist toward the side of the ulna (It is positive if pain is elicited.)
- vibration—256 cps tuning fork
- volumetry (See Schultz-Johnson, K. 1988. *Volumetrics: A literature review.* Santa Monica, CA: Upper Extremity Technology, 1988. Also available from Roylan Medical Products, P.O.B. 555, Menomonee Falls, WI 53051.)
- Moberg pick-up test
- Semmes-Weinstein calibrated monofilaments (See J.A. Bell. 1987. The repeatability of testing with Semmes-Weinstein monofilaments. *Journal of Hand Surgery* [monograph], or J.A. Bell-Krotoski. 1990. Light touch-deep pressure-testing using Semmes-Weinstein monofilaments. *Rehabilitation of the hand,* 3d ed., ed. J.M. Hunter, et al., 585-93. St. Louis: C.V. Mosby.)
- Minnesota Rate of Manipulation, by Minnesota Employment Stabilization Research Institute, Circle Pines, MN: American Guidance Services, 1967 (not an occupational therapist)
- Purdue Pegboard Test by J. Tiffin, Chicago, IL: Science Research Associates, 1947 (not an occupational therapist)
- Crawford Small Parts Dexterity Test by J.E. Crawford and D.M. Crawford (not occupational therapists)
- Nine-Hole Peg Test (See Mathiowetz, V., et al. 1985. Adult norms for the Nine Hole Peg Test of finger dexterity. *Occupational Therapy Journal of Research* 5(1):24–38.)
- WEST series (See L. Ogden-Niemeyer. 1989. Procedure guidelines for the WEST Standard Evaluation, Long Beach CA: West Evaluation System Technology, 1989.)
- Job Site Lifting Evaluation Worksheet by K. Schultz-Johnson, Upper extremity factors in the evaluation of lifting, *Journal of Hand Surgery*, 3(2):72–85, 1990.

PROBLEMS

Motor

- inflammation of the tendon (tendinitis) (Tendon may become thickened, bumpy, or irregular. Some fibers may fray or tear apart.)
- excessive synovial fluid accumulation in the tendon sheath (tenosynovitis)
- constriction of the tendon sheath (de Quervain's disease)

Sensory

- soreness or pain in the forearm or elbow (epicondylitis)
- burning or tingling pain in the shoulders (rotator cuff tendinitis)
- numbness, tingling, or "pins and needles" sensation in the hands or fingers (carpal tunnel syndrome or thoracic outlet syndrome)
- pale or ashen skin with intermittent numbness and tingling in the fingers (Raynaud's phenomenon)

Cognition

Cognitive faculties are not affected.

Intrapersonal

- The person may fear being unable to work.
- Pain may reduce effectiveness of judgment.
- The person may have a tendency to guard injured or painful body part.

Interpersonal

The person may make excuses for not participating in social activities because of pain or fatigue.

Self-Care

The person may be unable to perform some activities of daily living because of pain, loss of hand function, or loss of sensation.

Productivity

- The person may be unable to continue performing certain job tasks because of permanent disability.
- The person may be able to continue working only if performance requirements are changed.

Leisure

The person may be unable to engage in leisure activities that require similar motions or body positions as those related to the cumulative trauma disorder.

TREATMENT/MANAGEMENT

Treatment frequently is coordinated by workers' compensation or a private insurance company. Knowledge of workers' compensation regulations is important.

Motion

- Increase muscle strength, grip, and hand strength through use of graded activity.
- Increase range of motion.
- Decrease edema and swelling.
- Consider splinting to immobilize the body part or decrease motion at selected joints.
- Increase endurance and work tolerance.

Sensation

- Desensitize hypersensitivity, if present
- Reduce pain through use of paraffin bath, fluidotherapy, or other heat modality.

Cognition

- Instruct the person about principles of good posture and body mechanics.
- Instruct the person about energy-conservation and work-simplification concepts.
- Instruct the person regarding concepts of good tool handling and machine operation.

Self-Care
Gradually increase the person's performance of self-care and daily living activities.

Productivity
- Analyze the work site and make recommendations for job and tool modifications, if possible.
- If the person's return to his or her present job is not possible, encourage management to provide alternate job placements and/or the person to explore other vocational interests.

PRECAUTIONS
The use of cold as a modality has produced mixed results and should be used with caution in dealing with pain.

PROGNOSIS AND OUTCOME
- The person demonstrates normal muscle strength of the upper extremity for his or her sex, age, and occupation.
- The person demonstrates full range of motion of the upper extremity.
- The person demonstrates normal endurance.
- The person does not complain of pain in the upper extremity.
- The person demonstrates knowledge of good posture and body mechanics while performing activities.
- The person demonstrates knowledge of energy-conservation and work-simplification techniques.
- The person is able to perform self-care and daily living activities independently with self-help devices if needed.
- The person is able to perform productive activities, although a change of vocation may be necessary to avoid reinjury.
- The person is able to perform leisure activities.
- Recommendations to the employer to modify the person's job or tools have been made.

REFERENCES

Barrett, T. 1985. Description of repetition strain injury, and prevention. *Australian Occupational Therapy Journal* 32(3):113–7.

Blair, S.J., and J. Bear-Lehman. 1987. Editorial comment: Prevention of upper extremity occupational disorders. *Journal of Hand Surgery* 12A:821–2.

Bruening, L.A., and D. Beaulieu. 1990. The return to work phase for the patient with cumulative trauma. In *Rehabilitation of the hand*, 3d ed., ed. J.M. Hunter, et al., 1192–6. St. Louis: C.V. Mosby.

Chandani, A., P.J. Agnew, and F. Maas. 1986. Repetitive strain injury: Age, sex and activity patterns. *Australian Occupational Therapy Journal* 33(4):133–41.

Cummins, M. 1988. Profile of a population with occupational overuse injury. *Australian Occupational Therapy Journal* 35(2):73–80.

Dortch, H.L. 1990. The effects of education on hand use with industrial workers in repetitive jobs. *American Journal of Occupational Therapy* 44(9):777–82.

Flinn-Wagner, S., A. Mladonicky, and G. Goodman. 1990. Characteristics of workers with upper extremity injuries who make a successful transition to work. *Journal of Hand Therapy* 3(2):51–5.

Herbin, M.L. 1987. Work capacity evaluation for occupational hand injuries. *Journal of Hand Surgery* 12A(5, Pt. 2):958–61.

Mandel, S., S. Patterson, and C. Johnson. 1986. Overuse syndrome in a double bass player. *Problems of Performing Artists* 1(4):133–4.

Muffly, E.D., and W.S. Flinn. 1987. Proposed screening tool for the detection of cumulative trauma disorders of the upper extremity. *Journal of Hand Surgery (Am)* 12A(5 Pt 2):931–5.

Poole, B.C. 1988. Cumulative trauma disorder of the upper extremity from occupational stress. *Journal of Hand Therapy* 1(4):172–80.

Riggle, M. 1990. Cumulative trauma in the workplace. *Occupational Therapy Forum* 5(43):1, 3–4.

Tadano, P. 1990. A safety-prevention program for VDT operators: One company's approach. *Journal of Hand Therapy* 3(2):64–71.

Fractures of the Forearm and Wrist

DESCRIPTION

The most common fracture of the forearm is to the distal end of the radius (Colles' fracture), however fractures of the ulnar process and carpal bones do occur.

CAUSE

Typically the cause of these fractures is falling on the extended or outstretched hand or force of impact against the hand, as in an automobile accident. Usually the person is an older female. Falling on the flexed wrist (Smith's fracture) occurs usually in younger women. Crush injuries are also possible.

ASSESSMENT

Assessment should concentrate on (1) determining the person's ability and skill in performing activities with the involved arm, or exploring compensatory methods until function is restored, and (2) preventing recurrent falls through analysis and correction of unsafe situations.

Areas
- edema
- range of motion
- muscle strength
- hand functions
- fine motor coordination, manipulation, dexterity
- sensory registration
- sensory processing, especially tactile, vestibular, proprioceptive, and kinesthetic
- functional assessment—measure daily living activities and independent living tasks
- home and job assessment—measure performance capacity and safety considerations
- leisure assessment—measure leisure interests

Instruments
- volumeter
- goniometry

- manual muscle test
- hand function test
- dexterity test
- stereognosis
- activities of daily living scale
- occupational history
- leisure checklist

PROBLEMS

Motor
- The person may lose range of motion.
- The person may lose or have decreased wrist extension; occasionally wrist flexion.
- The person may have edema and swelling.
- The person may lose hand grasp functions.
- The person may lose forearm supination.
- The person may develop contractures.
- The person may have disuse atrophy.
- The person may have malunion.

Sensory
The person may experience pain with motion of the digits.

Cognitive
Cognitive functions are usually not affected directly by the disorder, but cognitive disorders may be present due to other causes.

Intrapersonal
- The person may fear loss of hand function.
- The person may fear loss of independence.
- The person may fear permanent disability.
- The person may be fearful of using the injured arm due to lack of knowledge about safe and unsafe use during recovery.

Interpersonal
- The person may withdraw from society to avoid explaining what happened.
- The person may become bossy and order others around.

Self-Care
- The person is unable to perform activities requiring hand grasp because of the cast initially, but also because of contractures or decreased wrist extension later on. Most problems occur when the dominant hand is involved.
- The person may have difficulty performing activities that require supination of the forearm because of the cast. Most problems occur in hand to face movements when the dominant hand is involved.

- The person may avoid performing some daily living activities due to lack of knowledge about how to deal with the problem, such as not taking a shower because of lack of knowledge about how to keep the cast dry. (A plastic bag pulled over the cast and taped to the arm above the cast would keep it dry while showering.)

Productivity
- The person may have difficulty performing some job tasks that require hand grasp or supination of the forearm.
- The person may avoid doing some homemaking tasks for fear of further injuring the arm.

TREATMENT/MANAGEMENT
There are usually two stages to management. Stage one begins immediately with reduction and immobilization and continues until healing has occurred (about six weeks). Stage two begins when immobilization stops (cast or pinning is removed) until return of function is achieved. The treatment model is based on the biomechanical (Trombly) or orthopedic model.

Motor
- Prevent edema (stages one and two) by use of elevation, retrograde massage, active movement, and compressive wraps.
- Maintain range of motion and mobility of joint within limits of immobilization (stage one), including shoulder, elbow, fingers, and thumb. Increase range of motion and mobility (stage two), especially forearm supination and pronation, wrist flexion and extension, MCP (metacarpal phalangeal) flexion, proximal interphalangeal and distal interphalangeal extension, forearm interosseous membrane tightness, wrist and finger extensor tendon tightness, wrist and finger flexor tendon shortening, finger collateral ligament shortening, and intrinsic muscle tightness.
- Maintain muscle strength and coordination within limits of immobilization (stage one). Increase muscle strength and coordination (stage two) through repetitive active motion activities first, followed by progressive resistive exercises, if needed.
- Consider splinting to maintain or enhance functional gains, such as a cock-up splint to maintain ligament length and reduce tendon tightness.

Sensory
Check the person's fingertips using light touch and two-point discrimination to monitor changes in sensibility.

Cognitive
- Teach one-handed techniques (stage one).
- Teach safety evaluation of the home and frequently traveled routes to reduce chances of another fall (stage one and two).

Intrapersonal
Encourage the person to verbalize concerns and provide realistic answers or solutions in order to allay the fears.

Interpersonal

Encourage the person to engage in social activities, such as group activities with persons who have upper extremity limitations.

Self-Care

- Recommend sleeping on the unaffected side with the affected arm placed on pillows or bolsters (stage one).
- Provide instruction in compensatory approaches, such as one-handed techniques when movement is required that the immobilized arm cannot perform, such as hand grasp or forearm supination (stage one).
- Encourage use of the immobilized arm for all activities in which active movement is possible and safe (stage one).
- Suggest adapted equipment that may be useful during immobilization and facilitate independence after recovery (stages one and two), such as elongated handles, elastic shoe-laces, and non-skid materials.

Productivity

- A home program to encourage the person to use homemaking activities where possible can support therapy gains and facilitate the return to performing normal homemaking activities.
- A work-hardening program may be necessary to regain the movements and motions necessary to perform job tasks effectively and safely.

Leisure

Leisure activities such as crafts and games may be useful in the therapy program to provide movements and motion patterns useful in regaining joint range, mobility, and strength.

PRECAUTIONS

- Watch for signs of peripheral nerve compression if the person's wrist is in flexion.
- Watch for signs of reflex sympathetic dystrophy.
- Watch for signs of shoulder-hand syndrome.

PROGNOSIS AND OUTCOME

Usually the prognosis is good since the radius has a good blood supply and bone union can be expected. Disuse atrophy, bony malunion, peripheral nerve compression, reflex sympathetic dystrophy, and shoulder-hand syndrome are the major complications that may prolong the rehabilitation process and delay the return to functional activities and independent living.

- The person demonstrates functional range of motion.
- The person demonstrates muscle strength necessary to perform daily activities.
- The person demonstrates basic hand functions.
- The person does not report chronic pain or swelling (edema) upon use of the arm or hand.
- The person demonstrates two-point discrimination and stereognosis.

- The person is able to perform daily living activities independently.
- The person is able to perform productive activities.
- The person is able to perform leisure activities.

REFERENCES

Nauton, D. 1987. Occupational therapy and the treatment of the Colles' fracture. *Occupational Therapy in Health Care* 4(3/4):109–124.

Neeman, R.L. 1988. Orthokinetic orthoses application treatment of patients with Colles' fracture post-immobilization hypokinesia: A single-subject design efficacy study. *Physiotherapy Canada* 40(5):286–95.

Opgrande, J.D., and S.A. Westphal. 1983. Fractures of the hand. *Orthopedic Clinics of North America* 14(4):779–91.

Polivy, K.D., L.H. Millender, A. Newerg, et al. 1985. Fractures of the hook of the hamate: A failure of clinical diagnosis. *Journal of Hand Surgery* 10A(1):101–4.

Turner, A. 1987. Upper limb injuries. In *The practice of occupational therapy*, 2d ed., ed. A. Turner, 568–70. Edinburgh, Scotland: Churchill Livingstone.

Fractures of the Hip and Hip Replacement

DESCRIPTION

A hip fracture is defined as a break in the femur in the neck region, trochanter, or upper shaft. Five types of fractures are recognized based on the location of the fracture: subcapital, transcervical, basilar, intertrochanteric, and subtrochanteric. Four classifications of fractures are recognized based on the degree of displacement of the bone segments: incomplete, complete with no displacement, partially displaced, and completely displaced. When healing does not occur, degeneration of bone continues or fractures have reoccurred, and replacement may be necessary.

Types of Hip Surgery

Intertrochanteric osteotomy—changes the alignment of the femur to alter the weight-bearing on the hip joint

Arthrodesis—fusing the hip joint at 30 degrees of flexion and 0 degrees of abduction and rotation

Hip arthroplasty—placement of a metal cup over the head of the femur

Total hip articular replacement with internal eccentric shells (THARIES)—placement of a shell over the reshaped head of the femur

Total hip arthroplasty (THA)—removal of the head and neck of the femur and replacement with a prosthetic appliance

CAUSE

The most common cause of fractures is trauma caused by a fall or sudden rotational force. Degeneration of the head of the femur, such as necrosis or loss of bone strength as in osteoporosis or osteoarthritis, contribute to the chance of a fracture. Fractures occur more frequently in men due to occupational injuries during their 30s or 40s and in women past the age of 65.

ASSESSMENT

Areas
- muscle strength
- range of motion of the lower extremities
- physical endurance
- sensory registration and processing
- pain
- orientation (especially important in older persons)
- self-concept
- social support
- daily living skills
- productivity history, skills, interests, and values
- leisure interests and skills
- architectural and environmental barriers
- home safety
- knowledge of community resources.

Instruments

No specific instruments developed by occupational therapists were identified in the literature. The following assessments may be used:

- manual muscle test
- goniometry
- activities of daily scale
- occupational history
- leisure interest checklist

PROBLEMS

Motor
- The person usually must limit hip flexion beyond 70 to 80 degrees for six to eight weeks after surgery to permit soft tissue healing and avoid internal rotation or adduction of the hip. These precautions apply especially to hip replacement.
- The hip is frequently limited to 90 degrees of hip flexion in hip replacement.
- Out-of-bed activities usually can begin for fractures within two to four days after surgery.
- Crutches or a walker will be needed for six to eight weeks and may be necessary for longer periods.

Sensory
- Pain may continue to be present.
- Tactile sensation may be diminished.

Cognitive
The person's thinking and problem-solving skills may be reduced due to chronic pain.

Intrapersonal
- The person may be depressed.
- The person may have lost self-esteem as an active, contributing member of society.
- The person may express feelings about being disabled and losing body image.
- The person may lose independence and autonomy, becoming dependent on others.

Interpersonal
The person may have stopped engaging in most social activities prior to surgery because of pain and limited mobility.

Self-Care
- The person may have reduced his or her performance of activities of daily living to a minimum prior to surgery.
- The person may be using unsafe techniques for performing bathing and dressing activities.

Productivity
The person may have limited or stopped performing productive activities prior to surgery.

Leisure
The person may have given up many leisure activities prior to surgery.

TREATMENT/MANAGEMENT
The model of treatment is based on the biomechanical (Trombly) or orthopedic model.

Motor
- Strengthen the person's upper extremities for crutch walking and assisting in pushing up to rise from a chair or bed.
- Increase range of motion gradually through walking.
- Maintain or increase endurance through physical activities.

Sensory
Help the person monitor and control pain, if needed.

Cognitive
- Instruct the person how to avoid or correct architectural or environment barriers, such as low chairs, soft sofas, and throw rugs.
- The person should learn to avoid forcing hip flexion, as in reaching down to put on socks and shoes.

- The person should learn to avoid strenuous exercise.
- Assist the person to arrange a time schedule to permit activity and rest cycles.
- Instruct the person in concepts of energy conservation and work simplification.
- Discuss the need for evaluating his or her home or apartment for safety considerations; for example, mats or rugs should lie flat and not skid, railing and banisters should be sturdy and tightly in place.

Intrapersonal
- Encourage the person to engage in activity that will maintain or increase self-esteem by assisting the individual to do familiar activities again, with modification if needed, and learn new activities.
- Encourage the person to express feelings and discuss ways of coping with those feelings.

Interpersonal
- The person should be encouraged to slowly return to social activities that are within safe limits.
- Encourage family members to participate in some treatment sessions to learn safe procedures and precautions.

Self-Care
- Provide self-help devices and opportunity to practice their use in activities that normally require hip flexion, such as putting on socks and shoes and picking up objects from the floor.
- Suggest that safety items, such as grab bars and nonskid tape, be installed in the bathroom to reduce the chance of falls.
- Recommend that dressing activities be done while sitting when possible to reduce problems of maintaining balance on one leg or with reduced vision as clothing is pulled over the head.
- Adapted equipment, such as a commode chair with armrests, a bench seat in the shower, and a bar stool for kitchen activities, may be recommended.

Productivity
- Assist the person to rearrange personal and homemaking items to decrease the need for bending, stooping, kneeling, or stretching overhead. For example, shoes can be put in hanging racks and canned goods should be put within easy arm reach.
- The person should be cautioned against performing heavy housework, such as vacuuming, lifting more than 20 pounds, or making beds.

Leisure
Assist the person to define what leisure activities would be useful and which ones must be avoided. For example, short walks are good; outside gardening is bad. Substitute raising houseplants.

PRECAUTIONS
- The person should be warned that infection in any part of the body should be treated promptly to decrease the chance of spreading to the hip joint.

• The person should be warned that strenuous activity, such as running, jumping, hopping, or lifting heavy objects, could result in reinjury of the hip.

PROGNOSIS AND OUTCOME
• The person demonstrates physical endurance to perform functional activities.
• The person demonstrates range of motion and muscle strength of hip necessary for walking and climbing stairs.
• The person is able to perform activities of daily living independently.
• The person is able to perform productive activities, such as light housekeeping or volunteer work.
• The person is able to perform leisure activities.
• The person and his or her support group are aware of community resources.
• The person demonstrates a knowledge of safety and an ability to minimize barriers.

REFERENCES

Babayov, D., H. Omer, and J. Menczel. 1985. Sensorimotor integration therapy for hip fracture and CVA patients. *Canadian Journal of Occupational Therapy* 52(3):133–7.

Meech, A.G. 1987. Rehabilitation equipment. In *The practice of occupational therapy*, 2d ed., ed. A. Turner, 177–206. Edinburgh, Scotland: Churchill Livingstone.

Parent, L.H. 1983. Fractures. In *Occupational therapy for physical dysfunction*, 2d ed., ed. C.A. Trombly, 365–75. Baltimore, MD: Williams & Wilkins.

Parent, L.H. 1989. Orthopedic conditions. In *Occupational therapy for physical dysfunction*, 3d ed., ed. C.A. Trombly, 531–42. Baltimore, MD: Williams & Wilkins.

Pitbladdo, K., J. Polon, H. Bobrove, et al. 1985. Hip fractures and total hip replacement. In *Occupational therapy: Practice skills for physical dysfunction*, 2d ed., ed. L.W. Pedretti, 379–89. St. Louis: C.V. Mosby.

Pitbladdo, K., E.M. Bianchi, S.L. Lieberman, et al. 1990. Hip fractures and total hip replacement. In *Occupational therapy: Practice skills for physical dysfunction*, 3d ed., ed. L.W. Pedretti and B. Zoltan, 553–64. St. Louis: C.V. Mosby.

Schofield, J. 1983. Fractured neck of femur. A criteria audit of occupational therapy treatment. *Australian Clinical Review* 7(11):17–9.

Seeger, M.S., and L.A. Finsher. 1982. Adaptive equipment used in the rehabilitation of hip arthroplasty patients. *American Journal of Occupational Therapy* 36(8):503–8.

Hands—Disabilities

DESCRIPTION
Hand disabilities are defined as loss of functional abilities and sensation in the hand. (See also sections on carpal tunnel syndrome, median nerve injuries, radial nerve injuries, ulnar nerve injuries, finger injuries, tendon injuries, and tendon transfers.)

CAUSE
The causes include amputation of any part of the hand, nerve injuries, joint deformities, joint dislocation, tendon injuries, contractures, cumulative trauma disorders, or fractures.

Factors Related to Skin Stress and Soft Tissue Damage

Degree of stress (measured in degrees of force or pressure)
- *low*—most likely to be damaging if duration is continuous and ischemia results
- *moderate*—most likely to be damaging if repetitive
- *high*—usually damaging, but size is likely to be the critical factor

Duration of stress (measured in time units, such as seconds, minutes, hours, days)
- continuous short/long
- intermittent short/long

Repetition of stress (measured in number of repeated cycles)
- infrequent
- frequent
- constant

Direction of force of stress (measured in weight units such as pounds, kilograms)
- direct (perpendicular to the surface)
- shear (lateral to the surface, may produce a tearing effect)

Size of stress (measured in surface units, such as inches, centimeters in diameter)
- localized
- large
- diffuse

Key locations of stress (described in relation to a body part)
- bony prominence in contact with a wrap, splint, or cast
- edges of a wrap, splint, or cast, including "windows" in casts

Source: Based on Bell-Krotoski, J.A., D.E. Breger, and R.B. Beach. 1990. Application of biomechanics for evaluation of the hand. In *Rehabilitation of the hand*, 3d ed., ed. J.M. Hunter, et al., 139–64. St. Louis: C.V. Mosby.

ASSESSMENT

Areas
- range of motion, including active, passive, and total
- hand functions
- grip and pinch strength
- muscle strength
- sensory registration
- sensory processing, including response to light touch, two-point discrimination, pressure sensitivity, point localization, and stereognosis, proprioception, and vibration
- fine motor skills, manipulation, dexterity, and bilateral coordination
- skin color and condition

- edema and swelling
- daily living skills
- productivity history, skills, interests, and values
- work capacity and tolerance
- leisure interests and skills

Instruments
- Jebsen Hand Function Test (See R.H. Jebsen, et al. 1969. An objective and standardized test of hand function. *Archives of Physical Medicine and Rehabilitation* 50:311–9.)
- finger goniometer (See American Society for Surgery of the Hand. 1990. *The hand: Examination and diagnosis*, 3d ed., 122–7. Edinburgh, Scotland: Churchill Livingstone.)
- dynamometer and pinch meter (For positioning, see American Society for Surgery of the Hand. 1990. *The hand: Examination and diagnosis*, 3d ed., 121–2. Edinburgh, Scotland: Churchill Livingstone.)
- manual muscle test
- Moberg pick-up test modified by A. Dellon (dexterity, stereognosis) (See A. Callahan in *Rehabilitation of the hand,* 3d ed., ed. J.M. Hunter, et al., 606, 1990, or A. Callahan in *Manual on management of specific hand problems,* ed. M.H. Malick and M.C. Kasch, 1984, 25. Pittsburgh: AREN Publications.)
- Moving Two-Point Discrimination Test by A. Dellon (See The moving two-point discrimination test: clinical evaluation of the quickly-adapting fiber receptor system. *Journal of Hand Surgery*, 3:474–81, 1978. Also see A. Callahan in *Rehabilitation of the hand*, 3d ed., ed. J.M. Hunter, et al., 1990, 605–6; or A. Callahan in *Manual on management of specific hand problems,* M.H. Malick and M.C. Kasch, 1984, 24.)
- Disk-Criminator or Boley gauge (static two-point discrimination) (See norms in section on evaluation or see A. Callahan in *Rehabilitation of the hand*, 3d ed., ed. J.M. Hunter, et al., 1990, 605, or A. Callahan in *Manual on management of specific hand problems,* ed. M.H. Malick and M.C. Kasch, 1984, 24.)
- Semmes-Weinstein calibrated monofilaments (light touch-deep pressure) (See J.A. Bell. 1987. The repeatability of testing with Semmes-Weinstein monofilaments. *Journal of Hand Surgery* 12:155–61, or J.A. Bell-Krotoski. 1990. Light touch-deep pressure testing using Semmes-Weinstein monofilaments. In *Rehabilitation of the hand*, 3d ed., ed. J.M. Hunter, et al., 585–93.)
- ninhydrin sweat (printing) test by Moberg (See P.E. Phelps, and E. Walker. 1977. Comparison of the finger wrinkling test results to established sensory test in peripheral nerve injury. *American Journal of Occupational Therapy* 31(9):565–72, or A. Callahan in *Rehabilitation of the hand*, ed. J.M. Hunter, et al., 1990, 608.)
- O'Riain wrinkle test (See S. O'Riain. 1973. New and simple test of nerve function in the hand. *British Medical Journal* 3:615–6. See also A. Callahan in *Rehabilitation of the hand*, ed. J.M. Hunter, et al., 1990, 608.)
- ridge sensitometer (See N.K. Poppen, et al. 1979. Recovery of sensibility after suture of digital nerves. *Journal of Hand Surgery* 4:212–26.)
- Tinel's sign (See American Society for Surgery of the Hand. 1990. *The hand: examination and diagnosis*, 3d ed., 93–95. Edinburgh, Scotland: Churchill Livingstone.)
- commercial hand-finger coordination/dexterity tests:
  1. Minnesota Rate of Manipulation, American Guidance Services, Circle Pines, MN, 1946
  2. Purdue Pegboard Test by J. Tippen, Chicago, IL: Science Research Associates, 1947

3. Crawford Small Parts Dexterity Test, revised by J.E. Crawford and D.M. Crawford, San Antonio, TX: The Psychological Corporation, 1981
4. Hand-Tool Dexterity Test by G.K. Bennett, Lafayette, IN: Lafayette Instrument
5. O'Connor Finger Dexterity Test by J. O'Connor, Wood Dale, IL: Stoelting Company
6. Lafayette Grooved Pegboard, Lafayette, IN: Lafayette Instrument
7. Pennsylvania Bi-Manual Work Sample by J. Roberts, Circle Pines, MN: American Guidance Service, 1945
8. Minnesota Manual Dexterity Test, San Diego, CA: Educational & Industrial Test Services or Lafayette, IN: Lafayette Instruments

- vibration: tuning forks, 30 cps and 245 cps, or Bio-Thesiometer (See A. Callahan in *Rehabilitation of the hand*, 3d ed., ed. J.M. Hunter, et al., 1990, 604.)
- finger and point identification (localization) (The finger is touched just enough to indent the skin with the point of a pencil. The person is asked to identify the finger that was touched and point to the finger where the pencil touched the skin. See Callahan in Malick and Kasch, 1984, 25.)
- physical or work capacities evaluation
- sensitivity test (See E.J. Yerxa, et al. 1983. Development of a hand sensitivity test for the hypersensitive hand. *American Journal of Occupational Therapy* 37(3):176–81.)
- Smith hand function evaluation (See H.B. Smith. 1973. Smith hand function evaluation. *American Journal of Occupational Therapy* 25:77–83.)
- Valpar work sample series, Tucson, AZ: Valpar Corporation.
1. Valpar whole body range of motion work sample
2. Valpar upper extremity range of motion work sample
3. Valpar small tools (mechanical) work sample
4. Valpar eye-hand-foot coordination work sample
5. Valpar clerical comprehension work sample
- volumetry (See K. Schult-Johnson, *Volumetrics: A literature review.* Santa Monica, CA: Upper Extremity Technology, 2210 Santa Monica Blvd. Suite A, 1988.)

PROBLEMS

Motor
- The person may have loss of range of motion.
- The person may have loss of joint mobility.
- The person may have loss of joint stability.
- The person may have loss of grip or pinch strength.
- The person may have loss of hand functions.
- The person may have loss of manipulation skills, dexterity, and bilateral coordination.
- The person may have vasomotor changes, such as changes in skin color and texture.
- The person may have edema and swelling.

Sensory
- The person may have loss of sensory registration in tactile, proprioceptive, pressure, temperature, and vibrator senses.
- The person may have loss of sensory processing, including tactile discrimination and localization.

- The person may have loss of perceptual skills, such as stereognosis and graphesthesia.
- The person may have hypersensitivity, especially touch.

Types of Injuries to the Hand

- joint injuries—puncture, infection, tearing of capsule
- joint dislocations
- joint deformities
- tendon injuries—rupture, tearing of sheath
- tendon dislocations
- bone fractures and dislocations
- nerve compression
- nerve severance (partial or complete)
- muscle weakness
- muscle paralysis (temporary or permanent)
- thermal injuries to the skin and soft tissue (burns, freezing)
- skin and soft tissue injuries—puncture, infection, abrasions
- amputation (traumatic, congenital)
- transplantation or replantation

Cognitive

Cognitive faculties are not usually affected directly by the hand disability, unless it is related to a closed or open head injury.

Intrapersonal

- The person may fear disability or disfigurement.
- The person may be angry at his or her employer or him- or herself for causing the injury.
- The person may fear being unable to return to work.
- The person may experience loss of self-esteem.
- The person may grieve over loss of function.
- The person may become depressed.
- The person may fear changes in role identity.

Interpersonal

- The person may withdraw from family or friends and social activities.
- The person may have changes in social roles.

Self-Care

The person usually is unable to perform some self-care and daily living tasks.

Productivity

- The person is usually unable to work during the acute phase of the disability.
- The person may be unable to continue employment in his or her current job.
- The person may be unable to perform some home-management tasks.

Leisure

The person may be unable to engage in his or her favorite leisure activities.

TREATMENT/MANAGEMENT

Models of treatment are based on biomechanical (Trombly) and orthopedic models.

Motor

- Increase the person's range of motion through daily living activities, creative activities, or prescribed exercises.
- Improve joint mobility through daily living activities.
- Increase grip and pinch strength using exercises on the weighted dumbbells, theraband, grippers, putty, spring-type clothes pins, or other household items and toys.
- Provide practice in the use of hand positions through activities or games that require various hand positions to perform a task.
- Increase coordination and dexterity through games or activities involving manipulation of small pieces or parts.
- Consider splinting to maintain the hand position, prevent deformity or contracture, or improve functional performance.
- Decrease edema and swelling through positioning or splinting.

Sensory

- Provide sensory re-education, if needed.
- Provide desensitization program, if needed.

Cognitive

- Provide instructions on a home program.
- Provide instruction in one-hand activities, if needed, during recovery period.
- Provide factual information on prognosis and outcome of specific injury or surgery.

Intrapersonal

- Encourage the person to express feelings about the appearance of the hand and his or her fears for the future.
- Permit the person to express feelings of anger or guilt about the injury or the situation in which the injury occurred.

Interpersonal

- Through scheduling or participation in a support group, encourage the person to share experiences with other clients who have had similar experiences.
- Encourage the person to continue participation in social activities. Provide ideas or techniques for adapting participation (in leisure activities, for example) if needed.

Self-Care

- Encourage performance of self-care activities.
- Provide self-help devices and training, if needed.

Productivity
- Provide work tolerance or work hardening programs, if needed.
- Provide opportunities to explore other vocational skills and interests if a return to the original job is impossible.
- Make recommendations to employers regarding job modifications that can reduce worker injury.
- Make recommendations for modification of homemaking activities to accommodate temporary or permanent disability.

Leisure
- Make recommendations for modifications of leisure activities for temporary or permanent disability.
- Assist the person to explore new or renew old interests to replace activities that cannot be continued, if necessary.

PRECAUTIONS
- Dynamometers must be recalibrated frequently to provide reliable data.
- A person without protective sensation (decreased proprioception and pressure feedback) tends to use too much force to perform simple activities, such as turning a key in a lock. The result is lacerations, abrasions, or other damage to soft tissue.
- A hand with decreased sensation may be used to grip or pinch objects repetitively beyond the point of tissue tolerance for which normal sensation would provide a warning (pain and redness). The result is blisters and bruises. Adapted grips are especially prone to cause such damage.
- Lack of sensation is usually accompanied by a lack of sweating. The result is dry, cracked skin, which is more likely to be damaged from daily use than skin that is soft and pliable.

Special Precautions for Reduced Sensation in Hand

- Avoid heat, cold, and sharp objects; use gloves.
- Avoid applying more force than necessary to grip a tool or object; consciously monitor grip force.
- Avoid using small handles; build up the handles to increased distribution of pressure over grip surface.
- Avoid holding or using one tool for long periods of time; either change tools frequently or take rest breaks.
- Observe skin for signs of stress, such as redness, edema, or warmth. If blisters, lacerations, or other wounds occur, treat promptly.
- Follow skin care routine daily using soaking and oil massage to keep moisture in skin.

Source: Adapted from Callahan, A.D.. 1990. Methods of compensation and reeducation for sensory dysfunction. In *Rehabilitation of the hand,* 3d ed., ed. J.M. Hunter, et al., 614. St. Louis: C.V. Mosby.

PROGNOSIS AND OUTCOME

- The person demonstrates grip strength within normal range for his or her sex, age, and type of work. (Note: Right-handed dominant people tend to have a 10% stronger grip in the right hand than the left, but left-handed dominant people tend to have equal strength.)
- The person demonstrates functional range of motion in the fingers, thumb, wrist, and forearm.
- The person demonstrates functional hand positions, including pinch and grasp positions.
- The person demonstrates tactile awareness and discrimination.
- The person demonstrates dexterity and coordination using injured hand alone and bilaterally.
- The person is able to perform activities of daily living independently.
- The person is able to perform productive activities.
- The person is able to perform leisure activities.

REFERENCES

Anderson, L.J., and J.M. Anderson. 1988. Hand splinting for infants in the intensive care and special care nurseries. *American Journal of Occupational Therapy* 42(4):222–6.

Barber, L.M. 1984. Desensitization of the traumatized hand. In *Rehabilitation of the hand*, 2d ed., ed. J.M. Hunter, et al., 493–502. St. Louis: C.V. Mosby. 3d ed., 1990, 721–30.

Baxter, P.L., and M.S. Ballard. 1984. Evaluation of the hand by functional tests. In *Rehabilitation of the hand*, 2d ed., ed. J.M. Hunter, et al., 91–100. St. Louis: C.V. Mosby.

Bear-Lehman, J. 1983. Factors affecting return to work after hand injury. *American Journal of Occupational Therapy* 37(3):189–94.

Bear-Lehman, J., and S. Flinn-Wagner. 1987. Hand rehabilitation and occupational therapy: Implications for practice. *Occupational Therapy in Health Care* 4(3/4):7–15.

Bear-Lehman, J., and B.C. Abreu. 1989. Evaluating the hand: Issues in reliability and validity. *Physical Therapy* 69(12):1025–33.

Bell-Krotoski, J.A., D.E. Breger, and R.B. Beach. 1990. Application of biomechanics for evaluation of the hand. In *Rehabilitation of the hand*, 3d ed., ed. J.M. Hunter, et al., 139–66. St. Louis: C.V. Mosby.

Beribak, L., et al. 1984. Trauma splinting. In *Current concepts in orthotics: A diagnostic-related approach,* ed. E.M. Ziegler, 123–65. Menomonee Falls, WI: Roylan Medical Products.

Bittinger, S. 1986. Sprains and joint injuries: Therapist's management. *Hand Clinics* 2(1):99–105.

Brown, D.M., and R.K. Ellis. 1986. Purposeful activities: Yesterday, today, tomorrow. *Physical Disabilities Special Interest Section Newsletter* 9(4):4–5.

Brown, F.E., M.P. Hamlet, and D.G. Tobin. 1990. Acute care and rehabilitation of the hand after cold injury. In *Rehabilitation of the hand*, 3d ed., ed. J.M. Hunter, et al., 858–66. St. Louis: C.V. Mosby.

Byron, P.M., and E.M. Muntzer. 1986. Therapist's management of the mutilated hand. *Hand Clinics* 2(1):69–79.

Colditz, J.C. 1984. Dynamic splinting of the stiff hand. In *Rehabilitation of the hand*, 2d ed., ed. J.M. Hunter, et al., 231–40. St. Louis: C.V. Mosby. Revised in 3d ed., 1990, 342–52.

Cole, I.C. 1988. Principles and guidelines in hand therapy and rehabilitation during recovery from small joint injuries. *Hand Clinics* 4(1):123–31.

Durand, L.G. 1989. Design and preliminary evaluation of a portable instrument for assisting physiotherapists and occupational therapists in the rehabilitation of the hand. *Journal of Rehabilitation Research and Development* 26(2):17–54.

English, C.B., R.A. Rehm, and R.L. Petzoldt. 1982. Slocking splints to assist finger exercise. *American Journal of Occupational Therapy* 36(4):259–62.

Enos, L., R. Lane, and B.A. MacDougal. 1984. Brief or new: The use of self-adherent wrap in hand rehabilitation. *American Journal of Occupational Therapy* 38(4):265–6.

Fess, E.E. 1984. Documentation: Essential elements of an upper extremity assessment battery. In *Rehabilitation of the hand*, 2d ed., ed. J.M. Hunter, et al., 49–78. St. Louis: C.V. Mosby. Revised in 3d ed., 1990, 53–81.

Flinn-Wagner, S., J. Maier, and R.J. Yetman. 1986. Hand rehabilitation: Today and looking ahead. *Clinics in Plastic Surgery* 13(2):301–9.

Grunert, B.K., et al. 1988. Flashbacks after traumatic hand injuries: Prognostic indicators. *Journal of Hand Surgery* 13A:125–7.

tion of the traumatized hand. In *Rehabilitation of the hand*, 3d ed., ed. J.M. Hunter, et al., 721–30. St. Louis: C.V. Mosby.)
- Moberg pick-up test modified by A. Dellon (sensory motor) (See A.D. Callahan. 1990. In *Rehabilitation of the hand*, 3d ed., ed. J.M. Hunter, et al., 606. St. Louis: C.V. Mosby, or A.D. Callahan. 1984. In *Manual on management of specific hand problems,* ed. M.H. Malick and M.C. Kasch, 25. Pittsburgh: AREN Publications.)
- hand function test
- fine motor dexterity tests, such as the Purdue pegboard, and the Pennsylvania Bimanual
- activities of daily living scale
- occupational history
- leisure interest checklist

PROBLEMS

Motor
- The person usually has loss of active and passive range of motion.
- The person usually has decreased grip and pinch strength.
- The person may have loss of specific hand functions, depending on type of injury.
- The person may have disuse atrophy if his or her fingers or thumb have not been used.
- The person may have contractures.

Sensory
- The person may have decreased tactile discrimination.
- The person may have increased hypersensitivity.
- The person may have pain.

Cognitive
Cognitive faculties are not affected directly by the injury or injuries.

Intrapersonal
- The person may express feelings of anger at his or her employer or the situation that caused the accident.
- The person may feel guilty about causing an accident.
- The person may fear that the fingers will be unuseable.
- The person may fear being unable to return to work.
- The person may fear that the hand and fingers will be disfigured.

Interpersonal
- The person may have difficulty participating in some social activities during rehabilitation because of the injury or requirement to wear a splint.
- The person may withdraw from social situations to avoid being seen with an injured hand or fingers in public.

Self-Care
The person may be unable to perform some activities of daily living due to an inability to use the fingers or thumb in the normal or accustomed manner.

Productivity

The person may be unable to perform some productive activities due to an inability to use the affected fingers or thumb in the normal or accustomed manner.

Leisure

The person may be unable to perform some favorite leisure activities due to an inability to use the affected fingers or thumb in the normal or accustomed manner.

TREATMENT/MANAGEMENT

Motor

- Increase the person's range of motion. For one-finger injuries, the involved finger can be taped to an uninvolved finger to increase passive motion.
- Increase the person's muscle strength through the handling of objects of increasing weight or the use of craft activities, such as macramé.
- Increase hand and finger functions through the use of activities that require using various hand positions to perform the activities.
- Consider splinting to maintain finger position, block certain movements, or promote selected movements.

Sensory

- Increase the person's tactile discrimination by using texture sticks or locating objects hidden in sand or a similar substance.
- Decrease hypersensitivity by using levels of desensitization techniques.

Levels of Treatment for the Desensitization of the Hypersensitive Hand

Level	Activity
1	tuning fork vibration paraffin gentle massage
2	battery operated vibration (23 cycles, 53 cycles, 83 cycles, 100 cycles, 125 cycles) friction massage constant touch/pressure
3	electric vibration textures splints
4	electric vibration object identification
5	work simulation

Source: Adapted from Hardy, M.A., C.A. Moran, and W.H. Merritt. 1982. Desensitization of the traumatized hand. *Virginia Medical* 109:134–7.

Samples of Textures and Contact Particles

Textures: burlap, velvet, felt, moleskin, Velcro loops, Velcro hooks, canvas cloth

Contact particles: macaroni, pinto beans, unpopped popcorn, dry rice, cotton, pieces of terry cloth, buckshot, or pebbles

---

Cognitive
- Instruct the person in a home program.
- Instruct the person in one-handed techniques if the injured hand cannot be used to assist in two-handed activities for a period of time.
- Assist the physician in providing factual information to the person about the recovery process of his or her particular type of hand injury or surgery.

Intrapersonal
- Permit the person to express feelings of anger or guilt about the injury or the situation in which the injury occurred.
- Dispel fears of disfigurement, inability to use the hand, or inability to return to work by providing factual information on the prognosis and outcome of the specific injury or surgery.

Interpersonal
Encourage the person to continue participation in social activities. Provide ideas or techniques for adapting participation (in leisure activities, for example) if needed.

Self-Care
Consider providing adapted self-help devices for use until the finger or thumb is healed.

Productivity
- Provide simulated work and home management activities to permit the person to try out the use of the hand or fingers in a controlled environment.
- Assist the person to explore alternative job or career choices if a return to his or her present job or vocation will not be possible.

Leisure
- Suggest alternate techniques or equipment for performing leisure activities, if necessary.
- Assist the person to explore new leisure interests if some favorite leisure activities cannot be continued due to injury.

PRECAUTIONS

If a splint is used, check frequently to assure proper fit and avoid skin or circulation damage.

PROGNOSIS AND OUTCOME

* The person demonstrates grip and pinch strength within normal range for his or her sex, age, and type of work.
* The person demonstrates functional range of motion in the fingers, thumb, and wrist.
* The person demonstrates functional hand positions including pinch and grasp positions.
* The person demonstrates manipulation skills, coordination, and dexterity in the injured hand alone and bilaterally.
* The person demonstrates tactile awareness and discrimination.
* The person is able to perform self-care skills independently.
* The person is able to perform productive activities.
* The person is able to perform leisure activities.

REFERENCES

Bell, J.A. 1984. Plaster cylinder casting for contractures of the interphalangeal joints. In *Rehabilitation of the hand*, 2d ed., ed. J.M. Hunter, et al., 875–80. St. Louis: C.V. Mosby.

Callahan, A.D., and P. McEntee. 1986. Splinting proximal interphalangeal joint contractures: A new design. *American Journal of Occupational Therapy* 40(6):408–13.

Casanova, J.S. 1989. Adult prehension: Patterns and nomenclature for pinches. *Journal of Hand Therapy* 2(4):231–44.

Colditz, J.C. 1983. Low profile dynamic splinting of the injured hand. *American Journal of Occupational Therapy* 37(3):182–8.

Colditz, J.C. 1984. Spring-wire splinting of the proximal interphalangeal joint. In *Rehabilitation of the hand*, 2d ed., ed. J.M. Hunter, et al., 862–74. St. Louis: C.V. Mosby.

Colditz, J.C. 1990. Anatomic considerations for splinting the thumb. In *Rehabilitation of the hand*, 3d ed., ed. J.M. Hunter, et al., 353–63. St. Louis: C.V. Mosby.

Dovelle, S., P.I. Heeter, and T.V. McFault. 1988. A dynamic finger flexion loop. *American Journal of Occupational Therapy* 42(8):535–7.

Dovelle, S., et al. 1988. Early controlled motion following flexor tendon graft. *American Journal of Occupational Therapy* 42(7):457–63.

Heithoff, S.J., L.H. Millender, and J. Helman. 1988. Bowstringing as a complication of trigger finger release. *Journal of Hand Surgery* 13A:567–70.

Kappel, D.A., and J.G. Durech. 1985. The cross-finger flap: An established reconstructive procedure. *Hand Clinics* 1(2):247–57.

McPhee, S.D. 1987. Extension block splinting for the proximal interphalangeal joint. *American Journal of Occupational Therapy* 41(6):389–90.

Parks, B.J., K.P. Barrett, and K. Voss. 1983. The use of Hexcelite in splinting the thumb. *American Journal of Occupational Therapy* 37(4):266–7.

Patel, M.R., S.S. Desai, and L. Bassini-Pipson. 1986. Conservative management of chronic mallet finger. *Journal of Hand Surgery* 11A(4):570–3.

Peimer, C.A., D.J. Sullivan, and D.R. Wild. 1984. Palmar dislocation of the proximal interphalangeal joint. *Journal of Hand Surgery* 9A:39–48.

Pidgeon, K.J., P. Abadee, R. Kanakamedala, et al. 1985. Posterior interosseous nerve syndrome caused by an intermuscular lipoma. *Archives of Physical Medicine and Rehabilitation* 66(7):168–71.

Robinson, S.M., and S.D. McPhee. 1986. Case report: Treating the patient with digital hypersensitivity. *American Journal of Occupational Therapy* 40(4):285–7.

Singer, M., and S. Maloon. 1988. Flexor tendon injuries: the results of primary repair. *Journal of Hand Surgery (Br)* 13(3):269–72.

Swanson, A.B., J.B. Leonar, and G.D. Swanson. 1986. Implant resection arthroplasty of the finger joints. *Hand Clinics* 2(1):107–17.

Hands—Tendon Injuries

DESCRIPTION

These injuries are defined as lacerations, avulsion-type injuries, and crush injuries to the flexor or extensor tendons of the hand. The injury may occur primarily to the tendons, but more often it is accompanied by fractures, nerve injuries, and soft tissue damage.

CAUSE

The most frequent causes of these tendon injuries are work-related or sports activities; however, injuries resulting from knives, glass, or other sharp objects also occur. Injury may occur because the tendon is overstretched or ruptured, or the tendon and part of its insertion onto the bone is avulsed or fractured, or the epiphysis is slipped from the bone shaft.

ASSESSMENT

Areas
- range of motion (Measure active range of motion, passive range of motion, total active motion for digits, and total passive motion for digits.)
- muscle testing
- grip and pinch strength
- edema
- hand functions
- daily living tasks
- productivity history, skills, interests, and values
- leisure interests and skills

Instruments
- goniometer (See N. Cannon. 1984. Tendon injuries. In *Manual on management of specific hand problems*, ed. M.H. Malick and M.C. Kasch, 32–5. Pittsburgh: American Rehabilitation Educational Network Publications.)
- manual muscle test (See N. Cannon. 1984. Tendon injuries. In *Manual on management of specific hand problems*, ed. M.H. Malick and M.C. Kasch, 36–7 Pittsburgh: American Rehabilitation Educational Network Publications.)
- dynamometer and pinch meters (See American Society for Surgery of the Hand. 1990. *The hand: Examination and diagnosis*, 3d ed., 121–2. New York: Churchill Livingstone.)
- volumeter (See N. Cannon. 1984. Tendon injuries. In *Manual on management of specific hand problems*, ed. M.H. Malick and M.C. Kasch, 39. Pittsburgh: American Rehabilitation Educational Network Publications.)
- Jebsen Hand Function Test (See R.H. Jebsen, N. Taylor, R.B. Trieschmann, et al. 1969. An objective and standardized test of hand function. *Archives of Physical Medicine and Rehabilitation* 50:311–319.)

- Froment's sign—forceful lateral pinch of the thumb against the lateral border of the index finger (See American Society for Surgery of the Hand. 1990. *The hand: Examination and diagnosis*, 3d ed., 29. New York: Churchill Livingstone.)
- activities of daily living scale
- occupational history
- leisure checklist

PROBLEMS

Motor

- flexor tendon injuries of the hand.
  1. Zone I (jersey finger)—lack of active flexion of the distal interphalangeal joint, most commonly in the ring finger
  2. Zone II—lack of active flexion of the proximal interphalangeal joint
  3. Zones III, IV, and V—lack of active flexion of fingers at all joints
- extensor tendon injuries of the hand
  1. mallet finger
     (a) inability to actively extend the distal interphalangeal (DIP) joint
     (b) may have flexion deformity
  2. boutonniere deformity
     (a) hyperextension of the metacarpophalangeal joint
     (b) flexion of proximal interphalangeal (PIP) joint
     (c) hyperextension of the distal interphalangeal joint
  3. dislocation of extensor digitorum communis hood
     (a) incomplete active extension

Flexor Zones of the Hand

Zone I—includes the fingertips, DIP joint, and distal half between the DIP and PIP joint

Zone II—includes the proximal half between the DIP and PIP joint, the PIP joint, the MCP point to the palmar crease

Zone III—includes the space between the palmar crease to a line drawn across the palm at the distal point where the thumb joins the hand

Zone IV—includes the space between the line drawn across the palm at the distal point where the thumb joins the hand to the crease at the wrist

Zone V—begins at the crease at the wrist up the forearm

Source: Based on Cannon, N.M. 1984. Tendon injuries. In *Manual on management of specific hand problems*, ed. M.H. Malick and M.C. Kasch, 44. Pittsburgh: American Rehabilitation Educational Network Publications.

Extensor Zones of the Hand

Zone I—distal interphalangeal joints of digits 2 to 5

Zone II—space between the distal and proximal interphalangeal joints of digits 2 to 5

Zone III—proximal interphalangeal joints of digits 2 to 5

Zone IV—space between the proximal interphalangeal joints and the metacarpal phalangeal joints of digits 2 to 5

Zone V—metacarpal phalangeal joints

Zone VI—space between the metacarpal phalangeal joints and the carpal bones of the wrist

Zone VII—carpal bones of the wrist

Source: Based on Cannon, N.M. 1984. Tendon injuries. In *Manual on management of specific hand problems*, ed. M.H. Malick and M.C. Kasch, 60. Pittsburgh: American Rehabilitation Educational Network Publications.

Zones of the Thumb

Zone T I—interphalangeal joint

Zone T II—space between the interphalangeal joint and the metacarpal phalangeal joint

Zone T III—metacarpal phalangeal joint

Zone T IV—space between the metacarpal phalangeal joint and the carpal bones of the wrist

Zone T V—area of the carpal bones on the thumb side

Sensory
- The person may have tenderness to touch.
- The person may experience pain with or without movement.

Cognitive

There are no specific cognitive problems related directly to the tendon injury.

Intrapersonal
- The person may express feelings of anger at his or her employer or the situation that caused the accident.
- The person may feel guilty about causing an accident.
- The person may fear that his or her fingers will be unuseable.
- The person may fear being unable to return to work.
- The person may fear that his or her hand and fingers will be disfigured.

Interpersonal
- The person may have difficulty participating in some social activities during rehabilitation because of the injury or a requirement to wear a splint.
- The person may withdraw from social situations to avoid being seen with an injured hand or fingers in public.

Self-Care
   The person may be unable to perform some activities of daily living due to an inability to use the fingers in the normal or accustomed manner.

Productivity
   The person is usually unable to perform some productive activities due to an inability to use the injured fingers in the normal or accustomed manner.

Leisure
   The person may be unable to perform some favorite leisure activities due to an inability to use the injured fingers in the normal or accustomed manner.

TREATMENT/MANAGEMENT

Motor
- flexor tendon repairs—single digit (Mason and Allen method, 1941. See Kuxhau in the reference section.)
  1. No treatment for three weeks while the hand and wrist are immobilized in flexion with a postoperative dressing.
  2. At three weeks, an extension blocking splint is applied after the dressing is removed.
  3. Active flexion exercises are initiated within the limits of the extension blocking splint, consisting of eight to ten repetitions of DIP and PIP flexion and five to ten full finger flexion repetitions.
  4. Scar massage is applied along the length of the healing incision beginning with gentle massage and increasing as the person can tolerate it in order to decrease adhesions.
  5. At four weeks, exercises are performed without the splint.
  6. At six to seven weeks, range of motion can be assessed to determine the amount of tendon gliding present.
  7. The person begins to use hand in light activities of daily living.
  8. Gradually the exercises are increased and the blocking splint is changed to permit more range of motion, but strenuous exercise and prolonged gripping is not permitted.
  9. At twelve weeks, the person is allowed unrestricted use of the hand and finger.
- flexor tendon repairs and controlled motion (Washington regimen.) (See Dovelle and Heeter, 1989, in the reference section.)
  1. No treatment for two to three days while hand is immobilized in bulky dressing and plaster splint.
  2. At three days after surgery, the dressing and splint are removed and a thermoplastic dynamic flexion assist splint (extension blocking splint) is made, which allows 2 to 3 mm of tendon glide. The wrist is positioned in 45 degrees of flexion and the metacarpal

phalangeal joint at 40 degrees flexion for tendon injuries in zones 1 to 4. For injuries to tendons in zone 5, the positions are 20 degrees of flexion in the wrist and 60 degrees of flexion in the metacarpal phalangeal joint. The splint is held by soft strapping material applied at the distal palmar crease, at the volar wrist crease, and midway on the forearm, and fastened by Velcro tabs. A palmar pulley dynamic traction system is constructed using safety pins attached to the straps on the forearm and distal palmar crease. A clothing hook is attached to the fingernail and a pulley is constructed of 10 lb. test nylon monofilament line and one and one-half #18 rubber bands. The splint and pulley are worn 24 hours per day for 28 days.

3. Active extension and passive flexion exercises are initiated using a single (half) rubber band strand (the double or full rubber band is removed). The person actively extends against the rubber band ten times every hour during waking hours. After each set of exercises the double rubber band is reattached. The exercises continue for four weeks.

4. The therapist applies passive flexion to extend the metacarpal phalangeal joints into full flexion (90 degrees) and simultaneously extends the proximal and distal interphalangeal joints for the first two weeks.

5. At five weeks, active extension and active flexion exercises begin and continue through the sixth week, beginning with gentle flexion. The rubber band traction is removed during the exercises. The person attempts to touch the distal crease in the palm with the fingertip 10 times. Also the person learns to passively flex the finger joints using the other (noninvolved) hand. Light activities of daily living may be started.

6. At six weeks, the dorsal splint is modified so the wrist is in a neutral position and the metacarpal phalangeal joints are in 20 degrees of flexion.

7. At seven weeks, the splint is removed. Hand activities are encouraged, but lifting is limited to 5 lbs. or less until the end of the 12th week.

8. At eight weeks, isolated blocking exercises of the involved fingers is begun, and deep friction massage over the scar is encouraged to break down scar adhesions.

• Extensor tendon repair and controlled motion (See S. Dovelle, et al., 1989, in the reference section.)

1. After surgery, the hand is wrapped in a bulky postoperative dressing with the wrist in 45 degrees dorsiflexion and the metacarpal phalangeal joints in 30 degrees flexion. The interphalangeal joints are not restricted.

2. On day two, a thermoplastic extension assist splint is designed. The static component maintains the wrist in 45 degrees dorsiflexion. The dynamic component holds the injured finger in +10 degrees hypertension at rest through the use of an outrigger with a monofilament line attached to a rubber band. The dynamic component permits full passive extension of the metacarpal phalangeal joint of the injured finger. Flexion of the digit is not restricted.

3. Active controlled motion exercises are begun immediately. The metacarpal phalangeal joint is to be flexed to 15 degrees 10 times every waking hour. A marker on the monofilament line indicates when the 15 degrees of flexion are obtained.

4. At postoperative day eight, the range of motion is increased to 30 degrees active flexion of the metacarpal phalangeal joint to allow 3 to 5 mm of tendon glide to avoid tendon adhesions. The frequency and number of repetitions remains the same.

5. At postoperative day 15, the range of active flexion is increased to 45 degrees at the metacarpal phalangeal joint. Unrestricted active flexion of the noninjured interphalangeal joints is permitted. Passive range of motion to the interphalangeal joints

of the injured finger is provided to decrease joint stiffness and prevent tendon adhesions.

6. At postoperative day 22, the range of active flexion is increased to 60 degrees at the metacarpal phalangeal joint.
7. At postoperative day 29, the person is permitted to make a fist and begin to actively extend the injured finger while in the dynamic extension splint.
8. At five weeks, the splint is removed and active extension of the middle finger is continued without the protection of the splint. An example exercise is to place the hand on a table, palm down, and hyperextend the injured finger from the table surface 10 times during every waking hour, and make a fist 10 times per hour. Light activities of daily living are encouraged, such as grooming, bathing, and dressing, but heavy resistive activities are not permitted.
9. At 12 weeks, unresisted activity is permitted.

• Flexor tenolysis surgery (removal of the peritendinous adhensions) (See Cannon, 1989, in the reference section.)

1. The hand is wrapped in a bulky compressive dressing postoperatively to decrease edema. Digits are positioned in a semi-flexed position.
2. At day one, bulky dressing is removed. Edema is controlled with light compressive dressings or Coban wraps. Controlled active and passive exercises are initiated, which must be done hourly during waking hours. Each position should be held for five seconds. The exercises should be completed as follows:
   (a) active wrist and finger flexion before active wrist and finger extension
   (b) active finger flexion before intrinsic minus position (metacarpal phalangeal joints extended and interphalangeal joints flexed), followed by full extension of the fingers
   (c) blocking exercises to the proximal and distal phalangeal joints of individual fingers to determine independent glide of both the flexor digitorum superficialis (FDS) and flexor digitorum profundus (FDP) muscle tendons
   (d) isolated blocking of the interphalangeal joint to allow for independent adaptations or modifications of job tasks that might enable the person to function satisfactorily in the job situation
3. A static extension positioning splint is recommended between exercises and for night wear.
4. At six to eight weeks, gentle strengthening exercises should begin using a hand exerciser or gripper, nerf ball, or putty. Strengthening may be delayed if tendons do not show good strength in active exercises without resistance.

Sensory
• The person may need a pain-management program.
• The person may need desensitization of the scar area.

Cognitive
• The person must be fully informed regarding the requirements of the program, the rationale for each exercise, the purpose of the splint, and the care and maintenance of the splint.

- The person must know the signs of problems in the healing process or skin damage caused by improper fit of the splint, and he or she must know how to report the problems promptly.

Intrapersonal
- Permit the person to express feelings of anger or guilt about the injury or situation in which the injury occurred.
- Dispel fears of disfigurement, inability to use the hand, or inability to return to work by providing factual information on the prognosis and outcome of the specific injury or surgery.

Interpersonal
Encourage the person to continue participation in social activities. Provide ideas or techniques for adapting participation (in leisure activities, for example) if needed.

Self-Care
- Consider providing self-help devices or adapted equipment for use until the hand or finger is healed.
- Consider instructing the person in the use of one-hand techniques to permit functional performance until the injured hand is healed or recovered from surgery.

Productivity
- Temporary job modification or reassignment may permit some persons to work during recovery.
- Provide simulated work and home-management activities to permit the person to try out the use of his or her hand or fingers in a controlled environment.
- Assist the person to explore alternative job or career choices if a return to his or her present job or vocation is not possible.

Leisure
- Suggest alternate techniques or equipment for performing leisure activities, if needed.
- Assist the person to explore new leisure interests if some favorite leisure activities cannot be continued due to the nature of the injury.

PRECAUTIONS
- Application of controlled stress to the healing tendon must be carefully evaluated both in timing (number of days since surgery) and excursion of the tendon relative to the movement of the joint.
- Stress to the person the importance of following the exercise plan carefully to avoid active, heavy resistive movements until healing has occurred to reduce chances of tendon rupture.
- Watch for signs of inflammation and synovitis.

PROGNOSIS AND OUTCOME
- The person has full range of motion in injured or surgically repaired tendons.

- The person has normal muscle strength in the affected muscles.
- The person has normal hand functions.
- The person has normal manipulation, dexterity, and bilateral coordination skills.
- The person does not report pain or hypersensitivity to touch.
- The person is able to perform self-care skills independently.
- The person is able to perform productive activities.
- The person is able to perform leisure activities.

REFERENCES

Browne, E.Z., and C.A. Ribik. 1989. Early dynamic splinting for extensor tendon injuries. *Journal of Hand Surgery* 14A:72–6.
Burkhalter, W.E., et al. 1987. Rehabilitation: Flexor and extensor tendons. In *Tendon surgery in the hand*, ed. J.M. Hunter, L.H. Schneider, and E.J. Mackin, 558–82. St. Louis: C.V. Mosby (panel discussion).
Cannon, N.M. 1984. Tendon injuries. In *Manual on management of specific hand problems*, ed. M.H. Malick and M.C. Kasch, 31–70. Pittsburgh: American Rehabilitation Educational Network Publications.
Cannon, N.M. 1989. Enhancing flexor tendon glide through tenolysis…and hand therapy. *Journal of Hand Therapy* 2(2):112–37.
Cannon, N.M., and J.W. Strickland. 1985. Therapy following flexor tendon surgery. *Hand Clinics* 1(1):147–65.
Chow, J.A., L.J. Thomes, S. Dovelle, et al. 1987. A combined regimen of controlled motion following flexor tendon repair in "no man's land." *Plastic and Reconstructive Surgery* 79(3):447–55.
Chow, J.A., L.H. Thomes, S. Dovelle, et al. 1988. Controlled motion rehabilitation after flexor tendon repair and grafting. A multi-centre study. *Journal of Bone and Joint Surgery (Br)* 70(4):591–5.
Chow, J.A., S. Dovelle, L.J. Thomes, et al. 1989. A comparison of results of extensor tendon repair followed by early controlled mobilisation versus static immobilisation. *Journal of Hand Surgery (Br)* 14B(1):18–20.
Dovelle, S., and P.K. Heeter. 1985. Early controlled mobilization following extensor tendon repair in zone V-VI of the hand: Preliminary report. *Contemporary Orthopedics* 11(4):41–4.
Dovelle, S., and P.K. Heeter. 1989. The Washington regimen: Rehabilitation of the hand following flexor tendon injuries. *Physical Therapy* 69(12):1034–40.
Dovelle, S., P.K. Heeter, and R.D. Phillips. 1987. A dynamic traction splint for management of extrinsic tendon tightness. *American Journal of Occupational Therapy* 41(2):123–5.
Dovelle, S., P.K. Heeter, and T.V. McFaul. 1988. A dynamic finger flexion loop. *American Journal of Occupational Therapy* 42(8):535–7.
Dovelle, S., P.K. Heeter, D.R. Fischer, et al. 1989. Rehabilitation of extensor tendon injury of the hand by means of early controlled motion. *American Journal of Occupational Therapy* 43(2):115–9.
Evans, R.B., and W.E. Burkhalter. 1986. A study of the dynamic anatomy of extensor tendons and implications for treatment. *Journal of Hand Surgery* 11A(5):774–9.
Evans, R.B. 1986. Therapeutic management of extensor tendon injuries. *Hand Clinics* 2(1):157–69.
Evans, R.B. 1989. Management of the healing tendon…What must we question? *Journal of Hand Therapy* 2(2):61–5.
Evans R.B. 1989. Clinical application of controlled stress to the healing extensor tendon: A review of 112 cases. *Physical Therapy* 69(12):1041–9.
Hunter, J.M., S.M. Blackmore, and A.D. Callahan. 1989. Flexor tendon salvage and functional redemption using the Hunter tendon implant and the superficialis finger operation. *Journal of Hand Therapy* 2(2):107–13.
Kuxhau, M. 1984. Flexor and extensor tendon repairs. In *Current concepts in orthotics: A diagnostic-related approach*, ed. E.M. Ziegler, 49–78. Menomonee Falls, WI: Roylan Medical Products.
Lopez, M.S., and K.F. Hanley. 1984. Splint modification for flexor tendon repairs. *American Journal of Occupational Therapy* 38(6):398–402.
Saldana, M.J., P.K. Ho, D.M. Lichtman, et al. 1987. Flexor tendon repair and rehabilitation in zone II, open sheath technique versus closed sheath technique. *Journal of Hand Surgery (Am)* 12(6):1110–4.
Schneider, L.H., and P. McEntee. 1986. Flexor tendon injuries: Treatment of the acute problem. *Hand Clinics*, 2(1):119–31.
Stone, R.G., E.L. Spencer, and E.E. Almquist. 1989. An evaluation of early motion management following primary flexor tendon repair: Zones 1-3. *Journal of Hand Therapy* 2(4):223–30.
Wehbe, M.A. 1987. Tendon gliding exercises. *American Journal of Occupational Therapy* 41(3):164–7.

Hands—Tendon Transfers

DESCRIPTION

Tendons usually are transferred to improve the function of a movement pattern that is weak due to injury or disease. An example is the transfer of the brachioradialis to the extensor carpi radialis brevis, which is performed to obtain or augment wrist extension strength and provide useful tenodesis function of the hand.

CAUSE

The decision to transfer tendons depends on multiple factors. The primary reasons for transfers in the hand are to regain opposition of the thumb and fingers, to regain thumb adduction for lateral pinch, to resolve claw hand, to regain finger or thumb flexion, or to regain finger and thumb extension.

ASSESSMENT

Areas

- range of motion (Measure active range of motion, passive range of motion, total active motion for digits, and total passive motion for digits.)
- muscle testing
- grip and pinch strength
- edema
- hand functions
- daily living skills
- productivity history, skills, interests, and values
- leisure interests and skills

Instruments

- goniometer (See N. Cannon. 1984. Tendon injuries. In *Manual on management of specific hand problems*, ed. M.H. Malick and M.C. Kasch, 32–5. Pittsburgh: American Rehabilitation Educational Network Publications. See also American Society for Surgery of the Hand. 1983. *The hand: Examination and diagnosis*, 2d ed., 106–11. Edinburgh, Scotland: Churchill Livingstone.)
- manual muscle test (See N. Cannon. 1984. Tendon injuries. In *Manual on management of specific hand problems*, ed. M.H. Malick and M.C. Kasch, 36–7. Pittsburgh: American Rehabilitation Educational Network Publications. See also American Society for Surgery of the Hand. 1990. *The hand: Examination and diagnosis*, 3d ed. Edinburgh, Scotland: Churchill Livingstone.)
- dynamometer and pinch meters (See American Society for Surgery of the Hand. 1990. *The hand: Examination and diagnosis*, 3d ed., 121–2. Edinburgh, Scotland: Churchill Livingstone.)
- volumeter (See N. Cannon. 1984. Tendon injuries. In *Manual on management of specific*

hand problems, ed. M.H. Malick and M.C. Kasch, 39. Pittsburgh: American Rehabilitation Educational Network Publications.)
- Jebsen Hand Function Test (See R.H. Jebsen, N. Taylor, R.B. Trieschmann, et al. 1969. An objective and standardized test of hand function. *Archives of Physical Medicine and Rehabilitation* 50:311–9.)
- Froment's sign (forceful lateral pinch of the thumb against the lateral border of the index finger) (See American Society for Surgery of the Hand. 1983. *The hand: Examination and diagnosis*, 3d ed., 29. Edinburgh, Scotland: Churchill Livingstone.)
- activities of daily living scale
- occupational history
- leisure checklist

PROBLEMS

Motor
- low median nerve palsy:
  1. paralysis of the thenar muscles (abductor pollicis brevis, opponens pollicis, flexor pollicis brevis, and lumbricals)
  2. inability of the thumb to abduct, pronate, flex, or oppose
  3. inability to use the thumb in opposition to grasp or release objects
- low ulnar nerve palsy:
  1. paralysis of the adductor pollicis (oblique and transverse fibers), deep head of the flexor pollicus brevis, lumbricals to the ring and small fingers, dorsal and volar interossei, and hypothenar muscles (adductor digiti quinti, flexor digiti quinti, and opponens digiti quinti)
  2. inability to pinch a piece of paper between the thumb and lateral border of the index finger (Froment's test)
  3. subluxation of the metacarpal phalangeal joint and hyperflexion of the interphalangeal joint
- low median and ulnar nerve palsy:
  1. paralysis of all the lumbricals and dorsal and volar interossei muscles
  2. hand position is hyperextension of the metacarpal phalangeal joint and flexion of the interphalangeal joints
  3. when finger flexion is attempted, the interphalangeal joints must flex completely before the metacarpal phalangeal joints can be flexed
- high median and ulnar nerve palsy such as C6-7 quadriplegia:
  1. paralysis of all the lumbricals and dorsal and volar interossei muscles
  2. loss of flexion of the interphalangeal joints of the thumb
  3. hand position is hyperextension of the metacarpal phalangeal joints and flexion of the interphalangeal joints
- dorsal tendon loss in the hand:
  1. paralysis of the extensors to the metacarpal phalangeal joints of the fingers and interphalangeal joints
  2. inability to actively extend the fingers
  3. inability to release objects by extending the fingers
- C5 quadriplegia—poor wrist extension:

1. zero to fair strength in active wrist extensors
2. fair-plus to normal deltoid and biceps strength
- C6 quadriplegia—poor elbow extension:
1. lack of active elbow extension
2. weak prehension strength

Sensory
Sensory registration of tactile, temperature, pressure, and proprioception may be decreased.

Cognitive
Cognitive faculties are not specifically involved in the disorder, although overall intelligence is a consideration in the decision to transfer.

Intrapersonal
- The person may be anxious about the surgery or outcome.
- The person may express fear of disfigurement.

Self-Care
Problems in the performance of self-care activities are major factors in the decision to recommend a tendon transfer.

Productivity
Problems in the performance of productive activities are major factors in the decision to recommend a tendon transfer.

Leisure
Problems in the performance of leisure activities are considerations in the decision to recommend a tendon transfer.

TREATMENT/MANAGEMENT

Motor
- median nerve correction—surgical transfer of flexor digitorum sublimis tendon from the ring (fourth) finger around the flexor carpi ulnaris (which acts as a pulley) to the abductor pollicis brevis for insertion (Note: Other transfers include use of the flexor digitorum sublimis to the base of the proximal phalanx, extensor indicus proprius to the proximal phalanx of the thumb, abductor digiti quini to insertion on the abductor policis brevis, and palmaris longus to the radial side of the metacarpal joint.)
1. No treatment for three and one-half to four weeks while hand remains in compressive dressing with the wrist in slight palmar flexion and thumb in abduction.
2. At three and one-half to four weeks the person is fitted with a dorsal blocking splint with wrist in 30 degrees palmar flexion and thumb in 45 degrees of abduction, opposite to the index finger, and the person is encouraged to grasp light cylindrical objects (plastic cups or cones) and perform isolated finger to thumb opposition exercises. Passive and active range of motion activities are to be performed every hour.

3. At six weeks, the splint is removed and functional activities requiring grasp and release patterns are encouraged.

4. At eight weeks, functional hand use is encouraged through muscle strengthening and performance of hand activities related to the person's activities of daily living, work, and leisure.

- ulnar nerve correction—surgical transfer of the extensor carpi radialis longus (ECRL) tendon routed through the third and fourth metacarpals and inserted into the adductor pollicis (Note: Other transfers include transfer of the flexor digitorum sublimis to the base of the adductor pollicus and extensor pollicis longus, transfer of the extensor digiti quinti to the adductor pollicis and first dorsal interossei, and transfer of the extensor indicis proprius to the adductor pollicis.)

  1. No treatment for four weeks while the hand remains in compressive dressing with the wrist in slight dorsiflexion and the thumb in 30 degrees abduction.

  2. At four weeks, a dorsal blocking splint is applied to hold the hand in the same position as the dressing (slight dorsiflexion of the wrist and 30 degrees abduction of the thumb). Passive and active range of motion activities are performed every hour, which require thumb adduction and lateral pinch to pick up and hold light objects.

  3. At six weeks, the splint is removed and functional activities are graded to increase resistance to thumb adduction and lateral pinch.

- low median and ulnar nerve correction—surgical transfer of the extensor carpi radialis longus elongated with a plantaris graft and splint into four parts, which are slid through the carpal canal to the volar side of the hand following the course of each lumbrical for insertion into the lateral bands of each digit except the index, which is inserted into the ulnar lateral band (Brand transfer) (Other transfers include the Stiles-Bunnell, Lasso procedure by Zancolli, and Goldner.)

  1. No treatment for four and one-half weeks while the hand remains in compressive dressing with the wrist in 30 to 40 degrees flexion, the metacarpal phalangeal joints in full flexion, and the interphalangeal joints extended.

  2. At four and one-half weeks, a dorsal blocking splint is made to hold the wrist in 30 degrees flexion, the metacarpal phalangeal joints in 65 to 70 degrees of flexion, and the interphalangeal joints in extension. No passive flexion is permitted to avoid stretching the transfer insertion into the lateral band. Active range of motion is encouraged with the limits of the splint.

  3. At six weeks, the splint is reduced to a metacarpal phalangeal extension block and is worn between exercise periods and at night. Active and passive range of motion activities are performed with the wrist and fingers.

  4. At eight weeks, the splint is discontinued. The person is encouraged to perform functional activities with the hand and increase muscle strength.

- high median and ulnar nerve correction—surgical transfer of the extensor carpi radialis longus, which is brought radially around the forearm and inserted into the tendons of the flexor digitorum profundus, and surgical transfer of the brachioradialis into the flexor pollicis longus

  1. No treatment for three and one-half weeks while the hand remains in postoperative dressing positioned in 30 degrees of wrist flexion, metacarpal phalangeal joints in 50 degrees flexion, and the interphalangeal joints in extension. The elbow should be in 90 degrees flexion.

  2. At three and one-half weeks, a dorsal blocking splint is made to hold the wrist flexed at

30 degrees, metacarpal phalangeal joints at 50 degrees, interphalangeal joints in extension, and the interphalangeal joints of thumb in slight flexion. Active and passive range of motion activities are started.

3. At six weeks, the splint is discontinued.

- digital extension—surgical transfer of the flexor carpi ulnaris, which is brought around ulnarly and dorsally and inserted in the tendons of the extensor digitorum communis

  1. No treatment for four and one-half weeks while the hand remains in postoperative dressing positioned in wrist and digit extension.
  2. At four and one-half weeks, an extension resting pan splint is made to position the wrist in 15 degrees of dorsiflexion, 10 degrees flexion at the metacarpal phalangeal joints, and extension of the interphalangeal joints.
  3. At eight weeks, the splint is discontinued.

- C5 quadriplegia (poor wrist extension)—surgical transfer of the brachioradialis to the extensor carpi radialis brevis

  1. The protected position is 30 degrees of wrist extension and 90 degrees of elbow flexion.
  2. At three weeks, passive range of motion and light activities are permitted.
  3. At six weeks, normal activities are permitted.

- C6 quadriplegia (poor elbow extension)—surgical transfer of the posterior deltoid to the triceps

  1. The protected position is full elbow extension and shoulder abduction.
  2. Through weeks four to six, the elbow flexion is increased 10 to 15 degrees each week.
  3. An elbow flexion block orthosis is used to limit elbow flexion to a present angle but allow full extension.
  4. Movements in passive range of motion or active activities can be monitored through palpation or biofeedback.
  5. Activities should be graded for increased endurance, coordination, and strength up to the 12th week.
  6. Activities should be balanced between static and dynamic activities. Static activities to increase endurance and maintain grasp include writing, drawing, and painting. Dynamic activities to promote active grasp and release include such games and crafts as chess or checkers, puzzles, stringing beads, or mosaics.

Sensory

- Sensory re-education may be necessary as part of the total hand rehabilitation program.
- Desensitization of the scar areas may be needed.

Cognitive

- Instruct the person in a home program.
- Provide instructions on one-handed activities, if needed, during recovery period.
- Assist the physician in providing factual information to the person about the recovery process of his or her particular tendon transfer procedure.

Intrapersonal

Permit the person to express concerns about how well the transfer will perform.

Self-Care
Encourage the performance of self-care activities as healing permits.

Productivity
Encourage the performance of productive activities as healing permits.

Leisure
Encourage the performance of leisure activities as healing permits.

PRECAUTIONS
- Do not overstretch joints through passive range of motion in early stages of postoperative recovery (about three to four and one-half weeks depending on the type of transfer).
- Check joints for tendon gliding action once extensor or dorsal blocking splints are removed. If gliding action is limited, consider initiating tendon gliding activities.

PROGNOSIS AND OUTCOME
- The person will have all movement patterns of which the hand is capable.
- The person will have muscle strength within normal limits in hand movement patterns.
- The person will be able to perform functional activities of daily living.
- The person will be able to perform essential hand tasks in work settings.
- The person will be able to perform functional hand tasks in leisure activities.

REFERENCES

Ainsley, J., C. Voorhees, and E. Drake. 1985. Reconstructive hand surgery for quadriplegic persons. *American Journal of Occupational Therapy* 39(11):715–21.

Bell-Krotoski, J.A. 1990. Preoperative and postoperative management of tendon transfers after ulnar nerve injury. In *Rehabilitation of the hand*, 3d ed., ed. J.M. Hunter, et al., 676–95. St. Louis: C.V. Mosby.

Horowitz, E.R., and P.T. Casler. 1986. Replantation. In *Hand rehabilitation*, ed. C.A. Moran, 91–116. New York: Churchill Livingstone.

Kelly, C.M., A.A. Freehalfer, P.H. Peckham, et al. 1985. Postoperative results of opponensplasty and flexor tendon transfer in patients with spinal cord injuries. *Journal of Hand Surgery* 10A(6 Pt.1):890–4.

Robbins, F., and T. Reece. 1985. Hand rehabilitation after great toe transfer for thumb reconstruction. *Archives of Physical Medicine and Rehabilitation* 66(2):109–11.

Rosenblum, N.I., and S.J. Robinson. 1986. Advances in flexor and extensor tendon management. In *Hand rehabilitation*, ed. C.A. Moran, 17–44. New York: Churchill Livingstone.

Schuster, K.D. 1987. Pre- and postoperative occupational therapy for a toe to hand transplantation. *Occupational Therapy in Health Care* 4(3/4):125–33.

Silverman, P.M., V. Willette-Gree, and J. Petrilli. 1989. Early protective motion in digital revascularization and replantation. *Journal of Hand Therapy* 2(2):84–101.

Smith, R.J., et al. 1987. Rehabilitation: Tendon transfers. In *Tendon surgery in the hand*, ed. J.M. Hunter, L.H. Schneider, and E.J. Mackin, 663–84. St. Louis: C.V. Mosby.

Toth, S. 1986. Therapist's management of tendon transfers. *Hand Clinics* 2(1):329–46.

Verran, A.G., J.M. Baumgarten, and K. Paris. 1987. Occupational therapy management of tendon transfers in persons with spinal cord injury quadriplegia. *Occupational Therapy in Health Care* 4(3/4):155–69.

Head Injuries

DESCRIPTION

Head injuries may result from penetration of the skull or from rapid acceleration or deceleration of the brain, which injures tissue at the point of impact, at the opposite pole (contrecoup), and along the frontal and temporal lobes. In addition, nerve tissue, blood vessels, and meninges may be torn or ruptured, resulting in disruption of neural transmission, intra- or extracerebral ischemia, hemorrhage, and cerebral edema. An alternate name is traumatic brain injury (TBI).

CAUSE

Automobile, motorcycle, or off-road vehicle accidents are the primary causes. Injuries are also possible from objects falling on the head or from a bullet entering the skull.

ASSESSMENT

Note: Head injuries rarely occur in isolation. Usually there is trauma to other parts of the body as well. Assessment may be complicated by the existence of additional injury sites.

Areas
- reflex/reaction integration
- postural control and balance
- range of motion and joint mobility
- muscle tone—abnormal tone
- gross motor skill—coordination and mobility
- hand functions
- fine motor manipulation, dexterity, and bilateral coordination
- physical endurance
- sensory registration—awareness and discrimination
- sensory processing
- perceptual skills, especially visual and auditory
- arousal level and alertness
- attending behavior, attention span, and concentration
- orientation to time, person, place
- memory
- comprehension
- reasoning and problem-solving skills
- judgment of personal safety
- learning skills
- coping skills
- social interaction skills
- daily living skills

- productivity history, interests, values, and skills
- leisure interests and skills

Instruments
- Loewenstein Occupational Therapy Perceptual Cognitive Assessment by T. Najenson, L. Rahmani, B. Elazar, and S. Averbuch. 1983. In *Behavioral assessment and rehabilitation of the traumatically brain-damaged*, ed. B.A. Edelstein and E.T. Couture, 315–324. New York: Plenum Press.
- Luria-Nebraska Neuropsychological Battery by C.J. Golden. Los Angeles: Western Psychological Service, 1980 (not an occupational therapist). Used mostly by neuropsychologists, but the results can be useful in program planning.
- Glasgow Outcome Scale by B. Jennett and M. Bond. 1975. *Lancet* 1(Mar.1):480–484 (not occupational therapists).
- Perceptual Evaluation Manual by the Study Group on the Brain-Damaged Adult. Ontario Society of Occupational Therapists: Toronto, Canada, 1977. (See also M. Boys, et al. 1989. Ontario Society of Occupational Therapists Perceptual Evaluation. *American Journal of Occupational Therapy* 43(2):92–98.)
- Rivermead Perceptual Assessment Battery by S. Whiting, et al. Windsor, England: NFER-Nelson, 1985.
- *Reflex testing methods for evaluating CNS development* by M.A. Fiorentino. Springfield, IL: Charles C Thomas, 1973.
- Routine Task Inventory (See L.R. Williams and C.K. Allen. 1985. Research with a nondisabled population. In *Occupational therapy for psychiatric diseases: Measurement and management of cognitive disabilities*, ed. C.K. Allen, 315–38. Boston: Little, Brown & Co. See also N.E. Heimann, C.K. Allen, and E.J. Yerxa. 1989. The Routine Task Inventory: A tool for describing the functional behavior of the cognitively disabled. *Occupational Therapy Practice* 1(1):67–74.)
- dexterity tests:
  1. Minnesota Rate of Manipulation Test, Circle Pines, MN: American Guidance Service, 1946.
  2. Purdue Pegboard Test by J. Tiffin, Chicago: Science Research Associates, 1947.
  3. Crawford Small Parts Dexterity Test, New York: Psychological Corporation, 1956.
- visual perception tests
  1. Motor-Free Visual Perception Test, Novato, CA: Academic Therapy Publications, 1972.
  2. Hooper Visual Organization Test, Los Angeles: Western Psychological Services, 1958.
- self-care activities (In *Head injury: A guide to functional outcomes in occupational therapy*, ed. K.M. Kovich and B.E. Bermann, 1988, 145–6. Gaithersburg, MD: Aspen Publishers, Inc.)
- occupational history
- leisure checklist

PROBLEMS

Motor
- The person may have return of primitive reflexes, such as the tonic labyrinthine, asymmetrical tonic neck, symmetrical tonic neck, positive supporting, and grasp.

- The person may have impaired gross motor skills and coordination in rolling, sitting, or standing without support, rotating the trunk, and reciprocal movements of the arms and legs for walking.
- The person may have muscle weakness in the extremities in part due to decreased innervation and disuse atrophy.
- The person may have impaired hand functions and loss of fine motor manipulation, dexterity, and bilateral coordination skills due to wrist tightness interfering with extension, hyperpronation of the forearm, and difficulty in releasing grasp.
- The person may have constructional apraxia and other difficulties in motor planning and sequencing.
- The person may have abnormal tone in trunk and extremities—hypertonicity (spasticity) or hypotonicity.
- The person may have impaired postural control and balance reactions. Posture in decerebrate rigidity is dorsiflexion of the neck, extension and internal rotation of the shoulders, flexion of the wrists, and extension of the lower extremities. Posture in decorticate rigidity is flexion of the upper extremities and extension of the lower.
- The person may have decreased physical conditioning—tires easily and has low endurance.
- The person may have stiffness in joints—lack of flexibility, joint mobility, and range of motion.
- The person may show asymmetry of movement or abnormal movement patterns.

Sensory
- The person may have decreased visual acuity.
- The person may have visual neglect in field of vision.
- The person may have impaired hearing.
- The person may have impaired body awareness and body image
- The person may have difficulty with discrimination tasks, especially visual.
- The person may have hypersensitivity to tactile, proprioceptive, vibratory, temperature, and vestibular stimuli.

Cognitive
- The person may be in any of seven levels of coma.
- The person may have reduced attention and concentration skills.
- The person may have decreased analysis skills.
- The person may have difficulty with sequencing tasks
- The person may have difficulty organizing tasks.
- The person may have difficulty categorizing information.
- The person may have difficulty integrating information.
- The person may have lapses in short- and long-term memory.
- The person may have difficulty learning or relearning skills.
- The person may demonstrate incomplete thought and action.
- The person may have difficulty planning ahead in time.
- The person may have difficulty with problem solving and decision making.
- The person may have decreased judgment regarding personal safety.

Levels of Cognitive Functioning

- *No response*: unresponsive to any stimuli
- *Generalized response:* inconsistent and nonpurposeful response to a stimulus
- *Localized response*: specific but inconsistent response to a stimulus; may follow simple commands but performance is delayed
- *Confused-agitated*: incoherent verbalization, no independence in activities of daily living, becomes easily agitated, requires constant supervision for safety, short attention span, no short-term memory
- *Confused-inappropriate*: responds to simple commands, becomes agitated when presented with unfamiliar situations, performs activities of daily living with assistance, requires frequent supervision for safety, highly distractible, can converse at automatic level, memory is impaired, unable to learn new material
- *Confused-appropriate*: independent in performing activities of daily living but is dependent on external input for direction, follows simple directions, remote memory better than recent, requires minimal supervision for safety
- *Automatic-appropriate*: person appears appropriate and oriented within familiar environment such as hospital or home, needs minimal supervision for learning and safety, can perform activities of daily living without prompting, judgment is impaired
- *Purposeful-appropriate:* person is alert and oriented, able to recall and integrate past and recent events, can function independently, needs no supervision, able to tolerate stress, and uses judgment in unfamiliar situations

Source: Adapted from Hagen, C. 1981. Language-cognitive disorganization following closed head injury: A conceptualization. In *Cognitive rehabilitation: Conceptualization and intervention*, ed. L. Trexler, 138–9. New York: Plenum Press

Intrapersonal
- The person may be confused.
- The person may be disoriented.
- The person may show disorganization of verbal and nonverbal activity.
- The person may have difficulty initiating goal-directed action.
- The person may have decreased inhibition control.
- The person may have decreased judgment skills, including lack of personal safety.
- Personality changes may occur.
- The person may become depressed.
- The person may be anxious.
- The person may have low self-esteem or self-perception.
- The person may be nonassertive or demonstrate faulty assertion.
- The person may demonstrate aggressive behavior.

Intrapersonal
- The person may act inappropriately in social situations.
- The person may have slurred or dysarthric speech.
- The person may react differently to friends after the injury.
- The person may create family discord.
- The person may have sexual dysfunction.
- The person may have impaired receptive language in reading comprehension, word recognition, or auditory comprehension.
- The person may have impaired expressive language in writing, word finding, fluency, or spelling.

Self-Care
- The person may be unable to perform certain activities of daily living because of muscle weakness or limited range of motion.
- The person may have difficulty remembering how to do certain activities of daily living or other basic skills, such as simple math calculations.
- The person may start an activity and be unable to complete certain activities of daily living.

Productivity
- Problems with memory, judgment, and organization may hinder a return to work.
- Personality changes may interfere with job performance.

Leisure
- The person may be unable to continue previous leisure activities because of cognitive dysfunction.
- Interests may need to change because motor, perceptual, and cognitive skills are reduced as an outcome of the head injury.

TREATMENT/MANAGEMENT

Motor
- Improve muscle tone for cocontraction, bilateral, reciprocal, and isolated movement.
  1. If low tone is a problem, use facilitating activities, such as irregular, rapid movements with sudden starts and stops, to increase tone.
  2. If high tone is a problem, use inhibitive or damping activities, such as rhythmic, slow, rocking movement, inverted position, weight bearing, neutral warmth, and rotation.
  3. Changing the position of the head (prone or supine) in relation to the body (extended, flexed, turned to right or left) may be used to change tone in bed and in sitting and standing positions.
- Increase gross motor skills and coordination. Use activities at the person's neuromuscular level of development: If rolling is a problem, use activities or games that emphasize rolling; if trunk rotation is a problem, use activities or games that emphasize rotating the trunk.
- Improve hand functions.

1. Begin with activities requiring gross grasp and release (full hand) with forearm in mid-position between supination and pronation.
2. As extension of the wrist improves (release improves), decrease the size of objects so that radial fingers are used (three digits, then two digits).

- Increase fine motor manipulation, dexterity, and coordination. Use activities or games requiring one hand at a time, then two, and then reciprocal movements.
- Improve postural control and balance.
    1. Begin with head control in midline position using external support, inhibiting abnormal tone, facilitating righting reactions of head and neck, placing object of interest at eye level directly in front of person, or joint approximation applied through the head and neck.
    2. Facilitate postural alignment through adaptive postural reactions (rotation, weight shift, parachute or protective reactions, tilt or equilibrium reactions).
    3. Facilitate sensory integration of two sides of the body, crossing midline of body through the use of sensory integrative techniques (see section on vestibular-bilateral disorder).
- Increase the person's endurance. Start with short, frequent sessions (15 to 20 minutes two or three times daily), then increase the length and provide a program to be carried out between therapist-directed sessions.
- Increase joint mobility and range of motion, especially in upper extremities.
    1. Use daily living activities, games, or dance that require use of range of motion, such as reaching high and low, throwing a ball, or placing objects left or right.
    2. Consider use of splints to maintain range of motion such as a resting night splint to avoid contractures.
    3. Consider use of serial casting to decrease contractures and increase range if needed.

Sensory
- Increase sensory registration, awareness, and arousal. Use the following modalities to provide sensory stimulation.
    1. touch (Rub skin with various textures.)
    2. tactile (Have the person explore or hunt for objects buried in sand, rice, or cereal.)
    3. vibration (Use a variety of vibrator heads and fast and slow vibration.)
    4. proprioception/kinesthesia (Have the person change positions from lying down to being on all fours, sitting, standing, walking, and maneuvering in an obstacle course.)
    5. equilibrium (Use tilt boards, balancing on inner tubes, and dance exercises.)
    6. sound (Listen to music with a variety of tempos, or play rhythm instruments.)
    7. vision (Look at a family album, or track moving objects or visual light, such as a flashlight.)
    8. smell—sweet (perfume, candy), acid (vinegar, lemon juice)
    9. taste—sugar, salt, spices, extracts
- improve sensory processing.
    1. tactile (Provide experiences with objects of different textures [soft, hard, smooth, rough], size [large, small], shape [round, square], composition [cloth, metal], sharpness [sharp, dull].)
    2. temperature—hot, lukewarm, cold, frozen
    3. visual discrimination—shapes, sizes, colors, composition, or gestalt
    4. auditory (Distinguish among words, sounds, and noises.)
- Improve sensory perception

1. stereognosis (Use a feely bag with two or three common objects in it and gradually increase the number of objects or bury objects in rice, cream of wheat, or other small textured substances and have the person locate and identify objects.)
2. body awareness or image
    (a) Use movement in space and tactile stimulation to increase body awareness.
    (b) Have the person name body parts in front of a mirror or name parts on another person or in a picture to increase body image.
3. visual perception (see also section on perception disorders)
    (a) Provide practice in visual fixation, tracking, and scanning.
    (b) Provide practice in form constancy, figure-ground perception, , visual memory, and visual integration with auditory and tactile (cross-modal transfer) perception.

Cognitive
- arousal (Use modalities to provide sensory stimulation. See sensory registration above.)
- attention
    1. Begin with simple tasks, such as copying simple designs with a pencil, pegs, or blocks.
    2. Use simple crafts, such as link belts, pot holders, mosaic tile, embroidery, or leather lacing.
    3. Use simple games or puzzles.
    4. Slowly increase the complexity of the task, number of steps in the task, and the amount of time needed to complete the task.
- distractibility
    1. Begin with a controlled environment (one on one in a small room with minimum visual, audio, or other distractions).
    2. Gradually increase the size of the room, the number of persons present, and the number of visual objects, sound levels, and smells.
- orientation
    1. Begin with the person, place, and time.
    2. Gradually increase complexity of learning, such as increasing the size of the room, increasing the number of persons present, and increasing the number of visual objects, sound levels, and smells.
    3. Expand beyond the immediate environment to include all living quarters, the community, reading maps, and reading time schedules.
- memory (see also section on memory disorders)
    1. Use consistent, concise instruction.
    2. Emphasize relevant information (use simple declarative sentences).
    3. Use compensatory techniques, such as memory books, lists, and visual or tactile cues.
    4. Have the person repeat steps before performing the task, then perform the task, and repeat steps after performing the task.
- problem solving and decision making
    1. Use real or simulated situations.
    2. Use small group discussion.
    3. Use cues to structure the situation, such as pictures or writing each answer given on a large easel.
    4. Use a problem-solving outline (state the problem, list possible solutions, organize solutions into a hierarchy, select the best solution, implement the solution, evaluate the results, and try again).

- sequencing of tasks and activities
  1. Grade the number of steps in the sequence, starting with three and increasing the number.
  2. Repeat the same task or routine to increase mastery (practice).
  3. Have the person outline the steps or sequence verbally or in writing.
  4. Provide compensatory techniques, such as visual pictures or lists.
- judgment of safety
  1. Structure the environment at home or work to promote safety. This may require a visit to the living situation to determine potential safety hazards and recommend changes.
  2. Use cues (visual, auditory, tactile) to alert the person to danger.
  3. Discuss possible consequences (ask "what if" questions) of an activity before starting that activity.
  4. Provide simulated dangerous situations and rehearse possible actions.
- ability to follow commands or directions
  1. Start with simple, single verbal commands, such as "Pick up the spoon." Demonstrate as needed to provide multisensory input.
  2. Gradually increase the number of commands to be performed in a single location.
  3. Next, include commands to be performed in different locations around the room, in different rooms, or outside.
  4. Use cues or a demonstration at first and then fade out prompts.
  5. Use rehearsal (person repeats commands), performance (person performs commands), summary (person repeats actions performed), and comparison (person compares initial commands with those performed).
- time management
  1. The person follows a predetermined schedule.
  2. The person participates in developing a schedule.
  3. The person is responsible for developing a schedule and reporting how well he or she has been able to follow that schedule.
- energy conservation/work simplification (Instruct the person and family caregivers in concepts and techniques of energy conservation and work simplification.)

Intrapersonal

- Increase the person's self-perception through creative activities, such as art, crafts, drama, music, or dance. Activities need to be simple and have cues and verbal support for people who function at a low cognitive level. Gradually increase the skill level required as the person's cognitive level improves.
- Improve coping skills and frustration tolerance through training in relaxation techniques and by talking about alternative strategies that are socially acceptable or through group discussions on handling frustration.

Interpersonal

- Increase social interaction skills through participation in role playing or role simulation, small task groups, or large discussion groups. Encourage the family to take the person on short outings and to invite friends into the home first (familiar setting), then accept invitations outside the home.
- Increase group participation skills through one on one sessions with the therapist, small

group (three or four people sessions), task groups (five to seven people), or large discussion groups (eight or twelve people).
- Increase role performance.
  1. The person is able to identify various roles by observing a film videotape or by role playing.
  2. The person is able to participate in role performance with assistance, such as role-playing or working in a task group.
  3. The person is able to perform roles independently and critique his or her performance.
- Encourage the person and family to participate in a self-help group, if available.

Self-Care
Increase independent performance of self-care skills.

- Provide maximal assistance initially in the skills that are most deficient. Provide cues using sensory input through senses that are less involved.
- Provide moderate assistance using continuous verbal cuing and close supervision.
- Provide minimal assistance to ensure safety and provide intermittent cuing. The person should be able to perform at least half of the activity independently.
- The person performs self-care activities with setups (the objects needed are in sight and a list of steps may be visible). The therapist or family member checks to determine if the activity was performed or assists if an unusual situation occurs.
- The person performs most self-care activities independently using self-help devices or adapted equipment if needed. No assistance is required except a final checkup.
- The person performs all self-care activities consistently without supervision or checkup by another person.

Productivity
- Improve the person's home-management skills. Grade activity based on amount of physical assistance needed, amount of on-site supervision needed, amount and type of cues needed, types of equipment used, the position in which the tasks are performed, and the amount of time needed to perform the tasks. The performance scale outlined in the self-care section above can be used to determine progression of the performance level.
- Improve work habits. Measure the person's ability to arrive on time, maintain attention and concentration, follow instructions, detect and correct errors, determine quality control, maintain a safe working environment, and work with others.
- Increase work tolerance. Determine the person's performance level in lifting, carrying, climbing, pushing, pulling, reaching, stooping, hand grasp and release, finger manipulation and dexterity, and bilateral hand and finger coordination.

Leisure
- Reestablish old interests.
- Explore with the person new interests and provide opportunities for practice.

PRECAUTIONS
- The person's response may vary from day to day. Recovery from head injury does not necessarily follow a smooth course. Expect some regression and plateaus in performance.

- Be aware of the drugs or medication the person is taking and their possible side effects. Be especially aware of their possible influence on performance skills, balance, and thinking processes.
- If splints, orthotic devices, or casts are used, check the skin frequently for signs of pressure on pressure points, such as bony prominences.

PROGNOSIS AND OUTCOME

- The person is able to control muscle tone to permit movement throughout a range of motion with minimal or no spasticity.
- The person has functional range of motion in all joints.
- The person is able to perform gross motor skills, including rolling, trunk rotation, sitting, standing on one or two feet, walking, and climbing.
- The person is able to perform fine motor skills, including use of both hands in asymmetrical, bilateral, and reciprocal movements.
- The person is able to adjust posture to maintain midline stability, head control, and balance in a variety of static and dynamic situations.
- The person is able to respond with normal range to all types of sensory input.
- The person is able to attend to tasks without becoming distracted.
- The person is oriented to time, place, and person.
- The person is able to take responsibility for personal safety.
- The person is able to learn and master new tasks.
- The person is able to plan, organize, and complete tasks on a daily schedule.
- The person and family caregiver demonstrate knowledge of techniques of energy conservation, pacing, and work simplification.
- The person is able to participate in social activities exhibiting socially acceptable behavior.
- The person is able to work cooperatively in a group situation.
- The person is able to perform activities of daily living independently.
- The person is able to perform productive activities at home, as a volunteer, or as a paid worker.
- The person is able to participate in leisure activities.

REFERENCES

Booth, B.J., M. Doyle, and J. Montgomery. 1983. Serial casting for the management of spasticity in the head-injured adult. *Physical Therapy* 63(12):1960–6.
Brooks, N., et al. 1987. The effects of severe head injury on patient and relatives within seven years of injury. *Journal of Head Trauma Rehabilitation* 2(3):1–13.
Brooks, N., et al. 1987. Return to work within the first seven years of severe head injury. *Brain Injury* 1(5):5–19.
Brown, S. 1987. Head injuries. In *The practice of occupational therapy*, 2d ed., ed. A. Turner, 399–417. Edinburgh, Scotland: Churchill Livingstone.
Cervelli, L. 1990. Re-entry into the community and systems of posthospital care. In *Rehabilitation of the adult and child with traumatic brain injury*, 2d ed., ed. M. Rosenthal, et al., 463–75. Philadelphia: F.A. Davis.
Cole, J.R., D.N. Cope, and L. Cervelli. 1985. Rehabilitation of the severely brain injured patient: A community-based low cost community model. *Archives of Physical Medicine and Rehabilitation* 66(1):38–40.
Crosson, B., et al. 1989. Awareness and compensation in postacute head injury rehabilitation. *Journal of Head Trauma Rehabilitation* 4(3):46–54.

Deaton, A.V., C. Poole, and D. Long. 1987. Improving the work potential of brain-injured adolescents and young adults: A model for evaluation and individualized training. *Occupational Therapy in Health Care* 4(2):147–59.

DePoy, E. 1987. Community-based occupational therapy with a head-injured adult. *American Journal of Occupational Therapy* 41(7):461–4.

Doughery, P.M., and M.V. Radomski. 1988. *The cognitive rehabilitation workbook: A systematic approach to improving independent living skills in brain-injured adults.* Gaithersburg, MD: Aspen Publishers, Inc.

Dow, P.W. 1989. Traumatic brain injuries. In *Occupational therapy for physical dysfunction,* 3d ed., ed. C.A. Trombly, 484–509. Baltimore, MD: Williams & Wilkins.

Epperson-Sebour, M.M., and E.W. Rifkin. 1985. Center for living: Trauma aftercare and outcomes. *Maryland Medical Journal* 34(12):1187–92.

Fussey, I., and G.M. Giles, eds. 1989. *The rehabilitation of the brain injured adult.* London, England: Croom Helm.

Giles, G.M., and J. Clark-Wilson. 1988. The use of behavioral techniques in functional skills training after severe brain injury. *American Journal of Occupational Therapy* 42(10):658–65.

Giles, G.M., I. Fussey, and P. Burgess. 1988. The behavioural treatment of verbal interaction skills following severe head injury: A single case study. *Brain Injury* 2(1):75–9.

Giles, G., and M. Shores. 1988. The role of the transitional living center in rehabilitation after brain injury. *Cognitive Rehabilitation* 6(1):26–31.

Giles, G.M., and M. Shores. 1989. A rapid method for teaching severely brain injured adults how to wash and dress. *Archives of Physical Medicine and Rehabilitation* 70(2):156–8.

Girvus, M. 1983. Occupational therapy for the brain injured patient. *Cognitive Rehabilitation* 1(3):8–10.

Guzik, J. 1986. Group treatment approaches to cognitive and social needs. In *Brain injury: Cognitive and prevocational approaches to rehabilitation,* ed. J. Kenig, A.R. Morse, M.A. Flaherty, et al., 121–44. New York: Tiresias Press.

Hill, J., and M. Carper. 1985. Greenery: Group therapeutic approaches with the head injured. *Cognitive Rehabilitation* 3(1):18–29.

Howard, P.A., S. Stephens, and R. Tyerman. 1985. Multidisciplinary organization of treatment for brain damaged patients. *British Journal of Occupational Therapy* 48(11):329–331.

Jaffe, M.B., et al. 1985. Intervention for motor disorders. In *Head injury rehabilitation: Children and adolescents,* ed. M. Ylvisaker, 167–94. San Diego, CA: College-Hill Press.

Johnson, D.A., and A. Newton. 1987. HIPSIG: A basis for social adjustment after head injury. *British Journal of Occupational Therapy* 50(2):47–52.

Johnson, R., and C. Garvie. 1985. The BBC microcomputer for therapy of intellectual impairment following acquired brain damage. *British Journal of Occupational Therapy* 48(2):46–8.

Johnston, M.V., and L. Cervelli. 1989. Systematic care for persons with head injury. In *Traumatic brain injury,* ed. P. Bach-y-Rita, 203–29. New York: Demos.

Kendig, J., et al. 1986. *Brain injury: Cognitive and prevocation approaches to rehabilitation.* New York: Tiresias Press.

Kovich, K.M. 1988. *Head injury: A guide to functional outcomes in occupational therapy.* Gaithersburg, MD: Aspen Publishers, Inc.

Krefting, L. 1989. Reintegration into the community after head injury: The results of an ethnographic study. *Occupational Therapy Journal of Research* 9(2):67–83.

Larkin, D. 1989. Movement laterality and its relationship to hemispheric specialization. *American Journal of Occupational Therapy* 43(5):308–12.

London, P.S. 1989. A long look at head injuries. *British Journal of Occupational Therapy* 52(3):101–2.

Lundgren, C.C., and E.L. Persechino. 1986. Cognitive group: A treatment program for head-injured adults. *American Journal of Occupational Therapy* 40(6):397–401.

Lyons, J.L., and A.R. Morse. 1988. A therapeutic work program for head-injured adults. *American Journal of Occupational Therapy* 42(6):364–70.

Lysaght, R., and E. Bodenhamer. 1990. The use of relaxation training to enhance functional outcomes in adults with traumatic head injuries. *American Journal of Occupational Therapy* 44(9):797–802.

Malkmus, D., B.J. Booth, and C. Kodimer, eds. 1980. *Rehabilitation of the head injured adult: Comprehensive cognitive management.* Downey, CA: Professional Staff Association of Rancho Los Amigos Hospital, Inc.

McNeny, R. 1990. Deficits in activities of daily living. In *Rehabilitation of the adult and child with traumatic brain injury,* 2d ed., ed. M. Rosenthal, et al., 193–205. Philadelphia: F.A. Davis.

Mercer, L., and M. Boch. 1983. Residual sensorimotor deficits in the adult head-injured patient. *Physical Therapy* 63(12):1988–91.

Minassian, P.H. 1986. Return to work: Prevocational assessment and training. In *Brain injury: Cognitive and prevocational approaches to rehabilitation,* ed. J. Kenig, A.R. Morse, M.A. Flaherty, et al., 145–86. New York: Tiresias Press.

Morse, A.M. 1986. Neuropsychological tools and techniques of cognitive assessment. In *Brain injury: Cognitive and prevocational approaches to rehabilitation*, ed. J. Kenig, A.R. Morse, M.A. Flaherty, et al., 51–88. New York: Tiresias Press.

Najenson, T., et al. 1984. An elementary cognitive assessment and treatment of craniocerebrally injured patients. In *Behavioral assessment and rehabilitation of the traumatically brain-injured*, ed. B.A. Edelstein and E.T. Couture, 313–37. New York: Plenum Press.

Newton, A., and D.A. Johnson. 1985. Social adjustment and interaction after severe head injury. *British Journal of Clinical Psychology* 24(Pt 4):225–34.

Panikoff, L.B. 1983. Recovery trends of functional skills in the head-injured adult. *American Journal of Occupational Therapy* 37(11):735–43.

Ponsford, J.L., and G. Kinsella. 1988. Evaluation of a remedial programme for attentional deficits following closed-head injury. *Journal of Clinical and Experimental Neuropsychology* 10(6):693–708.

Prigatano, G.P., et al. 1984. Neuropsychological rehabilitation after closed head injury in young adults. *Journal of Neurology, Neurosurgery and Psychiatry* 43:798–802.

Simon, K.B. 1988. Outpatient treatment for an adult with traumatic brain injury. *American Journal of Occupational Therapy* 42(4):247–51.

Soderback, I. 1988. A housework-based assessment of intellectual functions in patients with acquired brain damage. *Scandinavian Journal of Rehabilitation Medicine* 20:57–69.

Soderback, I. 1988. The effectiveness of training intellectual functions in adults with acquired brain damage: An evaluation of occupational therapy methods. *Scandinavian Journal of Rehabilitation Medicine* 20:47–56.

Soderback, I., and L.A. Normell. 1986. Intellectual function training in adults with acquired brain damage. Methods. *Scandinavian Journal of Rehabilitation Medicine* 18:139–47.

Soderback, I. and L.A. Normell. 1986. Intellectual function training in adults with acquired brain damage. Evaluation. *Scandinavian Journal of Rehabilitation Medicine* 18:148–53.

Soderback, I., and B. Ramund. 1988. Evaluation of an intellectual function assessment method for adults with acquired brain damage. *Scandinavian Journal of Caring Sciences* 2(1):11–8.

Spencer, E.A. 1988. Head injury. In *Willard and Spackman's occupational therapy*, 8th ed., ed. H.L. Hopkins and H.D. Smith, 474–80. Philadelphia: J.B. Lippincott.

Stoneman, R. 1985. The potential use of the microcomputer with patients suffering from cerebral vascular accident and head injury. *British Journal of Occupational Therapy* 48(6):163–6.

Strano, C.M. 1989. Effects of visual deficits on ability to drive in traumatically brain-injured population. *Journal of Head Trauma Rehabilitation* 4(2):35–43.

Sullivan, T., et al. 1988. Serial casting to prevent equineis in acute traumatic head injury. *Physiotherapy Canada* 40(6):346–50.

Timmons, M., L. Gasquoine, and J.W. Scibak. 1987. Functional changes with rehabilitation of very severe traumatic brain injury survivors. *Journal of Head Trauma Rehabilitation* 2(3):64–73.

Wahlstrom P.E. 1983. Occupational therapy evaluation. In *Rehabilitation of the head injured adult*, ed. M. Rosenthal, et al., 271–8. Philadelphia: F.A. Davis.

Weber, P.L. 1983. Closed head injuries. In *Occupational therapy for physical dysfunction*, 2d ed., ed. C.A. Trombly, 336–47. Baltimore, MD: Williams & Wilkins. 3d ed., 1989, 484–509.

Ylvisaker, M., et al. 1990. Rehabilitation assessment following head injury in children. In *Rehabilitation of the adult and child with traumatic brain injury*, 2d ed., ed. M. Rosenthal, et al., 558–92. Philadelphia: F.A. Davis.

Zablotny, C., M.F. Andric, and C. Gowland. 1987. Serial casting: Clinical applications for the adult head-injured patient. *Journal of Head Trauma Rehabilitation* 2(2):46–52.

Zoltan, B. 1990. Occupational therapy evaluation. In *Rehabilitation of the adult and child with traumatic brain injury*, 2d ed., ed. M. Rosenthal, et al., 284–93. Philadelphia: F.A. Davis.

Zoltan, B.B., and D.M. Ryckman. 1987. Head injury in adults. In *Occupational therapy: Practice skills for physical dysfunction*, 2d ed., ed. L.W. Pedretti, 436–61. St. Louis: C.V. Mosby.

Zoltan, B., and D.M. Ryckman. 1990. Head injury in adults. In *Occupational therapy: Practice skills for physical dysfunction*, 3d ed., ed. L.W. Pedretti and B. Zoltan, 623–47. St. Louis: C.V. Mosby.

Peripheral Nerve Injuries—
Median Nerve

DESCRIPTION

Median nerve injury is injury resulting to median nerve fibers from crushing, severance, or an inflammatory or degenerative process that results in loss of precision grip and pinch.

CAUSE

The causative factors may include (1) cervical cord and brachial plexus lesions, (2) complete or partial lacerations, dislocations, and fractures in the arm, forearm, wrist, or hand, (3) prolonged compression, (4) callus formation around a fracture, and (5) neuritis.

ASSESSMENT

Areas

- muscle, grip, and pinch strength
- functional range of motion
- hand functions
- fine motor skills, manipulation, and dexterity
- sensory registration
- sensory processing, including tactile two-point discrimination, sharp-dull discrimination, localization of stimuli, stereognosis, vibration, pressure (light touch), and deep pressure
- sympathetic functions—vasomotor, sudomotor (sweat), pilomotor (gooseflesh), and trophic (nourishment)
- daily living skills
- productive history, skills, values, and interests
- leisure skills and interests

Muscles Innervated by the Median Nerve

- pronator teres
- flexor carpi radialis
- flexor digitorum subimis
- flexor digitorum profundus
- flexor pollicis longus
- adductor pollicis brevis
- flexor pollicis brevis (1/2)
- opponens pollicis
- first lumbrical
- second lumbrical

Instruments

- dynamometer and pinch meter (For positioning protocol, see American Society for Surgery of the Hand. 1990. *The hand: Examination and diagnosis*, 3d ed., 121–2. New York: Churchill Livingstone.)

- manual muscle test (See American Society for Surgery of the Hand. 1990. *The hand: Examination and diagnosis*, 3d ed., chap. 2. New York: Churchill Livingstone; or A. Callahan in M.H. Malick and M.C. Kasch, *Manual on management of specific hand problems*, 1984, 19–20. Test pronation, wrist flexion, finger flexion, thumb tip flexion, palmar abduction of thumb, thumb opposition, metacarpophalangeal flexion of index and long fingers, and interphalangeal extension of index and long fingers.)
- goniometry (Figure total passive motion [TPM] and total active motion [TAM]. See American Society for Surgery of the Hand. 1990. *The hand: Examination and diagnosis*, 3d ed., 121. New York: Churchill Livingstone.)
- Tinel's sign (nerve regeneration) (Gently tap the skin [percuss] over the nerve trunk in a distal to proximal direction or use a 30 cps tuning fork. Test is positive at the most distal point at which the person perceives a tingling sensation.)
- Semmes-Weinstein monofilaments (light touch-deep pressure) (See J.A. Bell-Krotoski. 1990. Light touch-deep pressure testing using Semmes-Weinstein monofilaments. In *Rehabilitation of the hand*, 3d ed., ed. J.M. Hunter, et al., 585–93. St. Louis: C.V. Mosby.)
- Disk-Criminator or Boley gauge (static two-point discrimination) (See A. Callahan in Hunter, et al., eds. *Rehabilitation of the hand*, 1990, 605; or A. Callahan in M.H. Malick, and M.C. Kasch, *Manual on management of specific hand problems*, 1984, 24.)
- moving two-point discrimination (See A.L. Dellon. 1978. The moving two-point discrimination test: Clinical evaluation of the quickly-adapting fiber/receptor system. *Journal of Hand Surgery* 3:474–81. Also see A. Callahan in J.M. Hunter, et al., eds., *Rehabilitation of the hand*, 1990, 605–6; or A. Callahan in M.H. Malick, and M.C. Kasch, *Manual on management of specific hand problems*, 1984, 24.)
- localization test (See A. Callahan in J.M. Hunter, et al., eds., *Rehabilitation of the hand*, 1990, 605; or A. Callahan in M.H. Malick, and M.C. Kasch, *Manual on management of specific hand problems*, 1984, 25.)
- Moberg pick-up test, modified by A. Dellon (sensory motor) (See A. Callahan in J.M. Hunter, et al., eds., *Rehabilitation of the hand*, 1990, 606; or A. Callahan in M.H. Malick, and M.C. Kasch, *Manual on management of specific hand problems*, 1984, 25.)
- safety pin for pinprick test (sharp and dull sensation) (See A. Callahan in J.M. Hunter, et al., eds., *Rehabilitation of the hand*, 1990, 602; or A. Callahan in M.H. Malick, and M.C. Kasch, *Manual on management of specific hand problems*, 1984, 22.)
- tuning forks (30 cps and 256 cps) or vibrometer (vibration)
- ninhydrin sweat test (See A. Callahan in J.M. Hunter, et al., eds., *Rehabilitation of the hand*, 1990, 606–7.)
- wrinkle test by O'Rianin (See A. Callahan in J.M. Hunter, et al., eds., *Rehabilitation of the hand*, 1990, 608.)

PROBLEMS

Motor

- atrophy of the thenar eminence and flexor-pronator group
- loss or weakness of forearm pronation
- weakness in wrist flexion and radial abduction
- hand inclines to the ulnar side
- thumb is in the plane of hand (ape hand or hand of benediction)
- inability to oppose or flex the distal phalanx of the thumb or to abduct

- weak grip, especially in the thumb and index finger
- inability to flex the distal phalanx of the thumb and index finger
- weakness or loss of flexion in the fingers, depending on ulnar nerve distribution
- weakness of flexion in proximal and interphalangeal joints of the ring and little fingers
- loss of flexion in the index and long finger joints (sublimis and profundus)
- loss of flexion in the metacarpal phalangeal joint of the thumb

Sensory
- loss of sensation over the cutaneous destruction of the median nerve, especially the distal phalanges of the first two fingers
- pain, particularly in partial injuries (causalgia)

Cognitive
Cognitive faculties are not directly affected by the injury.

Intrapersonal
- The person may fear becoming permanently disabled.
- The person may fear disfigurement if the condition is or becomes permanent.
- The person may lose self-image and self-esteem.
- The person may lose self-confidence.

Interpersonal
- The person may refuse to participate in social activities because of the appearance of his or her hand.
- The person may change family roles.

Self-Care
The person may be unable to perform some activities of daily living.

Productivity
The person may be unable to perform some job tasks.

Leisure
The person may be unable to engage in some leisure activities.

TREATMENT/MANAGEMENT

Motor
- Consider splinting the hand with a short opponens to assist the function of the thumb for pinch, prevent overstretching of the antagonists, and prevent contracture of the first web space.
- If opponens splint is not indicated because the person can substitute other thumb motions for opposition, consider a web spacer splint to maintain the thumb in palmer abduction during the night.
- Provide passive range of motion to prevent contractures. Avoid stress to the collateral ligaments.

- As function returns, provide activities and games requiring various prehension patterns, such as three-point prehension (three jaw chuck) and tip prehension. Activities requiring objects to be picked up can be graded in weight and size. Other activities include lacing and stamping in leatherwork, making pinch pots, and macramé.
- If web space contracture has occurred, consider serial splinting to increase web space.
- As function returns, provide activities and games to increase coordination and dexterity.
- As function returns, provide activities and games to increase muscle strength in the forearm and wrist. Use bilateral activities to facilitate cross-stimulation.
- As function returns, provide activities and games to increase hand and pinch grip strength.
  1. Sessions should be brief to avoid fatigue until the muscles have achieved fair-plus or better strength.
  2. Begin by asking for isolated contraction of the muscle. Move the joint passively before requesting active movement.
  3. Begin with isometric and proceed to isotonic contractions.
  4. Use gravity-eliminated positions until muscle strength is graded fair-plus or better.
  5. Move toward activities that require groups of muscles to contract.
- Biofeedback may be useful to assist the person to locate (feel) a muscle or group of muscles and their movement.

Sensory
- Promote reeducation of tactile sensation.
  1. For stereognosis, have the person practice identifying objects, shapes, and textures with the eyes closed and then check by visual inspection.
  2. For discrimination, have the person identify textures that are the same or different, such as sandpaper on dowels, beaded or Velcro letters, types of cloth; locate objects in finely particled substances, such as rice, and graded substances so that the substances, such as styrofoam chips, are nearly as large as the objects to be located; and follow Braille or raised line shapes and mazes.
  3. For tactile awareness, use activities with high texture, such as clay or kneading dough.
  4. For locationization, start with a stimulus that is blunt and use firm pressure. Grade to finer or smaller size (not sharper) and use lighter pressure.
- Observe skin daily for signs of pressure or inflammation that could decrease sympathetic function.

Cognitive
- Instruct the person in safety techniques to avoid injury to skin due to lack of sensation on the palmar surface.
- Instruct the person in one-handed techniques that can be used temporarily until some function returns.

Self-Care
Provide self-help devices and training to assist in activities of daily living, which are usually a problem if the dominant hand is affected.

Productivity
- Objects used on the job may be useful in motor and sensory retraining, such as nuts and bolts or small tools.

- Objects used in the home may be useful in motor and sensory retraining if the person is familiar with using the objects.

Leisure
As strength returns, leisure activities may be useful to provide additional motor and sensory retraining.

PRECAUTIONS
Be aware of signs of carpal tunnel syndrome.

PROGNOSIS AND OUTCOME
- The person demonstrates hand strength within normal range of his or her sex, age, and type of work.
- The person has sensory awareness of touch, temperature, and two-point discrimination.
- The person has normal range of motion.
- The person demonstrates coordination and dexterity within normal range for his or her sex, age, and type of work.
- The person is able to perform functional skills and activities of daily living independently.
- The person is able to perform productive activities.
- The person is able to perform leisure activities.

REFERENCES

Arsham, N.A. 1984. Nerve injury. In *Current concepts in orthotics: A diagnosis-related approach to splinting*, ed. E.M. Ziegler, 79–100. Menomonee Falls, WI: Roylan Medical Products.

Barber, L.M. 1984. Desensitization of the traumatized hand. In *Rehabilitation of the hand*, 2d ed., ed. J.M. Hunter, et al., 493–502. St. Louis: C.V. Mosby.

Bell, J.A. 1984. Sensibility testing: State of the art. In *Rehabilitation of the hand*, 2d ed., ed. J.M. Hunter, et al., 390–8. St. Louis: C.V. Mosby. Revised in 3d ed., 1990, 575–84.

Callahan, A.D. 1984. Sensibility testing: Clinical methods. In *Rehabilitation of the hand*, 2d ed., ed. J.M. Hunter, et al., 407–431. St. Louis: C.V. Mosby. Revised in 3d ed., 1990, 594–610.

Callahan, A. 1984. Nerve injuries in the upper extremity. In *Manual on management of specific hand problems*, ed. M.H. Malick and M.C. Kasch, 2–30. Pittsburgh: American Rehabilitation Educational Network Publications.

Callahan, A.D. 1984. Methods of compensation and reeducation for sensory dysfunction. In *Rehabilitation of the hand*, 2d ed., ed. J.M. Hunter, et al., 432–42. St. Louis: C.V. Mosby. Revised in 3d ed., 1990, 611–21.

Callahan, A.D. 1987. Role of the therapist in rehabilitation of the paralysed hand. In *The paralysed hand*, ed. D.B. Lamb, 234–46. Edinburgh, Scotland: Churchill Livingstone.

Colditz, J.C. 1990. Splinting peripheral nerve injuries. In *Rehabilitation of the hand*, 3d ed., ed. J.M. Hunter, et al., 647–57. St. Louis: C.V. Mosby.

Fess, E.E. 1986. Rehabilitation of the patient with peripheral nerve injury. *Hand Clinics* 2(1):207–15.

Moran, C.A., and A.D. Callahan. 1986. Sensibility measurement and management. In *Hand rehabilitation*, ed. C.A. Moran, 45–68. New York: Churchill Livingstone.

Parker, B.C. 1988. Rehabilitation aspects of nerve injuries of the hand. *Orthopaedic Nursing* 7(1):29–34.

Pearson, S.O. 1984. Splinting the nerve-injured hand. In *Rehabilitation of the hand*, 2d ed., ed. J.M. Hunter, et. al., 452–6. St. Louis: C.V. Mosby.

Robinson, C. 1987. Peripheral nerve lesions (of the upper limb). In *Practice of occupational therapy*, 2d ed., ed. A. Turner, 498–511. Edinburgh, Scotland: Churchill Livingstone.

Waylett-Rendall, J. 1989. Sequence of sensory recovery: A retrospective study. *Journal of Hand Surgery* 2(4):245–51.

Peripheral Nerve Injuries— Radial Nerve

DESCRIPTION

Radial nerve injury is injury resulting to radial nerve fibers from crushing, severance, or an inflammatory or degenerative process. The most common sites of injury are at the elbow or distal end of the radius.

CAUSE

Causative factors include (1) cervical cord and brachial plexus lesions, (2) complete or partial lacerations, fractures, and dislocations in the shoulder, arm, or forearm, (3) prolonged compressions, (4) violent blows on the arm, (5) neuritis, (6) callus formation around a fracture, or (7) tuberculosis of the bone, tumors, or syphilis (rare).

ASSESSMENT

Areas
* joint range of motion and mobility
* muscle, grip, and pinch strength
* fine motor coordination, manipulation, and dexterity
* hand functions and prehension skills
* sensory registration
* sensory processing, including tactile stereognosis, localization and discrimination, and proprioception
* daily living skills
* productive history, skills, and interests
* leisure skills and interests

Instruments

No specific tests by occupational therapists were identified in the literature. The following instruments may be useful:

* goniometry
* manual muscle test
* dynamometer and pinch meter (For positioning protocol, see American Society for Surgery of the Hand. 1990. *The hand: Examination and diagnosis*, 3d ed., 121–2. New York: Churchill Livingstone.)
* Semmes-Weinstein monofilament (light touch-deep pressure) (See J.A. Bell-Krotoski. 1990. Light touch-deep pressure testing using Semmes-Weinstein monofilaments. In *Rehabilitation of the hand*, 3d ed., ed. J.M. Hunter, et al., 585–93. St. Louis: C.V. Mosby.)
* Disk-Criminator or Boley gauge (two-point discrimination [static] by Weber, modified by E. Moberg) (Methods for examining sensibility in the hand. In J.E. Flynn, *Hand surgery*,

Baltimore, MD: Williams & Wilkins, 1966, 435–9. See also Callahan in Hunter, et al., 1990, 605, or Callahan in Malick, 1984, 24.)
- Moberg pick-up test by E. Moberg (See Objective methods for determining the functional value of sensibility in the hand. *Journal of Bone and Joint Surgery*, 40B:454–66, 1958; or see Callahan in Hunter, et al., 1990, 606, or Callahan in Malick, 1984, 25.)
- Moving two-point discrimination by A.L. Dellon (See The moving two-point discrimination test: Clinical evaluation of the quickly-adapting fiber/receptor system. *Journal of Hand Surgery* 3:474–81, 1978. Also see Callahan in Hunter, et al., 1990, 605–6; or Callahan in Malick, 24.)

PROBLEMS

Motor
- loss of function in all or part of the muscles innervated by the radial nerve
- inability to extend the thumb, metacarpal phalangeal joints, or wrist if injury is below the elbow (Loss of supination and elbow extension should be added if the injury is above the elbow.)
- inability to grasp objects adequately or make a fist due to "wrist drop," which interferes with the action of the flexor muscles
- contractures
- loss of joint range

Muscles Innervated by the Radial Nerve

- triceps (all three heads)
- teres minor
- brachioradialis
- extensor carpi radialis brevis
- extensor carpi radialis longus
- supinator
- anconeous

- extensor digitorum
- extensor digiti minimi
- extensor carpi ulnaris
- abductor policis longus
- extensor policis longus
- extensor policis brevis
- extensor indicis

Sensory
The person may lose sensation on the dorsal radial surface of the hand.

Cognitive
Cognitive faculties are not affected directly by the injury.

Intrapersonal
- The person may fear permanent disability.
- The person may fear reconstructive surgery.
- The person may fear functional loss.

Interpersonal

The person may avoid social situations to avoid stares.

Self-Care

- The person may be unable to perform some activities of daily living.
- The person will experience difficulty performing any activity that requires power in the hand, such as opening caps or lids on new tubes, bottles, or jars.

Productivity

The person may be unable to perform some job tasks, especially those that require power or dexterity of the hand.

Leisure

The person may be unable to participate in some leisure activities, especially those that require power or dexterity of the hand.

TREATMENT/MANAGEMENT

Motor

- Increase muscle strength as innervation returns in wrist and finger extension and supination.
- Increase coordination and dexterity.
- Maintain joint mobility in the wrist and fingers.
- Increase range of motion as innervation returns.
- Prevent contractures.
- Consider dynamic splinting (dorsal forearm-based wrist cock-up or outrigger) to prevent wrist flexion deformity and reduce chances of overstretching weak extensors and begin muscle strengthening. (See Colditz articles in the reference section.)
- Increase grip strength by promoting stability in the wrist joint.
- Start muscle strengthening with light activities, such as pastry making, coil pottery, computer keyboard, and board games using elastic bands. Increase resistive activities, such as weaving on a floor loom, printing, using a pottery wheel, and wood working with hand tools.

Sensory

Usually no special sensory treatment is needed because the dorsum of the hand is affected.

Cognitive

- Instruct the person to care for extremity to avoid further injury.
- Instruct the person in the use of one-handed techniques during the recovery process.

Intrapersonal

Encourage the person to discuss fears.

Interpersonal

Encourage the person to maintain or reestablish social activities.

Self-Care
Provide the person with self-help devices as needed for self- care.

Productivity
Explore possible job opportunities if the person is unable to return to his or her previous occupation.

Leisure
- Maintain previous interests if feasible and incorporate them into a therapy program when possible.
- Identify and develop new interests, if previous interests cannot be continued.

PRECAUTIONS
Avoid injury to the skin that has lost sensation temporarily or permanently.

PROGNOSIS AND OUTCOME
The outcome is generally good. Reinnervation occurs in most cases.

- The person demonstrates normal range of elbow extension, forearm supination, wrist extension, and finger and thumb extension.
- The person is able to perform activities requiring elbow extension, forearm supination, wrist extension, and finger and thumb extension.
- The person demonstrates hand strength within normal range for his or her sex, age, and work activities.
- The person is able to perform productive activities at home and at work, paid or volunteer.
- The person is able to perform functional activities independently.
- The person has normal sensation on the dorsum of his or her hand.
- The person demonstrates coordination and dexterity in one- and two-handed activities within normal range of performance.
- The person is able to perform leisure activities.

REFERENCES

Arsham, N.A. 1984. Nerve injuries. In *Current concepts in orthotics: A diagnosis-related approach*, ed. E.M. Ziegler, 79–100. Menomonee Falls, WI: Roylan Medical Co.

Bell, J.A. 1984. Sensibility testing: State of the art. In *Rehabilitation of the hand*, 2d ed., ed. J.M. Hunter, et al., 390–8. St. Louis: C.V. Mosby. Revised in 3d ed., 1990, 575–84.

Callahan, A. 1984. Nerve injuries in the upper extremity. In *Manual on management of specific hand problems*, ed. M.H. Malick and M.C. Kasch, 1–30. Pittsburgh: American Rehabilitation Educational Network Publications.

Callahan, A.D. 1984. Sensibility testing: Clinical methods. In *Rehabilitation of the hand*, 2d ed., ed. J.M. Hunter, et al., 407–31. St. Louis: C.V. Mosby. Revised in 3d ed., 1990, 594–610.

Callahan, A.D. 1984. Methods of compensation and reeducation for sensory dysfunction. In *Rehabilitation of the hand*, 2d ed., ed. J.M. Hunter, et al., 432–42. St. Louis: C.V. Mosby. Revised in 3d ed., 1990, 611–21.

Callahan, A.D. 1987. Role of the therapist in rehabilitation of the paralysed hand. In *The paralysed hand*, ed. D.B. Lamb, 234–36. Edinburgh, Scotland: Churchill Livingstone.

Colditz, J.C. 1989. Splinting for radial nerve palsy. *Journal of Hand Therapy* 1(1):18–23. Also in *Physical Disabilities Special Interest Section Newsletter* 13(4):1–5, 1990.

Colditz, J.C. 1990. Splinting peripheral nerve injuries. In *Rehabilitation of the hand*, 3d ed., ed. J.M. Hunter, et al., 647–57. St. Louis: C.V. Mosby.

Fess, E.E. 1986. Rehabilitation of the patient with peripheral nerve injury. *Hand Clinics* 2(1):207–15.

Halar, E.M., et al. 1987. Sensory perception threshold measurement: An evaluation of semiobjective testing devices. *Archives of Physical Medicine and Rehabilitation* 68(8):499–507.

Moran, C.A., and A.D. Callahan. 1986. Sensibility measurement and management. In *Hand rehabilitation*, ed. C.A. Moran, 45–68. New York: Churchill Livingstone.

Parker, B. 1988. Rehabilitation aspects of nerve injuries of the hand. *Orthopedic Nursing* 7(1):29–34.

Pearson, S.O. 1984. Splinting the nerve-injured hand. In *Rehabilitation of the hand*, 2d ed., ed. J.M. Hunter, et al., 452–6. St. Louis: C.V. Mosby.

Turner, A. 1987. Upper limb injuries. In *Practice of occupational therapy*, 2d ed., ed. A. Turner, 568–76. Edinburgh, Scotland: Churchill Livingstone.

Waylett-Rendall, J. 1989. Sequence of sensory recovery: A retrospective study. *Journal of Hand Therapy* 2(4):245–51.

Peripheral Nerve Injuries— Ulnar Nerve

DESCRIPTION

Ulnar nerve injury is injury to the ulnar nerve from crushing, severance, or an inflammatory or degenerative process. Injuries are especially common from fractures of the medial epicondyle of the humerus and olecranon process of the ulna and from lacerations of the wrist.

CAUSE

Causative factors include: (1) cervical cord and brachial plexus lesions, (2) complete or partial lacerations, fractures, and dislocations to the arm, forearm, wrist, or hand, (3) prolonged compressions, (4) callus formation around a fracture, or (5) mononeuritis.

ASSESSMENT

Areas
- range of motion
- muscle strength, grip, and pinch strength
- hand functions and prehension skills
- fine motor coordination, manipulation, and dexterity
- sensory registration, including tactile awareness
- sensory processing, including tactile discrimination, proprioception, and vibration
- daily living skills
- productivity history, skills, values, and interests
- leisure interests and skills

Instruments
- goniometry
- manual muscle test
- dynamometer and pinch meters

- Tinel's sign using 30 cps tuning fork (See J. Tinel. 1978. The "tingling" sign in peripheral nerve lesions (translated by E. Kaplan). In *Injuries to the major branches of peripheral nerves of the forearm,* 2d ed., ed. M. Spinner. Philadelphia: W.B. Saunders.)
- Froment's sign (lateral pinch) (See American Society for Surgery of the Hand. 1990. The hand: Examination and diagnosis, 3d ed., 121–2. New York: Churchill Livingstone.)
- Semmes-Weinstein monofilaments (light touch-deep pressure) (See J.A. Bell-Krotoski. 1990. Light touch-deep pressure testing using Semmes-Weinstein monofilaments. In *Rehabilitation of the hand*, 3d ed., ed. J.M. Hunter, et al., 585–93. St. Louis: C.V. Mosby.)
- Moberg pick-up test by E. Moberg as modified by A. Dellon (sensory motor) (See Callahan in Hunter, et al., 1990, 606, or Callahan in Malick and Kasch, 1984, 25.)
- Moving two-point discrimination (See A.L. Dellon. 1978. The moving two-point discrimination test. *Journal of Hand Surgery* 3:474–81. See also Callahan in Hunter, et al., 1990, 605–6, or Callahan in Malick, 1984, 24.)
- Disk-Criminator or Boley gauge. Two-point discrimination (static) test by Moberg. (See norms in section on median nerve. See also Callahan in Hunter, et al., 1990, 605; or Callahan in Malick, 1984, 24.)

PROBLEMS

Motor
- loss or partial loss of function in all muscles innervated by the ulnar nerve.
- hyperextension of the metacarpal phalangeal joints in the ring and little fingers caused by extensor digitorum communis (innervated by radial nerve), but normal flexion of medial joint in the ring and little fingers caused by flexor digitorum sublimis (innervated by medial nerve) The result is called "claw" hand.
- decreased adduction of the thumb and fingers
- loss or decreased abduction of the fingers; abduction of the little finger is lost
- weakness of wrist flexion and loss of wrist stability
- contractures
- loss of grip strength
- loss of the ability to perform some gross motor activities, especially those requiring upper extremity power
- inability to fully extend the fingers in preparation for picking up objects
- inability to hold objects between the fourth and fifth fingers
- inability to fully flex the fingers into a spherical or cylindrical grip and flex the distal joints for hook grasp

---

Muscles Innervated by the Ulnar Nerve

• flexor carpi ulnaris	• opponens digiti minimi
• flexor digitorum profundud (1/2)	• flexor digiti minimi
• adductor pollicis	• dorsal interossei
• flexor pollicis brevis	• palmar interossei
• palmaris brevis	• third lumbrical
• abductor digiti minimi	• fourth lumbrical

Sensory
- loss of sensation on the ulnar side, palmar aspect of the forearm and hand, little finger, and ulnar side of the ring finger
- neuritis

Cognitive

Cognitive faculties are not affected directly by the disorder.

Intrapersonal
- The person may fear permanent disability and disfigurement.
- The person may fear loss of function if the injury is to dominant hand.

Interpersonal

The person may avoid social situations because of his or her appearance.

Self-Care

The person may be unable to perform some activities of daily living because of loss of intrinsics, which reduces the effect of total grasp and normal release patterns. The person may experience difficulty in writing with the dominant hand. Holding activities in the nondominant hand may be difficult.

Productivity

The person may be unable to perform some job tasks, such as heavy labor, driving a truck, typing or keypunching, or taking dictation.

Leisure

The person may be unable to perform some leisure activities, such as playing the piano or other musical instruments requiring finger dexterity and coordination.

TREATMENT/MANAGEMENT

Motor
- Increase muscle strength as innervation returns.
- Increase coordination and dexterity.
- Maintain and increase joint mobility.
- Increase range of motion.
- Consider splinting using a hand-based splint with a lumbrical bar to prevent hyperextension of the metacarpal phalangeal joints of the ring and small finger, and increase extrinsic extensors to extend the fingers and thus prevent contractures.
- Start with whole arm activities and as recovery occurs, use activities to engage grip, flexion of the metacarpal phalangeal joints and extension of the interphalangeal joints, thumb lateral pinch, and opposition of fingers to thumb.
- As function returns, provide activities and games that require cylindrical and hook grasp.

Sensory

Provide stimulation to the ulnar border of the hand.

Cognitive
* Instruct the person in use of one-handed activities.
* Instruct the person in safety techniques to avoid injury to skin while sensation is poor.

Intrapersonal
Encourage the person to express fears.

Interpersonal
Encourage the person to maintain or reestablish social activities.

Self-Care
Provide self-help devices and training as needed to perform self-care activities.

Productivity
Make recommendations regarding modifications in the work environment that would permit the person to continue productive activities during recovery.

Leisure
Explore leisure interests and make suggestions for modifications that would permit the person to enjoy leisure activities during recovery.

PRECAUTIONS
Protect deinnervated skin from injuries caused by friction, chemical agents, or heat.

PROGNOSIS AND OUTCOME
Generally the outcome is good. Reinnervation occurs in most cases.

* The person demonstrates hand functions and strength within normal range for his or her sex, age, and type of work, especially cylindrical and hook grasp.
* The person demonstrates coordination and dexterity.
* The person has functional range of motion of the hand and wrist.
* The person has sensation for touch, temperature, and two-point discrimination.
* The person demonstrates the ability to perform functional activities and activities of daily living.
* The person is able to perform productive activities.
* The person is able to perform leisure activities.

REFERENCES

Arsham, N.A. 1984. Nerve injuries. In *Current concepts in orthotics: A diagnostic-related approach*, E.M. Ziegler, 79–100. Menomonee Falls, WI: Roylan Medical Products.
Barber, L.M. 1984. Desensitization of the traumatized hand. In *Rehabilitation of the hand*, 2d ed., ed. J.M. Hunter, et al., 493–501. St. Louis: C.V. Mosby.
Bell, J.A. 1984. Sensibility testing: State of the art. In *Rehabilitation of the hand*, 2d ed., ed. J.M. Hunter, et al., 390–8. St. Louis: C.V. Mosby. Revised in 3d ed., 1990, 575–84.

Callahan, A. 1984. Nerve injuries in the upper extremities. In *Manual on management of specific hand problems*, ed. M.H. Malick and M.C. Kasch, 2–30. Pittsburgh: American Rehabilitation Educational Network Publications.

Callahan, A.D. 1984. Sensibility testing: Clinical methods. In *Rehabilitation of the hand*, 2d ed., ed. J.M. Hunter, et al., 407–31. St. Louis: C.V. Mosby. Revised in 3d ed., 1990, 594–610.

Callahan, A.D. 1984. Methods of compensation and reeducation for sensory dysfunction. In *Rehabilitation of the hand*, 2d ed., ed. J.M. Hunter, et al., 432–43. St. Louis: C.V. Mosby. Revised in 3d ed., 1990, 611–21.

Callahan, A.D. 1987. Role of the therapist in rehabilitation of the paralysed hand. In *The paralysed hand*, ed. D.B. Lamb, 234–46. Edinburgh, Scotland: Churchill Livingstone.

Colditz, J.C. 1990. Splinting peripheral nerve injuries. In *Rehabilitation of the hand*, 3d ed., ed. J.M. Hunter, et al., 647–57. St. Louis: C.V. Mosby.

Fess, E.E. 1986. Rehabilitation of the patient with peripheral nerve injury. *Hand Clinics* 2(1):207–15.

Halar, E.M., et al. 1987. Sensory perception threshold measurement: An evaluation of semiobjective testing devices. *Archives of Physical Medicine and Rehabilitation* 68(8):499–507.

Hooper, R.M., and E.R. North. 1982. Dynamic interphalangeal extension splint design. *American Journal of Occupational Therapy* 36(4):257–8.

Moran, C.A., and A.D. Callahan. 1986. Sensibility measurement and management. In *Hand rehabilitation*, ed. C.A. Moran, 45–68 New York.: Churchill Livingstone.

Parker, B. 1988. Rehabilitative aspects of nerve injuries of the hand. *Orthopedic Nursing* 7(1):29–34.

Pearson, S.O. 1984. Splinting the nerve-injured hand. In *Rehabilitation of the hand*, 2d ed., ed. J.M. Hunter, et. al., 452–6. St. Louis: C.V. Mosby.

Robinson, C. 1987. Peripheral nerve lesions. In *Practice of occupational therapy*, 2d ed., ed. A. Turner, 568–76. Edinburgh, Scotland: Churchill Livingstone.

Waylett-Rendall, J. 1989. Sequence of sensory recovery: A retrospective study. *Journal of Hand Therapy* 2(4):245–51.

Spinal Cord Injuries— Paraplegia

DESCRIPTION

Paraplegia is defined as loss of motor and sensory function below the level of a spinal cord lesion; usually about T10 or below. In an acute transverse cord lesion, the loss is permanent. Less complete lesions may result in partial motor or sensory loss. Hemisection (Brown-Séquard's syndrome) of the cord results in ipsilateral spastic paralysis and loss of postural sense, and contralateral loss of pain and thermal sense.

CAUSE

The causes of paraplegia include traumatic injuries from automobile or motorcycle accidents, sports injuries, gunshot, knife, or stabbing wounds, or accidental falls. Other causes include tumors or infectious diseases of the central nervous system. Traumatic injuries occur most frequently to adolescents or young adults.

ASSESSMENT

Areas
- muscle strength
- functional range of motion

- muscle tone (Check for spasticity.)
- reflexes present and lost
- sensory registration and processing, including level of tactile sensation and loss
- learning skills
- self-concept
- coping skills
- social and family support
- daily living skills
- productivity history, skills, interests, and values
- leisure interests and skills
- architectural and environmental barriers

Instruments

No instruments developed by occupational therapists for this condition were found in the literature. Some useful instruments are:

- manual muscle test
- goniometry
- sensory testing
- activities of daily living scale or functional assessment
- occupational history
- leisure interest checklist

PROBLEMS

Motor
- partial or total loss of muscle control below the level of lesion
- spasticity due to exaggeration of normal stretch reflexes
- extensor or flexor muscle spasms if the lumbosacral cord is intact
- contractures, especially if partial loss occurs
- loss of range of motion
- decreased vital capacity if the lesion is high

Sensory
- partial or total loss of touch and tactile sense
- partial or total loss of proprioception and kinesthesia
- partial or total loss of sense of temperature
- partial or total loss of postural and equilibrium reactions
- pain at the level of the injury
- diffuse pain below the level of injury
- sensory deprivation as a result of isolation to avoid infection

Cognition
- Cognition is not usually affected directly, although concomitant head injuries do occur.
- Secondary problems may include an inability to make decisions and solve problems.

Intrapersonal
- loss of sense of independence
- fear of becoming helpless
- anger or hostility (Why me?)
- depression and suicidal thoughts
- loss of self-image, especially masculinity or femininity
- hallucinations or delusions
- poor coping skills, especially if skills prior to injury were marginal (Level of education, cultural and social values, and family support structure are variables.)

Stages in Adjustment to Injury

Stage	Response
Shock	Disbelief at what happened Denial that anything serious or bad has actually occurred
Expectancy of Recovery	Hope that the injury is only temporary Bargaining as a means of ensuring a fast and complete recovery
Mourning	Recognition that the injury is permanent and that a self-image based on previous abilities has been lost Constriction of interests Focus on self-depreciating behavior, such as self-pity and expressions of hopelessness or worthlessness Depressive behavior, including turning away from the support system of family and friends
Defense	New self-image begins to form New behavior is tested and tried out, including angry, aggressive, or acting out behavior Dependence-independence struggle of adolescence is repeated Emphasis is placed on the here and now
Adjustment	New self-image is formed Goals and plans can be made for the future Interest in exploring the quality of life for him- or herself and significant others Ability to make decisions and solve problems

Source: Adapted from Seidel, A.C. 1982. Spinal cord injury. In *Adult rehabilitation: A team approach for therapists*, ed. M.K. Logigian, 325–46. Boston: Little, Brown & Co.

Interpersonal
- The person may withdraw and refuse to interact with friends or family.
- The person may take frustration out on others.

Self-Care
Depending on the level of the lesion, the person will be unable to perform some activities of daily living, especially those activities that usually require standing or walking.

Productivity
- The person may be unable to attain career goals because of injury, such as a desire to become a professional athlete or model.
- The person may be unable to continue in his or her job.

Leisure
The person may be unable to continue some leisure activities, such as certain sports, because of injury.

MANAGEMENT/TREATMENT

Motor
- Help the person maintain passive range of motion through stretching, especially in the trunk and legs, to provide flexibility and prevent contractures.
- Increase the person's active range of motion and joint mobility to facilitate performing self-care activities.
- Increase muscle strength in upper extremities to facilitate performance of self-care activities, including getting around in a wheelchair or walking on crutches and prepare for productive and leisure activities.
- Increase the person's endurance.

Sensory
Provide sensory stimulation to reduce effects of sensory deprivation.

- auditory—radio, television, tape recorder, compact disc player
- visual—games, page turner for magazines and books

Cognitive
- Assist in instructing the person on skin care procedures.
- Assist in instructing the person in bowel and bladder care.
- Assist in providing information on community and national resources.

Intrapersonal
- Assist in sexual counseling.
- Encourage the person to express feelings.
- Creative activities such as crafts can be useful to support development of a new self-image.

Interpersonal

Encourage participation in social activities, especially support groups for persons with spinal cord injuries and their families.

Self-Care

- Promote independence in self-care activities.
- Provide self-help devices and training designed to achieve independence in daily living activities.

Productivity

- Provide work tolerance or work hardening if needed.
- Provide opportunities for the person to identify work interests and explore career goals, if needed.
- Provide practice in home management, including suggestions for possible modifications that would permit greater independence.
- If needed, provide practice in child-care management.

Leisure

Encourage the person to identify interests and explore methods for using those interests.

PRECAUTIONS

- Check skin carefully and avoid pressure over bony prominences. Provide padding to prevent pressure sores.
- Observe the person for suppressed respiratory functions if morphine is given to reduce pain.
- Avoid overstretching joints, which might cause injury to joint support structures.

PROGNOSIS AND OUTCOME

- The person demonstrates maximum muscle strength in the upper extremities, shoulders, and upper trunk.
- The person demonstrates full range of motion in upper body joints.
- The person uses self-help devices to facilitate performance as needed.
- The person is independent in mobility.
- The person is knowledgeable about safety procedures used to decrease risk of injury at home or in the workplace.
- The person demonstrates good coping skills.
- The person and his or her family are knowledgeable about community resources and services.
- The person is able to perform self-care activities independently.
- The person is able to perform productive activities.
- The person is able to perform leisure activities.

REFERENCES

See also articles on spinal cord injuries listed under quadriplegia.

Arnott, G. 1984. The role of the occupational therapist. In *Progress in rehabilitation: Paraplegia*, ed. R. Capildeo and A. Maxwell, 61–77. London, England: Macmillan Press.

Decker, S.D., and R. Schulz. 1985. Correlates of life satisfaction and depression in middle-aged and elderly spinal cord-injured persons. *American Journal of Occupational Therapy* 39(11):740–5.

Garber, S. 1985. Wheelchair cushions for spinal cord-injured individual. *American Journal of Occupational Therapy* 39(11):722–5.

Harburn, K.L., and S.J. Spaulding. 1986. Muscle activity in the spinal cord-injured during wheelchair ambulation. *American Journal of Occupational Therapy* 40(9):629–36.

Spaulding, S.J., and K.L. Robinson. 1984. Electromyographic study of the upper extremity during bilateral sanding: Unresisted and resisted conditions. *American Journal of Occupational Therapy* 38(4):258–62.

Spencer, E.A. 1988. Specific considerations: Paraplegia. In *Willard and Spackman's occupational therapy*, 7th ed., ed. H.L. Hopkins and H.D. Smith, 498–502. Philadelphia: J.B. Lippincott.

Stanbury, J., and J. Mountford. 1985. Occupational therapy. In *Lifetime care of the paraplegic patient*, ed. G.M. Bedbrook, 198–201. Edinburgh, Scotland: Churchill Livingstone.

Spinal Cord Injuries— Quadriplegia

DESCRIPTION

Quadriplegia is defined as partial or complete paralysis of the upper and lower extremities caused by compression or dislocation of the spinal cord, which results in disruption of nerve impulses to and from the brain and spinal nerves.

CAUSE

The causes are accidents (automobile, diving), spinal cord tumors, or birth defects. Quadriplegia most frequently occurs in adolescents and children.

ASSESSMENT

Of special interest are the level of injury and remaining muscle strength. However, all areas of function must be assessed to provide a base level of function and identify interests to increase motivation.

Areas

- muscle strength
- range of motion
- muscle tone (Check for spasticity.)
- reflexes present and lost
- sensory registration
- sensory processing, including tactile sensation and proprioception
- temperature control
- pain
- problem-solving and decision-making skills

Levels of Spinal Cord and Function

C1–C3	Has face and neck muscles innervated by cranial nerves	Can chew, swallow, talk, see, hear, smell, taste, suck, blow, sense motion
C4	Has phrenic nerve to innervate diaphragm and trapezius	Can breathe independently and has shoulder girdle elevation
C5	Has biceps, brachialis, brachioradialis, deltoid, infraspinatus	Has shoulder external rotation and abduction to 90 degrees, and elbow flexion and supination
C6	Has latissimus dorsi, pectoralis major, serratus anterior, pronator teres, radial wrist extensors	Has shoulder internal rotation, flexion, extension, and adduction, forearm pronation, and wrist extension
C7	Has triceps, flexor carpi radialis, extrinsic finger extensors	Has elbow extension, wrist extension, and finger extension
C8, T1	Has ulnar wrist flexors and extensors, thumb flexors, extensors, abductors, adductors, circumduction, and finger intrinsics	Has power grasp, thumb movements, finger abduction and adduction, and fine motor coordination

---

- self-concept
- mood or affect
- social and family support
- communication skills
- daily living skills
- productive history, skills, values, and interests
- leisure skills and interests

Instruments
- Quadriplegia Index of Function (See Gresham, G.E., et al. 1986. The Quadriplegia Index of Function [QIF]: Sensitivity and reliability demonstrated in a study of thirty quadriplegic patients. *Paraplegia* 24:38–41.)
- Jebsen Hand Function Test (See Jebsen, R., and N. Taylor, et al. 1969. An objective and standardized test of hand function. *Archives of Physical Medicine and Rehabilitation* 50:311–9.)

- Klein-Bell ADL Scale (See Klein, R.M., and B.J. Bell. 1982. Self-care skills: Behavior measurement with the Klein-Bell ADL scale. *Archives of Physical Medicine and Rehabilitation* 63:335–8.)
- manual muscle test
- goniometry
- occupational history
- leisure interest checklist

PROBLEMS

Motor
- The person may have total or partial loss of movement of all the muscle groups affected.
- The person may have weakness or complete loss of strength in all muscle groups affected.
- The person usually has decreased cardiovascular fitness due to loss of skeletal muscle support, which leads to less energy reserve.

Sensory
- The person usually has loss of the sense of touch and tactile discrimination below the level of the lesion site.
- The person usually has loss of kinesthesia and proprioception in affected areas.
- The person usually has loss of temperature control in the affected areas.
- The person's vision, hearing, taste, and smell are usually not affected.

Cognitive
Cognitive faculties are not affected directly by the disorder, although people with high level spinal cord injuries may also have some injury to the brain that may go undetected unless the therapist notes and reports any observed cognitive disabilities.

Intrapersonal
- The person may express feelings of helplessness until the basic activities of daily living are relearned.
- The person may deny reality and expect to be walking independently in a few months.
- The person may become depressed when reality is accepted.
- The person may express feelings of hopelessness and wish to die.

Interpersonal
- The person may experience loss of loved ones or friends who cannot accept the person's change from physically able to physically challenged.
- The person may experience difficulty in finding new friends and interacting in group situations.

Self-Care
- The person will initially experience difficulty performing simple activities of daily living without assistance.
- The level of injury will determine in part the degree of self-care the person can achieve.

Productivity
- The person usually will be unable to perform most job tasks requiring physical motor performance, such as lifting, carrying, bending, stooping, climbing, or assembling.
- The person probably will need vocational assessment or reassessment.

Leisure

The person usually will be unable to perform leisure activities requiring physical motor performance, such as walking, running, jumping, climbing, kicking, throwing, swinging a bat, playing the piano, or playing a stringed or wind instrument.

TREATMENT/MANAGEMENT

Motor
- Strengthen remaining muscle groups.
- Teach compensatory or substitute motions.
- Provide splints to maintain the functional position of the wrist and hand and to assist in substitute motions (flexor hinge).
- Teach conservation of energy in all activities requiring motor activity.
- Assist in teaching wheelchair mobility skills.

Sensory
- Teach safety using visual inspection and hearing as substitutes for tactile and temperature sensation.
- Teach the importance of visual inspection of skin surfaces to avoid decubitus ulcers.

Cognitive

It may be useful to increase the person's memory skills so that he or she can remember the location of items since energy reserve is less.

Intrapersonal
- Use previous interests to motivate the person to learn and relearn useful skills.
- Encourage a positive outlook through demonstration of possibilities.

Interpersonal
- Provide opportunities for social interaction with handicapped and able-bodied persons.
- Teach the person how to instruct nonmedical personnel to assist in pushing a wheelchair safely, using ramps, and transferring from a wheelchair to a chair or bed.

Self-Care
- Teach the use of self-help devices.
- Teach alternate methods and body positions for performing self-care activities.
- Provide information on architectural requirements for the safe use of a wheelchair in the home and community.

- Assist the person and family in planning ahead for independent living.
- Consider the lifestyle of the person before encouraging the person to perform activities of daily living that require more time and energy to perform than would be expended by a normal person, such as dressing for level C6. The person may prefer to use the time and limited energy on productive or leisure activities.

Productivity
- Assist in determining vocational choices based on interests, cognitive abilities, and skill level.
- Assist in determining changes in the person's work environment needed to permit the person to work safely and effectively.

Leisure
- Assist the person to develop or expand leisure activities based on interests, cognitive abilities, and skill level.
- Assist in providing adaptations that may facilitate the person's participation in chosen leisure activities.

PRECAUTIONS
- Always observe skin for redness or indications of skin breakdown.
- Always observe temperature. Overheating is especially harmful. Time in the sun should be kept to a minimum. Body fluids should be maintained at all times.

PROGNOSIS AND OUTCOME
Successful rehabilitation depends on the person's willingness and ability to monitor fluid input and output and skin integrity and to observe safety rules to reduce disease and accidents. The person's general intelligence and variety of interests increase opportunities for education and work. Social support and leisure interests increase life satisfaction.

- The person demonstrates maximum muscle strength that can be obtained given the level of the lesion.
- The person demonstrates full range of motion given the level of the lesion.
- The person demonstrates the use of substitute and compensatory movements to increase functional performance.
- The person uses hand splints to augment performance, if needed.
- The person uses self-help devices to facilitate performance.
- The person is independent in mobility when using powered mobility.
- The person is able to communicate using a variety of communication devices.
- The person is able to control his or her environment using a variety of electronic devices.
- The person understands and uses energy-conservation and work-simplification techniques.
- The person is able to perform self-care activities independently but may have agreed to the use of an attendant to conserve energy and time for productive or leisure activities.
- The person is able to perform productive activities.
- The person is able to perform leisure activities.

REFERENCES

Adler, C. 1989. Equipment considerations. In *The management of high quadriplegia,* ed. G. Whiteneck, et al., 207–31. New York: Demos.

Adler, C., and L.W. Pedretti. 1990. Spinal cord injury. In *Occupational therapy: Practice skills in physical dysfunction,* 3d ed., ed. L.W. Pedretti and B. Zoltan, 502–602. St. Louis: C.V. Mosby.

Arnott, G. 1987. Spinal cord lesions. In *The practice of occupational therapy,* 2d ed., ed. A. Turner, 532–67. Edinburgh, Scotland: Churchill Livingstone.

Baumgarten, J.M. 1985. Upper extremity adaptations for the person with quadriplegia. *Clinics in physical therapy #6* 219–42. Edinburgh, Scotland: Churchill Livingstone.

Chorazy, A.J.L., et al. 1986. Rehabilitation of spinal cord injured children. *Spinal cord injuries in children,* ed. J.E. Wilberger, 189–234. Mount Kisco, NY: Futura Press.

Creighton, C. 1989. Pregnancy and quadriplegia: An occupational therapy home program. *American Journal of Occupational Therapy* 43(1):44–6.

Decker, S.D., and R. Schulz. 1985. Correlates of life satisfaction and depression in middle-aged and elderly spinal cord-injured persons. *American Journal of Occupational Therapy* 39(11):740–5.

DiPasquale, P.A. 1986. Exhaler class: A multidisciplinary program for high quadriplegic patients. *American Journal of Occupational Therapy* 40(7):482–5.

Frieden, L., and J.A. Cole. 1985. Independence: The ultimate goal of rehabilitation for spinal cord-injured person. *American Journal of Occupational Therapy* 39(11):734–9.

Garber, S.L. 1985. New perspectives for the occupational therapist in the treatment of spinal cord injured individuals. *American Journal of Occupational Therapy* 39(11):703–4.

Garber, S.L. 1985. Wheelchair cushions for spinal cord-injured individuals. *American Journal of Occupational Therapy* 39(11):722–5.

Garber, S.L., and T.L. Gregorio. 1990. Upper extremity assistive devices: Assessment of use by spinal cord-injured patients with quadriplegia. *American Journal of Occupational Therapy* 44(2):126–31.

Glass, K., and K. Hall. 1987. Occupational therapists' views about the use of robotic aids for people with disabilities. *American Journal of Occupational Therapy* 41(11):745–7.

Hage, G. 1985. Brief or new: Two pronation splints. *American Journal of Occupational Therapy* 39(4):265–7.

Hage, G. 1988. Makeup board for women with quadriplegia. *American Journal of Occupational Therapy* 42(4):253–5.

Hammel, J., et al. 1989. Clinical evaluation of a desktop robotic assistant. *Journal of Rehabilitation Research and Development* 26(3):1–16.

Harburn, K.L., and S.J. Spaulding. 1986. Muscle activity in the spinal cord-injured during wheelchair ambulation. *American Journal of Occupational Therapy* 40(9):629–36.

Henshaw, J., D. Grundy, and J. Russell. 1986. ABC of spinal cord injury: Occupational therapy. *British Medical Journal* 292(Feb. 15):473–5.

Hill, J. 1986. *Spinal cord injuries.* Gaithersburg, MD: Aspen Publishers, Inc.

Johnstone, B.R., C.J. Jordan, and J.A. Buntine. 1988. A review of surgical rehabilitation of the upper limb in quadriplegia. *Paraplegia* 26:317–39.

Kanellos, M.C. 1985. Enhancing vocational outcomes of spinal cord-injured persons: The occupational therapist's role. *American Journal of Occupational Therapy* 39(11):726–33.

Kelly, S.N. 1983. Adaptations for independent use of cassette tape recorder/radio by high-level quadriplegic patients. *American Journal of Occupational Therapy* 37(11):766–7.

Keppler, J.P. 1987. Rehabilitation in spinal cord injury. *Critical Care Clinics* 3(3):637–54.

Krouskop, T.A., S.L. Garber, N.P. Peddy, et al. 1986. A synthesis of the factors that contribute to pressure sore formation. In *Spinal cord injury medical engineering,* ed. D.N. Ghista and H.L. Frankel, 247–67. Springfield, IL: Charles C Thomas.

Lathem, P.A., T.L. Gregorio, and S.L. Garber. 1985. High-level quadriplegia: An occupational therapy challenge. *American Journal of Occupational Therapy* 39(11):705–14.

Lee, A.C. 1988. Survey of Rancho flexor hinge splint users. *British Journal of Occupational Therapy* 51(6):197–8.

McDonald, D.W., M.A. Boyle, and T.L. Schumann. 1989. Environmental control unit utilization by high-level spinal cord injured patients. *Archives of Physical Medicine and Rehabilitation* 70(8):621–23.

McGibbon, J. 1987. Paramedical aspects of spinal cord injured patients. *Paraplegia* 25(3):270–4.

Mildenberger, L.A. 1985. Brief or new: Disk hand control for persons with high-level spinal cord injuries. *American Journal of Occupational Therapy* 39(3):200–1.

Nawoczenski, D.A., et al. 1987. Physical management. In *Spinal cord injury: Concepts and management approaches*, ed. L.E. Buchanan and D.A. Nawoczenski, 123–84. Baltimore, MD: Williams & Wilkins.

Perinchief, J.M., G. Miller, T.L. Askcom, et al. 1984. Rehabilitation. In *Current therapy in physiatry: Physical medicine and rehabilitation*, ed. A.P. Ruskin, 426–37. Philadelphia: W.B. Saunders.

Ryan, J., A.M. Werner, and J.W. Lipton. 1988. Technological applications to promote independent living in the elderly. *Physical and Occupational Therapy in Geriatrics* 6(2):13–23.

Sargant, C., and M.A. Braun. 1986. Occupational therapy management of the acute spinal cord-injured patient. *American Journal of Occupational Therapy* 40(5):333–7.

Seidel, A.C. 1982. Spinal cord injury. In *Adult rehabilitation: A team approach for therapists*, ed. M.K. Logigian, 325–46. Boston: Little, Brown & Co.

Seplowitz, C. 1984. Technology and occupational therapy in the rehabilitation of the bedridden quadriplegic. *American Journal of Occupational Therapy* 38(11):743–7.

Smith, R. 1989. Mouth stick design for the client with spinal cord injury. *American Journal of Occupational Therapy* 43(4):251–5.

Smith, R. 1988. Quality assurance in equipment ordering for the spinal cord-injured client. *American Journal of Occupational Therapy* 42(1):16–9.

Spaulding, S.J., and K.L. Robinson. 1984. Electromyographic study of the upper extremity during bilateral sanding: unresisted and resisted conditions. *American Journal of Occupational Therapy* 38(4):258–62.

Spencer, E.A. 1988. Spinal cord injury. In *Willard and Spackman's occupational therapy*, 8th ed., ed. H.L. Hopkins and H.D. Smith, 486–502. Philadelphia: J.B. Lippincott.

Pedretti, L.W. 1987. Spinal cord injuries. In *Occupational therapy: Practice in skills for physical dysfunction*, 2d ed., ed. L.W. Pedretti, 403–18. St. Louis: C.V. Mosby.

Staas, W.E., et al. 1988. Rehabilitation of the spinal cord injured patient. In *Rehabilitation medicine: Principles and practices*, ed. J.A. DeLisa, 635–59. Philadelphia: J.B. Lippincott.

Trombly, C.A. 1983. Spinal cord injury. In *Occupational therapy for physical dysfunction*, 2d ed., ed. C.A. Trombly, 385–98. Baltimore, MD: Williams & Wilkins. 3d ed., 1989, 555–70.

Turnks, E., N. Bahry, and M. Basbaum. 1986. The resocialization process after spinal cord injury. In *Management of spinal cord injuries,* ed. R.F. Block and M. Basbaum, 387–409. Baltimore, MD: Williams & Wilkins.

Vaugeois, A. 1986. Occupational therapy in the treatment of spinal cord injuries. In *Management of spinal cord injuries*, ed. R.F. Block and M. Basbaum, 348–66. Baltimore, MD: Williams & Wilkins.

Verran, A.G., J.M. Baumgarten, and K. Paris. 1987. Occupational therapy management of tendon transfers in persons with spinal cord injury quadriplegia. *Occupational Therapy in Health Care* 4(3/4):155–69.

Weingarden, S.E., and C. Martin. 1989. Independent dressing after spinal cord injury: A function time evaluation. *Archives of Physical Medicine and Rehabilitation* 70(7):518–9.

Welch, R.D., et al. 1986. Functional independence in quadriplegia: Critical levels. *Archives of Physical Medicine and Rehabilitation* 67(4):235–40.

Wilson, D.J., et al. 1984. *Spinal cord injury: A treatment guide for occupational therapists*, rev. ed. Thorofare, NJ: Slack Incorporated.

Yerxa, E.J., and S. Baum. 1986. Engagement in daily occupations and life satisfaction among people with spinal cord injuries. *Occupational Therapy Journal of Research* 6(5):271–83.

Yerxa, E.J., and S.B. Locker. 1990. Quality of time use by adults with spinal cord injuries. *American Journal of Occupational Therapy* 44(4):318–26.

Part VI

Musculoskeletal Disorders

Arthritis—Arthritic Hand

DESCRIPTION

Arthritic hand is defined as skeletal, joint, and functional changes of the hand in persons with arthritis.

CAUSE

Arthritic hand is associated with the factors involved in rheumatoid and osteoarthritis, including synovitis and tenosynovitis.

Stages of Rheumatoid Arthritis in the Hand

Stage 1—Acute stage: Characterized by inflammation but no obvious signs on X-ray of osteoporosis, demineralization, or other bony changes.

Stage 2—Subacute stage: Characterized by proliferation in which the synovium within the joint begins to invade the soft tissues nearby, usually where the ligament attaches to the bone. X-ray shows bone destruction but observation of the hand does not show gross deformity. Range of motion in flexion or extension of the fingers may be slightly limited due to increase in tenosynovitis affecting tendon glide, and muscle atrophy of the intrinsics may be detected.

Stage 3—Destructive stage: Characterized by chronic disease, muscle imbalance, and soft tissue distention. X-ray shows obvious destruction of cartilage and bone. Joint deformities include subluxation, ulnar deviation, and hyperextension. Passive range of motion is limited.

Stage 4—Skeletal collapse and deformity: Characterized by gross dislocation and instability of the joint with fibrous or bony ankylosis causing permanent loss in range of motion. Hand dysfunction is severe.

ASSESSMENT

Areas

- grip and pinch strength (An average grip strength of 20 pounds and an average of 5 to 7 pounds of pinch strength are considered necessary to perform most daily living activities.)
- muscle strength based on performance of functional activities
- range of motion: active, passive, and total
- fine motor skills, manipulation, and dexterity
- hand functions
- joint stability
- vasomotor changes, such as redness or warm to touch

- trophic changes, such as brittle nails, pulp atrophy, and hyperemia
- pain and swelling
- sensory registration
- daily living skills
- productivity history, skills, interests, and values
- leisure skills and interests

Instruments
- dynamometer or sphygmomanometer and pinch meter
- goniometry
- activities of daily living scale
- productive history, skills, and values
- leisure checklist

PROBLEMS

Motor
- The person may have weak grip and pinch strength below the minimum required to perform daily living activities.
- The person may have limited range of motion.
- The person may have deformities, such as ulnar deviation of the wrist, swan neck deformity, boutonniere deformity, nodules, joint subluxation, joint dislocation, and bone spurs.
- The person may have poor manipulative and dexterity skills.
- The person may have instability in joints, such as the carpometacarpal joint of the thumb.
- The person may have muscle atrophy (intrinsics).
- Some joints may become immobile due to the disease process (tightness of the intrinsics), other joints may be immobilized by the person to reduce pain.

Sensory
The person usually has pain.

Cognitive
- Chronic pain may reduce problem-solving skills.
- The person may have cognitive disorders not directly related to the disorder.

Intrapersonal
See section on rheumatoid arthritis.

Interpersonal
See section on rheumatoid arthritis.

Self-Care
The person usually has experienced difficulty performing self-care and daily activities because of pain, loss of range of motion, or loss of grip or pinch strength.

Productivity
- The person usually has experienced difficulty performing productive activities in the home or at work due to pain, loss of range of motion, or loss of grip or pinch strength.
- The person may be performing productive activities in a manner that is harmful to the joints.

Leisure
- The person may be performing leisure activities that are harmful to the joints.
- The person may have given up many leisure activities because of pain, loss of range of motion, or loss of grip or pinch strength.

TREATMENT/MANAGEMENT

Motor
- Maintain or increase muscle, grip, and pinch strength through performance of daily living activities and selected exercise and activities as needed.
- Maintain or increase range of motion through the performance of daily living activities and selected exercise and activities as needed.
- Maintain or increase manipulative and dexterity skills.
- Consider splinting to maintain good position or alignment, such as a resting splint, to limit range of motion, such as an ulnar deviation splint, and to provide joint stabilization, such as a thumb splint.

Sensory
Consider splinting to relieve pain, such as a cock-up splint.

Cognitive
- Instruct the person in the concepts of joint protection, especially of the hand.
- Instruct the person in the concepts of energy conservation and work simplification to reduce stress on the hands.
- Instruct the person in the progress of the disease, including the role of synovitis and tenosynovitis as related to hand dysfunction and the importance of preventive mainte-nance.

Intrapersonal
See section on rheumatoid arthritis.

Interpersonal
See section on rheumatoid arthritis.

Self-Care
Self-help aids, such as enlarged handles or extended handles, should help improve performance of self-care and daily living skills.

Productivity
Adapted equipment, such as grippers to open jars, should help productivity.

Leisure
* Explore and develop leisure activities that do not aggravate the disorder.
* The person's favorite leisure activities may be adapted to eliminate or decrease the undesirable aspects of the activity.

PRECAUTIONS
* Person should avoid static holding positions of the hands, such as handwriting. Activity should be divided into short sessions of about 10 minutes followed by a short break to move the fingers (flex and extend); or avoid the activity by using a device to hold the object, such as a book holder.
* The person should avoid placing weight on the radial side of the hand. The person should use the heel of the palm.
* The person should avoid holding small objects that require a strong grip. Provide enlarged handles.
* The person should avoid pulling himself or herself to a standing position with the hands.

PROGNOSIS AND OUTCOME
* The person is able to maintain or increase grip and pinch strength.
* The person is able to maintain or increase range of motion.
* The person is able to use his or her hand for functional activities.
* The person is wearing splint(s), if prescribed, for the purpose specified.
* The person demonstrates knowledge of joint protection techniques.
* The person demonstrates knowledge of energy-conservation and work-simplification techniques.
* The person is able to perform self-care and daily activities independently with self-help devices, if needed.
* The person is able to perform productive activities using adapted equipment if needed.
* The person is able to perform leisure activities.

REFERENCES

Anderson, K., and F. Maas. 1987. Immediate effect of working splints on grip strength of arthritic patients. *Australian Occupational Therapy Journal* 34(1):26–31.

Backman, C. 1988. Spandex wrist splint: An alternative for the client with arthritis. *Canadian Journal of Occupational Therapy* 55(3):115–6.

Backman, C.L., and J.C. Deitz. 1988. Static wrist splint: Its effect on hand function in three women with rheumatoid arthritis. *Arthritis Care and Research* 1(3):151–60.

Chawla, R. 1984. Occupational therapy for the rheumatoid hand. In *Current therapy in physiatry: Physical medicine and rehabilitation,* ed. A.P. Ruskin, 268–71. Philadelphia: W.B. Saunders.

Colditz, J.C. 1984. Arthritis. In *Manual on management of specific hand problems*, ed. M.H. Malick and M.C. Kasch, 111–36. Pittsburgh: American Rehabilitation Education Network Publications.

DeVore, G.L. 1984. Preoprative assessment and postoperative therapy and splinting in rheumatoid arthritis. In *Rehabilitation of the hand,* 2d ed., ed. J.M. Hunter, et al., 695–704. St. Louis: C.V. Mosby. 3d ed., 1990, 942–9.

Geisser, R.W. 1984. Splinting the rheumatoid arthritic hand. In *Current concepts in orthotics: A diagnosis-related approach to splinting*, ed. E.M. Ziegler, 29–84. Menomonee Falls, WI: Rolyan Medical Products.

Gruen, H. 1986. Splinting in the rheumatic diseases. In *Rehabilitation management of rheumatic conditions*, 2d ed., ed. G.E. Ehrlich, 257–63. Baltimore, MD: Williams & Wilkins.

Hasselkus, B.R., K.K. Kshepakaran, and M.J. Safrit. 1981. Handedness and hand joint changes in rheumatoid arthritis. *American Journal of Occupational Therapy* 35(11):705–10.

Hillender, L.H., et al. 1987. Hand therapist's role in the management of rheumatoid hand patients. In *Tendon surgery in the hand*, ed. J.M. Hunter, L.H. Schneider, and E.J. Mackin, 612–35. St. Louis: C.V. Mosby.

McKnight, P.T., 1988. Splinting and joint protection. In *Physical therapy management of arthritis*, ed. B.F. Banwell and V. Gall. *Clinics in Physical Therapy* 16:125–57.

Melvin, J.L. 1984. Hand dysfunction associated with arthritis. In *Rheumatic diseases: Rehabilitation and management*, ed. G.K. Riggs and E.P. Gall, 361–82. Boston: Butterworth Publications.

Nalebuff, E.A., and C.A.Philips. 1984. The rheumatoid thumb. In *Rehabilitation of the hand*, 2d ed., ed. J.M. Hunter, et al., 681–93. St. Louis: C.V. Mosby. 3d ed., 1990, 929–41.

Philips, C.A. 1989. Rehabilitation of the patient with rheumatoid hand involvement. *Physical Therapy* 69(12):1091–8.

Philips, C.A. 1989. Management of the patient with rheumatoid arthritis: The role of the hand therapist. *Hand Clinics* 5(3):291–309.

Rayan, G.M., et al. 1987. Functional assessment of bilateral wrist arthrodeses. *Journal of Hand Surgery* 12A(6):1020–4.

Sofer, S., A. Pagnotta, and N. Korner-Bitensky. 1987. Ulnar deviation adaptation for the wrist cock-up splint. *Canadian Journal of Occupational Therapy* 54(2):81–7.

Steadman, A.K., and D.A. Netscher. 1990. A detachable thumb spica combined with an outrigger brace simplifies postoperative management of the rheumatoid hand. *Journal of Hand Therapy* 3(4):205–8.

Swanson, A.B., G. Swanson, and J. Leonard. 1984. Postoperative rehabilitation programs in flexible implant arthroplasty of the digits. In *Rehabilitation of the hand*, 2d ed., ed. J.M. Hunter, et al., 912–28. St. Louis: C.V. Mosby. Revised in 3rd ed., 1990, 912–28.

Wood, V.E., D.R. Ichtertz, and H. Yahiku. 1989. Soft tissue metacarpophalangeal reconstruction for treatment of rheumatoid hand deformity. *Journal of Hand Surgery* 14A(2 Pt 1):163–74.

Arthritis—Juvenile Rheumatoid

DESCRIPTION

Juvenile rheumatoid arthritis (JRA) is a chronic syndrome characterized by nonspecific, usually systemic, inflammation of the peripheral joints that begins before the person reaches 16 years of age. It can be divided into three types: (1) systemic onset (Still's disease) affects multiple joints plus other organ systems, including the spleen, liver, and lymph nodes,   (2) pauciarticular onset usually affects only a limited number of joints, such as the knee, hip, ankle, or elbow joints, often asymmetrically, and is accompanied by iridocyclitis, an inflamed condition of the iris and ciliary body of the eye that can lead to blindness if not treated, and (3) polyarticular onset may be abrupt and painful with symmetrical involvement of the joints, such as hands, wrists, feet, ankles, knees, and sometimes the cervical vertebrae of the spine, plus other symptoms, such as weight loss, low-grade fever, and general malaise.

CAUSE

The cause is unknown. Possible causes include genetic disorders, psychological trauma, viruses, histocompatibility antigents, and antigen-antibody immune complexes. Girls are affected more often than boys. The percentage of cases is about 20% systemic, 40% pauciarticular, and 40% polyarticular.

ASSESSMENT

Areas

- range of motion, passive and active
- muscle strength, grip, and pinch strength
- muscle spasms
- gross motor development, coordination, and skills
- fine motor development, coordination, manipulation, dexterity
- physical endurance
- mobility and gait
- joint stiffness, inflammation, or swelling
- joint integrity and stability (Note laxity, tendon alignment, rheumatoid nodules, crepitation, or subluxation.)
- reflex maturation (Note especially the development of equilibrium and protective and righting reactions.)
- balance and postural control
- posture (Note leg length, position of pelvis, and any deformities.)
- motor planning or praxis
- pain
- sensory registration
- self-concept
- affect or mood
- social skills
- communication skills, especially assertiveness
- daily living skills
- productive history, values, skills, and interests
- play skills
- leisure skills and interests
- architectural or environmental barriers or accessibility
- home safety

Instruments

- manual muscle test
- goniometry
- dynamometer and pinch meter
- reflex testing
- developmental testing
- occupational and physical therapy evaluation of the JRA patient (See Emery and Kucinski in reference section, pp. 21–22.)

PROBLEMS

Motor

- The person may have limited joint range of motion.
- The person may have tightness or flexion contractures of hips, knees, or elbows.

- The person may have morning stiffness, inflammation, and swelling of the joints.
- The person may have difficulty walking due to unequal growth in the long bones, instability of the pelvis, scoliosis, or pain.
- The person may fatigue easily and have low endurance.
- The person may have weak hand grasp and weakness in affected joints, especially the hips, neck, quadriceps, wrist extensors, and finger flexors and extensors.
- The person may have ligament (joint) instability, subluxation, or dislocation.
- The person may have developmental delays in gross motor skills, especially in running, hopping, and standing on one leg.
- The person may have developmental delays in fine motor skills.
- The person may have muscle spasms, especially in the wrist flexors and knee extensors.
- The person may have poor posture.
- The person may have underdeveloped equilibrium and protective and righting reactions.

Sensory
- The person may have loss of sight (pauciarticular form).
- The person frequently has pain in affected joints.

Cognitive
   Cognitive faculties are usually not affected directly by the disorder, but taking notes regarding the person's attending behavior, concentration, and interest in learning will be useful in program management.

Intrapersonal
- The person may feel a loss of self-esteem and self-confidence.
- The person may have feelings of being different.
- The person may become depressed.
- The person may become irritable.
- The person may become listless.

Interpersonal
- The person may develop a dependency on others.
- The person may express hostility.
- The person may be uncooperative during treatment.

Self-Care
- The person may be unable to perform certain activities of daily living due to wrist or hand involvement.
- The person may be behind his or her chronological age in developmental skills associated with self-care, especially dressing skills.

Productivity
- The person may have difficulty performing hand and wrist activities, such as holding a pencil or pen.
- The person may have difficulty sitting comfortably for productive activities.

Leisure

The person may be unable to participate in sports that require standing or walking for long periods of time, or running, jumping, or climbing.

TREATMENT/MANAGEMENT

Models of treatment are based on neurodevelopmental treatment (Bobath), sensory integration (Ayres), biomechanics, and rehabilitation

Motor

- Consider splinting the affected joints to prevent flexion contractures and increase function, such as the use of a resting splint, cock-up splints, ulnar gutter splints, or stabilizing splints (see Emery and Kucinski in the reference section).
- Maintain or increase range of motion using active activities and exercises, such as swimming, riding a tricycle or bicycle, creative dance, and hitting soft balls, but use with care activities or exercises that force the joints or require resistive exercises.
- Increase muscle strength using isometric exercises or normal activities rather than resistive exercises.
- Increase physical endurance and cardiovascular fitness through such activities and exercises as walking, swimming, or cycling.
- Promote reflex maturation through the use of tilt boards, rocking boards, large balls, and bicycle riding.
- Promote gross motor development through the use of games, such as hopscotch, obstacle courses, and kick ball.
- Promote fine motor development through activities and games requiring manipulation, various hand grasps, and dexterity, such as pop beads, squeezing and rolling clay, and lacing cards.

Sensory

- Splints may be useful to decrease pain in inflamed joints.
- Provide sensory stimulation, including tactile, proprioceptive, and vestibular.
- A pain management program may be useful to control pain.

Cognitive

- Instruct the person and his or her family on how to use warm compresses and a paraffin bath, if indicated.
- Instruct the person and his or her family in the concepts of joint protection and positioning techniques; for example lying prone for 20 minutes to relax joints and prevent flexion contractures of the knees.
- Instruct the person and his or her family in the concepts of time management to organize self-care, resting, productivity and leisure activities.
- Instruct the person and his or her family in the concepts of energy conservation, pacing, and work simplification.
- Instruct the person and his or her family in a home therapy program and encourage compliance. Videotaping the home program may be useful.

Intrapersonal
- Provide the person with opportunities to increase self-concept and self-esteem through creative activities, such as art, crafts, dance, drama, or music.
- Provide opportunities to express feelings and emotions through discussion, role playing, or creative outlets.
- Use behavior modification techniques to achieve cooperation with specific objectives of treatment (see Emery and Kucinski in the reference section, p. 18.)

Interpersonal
- Encourage the person to participate in social activities.
- Encourage the person and his or her family to participate in a self-help group and use other community resources.

Self-Care
- Provide adaptive equipment, such as reachers and elongated handles, for limited range of motion.
- Provide enlarged handles for weakened grasp or back packs to reduce the need for grasp.

Productivity
- Provide opportunities to develop play skills and promote play development.
- Assist in exploring vocational interests in view of physical limitations for persons who have not worked or need to change vocation.
- Assist in evaluating and recommending changes in living quarters (home or apartment).
- Assist in reorganizing the person's kitchen to permit easier reach of utensils and food items.
- Assist teachers to develop routines that permit the person to change positions and activities every 20 to 30 minutes to decrease static positioning.

Leisure
- Encourage continuous motion activities, such as creative dance, bicycle riding, swimming, or walking.
- Explore and assist in developing interests that may be used during the rest periods required when exacerbations occur.

PRECAUTIONS
- Watch for signs of deformity.
- Watch for signs of tendon rupture.
- Generally, have the person avoid activities that require placing total body weight on non-weight bearing joints, such as hand stands, cartwheels, or crutch walking.
- Generally, have the person avoid activities that require repeated pounding of a joint, such as jumping rope, jumping jacks, or jogging.
- Generally, contact sports, such as football or boxing, should be avoided, but cycling and swimming may be tolerated
- Have the person avoid static positions for long periods of time. Break routines into short periods of time.

PROGNOSIS AND OUTCOME

Most children recover completely within one to two years from the pauciarticular type of juvenile rheumatoid arthritis. About 15% of those with the polyarticular type have permanent disabilities.

- The person has normal range of motion for his or her age or functional range of motion if permanent disability remains.
- The person has normal muscle strength in all muscle groups or maximum muscle strength given the degree of permanent disability.
- The person has normal endurance and cardiovascular fitness.
- The person has functional mobility whether by ambulation or powered mobility.
- The person has achieved normal developmental levels for his or her age.
- The person demonstrates knowledge and use of joint protection techniques.
- The person demonstrates knowledge and use of energy conservation, pacing, and work simplification techniques.
- The person demonstrates knowledge of a home program, if needed, including the use of heat modalities, wearing splints, and taking medications.
- The person is able to perform daily living activities with self-help devices if needed.
- The person is able to perform productive activities.
- The person is able to perform leisure activities.
- The person and his or her family are knowledgeable about community resources.

REFERENCES

Atwood, M.J. 1985. Occupational therapy intervention for the adolescent with juvenile rheumatoid arthritis. *Occupational Therapy in Health Care* 2(3):109–26.

Chronic, C.L. 1985. Juvenile rheumatoid arthritis: The occupational therapist's role. *Developmental Disabilities Special Interest Section Newsletter* 8(4):1–2.

Emery, H.M., and J. Kucinski. 1987. *Management of juvenile rheumatoid arthritis: A handbook for occupational and physical therapists.* Chicago: La Rabida Children's Hospital.

Erlandson, D.M. 1989. Juvenile rheumatoid arthritis. In *A team approach for therapists: Pediatric rehabilitation*, ed. M.K. Logigian and J.D. Ward, 195–227. Boston: Little, Brown & Co.

Melvin, J.L., and M. Atwood. 1989. Juvenile rheumatoid arthritis. In *Rheumatic disease in the adult and child: Occupational therapy and rehabilitation*, 3d ed., ed. J.L. Melvin, 135–87. Philadelphia: F.A. Davis.

Minnis, R.J., et al. 1988. A new motorized seat for a patient with juvenile polyarticular arthritis. *Clinical Rehabilitation* 2:17–21.

Scull, S.A., M.B. Dow, and B.H. Arthreya. 1986. Physical and occupational therapy for children with rheumatic diseases. *Pediatric Clinics of North America* 33(5):1053–77.

Arthritis—Osteoarthritis

DESCRIPTION

Osteoarthritis is primarily a disorder of hyaline cartilage and subchondral bone, although all tissues in and around involved joints are hypertrophic. It is also called degenerative joint disease.

CAUSE

Osteoarthritis appears to be the result of a complex system of interacting mechanical, biologic, biochemical, and enzymatic feedback loops. Factors include congenital joint abnormalities; genetic defects; infections; metabolic, endocrine, and neuropathic diseases; diseases of the hyaline cartilage, such as rheumatoid arthritis or gout; acute trauma, such as a fracture; and chronic trauma that may occur in certain occupations. Traditionally, osteoarthritis has been divided into two broad groups, primary or idiopathic and secondary, which is due to a known cause. Onset usually begins when the person is in his or her 20s and 30s, but is almost universal by age 70. Both men and women are affected but loss of hand function is greatest in women.

ASSESSMENT

Areas
- range of motion
- muscle strength, including grip and pinch
- hand functions
- fine motor coordination, manipulation, and dexterity
- functional mobility, especially walking
- work tolerance, especially bending, lifting, and carrying
- physical endurance
- pain and swelling
- self-concept
- self-care and daily living skills
- productivity history, skills, and interests
- leisure skills and interests
- architectural or environmental barriers
- home safety

Instruments
- goniometry
- manual muscle test, dynamometer, and pinch meter
- Smith hand function evaluation (See H.B. Smith. 1973. Smith hand function evaluation. *American Journal of Occupational Therapy* 27:244–51.)
- fine motor dexterity tests, such as the Purdue Pegboard
- Stanford Health Assessment Questionnaire (See J.F. Fries, R. Spitz, R.G. Kraines, et al. 1980. Measurement of patient outcome in arthritis. *Arthritis and Rheumatology* 23: 137–45.)
- activities of daily living scale
- occupational history
- leisure checklist

PROBLEMS

Motor
- The person usually has limited of range of motion. In the hand, the joints that are most commonly involved are the distal interphalangeal joints and the trapeziometacarpal joint

of the thumb. The proximal interphalangeal joints may be involved but rarely the metacarpal phalangeal joints. In the wrist, loss of motion is greatest in wrist flexion.
- Morning stiffness follows inactivity but improves with exercise. Stiffness also occurs after 15 to 30 minutes of static positioning.
- Flexion contractures may be present.
- Joints may be enlarged and deformed.
- Heberden's or Bouchard's nodes (bone overgrowths) may be present.
- Muscle spasm and muscle inhibition may occur.
- The person may experience crepitation upon movement.
- The person may have muscle weakness and disuse atrophy.
- The person may have inflammation of the joint.

Sensory
- The person usually has pain upon movement of certain joints, especially in certain motions or exercises.
- The person may experience aching during cold weather.
- The person's body image (sense of self) may be altered.

Cognitive
Cognitive faculties are not affected directly by the disorder, but cognitive disorders may be present due to other causes.

Intrapersonal
- The person may complain of feeling old because of movement limitations.
- The person may feel less able to cope.
- The person may experience loss of self-concept.

Interpersonal
- Emotional and physical dependency on others may occur.
- The person may become demanding.

Self-Care
Performance of self-care and daily living activities may become more difficult, especially in the morning.

Productivity
- Performance of some job tasks may become impossible or very difficult.
- The person may not be able to continue in his or her present job.

Leisure
- The person may find engaging in rigorous sports causes excessive pain.
- Activities that require static holding may also become painful.

TREATMENT/MANAGEMENT
The model of treatment is based on the biomechanical model (Trombly) or the orthopedic model.

Motor
- Maintain or increase functional range of motion. In the hand, immersion in warm water, or paraffin wax treatments followed by range of motion exercises may be useful. Stiffness may be helped by use of pressure gradient or cotton stretch gloves.
- Consider splints to prevent flexion contractures of the fingers (finger gutter splint) and provide thumb stability at the carpometacarpal joint for better pinch grasp (thumb post splint). Other commonly used splints are the wrist cock-up splint and volar resting hand splint.
- Mild graded physical activities and exercises can improve movement patterns and reduce stiffness.
- Increase muscle strength, especially around the affected joints, to increase stability.
- Reduce joint stress and practice correct joint use for lifting, or suggest alternate methods for accomplishing a task.
- Maintain mobility, especially in walking, by encouraging the person to take daily walks.

Sensory
- A pain-management program may be useful.
- Body image may respond to the increased ability to move.
- The use of splints, especially for the hand and neck, may reduce pain.

Cognitive
- Instruct the person in concepts of energy conservation and work simplification.
- Instruct the person in concepts of joint protection.
- Instruct the person on home safety and reduction of architectural barriers.

Intrapersonal
- Increase self-concept and sense of mastery.
- Provide training in relaxation techniques to reduce muscle tension and pain.

Interpersonal
Encourage the person to continue social activities.

Self-Care
- Increase or maintain the person's ability to perform activities of daily living but with less trauma to the joints.
- Provide self-help devices to assist in performing activities of daily living, such as built-up handles, elongated handles, or reachers. Alternate techniques, such as using both hands to lift should also be considered.
- Suggest modifications of furniture, such as elevated chairs, high beds, sofas with firm padding, and arm rests, to assist in getting up.

• Suggest wearing loose fitting clothing with front openings to make dressing and undressing easier.

Productivity
Encourage the person to participate in productive activities, including volunteer activities, paid employment, home management, or attending classes or senior citizens meetings.

Leisure
Encourage the person to explore and develop old and new interests.

PRECAUTIONS
• The person should not be encouraged to overdo any activity.
• If splints are provided, check for redness or discomfort.
• Discourage the person from sleeping prone, using more than one pillow, or using other unusual sleeping positions. Recommend a cervical pillow instead.

PROGNOSIS AND OUTCOME
Osteoarthritis is a slowly progressive disorder. Management depends on the person's willingness to avoid activities and situations that tend to accelerate the progression and to learn to live within the limitations of the disorder.

• The person has maintained functional range of motion using splints if necessary.
• The person has maintained hand functions, pinch, and grasp, using splints if necessary.
• The person demonstrates knowledge and use of joint protection techniques.
• The person demonstrates knowledge and use of energy-conservation and work-simplification techniques.
• The person continues to be independently mobile in walking.
• The person is able to perform daily living skills using self-help devices if needed.
• The person is able to perform productive activities using splints or other adaptations if needed.
• The person is able to perform leisure activities.
• The person has a modified living environment to promote safety, mobility, and functional performance of self-care and home-management activities.

REFERENCES

Baron, M., et al. 1987. Hand function in the elderly: Relation to osteoarthritis. *Journal of Rheumatology* 14(4):815–9.

Doyle, D.V., and J.G. Lanham. 1984. Routine drug treatment of osteoarthritis. *Clinics in Rheumatic Diseases*, 10(2):277–91.

Lewis, R.B., and J.W. Applin. 1990. Degenerative joint disease. *Physical Medicine and Rehabilitation: State of the Art Reviews* 4(1):49–55.

Melvin, J.L. 1989. Osteoarthritis (degenerative joint disease). In *Rheumatic disease in the adult and child: Occupational therapy and rehabilitation*, 3d ed., ed. J.L. Melvin, 49–61. Philadelphia: F.A. Davis.

Moratz, V., H.L. Muncie, and H. Miranda-Walsh. 1986. Occupational therapy in the multidisciplinary assessment and management of osteoarthritis. *Clinical Therapeutics* 9(Suppl 1):B24–9.

Palmieri, T.J. 1987. Treatment of osteoarthritis in the hand and wrist: Nonoperative treatment. *Hand Clinics* 3(3):371–81.

Schumacher, H.P., K. Moutevelis, and N. Wolchsty. 1984. Osteoarthritis. In *Rheumatic diseases: Rehabilitation and management*, ed. G.K. Riggs and E.P. Gall, 419–27. Boston: Butterworth Publications.

Turner, A. 1987. Osteoarthritis. In *The practice of occupational therapy: An introduction to the treatment of physical dysfunction*, 2d ed., ed. A. Turner, 440–9. Edinburgh, Scotland: Churchill Livingstone.

Arthritis—Rheumatoid

DESCRIPTION

Rheumatoid arthritis is a chronic disorder characterized by inflammation of the distal joints that can lead to progressive destruction of the articular and periarticular structures.

CAUSE

The cause is unknown. Multiple factors may be involved, including autoimmune reactions. The disorder is more common in women. Onset usually occurs between age 25 and 50.

ASSESSMENT

Areas

- range of motion, active and passive
- grip and pinch strength
- muscle strength
- hand deformities
  1. ulnar deviation/drift
  2. boutonniere deformity
  3. swan-neck deformity
  4. subluxation of wrist or metacarpal phalangeal joint
  5. thumb deformities (See section on the arthritic hand.)
- hand functions
- physical endurance/fitness
- sensory functions
- memory
- goal-directed behavior/motivation
- self-concept
- coping skills
- interpersonal/social skills
- communication skills
- support structure
- activities of daily living
- productivity skills and interests
- leisure skills and interests

Instruments
- manual muscle test
- goniometry
- dynamometer and pinch meter
- Stanford Health Assessment Questionnaire (See F. Wolfe, et al. 1988. The clinical value of the Stanford Health Assessment Questionnaire Functional Disability Index in patients with rheumatoid arthritis. *Journal of Rheumatology* 15(10):1480–88.)
- Robinson Bashall Functional Assessment (See H.S. Robinson and D.A. Bashall. 1962. Functional assessment in rheumatoid arthritis. *Canadian Journal of Occupational Therapy* 29:123–138. See also L. McCloy and L. Jongbloed. 1987. Robinson Bashall functional assessment for arthritis patients: Reliability and validity. *Archives of Physical Medicine and Rehabilitation* 68(8):486–9.)
- productivity history, skills, and interests
- leisure interests

PROBLEMS

Motor
- limited/decreased range of motion of major joints
- joint deformities, especially in the hand and wrist
- muscle weakness in major muscle groups
- swelling in the major joints
- stiffness in the morning
- fatigue

Sensory
The person may experience pain and tenderness in joints.

Cognitive
Cognitive faculties undergo no major changes.

Intrapersonal
- The person may have feelings of hopelessness and helplessness.
- The person may have a poor self-concept.
- The person may have anxiety.
- The person may become depressed.

Interpersonal
The person may exhibit manipulative behavior.

Self-Care
The person may be unable to perform various activities of daily living because of motor limitations, especially those related to bending, reaching, lifting, and carrying.

Productivity

The person may be unable to perform some job tasks when pain and swelling intensify, especially those related to bending, reaching, lifting, or carrying.

Leisure

The disorder limits the variety of leisure pursuits in which the person can participate.

TREATMENT/MANAGEMENT

Motor
- Maintain or increase joint range of motion and mobility.
- Consider splints, such as a resting splint, to maintain wrist extension of the hand.
- Consider night leg splints to maintain knee extension.
- Maintain or increase muscle strength.
- Maintain or improve positioning. Consider a splint to prevent ulnar deviation deformity of the hand and wrist.
- Maintain or improve endurance.
- Maintain or improve functional ability.
- Prevent or correct joint deformity.

Sensory

Decrease the person's response to pain.

Cognitive
- Teach the person safe limits of activity to avoid overexertion.
- Teach the person conservation of energy and work-simplification tasks.
- Teach the principles of joint protection.
- Develop problem-solving skills to enable the person to apply the concepts of modifying daily activities, protecting joints, and conserving energy.

Intrapersonal
- Promote acceptance of chronic disability.
- Teach stress-management techniques.

Interpersonal

Promote social activities.

Self-Care

Provide self-help devices, if needed, and teach their use.

Productivity
- Suggest possible modifications or adaptation in the workplace that will facilitate the person performing job tasks.
- Suggest modifications or adaptation in the home that will improve safety and facilitate performing household tasks.

Leisure
- Explore interests and develop leisure activities based on interests and physical abilities.
- Suggest possible modification of existing activities that might make continued participation possible.

PRECAUTIONS
- Persons with arthritis are known to not comply with treatment/management regimes. Increased compliance can be obtained by using good learning or teaching techniques, sharing expectations of treatment and management, encouraging personal assumption of responsibility, and maintaining a relaxed, friendly atmosphere to encourage communication.
- Observe hand functions for signs of carpal tunnel syndrome.

PROGNOSIS AND OUTCOME
The prognosis varies and cannot be predicted early in the course of the disease.

- The amount of joint inflammation has decreased.
- Range of motion has been maintained or increased.
- Muscle strength and tone have been maintained or increased.
- The person demonstrates knowledge of joint protection concepts.
- The person demonstrates knowledge of work-simplification and energy-conservation techniques.
- The person demonstrates knowledge of proper body positioning techniques during work, rest, and play.
- The person has been provided with a hand splint and wears the splint as prescribed, if needed.
- The person has been provided with adapted aids and equipment and uses the devices, if needed.
- The person can describe the problems of living with arthritis and the resources available to assist in coping with the disabilities to minimize handicaps.
- The person demonstrates coping skills to decrease the stresses of living with a chronic disability.
- The person maintains social relations and support.
- The person is able to perform activities of daily living within the limits of his or her disability.
- The person is able to perform productive activities within the limits of his or her disability.
- The person is able to perform leisure activities that are of interest and provide satisfaction within the limits of his or her disability.

REFERENCES

Birnbaum, N.S., L.H. Gerber, and R.S. Panush. 1989. Self-help for arthritis patients. *Patient Care* 23(Aug 15): 69–72,77,80–82,84,91.

Brown, D. 1983. A community model for arthritis rehabilitation. *Canadian Journal of Occupational Therapy* 50(4):115–8.

Clarke, A.K. 1982. Community care in the management of rheumatoid arthritis. *International Rehabilitation Medicine* 4(3):144–7.

Cosgrove, J.L., et al. 1988. Team treatment. Does a specialized unit improve team performance? *American Journal of*

Physical Medicine and Rehabilitation 67(6):253–60.

Dickey, R., and S.H. Shealey. 1987. Using technology to control the environment. *American Journal of Occupational Therapy* 41(11):717–21.

Feinberg, J., and K.D. Brandt. 1981. Use of resting splints by patients with rheumatoid arthritis. *American Journal of Occupational Therapy* 35(3):173–8.

Feinberg, J., and K.D. Brandt. 1984. Allied health team management of rheumatoid arthritis patients. *American Journal of Occupational Therapy* 38:613–20.

Feinberg, J. 1988. The effect of patient-practitioner interaction on compliance: A review of the literature and application in rheumatoid arthritis. *Patient Education and Counseling* 11:171–87.

Furst, G.P., et al. 1987. A program for improving energy conservation behaviors in adults with rheumatoid arthritis. *American Journal of Occupational Therapy* 41(2):102–11.

Furst, G. 1985. *Rehabilitation through learning: Energy conservation and joint protection: A workbook for persons with rheumatoid arthritis.* Washington, DC: Superintendent of Documents, Government Printing Office.

Helewa, A., et al. 1987. The total assessment of rheumatoid polyarthritis—evaluation of a training program for physiotherapists and occupational therapists. *Journal of Rheumatology* 14(1):87–92.

Jacobs, S.R. 1984. Rehabilitation of the person with arthritis of the ankle and foot. *Clinics in Podiatry* 192:373–99.

Kulp, C.S., et al. 1988. Inpatient arthritis rehabilitation programs in the US: Results from a national survey. *Archives of Physical Medicine and Rehabilitation* 69(10):873–6.

Kulp, C.S. 1988. Changes in mobility and daily living skills. In *A guide to arthritis home health care*, ed. J.K. Sands and J.H. Matthews, 75–117. New York: Wiley & Sons.

Melvin, J.L. Rheumatoid arthritis. In *Rheumatoid disease in the adult and child: Occupational therapy and rehabilitation*, 3d ed., ed. J.L. Melvin, 75–87. Philadelphia: F.A. Davis.

Navarro, A.H., and J.D. Sutton. 1982. Rheumatoid arthritis VIII: The approach of the allied health professional. *Maryland State Medical Journal* 31(12):27–8.

Pedretti, L.W., and M.C. Kasch. 1987. Rheumatoid arthritis. In *Occupational therapy: Practice skills for physical dysfunction*, 2d ed., ed. L.W. Pedretti, 291–306. St. Louis: C.V. Mosby.

Pedretti, L.W., J.M. Hittle, and M.C. Kasch. 1990. Rheumatoid arthritis. In *Occupational therapy: Practice skills for physical dysfunction*, 3d ed., ed. L.W. Pedretti and B. Zoltan, 458–76. St. Louis: C.V. Mosby.

Philips, C.A. 1990. The management of patients with rheumatoid arthritis. In *Rehabilitation of the hand*, 3d ed., ed. J.M. Hunter, et al., 903–7. St. Louis: C.V. Mosby.

Podgorski, M., and J. Edmonds. 1985. Non-pharmacological treatment of patients with rheumatoid arthritis. *Medical Journal of Australia* 143(11):511–6.

Seeger, M.S. 1984. Splints, braces, and casts. In *Rheumatic diseases: Rehabilitation and management*, ed. G.K. Riggs and E.P. Gall, 151–85. Boston: Butterworth Publications.

Shapiro-Slonaker, D.M. 1984. Joint protection and energy conservation. In *Rheumatic diseases: Rehabilitation and management*, ed. G.K. Riggs and E.P. Gall, 253–61. Boston: Butterworth Publications.

Simpson, C.F. 1985. Physical and occupational therapy for arthritis. *Western Journal of Medicine* 142:562–4.

Singer, C.F., et al. 1982. The use of questionnaires in the evaluation of the functional capacity in rheumatoid arthritis. *Clinical Rheumatology* 1(4):251–61.

Speigel, J.S., M.S. Hirshfield, and T.M. Speigel. 1985. Evaluating self-care activities: Comparison of a self-reported questionnaire with an occupational therapist interview. *British Journal of Rheumatology* 24(4):357–61.

Tan, P.O. 1984. Dressing techniques and adaptations for patients with rheumatoid arthritis. In *Current therapy in physiatry: Physical medicine and rehabilitation*, ed. A.P. Ruskin, 240–53. Philadelphia: W.B. Saunders.

Trombly, C.A. 1983. Arthritis. In *Occupational therapy for physical dysfunction*, 2d ed., ed. C.A. Trombly, 376–84. Baltimore, MD: Williams & Wilkins,. 3d ed., 1989. 543–54.

Van Deusen, J., and D. Harlowe. 1987. The efficacy of the ROM Dance Program for adults with rheumatoid arthritis. *American Journal of Occupational Therapy* 41(2):90–5.

Wegener, S.T., and C.S. Kulp. 1988. Fatigue and sleep disturbance in arthritis. In *A guide to arthritis home health care*, ed. J.K. Sands and J.H. Matthews, 185–95. New York: Wiley & Sons.

Wegener, S.T., and C.S. Kulp. 1988. The management of arthritis pain. In *A guide to arthritis home health care*, ed. J.K. Sands and J.H. Matthews, 145–83. New York: Wiley & Sons.

Weinberger, M., M.K. Potts, and K.D. Brandt. 1985. Diagnosis-related group regulations. Implications for the practicing rheumatologist. *Arthritis and Rheumatism* 28(2):204–9.

Wolfe, F., S.M. Kleinheksel, P.W. Spitz, et al. 1986. A multi-center study of hospitalization in rheumatoid arthritis: Frequency of medical-surgical admissions, and charge. *Arthritis and Rheumatism* 29:614–9.

Wolfe, F., S.M. Kleinheksel, and M.A. Khan. 1988. Familial vs sporadic rheumatoid arthritis: A comparison of the demographic and clinical characteristics of 956 patients. *Journal of Rheumatology* 15(3):400–4.

Myasthenia Gravis

DESCRIPTION
Myasthenia gravis is a chronic progressive disorder of striated muscles that leads to weakness in the voluntary muscles, especially those innervated by the bulbar nucleus.

CAUSE
Myasthenia gravis appears to be an autoimmune disorder. Two possible explanations exist: (1) immunoglobulin G autoantibodies block acetylcholine receptors on the post-synaptic membrane at the myoneurojunction or (2) there is a defect in the resynthesis of acetylcholine on the presynaptic membrane. The disorder occurs more frequently in 20- to 30-year-old women than in men. After the age of 40, the frequency is about the same. Surgical removal of the thymus gland helps some patients, although the reasons for the improvement are not well understood. Remissions and exacerbations occur.

ASSESSMENT

Areas
- muscle strength (Note that muscle testing adds to fatigue. Testing a few muscles at a time may be necessary.)
- oral-motor skills
- range of motion
- physical endurance
- fine motor skills, dexterity, and manipulation
- ocular-motor skills (tracking, scanning)
- balance and equilibrium reactions
- mood or affect
- daily living skills
- productivity
- leisure

Instruments
No tests have been identified in the literature as developed by occupational therapists. The following types of tests may be useful:

- manual muscle test
- goniometry
- activities of daily living scale
- occupational history
- leisure checklist

PROBLEMS

Motor
- muscle fatigue and weakness, especially after exertion or at the end of the day
- extraocular muscles: diplopia (double vision), ptosis, ocular paralysis
- facial: person looks tired, jaw may be open, attempts to smile look like snarling
- chewing: person tires from chewing
- speech: voice may become a whisper
- neck: head may fall forward because of weak neck muscles
- upper extremities: difficult for person to reach overhead
- hand muscles: fine motor activities may be impaired and muscles fatigue quickly
- swallowing: may drool or have difficulty managing saliva
- respiratory: may have respiratory insufficiency because intercostals and diaphragm are involved
- low physical endurance: tires easily

Sensory
- Visual problems may occur because of diplopia and ocular paralysis.
- Kinesthesia and proprioception may be affected in the upper extremities and hands.

Cognitive
Cognitive faculties are not affected directly by the disorder.

Intrapersonal
- The person may express feelings of hopelessness or helplessness.
- The person may become depressed.
- The person may express anger at being unable to do what others can do easily.

Interpersonal
- The person may try to deny to others that anything is wrong.
- The person may make excuses to avoid social situations.

Self-Care
- Note potential difficulties with chewing and swallowing during meals.
- The person may have difficulty with overhead arm raising during dressing.
- The person may experience fine motor impairment in performing buttoning, writing, and typing activities.

Productivity
The job tasks that require physical exertion or fine motor performance may become impossible to continue or must be curtailed.

Leisure
See notes on productivity.

TREATMENT/MANAGEMENT

Motor
- Increase muscle strength and endurance through gentle, nonresistive activities and games.
- Maintain range of motion.
- Use overhead slings or mobile arm supports if upper extremity muscles are too weak to permit hand functions. If the person is bedridden, electronic aids may be needed.

Cognitive
- Help the person determine what tasks need to be done, decide when during the day or week the tasks should be done, and develop a time-management program.
- Teach the person energy-conservation and work-simplification techniques.
- Teach the person to examine his or her home for architectural barriers and how to use grab bars or railings to increase safety.

Intrapersonal
Provide stress-management training.

Interpersonal
- Encourage the person to continue social activities but modify plans to permit rest breaks or shorten the length of the outing.
- Consider expanding communication systems in the home, such as a voice-activated telephone or intercom to permit easier communication with the family and community agencies.

Self-Care
- Provide self-help aids that will facilitate performing activities of daily living. If the person is bedridden, arm supports or electronic devices that can control the environment may be useful.
- Teach the person to cut pieces of meat into small bites, take small bites, and drink plenty of liquid to aid swallowing.
- Assist the person to plan and prepare meals that contain soft foods that are easy to swallow.

Productivity
- Explore job interests if the person's present job situation cannot be continued.
- Recommend modifications in job tasks or physical environment that could permit the person to continue his or her present job.

Leisure
- Recommend modifications of leisure activities that might permit continuation of the person's favorite activities.
- Explore interests to develop new leisure activities that are within the person's physical capacity.

PRECAUTIONS
- Avoid overexertion. Watch the person for signs of fatigue by observing the face and eyes.
- Observe the person for changes in respiration. Encourage relaxation.
- Do not use strenuous or resistive activities.
- Do not use activities that aggravate respiratory problems.

PROGNOSIS AND OUTCOME
- The person maintains muscle strength consistent with the stage of the disease.
- The person maintains range of motion consistent with the stage of the disease.
- The person maintains hand function and use of upper extremities consistent with the stage of the disease.
- The person uses assistive devices, if needed, to perform activities.
- The person demonstrates knowledge of concepts of energy conservation and work simplification.
- The person demonstrates knowledge of safety procedures.
- The person is able to perform daily living tasks with self-help devices if needed.
- The person is able to perform productive activities.
- The person is able to perform leisure activities.

REFERENCES

Spencer, E.A. 1988. Lesions of the myoneural junction: Myasthenia gravis. In *Willard and Spackman's occupational therapy*, 7th ed., ed. H.L. Hopkins and H.D. Smith, 502–3. Philadelphia: J.B. Lippincott.

Osteoporosis

DESCRIPTION
Osteoporosis is a metabolic bone disorder in which the rate of bone resorption accelerates while the rate of bone formation slows down, causing a loss of bone mass. Bones affected by the disease lose calcium and phosphate salts and thus become porous, brittle, and vulnerable to fracture.

CAUSE
The cause of primary osteoporosis is unknown. Types of primary osteoporosis include involutional (type 1, ages 50 to 70, and type 2, age 70 or greater), idiopathic, and juvenile osteoporosis. Risk factors include inadequate intake of calcium, declining gonadal adrenal function, estrogen deficiency, and a sedentary lifestyle. The causes of secondary osteoporosis are related to alcoholism, immobilization, hyperthyroidism, lactose intolerance, malnutrition, malabsorption, osteogenesis imperfecta, Sudeck's atrophy, or prolonged therapy with steroids or heparin. Caucasian women 50 years or older who are postmenopausal with inadequate dietary calcium intake, small bone structure, and a sedentary lifestyle are most frequently affected.

ASSESSMENT

Areas
* muscle strength
* range of motion
* balance and postural control
* learning skills
* self-concept
* coping skills
* social skills
* daily living skills
* productive history, skills, interests, and values
* leisure skills
* home safety
* architectural and environmental barriers

Instruments
No instruments developed by occupational therapists for this disorder were identified in the literature.

* manual muscle test
* goniometry
* activities of daily living scale
* occupational history
* leisure checklist

PROBLEMS

Motor
* The person usually has dorsal kyphosis in the thoracic region.
* The person usually has lordosis in the cervical region.
* The person usually has loss of height.
* The person may have marked changes in posture and increased anterior flexion.
* The person may have vertebral crush fractures at T-8 or below.
* The person usually has decreased bone strength.
* The person may have decreased neuromuscular stability.
* The person may have decreased postural control and balance.

Sensory
The person may have pain in the lower back that radiates around the trunk.

Cognitive
Cognitive faculties are not affected directly by the disease.

Intrapersonal
The person may feel and act old because of changes in appearance.

Interpersonal

The person may withdraw from social contacts.

Self-Care

The person may experience difficulty performing some activities of daily living because of changes in skeletal function.

Productivity

The person may avoid home-management activities that require upright position and weight bearing.

Leisure

The person may have limited interests that can be done primarily in a sitting-reclining position rather than requiring upright position and weight bearing.

TREATMENT/MANAGEMENT

Motor

- Provide graded activities to exercise joints, especially hyperextension of the back by raising arms overhead.
- Encourage good positioning in performing any activity.
- Encourage weight-bearing activities, such as walking and social dancing, which can maintain or increase muscle strength around the hip joint.

Sensory

- Decrease pain by promoting better posture and increased level of physical activity.
- Provide activities to promote the use of protective reflexes in a safe environment.

Cognitive

- Instruct the person in safety procedures, including the use of grab bars and handrails, the elimination of floor hazards, such as rugs or cords, and the value of good lighting and contrast.
- Instruct the person in basic body mechanics, especially those related to lifting and carrying techniques, to avoid back strain.
- Instruct the person in selecting furniture that will provide good support for back and neck as well as solid armrests to facilitate sitting and standing.
- Instruct the person in concepts of energy conservation and work simplification. Emphasize task analysis for safety.
- The person may benefit from a discussion of an activity schedule that provides for alternate cycles of activity and rest.

Intrapersonal

- The person may find increased physical activity reduces the feeling of being old.
- Use creative crafts, music, drama, or dance to improve the person's self-concept.

Interpersonal

If withdrawal has occurred, encourage the person to reestablish or make new contacts in the community who may also need more physical activities.

Self-Care

Provide self-help devices that will facilitate performance of activities of daily living safely, such as long-handled items, reachers, seats for toilet and bath, and remote control devices for lighting.

Productivity

Explore with the person home management activities that can be used to achieve the need for more physical activity (and can be performed safely), such as cleaning, washing, folding sheets, and hanging up garments.

Leisure

Explore with the person possible leisure interests that can be used to achieve need for more physical activity, such as shopping, visiting art galleries or museums, and going on garden tours or nature walks.

PRECAUTIONS

Fractures of the hip and radius may occur from minor falls. Insist on safety measures.

PROGNOSIS AND OUTCOME

- The person's posture will improve toward upright standing position.
- The person will increase the level of physical activities associated with weight bearing.
- The person demonstrates knowledge of safety issues and takes actions to reduce hazards.
- The person is able to adjust cycles of activity and rest to increase physical activity but not pain.
- The person is able to use self-help devices to perform activities that would otherwise lead to back strain or excess body flexion.

REFERENCES

Ages, S., and D. Reid. 1988. Osteoporosis in post-menopausal women: Implications for occupational therapy practice. *Canadian Journal of Occupational Therapy* 55(2):82–8.

Asato, M.R. 1988. Clinical management of osteoporosis using environmental adaptations. *Occupational Therapy Forum* 3(40):9–11.

Polymyositis/Dermatomyositis

DESCRIPTION

Polymyositis/dermatomyositis is a systemic connective tissue disease characterized by inflammatory and degenerative changes in the muscles (polymyositis) or skin (dermatomyositis) leading to symmetric weakness and some degree of muscle atrophy, usually in the limb girdles.

CAUSE

The cause is unknown. The disease may be caused by an autoimmune reaction or a virus. Females are affected twice as frequently as males. The disease may appear at any age but is most common between age 40 and 60. Onset usually is rapid in children but insidious in adults.

ASSESSMENT

Areas
- muscle strength
- range of motion
- endurance
- balance and postural control
- fine motor coordination, manipulation, and dexterity
- pain
- daily living skills
- productive history, skills, and interests
- leisure skills and interests

Instruments

No instruments developed by occupational therapists were identified in the literature. The following types of tests may be useful:

- manual muscle test
- goniometry
- activities of daily living scale
- occupational history
- leisure checklist

PROBLEMS

Motor
- decreased muscle strength especially in the girdle muscles of the shoulder and hip (proximal muscles) (The person may be unable to raise his or her arms above the shoulders, climb steps, rise from a sitting position, or raise his or her head from a pillow.)
- decreased range of motion, especially in the girdle joints
- decreased muscle control
- decreased coordination
- decreased physical endurance
- muscle atrophy
- muscular stiffness
- deformities

Sensory
- pain in muscles
- muscle tenderness
- decreased tactile and touch sensation occur due to rash

Cognitive
Cognitive faculties are not directly affected.

Intrapersonal
- fear of dying
- loss of self-concept and self-esteem
- depression

Interpersonal
Dysphonia may occur due to weak laryngeal muscles.

Self-Care
- Dysphagia may decrease the ability to swallow, which interferes with eating and drinking.
- Muscle weakness and joint limitations will decrease the ability to perform activities of daily living that require above-the-shoulder motions and most activities that require hip stability in the standing position.

Productivity
- The person may be unable to perform most productive activities, except very light work tasks, during the acute stage.
- The amount of productive work tasks the person can perform depends on some recovery of muscle strength, range of motion, and physical endurance.

Leisure
- The person probably will only be able to engage in passive leisure activities during the acute stage.
- Activity limitations depend on the degree of recovery.

TREATMENT/MANAGEMENT

Motor
- Increase muscle strength (stability) of upper extremities through selected activities designed for the shoulder girdle and shoulder joint.
- Increase range of motion of upper extremities (flexibility) through the use of functional and selected activities.
- Improve muscle control (stability) through functional activities.
- Increase coordination and dexterity (flexibility) through selected activities.
- Provide functional activities for general strengthening and endurance.
- Maintain active movement to decrease muscle atrophy.
- Encourage activity to decrease muscle stiffness.
- Provide positioning equipment, including chair modifications and splints, to decrease or prevent deformities.
- Assist in providing powered mobility for persons without sufficient strength to stand and walk.

Sensory
The person may benefit from a pain-management program.

Cognitive
- Instruct the person in the concept of levels of activity, such as MET (metabolic equivalent table) units as a means of determining safe limits of energy expenditure.
- Instruct the person in concepts of work simplification and energy conservation, especially in performing self-care activities.
- Instruct the person in concepts of safety designed to decrease injuries from falls or other household dangers.

Intrapersonal
- Increase the person's self-concept (mastery) through the use of selected craft or game activities.
- Encourage the person to express his or her feelings, including hopelessness, helplessness, and dying.

Interpersonal
- Encourage the person to engage in social activities within limitations of safe level of activity.
- Assist the family or support group to adjust role expectations as the person's performance permits.

Self-Care
Provide adaptive devices to assist the person to perform activities of daily living as independently as possible, including extension handles and reachers.

Productivity
Encourage the person to perform productive activities with limitations on the level of activity.

Leisure
- Encourage the person to continue leisure activities that are within his or her level of activity or can be modified to permit performance.
- Assist the person to explore new interests that are within his or her level of activity.

PRECAUTIONS
- Cardiac arrhythmias or other conduction disorders may occur and require curtailment of activity.
- Acute renal failure may occur and require curtailment of activity.
- If a skin rash is present, avoid use of substances that may further irritate the skin and avoid pressure over areas of the rash.

PROGNOSIS AND OUTCOME
Some persons do recover, especially children. Adults may die following severe and

progressive muscle weakness. When malignancy occurs, prognosis depends on the course of cancer therapy.

- The person demonstrates sufficient muscle strength and range of motion in upper extremities to permit performance of activities requiring shoulder stability and movement.
- The person demonstrates sufficient general strength and endurance to participate in functional activities.
- The person performs activities of daily living at his or her maximum level of independence.
- The person demonstrates knowledge of his or her level of activity and adheres to performing functional tasks within the recommended activity level in self-care, productive, and leisure tasks.
- The person is able to use adaptive equipment and positioning devices, if provided, to facilitate performance of functional activities.

REFERENCES

Melvin, J.L. 1989. Polymyositis and dermatomyositis. In *Rheumatic disease in the adult and child: Occupational therapy and rehabilitation*, 3d ed., ed. J.L. Melvin, 118-22. Philadelphia: F.A. Davis.

Part VII

Systemic Disorders

Diabetes Mellitus—Type II

DESCRIPTION

Diabetes mellitus type II is a disorder with hereditary and environmental factors character-ized by abnormal insulin secretion, elevated blood glucose levels, and a variety of potential complications of various organ systems. A person with type II diabetes mellitus is not dependent on insulin (noninsulin-dependent diabetes mellitus, NIDDM) as is someone with type I (insulin-dependent diabetes mellitus, IDDM). Diabetes may be a primary or secondary diagnosis.

CAUSE

This disease has no distinct etiology, pathogenesis, specific clinical findings, or laboratory tests. The clinical syndrome always involves hyperglycemia, large vessel disease, disease of the retina and kidney, and neuropathy. Onset is usually after age 30.

ASSESSMENT

Areas

- muscle strength by groups of muscles
- fine motor skills, manipulation, dexterity, and bilateral coordination
- grip and pinch strength
- balance and postural control
- sensory registration
- sensory processing (tactile, pain, proprioceptive, vibration) of the feet, hands, and limbs
- perception skills, especially visual
- self-concept
- role behavior
- daily living skills
- productivity history, skills, interests, and values
- leisure interests and skills

Instruments

No specific instruments developed by occupational therapists were identified in the literature. The following types of instruments may be useful:

- dynamometers and pinch meters
- two-point discrimination tool, such as a Disk-Criminator or Boley gauge
- coordination/dexterity tests, such as the Purdue Pegboard Dexterity Test
- balance beam and tilt board
- activities of daily living scale
- occupational history
- leisure checklist

PROBLEMS

Motor
- The person may have general weakness and loss of weight.
- The person usually has decreased endurance and physical tolerance and fatigues easily.
- The person may have loss of reflexes or reactions.
- The person may have muscle aches and pains.
- The person may have specific muscle weaknesses, such as in the intrinsics of the foot (diabetic neuropathy).
- The person may have flexion contractures in the hand.
- The person may have limited grasp and release in the hand.
- The person may have impaired circulation associated with diabetes, which may cause myocardial or cerebral infarction or result in amputation of a leg.
- The person may have renal disease associated with diabetes.

Sensory
- The person may have loss of vision and other eye changes (diabetic retinopathy, diabetic retinitis, or diabetic cataract).
- The person may have loss of the sense of touch.
- The person may experience paresthesia, hyperesthesia, or hypoesthesia.
- The person may lose vibration and position sense.
- The person may have decreased sensitivity to pain in the extremities but experience chronic pain in other body parts.
- The person may have decreased temperature sensation.

Cognitive
Cognitive faculties are not affected directly by the disorder.

Intrapersonal
- The person may fear being dependent on insulin.
- The person may have anxiety about living with diet restrictions.
- The person may become depressed or angry. (Why me?)
- The person may become irritable.
- The person may be easily discouraged.
- The person may worry about the future.

Interpersonal
The person may have decreased social activities due to fatigue or diet restrictions.

Self-Care
The person must learn to administer insulin, whether orally or by injections.

Productivity
The person may be unable to perform productive activities due to fatigue.

Leisure

The person may have stopped participating in his or her favorite leisure activities due to fatigue.

TREATMENT/MANAGEMENT

Models of treatment do not appear to be well established but include aspects of compensation/substitution, biomechanical, and human occupation models.

Motor
- Increase muscle strength through the use of specific activities.
- Increase endurance and physical tolerance through the use of functional activities.
- Provide a home program to maintain movements of feet and ankles and decrease edema, such as picking up small objects with the toes or rolling a bottle back and forth with the feet.
- Biofeedback may be helpful in increasing circulation, maintaining temperature in the extremities, decreasing heart rate and pressure, and maintaining or increasing muscle contraction.
- Serial casting may be used to prevent contractures and increase joint mobility during or after ulcer healing of the foot.

Sensory
- Maintain sensory awareness, especially in the feet, through the use of foot activities and games or biofeedback.
- If sensory loss has occurred, provide opportunity to practice compensatory skills using remaining sensory systems as backups or substitutes.

Cognitive
- Instruct the person on concepts of energy conservation and work simplification.
- If sensory loss has occurred, instruct the person on safety requirements necessary to avoid injury.
- Instruct the person in time management to organize cycles of rest and activity.
- Assist in instructing the person to modify diet according to recommended guidelines, including changing recipes and planning meal menus.
- Assist in instructing the person about the secondary complications of diabetes, such as decreased tactile awareness (routine visual inspection especially of the feet needed), circulation impairment (shoes designed to protect against pressure should be worn), and visual problems (relationship of increased systolic pressure to retinal aneurysms).
- Instruct the person on the relationship of exercise to blood sugar level.

Intrapersonal
- Maintain or increase the person's self-concept and sense of mastery.
- Maintain or increase the person's self-identity and sense of self-responsibility.
- Increase the person's coping skills needed to adjust to life with a disability but not a handicap.
- Provide instruction and practice in relaxation techniques to reduce stress.

Interpersonal
- Encourage the person to maintain dyadic relationships.
- Support group interaction, including a support self-help group for persons and families with diabetes.
- Assist the family to adjust roles and functions to maintain the person's active participation in the family unit.

Self-Care
- Provide adapted equipment, if necessary, to facilitate performance of self-care activities.
- Encourage the person to maintain independence in activities of daily living.

Productivity
- Explore possible needs for modifications in the work or home environment to conserve energy and simplify work tasks.
- If the current job situation is dangerous to the person's health, explore alternative vocational interests.
- Encourage the person to participate in home-management tasks.

Leisure
- Assist the person to determine which leisure interests must be modified or discontinued.
- Assist the person to explore new interests to replace those that cannot be continued.
- Provide information on available community programs and resources.

PRECAUTIONS
- Observe the person for symptoms of insulin shock.
- Observe safety rules.

PROGNOSIS AND OUTCOME
- The person has sufficient strength and endurance to perform activities of daily living.
- The person demonstrates the use of good energy-conservation and work-simplification techniques during functional activities.
- The person demonstrates time-management skills in regulating physical activities according to rest and activity cycles based on insulin and diet considerations.
- The person demonstrates knowledge regarding skin care to prevent skin breakdown.
- The person has learned compensatory skills for any sensory loss and can perform activities safely.
- The person has learned coping skills to live within restrictions of the disease without becoming handicapped.

REFERENCES

Andrew, M. 1987. The occupational therapist's role in the management of diabetes. *Canadian Journal of Occupational Therapy* 54(1):11–5.
Dean, E. 1984. Temperature biofeedback training to improve peripheral blood flow in the upper extremities of diabetic patients. *Canadian Journal of Occupational Therapy* 51(5):219–24.

Helm, P.A., S.C. Walker, and G. Pullium. 1984. Total contact casting in diabetic patients with neuropathic foot ulcerations. *Archives of Physical Medicine and Rehabilitation* 65:691–3.

Herbert-Green, C. 1986. Developing exercise programs for the elderly person with diabetes. *Gerontology Special Interest Section Newsletter* 9(4):2–3.

Nakada, M., and A.L. Dellon. 1989. Relationship between sensibility and ability to read Braille in diabetics. *Microsurgery* 10:136–41.

Peterson, P., and D. Comello. 1983. Rehabilitation guidelines for the geriatric patient with diabetes. *Physical and Occupational Therapy in Geriatrics* 3(2):17–34.

Walker, S.C., P.A. Helm, and G. Pullium. 1987. Total contact casting and chronic diabetic neuropathic foot ulcerations: Healing rates by wound location. *Archives of Physical Medicine and Rehabilitation* 68(4):217–21.

Kidney Disease with Dialysis

DESCRIPTION

Diseased kidneys are unable to maintain homeostatic balance of water, minerals, and excretion. Toxic end-products accumulate in the blood and tissue. The kidney also is no longer able to function as an endocrine organ. Dialysis is the process of separating elements in a solution by diffusion across a semipermeable membrane. The purpose is to reestablish homeostatic balance and decrease the toxic end-products.

CAUSE

Acute or chronic kidney failure may occur as a result of numerous disorders, including uremic encephalopathy, pericarditis, intractable metabolic acidosis, congestive heart failure, and hyperkalemia. Persons affected may be of any age. Both sexes are affected equally.

ASSESSMENT

Areas
- developmental profile
- muscle strength
- range of motion
- endurance
- fine motor skills, manipulation, dexterity, and bilateral coordination
- sensory registration
- sensory processing
- attention span
- learning skills
- self-concept
- sense of self-mastery or self-control
- mood or affect, especially signs of depression
- social skills
- coping skills
- daily living skills

- productive history, values, skills, and interests, including academic and play skills
- leisure skills and interest

Instruments
No specific instruments developed by occupational therapists were identified in the literature. The following types of tests may be useful:

- developmental testing
- manual muscle test by groups of muscles
- goniometry
- activities of daily living
- play history
- leisure checklist

PROBLEMS

Motor
- The person may have decreased muscle strength.
- The person may have decreased physical endurance and rapid fatigue.
- The person may have loss of range of motion.
- The person may have decreased muscle control.
- The person may have decreased fine motor coordination and dexterity.
- The person may have foot drop, tremor, or other signs of peripheral neuropathy.

Sensory
- Loss of sensation may occur.
- Loss of vision or decreased visual acuity may occur.

Cognitive
- The person may have loss of attention span and concentration.
- The person may experience drowsiness.

Intrapersonal
- The person usually experiences a decrease or loss of self-concept, especially mastery and autonomy.
- The person may have lost self-esteem or feelings of self-worth.
- The person may express anger and frustration.
- The person may experience loss of effective coping skills.
- The person may have an increased sense of dependency.
- The person may be depressed.
- The person may express fear of death.
- The person may become irritable and uncooperative.
- The person may become confused and anxious.
- A preschool child may perceive painful medical procedures, hospitalization, and separation from parents as punishment.

- A school-age child may perceive him- or herself as different from others.
- The parent or parents may have many of the same problems that the child experiences.

Interpersonal
- The person may experience difficulty relating to authority figures.
- The person may withdraw from social group interaction.
- The person may experience conflict with his or her family related to changing roles.

Self-Care
The person may be unable to perform some activities of daily living due to limited energy or decreased range of motion.

Productivity
The person may be unable to perform productive activities, such as academic work, play, and chores, due to reduced energy level or decreased strength.

Leisure
The person may not engage in favorite leisure activities because of decreased functional abilities.

TREATMENT/MANAGEMENT

Motor
- Increase muscle strength through graded activities.
- Increase functional range of motion through selected activities within the person's normal activities if possible.
- Increase the person's muscle control.
- Increase coordination and dexterity through selected activities.
- Increase physical endurance through gentle exercises.

Sensory
No specific sensory treatment or management is recommended.

Cognitive
- Instruct the person in concepts of energy conservation and work simplification.
- Instruct the person in concepts of safety associated with dialysis.
- Assist in instructing the person on recommended diet changes and necessary modifications in food preparation.
- Instruct the person in the development of a time-management schedule that includes cycles of rest and exercise.
- Select projects that are quick and require a short attention span, such as games, puzzles, mazes, or crosswords for children.

Intrapersonal
- Increase self-concept through successful accomplishment of art, craft, educational, creative writing, or game activities.

- Increase the person's sense of mastery through knowledge about and performance of activities.
- Encourage the person and family members to verbalize feelings of hopelessness, helplessness, and fear of dying.

Interpersonal
- Encourage the person to engage in social activities.
- Assist the person and family to reorganize roles within the family unit, if necessary.
- Encourage the person and family to participate in a self-help group, if available, in their hospital or community.
- Encourage the person to maintain contact with the outside world if hospitalization is required. Field trips may be useful.

Self-Care
- Maintain or increase independence in self-care activities through the use of work-simplification or time-management techniques.
- Provide adapted equipment to assist the person in the performance of self-care activities when indicated.
- Cooking may be useful to increase appetite and reinforce concepts of good nutrition. Check dietary restrictions, such as avoiding salt and chocolate.
- Young children may need to develop skills in dressing and grooming.

Productivity
- Assist the person to modify his or her home and work environment if needed.
- Assist the person to explore alternate interests if current vocation cannot be continued.
- Assist the person to perform other productive roles, including home manager, volunteer, or student, as indicated.
- Encourage the person to continue studies, if a student.
- Increase development of play skills. Role-playing as a doctor or nurse may relieve a child's fears and anxieties and provide outlet for feelings.

Leisure
- Assist the person to modify existing leisure interests to conform to physical capacities.
- Assist the person to explore new interests that can be performed within physical capacities.

PRECAUTIONS
Avoid messy or dirty activities since persons with renal disorders may be in poor general health or have a poor immune system.

PROGNOSIS AND OUTCOME
- The person has maintained or increased muscle strength.
- The person has maintained or increased range of motion.
- The person has maintained or increased fine motor dexterity and bilateral coordination.

- The person has maintained or increased physical endurance.
- The person has maintained or increased balance and postural control.
- The person demonstrates use of energy-conservation and work-simplification techniques.
- The person demonstrates knowledge of safety factors associated with dialysis.
- The person is able to express feelings about dying.
- The person demonstrates a positive self-concept and internal locus of control.
- The person demonstrates stress-management and coping skills.
- The person maintains or increases social interaction skills.
- The person is independent in self-care and daily living skills.
- The person demonstrates productive skills.
- The person demonstrates leisure skills.

REFERENCES

Bewley, R. 1985. Occupational therapy for children with renal failure. *Australian Occupational Therapy Journal* 32(1):10–6.

Birnbaum, A.S., and J.M. Phillips. 1983. Occupational therapy in the rehabilitation of nephrology patients. *AANNT Journal* 10(6):48–50,54.

Kobe, C.T. 1981. Shunt splint for adult renal patients. *American Journal of Occupational Therapy* 35(3):195–6.

Menninger, B. 1985. Psychosocial needs of children with end-stage renal disease. *Developmental Disabilities Special Interest Section Newsletter* 8(4):3.

Norman, S.B. 1982. Occupational therapy in the treatment of children undergoing renal dialysis. *Australian Occupational Therapy Journal* 29(1)3–7.

Wallace, S. 1989. Clinical perspective. Activity groups in a renal dialysis unit. *Australian Occupational Therapy Journal* 36(3):142–8.

Scleroderma/Systemic Sclerosis

DESCRIPTION

Scleroderma is a progressive disorder characterized by diffuse fibrosis, degenerative changes, and vascular abnormalities in the skin, articular structures, and internal organs (especially the esophagus, intestinal tract, lung, heart, and kidney). The disease varies in degree of severity and rate of progression. The subtype sclerodactyly is confined to the hands for many years. The subtype diffuse scleroderma may progress to total body involvement within one year. It is frequently associated with the CREST syndrome (calcinosis, Raynaud's phenomenon, esophageal dysfunction, sclerodactyly, and telangiectasis). Symptoms may subside for many months, but the course of the disease is not reversed. Death usually occurs because of visceral involvement.

CAUSE

The cause is unknown. The ratio of women to men is about 4:1. Diagnosis usually occurs between the ages of 30 to 50. The disorder is rare in children and the elderly. Involvement usually is symmetrical, beginning in the hands and progressing proximally to the arms, neck, and face, followed by involvement of the trunk and lower extremities.

ASSESSMENT

Areas
- range of motion, active and passive
- hand functions
- fine motor skills, manipulation, dexterity, and bilateral coordination
- physical endurance
- functional mobility
- affect or mood
- social skills
- social roles
- daily living skills
- productivity history, skills, interests, and values
- leisure skills and interests

Instruments
No specific instruments developed by occupational therapists were identified in the literature. The following types of instruments may be useful:

- goniometry
- dynanometers and pinch meters
- dexterity and coordination tests, such as the Purdue Pegboard Dexterity Test
- activities of daily living
- occupational history
- leisure checklist

PROBLEMS

Motor
- The person may have decreasing range of motion and loss of joint mobility.
- The person may have decreased physical endurance.
- The person may have stiffness and swelling of the joints, especially in the hands and feet.
- Flexion contractures of the wrists and elbows may occur.
- Claw hand deformity may occur (metacarpophalangeal joints in extension, proximal interphalangeal joints in flexion, and adduction of the thumb, which results in loss of opposition).
- The person may have myopathy, including muscle weakness and wasting.
- The person may develop ulcers on the fingertips and dorsum of the knuckles due to repeated ischemic attacks related to vasospasms (see sensory problems below).
- The person may lose fine motor skills due to bony resorption, which results in shortening of the fingers or calcium deposits that occur subcutaneously or intracutaneously.

Sensory
- Affected persons frequently have episodic vasospasms of the peripheral arteries that result in balancing and cyanosis of the hands (loss of temperature control) during spasms and erythema following spasm (Raynaud's phenomena). The disorder may also affect the toes, earlobes, tip of the nose, and tongue.
- Polyarthralgia (pain in multiple joints) may occur.
- Changes in body image usually occur.
- The person may have pain and paresthesia.
- The skin may become puffy, swollen, and edematous. Thickening may occur and finally atrophy and deformity.
- Hands may become hypersensitive. The person may respond by keeping his or her hands in a protected position (elbows and wrists flexed).

Cognitive
Cognitive faculties are not directly affected.

Intrapersonal
- The person may have fear of or difficulty adjusting to what others will think about his or her changing body image.
- The person may have fear of or difficulty dealing with dying.
- The person may have fear of or difficulty adjusting to becoming increasingly helpless.
- The person may have fear of or difficulty adjusting to facial and upper extremity disfigurement.

Interpersonal
- The person may withdraw from social situations.
- The person may experience difficulty speaking clearly if mouth, lips, and respiratory system are involved.
- The person may experience changes in roles and role performance.

Self-Care
- The person usually experiences increasing difficulty performing activities of daily living, especially those requiring range of motion or reaching, such as dressing, grooming, housekeeping, and cleaning.
- The person may experience regurgitation of food.
- Decreased size of the mouth opening (oral aperture) may restrict oral hygiene, dental care, and the ability to chew solid food.
- The person may experience dry mouth (sicca syndrome), which interferes with chewing and swallowing.

Productivity
- The person may become increasing unable to perform certain job tasks due to limited range of motion, endurance, or pain.
- The person may be unable to continue working in a specific job due to inability to perform the required job tasks.

Leisure
The person may find certain leisure activities are difficult to continue due to limited range of motion, endurance, or pain.

TREATMENT/MANAGEMENT
Models of treatment are based on biomechanical (Trombly) and rehabilitation models.

Motor
- Maintain range of motion and joint mobility as long as possible. Special attention should be paid to maintaining metacarpophalangeal joint flexion, proximal interphalangeal joint extension, thumb abduction to maintain web space and opposition, and wrist extension. (Avoid claw hand deformity.)
- Consider providing hand splints if the person is unable to carry out range of motion exercises. Metacarpophalangeal flexion may be maintained by using cock-up splints with dynamic finger flexion slings added and using rubber bands to apply tension. The person wears a splint for 15 to 30 minutes while performing daily activities. A splint with a C-bar may be used to maintain web space. This splint may be worn at night. Watch for signs of edema, decreased circulation, and skin changes.
- Maintain physical endurance as long as possible.
- Slow the process of contracture development and prevent contractures due to poor positioning, disuse, or inadequate range of motion exercise.
- Maintain facial mobility (oral aperture, lip closure, and temporomandibular joint excursion) through exercises (see Melvin, 1989, pp.13–4 in the reference section). Massage with a warm washcloth or use of a vibrator may facilitate performance of the exercises.

Sensory
- Wearing gloves or mittens for hands and socks for feet may decrease temperature loss.
- Biofeedback may be useful to control symptoms, relieve pain, and improve function.

Cognitive
- Instruct the person about symptoms, progression of the disorder, and treatments that are effective versus those with no known effectiveness.
- Instruct the person on joint protection and the best postures for activities requiring standing, sitting, and lying down.
- Instruct the person on energy conservation, pacing, and work simplification.
- Provide the person with an objective system for checking range of motion to permit self-monitoring of the progress of the disorder, such as templates of the hands and fingers drawn from the most recent visit (see the Melvin article in the reference section).
- Provide a home program of daily exercises. Check to ensure that the person understands how the exercise is to be performed and why the exercise is important (to maintain range of motion and joint mobility). Pay special attention to metacarpophalangeal flexion, followed by thumb abduction and opposition, and finger proximal interphalangeal extension.

Intrapersonal
- Permit the person to voice fears about changing body image, possible disfigurement, death and dying, and the reaction of family and friends.

- Assist in providing counseling to the person and family or friends regarding the need for physical and emotional support.
- Provide training in stress-management and relaxation techniques. Deep breathing is especially useful since it reinforces breathing exercises. Biofeedback may be useful to develop relaxation skills.

Interpersonal
- Encourage the person to continue socialization.
- Encourage the person to seek social support from family and friends.
- Encourage the person and family to participate in a self-help group if available and use other community resources as needed.

Self-Care
- Encourage the person to maintain independence in self-care activities.
- Recommend self-help devices and provide training in their use if needed. If ulcers or calcium deposits limit functional ability, pressure on sensitive areas may be relieved by using padding on utensils or using strap loops, faucet turners, button hooks, and pencil holders.
- For hypomotility, reflux esophagitis (regurgitation), and dysphagia, suggest sitting very erect during meals, using relaxation techniques before eating, eating smaller and more frequent meals, remaining erect for 15 to 20 minutes after eating, sleeping with the head elevated eight inches above the body, and using antacids.

Productivity
- Make recommendations for modification in work setting that might enable the person to continue working.
- Provide opportunities for exploring interests and career options if present job cannot safely or effectively be continued.
- Make recommendations for modifications in the home that might enable the person to function more independently and contribute to home management.

Leisure
Encourage the person to identify interests and explore leisure activities that can be pursued within the limitations of the disability.

PRECAUTIONS
- Provide information on the need to avoid or limit contact with household detergents because of their drying effect on the skin.
- Provide information on the need to avoid or limit contact with cold or tobacco because of their effect on vasoconstriction.
- Provide information on the need to avoid or limit contact with abrasives that may irritate the skin and lead to infection.
- Watch for signs of carpal tunnel syndrome, which may occur due to dorsal or volar wrist tenosynovitis.

PROGNOSIS AND OUTCOME

The prognosis varies. The person may have remission and lead a relatively healthy life or may become chronically ill and have multiple systemic involvement.

- The person is able to maintain range of motion and joint mobility, especially in the hands, upper extremities, and oral musculature.
- The person demonstrates the use of joint protection techniques in the performance of all daily activities.
- The person demonstrates the use of energy-conservation and work-simplification techniques.
- The person demonstrates the use of coping strategies or stress-management techniques to reduce stress.
- The person maintains social interaction with family and friends.
- The person has social support of family and friends.
- The person performs daily living activities independently using self-help devices as needed.
- The person performs productive activities.
- The person performs leisure activities.

REFERENCES

Melvin, J.L., K.L. Brannan, and E.C. LeRoy. 1984. Comprehensive care for the patient with systemic sclerosis (scleroderma). *Clinical Rheumatology in Practice* 2(3):112–117.

Melvin, J.L. 1989. Systemic sclerosis (scleroderma). In *Rheumatic disease in the adult and child: Occupational therapy and rehabilitation*, 3d ed., ed. J.L. Melvin, 106–17. Philadelphia: F.A. Davis.

Seeger, M.W., and D.E. Furst. 1987. Effects of splinting in the treatment of hand contractures in progressive systemic sclerosis. *American Journal of Occupational Therapy* 41(2):118–21.

Part VIII

Immunologic Disorders

Acquired Immunodeficiency Syndrome (AIDS)

DESCRIPTION

AIDS is a secondary immunodeficiency syndrome caused by a virus and characterized by severe immune deficiency that permits opportunistic infections, malignancies, and neurologic lesions in individuals without a prior history of immunologic abnormality.

CAUSE

The cause is a retrovirus that is called the human immunodeficiency virus (HIV). Other names include the human T-lymphotrophic virus type III (HTLV-III), lymphadenopathy-associated virus (LAV), and the AIDS-associated retrovirus (ARV). Transmission to another person requires transmission of body substances containing infected cells such as blood, plasma, and plasma-containing fluids (saliva). Secondary disorders include pneumocystis and Karposi's sarcoma. Additional disorders caused by the AIDS virus include segmental demyelination, mononeuritis multiplex, polyneuropathy, ganglioneuronitis, and radiculopathy. The groups most affected are sexually active homosexual and bisexual men, intravenous drug users, hemophiliacs infected by blood transfusions, and Haitians.

ASSESSMENT

Areas
- muscle tone
- muscle strength
- fine motor skills, manipulation, dexterity, and coordination
- balance and postural control
- praxis or motor planning skills
- sensory registration and processing
- visual perception
- pain
- organizational skills
- memory
- reality orientation
- coping skills
- safety awareness
- judgment
- quality of life
- self-concept or self-esteem
- support system and family relationships
- communication skills
- knowledge of community management resources

- daily living skills (include medication schedule)
- work capacity or activity tolerance
- productivity history, skills, values, and interests
- leisure interests and skills
- architectural or environmental barriers

Instruments

No specific instruments developed by occupational therapists for this disorder were identified in the literature. The following types of instruments may be useful:

- manual muscle test
- dexterity and coordination test, such as the Purdue Pegboard Dexterity Test
- activities of daily living scale
- work capacities evaluation
- occupational history
- leisure checklist

PROBLEMS

Motor
- The person usually has loss of physical endurance.
- The person usually has weight loss.
- The person usually has progressive loss of muscle strength.
- The person may experience gait ataxia.
- The person may experience loss of coordination.

Sensory
- The person may have pain.
- The person may have loss of sensation.
- The person may have loss of perceptual skills.

Cognitive
The person may experience signs of dementia, including confusion and loss of problem-solving skills.

Intrapersonal
- The person may express fear of death.
- The person may become depressed.
- The person may have feelings of hopelessness and helplessness.
- The person may have loss of self-esteem and self-worth.
- The person may express anxiety about finances, relationships, and care.
- The person may have loss of coping skills.

Interpersonal
The person may experience loss of friends or rejection by lover and family members.

Self-Care

As loss of strength increases, the person may be unable to perform activities of daily living.

Productivity

- The person may be terminated from employment because of disease.
- The person may be unable to continue job tasks because of weakness and recurrent illness.

Leisure

The person may be unable to continue leisure activities.

TREATMENT/MANAGEMENT

Models of treatment are not well defined but appear to be based on neurodevelopmental (child), biomechanical, rehabilitation, and human occupation. (Note: This section does not include information on treating children born with AIDS. Literature on occupational therapy for infants or children born with AIDS is very limited. See Anderson et al., 1990 and Pizzi, 1989, in the reference section.)

Motor

- Maintain the person's physical endurance.
- Maintain muscle strength.
- Maintain normal muscle tone.
- Assist in gait training and the use of ambulation aids.

Sensory

- Provide techniques for pain management, including relaxation techniques.
- Provide sensory stimulation.

Cognitive

- Provide the person with facts about the disease and the resources available for care and treatment.
- Encourage the person to engage in purposeful activities.
- Stress the importance of maintaining the immune system through the use of good body mechanics, proper nutrition, and an adequate exercise program.
- Provide instruction about safety issues associated with protecting the person from opportunistic infections and other diseases.

Intrapersonal

- Improve the person's self-concept and sense of mastery through the use of creative activities, such as crafts, music, drama, or dance.
- Decrease anxiety by permitting the person to voice concerns and work on solutions.
- Provide training in stress-management techniques, including such relaxation techniques as visualization, Yoga, meditation, and biofeedback.

Interpersonal

Encourage communication among the person's family, friends, and lover.

Self-Care
- Maintain skills the person needs to perform activities of daily living.
- Provide adaptive equipment, if needed, to perform self-care skills.
- Assist the person to prepare and eat nutritious meals.

Productivity
- Encourage the person to maintain productive activities.
- Suggest modifications of the work or home environment that will permit the person to continue productive activities.

Leisure
Encourage the person to explore and develop new leisure interests to replace those that cannot be continued.

PRECAUTIONS
- Protect the person from communicable diseases. The therapist should wear a mask if he or she has cold or flu symptoms.
- Wash hands before and after working with the person.
- The therapist should use gloves if he or she will be exposed to body fluids.
- Be alert when using sharp objects to avoid pricking or puncturing oneself.
- If a therapy pool is used, be sure the pool is properly maintained and disinfected.
- The person's house, apartment, or room should be cleaned regularly with bleach.
- Detergent and bleach should be used for cleaning laundry.
- Food preparation surfaces should be cleaned frequently.

PROGNOSIS AND OUTCOME
The outcome is poor. Most persons die of opportunistic infections.

- The person demonstrates knowledge of how to maintain physical fitness and endurance as long as possible.
- The person demonstrates knowledge of work-simplification, pacing, and energy-conservation techniques.
- The person demonstrates knowledge of stress-management techniques, including relaxation.
- The person demonstrates a positive self-concept.
- The person is able to maintain independence in daily living skills using self-help devices as needed.
- The person is able to maintain productive activities at work and at home.
- The person has a variety of leisure activities.

REFERENCES

Anderson, J., J. Hinojosa, G. Bedell, et al. 1990. Occupational therapy for children with perinatal HIV infection. *American Journal of Occupational Therapy* 44(3):249–55.
Bakland, L.K., 1989. Health care professionals' role in the treatment of AIDS. In *AIDS and the allied health professions*, ed. J.W. Hopp and E.A. Rogers, 209–61. Philadelphia: F.A. Davis.

Bonck, J. 1988. The neurological sequelae of AIDS: Treatment issues for occupational therapy. *Physical Disabilities Special Interest Section Newsletter* 10(3):1,6–7.

Bonck, J., and A. MacRae. 1990. Part II Human immunodeficiency virus (HIV) illness. In *Neurological rehabilitation*, 2d ed., ed. D.A. Umphred, 518–29. St. Louis: C.V. Mosby.

Castle, S.M. 1986. The emerging role of occupational therapy with AIDS. *Occupational Therapy Forum* 1(9):12–13.

Coates, R., and J. Barratt. 1990. HIV infection, AIDS and occupational therapy. *British Journal of Occupational Therapy* 53(5):178–80.

Cornblatt, M.S., M.J. Ayres, and E.L. Kolodner. 1990. A legal perspective on AIDS. *American Journal of Occupational Therapy* 44(3):244–6.

Cusack, L., L. Phillips, and S. Singh. 1990. The role of the occupational therapist in HIV disease and AIDS. *British Journal of Occupational Therapy* 53(5):181–3.

Denton, R. 1987. AIDS: Guidelines for occupational therapy intervention. *American Journal of Occupational Therapy* 41(7):427–32.

Giles, G.M., and M.E. Allen. 1987. Safety issues in the treatment of the AIDS patient. *Occupational Therapy Forum* 2(16):4–7.

Gordon, L. 1987. An occupational therapy protocol for the AIDS patient. *Physical Disabilities Special Interest Section Newsletter* 10(3):4–6.

Guindon, K.R., et al. 1989. Supportive measure: Living with AIDS. In *AIDS and the allied health professions*, ed. J.W. Hopp and E.A. Rogers, 151–69. Philadelphia: F.A. Davis.

Gutterman, L. 1990. A day treatment program for persons with AIDS. *American Journal of Occupational Therapy* 44(3):234–7.

Hansen, R.A. 1990. The ethics of caring for patients with HIV or AIDS. *American Journal of Occupational Therapy* 44(3):239–42.

Human immunodeficiency virus (position paper). 1989. *American Journal of Occupational Therapy* 43(12):803–4.

Johnson, C.D., and S.Z. Glickel. 1989. AIDS and the hand therapist. *Journal of Hand Therapy* 2(3):157–63.

Madill, H.M. 1988. Position paper on the human immunodeficiency virus (HIV): The implications for occupational therapy practice. *Canadian Journal of Occupational Therapy* 55(5):Centrefold,1–6.

O'Rourke, G.C. 1990. The HIV-positive intravenous drug abuser. *American Journal of Occupational Therapy* 44(3):280–3.

Peoloquin, S.M. 1990. AIDS: Toward a compassionate response. *American Journal of Occupational Therapy* 44(3):271–8.

Person-Karell, B. 1987. The role of the occupational therapist in an AIDS clinic: Two case reviews. *Physical Disabilities Special Interest Section Newsletter* 10(3):4–5.

Piemme, J.A., and J.L. Bolle. 1990. Coping with grief in response to caring for persons with AIDS. *American Journal of Occupational Therapy* 44(3):266–9.

Pizzi, M. 1989. Occupational therapy: Creating possibilities for adults with HIV infection, ARC, and AIDS. *AIDS Patient Care* 3:18–23.

Pizzi, M. 1989. Occupational therapy: Creating possibilities for children with HIV infection, ARC, and AIDS. *AIDS Patient Care* 3:31–6.

Pizzi, M. 1990. Nationally speaking—The transformation of HIV infection and AIDS in occupational therapy: Beginning the conversation. *American Journal of Occupational Therapy* 44(3):199–203.

Pizzi, M. 1990. The model of human occupation and adults with HIV infection and AIDS. *American Journal of Occupational Therapy* 44(3):257–64.

Schindler, V.J. 1988. Psychosocial occupational therapy intervention with AIDS patients. *American Journal of Occupational Therapy* 43(8):507–12.

Sladyk, K. 1990. Teaching safe sex practices to psychiatric patients. *American Journal of Occupational Therapy* 44(3):284–6.

Vincent, T.A., and J.K. Schkade. 1990. Knowledge and attitudes of occupational therapy students regarding AIDS. *American Journal of Occupational Therapy* 44(3):205–17.

Weinstein, B.D. 1990. Assessing the impact of HIV disease. *American Journal of Occupational Therapy* 44(3):220–6.

Weinstein, B.D., and L.S. De Neffe. 1990. Hemophilia, AIDS, and occupational therapy. *American Journal of Occupational Therapy* 44(3):228–32.

Cancer/Neoplasms

DESCRIPTION
A neoplasm or cancer is a cellular structure that has lost normal controls. The result may be unregulated growth, lack of differentiation, and the ability to invade surrounding tissue and metastasize to other sites.

CAUSE
Age is a significant factor in the incidence and mortality of cancer. Certain cancers are associated with children, such as acute lymphoblastic leukemia; others are associated with young adults, such as Hodgkin's disease; while still others are associated with old age, such as cancer of the prostate, stomach, and colon. The exact cause is unknown but related to genetic susceptibility, chromosome breakage disorders, viruses, environmental factors (chemical carcinogens or radiation), and immunologic disorders.

ASSESSMENT

Areas
- range of motion
- muscle strength
- postural control and balance
- fine motor skills, manipulation, dexterity and coordination
- sensory registration and processing
- perceptual skills
- self-concept
- coping skills
- social skills
- communication skills
- daily living skills
- productivity history, skills, interests, and values
- work or physical capacities evaluation
- leisure interests and skills
- architectural and environmental barriers
- home safety

Instruments
No instruments developed by an occupational therapist for this disorder were found in the literature. The following types of instruments may be useful:

- manual muscle test
- goniometry
- dexterity and coordination tests, such as the Purdue Pegboard Dexterity Test

- activities of daily living scale
- occupational history
- work capacities evaluation
- leisure checklist

PROBLEMS

Motor
- The person may lose muscle strength.
- The person may lose range of motion.
- The person may lose joint mobility.
- The person may have low physical tolerance and fatigue easily.

Sensory
- The person may experience a variety of types of pain or a single intense type of pain.
- The person may lose one or more sensory systems depending on the type of cancer.

Cognitive
- If the tumor is in the brain, cognitive functions may be adversely affected.
- Drug therapy may cause some cognitive dysfunction.

Intrapersonal
- The person may express fear of pain, suffering, and dying.
- The person may fear loss of independence and control of his or her life.
- The person may be depressed and express a sense of despair.
- The person may suffer loss of self-esteem.
- The person may feel hopeless and helpless.
- The person may express feelings of anger. (Why me?)
- The person may become tense and overanxious.
- The person may become highly defensive or deny anything is wrong.

Interpersonal
The person may lose social support as friends find excuses for not visiting a person with cancer or a person who is dying.

Self-Care
The person may be unable to perform certain activities of daily living, depending on the type of cancer and resulting disability.

Productivity
The person may be unable to continue productive roles formerly occupied.

Leisure
The person may be unable to continue leisure activities formerly enjoyed.

TREATMENT/MANAGEMENT

The approach to treatment and management must be individualized to the needs of the person, to the specific disease state, and to the degree of disability. The model of treatment is occupational behavior (Reilly).

Motor

- Assist the person to maintain as much physical strength as possible through organization of rest and activity cycles.
- Maintain or increase range of motion through activities selected to promote the use of joints.
- Provide orthotic devices, such as splints and other positioning support as needed, to reduce deformity and promote function.
- Maintain or increase muscle strength through the use of graded activities.
- Provide pre- and post-prosthesis training if needed. (See the section on amputations.)

Sensory

- Assist the person to reduce response to pain, if present.
- The use of therapeutic touch may promote relaxation or promote a sense of caring.
- Provide sensory stimulation to the vestibular, tactile, proprioceptive, and visual senses to facilitate maintenance of sensorimotor integration.

Cognitive

- Teach the person the concepts of work simplification and energy conservation.
- Teach concepts of safety in the home and workplace to reduce the possibility of added injury.
- Assist in explaining possible side effects of treatment from surgery, chemotherapy, or radiation therapy.
- Teach the person and family about the disease.

Intrapersonal

- Maintain or improve the quality of life, including present lifestyle, past experiences, hope for the future, and ambitions.
- Provide stress-management training, including relaxation techniques, if not contraindicated.
- The use of craft activities may be useful to maintain self-esteem. Crafts selected should be chosen based on the person's age, level of function, stage of illness, and degree of disability.
- The use of music may be helpful in promoting relaxation or arousal by changing respiration, pulse rate, or blood pressure.
- The use of humor may be helpful in changing a person's outlook on the situation and as a means of interacting with others.

Interpersonal

- Maintain or improve social support system.
- Provide training in the use of alternative communication systems, especially if the ability to talk is impaired or lost.

• Assist the family to provide caregiving, cope with problems, and set realistic goals.

Self-Care
• Maintain or increase the person's ability to independently perform activities of daily living (dressing, eating, hygiene) and functional skills (writing, cooking, driving).
• Provide adaptive equipment and train the person in its use, if needed. Adapted devices for eating or grooming and installation of grab bars and non-skid materials may be useful.
• Provide recommendations about modification of the living environment that may increase the ability of the person to function independently or make caregiving easier, including elimination of architectural barriers and making provisions for safety.

Productivity
• Maintain participation in productive activities as long as possible, including participation in homemaking, work for pay, or student or volunteer roles.
• Make recommendations for modifications of the work environment to provide easier access, promote task performance, and increase safety.

Leisure
Explore leisure interests and encourage the development or expansion of leisure activities that are within the person's physical and psychosocial abilities.

PRECAUTIONS
Be alert to possible side effects of medication and radiation treatments, such as nausea.

PROGNOSIS AND OUTCOME
• The person can demonstrate knowledge of his or her health status and disabilities, if any.
• The person performs self-care activities independently with self-help devices if needed.
• The person performs productive activities within the range of his or her health status.
• The person performs leisure activities that require active participation.
• The person can demonstrate knowledge of community support services.
• Family and friends encourage the person to perform as independently as possible within his or her health status.

REFERENCES

Bieringer, A. 1981. Cancer and impaired independence. In *Physical disabilities manual*, ed. B. Abreu, 285–93. New York: Raven Press.

Cusick, A., R. Lawler, and M. Swain. 1987. Chemotherapy, cancer, and the quality of life: An occupational therapy approach. *Australian Occupational Therapy Journal* 34(3):105–13.

Lloyd, C., and J. Neven. 1988. Occupational therapy and the elderly cancer patient. *Physical and Occupational Therapy in Geriatrics* 6(3/4):87–97.

Lloyd, C., and L. Coggles. 1988. Contribution of occupational therapy to pain management in cancer patients with metastatic breast disease. *American Journal of Hospice Care* 5(6):36–8.

Lloyd, C., and L. Coggles. 1989. Occupational therapy and the cancer patient: An occupational behavior perspective. *Physical and Occupational Therapy in Geriatrics* 7(4):59–69.

Lloyd, C., and L. Coggles. 1990. Psychosocial issues for people with cancer and their families. *Canadian Journal of Occupational Therapy* 57(4):211–5.

Logigian, M.K. 1982. Oncological rehabilitation. In *Adult rehabilitation: A team approach for therapists*, ed. M.K. Logigian, 41–69. Boston: Little, Brown & Co.

Lynch, P.D., S. Schaefer, and D. Eckert. 1983. Cancer rehabilitation issues for occupational and physical therapists: A conference report. *Progress in Clinical and Biological Research* 130:443–53.

Mehls, J.D. 1983. Occupational therapy as a component of cancer rehabilitation. *Progress in Clinical and Biological Research* 121:231–40.

Nordstrom, D.B. 1988. The autosyringe backpack for children with cancer: A device that permits mobility. *Occupational Therapy in Health Care* 5(2/3):77–86.

Romsaas, E.P., and S.A. Rosa. 1985. Occupational therapy intervention for cancer patients with metastatic disease. *American Journal of Occupational Therapy* 39(2):79–83.

Stowell, M.S. 1987. Psychosocial role of the occupational therapist with pediatric bone marrow transplant patients. *Occupational Therapy in Mental Health* 7(2):39–50.

Strong, J. 1987. Occupational therapy and cancer rehabilitation. *British Journal of Occupational Therapy* 50(1):4–6.

Tigges, K.N., and L.M. Sherman. 1983. The treatment of the hospice patient: From occupational history to occupational role. *American Journal of Occupational Therapy* 37(4):235–8.

Tigges, K.N., and W.M. Marcill. 1988. Cancer and AIDS. In *Terminal and life-threatening illness: An occupational behavior perspective*, ed. K.N. Tigges and W.M. Marcil, 45–90. Thorofare, NJ: Slack, Inc.

Wescott, L.A. 1989. Occupational therapy protocol for Cancer Rehabilitation Program. *Occupational Therapy Forum* 4(July, 17):4.

Wingate, L. 1989. Rehabilitation of the mastectomy patient: A randomized, blind, prospective study. *Archives of Physical Medicine and Rehabilitation* 70(1):21–4.

Part IX

Skin Disorders

Burns—Adult

DESCRIPTION

Burns are tissue injury that results in protein denaturation, burn wound edema, and loss of intravascular fluid volume due to increased vascular permeability.

CAUSE

The causes include thermal (heat or cold), chemical (acids or alkalis), or electrical contact.

ASSESSMENT

Description

- Severity—percentage of body surface area (BSA) burned
  1. small—< 15% BSA
  2. moderate—15 to 49% BSA
  3. large—50 to 69% BSA
  4. massive—> 70% BSA
- depth—layers of skin burned
  1. first degree—burns are red, very sensitive to the touch, blanche to light pressure, and usually moist but there are no blisters
  2. second degree—the wound is sensitive to touch and may blanch to pressure. There may be blisters.
  3. third degree—surface may be white and pliable or black, charred, and leathery. Subdermal vessels do not blanch to pressure and generally the wound is anesthetic or hypoesthetic. Hairs may be pulled from their follicles easily.

Areas

- burned areas, including type, percentage, depth, and location
- range of motion, active and passive
- muscle strength
- pain
- sensory registration and processing
- affect or mood
- self-concept
- daily living skills
- productivity history, skills, interests, and values
- leisure skills and interests

Instruments

No instruments developed by occupational therapists for this disorder were identified in the literature. The following types of instruments may be useful:

- goniometers
- manual muscle test
- pain questionnaire
- activities of daily living scale
- occupational history
- leisure checklist

PROBLEMS

Motor
- The person may have limitations in range of motion.
- The person may have muscle weakness and disuse atrophy.
- The person may have contractures.
- The person may have faulty posture.
- The person may have deformities.

Sensory
- The person usually has severe physical pain and discomfort.
- The person may have loss of sensory registration and processing in tactile, proprioceptive, temperature, and pressure senses.

Cognitive
Cognitive faculties are not affected directly but pain and discomfort limit attention span and concentration.

Intrapersonal
- The person may fear permanent physical deformity and disfigurement.
- The person may fear chronic pain.
- The person may express feelings of inadequacy and physical helplessness.
- The person may feel injury is a punishment for misdeeds.
- The person may have loss of self-esteem.
- The person may become dependent or regress.
- The person may become depressed.
- The person may become irritable.
- The person may express anger or hostility at his or her employer for permitting situation to occur that led to burns.

Interpersonal
- The person may have limited verbal communication ability if face is burned.
- The person may withdraw and express feelings of being rejected.

Self-Care
The site of injury and degree of injury usually determine the degree of loss of performance of activities of daily living. Burns to the hands and arms result in greater loss of skills.

Productivity

The person usually will be unable to work for several months and may be unable to return to his or her former occupation.

Leisure

- If the lower limbs are injured, sports activities may be limited.
- If the hands are injured, the person may be unable to perform fine motor skills.

TREATMENT/MANAGEMENT

Motor

Pregrafting Stage

- Provide positioning devices as needed, such as
  1. foam head donut to prevent neck flexion contracture
  2. foam ear protector to prevent pressure on ear that is burned
  3. arm trough to maintain abduction of shoulder
  4. foot board to maintain ankle in neutral position
- Provide splints as needed, such as
  1. neck conformer or soft cervical collar to prevent contractures of neck tissue
  2. axillary or airplane splint to maintain shoulder abduction
  3. elbow conformer or three-point extension splint to maintain elbow extension
  4. cock-up splint to maintain wrist extension with or without C-bar to maintain web space
  5. abductor wedge to maintain hip abduction
  6. knee conformer or three-point extension splint to maintain knee extension
  7. foot drop splint to maintain ankle in neutral position
- Encourage active range of motion when changing positioning device, splint, or bandage.
- Use of continuous passive motion may be useful to prevent contractures and decrease deformity.
- Maintain or increase muscle strength in unaffected areas through activities that provide progressive-resistive exercise.

Grafting Stage

Additional positioning devices or splints may be needed, depending on the graft site.

Postgrafting Stage

Minimize scarring by applying pressure to the person's skin through the use of pressure garments.

Sensory

Provide sensory stimuli according to the person's needs to prevent environmental deprivation.

Cognitive

Provide instruction to the person and his or her family about recovery from burns and the assistance available.

Intrapersonal
Use craft or game activities to enhance self-esteem and provide purposeful activity. Generally avoid skin irritants or hazardous tools. While the person is in bed or confined to room, avoid dirty or messy activities or ones that require many parts. Consider ceramic tiles, painting, needlework, leather lacing, board games, and puzzles.

Interpersonal
Provide communication board for person who is intubated and cannot talk.

Self-Care
Facilitate performance of activities of daily living by providing self-care devices and instruction if needed, such as built-up handles to compensate for lack of grasp.

Productivity
- Assist the person to prepare for a return to productive activities as stages of recovery permit.
- Explore the need for changes in productive environment that might permit earlier return to productive tasks.

Leisure
Assist the person to explore leisure interests that are within functional capacity at various stages of recovery.

PRECAUTIONS
- Watch for signs of infection. Splints can be a source of microorganisms. They should be cleaned whenever removed from the person with a disinfecting agent, such as a quaternary ammonia solution.
- Watch for signs of skin breakdown (decubitus ulcer) or failure of grafts.
- Watch for signs of heterotopic ossification (calcium deposits in a joint, such as the elbow).
- Watch for signs of peripheral nerve injury from compression.
- Watch for signs of hypertrophic scarring.
- Watch for signs of contracture formation.

PROGNOSIS AND OUTCOME
- The person demonstrates maximum level of independence in performance of activities of daily living.
- The person is able to control pain to permit maximum function in performing daily tasks.
- The person is able to control skin sensitivity to permit maximum function in performing daily tasks.
- Deformities are eliminated or minimized to the degree possible.
- Hypertrophic scarring is reduced to the minimum possible and does not interfere with functional performance of daily tasks.
- The person is able to perform productive activities.

REFERENCES

Apfel, L. 1984. Occupational therapy techniques for the patient with thermal injuries of the head and neck. In *Burns of the head and neck*, ed. T.L. Wachtel and D.H. Frank, 133–52. Philadelphia: W.B. Saunders Co.

Apfel, L.M., T.A. Synstegard, T.L. Wachtel, et al. 1984. Functional hand assessment after enzymatic debridement and early autografting. *Journal of Burn Care and Rehabilitation* 5(4):438–45.

Apfel, L.M., et al. 1987. Functional electrical stimulation in intrinsic/extrinsic imbalanced burned hands. *Journal of Burn Care and Rehabilitation* 8(2):97–102.

Apfel, L.M., et al. 1988. Computer-drafted pressure support gloves. *Journal of Burn Care and Rehabilitation* 9(2):165–8.

Bruster, J.M., and G. Pullium. 1983. Gradient pressure. *American Journal of Occupational Therapy* 37(7):485–8.

Chan, S.W., and L.W. Pedretti. 1985. Burns. In *Occupational therapy: Practice skills for physical dysfunction*, 2d ed., ed. L.W. Pedretti, 279–90. St. Louis: C.V. Mosby. 3d ed., 1990, 445–56.

Cheng, S., and J.C. Rogers. 1989. Changes in occupational role performance after a severe burn: A retrospective study. *American Journal of Occupational Therapy* 43(1):17–24.

Cooper, F.C., and E.J. Yerxa. 1984. Denial: Implications of a pilot study on activity level related to sexual competence in burned adults. *American Journal of Occupational Therapy* 38(8):529–34.

Covey, M.H. 1987. Occupational therapy. In *The art and science of burn care*, ed. J.A. Boswick, 285–98. Gaithersburg, MD: Aspen Publishers, Inc.

Covey, M., K.D. Dutcher, D.M. Heimbach, et al. 1987. Return of hand function following major burns. *Journal of Burn Care and Rehabilitation* 8(3):224–6.

Covey, M. 1988. Application of CPM devices with burn patients. *Journal of Burn Care and Rehabilitation* 9(5):496–7.

Covey, M., K.D. Dutcher, J.A. Marvin, et al. 1988. Efficacy of continuous passive motion (CPM) devices with hand burns. *Journal of Burn Care and Rehabilitation* 9(4):397–400.

Dobner, D., and M. Mitani. 1988. Community reentry program. *Journal of Burn Care and Rehabilitation* 9(4):420–1.

Duncan, C.E., and M.E. Cathcart. 1988. A multi-disciplinary model for burn rehabilitation. *Journal of Burn Care and Rehabilitation* 9(2):191–2.

Eles, A., and J.A. Marvin. 1985. Burn patient cooperation in physical and occupational therapy. *Journal of Burn Care and Rehabilitation* 6(3):246–9.

Engrav, L.H., L.B. Macdonald, M.H. Covey, et al. 1983. Do splinting and pressure devices damage new grafts? *Journal of Burn Care and Rehabilitation* 4(2):107–8.

Fader, P. 1985. A self-instructional package: Neck conformer. *Journal of Burn Care and Rehabilitation* 6(2):124–7.

Fowler, D. 1987. Australian occupational therapy: Current trends and future considerations in burn rehabilitation. *Journal of Burn Care and Rehabilitation* 8(5):415–7.

Goldberg, N., P. Stadler, and M. Kaplan. 1984. Occupational therapy: Splinting, positioning and exercise. In *Rehabilitation of the burn patient*, ed. V.R. DiGregorio, 33–54. New York: Churchill Livingstone.

Heitman, J., and P. Parshley. 1987. Burns. In *Interdisciplinary rehabilitation in trauma*, ed. J.J. Gerhardt, et al, 320–9. Baltimore, MD: Williams & Wilkins.

Helm, P.A., C.G. Kevorkian, M. Lushbaugh, et al. 1982. Burn injury: Rehabilitation management in 1982. *Archives of Physical Medicine and Rehabilitation* 63(1):6–16. Reprinted in *Journal of Burn Care and Rehabilitation* 4(6):411–22, 1983.

Hill, C. 1985. Psychosocial adjustment of adult burns patients: Is it more difficult for people with visible scars? *British Journal of Occupational Therapy* 48(9):281–3.

Howard, W. 1987. Burns. In *The practice of occupational therapy*, 2d ed., ed. A. Turner, 310–18. Edinburgh, Scotland: Churchill Livingstone.

Johnson, C.L., and R. Underwood. 1986. Harborview: A view of a rehabilitation team. *Journal of Burn Care and Rehabilitation* 7(3):261–5.

Kaplan, S.H. 1985. Patient education techniques used at burn centers. *American Journal of Occupational Therapy* 39(10):655–8.

Knothe, B. 1990. Returning to work after burn injury. *Work Programs Special Interest Section Newsletter* 4(3):1–3.

Logigian, M.K. 1989. Medical disorders: Burns. In *A team approach for therapists: Pediatric rehabilitation*, ed. M.K. Logigian and J.D. Ward, 258–68. Boston: Little, Brown & Co.

McGourty, L.K., A. Givens, and P.B. Fader. 1985. Roles and functions of occupational therapy in burn care delivery. *American Journal of Occupational Therapy* 39(12):791–4. Also in *Journal of Burn Care and Rehabilitation* 7(5):431–3, 1986.

Miles, W.K. 1984. Remodeling of scar tissue in the burned patient. In *Rehabilitation of the hand*, 2d ed., ed. J.M.

Hunter, et al., 596–610. St. Louis: C.V. Mosby. Revised in 3d ed., 1990, 841–57.

Ngim, R.C., S.T. Lee, and A. Tang. 1983. Rehabilitation of burns of the upper limb. *Annals of the Academy of Medicine Singapore* 12(3):350–7.

Neeman, R.L. 1985. Case reports of burn injury rehabilitation: Hand dyskinesia and finger pain—treatment by orthokinetic orthoses. *Journal of Burn Care and Rehabilitation* 6(3):495–500.

Northdurft, D., P.S. Smith, and J.E. LeMaster. 1984. Exercise and treatment modalities. In *Comprehensive rehabilitation of burns*, ed. S.V. Fisher and P.A. Helm, 96–147. Baltimore, MD: Williams & Wilkins.

Ostergren, G. 1984. Burn care. In *Current concepts in orthotics: A diagnosis-related approach to splinting*, ed. E.M. Ziegler 101–122. Menomonee Falls, WI: Roylan Medical Products.

Parent, L.H. 1983. Burns. In *Occupational therapy for physical dysfunction*, 2d ed., ed. C.A. Trombly 399–408. Baltimore, MD: Williams & Wilkins. 3d ed., 1989, 571–80.

Questad, K.A., et al. 1988. Relating mental health and physical function at discharge to rehabilitation status at three months postburn. *Journal of Burn Care and Rehabilitation* 9(1):87–9.

Reeves, S.U. 1983. Occupational therapy in burn treatment. In *Manual on burn therapeutics*, ed. R.E. Sallsbury, N.M. Newman, and G.P Dingeldein, 179–95. Boston: Little, Brown & Co.

Rivers, E.A. 1984. Management of hypertrophic scarring. In *Comprehensive rehabilitation of burns*, ed. S.V. Fisher and P.A. Helm, 177–217. Baltimore, MD: Williams & Wilkins.

Rivers, E. 1984. A compression hand wrap. *Journal of Burn Care and Rehabilitation* 5(4):291–3.

Rivers, E.A. 1987. Rehabilitation management of the burn patient. In *Advances in Clinical Rehabilitation*, vol. 1, ed. M.G. Eisenberg and R.C. Grzesiak, 177–214. New York: Springer Publications.

Salisbury, R.E., S. Reeves, and P. Wright. 1984. Acute care and rehabilitation of the burned hand. In *Rehabilitation of the hand*, 2d ed., ed. J.M. Hunter, et al., 585–95. St. Louis: C.V. Mosby. 3d ed., 1990, 831–40.

Smith, K., and K. Owens. 1985. Physical and occupational therapy burn unit protocol: Benefits and uses. *Journal of Burn Care and Rehabilitation* 6(6):506–8.

Stramba, L.M. 1981. Early motion and splinting of hands following burns: A literature review. *Canadian Journal of Occupational Therapy* 48(1):27–32.

Turner, D.G., C. Leman, and M.H. Jordan 1989. Cooking-related burn injuries in the elderly: Preventing the "granny gown" burn. *Journal of Burn Care and Rehabilitation* 10:356–9.

van Straten, O. 1986. The use of games in occupational therapy of hand burns. *Burns: Including Thermal Injury* 12(7):521–5.

van Straten, O., and D. Mahler. 1984. Pressure garments in the control of hypertrophic scarring and rehabilitation of the burn patients: An occupational therapy approach. *Israel Journal of Medical Sciences* 20(4):320–2.

van Straten, O., P. Ben-Meir, B. Greber, et al. 1987. New ideas in splinting of burns. *Burns* 13(1):66–8.

Wright, M.P., et al. 1989. The microbiology and cleaning of thermoplastic splints in burn care. *Journal of Burn Care and Rehabilitation* 10(1):79–83.

Burns—Child

DESCRIPTION

Burns in children are defined as tissue injury to the layers of skin and in some cases the soft-tissue structure under the skin resulting in protein denaturation, burn wound edema, and loss of intravascular fluid volume due to increased vascular permeability. Systemic effects, such as hypovolemic shock, infection, or respiratory tract injury, pose a greater threat to life than does the injury to the skin and soft tissue directly.

CAUSE

The most common sources of burns in children are fire and hot water. Other sources are electrical burns that occur from biting an electrical cord, sunburn, various caustic chemicals, or radiation. Young children ages one to three are likely to be burned by hot water, while children older than three are more likely to be burned by fire in their clothing or their home.

ASSESSMENT

Areas
• developmental profile
• range of motion
• muscle strength
• fine motor skills, manipulation, dexterity, and bilateral coordination
• sensory registration and processing
• self-concept
• coping skills
• communication skills
• daily living skills
• play skills
• academic skills
• leisure interests

Instruments
No specific instruments developed by occupational therapists for this disorder were identified in the literature. The following types of instruments may be useful:

• developmental tests
• goniometers
• manual muscle test
• dexterity and coordination tests, such as the Purdue Pegboard Dexterity Test
• activities of daily living scale
• play history
• leisure checklist

PROBLEMS

Motor
• The child usually has limited range of motion.
• The child usually has loss of muscle strength.
• The child may have loss of dexterity and coordination.
• The child may have contractures.
• The child may have deformities.

Sensory
• The child may have hypertrophic scar formation.
• The child may have distorted body image.
• The child usually has pain.

Cognitive
The child may have difficulty concentrating on tasks due to pain and/or pain medication.

Intrapersonal
- The child may have fear of dying.
- The child may have anxiety about what is happening.
- The child may have guilt that burns are his or her fault or are a punishment.
- The child may be angry and irritable.
- The child may become depressed, listless, or apathetic.
- The child may have low self-esteem.

Interpersonal
- The child may suffer loss and separation from his or her family.
- The child may have loss of verbal communication if intubated or microstomia splint is used.

Self-Care
The child may lose the ability to perform self-care skills or fall behind in development of self-care activities.

Productivity
- The child may lose play skills or fall behind in play skill development.
- The child may fall behind in academic skills.

Leisure
The child may be unable to participate in favorite leisure activities.

Splinting Positions

Location	Position
Neck	0 degrees or neutral
Shoulder	90 to 150 degrees abduction with slight external rotation
Elbow	5 to 10 degrees flexion (reduces incidence of bony blocks in the elbow joint)
Wrist	30 degrees hyperextension, 0 degrees ulnar or radial deviation
Metacarpophalangeal	45 to 60 degrees flexion
PIP and DIP	0 degrees or full extension; child under four, slight flexion
Knee	0 degrees or neutral—no hyperextension
Ankle	70 to 90 degrees dorsiflexion

Source: Based on C.B. Doane. In P.N. Pratt and A.S. Allen, eds. *Occupational therapy for children*, 2d ed. St. Louis: C.V. Mosby, 1989, 528.

TREATMENT

Motor
- Assist in positioning of body parts through the use of splints to prevent contractures and deformities. Common splints include: (1) anterior neck conformer for neck, (2) pan splint for hands, (3) axillary splint for shoulders, (4) bivalue splint for elbow or knee, or (5) posterior knee splint. Less common is the transparent face mask and microstomia splint to maintain the size of the mouth.
- Provide exercises for the burned hand to avoid possible damage to the extension mechanisms: tabletop (metacarpophalangeal [MCP] flexion, proximal and distal interphalangeal [PIP and DIP] extension), and curl (MCP extension, PIP and DIP flexion).

Sensory
Provide pressure garments to reduce scar hypertrophy.

Cognitive
- Provide instructions to family members on the care of burns and progress of rehabilitation.
- Assist the physician in providing factual information on the prognosis and outcome of the burn sites.

Intrapersonal
- Provide opportunities for self-expression, such as storytelling, simple craft projects, or games.
- Provide stress-management techniques, including relaxation training.

Interpersonal
Provide a communication board if needed to facilitate communication.

Self-Care
Provide adapted self-care equipment as needed, such as built-up handles, one-handed devices, prism glasses, reachers, large hook handles, nonslip devices or material, long straws, or long handles.

Productivity
- Provide opportunities to maintain or develop play skills.
- Assist in promoting academic development by providing suggestions for adapted devices or equipment.

Leisure
Promote participation in leisure activities using adapted devices or techniques if needed.

PRECAUTIONS
- Watch for signs of infection. Clean splints with approved solution.
- Watch for skin breakdown or graft site failure.
- Watch for heterotopic ossification.

- Watch for peripheral nerve injury from compression, which may occur from a splint.
- Watch for hypertrophic scarring.
- Watch for contractures.

PROGNOSIS AND OUTCOME
- The child maintains or improves developmental profile to his or her chronological age.
- The child maintains or improves muscle strength in muscle groups affected by burns.
- The child maintains or improves range of motion in joints affected by burns.
- The child maintains or improves fine motor dexterity and bilateral coordination.
- The child maintains or improves sensory registration and processing of sensory information.
- The child demonstrates positive self-concept and self-esteem.
- The child demonstrates coping techniques.
- The child is able to perform self-care activities independently using self-help devices if needed.
- The child demonstrates age-appropriate play skills.
- The child is able to maintain or improve academic skills with adapted devices or equipment if needed.
- The child is able to participate in leisure activities.

REFERENCES

Cooney, M.A. 1984. Splinting the pediatric patient with multiple joint involvement. *Journal of Burn Care and Rehabilitation* 5(3):215–7.

Doane, C.B. 1985. Children with severe burns. In *Occupational therapy for children*, ed. P.N. Clark and A.S. Allen, 419–29. St. Louis: C.V. Mosby. P.N. Pratt and A.S. Allen, eds., 2d ed., 1989, 524–34.

Fader, P. 1988. Preserving function and minimizing deformity: The role of the occupational therapist. In *Burns in children: Pediatric burn management*, ed. H.F. Carvajal and D.H. Parks, 324–44. Chicago: Year Book Medical Publications.

Macdonald, L.B., M.H. Covey, and J.A. Marvin. 1985. The papoose: Device for positioning the burn child's axilla. *Journal of Burn Care and Rehabilitation* 6(1):62–3.

Rose, M.P., and E.A. Deitch. 1983. The effective use of a tubular compression bandage, tubigrip, for burn scar therapy in the growing child. *Journal of Burn Care and Rehabilitation* 4(3):197–201.

Stap, L., R. Brock, and L. Zissermann. 1983. The tactile functions of burned children. *Journal of Burn Care and Rehabilitation* 4(4):291–302.

Part X

Cognition and Psychomotor Disorders

Alzheimer's Disease

DESCRIPTION

Alzheimer's disease is a degenerative disorder of the cerebral cortex and other areas of the brain characterized by gradually increasing impairment of function. Loss of memory and intelligence are usually noticed first. Age of onset is 45 years or older.

Stages of Cognitive Decline

Normal: No objective evidence of impairment. Activities of daily living (ADLs) are performed without difficulty.

Forgetfulness: No objective evidence of impairment, but the person may express concern about forgetting the location of familiar objects or forgetting names and words. No problem with ADLs.

Borderline Alzheimer's Disease: Objective evidence is hard to obtain, but the family and associates confirm problems, such as the person gets lost, job performance has declined, person forgets what has just been said and has difficulty finding words in conversation, and individual expresses anxiety about memory problems. No problem with ADLs.

Mild Alzheimer's Disease: Objective evidence of cognitive deficit is apparent, such as decreased ability to handle finances or shop for supplies, decreased knowledge of current events, and deficits in memory of personal history and ability to concentrate on a task. No consistent problems with ADLs.

Moderate Alzheimer's Disease: Objective evidence of dementia is apparent, such as inability to recall address and telephone number, names of family members, or date of graduation from high school. ADLs are beginning to be affected, such as difficulty choosing proper clothing or remembering to bathe, although eating and toileting skills can still be performed independently.

Moderately Severe Alzheimer's Disease: Objective evidence of dementia is readily apparent, such as difficulty in remembering the name of the primary caregiver although the person can distinguish between strangers and friends. The person is generally unaware of current events, is not oriented to time and place, and cannot travel alone. The person is semi-dependent in most ADLs, has difficulty putting on clothes, needs assistance in bathing and toileting, and may be incontinent. The person may still be independent in eating if food is placed on plate.

Severe Alzheimer's Disease: The brain no longer directs voluntary activities. Verbal and psychomotor skills are severely limited or lost. The person may be in a stupor or coma. The person is totally dependent in all ADLs.

Source: Based on Reisberg, B. 1984. Stages of cognitive decline. *American Journal of Nursing* 84(2):227.

CAUSE
The cause is unknown, but may be a combination of any of the following: neurochemical, environmental, viral, trauma, or genetic immunologic factors.

ASSESSMENT

Areas
- gross motor skills and coordination
- fine motor skills, manipulation, dexterity, and bilateral coordination
- postural control and balance
- mobility
- motor planning or praxis
- sensory registration
- sensory processing
- perceptual skills
- attending behavior
- attention span
- orientation
- conceptualization or abstract reasoning
- learning skills
- mood or affect
- judgment of safety
- communication skills
- social skills
- daily living skills
- productivity history, skills, interests, and values
- leisure skills and interests
- home safety

Instruments
Activities of Daily Living (ADL) Situational Test (See E. Skurla, J.C. Rogers, and T. Sunderland, 1988. Direct assessment of activities of daily living in Alzheimer's Disease. *Journal of the American Geriatrics Society* 36:97–103.)

PROBLEMS

Motor
- The person usually has increasing loss of gross motor skills and coordination.
- The person usually has increasing loss of balance and equilibrium reactions.
- The person usually has increasing loss of fine motor skills, manipulation, dexterity, and bilateral coordination.
- The person may have gait disturbances such as stumbling, wide based gait, or shuffling feet.
- The person may have contractures in advanced or terminal stages.
- Positioning may be an issue in advanced or terminal stages.

Sensory

- The person may have increasing loss of sensory awareness and registration.
- The person may have increasing loss of sensory processing.
- The person may have reduced ability to monitor (inhibit) incoming stimuli, which leads to overstimulation.
- The person may have increasing loss of spatial relations and spatial visualization.
- The person may lose binocular vision or visual accommodation, which affects depth perception.

Cognitive

- The person usually has increasing memory loss, which begins with recent events and increases to include remote events.
- The person usually has increasing forgetfulness and disorientation.
- The person usually has increasing difficulty learning and remembering new information.
- The person usually has increasing inability to concentrate.
- The person usually has increasing loss of abstract thinking skills.

Intrapersonal

- The person may become restless, especially at night.
- The person may become increasingly irritable.
- The person usually becomes increasingly disoriented to time, place, or person.
- The person may experience emotional lability and moodiness.
- The person usually has loss of judgment about personal safety.
- The person usually has loss of spontaneity.
- The person may be hypochondriacal.

Interpersonal

- The person usually experiences decreased ability to write or speak.
- The person may blame others for personal problems, such as accusing others of stealing items that have been misplaced or discarded many years ago.

Self-Care

The person may experience loss of self-care skills, especially those requiring fine motor hand skills.

Productivity

- The person may have loss of productive skills because of memory loss and other cognitive impairments.
- The person may lose his or her job or be forced to take early retirement.

Leisure

- The person may lose interest in activities that used to be important leisure pursuits.
- Loss of motor coordination may limit some leisure pursuits.

TREATMENT/MANAGEMENT

Treatment goals can be divided into four stages of treatment: early, middle, advanced, and terminal. Models of treatment are cognitive levels (Allen) and human occupation (Kielhofner).

- *Early.* Enable the person to maintain as much independence as possible and teach caregivers how to cope with the stress of dealing with a person who has Alzheimer's.
- *Middle.* Encourage physical fitness, facilitate socialization and communication, and promote adjustment to the environment.
- *Advanced.* Maximize the quality of life, promote awareness of self and others, maintain overall fitness, and increase sensory stimulation.
- *Terminal.* Prevent or decrease contractures and make the person comfortable.

Motor

- Encourage exercise to maintain mobility and general fitness.
- Use more gross motor or large motor activities when fine motor activities become difficult or impossible. Examples include walking groups, bowling, a rhythm band, musical chairs games, balloon volleyball, or exercise groups.
- Consider splints to prevent contractures.

Sensory

- Stimulate sensory systems to maintain contact with the environment.
- Maintain balance and equilibrium reactions as long as possible to reduce possible falls and injuries. Examples include the use of vestibular boards, large balls or inflatables, swings, teetertotters, or merry-go-rounds.

Cognitive

- Teach compensatory memory techniques, such as writing down a daily schedule and keeping a notebook of important personal information.
- In conjunction with sensory stimulation, have the person name the type of stimulation and review a past experience with the same or similar sensory input.
- Use simple one- or two-step commands when providing instructions to reduce confusion and anxiety.

Intrapersonal

- Orient the person to the environment through reality orientation sessions, including the name, place, date, day, and weather. Use memory aids if the person can read.
- Promote self-esteem by praising the person for maintaining self-care skills (dressing and grooming nicely), for completing a task as requested, or for engaging in a leisure activity.
- Reduce anxiety by providing a structured, organized, and scheduled environment, telling the person what is going to happen in advance of a scheduled event and what behavior is expected of the individual (e.g., wash hands before sitting at the table for lunch).

Interpersonal

- Increase opportunities for socialization through such programs as pet therapy, sing-a-longs, field trips, show-and-tell sessions, parties, and entertainment.

- Promote vocalization and interaction skills through such activities as word games, object identification games, remember-when games, or name that tune. Modify according to the person's ability level.

Self-Care
- Encourage the person to maintain independent performance of daily living activities as long as possible.
- Provide assistive devices and instruct the person in the use of the devices if their use will prolong independent or semi-independent performance.
- Instruct the caregiver (family member or home health aide) on assisting the person to perform those daily living activities that the individual can no longer perform independently in a satisfactory or safe manner.

Productivity
- Encourage the person to participate in productive activities (work, homemaking, volunteering) as long as possible; that is, the person performs at a satisfactory level or meets an acceptable standard set by an employer or other person charged with establishing and maintaining a criterion level.
- Modify productive tasks (simplify or redesign) if such changes will permit the individual to continue productive activity at a level of performance that is satisfactory or meets an acceptable standard.

Leisure
- Maintain the person's leisure interests as long as possible by offering opportunities to engage in favorite leisure activities.
- Modify leisure activities within the scope of the person's leisure interests if original activities are no longer possible or practical.

PRECAUTIONS
- The person can become lost even in familiar environments. Do not leave unattended.
- Avoid giving false expectations of the person's performance ability.
- Avoid overstimulating the person and provide a quiet space if overstimulation occurs.
- Observe for changes in sensory acuity that affect safety, such as decreased depth perception, decreased response to warning sounds, or decreased sense of tactile perception and touch to heat.
- In an advanced stage, avoid stairs or climbing when possible because of balance and gait problems.
- In the terminal stage, avoid the use of sharp objects, especially feeding utensils, to reduce possible injury.
- In the terminal stage, if splints are used, observe the person's skin frequently for changes in blood circulation, since the person may be unaware or not report sensory changes him- or herself.

PROGNOSIS AND OUTCOME
Progressive loss of cognitive functions generally occurs. The physical body may remain in

relatively good health for years after the cognitive functions are lost. Outcomes apply to early stages of the disorder. In advanced and terminal stages, loss of skills is unavoidable.

- The person maintains or improves gross motor skills, including rolling, sitting, and standing.
- The person maintains or improves fine motor skills, including dexterity and bilateral coordination.
- The person maintains or improves postural control and balance.
- The person maintains or improves functional mobility.
- The person maintains or improves sensory registration and processing.
- The person maintains or improves perceptual skills, especially vision.
- The person maintains or improves attending behavior and attention span.
- The person maintains or improves memory skills.
- The person maintains or improves learning skills.
- The person maintains or improves orientation to person, place, and time.
- The person maintains or improves communication skills.
- The person demonstrates the ability to perform self-care activities.
- The person demonstrates the ability to perform productive activities.
- The person demonstrates the ability to perform leisure activities.

REFERENCES

Arshonsky, L., H. Adelstein, and K. Stauber. 1988. The forgotten victims: Adolescents and young adults dealing with Alzheimer's disease. In *Understanding Alzheimer's disease: What it is, how to cope with it, future directions,* ed. M.K. Aronson, 173–87. New York: Charles Scribner's Sons.

Baum, C.M., et al. 1988. Performance components in senile dementia of the Alzheimer type: Motor planning, language, and memory. *Occupational Therapy Journal of Research* 8(6):356–68.

Bonder, B.R. 1986. Family systems and Alzheimer's disease: An approach to treatment. *Physical and Occupational Therapy in Geriatrics* 5(2):13–24.

Coons, D.H., and S.E. Weaverdyck. 1986. Wesley Hall: A residential unit for persons with Alzheimer's disease and related disorders. *Physical and Occupational Therapy in Geriatrics* 4(3):29–53.

Davis, C.M. 1986. The role of the physical and occupational therapist in caring for the victim of Alzheimer's disease. *Physical and Occupational Therapy in Geriatrics* 4(3):15–28.

Kern, T. 1986. Safety first: Modifying and adapting the environment for the patient with Alzheimer's disease. *Gerontology Special Interest Section Newsletter* 9(3):4–5.

Mace, N. 1986. Home and community services for Alzheimer's disease. *Physical and Occupational Therapy in Geriatrics* 4(3):5–13.

Occupational therapy services for Alzheimer's disease and related disorders (position paper). 1986. *American Journal of Occupational Therapy* 40:822–24.

Rabinowitz, E. 1986. Day care and Alzheimer's disease: A weekend program in New York City. *Physical and Occupational Therapy in Geriatrics* 4(3):95–103.

Rheaume, Y.L., K.J. Fabiszewski, J. Brown, et al. 1988. Education and training of interdisciplinary team. In *Clinical management of Alzheimer's disease,* ed. L. Volicer, K.J. Fabiszewski, Y.L. Rheaume, et al., 201–22. Gaithersburg, MD: Aspen Publishers, Inc.

Williams-Schroeder, M.L. 1984. Meeting the needs of the Alzheimer's caregiver. *Physical and Occupational Therapy in Geriatrics* 3(4):33–8.

Zachary, R.A. 1984. Day care within an institution. *Physical and Occupational Therapy in Geriatrics* 3(4):61–67.

Zgola, J.M. 1987. *Doing things: A guide to programing activities for persons with Alzheimer's disease and related disorders.* Baltimore, MD: Johns Hopkins University Press.

Zgola, J. 1988. Therapeutic companionship: The occupational therapist's role in a home based program for clients with Alzheimer's disease. *Canadian Journal of Occupational Therapy* 55(1):26–30.

Apraxia

DESCRIPTION

Apraxia is the inability to perform purposeful learned motor acts in the absence of paresis, ataxia, or disturbance of muscle tone, such as spasticity. Typically, the person is unable to follow a motor command even though he or she understands it and is physically able to execute the individual component movements. Subtypes of apraxia include

- ideational apraxia—disturbance in the conceptual organization of complex actions
- ideomotor apraxia—difficulty in producing or programming a correct movement in response to a verbal command or by imitation
- constructional apraxia—inability to draw, build, or assemble simple constructions
- developmental apraxia or dyspraxia—difficulty performing gross and fine motor skills in children (See section on developmental dyspraxia.)
- akinesia or dyskinesia—a behavioral state of diminished motor and psychic spontaneity
- dressing apraxia—difficulty organizing the sequence of actions necessary to put on one's clothes
- sequential apraxia or sequencing apraxia—difficulty organizing the sequence of actions necessary to perform a task
- oral-motor apraxia—inability to program the position of the oral muscles and sequence of muscle movements necessary to produce chewing, swallowing, and vocalization
- kinetic apraxia—inability to coordinate a limb or part of limb, such as the wrist and fingers.

CAUSE

The cause apparently is a lesion in the neural pathways that retain the memory of learned patterns of movement so that the person has difficulty with any or all the following:

- developing a plan or intention to move
- selecting the correct or effective motor or movement response
- organizing the components (velocity, muscle tension, limb placement, sequence) of the movement
- analysis and making corrections based on the feedback received during the execution of the movement

In other words, the person has difficulty conceptualizing and organizing the necessary movement patterns and translating them into purposeful action. Apraxia is common in many metabolic and structural diseases that involve diffuse areas of the brain. Ideational and ideomotor apraxia are associated with left-sided lesions while constructional apraxia is associated with right-side lesions.

Characteristics of Different Apraxias

Ideational apraxia—frontal lobe involvement
- difficulty with intention to move
- expressive and gestural language are affected
- oral motor musculature is affected
- inability to recognize objects and their uses through vision alone (object agnosia)
- bilateral apraxic involvement
- attention deficit

Ideomotor apraxia—premotor area of the cortex involvement
- inability to execute a series of goal-directed movements although intention is preserved
- dyskinesia is present, movement is awkward and clumsy
- inability to use feedback, i.e., analyze, synthesize, and monitor body scheme and motions in progress to make corrections
- no sensory involvement

Kinetic apraxia—precentral zone involvement
- akinesia or difficulty in differentiating between movements
- marked disturbances of fine motor coordination when eyes are closed
- imitative and gestural language are affected

Constructional apraxia—retrolandic lesions of the cerebral cortex
- right hemisphere lesions result in visual-spatial agnosia
- left hemisphere lesions result in motor execution problems
- difficulty performing tasks that require assembly or sequential order of steps
- may be bilateral or unilateral

Source: Based on Okoye, R. The apraxias. In *Physical disabilities manual,* ed. B.C. Abreu, 241–56.

ASSESSMENT

Areas

(Rule out problems due to spasticity, ataxia, or paresis.)
- muscle tone
- range of motion
- coordination—reciprocal, bilateral, and visual motor
- gross motor skills
- fine motor skills, manipulation, and dexterity
- postural control and balance
- functional mobility
- sensory registration
- sensory sensibility or processing
- perceptual skills

- attending behavior
- imitation of movement
- expressive and receptive language
- social skills

Instruments
- Sensory Integration and Praxis Tests by A.J. Ayres, Los Angeles: Western Psychological Services, 1989.
- Constructional Praxis Tests by A. Benton, in *Tests of three-dimensional block construction*, New York: Oxford University Press, 1973 (See also A.L. Benton, and M.L. Fogel, 1987. Three-dimensional constructional praxis: A clinical test. *Archives of Neurology* 7:347–54) (not occupational therapists).
- Block construction portion of the Boston Diagnostic Aphasia Examination (See H. Goodglass and E. Kaplan. 1972. *The assessment of aphasia and related disorders.* Philadelphia: Lea & Febiger) (not occupational therapists).
- Kohs Block Test (See S.C. Kohs. 1923. *Intelligence measurement: A psychological and statistical study based upon the block-design test.* New York: Macmillan Company) (not an occupational therapist).
- activities of daily living scale
- occupational history
- leisure checklist

PROBLEMS

Motor
- The person has difficulty planning or carrying out motor movements.
- The person may appear clumsy, especially when performing a series of movements (ideomotor).
- The person may appear uncoordinated, especially when trying to perform a task that requires the use of both sides of the body at the same time (ideational).
- The person may have difficulty with manipulation and dexterity (kinetic apraxia).
- The person may have loss of range of motion, including contractures.
- The person may have sparing of some movements that are performed in isolation.
- The person may have muscle weakness or atrophy due to disuse.

Sensory
- The person may have decreased sensory registration.
- The person may have loss of sensory sensitivity.
- The person may have associated perceptual disorders, such as visual or auditory perceptual dysfunction, dyskinesia, agraphia, astereognosis, and tactile defensiveness.

Cognitive
- The person may have decreased or poor visualization skills.
- The person may have decreased ability to imitate.

Intrapersonal
The person may have low self-esteem and self-confidence.

Interpersonal
- The person may have difficulty making and keeping friends because of odd behavior (clumsy and uncoordinated).
- The person may not be permitted to assume certain roles within the family because of clumsiness.
- The person may have expressive or receptive aphasia or both.

Self-Care
The person usually has some difficulty performing activities of daily living, such as dressing, grooming, or writing.

Productivity
The person may be unable to perform some job tasks that require use of both hands simultaneously.

Leisure
The person may be unable to do some leisure activities that require highly skilled coordinated movements.

TREATMENT/MANAGEMENT
The model of treatment is based on sensory integration (Ayres).

Motor
- Improve gross motor skills through guided practice.
- Maintain or increase range of motion (ideational apraxia).
- Prevent atrophy by facilitating whatever movements are possible (ideational apraxia).
- Use developmental sequence of postural reflexes to evoke movements (ideomotor apraxia).
- Have the person perform a movement using noninvolved side first and then try to copy or imitate the movement on the involved side (kinetic apraxia).

Sensory
- Provide sensory input through the tactile and touch systems using deep pressure, neutral warmth, discrimination of objects in other media such as sand, a variety of textures on the skin, and alternating passive touch and active tactile activities.
- Provide sensory input through the kinesthetic and proprioceptive systems using movement of body parts and resistance to movement.
- Provide sensory input through the vestibular system using rocking, swinging, turning, jumping, forward and backward acceleration, and deceleration.
- Provide sensory input through the visual system using familiar objects when possible (kinetic apraxia) to assist the haptic sense. Begin with models or actual objects and progress to drawings or schematic representations as improvement occurs (constructional apraxia).
- Provide sensory input through the auditory system using familiar sounds or music when possible.

- Provide sensory input through the gustatory and olfactory senses.
- Combine sensory input, such as tactile and vision, when possible.
- The use of sensorimotor (Rood) techniques may be helpful with ideomotor apraxia, including tapping, icing, brushing, rubbing, kneading, and vibration (see treatment section on inhibitatory and facilitation techniques).

Cognitive
Instruct the family and caregivers in techniques found to be effective for the person.

Self-Care
Use environmental cues and knowledge of the person's previous habits to invoke self-care skills. For example, if the person brushed his or her teeth in the morning upon rising then take the person to the bathroom sink where toothbrush and toothpaste have been placed. Placing a familiar object in the person's hand may also be helpful in evoking the desired movement (ideational apraxia).

Productivity
- The work situation may require modification to eliminate or reduce the need for praxis skills that the person cannot perform reliably.
- The person may need to explore interests, career goals, and vocational choices that do not require praxis skills that the person cannot perform.

Leisure
Explore with the person leisure interests and activities that are within the person's ability to perform.

PRECAUTIONS
Test performance varies with the type and method of test administration. Drawings or photographs produce different results than three-dimensional models, and the time permitted for performance is important for older persons (see Fall article in the reference section).

PROGNOSIS AND OUTCOME
The prognosis and outcome vary depending on the type of apraxia and the causative factors. In degenerative disorders, the prognosis is poor, but in other disorders, such as head injury, the prognosis may be good. Therefore, the outcomes listed below are examples of possible outcomes rather than typically expected outcomes. Outcome statements should be selected on the basis of expectation for the individual person.

- The person is able to plan, organize, and execute a motor act requiring motor planning with which the person is unfamiliar.
- The person is able to perform a motor act requiring motor planning in a smooth (not jerky) and coordinated (using two sides of the body together) manner.
- The person's resting muscle tone is within normal limits with no evidence of hyper- or hypotonicity.
- The person's muscle tone is balanced between flexion and extension, not biased toward

flexion or extension.

- The person can perform motor acts requiring motor planning through the range of motion, not within a narrow arc of motion.
- The person is able to perform motor acts requiring motor planning and bilateral or reciprocal coordination.
- The person can perform motor acts requiring motor planning and execution through the use of postural control and balance reactions in a variety of body positions.
- The person is able to perform motor acts requiring motor planning and execution of constructional or assembly tasks.
- The person can perform motor acts requiring motor planning and execution of a prescribed series of sequential or ordered tasks.
- The person is able to perform motor acts requiring motor planning and execution of rapidly alternating movement of body parts, such as the hand, wrist, tongue, or mouth.

REFERENCES

Ayres, A.J. 1985. *Developmental dyspraxia and adult-onset apraxia.* Torrance, CA: Sensory Integration International.

Baum, B., and K.M. Hall. 1981. Relationship between constructional praxis and dress in the head-injured adult. *American Journal of Occupational Therapy* 35:438–42.

Baum, C.M., et al. 1988. Performance components in senile dementia of the Alzheimer type: Motor planning, language, and memory. *Occupational Therapy Journal of Research* 8(6):356–68.

Bjorneby, E.R., and I.R. Reinvang. 1985. Acquiring and maintaining self-care skills after stroke: The predictive value of apraxia. *Scandinavian Journal of Rehabilitation* 17:75–80.

Bradley, K.P. 1982. Brief: the effectiveness of constructional praxis tests in predicting upper extremity dressing ability. *Occupational Therapy Journal of Research* 2(3):184–5.

Cermak, S.A. 1984. Constructional apraxia. *Sensory Integration Special Interest Section Newsletter* 7(3):1,3–4.

Concha, M.J. 1987. A review of apraxia. *British Journal of Occupational Therapy* 50(7):222–6.

Fall, C.C. 1987. Comparing ways of measuring constructional praxis in the well elderly. *American Journal of Occupational Therapy* 41(8):500–4.

Kowalski-Lundi, M.H., and M.D. Mitcham. 1984. Brief: The relationship of constructional praxis to an upper extremity dressing task. *Occupational Therapy Journal of Research* 4(4):313–5.

Lamm-Warburg, C. 1988. Assessment and treatment planning strategies for perceptual deficits. In *Physical rehabilitation: Assessment and treatment*, 2d ed., ed. S.B. O'Sullivan and T.J. Schmitz, 93–120. Philadelphia: F.A. Davis.

Neistadt, M.E. 1989. Normal adult performance on constructional praxis training tasks. *American Journal of Occupational Therapy* 43(7):448–55.

Okoye, R. 1981. The apraxias. In *Physical disabilities manual*, ed. B.C. Abreu, 241–56. New York: Raven Press.

Quintyn, M., and E. Cross. 1986. Factors affecting the ability to initiate movement in Parkinson's disease. *Physical and Occupational Therapy in Geriatrics* 4(4):51–60.

Siev, E., B. Freishtat, and B. Zoltan. 1986. The apraxias. In *Perceptual and cognitive dysfunction in the adult stroke patient*, ed. E. Siev et al., rev. ed., 35–50. Thorofare, NJ: Slack, Inc.

Wareen, M. 1981. Relationship of constructional apraxia and body scheme disorders to dressing performance in adult CVA. *American Journal of Occupational Therapy* 35(7):431–7.

Cognition Disorders

DESCRIPTION

Cognition disorders or cognitive dysfunction are difficulties in information processing due to brain damage, which alters a person's experiences and responses to stimuli and interferes with the performance of everyday living tasks. Cognition disorders include problems in awareness, orientation, attention and concentration, memory, problem-solving, decision-making, abstraction, and organization. The deficits may be global, specific, or both and they affect the brain, especially the cerebral hemispheres, although lower level structures are involved in some skills. Treatment to remediate problems in cognition had been studied sporadically in persons with strokes for many years but renewed interest began in 1966 when Ben-Yishay was asked by the Israeli government to develop a program for soldiers with head injuries suffered during the 1967 war (see also sections on memory disorders and dementia).

CAUSE

Cognition disorders may be due to developmental delay, an affective disorder, or organic impairment. These problems are frequently seen in adults with mental retardation, schizophrenia, bipolar disorders, head injuries, and cerebrovascular disorders.

ASSESSMENT

Areas
- awareness or level of consciousness
- orientation—temporal, personal, environmental, situational, and left-right
- attention or concentration—arousal, span or length of attention, and distractibility
- sensory acuity and discrimination—tactile, visual, and auditory
- memory functions—immediate, delayed, and remote
- learning and fund of information
- problem solving
- decision making
- cause and effect
- organization of tasks and sequencing
- judgment of safety
- insight—especially awareness of disability
- abstraction
- concept formation and categorization
- motivation or goal-directed behavior
- frustration tolerance and coping behavior
- behavioral control

Instruments
- See I. Soderback, and B. Ramund. 1988. Evaluation of an intellectual functional assessment method in adults with acquired brain damage. *Scandinavian Journal of Caring Sciences* 2(1):11–8.
- Riverdale Hospital's Home and Community Skills Assessment (See Brown, H. 1988. The standardization of the Riverdale Hospital's Home and Community Skills Assessment. *Canadian Journal of Occupational Therapy* 55(1):9–14.)
  - assessment of attention scales—These tests are usually not administered by occupational therapists but the information from them can be useful in program planning.
    1. Wechsler Memory Scale—Revised (WMS-R) by D. Wechsler, San Antonio, TX: Psychological Corporation, 1987 (Subtests: digit span and mental control)

2. Wechsler Adult Intelligence Scale—Revised (WAIS-R) by D. Wechsler, San Antonio, TX: Psychological Corporation, 1981 (Subtests: digit span and arithmetic)
- assessment of organization and planning—These tests are not usually administered by occupational therapists.
  1. Wisconsin Card Sorting Test (WCST) by D.A. Grant and E.A. Berg, San Antonio, TX: Psychological Corporation, 1980
  2. WAIS-R (picture arrangement subtest)
  3. Porteus Maze Test by S.D. Porteus, San Antonio, TX: Psychological Corporation, 1965

PROBLEMS

Motor
- The person may have difficulty with the execution or imitation of simple motor acts on command.
- The person may have difficulty combining or integrating sensory or perceptual information with motor skills, such as seeing a red light and stopping on the curb or seeing an elevator door open and moving into the elevator.
- The person may have difficulty with motor impersistence.

Sensory
- The person may have specific deficits in the registration of sensory input, especially in the auditory, visual, proprioceptive, or tactile modalities.
- The person may have difficulty with integrating cross-modal information, such as tactile-kinesthetic, tactile-visual, or auditory-visual input.

Cognitive
- The person may have difficulty maintaining attention and concentration (or freedom from distraction) in performing
  1. psychomotor tasks
  2. organizing, assembling, and sequencing routines
  3. reasoning and learning activities
  4. following directions or other structured interaction
  5. unstructured situations
  6. modulation of response to stimuli (disinhibition, hyperresponsiveness)
- The person may have difficulty with memory, such as problems with
  1. time span (immediate, short-term, and remote)
  2. retention of content (simple instructions, basic routines of daily life, simple assignments or chores or commitments, and resolutions and promises to significant others)
  3. learning, assimilating, and retaining new information at mastered criterion level
- The person may have problems in thinking, such as difficulty
  1. articulating thoughts
  2. comprehending the main idea
  3. weighing alternatives
  4. planning a course of action
  5. arriving at conclusions
  6. drawing inferences

7. thinking in symbolic terms

8. thinking abstractly, using abstract reasoning

- The person may have difficulty in problem solving, such as

  1. carrying out routine self-care and household chores

  2. carrying out basic adaptive behaviors, such as making a phone call, asking for directions, or using public transportation

  3. using convergent reasoning, i.e., formulating the problem, determining the objective sought, and considering the relevant factors

  4. using divergent reasoning, i.e., considering alternatives systematically and choosing a strategy

  5. using "executive" abilities, i.e., formulating a plan, prioritizing the details, executing the plan, monitoring the performance, and verifying the solution obtained against the original plan

- The person may have difficulty with judgment, such as

  1. appropriateness in manner of dress, use of verbal and nonverbal expression or gestures, awareness of what "fits" the occasion

  2. propriety concerning privacy, invasion of privacy, friendliness or chumminess

- The person may have difficulty understanding roles, such as

  1. family roles: wife, husband, child, parent

  2. work roles: employee, volunteer, student

  3. social or community roles: traveler, shopper, customer, theater-goer

Intrapersonal

- The person may lack self-initiative or be unable to self-induce even simple acts, routines, or communications without the help of others.

- The person may lack the ability to maintain or sustain an act or routine independently without prodding or reminding by others.

- The person may manifest behavioral lag, delay of response, or slowed-down rhythm.

- The person may manifest reduced rate of behavioral performance and/or increased passivity.

- The person may exhibit flat affect, lack of emotion.

Interpersonal

- The person may have difficulty with speech production, such as dysarthria and verbal or oral apraxia.

- The person may have difficulty with language, such as word substitution, anomia, or grammatical errors.

- The person may have difficulty with written communication.

Self-Care

The person may have difficulty performing self-care routines without prompting.

Productivity

The person may have difficulty performing complex routines, such as driving, shopping, preparing meals, and serving.

Leisure
- The person may have difficulty performing the complex coordination skills required in some sports.
- The person may have difficulty with the attention and concentration required in many table games.

TREATMENT/MANAGEMENT

The treatment focus is on cognitive retraining and a systematic attempt to improve intellectual deficits that interfere with the processing of information at some level. Approaches are based primarily on the work of Luria. (Note: Most treatment and management in occupational therapy is based on the concept of cognitive rehabilitation, which is broader in scope than cognitive retraining because the goal is functional adaptation to daily living activities. The limited focus on cognitive retraining in this section permits more in-depth focus on the cognitive aspects.)

Theories of Recovery from Brain Injuries

Jackson's Compensatory Principle (named for J.H. Jackson, neurologist): In head or brain injuries, higher level cortical processes are released to the lower level cortical centers from which they originated (ontogenesis of function). The lower level centers resume control and carry out, to some extent, the functions controlled by the higher centers before the injury occurred.

"Substitutionist" or "Replacement" Theory: Recovery from head or brain injury is possible because existing, intact behavioral strategies can replace the functions destroyed by the head or brain damage by "shunting" around a brain lesion and using a different part of the brain to solve a cognitive problem. Thus substitute habits may be used to replace previously acquired habits.

Shock and Shut-down Theory: Damage to a focal region of the brain causes a shock or diaschisis (loss of function) to other regions, which are then deprived of the normal amount of afferent stimulation and thus a general shut down occurs. As the shock dissipates over time, the intact regions resume their normal state and function as before the injury occurred. Residual symptoms following recovery from shock are the direct result of the focal lesion.

Luria's Retraining Theory (named for A.R. Luria): Areas of the brain spared by the injury reorganize so they carry out the affected or lost functions in new (compensatory) ways. The retraining process should follow the ontogenesis of function.

Source: Based on Ben-Yishay, Y., and L. Diller. 1983. Cognitive remediation. In *Rehabilitation of the head injured adult*, ed. M. Rosenthal, et al., 367–80. Philadelphia: F.A. Davis.

Motor
See sections on apraxia and head injuries.

Sensory
See sections on perceptual disorders, sensory integration, and head injuries.

Cognitive

Teaching Methods
- substitution—teaching a new set of responses to a given cognitive demand
- compensatory—teaching an alternate response (usually already available in the behavior repertoire) to a given cognitive demand
- saturation cuing—giving the person increasingly more information on successive trials to the point that success is virtually assured, then incrementally removing the cues (fading out) so the person learns to perform a task with less and less cuing
- error prevention—giving the person a task that is virtually error proof
- response pacing—having the person talk aloud or talk through the steps or sequence of a response
- control of stimulus complexity—controlling the environmental situation to limit or increase the number or amount of stimulus input
- repetitive practice—using the same or similar materials in different situations
- repetitive practice—using diverse materials related to the person's living environment or controlled situation
- anchoring—providing a person with a cue as to where to begin a task
- elaboration—providing visual images or verbal mediation to assist the person to pursue a task
- self-evaluation—having the individual review his or her own performance

Teaching Modalities
- computer programs—practicing specific skills (educational programs) or planning strategies (games)
- group activities—practicing decision making, problem solving, and awareness of others
- gross and fine motor activities—practicing responding to environmental or interpersonal demands
- survival skills—reading and obeying street signs, making change, writing checks, reading bus or train schedules
- games and crafts—practicing planning strategies

Levels or Phases of Treatment
1. stimulation—activities that require detecting and responding appropriately to the environment (sensory registration and motor response); responses should be at the automatic level (lower brain function) with little or no processing required
2. structure—activities that require discrimination, simple analysis, and manipulation of information from the environment; responses require moderate processing capacity
3. integration—activities that require planning, organization, and problem solving in thoughts, emotions, and ideas; responses require maximum effort, concentration, and analysis

Intrapersonal

See sections on head injuries and schizophrenia.

Interpersonal

See sections on head injuries and schizophrenia.

Self-Care

Self-care activities can be used at level 1 because they are performed at an automatic level (see section on coma and stupor—Glasgow Coma Scale).

Productivity

Productive activities can be used at level 2 to provide structured activities, such as sorting, matching, and counting; and at level 3 to provide integrated activities, such as planning and organizing work activities, or solving a problem in the work environment (see section on coma and stupor—Rancho Los Amigos Cognitive Functioning Scale).

Leisure

Leisure activities can be used at all three levels. Simple, non-competitive games can be used at level 1. Games with rules and simple crafts can be used at level 2. Games requiring strategy, craft projects requiring planning, and community outings requiring organization can be used at level 3 (see section on coma and stupor—Rancho Los Amigos Cognitive Functioning Scale).

PRECAUTIONS

- Studies using computer-assisted cognitive retraining have not been shown to be superior to standard cognitive rehabilitation approaches.
- Persons who are confused or disoriented should be supervised at all times. Do not leave them unattended.
- If an activity is not working, do not pursue the activity; change focus.
- Avoid continuous stimulation, such as playing the radio or TV continuously, to reduce habituation.

PROGNOSIS AND OUTCOMES

- The person will be able to generalize learning to improve performance of everyday tasks.
- The person can demonstrate or articulate cognitive strategies (organized sets of rules) used to process information and organize a plan to approach the problem or situation.

REFERENCES

Abreu, B. 1985. Perceptual-cognitive rehabilitation: An occupational therapy model. *Physical Disabilities Special Interest Section Newsletter* 8(1):1–2.

Abreu, B.C., and J.P. Toglia. 1987. Cognitive rehabilitation: A model for occupational therapy. *American Journal of Occupational Therapy* 41(7):439–48.

Allen, C.K. 1985. *Occupational therapy for psychiatric diseases: Measurements and management of cognitive disabilities.* Boston: Little, Brown & Co.

Averbuch, S., and N. Katz. 1988. Assessment of perceptual cognitive performance: Comparison of psychiatric and brain injured adult patients. *Occupational Therapy in Mental Health* 8(1):57–71.

Batt, R.C., and P.A. Lounsbury. 1990. Teaching the patient with cognitive deficits to use a computer. *American Journal of Occupational Therapy* 44(4):364–7.

Carter, L.T., B.E. Howard, and W.A. Oneil. 1983. Effectiveness of cognitive skill remediation in acute stroke patients. *American Journal of Occupational Therapy* 37(5):320–6.

Carter, L.T., D.O. Oliveira, J. Duponte, and S.V. Lynch. 1988. The relationship of cognitive skills performance in activities of daily living in stroke patients. *American Journal of Occupational Therapy* 42(7):449–55.

Creek, J. 1990. Cognitive approaches. In *Occupational therapy and mental health: Principles, skills and practice*, ed. J. Creek, 179–92. Edinburgh, Scotland: Churchill Livingstone.

Diller, L. 1985. Results of cognitive rehabilitation. *Physical Disabilities Special Interest Section Newsletter* 8(1):1,4–5.

Flaherty, M.A. 1986. Therapy strategies for cognitive skills training. In *Brain injury: Cognitive and prevocational approaches to rehabilitation*, ed. J. Kenig, A.R. Morse, and P.A. Morse, 89–120. New York: Tiresias Press.

Harbauer-Krupa, J., L. Moser, G. Smith, et al. 1984. Cognitive rehabilitation therapy: Middle states of recovery. In *Head injury rehabilitation: Children and adolescents*, ed. M. Ylvisaker, 287–310. San Diego: College-Hill Press.

Katz, N., N. Josman, and N. Steinmetz. 1988. Relationship between cognitive disability theory and the model of human occupation in the assessment of psychiatric and nonpsychiatric adolescents. *Occupational Therapy in Mental Health* 8(1):31–43.

Kirsch, N.L., et al. 1987. Focus on clinical research: The microcomputer as an "orthotic" device for patients with cognitive deficits. *Journal of Head Trauma Rehabilitation* 2(3):77–86.

Kreutzer, J., et al. 1986. A glossary of cognitive rehabilitation terminology. *Cognitive Rehabilitation* 4(3):10–3.

Lundgren, C.C., and E.L. Persechino. 1986. Cognitive group: A treatment program for head-injured adults. *American Journal of Occupational Therapy* 40(6):397–401.

Morse, A.R. 1986. Neuropsychological tools and techniques of cognitive assessment. In *Brain injury: cognitive and prevocational approaches to rehabilitation*, ed. P.A. Morse, 51–88. New York: Tiresias Press.

Prigatano, G.P., et al. 1986. The outcome of neuropsychological rehabilitation efforts. In *Neuropsychological rehabilitation after brain injury*, ed. G.P. Prigatano, 119–33. Baltimore, MD: Johns Hopkins University Press.

Siev, E., B. Freishtat, and B. Zoltan. 1986. *Perceptual and cognitive dysfunction in the adult stroke patient: A manual for evaluation and treatment*, rev. ed. Thorofare, NJ:Slack, Inc.

Skinner, A.D., and L.H. Trachtman. 1985. Brief or new: Use of a computer program (PC Coloring Book) in cognitive rehabilitation. *American Journal of Occupational Therapy* 39(7):470–2.

Smith, G.J., and M. Ylvisaker. 1985. Cognitive rehabilitation therapy: Early stages of recovery. In *Head injury rehabilitation: Children and adolescents*, ed. M. Ylvisaker, 275–86. San Diego: College-Hill Press.

Soderback, I., and L.A. Normell. 1986. Intellectual function training in adults with acquired brain damage. Evaluation. *Scandinavian Journal of Rehabilitation Medicine* 18(4):147–53.

Soderback, I., and L.A. Normell. 1986. Intellectual function training in adults with acquired brain damage: An occupational therapy method. *Scandinavian Journal of Rehabilitation* 18(4):139–46.

Yarkony, G.M., H.G. Betts, and V. Sahgal. 1983. Rehabilitation of craniocerebral trauma. *Annals of the Academy of Medicine, Singapore* 12(3):417–27.

Cognition Disorders—Dementia

DESCRIPTION

Dementia is a structurally caused permanent or progressive decline in several dimensions of intellectual function that interferes substantially with the individual's normal social or economic activity. There are two types: static or fixed dementia and progressive dementia.

CAUSE

The cause of static dementia usually is a single major injury, such as severe head trauma, cardiac arrest, or cerebral hemorrhage. The causes of progressive dementia include Alzheimer-type dementia, multi-infarct dementia, chronic hydrocephalus with normal pressure, chronic progressive traumatic encephalopathy, chronic drug-alcohol-nutritional abuse, brain tumor, Huntington's disease, dementia paralytica, Creutzfeldt-Jakob disease, Wilson's disease, parkinsonism, multiple sclerosis, and amyotrophic lateral sclerosis.

ASSESSMENT

Areas
- range of motion, functional
- muscle tone
- fine motor coordination, manipulation, dexterity
- mobility skills
- visual motor integration (Note the person's ability to copy figures or draw simple objects, such as a clock.)
- orientation skills (Note response to unfamiliar surroundings.)
- memory (Note changes in recent memory.)
- personality changes (Note paranoid ideation.)
- mood or affect (Note signs of depression or emotional outbursts.)
- communication skills (Note changes in handwriting.)
- daily living skills (Note changes in the person's ability to perform self-care skills, manage finances, and balance a checkbook.)
- productivity history, skills, and interests
- leisure skills and interests
- accessibility and safety in the home

Instruments
- goniometry
- Barthel Self-Care Index (See B. Hasselkus. 1982. Barthel Self-Care Index and geriatric home care patients. *Physical and Occupational Therapy in Geriatrics* 1(4):11–22; and F. Mahoney, and D. Barthel. 1965. Functional evaluations: The Barthel index. *Maryland State Medical Journal* 14:61–5.)
- Household Management Screening Assessment (See D.W. Olin. 1984. Assessing and assisting the persons with dementia: An occupational behavior perspective. *Physical and Occupational Therapy in Geriatrics* 3(4):30.)
- Evaluation for Furniture Riser Modifications (See D.W. Olin. 1982. *Physical and Occupational Therapy in Geriatrics* 1(4):55–8.)
- Clinical Dementia Rating (CDR) (See L. Berg. 1988. Clinical dementia rating (CDR). *Psychopharmacology Bulletin* 24:637–9.)
- Zarit Burden Interview (See S.H. Zarit, N.K. Orr, and J.M. Zarit. 1985. *The hidden victims of Alzheimer's disease: Families under stress*, 84. New York: New York University Press.)
- Memory and Behavior Problems Checklist (See S.H. Zarit, N.K. Orr, and J.M. Zarit. 1985. *The hidden victims of Alzheimer's disease: Families under stress.* New York: New York University Press.)

PROBLEMS

Motor
- Apraxia may be a coexisting condition but is not a specific problem of dementia.
- Limb rigidity may be present.
- Flexed posture may occur.

Sensory
- Agnosia or recognition of perceptions may be a coexisting problem but is not a specific problem of dementia.
- Spatial disorientation may be a coexisting problem.

Cognitive
- Familiar tasks may be performed well but learning new skills is very difficult.
- The person is distractible and his or her attention span is short.
- Conceptual thinking is decreased.
- The person may have poverty of thought.
- Recent memory impairment increases, beginning with problems in recalling recent events or remembering names.
- Remote memory may be spared in fixed dementia but becomes involved in progressive dementia.
- The person may have acute episodes of severe confusion, especially in response to an immediate stressful situation.

Intrapersonal
- The person may become depressed.
- The person may become anxious or restless.
- The person may show signs of paranoia.
- Insight is impaired.
- Judgment is impaired.
- Affect may be exaggerated and then become blunted or flat.
- Initiative usually decreases.
- Changes in personality structure may occur.
- The person may have acute episodes of severe emotional disturbance, especially in response to an immediate stressful situation.
- The person may be aware of decreasing abilities and suffer loss of self-esteem.

Interpersonal
- The person may lose social interaction skills.
- The person may demonstrate echolalia (parroting words or phrases said by others).
- The person may demonstrate palilalia (repeating part or all of a sentence while speaking).
- The person may speak nonsensical sentences or include jargon (a string of nonsense words) in a sentence.
- The person may become mute.

Self-Care
Habits of self-care deteriorate.

Productivity
The person is unable to perform or neglects job tasks and usually cannot continue to function productively without supervision.

Leisure
- The person may lose interest in leisure activities.
- The person may be unable to perform activities previously enjoyed.

TREATMENT/MANAGEMENT

Motor
Plan activities within the person's level of function. Emphasize gross motor rather than fine motor activities. Use familiar rather than novel movements.

Sensory
- Provide sensory stimuli, including nightlights, a radio, or television; avoid sensory deprivation but do not overstimulate.
- Maintain familiar settings when possible to assist in spatial orientation.
- Minimize distractions, such as the background noise of a radio or television during a treatment session. Reduce visual distractions too, if possible.
- Be aware of sensory deficits. Check to make sure the person has glasses on and his or her hearing aid is functioning.

Cognitive
- Keep explanations brief and simple. Use short, simple, and concrete statements that are literal and direct.
- Give one instruction at a time and repeat it if necessary. Break complex activities into simple, easy-to-follow steps.
- Ask questions that can be answered with yes or no to reduce the problem of trying to organize ideas for a response.
- Orientation to time may be helped by using calendars and clocks.
- Call the person by name or touch the person and establish eye contact to get the individual's attention before giving instructions.
- Expect poor recall of treatment program. Review any instructions that must be followed from one treatment session to the next.
- Anticipate poor independent practice. Caregiver will need to monitor exercises in a home program.

Intrapersonal
Anticipate denial of the disability. The person may be unaware of his or her limitations. Plan activities within the person's level of function.

Interpersonal
- Include the person in any discussion about his or her condition with caregivers. Do not speak as if the person were not aware of what is happening.
- Be aware that the person may comprehend nonverbal gestures much longer than verbal language. Monitor your facial expressions and tone of voice to project positive signals.
- Anticipate the need to interpret what the person says. Rephrase the message and ask for confirmation rather than ignoring an apparent rambling sentence.

Self-Care
- Develop and maintain a routine of daily living tasks.
- Printing a schedule of the tasks may be helpful. Pictures or photographs may help.
- Expect difficulty in learning any new routines in later stages of the disorders. Anticipate needed changes early, if possible, when learning is still possible.

Productivity
- Provide constant or frequent supervision if the person is helping with household activities or volunteering services.
- Alert the family that activities done many times by the person may be performed poorly because of memory lapses and inattention. (For example, baking cookies. The person may have baked cookies successfully for 50 years but now leaves out some critical ingredients. Suggest doing the activity together so that monitoring can occur.)

Leisure
If reading is a favorite activity of the person, be aware that his or her comprehension is decreasing. Short stories rather than novels may be helpful. More photos and less text may be useful. Talking books may aid comprehension.

PRECAUTIONS
- The person should not be left unattended.
- Avoid teasing the individual since the person may not comprehend.
- Avoid high-level humor, such as a play on words that the person may not understand and think someone is making fun of him or her.
- Avoid being over optimistic about his or her condition. State the facts.

PROGNOSIS
The prognosis is not good. The person's course continues downhill until death.

- The person is able to perform motor skills consistent with the stage of the disorder.
- The person is aware and registers sensory input in all major senses consistent with the stage of the disorder.
- The person is able to remember and to orient him- or herself using assistive devices or techniques consistent with the stage of the disorder.
- The person has maintained social skills consistent with the stage of the disorder.
- The person is able to perform daily living skills using assistive devices or techniques, as needed, in a supervised environment consistent with the stage of the disorder.
- The person is able to perform productive activities consistent with the stage of the disorder.
- The person is able to perform leisure activities consistent with the stage of the disorder.
- The person's living environment has been modified to provide maximum opportunity for independence consistent with safety considerations.
- The person and caregiver demonstrate knowledge of community resources, such as mobile meal programs, self-help groups, and respite care.

REFERENCES

Carnes, M. 1984. Diagnosis and management of dementia in the elderly. *Physical and Occupational Therapy in Geriatrics* 3(4):11–24.

Edwards, D.F., and C.M. Baum. 1990. Caregiver burden across states of dementia. *Occupational Therapy Practice* 2(1):17–31.

Griffin, R.M., and M.U. Matthews. 1986. The selection of activities: A dual responsibility. Special issue: Therapeutic interventions for the person with dementia. *Physical and Occupational Therapy in Geriatrics* 4(3):105–12.

Griffin, R.M., and F. Mouheb. 1987. Work therapy as a treatment modality for the elderly patient with dementia. *Physical and Occupational Therapy in Geriatrics* 5(4):67–72.

Griffin, R.M. 1990. *Protocols for adapting activities to the changing needs of people with dementia.* Baltimore, MD: CHESS Publishing.

Hanley, O., and K. Peele. 1985. An active occupational therapy programme for the severely demented patient in a psychogeriatric day hospital. *British Journal of Occupational Therapy* 48(11):336–8.

Levy, L.L. 1987. Psychosocial intervention and dementia: I. State of the art, future direction. *Occupational Therapy in Mental Health* 7(1):69–107.

Levy, L.L. 1987. Psychosocial intervention and dementia: II. The cognitive disability perspective. *Occupational Therapy in Mental Health* 7(4):13–36.

Macdonald, K.G. 1985–86. Occupational therapy approaches to treatment of dementia patients *Physical and Occupational Therapy in Geriatrics* 4(2):61–72.

Mace, N.L. 1987. Principles of activities for persons with dementia. *Physical and Occupational Therapy in Geriatrics* 5(3):13–27.

Maloney, C.C., and T. Daily. 1985–86. An eclectic group program for nursing home residents with dementia. Special issue: Therapeutic interventions for the person with dementia. *Physical and Occupational Therapy in Geriatrics* 4(3):55–80.

Nolen, N.R. 1988. Functional skill regression in late-stage dementias. *American Journal of Occupational Therapy* 42(10):666–9.

Olin, D.W. 1984. Assessing and assisting the persons with dementia: An ocupational behavior perspective. *Physical and Occupational Therapy in Geriatrics* 3(4):25–32.

Rogers, J.C., C.L. Marcus, and T.L. Snow. 1987. Maude: A case of sensory deprivation. *American Journal of Occupational Therapy* 41(10):673–6.

Skolaski-Pellitteri, T. 1983. Environmental adaptations which compensate for dementia. *Physical and Occupational Therapy in Geriatrics* 3(1):31–44.

Skolaski-Pellitteri, T. 1984. Environmental intervention for the demented person. *Physical and Occupational Therapy in Geriatrics* 3(4):55–9.

Wohl, L.M. 1989. Understanding dementia: Communicating with the demented patients in treatment. *Occupational Therapy Forum* 4(12)12–16.

Cognition Disorders—Memory Disorders

DESCRIPTION

Memory disorders are defined as partial or total inability to encode (process), store, or retrieve (recall) information. Encoding determines which stimuli are noticed or attended to and which ones are selected for storage. Storage concerns the saving of information. Retrieval concerns the recall of information from a memory store.

CAUSE

The causes of memory disorders can be divided into four types:

1. supratentorial mass lesions, including epidural and subdural hematoma, cerebral infarct or hemorrhage, brain tumor or abscess

2. subtentorial lesions including brainstem infarct, tumor, hemorrhage, or trauma, and cerebellar hemorrhage
3. diffuse and metabolic cerebral disorders, such as trauma, epilepsy, post-epileptic states, infection, toxins, and subarachnoid hemorrhage
4. psychiatric disorders, such as malingering, hysteria, and catatonia

---

Causes of Memory Disorders

Type or Component of Memory	*Probable Lesion Site*
Recognition	Thalamus
Short-term memory	Frontal lobe
Long-term memory	
• consolidated	Hippocampus or thalamus (limbic)
• storage	Temporal lobe
• recall	Temporal lobe

Source: Based on Siev, E., B. Freishtat, and B. Zoltan. 1986. Memory. In *Perceptual and cognitive dysfunction in the adult stroke patient: A manual for evaluation and treatment*, rev. ed., 116–17. Thorofare, NJ: Slack, Inc.

ASSESSMENT

Areas
(Any or all of the memory functions listed below may be assessed.)
- immediate memory—memory held consciously for less than one minute
- short-term memory—memory held for more than a minute
- long-term memory—memory held for more than a few minutes
- recent memory—memory held for several hours or months (It overlaps with the concept of long-term memory.)
- remote memory—memory held for many years, including back to childhood
- episodic memory—memory of one's personal history
- semantic memory—personal knowledge of the physical environment or world through language
- retrograde amnesia—loss of memory of events prior to a traumatic situation
- anterograde amnesia—loss of or decreased memory of events after a traumatic situation
- posttraumatic amnesia—decreased memory function (storing and retrieving information), confusion, and disorientation in the period following trauma
- verbal memory—memory of words and sentences
- semantic memory—memory of linguistic concepts
- visuospatial memory—memory of objects, spatial relationships, and configurations
- motor memory—memory of movements
- temporal memory—memory of the timing of events, their duration and sequence
- sensory memory—memory of sensory information (It may be specific to a single sensory

system, such as auditory, olfactory, or taste.)
* emotional memory—memory of all types of affect

Instruments

Generally occupational therapists have not tested for memory functions using published tests. Most testing is done by psychologists or neuropsychologists using the Wechsler Memory Scale or a similar instrument.

PROBLEMS

Motor

Motor problems, such as reduced range of motion, muscle weakness, and contractures, may exist depending on the brain disorder.

Sensory

Sensory problems such as loss of vision, hearing, touch, proprioception, taste, or smell may exist depending on the brain disorder.

Cognitive

* The person may have loss of immediate memory covering the past few seconds.
* The person may have loss of intermediate (short-term or primary) memory covering the period from a few seconds to a few days before.
* The person may have loss of recent (long-term or secondary) memory covering the period from hours to months.
* The person may have loss of remote (very long) memory covering events back to early childhood.
* The person may have retrograde amnesia for the period of time immediately preceding concussion or traumatic head injuries.
* The person may have anterograde or posttraumatic amnesia for the time period following concussion or severe head trauma.
* The person may confabulate to fill in memory gaps (Korsakoff's syndrome).
* The person may be unable to learn any new tasks but may be able to carry out complex tasks learned before the illness or injury.
* The person may have lost episodic memory or memory of his or her personal history, such as what clothes were worn yesterday.
* The person may have lost semantic memory, which includes linguistic concepts such as colors, sizes, and mammals.
* The person may have lost verbal memory, which includes words and sentences.
* The person may have lost visuospatial memory and be unable to recognize faces, familiar objects, or environmental surroundings.
* The person may have lost motor memory and be unable to remember how to do the movements of a once familiar task, such as typing, putting on clothes, or setting a table.
* The person may have lost temporal memory and be unable to remember when events occur, how long an event usually lasts, or the sequence of tasks within an event, such as going to a football game.
* The person may have lost sensory memory and be unable to remember common sounds, such as a bell or whistle, and be unable to remember common smells, such as perfume.

- The person may have lost emotional memory and be unable to remember what affect is appropriate for joy, anger, or sadness.

Intrapersonal
- The person may become angry or frustrated if he or she is aware of the decreased memory ability.
- The person may lose self-confidence because he or she is aware of memory failures.
- The person may become depressed.

Interpersonal
- The person may not recognize family or friends.
- The person may be unable to carry on a social conversation because the person had forgotten many of the subjects used to initiate and maintain a conversation.

Self-Care
If loss of remote memory is involved, the person may not remember how to perform basic activities of daily living.

Productivity
- The person may be able to perform some job tasks if remote memory is intact.
- The person may be unable to perform new job tasks because he or she is unable to learn them.

Leisure
- The person may be able to enjoy leisure activities learned many years ago.
- The person may be unable to enjoy new leisure activities because he or she is unable to learn how to do them.

TREATMENT/MANAGEMENT
Models of treatment are based on retraining the memory, if possible, by improving encoding, increasing attention, and aiding retrieval or by adaptive techniques designed to compensate for the loss of memory functions.

Motor
Motor routines can assist memory by using motor habits, such as always putting the checkbook in the same place on the desk or putting the egg slicer in the same drawer.

Sensory
Visual imagery may be useful. The person consolidates information by making a mental picture of the information to be remembered.

Cognitive
- Storage devices may be helpful as external memory aids, including lists, schedules, notebooks, calculators, diaries, or computers. Training in the use of memory aids is necessary, such as reminding the person to look at the list.
- Computers can be used to provide practice in memory tasks.

- Games, such as remembering objects on a tray and Twenty Questions, may be used in groups.
- The person with left-hemisphere problems may find visual cues more useful, while a person with right hemisphere problems may find linguistic cues more helpful.
- First letter mnemonics may be helpful to remember a list of items such as "mice" for milk, ice cream, cheese, and eggs.
- PQRST is a memory rehearsal system in which Preview stands for skimming the material for general content. Questions are then asked about the content. The person Reads to answer the questions. He or she then States, rehearses, or repeats the information read and finally Tests him- or herself by answering the questions.
- Semantic elaboration is a memory technique in which a person makes up a simple story about information to be remembered, such as "Tom needs a clean suit to go to the Pilgrim's Ball" for "Go pick up Tom's suit at Pilgrim Cleaners."

Intrapersonal

Increase self-confidence and decrease depression by providing opportunities for success.

Interpersonal

Family or friends may assist the person by providing cues regarding the memory assistive devices, such as asking if the person has checked the daily schedule board to determine the next task to be done.

Self-Care

Behavior modification techniques have been used successfully in assisting persons to relearn tasks with fixed sequences of steps, such as washing and dressing.

Productivity

- Job tasks with repetitive motor sequences, visual cues, or step-by-step instruction may assist the person to function in a job situation.
- A notebook, chalkboard, or computer schedule may provide reminders of tasks to be performed.

Leisure

The use of leisure activities learned long ago (remote memory) may be remembered better and thus be useful leisure activities and skills.

PRECAUTIONS

- Do not confuse decreased attention span or poor concentration with memory disorders. Attention span and concentration affect performance but not the actual memory.
- Persons with brain injuries have difficulty using internal strategies that require learning to use. External strategies may be more successful, especially during the early stages of recovery.

PROGNOSIS AND OUTCOME

The literature is mixed regarding improvement of memory in general or for specific types of memory.

- The person is able to perform self-care and daily living activities with or without memory aids.
- The person is able to perform productive activities with or without memory aids.
- The person is able to perform leisure activities with or without memory aids.

REFERENCES

Giles, G.M., and J. Clark-Wilson. 1988. The use of behavioral techniques in functional skills training after severe brain injury. *American Journal of Occupational Therapy* 42:658–65.

Giles, G.M., and M. Shore. 1989. The effectiveness of an electronic memory aid for a memory-impaired adult of normal intelligence. *American Journal of Occupational Therapy* 43(6):409–11.

Roberts, C. 1985. The management of memory disorders. *British Journal of Occupational Therapy* 48(3):76–8.

Robertson, L. 1987. Memory functioning in those who age normally and abnormally: A literature review. *British Journal of Occupational Therapy* 50(2):53–8.

Siev, E., B. Freishtat, and B. Zoltan. 1986. Memory. In *Perceptual and cognitive dysfunction in the adult stroke patient: A manual for evaluation and treatment*, ed. E. Siev et al., rev. ed., 113–21. Thorofare, NJ: Slack, Inc.

Strong, J. 1984. Memory function following traumatic head injury. *British Journal of Occupational Therapy* 47(9):281–6.

Deglutition Disorders/Dysphagia

DESCRIPTION

Deglutition disorders are defined as difficulty in the consumption (chewing and swallowing) of solids or liquids. They are also called dysphagia, swallowing dysfunction, pharyngeal motility disorders, or esophageal transport disorders. The process of chewing and swallowing can be divided into phases. The oral or mechanical phase occurs when there is difficulty moving the bolus or ball of food or liquid from the front or anterior of the mouth or oris to the back or posterior of the mouth or oris. The pharyngeal phase occurs when the bolus is swallowed and passes through the pharynx. The esophageal phase occurs when the bolus moves through the esophagus into the stomach.

CAUSE

There are multiple causes. Mechanical dysphagia may be congenital, such as cleft palate, or it may result from surgery for cancer of the mouth. Other mechanical causes include dysphagia constricta, which occurs when there is stenous of the pharynx or esophagus, and dysphagia lusoria, which occurs when there is compression of the esophagus by a persistent right aortic arch, a double aortic arch, or an anomalous right subclavian artery. Dysphagia paralytica occurs when there is disease or trauma to the brain stem or cranial nerves, which weakens the muscles of the face and mouth and diminishes the reflexes of the palate and pharynx, such as may occur in muscular dystrophy, tumor in the brain stem, or head injury to the brain stem. Pseudobulbar dysphagia occurs when there are lesions in the upper motor neuron system or cortex, which may result in the inability to initiate the act of swallowing or coordinate the various steps involved, such as occurs from a cerebrovascular accident, Parkinson's disease, multiple sclerosis, amyotrophic lateral sclerosis, myasthenia gravis, tumor in the cortex, or head injury to the cortex.

ASSESSMENT

Areas
• positioning
• muscle strength—oral motor muscles
• motor control and coordination of the oral musculature—jaw and tongue movements
• reflexes—oral motor, including rooting, bite, sucking, gag, and cough
• chewing skills
• swallowing initiation
• coordination of breathing with swallowing
• sensory registration and discrimination of taste, smell, and proprioception
• memory of food and eating
• ability to follow verbal instructions

Instruments
• Dysphagia Profile, St. Mary Medical Center (See N. O'Sullivan, ed., *Dysphagia Care* in the reference section.)
• Dysphagia Evaluation, Mount Zion Hospital and Medical Center (See N. O'Sullivan, ed., *Dysphagia Care* in the reference section.)
• Dysphagia Evaluation (See N. O'Sullivan, ed., *Dysphagia Care* in the reference section.)
• Dysphagia Assessment (See N. O'Sullivan, ed., *Dysphagia Care* in the reference section.)
• Oral Motor/Feeding Evaluation (See N. O'Sullivan, ed., *Dysphagia Care* in the reference section.)
• Restorative Dining Program Assessment: Dysphagia Program Assessment and Progress (See N. O'Sullivan, ed., *Dysphagia Care* in the reference section.)
• Referral for Swallowing Evaluation, Caswell Center (See C.A. Lust, D.E. Fleetwood, and E.L. Motteler. 1989. Developmental and implementation of a dysphagia program in a mental retardation residential facility. *Occupational Therapy in Health Care* 6(2/3):171–2.)
• Behavioral Assessment Scale of Oral Function in Feeding (See M. Stratton. 1981. *American Journal of Occupational Therapy* 35:719–22.)
• Pre-Feeding Evaluation (See E.H. Silverman and I.L. Elfant. 1979. Dysphagia: An evaluation and treatment program for the adult. *American Journal of Occupational Therapy* 33(6):388–90.)
• Fleming Index of Dysphagia (See S.M. Fleming. 1987. Index of dysphagia: A tool for identifying deglutition problems. *Dysphagia* 1:206–8.)

PROBLEMS

Motor
• The person may experience choking.
• The person may experience coughing.
• The person may have difficulty managing or controlling saliva and drooling.
• The person may "pocket" or "squirrel" food between his or her cheeks and gum (oral retention).
• The person may have difficulty moving bolus in the mouth from front to back or side to side.

- The person may have difficulty chewing.
- The person may experience aspiration.
- The person may have muscle weakness or paralysis of cranial nerves.
- The person may have hyper- or hypotonicity.
- The person may have instability of the jaw.
- The person may experience difficulty in sequencing the movements of chewing, swallowing, and breathing.
- The person may display an inability to sustain an action or activity (motor impersistence).
- The person may experience oral apraxia (the inability to perform an intended action or execute an act on command with the mouth or lips).
- The person may have abnormal oral reflex activity in rooting, biting, sucking, gag, or cough.
- The person may have nasal reflux.

Sensory
- The person may lack or have decreased sensation and discrimination of smell.
- The person may lack or have decreased sensation and discrimination of taste.
- The person may lack or have decreased sensation and discrimination of proprioception.
- The person may lack or have decreased sensation to temperature.
- The person may be hyperresponsive to tactile stimuli to the face, mouth, and lips.
- The person may experience pain during chewing or swallowing.

Cognitive
- The person may have difficulty maintaining an alert state.
- The person may be disoriented or confused.
- The person may have difficulty maintaining attention and be easily distracted.

Intrapersonal
- The person may fear coughing, choking, or aspiration.
- The person may show poor judgment regarding personal safety with utensils or the size of bites to be placed in the mouth.

Interpersonal
- The person may have difficulty interacting with the therapist due to aphasia, confusion, disorientation, or dementia.
- The person may try to talk with food in the mouth.

Self-Care
The person has difficulty performing feeding and eating activities without assistance.

Productivity
Difficulty in eating and swallowing may prevent return to productive occupations.

Leisure
Difficulty in eating and swallowing may prevent participation in leisure activities, such as going to a restaurant with family or friends.

TREATMENT/MANAGEMENT

Treatment/management techniques are based on sensorimotor (Rood), proprioceptive neuromuscular facilitation (Knott and Voss), and sensory integration (Ayres) models.

Motor

Positioning

The person should be positioned in a sitting position with the head slightly flexed, chin in the tucked position, shoulders slightly forward, trunk leaning slightly forward, hips flexed at slightly more than 90 degrees, knees flexed at 90 degrees, and feet flat on the floor. The upper extremities should be placed so elbows can be used to increase stability if needed. Body alignment should be maintained so that weight is evenly distributed. Pillows, trunk supports, lap boards, or chair arms may be useful to assist in maintaining posture so the person can concentrate on chewing and swallowing.

Muscle Strength and Control

- head and neck—Use diagonal, rotational patterns to increase head control. In supine or semi-reclining position, have the person raise his or her head against gravity (neck flexion) to look up over one shoulder and down toward the opposite elbow. Then do the opposite motion. In sitting, the therapist applies downward pressure (proprioceptive input) to the top of the head to give the person awareness of the position. Then ask the person to hold the position.
- lips—Icing or vibration may be used to stimulate the obicularis oris. Lip exercises may include asking the person to grin, smile, sneer, grit the teeth, or hold a tongue depressor between the lips. Alternating motions can be obtained by having the person say "OOO" followed by "EEE" followed by "OOO" and repeated. Women can stimulate the lips by putting on lipstick, lip gloss, or chapstick. It may be necessary to assist the involved side through movements during early phases.
- cheek—Tongue depressors may be used to increase cheek control. Place the tongue depressor in the mouth between the cheek and gum. Pull the cheek out with the tongue depressor and ask the person to pull the cheek in. It may be easier to use a tongue depressor on both the right and left to take advantage of bilateral activity. If two depressors are used, the therapist should hold the one placed in the right cheek with his or her right hand and the one in the left cheek with the left hand. Although the therapist's hands are crossed, the person will be more comfortable.
- jaw—To increase jaw control, resist jaw opening and closing, both in vertical and diagonal patterns through the full range of active motion but do not stress the temporomandibular joint. Work for symmetry. Jaw control can also be increased through external control. The therapist sits in front of the person, placing the thumb on the chin midway between the lips and the end of the jaw bone, placing the extended index finger along the jaw line and placing the flexed middle finger under the jaw at the midline.
- tongue—Before meals, have the person do range of motion exercises to the tongue. The person should grip the tongue gently but firmly with the thumb and index fingers using a piece of gauze on the top and bottom. Pull the tongue forward, then roll it out to the left and then to the right. Release the tongue. Resistance can be applied by using tongue depressors or lollipops. Resistance can be applied while the tongue is in the mouth (right, left, up, or down) or while the tongue is extended forward. Also have the person practice

licking by spreading food on the lips, on the teeth, and between the gums and cheek. Start with easy foods, such as a small piece of cracker, and increase difficulty to sticky foods, such as peanut butter or jam.
* soft palate—Stroke the palate with an iced Q-tip or laryngeal mirror three to five times and ask the person to say "A-H-H-H" or ask the person to swallow a small piece of food. An alternate method is to manually pinch the nose closed and ask the person to blow out a match or candle, blow bubbles, blow up a balloon, or blow through a tube.

Reflexes
* sucking—The person can practice sucking through a straw starting with a six-inch straw and thin liquids, gradually increasing the length of the straw and the thickness of the liquid.
* gag—A hyperactive gag reflex may be normalized by having the person begin to desensitize him- or herself. Use the person's finger or a tongue depressor and gradually "walk" or slowly press toward the back of the tongue.

Chewing Skills
Have the person chew on a tongue depressor wrapped with gauze or on crunchy foods, such as Melba toast or crackers. Note the person's alertness and level of control. Do not give crunchy foods to a person whose level of alertness drops. Be sure the person practices chewing on both sides. Alternate right and left chewing can promote symmetry.

Swallowing and Breathing
Breathing exercises may include blowing a whistle, blowing through straws of various diameters at ping pong balls or cotton balls, or blowing a party favor, such as a kazoo.

Sensory
* Place food in the most sensitive area of the mouth initially.
* A mirror or verbal cues by the therapist may be used to increase awareness of the location of food in the mouth. Check frequently for "pocketing" or "squirreling" of food between the gum and cheek.
* Firm pressure may be applied to the perioral area to reduce hypersensitivity. Firm pressure may be applied to the philtrum between the nose and upper lip, to the cheeks and temples, or to the dorsum of the tongue in the midline.

Cognitive
* Stimulation techniques may assist in maintaining an alert state, such as eating in a well-lit room and in an upright sitting position. Music and talking may provide additional multisensory input. Avoid overstimulation. Observe the person's response carefully.
* Attention may be easier to maintain if eating or feeding occurs in the normal routine for the person.
* Orient the person to eating or feeding activities by explaining what is happening and what foods are to be eaten. Remind the person frequently if disorientation or confusion is present.
* A home program of exercises may be useful if a caregiver is available to monitor the program. Provide written instructions and go over the instructions with the caregiver. Copies of home instructions are available in the O'Sullivan text listed in the reference section.

Diet Progression

Food

Step 1: ice chips (crushed ice or popsicles on a stick)

Step 2: stiff jelled foods (Jell-O, custard, yogurt, pudding)

Step 3: pureed foods (applesauce, ice cream, sherbet, mashed potatoes with gravy or butter, baby foods)

Step 4: semi-solid foods (hot cereal, macaroni and cheese, poached eggs, cottage cheese, ground, moistened meat)

Step 5: solid chunk foods (tuna, French toast, diced meats and vegetables, soups)

Step 6: regular foods (apples, fresh vegetables, corn on the cob, salad, steak)

Liquids

Step 1: thin liquids (clear broth, water, coffee, sodas)

Step 2: medium thick liquids (milk shakes, cream soups, tomato juice, or egg nog)

Step 3: thick liquids (thickened cream soups, thick shakes, or sherbet)

Source: O'Sullivan, N. 1990. *Dysphagia care: Team approach with acute and long-term patients (Los Angeles: Cottage Square):121-23.*

Interpersonal

- Exercises for facial expression may assist in communication as well as facilitating lip and mouth movements, such as "pucker your mouth," "press your lips together tightly," "keep your teeth together and open your lips."
- Many of the activities and exercises above can be done in small group sessions, which may increase cooperation. For sample programs see the O'Sullivan text listed in the reference section.

Self-Care

- If the person is fully alert and aware, he or she may be able to take responsibility for the exercises needed before eating. Always have the staff or caregiver check with the person to be sure the exercises were done.
- The use of selected self-help devices may be needed to further facilitate feeding, such as a glossectomy spoon, vacuum feeding cup, feeding syringe, or nosey cup.

PRECAUTIONS

- If food remains in the mouth at the end of a feeding session, it should be removed with a swab. Food should never be washed down with a drink.
- The person should remain in an upright or semiupright position for 15 to 20 minutes after eating as a precaution against regurgitation or aspiration.

- Do not schedule feeding sessions immediately after strenuous activity, such as in physical therapy or lengthy test procedures that are likely to reduce the sensation of hunger.
- Avoid overstimulation, which results in confusing or disorganizing the person. Too much noise, clutter, or bustling activity decreases attention and focus on eating.
- Observe safety precautions regarding hot foods or too large a bite in the mouth, biting the tongue or lip because of poor motor control or sequencing, injury from jabbing a fork accidentally into the cheek or gum, or cutting the mouth with a knife.
- Do not use foods that have multiple textures, are sticky or greasy, tough to chew, or spicy, have seeds or nuts, are fibrous, or break up in the mouth.

PROGNOSIS AND OUTCOME
- The person is able to chew and swallow selected foods without coughing, choking, or aspirating.
- The person is able to drink selected liquids without coughing, choking, or aspirating.

REFERENCES

Asher, I.E. 1984. Management of neurologic disorders: The first feeding session. In *Dysphagia: Diagnosis and management*, ed. M.E. Groher, 133–55. Boston: Butterworths.

Groher, M.E., and R. Bukatman. 1986. The prevalence of swallowing disorders in two teaching hospitals. *Dysphagia* 1(1):3–6.

Layne, K.S., F.D. Losinski, B.A. Zenner, et al. 1989. Using the Fleming Index of Dysphagia to establish prevalence. *Dysphagia* 4:39–42.

Lust, C.A., D.E. Fleetwood, and E.L. Motteler. 1989. Development and implementation of a dysphagia program in a mental retardation residential facility. *Occupational Therapy in Health Care* 6(2/3):153–72.

Mody, M., and J. Majai. 1990. A multidisciplinary approach to the development of competency standards and appropriate allocation for patients with dysphagia. *American Journal of Occupational Therapy* 44(4):369–72.

Nelson, K.L. 1990. Dysphagia: Evaluation and treatment. In *Occupational therapy: Practice skills in physical dysfunction*, 3d ed., ed. L.W. Pedretti and B. Zoltan, 146–76. St. Louis: C.V. Mosby.

O'Sullivan, N., ed. 1990. *Dysphagia care: Team approach with acute and long term patients.* Los Angeles: Cottage Square.

Rogers, J.C., and T. Snow. 1982. An assessment of the feeding behaviors of the institutionalized elderly. *American Journal of Occupational Therapy* 36(6):375–80.

Silverman, E.H., and I.L. Elfant. 1979. Dysphagia: An evaluation and treatment program for the adult. *American Journal of Occupational Therapy* 33(6):382–92.

Stallons, K.M. 1987. The evaluation and treatment of swallowing disorders. *Physical Disabilities Special Interest Section Newsletter* 10(2):4–5.

Stratton, M. 1989. Clinical management of dysphagia in the developmentally disabled adult. *Occupational Therapy in Health Care* 6(2/3):143–52.

Zerilli, K.S., V.A. Stefans, and M.A. DiPietro. 1990. Protocol for the use of videofluoroscopy in pediatric swallowing dysfunction. *American Journal of Occupational Therapy* 44(5):441–6.

Perception and Vision Disorders—Adult

DESCRIPTION
Perception disorders involve difficulty perceiving and understanding information from the visual system because of dysfunction in the cortex. Vision disorders involve dysfunction in

the visual organs or system itself, such as the eye, optic nerve, or optic lobe. The two disorders have been combined because they usually occur together and often must be treated together.

CAUSE

The usual cause of perception and vision disorders is injury or damage to the association areas of the brain or the nerve tracts leading to the association areas, especially the optic lobe. Injury or damage to the right hemisphere is thought to produce greater problems in visual perception than similar injury or damage to the left hemisphere. However, recent studies suggest that visual perception disorders occur in left and right hemiplegia following a stroke (Edmans, 1987—see reference section). Causes in adults are related to brain lesions that result from trauma, such as a stroke, head injury, tumor, or dementia.

ASSESSMENT

Areas

Visual Perceptual Tasks
- spatial relations (ability to perceive and deal with the relation of objects to each other or an object to the self or body)
- position in space (ability to perceive, interpret, and act on concepts that deal with the position of objects in space, such as up, down, behind, in front of, or beside)
- figure-ground discrimination (ability to distinguish the important object or detail from the background or unimportant details)
- visualization (ability to see in one's mind an object or situation without the benefit of immediate visual input)
- visual recognition (ability to perceive and determine what an object is or who a person is based on visual cues only)
  1. matching same and different objects or colors (ability to determine that two or more objects or colors are the same or different based on their physical properties)
  2. size, color, and shape recognition or discrimination (ability to determine objects based on size, color, or shape)
  3. form constancy (recognition of objects based on their visual form or shape)
- part/whole discrimination (ability to perceive and determine that certain parts make up a whole or that a whole may be composed of identifiable parts)
- depth or distance perception (ability to interpret information from the environment that gives cues as to how deep, how low, how high, or how far away an object is in the environment)
- position in space (ability to perceive and interpret spatial concepts, such as up, down, under, over, in, out, front, and back)

Eye Movement Tasks (Vision Disorders)
- visual field (the amount of visual space measured in degrees that one or both eyes can see while fixating on a point so as not to move the eyes; includes peripheral and focal vision)
- convergence/adaptation (ability to move the eyes together by contracting the muscles of the eyeball and cornea simultaneously)

- fixation (ability to focus gaze on a specific object or target)
- tracking or pursuit (ability to follow a moving object or target)
- visual scanning (awareness of the visual field and any new or novel stimulus that appears in the field)

Eye Teaming
- binocular vision or binocularity (ability to direct or use both eyes simultaneously to receive input from a single source or point, which permits the development of depth perception)

Cognitive Aspects
- visual attention (attending to a visual stimulus on verbal command)
- topographical orientation (understanding or remembering the relations of places to one another, which permits a person to negotiate space without becoming lost)

Instruments
- Ontario Society of Occupational Therapists Perceptual Evaluation Manual, Toronto, Canada: Study Group on the Brain-Damaged Adult, 1977 (See M. Boys, P. Fisher, C. Holzberg, and D.W. Reid. 1988. The OSOT Perceptual Evaluation: A research perspective. *American Journal of Occupational Therapy* 42(2):92–8.)
- St. Mary's CVA evaluation (See D. Harlowe, and J. Van Deusen. 1984. Construct validation of the St. Mary's CVA Evaluation: Perceptual measures. *American Journal of Occupational Therapy* 38(3):184–6; and J. Van Deusen, and D. Harlowe. 1987. Continued construct validation of the St. Mary's CVA Evaluation: Bilateral Awareness Scale. *American Journal of Occupational Therapy* 41(4):242–5. See erratum *American Journal of Occupational Therapy* 41(10):637, 1987.)
- Mohl, E., H. Kurten, and H.H. Janzik. 1987. Perceptual evaluation in occupational therapy. *International Journal of Rehabilitation Research* 10(4 Suppl 5):271–6.
- The Rivermead Perceptual Assessment Battery by S. Whiting, et al., Windsor, England: NFER-Nelson, 1985 (See also N.B. Lincohn, and D. Clarke. 1987. The performance of normal elderly people on the Rivermead Perceptual Assessment Battery. *British Journal of Occupational Therapy* 50(5):156–7.)
- Motor-Free Visual Perception Test (See M.J. Bouska. 1985. Application of the motor-free visual perception test. *Physical Disabilities Special Interest Section Newsletter* 8(1):6–7, Adult version.)
- The Behavioral Inattention Test (See S.A. Cermak and J. Hausser. 1989. *Physical and Occupational Therapy in Geriatrics* 7(3):43–53.)
- Visual Attention Test (See D.A. Lister. 1984. Apparatus for assessing vision after stroke. *Canadian Journal of Occupational Therapy* 51(5):237–40.)
- Southern California Figure-Ground Visual Perception Test by A.J. Ayres, Los Angeles: Western Psychological Services, 1966 (See P. Petersen, and R.L. Wikoff. 1983. The performance of adult males on the Southern California Figure-Ground Visual Perception Test. *American Journal of Occupational Therapy* 37(8):554–60; and P. Petersen, D. Goar, and J. Van Deusen. 1985. Performance of female adults on the Southern California Visual Figure-Ground Perception Test. *American Journal of Occupational Therapy* 39(8):525–30.)

- See Anton, H.A., C. Hershler, P. Lloyd, et al. 1988. Visual neglect and extinction: A new test. *Archives of Physical Medicine and Rehabilitation* 69(12):1013–16 (test has no formal name).

PROBLEMS

Motor (eye-hand coordination, eye-foot coordination)

The person has an inability to "steer" the body part in response to visual input. Problems may occur in the visual motor system or the extremity neuromuscular system or both.

- The person may lack awareness of body structure and relationship of body parts (somatagnosia).
- The person has difficulty staying within the lines if writing on ruled paper or cutting on the line if cutting out a pattern (eye-hand or visual-motor coordination).
- The person has difficulty planning, executing movements, or manipulating objects to perform simple tasks, and thus appears clumsy. See section on apraxia.
- The person may have difficulty switching or changing from one task to another.

Sensory

(Note: Division of problems between motor and sensory systems is arbitrary.)
- visual perceptual difficulties or problems
  1. The person may have difficulty negotiating the environment due to problems with spatial relationships, which reduce the ability to perceive the environment (relation of objects to the self or body) and respond accordingly.
  2. The person may have difficulty focusing, finding, and identifying an object (foreground) from the environment (background) in order to act to the object only.
  3. The person may be unable to "see in the mind's eye," thus limiting imagery. Body image is an example. Person has difficulty visualizing an accurate image of the body.
  4. The person may have difficulty recognizing objects or people based on visual input alone.
  5. The person may be unable to identify part of an object and its relation to the whole (object) or place in the whole. Conversely, the person may be unable to perceive that a whole (object) is composed of parts.
  6. The person may have difficulty judging the depth or height of a vertical surface or horizontal distance between the self and an object or between two objects.
  7. The person may have difficulty perceiving and interpreting spatial concepts, such as up, down, under, over, in, out, right, or left.
  8. The person may have difficulty understanding and remembering the relationship of one place to another.
- eye movements (ocular motility) The person has an inability to move the eyes, via the eye muscles, in a smooth, coordinated manner that permits tracking (following a specific target) and scanning (looking, observing the visual scene to determine if the object is present). These are vision disorders.
  1. The person may neglect, be unaware of, or ignore objects in his or her left field of vision (visual field neglect, unilateral field neglect).
  2. The person may be unable to locate (see, identify) objects in half of the visual field (hemianopia, visual extinction).

3. The person may have difficulty maintaining the place while reading, writing, or copying (tracking).
4. The person may skip lines or repeat lines while reading, writing, or copying (tracking).
5. One or both eyes may "jump" when crossing the midline or center of the visual field while moving horizontally or vertically (tracking).
6. The person may be unable to move one or both eyes across or up and down the visual field without moving the head (paralysis of gaze).
7. The person may be unable to locate objects visually in space, especially when the body is moving (scanning and fixation).
8. The person may be unaware of objects moving into the field of vision from the periphery due to difficulty in scanning.
- eye teaming (binocularity) The person has an inability to focus both eyes, via the eye muscles, on the same spot at the same time because of muscle tone imbalance, which results in failure of the eye muscles to pull (contract) at the same degree of strength in the vertical or horizontal plane. These are vision disorders.
1. The person may misalign numbers or words in columns due to difficulty in maintaining vertical or horizontal visual alignment.
2. The person may have double vision or diplopia due to decreased range of motion of one eye.
3. The person may lack depth or distance perception due to lack of focus of one eye.
4. The person may squint (partially close) one eye or cover the eye altogether.

Cognitive (see also cognition disorders)
- The person may have difficulty following (getting meaning from) written instructions because of the visual perceptual disorders.
- The person may have short attention span because the eyes bother the person.
- The person may have difficulty with topographical orientation (locating the top left of a page to begin reading, writing, or copying, or becomes lost in space because of difficulty using environmental cues to orient self).
- The person may repeat the same error over and over again and does not learn or has difficulty learning from experience.
- The person may take an inordinately long time to complete a task or may quickly complete it without checking for accuracy.
- The person may exhibit poor organizational skills because he or she is unable to determine or remember what the pieces or parts of an object do and how they fit together.

Intrapersonal
- The person may fear failure or ridicule.
- The person may have poor self-concept, low self-esteem.
- The person may have difficulty initiating or completing a task.
- The person may become easily frustrated and refuse to continue working on a task.
- The person may deny that anything is wrong with his or her functional skills or behavior or that any disability exists.

Interpersonal
The person may avoid social situations to avoid embarrassment because of clumsy behavior.

Self-Care
The person may fail to complete some tasks, such as eating food on the left side of the plate or shaving the left side of the face, due to a lack of awareness of items in left field of vision.

Productivity
- The person may be unable to perform some job tasks, such as visual inspector, because of perceptual disorders.
- The person may perform some home-management activities poorly, such as dusting, because of poor eye-hand coordination (breaking objects) or poor visual scanning to determine that dust is removed.

Leisure
The person usually avoids participation in leisure activities that require good performance of perceptual tasks which the person performs poorly.

TREATMENT/MANAGEMENT
Note: Two types of treatment/management exist—adaptive and remedial. Adaptive techniques or methods teach coping skills to aid adjustment to the environment using the person's strengths or assets to "cover" or "work around" the problem areas. Remedial techniques or methods attempt to improve or increase the person's ability to function by retraining or reteaching previously known perceptual skills based on the assumption that the central nervous system is plastic and can reestablish connecting links that have been damaged or establish collateral or alternate links to bypass or substitute for damaged areas of the brain. Models of treatment include sensory integration or sensorimotor (Ayres), neuro-developmental therapy (Bobath), transfer of training (learning theory), and functional training (compensation).

Motor
- somatagnosia or body scheme training to increase awareness of the relationship between body segments using games (Simon says) or obstacle courses
- eye-hand or eye-foot coordination or visual motor coordination (Games requiring gross motor actions with a ball and target may be useful to reestablish basic eye-hand or eye-foot coordination.)

Sensory
- visual perception
  1. spatial relations
     a. Provide opportunities to reproduce designs to reestablish part-whole perception and position in space. Parquetry blocks, puzzles, and pegboards are useful.
  2. figure-ground
     a. Embedded figures may be useful in reestablishing foreground-background ability.
     b. Compensation—Instruct the person to use other senses, such as tactile/touch to examine objects rather than relying on vision.
     c. Adaptation—Reduce the number of objects in the environment. Add color strips to objects to assist in identifying and locating them.
  3. visualization

      a. Start by having the person look at pictures of the body and identify whether the person is fat, thin, or normal.

      b. Have the person look at him- or herself and others in the mirror and indicate whether the person is fat, thin, or normal.

  4. visual recognition

      a. Practicing with tasks involving block design, visual scanning, and visual cancellation (crossing out a particular letter every time it appears in a random list of letters) may assist in reading and writing tasks.

      b. Assemble a number of objects that are similar in shape or size or color and ask the person to identify each object.

  5. part/whole discrimination

      a. Start with simple puzzles with few pieces and gradually increase the complexity of the puzzles.

      b. Use objects with few pieces, such as a canister and lid. Have the person put the lid on the canister. Gradually increase the number of pieces until the person can reassemble a coffee pot or similar item with five to seven pieces.

  6. position in space

      a. Place three or four identical objects in the same orientation and one in a different orientation and ask the person to identify the one that is in a different orientation. The orientation may be up, down, right, or left. To confirm the selection, ask the person to place an object in the same orientation as the others.

  7. topographic disorientation

      a. Start with simple directions, asking the person to go from one place to another in a room, to another room, outside, or in the community. Gradually increase the complexity of the directions. Using familiar or expected patterns may support learning and remembering.

      b. Frequently used routes may be marked with colored dots or other symbols to assist the person in locating a particular place. The symbols should be placed frequently (inches apart) initially and then gradually increased (feet apart, yards apart) as the learning occurs.

- eye motility

  1. visual neglect—The person should be taught to be aware of the deficit through the use of visual scanning. Teach the person to look to the left to check for objects in the left field, such as food on the left side of the plate or differences between the two sides, as would occur if only the right side of the face is shaved.

  2. hemianopsia—During early phases of treatment, place objects within the field of vision where the person is most likely to see them, such as eating utensils, a telephone, or a pencil. Then progressively move the items toward and across the midline.

  3. tracking

      a. Use brightly colored objects and request the person to follow the object (track) while the therapist moves the object horizontally, vertically, and diagonally.

  4. scanning

      a. Use familiar photographs or pictures and ask the person to identify what or who is in the photograph or picture. Generally, line drawings or photographs of faces are used first and then more complex items are introduced.

      b. A tray of common objects can be placed in front of the person and the person asked to find a specific object.

- eye teaming
  1. Provide matching tasks. Generally, matching objects by color and shape are used before matching of letters, words, or numbers as individual units or in sequences.

Cognition (see also section on cognition disorders)
- Teach compensatory techniques (the person changes behavior): (a) explain the problem and use simple directions to correct the problem, (b) establish and carry out a routine, (c) do each activity in a consistent manner, and (d) employ repetition as needed.
- Teach adaptation (alter the environment): use color, such as colored ribbons, or sound, such as bells, to alert or increase attention to the involved side of the body or neglected visual field.
- Teach organization sequence. Puzzles that illustrate the steps in a task may be used to facilitate relearning the organization and sequence of an activity.

Intrapersonal
No specific techniques were mentioned in the literature. Use of compensatory and adaptational techniques should reduce fear, frustration, and anxiety.

Interpersonal
Communication may be enhanced through the use of visual cues or demonstration.

Self-Care
Training in block design may help with organization of eating behavior.

Productivity
Objects with which the person is familiar from home or work should be used in treatment sessions when possible.

Leisure
Objects that the person is familiar with from leisure activities may be useful in treatment sessions.

PRECAUTIONS
- Persons with perceptual disorders should be watched carefully to avoid injury. The person may be unable to determine the height of a stair riser or small curb. The person with field neglect may not see a danger that is close to him or her.
- Perceptual disorders are not always readily apparent to family members, friends, supervisors, or coworkers. Small changes in the environment, such as lighting, may increase significantly the degree of dysfunction. People who live, work, and play with the person should be informed about the dysfunction to increase safety and reduce embarrassment, such as running into unseen objects.

PROGNOSIS AND OUTCOME
- The person shows improvement in his or her scores on perceptual functions originally assessed as deficient.

- The person is able to perform self-care and daily living activities independently.
- The person is able to perform productive activities.
- The person is able to perform leisure activities.

REFERENCES

Abreu, B.C. 1981. Interdisciplinary approach to the adult visual perceptual function-dysfunction continuum. In *Physical disabilities manual*, ed. B.C. Abreau, 151–81. New York: Raven Press.

Bechinger, D., and R. Tallis. 1986. Perceptual disorders in neurological disease. *British Journal of Occupational Therapy*, Part 1. 49(9):282–4. Part 2. 49(10):327–30.

Bernspang, B., M. Vitansen, and S. Eriksson. 1989. Impairments of perceptual and motor functions: Their influence on self-care ability 4 to 6 years after a stroke. *Occupational Journal of Research* 9(1):27–37.

Bouska, M.J., N.A. Kauffman, and S.E. Marcus. 1985. Disorders of the visual perceptual system. In *Neurological rehabilitation*, ed. D.A. Umphred, 552–85. St. Louis: C.V. Mosby. 2d ed., 1990, 705–40.

Carter, L.T., B.E. Howard, and W.A. O'Neil. 1983. Effectiveness of cognitive skill remediation in acute stroke patients. *American Journal of Occupational Therapy* 37(5):320–6.

Dudgeon, B.M., J.A. DeLisa, and R.M. Miller. 1985. Optokinetic nystagmus and upper extremity dressing independence after stroke. *Archives of Physical Medicine and Rehabilitation* 66(3):164–7.

Edmans, J.A., and N.B. Lincoln. 1987. The frequency of perceptual deficits after stroke. *Clinical Rehabilitation* 1(4):273–81.

Edmans, J.A., and N.B. Lincoln. 1989. Treatment of visual perceptual deficits after stroke: Four single case studies. *International Disabilities Studies* 11:25–33.

Eriksson, S., B. Bernspang, and A.R. Fugl-Meyer. 1988. Perceptual and motor impairment within 2 weeks after a stroke; A multifactorial statistical approach. *Occupational Therapy Journal of Research* 8(2):114–25.

Fox, J.W. 1983. Unilateral neglect: Evaluation and treatment. *Physical and Occupational Therapy in Geriatrics* 2(4):5–15.

Kaiser, F., et al. 1988. Response time of stroke patients to a visual stimulus. *Stroke* 19:335–9.

Kaplan, J., and D.B. Hier. 1982. Visuospatial deficits after right hemisphere stroke. *American Journal of Occupational Therapy* 36(5):314–21.

Lamm-Warberg, C. 1988. Assessment and treatment planning strategies for perceptual deficits. In *Physical rehabilitation: Assessment and treatment*, 2d ed., ed. S.B. O'Sullivan and T.J. Schmitz, 93–120. Philadelphia: F.A. Davis.

Lincoln, N.B., S.E. Whiting, J. Cockburn, et al. 1985. An evaluation of perceptual retraining. *International Rehabilitation Medicine* 7(3):99–191.

Loverro, J., and M. Reding. 1988. Bed orientation and rehabilitation outcome for patients with stroke and hemianopsia or visual neglect. *Journal of Neurologic Rehabilitation* 2(4):147–50.

Mohl, E., H. Kurten, and H.H. Janzik. 1987. Perceptual evaluation in occupational therapy. *International Journal of Rehabilitation Research* 10(Suppl 5):271–6.

Neistadt, M.E. 1988. Occupational therapy for adults with perceptual deficits. *American Journal of Occupational Therapy* 42(7):434–40.

Neistadt, M.E. 1990. A critical analysis of occupational therapy approaches for perceptual deficits with brain injury. *American Journal of Occupational Therapy* 44(4):299–304.

Polland, M. 1986. Unilateral neglect: Visual field, oculomotor dysfunction or body scheme disorder. *Sensory Integration Special Interest Section Newsletter* 9(4):1,5.

Siev, E., B. Freishtat, and B. Zoltan. 1986. *Perceptual and cognitive dysfunction in the adult stroke patient: A manual for evaluation and treatment*, rev. ed. Thorofare, NJ: Slack, Inc.

Simms, B. 1985. Perception and driving: Theory and practice. *British Journal of Occupational Therapy* 48(12):370–4.

Smith, A., and N.B. Lincoln. 1989. The relation between perceptual and language deficits in stroke patients. *British Journal of Occupational Therapy* 52(1):8–10.

Van Deusen, J. 1988. Unilateral neglect: Suggestions for research by occupational therapists. *American Journal of Occupational Therapy* 42(7):441–8.

Van Deusen, J. 1989. Alcohol abuse and perceptual-motor dysfunction: The occupational therapist's role. *American Journal of Occupational Therapy* 43(6):384–90.

Wahlstrom, P.E. 1983. Remediation of perceptual dysfunction. In *Rehabilitation of the head injured adult*, ed. M. Rosenthal, et al., 335–44. Philadelphia: F.A. Davis.

Walker, K.F. 1989. Clinically relevant features of the visual system. *Journal of Head Trauma Rehabilitation* 4(2):1–8.

Wold-Tortelli, N., S. Chioteli, S. Miron-Bernstein, et al. 1981. Adult perceptual motor evaluation and management. In *Physical disabilities manual*, ed. B. Abreu, 307–20. New York: Raven Press.

Yarnell, P.R., and B.B. Fiedman. 1987. Left "hemi" ADL learning and outcome: Limiting factors. *Journal of Neurologic Rehabilitation* 1(3):125–30.

Young, G.C., D. Collins, and M. Hren. 1983. Effect of pairing scanning training with block design training in the remediation of perceptual problems in left hemiplegics. *Journal of Clinical Neuropsychology* 5(3):201–12.

Zoltan, B. 1990. Remediation of visual-perceptual and perceptual-motor deficits. In *Rehabilitation of the adult and child with traumatic brain injury*, 2d ed., ed. M. Rosenthal et al., 351–65. Philadelphia: F.A. Davis.

Perception and Vision Disorders—Child

DESCRIPTION

These disorders are defined as difficulty perceiving and understanding information from the visual system (see also section on adults).

CAUSE

The causes in children include eye muscle imbalance, damage to one or more of the optic nerves or cranial nerves III, IV, or VI, or dysfunction of the association areas of the brain, especially the optic lobe. Strabismus is an example of muscle imbalance of the extraocular muscles resulting in deviation of one eye from parallelism with the other. The result is failure of one or the other eye to converge properly on an image. Two major causes are (1) a specific oculomotor nerve lesion that results in paralysis of one or more ocular muscles (paralytic or nonconcomitant strabismus) or (2) a supranuclear defect within the central nervous system that results in unequal ocular muscle tone (nonparalytic or concomitant strabismus). Concomitant strabisma may be further divided into convergent (esotropia), divergent (exotropia), or vertical (hypertropia or hypotropia). Children with learning disorders may have dysfunctions in the association areas of the brain that interfere with the processing and use of visual perceptual input.

ASSESSMENT

Areas

- gross motor development, coordination, and skills
- fine motor development, coordination, manipulation, and dexterity
- hand grasp functions
- reflex maturation
- postural control and balance
- praxis or motor planning skills
- visual motor integration
- eye motility—fixation, ocular saccadics, tracking (pursuit), scanning, nystagmus, accommodation (eye focusing), binocularity (fusion) or monocularity (no fusion), ocular posture
- visual perception, including spatial relations, position in space, form perception and

constancy, figure-ground discrimination
- sensory registration, awareness—tactile, vestibular, and auditory
- sensory processing—tactile, vestibular, proprioception (body schema and directionality), and auditory
- self-concept
- social skills
- academic achievement (obtained from school reports)
- play skills
- leisure skills and interests

Instruments
- cover test—Have the person fix on a pencil or flashlight held in front of him or her. Alternately cover and uncover an eye. Watch for a shift in the eye that is being uncovered as that eye picks up fixation on the object. In esotropia, the eye that was covered will turn in to achieve fixation, while in exotropia the eye will rotate out to fixate.
- tracking (ocular pursuit) test—Have the person watch the tip of a pencil or finger puppet held about 12 inches from the face. Move the pencil to the right and left, up and down, and diagonally. Note which eye is focusing and when the focus changes, if ever. Usually the change of focus occurs at the midline. (For scoring, see Duckman, 1984, p. 79 in the reference section)
- Southern California Postrotary Nystagmus Test by A.J. Ayres, Los Angeles: Western Psychological Services, 1972
- Southern California Sensory Integration Tests by A.J. Ayres, Los Angeles: Western Psychological Services, 1980 (limited in visual perception test items)
- Test of Visual-Perceptual Skills by M.F. Gardner, Seattle: Special Child Publications, 1982 (not an occupational therapist)
- Developmental Test of Visual Motor Integration, revised by K.E. Beery and N.A. Buktenica, Cleveland, OH: Modern Curriculum Press, 1980 (not occupational therapists)
- Primary Visual Motor Test by M. Haworth, New York: Grune & Stratton, 1970 (not an occupational therapist)
- Motor Free Visual Perception Test by R.P. Colarusso and D.D. Hammill, Novato, CA: Academic Therapy Publications, 1972 (not occupational therapists)

PROBLEMS

Motor
- The person may be clumsy or have motor incoordination when visual perception is required. The person has difficulty coordinating eye and hand to hit a ball or eye and foot to kick a ball.
- The person may have a history of delayed developmental milestones.
- The person may have difficulty with fine motor skills.

Sensory
- visual perception dysfunction—The person may reverse letters or words in reading.
- visual motor dysfunction—See the first problem under motor problems.

- visual spatial dysfunction—The person may misjudge distance or height in relation to body orientation; he or she bumps into doorways or falls while walking up stairs or inclines.
- visual tracking (pursuit) skills—The person usually has difficulty tracking an object from side to side or up and down, especially as the object crosses the midline.
- depth perception—The person usually lacks depth perception because the two eyes are unable to focus together.
- nystagmus—The person may have prolonged postrotary nystagmus.

Cognitive

The disorders may interfere with learning. Strabismus is a factor in learning disabilities and learning difficulties associated with cerebral palsy or other neurological disorders.

Intrapersonal

- The person may have loss of self-confidence and self-esteem because of repeated failure.
- The person may have feelings of being a failure, not being able to keep up with peers.
- The person may have feelings of being different, not like other kids.

Interpersonal

- The child may experience rejection by peers, such as being told he or she is a dummy, retarded, or a klutz, or alternately become the class clown and take advantage of being different.
- Social interaction skills may be delayed.

Self-Care

The child may have developed visually dependent skills slower than normal.

Productivity

Play skills may be delayed.

Leisure

The child may have developed few interests.

TREATMENT/MANAGEMENT

The model of treatment is based on normal growth and development and sensory integration (Ayres).

Motor

- Improve the child's motor planning skills. Activities include throwing a ball or beanbag at a target at various distances, performing animal walks (frog, duck, inchworm, crab), or climbing a jungle gym.
- Improve balance and postural control. Activities include balancing on a t-stool while throwing a beanbag or kicking a ball, walking on "stepping stones" (carpet or colored squares placed at irregular intervals on the floor), or playing hopscotch.
- Improve visual motor integration. Activities include throwing at a target (balls, darts), kicking at a target, jumping and landing on a target (hopscotch or "parachute jump"), parachute games (running into the open space).

Sensory
- Provide vestibular stimulation, such as swinging, rocking, or jumping on inner tubes.
- Activities for figure-ground discrimination include picking out all of one color or shape from a box of assorted pegs, beads, or shapes, arranging blocks of one color in a pattern surrounded by blocks of another color, putting together puzzles with backgrounds that compete with the foreground, or locating hidden figures in line drawings.
- Activities for form and shape constancy include stringing beads of one shape that vary in size or color, using formboard puzzles that outline shapes or objects, and copying pegboard forms or dot to dot forms.
- Activities for position in space include stringing beads in a specified sequence, copying a set of blocks (4, 6, or 9) with colors in the correct position, doing puzzles that require rotation to get the pieces to fit in the space, copying pegboard designs that emphasize left versus right or top versus bottom, and games, such as dominos or tanograms.
- Activities for spatial relations include copying pattern cards showing different shapes and sizes, copying pattern cards showing three dimensional block designs, putting together interlocking puzzles, and copying abstract designs.
- Activities for body schema include obstacle courses, Simon Says, Hokeypokey, and passing a beanbag behind the back or under the knee.
- Activities for eye-hand coordination include hitting a target (start with large target and decrease size), stringing beads (start with large holes), and placing pegs (start with large pegs).

Cognitive

It is assumed that cognitive skills, such as attention span and problem solving, will improve as a result of improved ocular and visual perceptual skills. Therefore, no specific objectives or goals are selected for cognition.

Intrapersonal

Encourage the child to select and choose activities. The therapist assists and clarifies rather than controls and directs.

Interpersonal

As skills improve, small group situations may increase the level of interest.

Self-Care

See note on cognition.

Productivity

See note on cognition.

Leisure

See note on cognition.

PRECAUTIONS
- Perceptual problems in children are not consistent from day to day. Expect to see uneven performance that is better one day and worse the next. Illness frequently increases, temporarily, the severity of the perceptual disorder.

- Perceptual disorders in vision may distort perception of height. Make the child aware of heights from which it is unsafe to jump.

PROGNOSIS AND OUTCOME
Surgical correction, optometric therapy, and the use of prisms in glasses all may reduce the problems and severity of strabismus.

- The child is able to use judgment of personal safety in a choice of activities.
- The child is able to perform self-care activities independently.
- The child is able to perform education activities at expected grade level for his or her chronological age.
- The child is able to participate in leisure activities.

REFERENCES

Duckman, R.H. 1984. Effectiveness of optometric visual training in a population of severely involved cerebral palsied children utilizing professional, non-optometric therapists. *Physical and Occupational Therapy in Pediatrics* 4(4):75–86.

Mayberry, W., and M.B. Gilligan. 1985. Ocular pursuit in mentally retarded, cerebral-palsied, and learning-disabled children. *American Journal of Occupational Therapy* 39(9):589–95.

Menken, C., S.A. Cermak, and A. Fisher. 1987. Evaluating the visual-perceptual skills of children with cerebral palsy. *American Journal of Occupational Therapy* 41(1):646–51.

Murphy, J.B., and J.A. Gliner. 1988. Visual and motor sequencing in normal and clumsy children. *Occupational Therapy Journal of Research* 8(2):89–113.

O'Brien, V., S.A. Cermak, and E. Murray. 1988. The relationship between visual-perceptual motor abilities and clumsiness in children with and without learning disabilities. *American Journal of Occupational Therapy* 42(6):359–63.

Polatajko, H.J. 1987. Visual-ocular control of normal and learning-disabled children. *Developmental Medicine and Child Neurology* 29:477–85.

Reid, D., and S. Drake. 1990. A comparative study of visual perceptual skills in normal children and children with diplegic cerebral palsy. *Canadian Journal of Occupational Therapy* 57(3):141–6.

Slavik, B.A. 1982. Vestibular function in children with nonparalytic strabismus. *Occupational Therapy Journal of Research* 2(4):220–3.

Part XI

Mental Health Disorders

Autism

DESCRIPTION

Autism is a disorder of early childhood characterized by one or more of the following:

- lack of responsiveness to other people
- gross deficit in communicative or language skills
- bizarre responses to various aspects of the environment
- peculiar speech patterns, such as immediate and delayed echolalia, metaphorical language, pronominal reversal, such as "you" for "I"
- onset within the first 30 months of life

Intellectual development is uneven. The disorder was originally defined in 1943 by L. Kanner who thought it was due to psychogenic factors related to cold and unloving parents.

CAUSE

The exact cause is unknown. Current theory classifies autism as a neurological disorder. The central nervous system is involved, probably in relation to problems in the reticular activating system, but the role of genetic, biochemical, metabolic, and viral disease or birth factors is unclear. The ratio of male to female cases is 4:1. The incidence is four to five per 10,000 births.

ASSESSMENT

Areas
- muscle tone
- gross motor skills
- fine motor skills, manipulation, dexterity, and bilateral coordination
- activity level (hyperactivity)
- reflex development and maturation
- postural control and balance
- praxis or motor planning
- stereotypical patterns (unusual use of the hands, feet, or body)
- sensory registration or orienting behavior
- sensory sensitivity (hyporesponsive or hyperresponsive)
- perceptual skills
- attending and arousal behavior
- concentration or attention span
- learning skills, such as imitation
- object relations, human and nonhuman
- social skills
- communication skills

- daily living activities
- play skills
- academic skills

Instruments
- Autism Screening Instrument for Education Planning (ASIEP) by D.A. Krug, J.R. Arick, and P.J. Almond, Portland, OR: ASIEP Ed. Co., 1980 (not occupational therapists)
- Southern California Postrotary Nystagmus Test by A.J. Ayres, Los Angeles: Western Psychological Services, 1975
- Sensory Integration and Praxis Tests by A.J. Ayres, Los Angeles: Western Psychological Services, 1989 (Note: Not appropriate for some autistic children. Check criteria before administering.)
- Response to Sensory Input (See A.J. Ayres and L.S. Tickle. 1980. Hyper-responsivity to touch and vestibular stimuli as a predictor of positive response to sensory integration procedures by autistic children. *American Journal of Occupational Therapy* 34(6):375–81.)

PROBLEMS

Motor
- The child exhibits stereotyped body movements, such as hand-flicking, body spinning, head banging, rocking, and twirling. These behaviors are classified as self-stimulating or self-abusive behaviors.
- The child may have poor gross and fine motor coordination.
- The child may have delayed response to reflex stimulation.
- The child may have low tone in extensors and/or flexors.
- The child may have poor cocontraction and joint stability, especially in the neck muscles.
- The child may have shortened postrotary nystagmus.

Sensory
Usually the sensory systems are not damaged, but the response to sensory input (sensory registration) is altered from hyper- to hyporesponsive behavior or sensitivity.

- Apparent deafness is often mentioned because the child does not respond or delays response to the human voice.
- The child may not respond to touch or have an aversion to touch (tactile defensiveness) but seek certain tactile input.
- The child may appear not to see humans but responds to objects readily.
- The child may not respond to pain.
- The child may not respond to certain visual or auditory stimuli but overrespond to other visual or auditory stimuli (insist on sameness or be upset by minor inconsistencies).
- The child may seek certain vestibular stimulation while avoiding other stimuli. He or she may show gravitational insecurity, for example.
- The child may have poor spatial relationships (insist on maintaining the same organization or relation of objects in the environment).

Cognitive
- Intelligence ranges from normal to severe retardation. Children with IQs below 50 have a poor prognosis.
- Learning disorders are common, such as dyslexia.
- The child may have poor attending or orienting behavior and poor eye contact (poor orienting reflex).
- The child may have short attention span and poor concentration skills.

Intrapersonal
- The child shows strong resistance to change in the environment and responds with crying or screaming.
- The child insists on following routines in precise detail.
- The child may repeat or perseverate certain behaviors, such as twirling objects.

Interpersonal
- The child has marked lack of awareness of the existence or feelings of others, and a lack of attachment to caregivers.
- The child usually fails to cuddle when held and does not seek comfort at times of distress.
- The child stiffens his or her body when being picked up.
- The child usually avoids eye gaze or seems to stare through a person rather than at the person.
- The child may be mute or have idiosyncratic speech, such as echolalia.
- The child may have strong attachment to objects but not to humans.
- The child does not imitate social behaviors, such as waving or copying parent's activities around the house.

Self-Care
Although the motor skills exist to perform activities of daily living, the cognitive directions do not activate the process. Usually the person must be directed to perform self-care activities.

Productivity
- The child has difficulty learning to consistently perform job tasks as required.
- The child has no or impaired social play skills and prefers to play alone.
- The child does not show imagination in play activities.

Leisure
The child has difficulty developing interests beyond those involved in ritual or perseverate behaviors.

TREATMENT/MANAGEMENT
Treatment is based on the model of sensory integration (Ayres), neurodevelopmental therapy (Bobath), behavior modification, and play therapy.

Motor
- Improve the child's gross motor skills through directed practice in a variety of play activities.

- Increase muscle tone and cocontraction to promote stability, especially in the midline trunk muscles and shoulder and hip joints using linear vestibular input (in a hammock or on a large ball), proprioception (all-fours position), prone extension position during play activities (scooter board), and sucking.
- Increase motor planning skills using mazes or obstacle courses.
- Self-abusive or self-stimulating behaviors are assumed to be related to stress and therefore are treated by reducing stress, such as reducing the noise level, reducing the number of people in the environment, or reducing the complexity of the environment. The behaviors may also indicate what sensory information is lacking, not registering, and is needed to increase sensitivity and discrimination.

Sensory
- For hyperresponsiveness and hyperactivity, reduce environmental visual and auditory stimuli while providing vestibular, proprioceptive, and tactile input.
- Provide vestibular stimulation, such as swinging, riding, or rocking. For hyperresponsiveness, use slow, regular input; for hyporesponsiveness use rapid, irregular input.
- Increase body awareness (proprioceptive and kinesthetic) through the use of obstacle courses or resistive activities and joint compression and traction, beginning with symmetrical flexion patterns organized at the midline, such as holding on to a bolster swing.
- Decrease tactile defensiveness, if present, and increase tactile discrimination through activities and games that use deep pressure (rolling in a blanket, sandwiching between mats, or swaddling), and the opportunity to experience a variety of tactile sensations (feeling a variety of textured cloth, locating articles buried in sand, pulling objects out of a "feely" bag). See also section on tactile defensiveness.
- Increase skills in spatial relations by creating mazes for the scooter board or navigating a pathway around the room; then use fine motor mazes and finally paper and pencil mazes.

Cognitive
- Provide directive commands and repeat them frequently to assist the person to focus attention on the activity or listen to directions, such as "Look at me," or "Look at the picture."
- Increase attending behavior and attention span by decreasing extraneous visual and auditory stimuli.

Intrapersonal
- Decrease dependence on routines or repetitive behaviors by encouraging the person to engage in novel behavior.
- Teach relaxation techniques and other stress reduction behaviors.

Interpersonal
- Encourage social skills through games and sports.
- Assist in the promotion of language. Sign language is frequently used. Music may be useful. Vestibular stimulation has been correlated with increased verbalization (Ray, 1988), as have fine motor skills (Reilly, 1983).

Self-Care
- Increase independence in performance of activities of daily living.
- In adolescence, increase independence in daily living skills to permit living in a group home.

Productivity
- Increase the level of play skills from solitary to parallel and cooperative play.
- Reinforce school work whenever possible. Examples might include reading simple directions for baking cookies or figuring the costs of items in a grocery list.
- In adolescence, promote vocational readiness skills.
- Increase home-management skills, including meal preparation, shopping, budgeting, and housecleaning.

Leisure
Explore interests that could be developed into leisure activities.

PRECAUTIONS

No specific precautions are mentioned. If sensory integration techniques are used, check the type of sensory integration technique for precautions. If behavior modification techniques are used, be aware that behavioral change often does not generalize to situations or environments other than the ones in which the behavior modification techniques were used.

PROGNOSIS AND OUTCOME

The prognosis is guarded. Response to treatment varies. Some individuals may be able to function in a semi-independent environment, such as a group home. Others will need a highly structured environment, such as a nursing home or state hospital. Children with higher intelligence, early language development, hyperresponsiveness, and good play skills seem to do better.

- The child demonstrates increased muscle tone, cocontraction, and joint stability.
- The child demonstrates increased discriminative skills to sensory stimuli.
- The child demonstrates increased ability to orient or attend to stimuli.
- The child demonstrates increased attention span or concentration.
- The child spends less time on ritual and repetitive behavior.
- The child is more tolerant of changes in the environment.
- The child demonstrates improved social skills.
- The child is able to perform daily living skills without assistance.
- The child is able to play with other children in parallel or cooperative play at or near his or her own age-appropriate level.
- The child is progressing in academic skills.

REFERENCES

Ayres, A.J. 1979. The autistic child. In *Sensory integration and the child*, ed. A.J. Ayers, 123–30. Los Angeles: Western Psychological Services.

Ayres, A.J., and Z.K. Mailloux. 1983. Possible pubertal effect on therapeutic gains in an autistic girl. *American Journal of Occupational Therapy* 37(8):535–40.

Bloomer, M.L., and C.C. Rose. 1989. Frames of reference: Guiding treatment for children with autism. *Occupational Therapy in Health Care* 6(2/3):5–26 (review article).

Clark, F. 1983. Research on the neuropathophysiology of autism and its implications for occupational therapy. *Occupational Therapy Journal of Research* 3(1):3–22 (review article).

Dunn, W., and A.G. Fisher. 1983. Sensory registration, autism and tactile defensiveness. *Sensory Integration Special Interest Section Newsletter* 6(2):3–4.

King, L.J. 1987. A sensory integrative approach to the education of the autistic child. *Occupational Therapy in Health Care* 4(2):77–85.

Lawton-Shirley, N. 1990. Craniosacral/myofascial techniques combined with sensory integration for autistic children. *Sensory Integration Special Interest Section Newsletter* 13(2):5–6.

Nelson, D.L. 1984. *Children with autism and other pervasive disorders of development and behavior: Therapy through activities.* Thorofare, NJ: Slack, Inc.

Peterson, T.W. 1986. Recent studies in autism: A review of the literature. *Occupational Therapy in Mental Health* 6(4):63–75 (bibliography).

Ramm, P.A. 1988. Autism. In *Willard and Spackman's occupational therapy,* 7th ed., ed. H.L. Hopkins and H.D. Smith, 661–5. Philadelphia: J.B. Lippincott.

Ray, T.C., L.J. King, and T. Grandin. 1988. The effectiveness of self-initiated vestibular stimulation in producing speech sounds in an autistic child. *Occupational Therapy Journal of Research* 8(3):186–90.

Reilly, C., D.L. Nelson, and A.C. Bundy. 1983. Sensorimotor versus fine motor activities in eliciting vocalization in autistic children. *Occupational Therapy Journal of Research* 3(4):199–212.

Royeen, C.B. 1983. Evaluation of autistic adolescents. *Sensory Integration Special Interest Section Newsletter* 6(4):5.

Royeen, C.B., and L.F. Little. 1985. Autistic adolescents: Developmental milestones and a model treatment program. *Occupational Therapy in Health Care* 2(3):59–69.

Slavik, B.A., J. Kitsuwa-Lowe, P.T. Danner, et al. 1984. Vestibular stimulation and eye contact in autistic children. *Neuropediatrics* 15:33–6.

Depression

DESCRIPTION

Depression is a psychopathologic state in which the disturbance of mood or affect is characterized by agitation, weight loss, guilt, insomnia, decreased activity, and an inability to experience pleasure. The state may be part of a bipolar disorder in which depression alternates with mania or the condition may be unipolar in which depression is the major disorder.

CAUSE

The cause may be singular or multiple depending on the theory. Psychoanalytic theories view depression as a result of the loss of a loved object. Behavioral theories emphasizing reinforcement view depression as the result of negative person-environment interaction. Behavioral theories emphasizing cognition view depression as the result of negative cognitive patterns of thinking. Biochemical theories focus on depression as the result of decreased neurotransmitter amines at the synaptic junction. Sociological theories focus on life roles, the stresses related to these roles, and the individual's ability to cope with stress.

Existential theories view depression as an inability to find meaning in life. About one in four persons experiences some form of affective disturbance in their lifetime. Women are affected more frequently than men. Bipolar disorders usually begin in the person's teens, 20s, or 30s. Unipolar forms occur throughout the person's lifespan.

ASSESSMENT

Areas
- postural control and balance
- posture during gross motor activities
- physical fitness and endurance
- fine motor skills, manipulation, dexterity, and bilateral coordination
- perceptual skills
- attending behavior
- attention span and concentration
- understanding and following direction
- memory
- problem solving and decision making
- conceptualization
- categorization
- organizational skills—time and materials
- ability to abstract
- mood or affect
- self-concept
- independence or dependence
- goals and values
- communication skills
- social roles
- daily living skills
- productivity history, skills, and interests
- leisure skills and interests

Instruments
- Allen Cognitive Level Test (See C.K. Allen, ed. 1985. *Occupational therapy for psychiatric diseases: Measurement and management of cognitive disabilities*, ed. C.K. Allen, 108–113. Boston: Little, Brown & Co. See also C.K. Allen. 1988. Occupational therapy: Functional assessment of the severity of mental disorders. *Hospital and Community Psychiatry* 39(3):140–2.)
- Riska Object Classification Test by L.R. Williams (See C.K. Allen. 1985. Research with a nondisabled population. In *Occupational therapy for psychiatric diseases: Measurement and management of cognitive disabilities*, ed. C.K. Allen, 315–38. Boston: Little, Brown & Co.)
- Occupational Therapy Assessment for Older Adults with Depression (See J.C. Rogers. 1986. *Physical and Occupational Therapy in Geriatrics* 5(1):13–33.)
- Bay Area Functional Performance Evaluation, 2d ed., by S.L. Williams and J.S. Bloomer, Palo Alto, CA: Consulting Psychologists Press, 1987 (See also R. Thibeault and E. Black-

mer. 1987. Validating a test of functional performance with psychiatric patients. *American Journal of Occupational Therapy* 41(8):515–21; and S.L. Williams and D. Houston. 1986. Use of the Bay Area Functional Performance Evaluation (BAFPE) with the depressed patient: A preliminary impression. In *Depression: Assessment and treatment update: Proceedings*, 22–35. Rockville, MD: American Occupational Therapy Association.)

- Stress Management Questionnaire (See F. Stein and J. Smith. 1989. Short-term stress management programme with acutely depressed in-patients. *Canadian Journal of Occupational Therapy* 56(4):185–92.
- Role Performance Assessment Scale (See M. Good-Ellis. 1986. Quantitative role performance assessment: Implications and application to treatment of depression. In *Depression: Assessment and treatment update: Proceedings*, 36–48. Rockville, MD: American Occupational Therapy Association; and M.A. Good-Ellis, S.B. Fine, J.H. Spencer, et al. 1987. Developing a role activity performance scale. *American Journal of Occupational Therapy* 41(4):232–41.)
- Occupational History (See L.C. Moorhead. 1969. The occupational history. *American Journal of Occupational Therapy* 23:329–34.)

PROBLEMS

Motor
- The person may exhibit psychomotor retardation (difficulty initiating the action of moving the body or parts of the body).
- The person may have psychomotor agitation with restlessness and wringing of the hands.
- The person may lack physical endurance and fatigue easily.

Sensory
The person may have hallucinations; auditory and visual hallucinations are the most common but occasionally tactile or olfactory hallucinations occur as well.

Cognitive
- The person may have difficulty in attending to a task.
- The person may express recurrent thoughts of death and suicide.
- The person may have difficulty making decisions and solving problems.
- The person may have difficulty in finding activities of interest.

Intrapersonal
- The person may have a poor self-concept or be self-denigrating.
- The person may express feelings of helplessness and hopelessness.
- The person may be preoccupied with feelings of guilt.
- The person may be unable to feel or express emotions.
- The person may express fear of going insane or losing his or her mind.
- The person may be irritable.
- The person may appear agitated.
- The person may lack self-confidence.
- The person may be dependent.

- The person may express feelings of worthlessness.
- The person may cry for no apparent reason.

Interpersonal
- The person may become socially withdrawn.
- The person may not speak or speaks with great effort.

Self-Care
- The person is usually disinterested in most activities of daily living.
- The person may refuse to eat, become anorexic, or lose weight.
- The person may have insomnia and awaken early in the morning.

Productivity
The person may be unable to perform job tasks.

Leisure
The person may lose interest in leisure activities formerly enjoyed.

TREATMENT/MANAGEMENT
Models of treatment include occupation behavior (Reilly) and human occupation (Kielhofner).

Motor
Increase the person's energy through participation in activities, including recreation.

Sensory
Maintain or increase sensory stimulation through participation in activities.

Cognitive
- Provide opportunities to make choices, solve problems, and make decisions in the selection of color, type of activity, or amount of time devoted to an activity.
- Provide instruction in time management and activity scheduling.
- Provide learning groups that discuss subjects, such as problems of depression, growing old, and managing emotions.

Intrapersonal
- Increase self-concept (self-mastery, sense of competence, self-confidence) through creative activities, such as art, crafts, drama, dance, or music, that can result in task accomplishment.
- Provide training in stress reduction, including discussion about life stresses, assertion, and relaxation training.
- Relate present activities to immediate feelings and goals to increase concept of purposeful activity and goal-directed behavior.

Interpersonal
- Provide opportunities to develop social skills and participate in group activities through structured task groups, discussion groups, or informal work-related groups.
- Encourage interpersonal relationships through group activities. Encourage the person to join a group in the community.
- Increase communication skills, verbal and nonverbal, through practice in group situations, role playing, discussion, and review.

Self-Care
- Express expectations that the person will perform activities of daily living.
- Provide instruction in daily living skills, such as money management, locating living quarters, shopping, or preparing meals.

Productivity
- Encourage the person to participate in home-management tasks. The family can be encouraged to assign specific tasks for the person to perform.
- If the person is working, explore career goals and interests.
- If the person is retired, explore the possibility of volunteer activities.

Leisure
Encourage the person to explore interests and develop enjoyable leisure activities.

PRECAUTIONS
- Watch the person to avoid self-inflicted injuries and suicide attempts.
- Observe for signs of overmedication, such as tremor and loss of visual acuity.

PROGNOSIS AND OUTCOME
Between episodes of depression or mania, there is full recovery of function.

- The person is able to resume his or her previous level of participation in the community.
- The person is able to perform activities of daily living and functional skills independently.
- The person is able to test reality and control his or her mood and activity level independently.
- The person is able to perform cognitive activities, including using judgment for personal safety, decision making, problem solving, and time management.
- The person is able to perform productive activities while setting realistic goals, conserving energy, and setting limits.
- The person assumes responsibility for performing leisure activities.
- The person is able to function in one-to-one and group situations.

REFERENCES

Boswell, S. 1989. A social support group for depressed people. *Australian Occupational Therapy Journal* 36(1):34–41.
Centoni, M., and B. Tallant. 1986. The projective use of drawings as a treatment technique with the depressed unemployed male. *Canadian Journal of Occupational Therapy* 53(2):81–7.

Davis-Kosaka, A., et al. 1986. Using purpose to engage the patient with depression. *Occupational Therapy in Health Care* 3(1):41–53.

Davison, J. 1987. Health education in a psychiatric setting. *British Journal of Occupational Therapy* 50(9):313–5.

Devereaux, E.B. 1986. Current issues in the assessment and treatment of depression. In *Depression: Assessment and treatment update: Proceedings*, 3–13. Rockville, MD: American Occupational Therapy Association.

Dotherty, F. 1986. Steps in the progressive treatment of depression in the elderly. *Physical and Occupational Therapy in Geriatrics* 5(1):59–76.

Eilenberg, A.O. 1986. An expanded community role for occupational therapy: Preventing depression. *Physical and Occupational Therapy in Geriatrics* 5(1):47–58.

Heine, D., and M. Steiner. 1986. Standardized paintings as a proposed adjunct instrument for longitudinal monitoring of mood states: A preliminary note. *Occupational Therapy in Mental Health* 6(3):31–7.

Johnston, M. 1986. Use of cognitive behavioral techniques with depressed adults in day treatment. In *Depression: Assessment and treatment update: Proceedings*, 49–61. Rockville, MD: American Occupational Therapy Association.

Katz, N. 1985. Research on major depression. In *Occupational therapy for psychiatric diseases: Measurement and management of cognitive disabilities*, ed. C.K. Allen, 299–313. Boston: Little, Brown & Co.

Larson, K.B. 1990. Activity patterns and life changes in people with depression. *American Journal of Occupational Therapy* 44(10):902–6.

Miller, P. 1986. Models for treatment of depression. *Physical and Occupational Therapy in Geriatrics* 5(1):3–11.

Neville, A. 1986. The model of human occupation and depression. *Mental Health Special Interest Section Newsletter* 8(1):1,3–4.

Neville, A. 1986. Depression and the model of human occupation: Theory and research. In *Depression: Assessment and treatment update: Proceedings*, 14–21. Rockville, MD: American Occupational Therapy Association.

Pedersen, I.D. 1986. Treatment of depression in institutionalized older persons. *Physical and Occupational Therapy in Geriatrics* 5(1):77–89.

Smith, H. 1986. Mastery and achievement: Guidelines using clinical problem solving with depressed elderly clients. *Physical and Occupational Therapy in Geriatrics* 5(1):35–46.

Stein, F., and J. Smith. 1989. Short-term stress management programme with acutely depressed in-patients. *Canadian Journal of Occupational Therapy* 56(4):185–92.

Watson, L.J. 1986. Psychiatric consultation-liaison in the acute physical disabilities setting. *American Journal of Occupational Therapy* 40(5):338–42.

Eating Disorders—Anorexia Nervosa

DESCRIPTION

The disorder is characterized by a refusal to maintain normal body weight for age and height, intense fear of gaining weight or becoming fat, a distorted body image, and amenorrhea in women.

CAUSE

The cause is unclear but may be related to a stressful life situation. The history of the person may suggest a model child. The disorder is more common among sisters and mothers of those with the disorder than among the general population. Onset usually occurs in early to late adolescence, but onset in the 20s also occurs. The disorder is predominant among females (95%).

ASSESSMENT

Areas
- motor activity level, especially hyperactivity
- body scheme or body image
- problem solving or decision making
- goals and values
- reality testing
- affect or mood
- self-concept and self-esteem
- social skills
- social roles
- daily living skills
- productivity in school, home, and job, including history, skills, values, and interests
- leisure skills and interests

Instruments
- Role Checklist (See F. Oakley, G. Kielhofner, and R. Barris. 1985. An occupational therapy approach to assessing psychiatric patients' adaptive functioning. *American Journal of Occupational Therapy* 39(3):47–54. See also F. Oakley, et al. 1986. The Role Checklist: Development and empirical assessment of reliability. *Occupational Therapy Journal of Research* 6(3):57–70.)
- Role Performance Scale (See M.A. Good-Ellis, S.B. Fine, and J.H. Spencer, Jr., et al. 1987. Developing a role activity performance scale. *American Journal of Occupational Therapy* 41(4):323–41. See also M.A. Good-Ellis. 1986. Quantitative role performance assessment: Implications and application to treatment of depression. In *Depression: Assessment and treatment update: Proceedings*, 36–48. Rockville, MD: American Occupational Therapy Association.)

PROBLEM

Motor
- Body weight is 15% or more below that expected for a person of a given age and height.
- The person has increased motor activity and frequently overexercises to "keep the calories off" or stands in preference to sitting for such activities as reading and watching television.

Sensory
The person has a distorted body schema. The body is seen as fatter and larger than it actually is.

Cognitive
- The person may use the need to study school subjects as a tool to avoid confronting problems.
- Cognitive skills are diminished but may be used as devices for avoidance behavior as suggested above.

- The person may base decisions on incorrect information about nutrition, digestion, and metabolism.
- The person may have great difficulty making decisions; for example, making choices from restaurant menus.
- Time spent on preparing and eating food may be out of balance with other activities.

Intrapersonal

- The person has intense fear of gaining weight or becoming fat even though he or she is underweight.
- Reality testing and belief systems may be distorted and not based on reality or fact.
- The person may have bulimic episodes (eating binges), often followed by vomiting.
- The person may hoard, conceal, crumble, or throw away food.
- The person usually denies or minimizes the severity of the illness and his or her emaciated body. He or she may be uninterested or resistant to therapy because "nothing is wrong."
- Compulsive or ritualistic behavior may be present, such as cutting food into minute pieces, putting food in bowls, eating with teaspoons, heavily spicing food, rearranging food so it appears to take up less space, and drawing meals out over long periods of time. (See Kerr, 1990, in the reference section.)
- Phobic behavior may be present so that certain foods are viewed as "bad" or "forbidden," such as sweets.
- Anxiety behavior may occur if the person has to handle certain foods, such as meats or fats.
- The person may have delayed psychosexual development.
- The person may undervalue him- or herself (poor self-concept), even though the person has numerous abilities.
- The person's feelings or beliefs about pleasure may be distorted.

Interpersonal

- The person may prepare an elaborate meal for others but limit him- or herself to eating low-calorie foods.
- The person may have poorly developed social skills, especially in group situations where food and eating are involved.

Self-Care

- The person may avoid performing some daily living activities, such as grooming.
- The person usually has periods of fasting when all food is refused.

Productivity

The person may fail to perform home-management tasks, including feeding and caring for the children, if present.

Leisure

The person neglects previously enjoyed activities; instead, leisure time may be characterized by boredom, restlessness, and aimlessness.

TREATMENT/MANAGEMENT

Models of treatment include cognitive behavioral (see Giles in the reference section) and human occupation (Kielhofner). Other models described in the literature are the medical model, behavior model, family therapy approach, and psychoanalytic approach.

Motor

Encourage daily participation in a physical fitness program designed to improve muscle tone, strength, and cardiopulmonary conditioning but in moderation. Yoga exercises may be useful to combine exercise and relaxation.

Sensory

Videotaping may be useful in confronting the person with a realistic appraisal of his or her body image and its relationship to the illness.

Cognitive

- Instruct the person in concepts of time and activity management to create a balance of self-care, productivity, and leisure.
- Instruct the person in the role of food in metabolism and the adverse effects of abnormal eating behavior.

Intrapersonal

- Provide opportunities for mastery, control, and self-expression through creative crafts, art activities, games, dance, or drama.
- Provide training in relaxation techniques to reduce anxiety and deal with stress.
- A contract may be useful to assist the person to set objectives or goals and work toward them.
- Assertiveness training may be useful to encourage the person to understand and control aggressive behavior and validate feelings.

Interpersonal

- The therapist should establish a trusting relationship that accepts the person and permits discussion of feelings and opinions.
- Improve interpersonal skills, especially regarding how others see the individual, to permit a realistic comparison between self-perception and the perception of others.
- Encourage the person to participate in social situations that include food and practice eating with others, such as dining at a restaurant.

Self-Care

- Provide opportunities for practicing shopping, preparing, and eating in a controlled setting, and then slowly releasing control as the person is able to gain responsibility for his or her actions and channel anxiety associated with food into more acceptable activities.
- The therapist may accompany the person to shop for new clothes after some weight has been regained to assist the person to realistically respond to being "fat" in public. An alternate approach could be sewing new clothes.
- Beauty and makeup sessions may be useful to assist in developing a new, positive image.

Productivity
- Assist the person to explore possible career options to promote self-concept.
- Encourage the person to continue school work and education but as part of a balanced program of self-care, productive, and leisure activities.

Leisure
- Explore with the person new interests to substitute for food behaviors that must be given up.
- Encourage the person to find interests that permit relaxation, fun, humor, and variety.

PRECAUTIONS
- Monitor cardiac performance for arrhythmias, such as ventricular fibrillation associated with hypokalemia.
- The variety of models and treatment approaches suggests that the disorder is not well understood. Therapists should be aware of changing viewpoints in working with such persons.

PROGNOSIS AND OUTCOME
- The person is able to maintain body weight at an established level.
- The person correctly describes body image.
- The person demonstrates improved ability to express feelings and thoughts.
- The person participates in social group activities.
- The person is able to prepare and eat food in a group setting.
- The person demonstrates knowledge of individual skills and assets.
- The person has increased the number of leisure skills performed.

REFERENCES

Alexander, N. 1986. Characteristics and treatment of families with anorectic offspring. *Occupational Therapy in Mental Health* 6(1):117–35.

Bailey, M.K. 1986. Occupational therapy for patients with eating disorders. *Occupational Therapy in Mental Health* 6(1):89–116.

Ericson, L.L. 1987. Anorexia nervosa. *Occupational Therapy Forum* 2(7):1,3–7.

Giles, G.M. 1985. Anorexia nervosa and bulimia: An activity oriented approach. *American Journal of Occupational Therapy* 39(8):510–7.

Giles, G.M., and M.E. Allen. 1986. Occupational therapy in the rehabilitation of the patient with anorexia nervosa. *Occupational Therapy in Mental Health* 6(1):47–66.

Giles, G.M., and C.L. Chng. 1984. Occupational therapy in the treatment of anorexia nervosa: A contractual coping approach. *British Journal of Occupational Therapy* 47:138–141.

Kerr, A.G. 1990. Occupational therapy. In *A day hospital group treatment program for anorexia nervosa and bulimia nervosa*, ed. N. Piran and A.S. Kaplan, 110–27. New York: Brunner/Mazel.

Martin, J.E. 1985. Occupational therapy in anorexia nervosa. *Journal of Psychiatric Research* 19(2/3):459–63.

Martin, J.E. 1985. Anorexia nervosa: A review of the theoretical perspectives and treatment approaches. *British Journal of Occupational Therapy* 48(8):236–40.

McColl, M.A., J. Friedland, and A. Kerr. 1986. When doing is not enough: The relations between activity and effectiveness in anorexia nervosa. *Occupational Therapy in Mental Health* 6(1):137–50.

McGee, K., and J. McGee. 1986. Behavioral treatment of eating disorders. *Occupational Therapy in Mental Health* 6(1):15–25.

Rockwell, L.E. 1990. Frames of reference and modalities used by occupational therapists in the treatment of patients with eating disorders. *Occupational Therapy in Mental Health* 10(2):47–59.

Stockwell, R., S. Duncan, and M. Levens. 1988. Occupational therapy with eating disorders. In *Occupational therapy in mental health: Principles in practice*, ed. D.W. Scott and N. Katz, 206–18. London, England: Taylor & Francis.

Van Deusen, J., and L. Allen. 1985. Is there perceptual-motor dysfunction in anorexia nervosa? Suggestions for research by therapists. *Physical and Occupational Therapy in Pediatrics* 5(4):51–8.

Waltos, D.L. 1986. Historical perspectives and diagnostic considerations. *Occupational Therapy in Mental Health* 6(1):1–13.

Eating Disorders—Bulimia

DESCRIPTION

Bulimia is characterized by recurrent episodes of binge eating in which large amounts of food are consumed in a short period of time; a feeling of lack of control over eating behavior during the eating binges; self-induced vomiting, use of laxatives or diuretics, strict dieting or fasting, or vigorous exercise in order to prevent weight gain; and persistent overconcern with body shape and weight.

CAUSE

Mood swings, disturbed family dynamics, impulsivity, lack of internal control, high anxiety, and low self-esteem are predisposing factors, but the exact etiology is unknown. Both men and women are affected, but the typical person is a young woman in her 20s.

ASSESSMENT

Areas

- gross motor skills
- fine motor coordination, manipulation, and dexterity
- attention span
- ability to follow directions
- problem-solving and decision-making skills
- goals and values awareness
- self-concept and self-esteem
- group interaction skills
- daily living skills
- productivity history, skills, and interests
- leisure interests and skills

Instruments

Information on published tests used by occupational therapists is lacking. See the interview process by C. Shaw, in *The evaluative process in psychiatric occupational therapy*, ed. B. Hemphill. Thorofare, NJ: Slack, Inc., 1982.

PROBLEMS

Motor
The person may engage in vigorous exercise in order to prevent weight gain.

Sensory
The person may have distortion of body scheme.

Cognitive
- The person may have difficulty concentrating on a task.
- Time may be managed more by food than any other aspect.
- The person usually has difficulty planning ahead.

Intrapersonal
- The person feels a lack of control over eating behavior, especially during eating binges.
- The person is overconcerned with body shape and weight and usually has a distorted body image.
- The person may feel that his or her life is dominated by conflicts about eating.
- The person has poor reality testing as evidenced by life-threatening behaviors, such as starvation, use of laxatives, and induced vomiting.
- The person may exhibit suicidal behavior by slashing wrists or overdosing.
- The person may describe feelings of sadness or depression.
- The person usually has low self-esteem and a feeling of being a failure.
- The person usually is a perfectionist.

Interpersonal
- The person may avoid interpersonal situations, when possible, to reduce chances of being found out.
- The person may engage only in social activities that the person can control.
- The person may be fearful of sustained closeness or intimacy.

Self-Care
- The person has a history of recurrent episodes of binge eating in which large amounts of food are consumed with little chewing.
- The person may engage in self-induced vomiting.
- The person may use laxatives or diuretics excessively.
- The person may attempt strict dieting or fasting.
- The person may lack independence in several self-care areas.

Productivity
- The person may have poorly developed vocational interests or consider only those related to food, fitness, modeling, dance, or caregiver occupations.
- The person may have difficulty in accepting supervision and following directions.
- The person may have a history of underproductivity and excessive absences.

Leisure
The person may have few leisure interests other than food, eating, binging, or dieting.

TREATMENT/MANAGEMENT

Models of treatment have been based on human occupation (Kielhofner) and cognitive behavior (activity approach).

Motor

Provide movement and exercise experiences emphasizing body toning, general strengthening, and general fitness.

Cognitive

- Instruct the person about body weight regulation, including caloric intake, homeostasis, and eating a balanced diet.
- Assist the person to organize an activity schedule designed to provide specific tasks to do, especially during times of the day or week when binge eating is most likely to occur.
- Instruct the person in stress-management techniques, including the use of exercise, yoga, and other relaxation techniques.
- Videotapes may be useful in discussing disturbances of body image. Reading materials may provide factual information about the disorder and its effects on a person's life, which can facilitate discussion with the therapist or in group therapy.

Intrapersonal

- Assist the person to set graded goals related to eating and select rewards for not binging.
- Increase self-esteem through activities that will provide a sense of mastery, such as leatherwork or ceramics. Art, drama, or music may also be useful.
- Encourage the person to verbalize feelings. Role-playing may be a useful technique.
- Correct dysfunctional thinking patterns or faulty constructions of reality, such as overgeneralization, all-or-none reasoning, superstitions, or attaching too much significance to specific events. Keeping a diary of dysfunctional thoughts may assist in identifying the thoughts as well as participation in group discussions.
- Identify and help the person evaluate automatic (ritualistic, obsessive) thoughts or images by examining the advantages, disadvantages, or logical inconsistencies of such thoughts.
- Increase coping skills and strategies through stress-management techniques.

Interpersonal

- Provide a group situation in which beliefs and values can be identified and examined.
- Provide opportunities to be assertive and enjoy creativity within a safe group setting, such as role-playing, drama, or dance.
- Encourage the person to participate in group activities outside of the treatment situation.

Self-Care

- Increase independence skills in self-care and daily living based on problem areas identified in the original assessment.
- A cooking class is useful to correct misinformation about food, such as caloric value and nutritionally balanced meals. Planning meals in advance and shopping may be helpful to control binge eating. Later on in treatment, eating at a restaurant may be useful to help the person practice self-control.

- The person may need to shop for new clothes when weight has been stabilized because his or her existing wardrobe does not fit. Practice in making decisions about and planning a wardrobe for work activities as well as leisure activities can be stressed.

Productivity

- Increase skills in independent living, such as money management, or living in an apartment.
- Provide work adjustment programs that develop work habits and skills.
- The person may need assistance in looking for job opportunities, developing interview techniques, and practice in completing an application form.

Leisure

- Provide opportunities to explore and develop leisure skills and activities. In later stages of treatment, the person should be encouraged to use community resources for leisure activities, rather than the hospital, to practice independence skills.
- Leisure activities should be directed away from food and eating interests.

PRECAUTIONS

- Watch for signs of relapse into binge eating.
- Follow-up programs are important to maintain short term gains.

PROGNOSIS AND OUTCOME

- The person is able to express, verbally and nonverbally, a positive sense of self.
- The person is able to set goals and perform activities without resorting to binge eating behaviors.
- The person is able to eat regular, normal meals independently, without supervision.
- The person is able to express opinions and accept feedback without withdrawing or becoming hostile.
- The person has increased skills toward independence or achieved independence in self-care activities.
- The person has increased skills in home management and career choice.
- The person demonstrates regular performance of leisure skills.

REFERENCES

Bailey, M.K. 1986. Occupational therapy for patients with eating disorders. *Occupational Therapy in Mental Health* 6(1):89–116.

Barris, R. 1986. Occupational dysfunction and eating disorders: Theory and approach to treatment. *Occupational Therapy in Mental Health* 6(1):27–45.

Giles, G.M. 1985. Anorexia nervosa and bulimia: An activity-oriented approach. *American Journal of Occupational Therapy* 39(8):510–7.

Roth, D. 1986. Treatment of the hospitalized eating disorder patient. *Occupational Therapy in Mental Health* 6(1):67–87.

Stockwell, R., S. Duncan, and M. Levens. 1988. Occupational therapy with eating disorders. In *Occupational therapy in mental health: Principles in practice*, ed. D.W. Scott and N. Katz, 206–218. London: Taylor & Francis.

Elder Abuse

DESCRIPTION
Elder abuse is defined as abuse, neglect, or maltreatment of older persons by family members, relatives, or friends who are responsible for part or all of the care received by an elderly person.

CAUSE
The causes of abuse have been grouped into six categories:

1. physical abuse
2. physical neglect
3. psychological or emotional abuse
4. psychological neglect
5. material abuse or exploitation
6. violation of personal rights or exploitation

One or more causes may be present in a specific case. Women are more often victims than men. Usually the person is over age 75, Caucasian, lives with a relative, and has a physical or mental impairment.

ASSESSMENT

Areas
Although an individual may be referred for specific treatment, a complete assessment is important. Many problems may exist that were not observed when the person was first seen by medical staff. Elder abuse is not a single disorder; all major problems should be evaluated.
- muscle strength
- range of motion
- endurance and physical fitness
- postural control and balance
- sensory awareness and processing
- perceptual skills
- memory and learning skills
- orientation
- values and goals
- self-concept or self-esteem
- social roles
- self-care and daily living skills
- productive history, skills, and interests
- leisure skills and interests
- architectural and environmental barriers
- home safety

Instruments

No specific instruments used by occupational therapists were identified in the literature. An elder abuse and neglect protocol is provided in the reference section (Tomita, 1982, pp. 45–50.) Some instruments that should be useful include

- manual muscle test
- goniometry
- activities of daily living scale
- occupational history
- leisure checklist

PROBLEMS

Motor
- The person may have general muscle weakness.
- The person may have decreased physical tolerance and endurance.
- The person may have decreased range of motion.
- The person may have residual motor problems from a previous illness, such as hemiplegia, arthritis, or other disorders.
- The person may have decreased balance and equilibrium reactions that may have been treated by drugs or a physical appliance, such as a cane, or that have remained untreated.
- The person may have decreased reaction time.

Sensory
- The person may have decreased visual acuity that is corrected with glasses or surgery (cataracts) or has remained untreated.
- The person may have a hearing loss that is corrected with a hearing aid or has remained untreated.
- The person may have decreased sense of touch and tactile responses.
- The person may have decreased kinesthesia and proprioception.
- The person may have decreased sense of taste and/or smell.

Cognitive
- The person may have poor short-term memory.
- The person may have poor judgment of personal safety.
- Alerting responses may be diminished.
- The person may have difficulty learning new information.

Intrapersonal
- The person may be depressed.
- The person may feel hopeless and helpless.
- The person may express suicidal thoughts.
- The person may be angry or hostile.
- The person frequently has problem behaviors, such as belligerence, combativeness, and incontinence.

- The person may have a psychiatric disorder.
- The person may be abusing drugs or alcohol.
- The person usually has a poor self-concept and low self-esteem.
- The person usually has ineffective coping skills.

Interpersonal
- The person may withdraw from others.
- The person may have lost or forgotten some social skills.
- The person usually has a poor relationship with the caregiver.
- The person usually is dependent on the caregiver for food, lodging, and money.

Self-Care
- The person may be unable to perform some activities without assistance from others or assistive devices.
- The person may neglect to perform some activities without reminders.

Productivity
The person may have ceased to perform any productive activities.

Leisure
- The person may have ceased most active pursuits.
- The person may have few passive activities beyond watching television.

TREATMENT/MANAGEMENT
Models of treatment used by occupational therapists do not appear in the literature. The objectives and goals listed below are drawn from suggestions, not from actual treatment plans.

Motor
- Increase endurance and general muscle strength through gentle exercise, such as walking, if possible.
- Increase or maintain range of motion and joint mobility where possible.

Sensory
Provide sensory stimulation through activities and games.

Cognitive
- Teach concepts of energy conservation and work simplification to the person and caregivers.
- Assist the person to develop an activity schedule so the person knows what to do when, and can maintain better orientation.
- Provide information on community resources that may decrease the amount of caregiving required of the family and, if possible, increase the amount of independence of the elder person.

Intrapersonal

Improve the person's self-concept and increase self-esteem by encouraging participation in craft activities, psychodrama, music, art, or games.

Interpersonal

- Encourage the caregiver to talk about problems in providing care and suggest modifications or alternatives, such as adult day care, meals on wheels, or senior recreation facilities.
- Assist the caregiver to modify the elderly person's environment to increase safety and reduce the risk of injuries.
- Encourage the individual to participate in social activities.

Self-Care

- Increase the person's ability to perform activities of daily living through modification of tasks or use of assistive devices.
- Provide instruction in the use of safety items, such as grab bars and railings.

Productivity

Establish or increase the role of the person as a productive member who contributes by performing some homemaking tasks, such as assisting in food preparation, sorting laundry, dusting, or doing simple repairs.

Leisure

Assist the person to identify and explore leisure interests, including forgotten or neglected activities as well as new ones.

PRECAUTIONS

Family dynamics must be considered whenever intervention and changes are made.

PROGNOSIS AND OUTCOME

- The person is able to perform self-care and daily activities independently with self-help devices if needed.
- The person has identified a productive role in the family, usually related to home management, and performs that role.
- The person demonstrates performance of leisure activities.
- The person and family demonstrate knowledge of community resources.

REFERENCES

Holland, L.R., K.R. Kasraian, and C.A. Leonardelli. 1987. Elder abuse: An analysis of the current problem and potential role of the rehabilitation professional. *Physical and Occupational Therapy in Geriatrics* 5(3):41–50.

Hooyman, N.R. 1982. Mobilizing social networks to prevent elderly abuse. *Physical and Occupational Therapy in Geriatrics* 2(2):21–35.

Tomita, S.K. 1982. Detection and treatment of elderly abuse and neglect: A protocol for health care professionals. *Physical and Occupational Therapy in Geriatrics* 2(2):37–51.

Emotionally Disturbed—
Child/Adolescent

DESCRIPTION
The definition of this disorder includes a broad group of potential diagnoses. The common factor in the description of emotionally disturbed children is the label applied by educational institutions to children who (1) are under 19 years of age and (2) have emotional or behavioral problems that are difficult or impossible for teachers to handle in regular school classrooms. Actual diagnoses may include conduct disorders, anxiety disorders, eating disorders, stereotyped movement disorders, substance abuse, and others. See specific sections for descriptions of attention deficit disorder and autism.

CAUSE
The causative factors may be singular or multiple but generally can be organized into four areas: primary, such as a neurological disorder; predisposing, such as failure to learn adaptive behavior; precipitating, such as an unstable home life; and reinforcing, such as being rewarded by a parent or sibling for stealing or selling drugs.

ASSESSMENT

Areas
• muscle tone
• range of motion
• reflex development, especially continuing existence of primitive reflexes
• physical endurance
• motor skills, including gross and fine skills
• developmental milestones—delayed or normal achievement
• sensation—normal, hypersensitive, or hyposensitive
• sensory integrative skills, including visual, tactile, proprioceptive, auditory, and vestibular
• cognitive skills, including intellectual and memory
• behavior patterns, including type, frequency, and location
• temperament, including locus of control, autonomy, motivation, affect, and expectancy
• emotional function, including fear, hostility, aggression, and withdrawal
• family dynamics, including parent-child interactions, appearance, attitudes, and concerns
• environmental influences, including home, school, parents, and peers
• role history
• daily living skills
• play history and skills and/or productivity history, skills, and interests
• leisure interests and skills

Instruments
• Developmental Test of Visual-Motor Integration by K.E. Berry and N.A. Buktenica, Cleveland, OH: Modern Curriculum Press, 1982

- Bruininks-Oseretsky Test of Motor Proficiency, Circle Pines, MN: American Guidance Services, 1978
- Test of Viusal-Perceptual Skills by M.F. Gardner, Seattle, WA: Special Child Publication, 1982
- Southern California Sensory Integration Test by A.J. Ayres, Los Angeles: Western Psychological Services, 1980
- The Interest Checklist (See J. Matsutsuya. 1969. *American Journal of Occupational Therapy* 23:368-73. See also J.C. Rogers, J.M. Weinstein, and J.J. Figone. 1978. The interest checklist: An empirical assessment. *American Journal of Occupational Therapy* 32(10):628-30.)
- Kohlman Evaluation of Living Skills by L.K. McGourty, Seattle, WA: KELS Research, 1979
- The Role Checklist (See F. Oakley, G. Kielhofner, and R. Barris. 1985. An occupational therapy approach to assessing psychiatric patients' adaptive functioning. *American Journal of Occupational Therapy* 39(3):47–54. See also F. Oakley, et al. 1986. The Role Checklist: Development and empirical assessment of reliability. *Occupational Therapy Journal of Research* 6(3):57–70.)
- Piers-Harris Children's Self-Concept Scale by E.V. Piers, Los Angeles: Western Psychological Services, 1984
- Pre-vocational Evaluation of Rehabilitation Potential by D.A. Ethridge, *American Journal of Occupational Therapy* 22:161–7, 1968
- Vineland Adaptive Behavior Scale by S.S. Sparrow, P.A. Balla, and D.V. Cicchetti, Circle Pines, MN: American Guidance Services, 1973
- Nowicki-Strickland Locus of Control Scale (See B.R. Strickland and S. Nowicki. 1973. *Journal of Consulting and Clinical Psychology* 40:148–54.)
- Adolescent Role Assessment (See M. Black. 1976. *American Journal of Occupational Therapy* 30(2):73–9.)
- Goodenough-Harris Drawing Test by D.B. Harris, Orlando, FL: Harcourt Brace Jovanovich, 1963
- Kinetic Family Drawing by R. Burns and H. Kaufman, in *Actions, styles, and symbols in kinetic figure drawing (K.F.D.)*, New York: Brunner/Mazel, 1972
- Expectancy Questionnaire (See S. Farnham-Diggory. 1966. Self, future, and time: A developmental study of the concepts of psychotic, brain damaged, and normal children. *Monographs of the Society for Research in Child Development* 31:1-63.)
- See L. Florey and S. Michelman. 1978. Occupational role history. *1978. American Journal of Occupational Therapy* 32(5):301-8.
- Play Skills Inventory by J.M. Hurff, *American Journal of Occupational Therapy* 34(10):651–6, 1980 (See also N.P. Bledsoe and J.T. Shepherd. 1983. A study of reliability and validity of a preschool play scale. *American Journal of Occupational Therapy* 36:783–8, 1982. See correction in 37(2):119.)

PROBLEMS

This section describes actually a group of childhood disorders that have specific names according to some classification schemes, such as conduct disorders, school phobia, childhood schizophrenia, and others. The problems are a composite from the literature in occupational therapy.

Motor
- The child may have poor fine motor skills.
- The child may show developmental delay in gross motor skills.
- The child may have impaired postural control and balance.
- The child may have injuries from physical abuse that result in loss of muscle strength and/or range of motion.
- The child may have poor motor planning skills.

Sensory
- The child may have had limited tactile stimulation and/or be tactilely defensive.
- The child may have difficulty with visual scanning and tracking.
- The child may have poor perception of spatial relationships.
- The child may have poor stereognosis.
- The child may be hyper- or hyporesponsive to vestibular stimulation.

Cognitive
- The child may have poor attending behavior.
- The child may have difficulty following directions.
- The child may have difficulty with problem solving and decision making.
- The child may have poor time-management skills.

Intrapersonal
- The child may have a poor self-concept.
- The child may have had inadequate or faulty discipline.
- The child may have suffered continued stress.
- The child may have been overprotected.
- The child may lack goal-directed behaviors or skills.

Interpersonal
- The child may have had faulty (verbal abuse) or little communication with adults.
- The child may lack social skills.
- The child may lack group interaction skills.

Self-Care
The child may not have learned self-care skills.

Productivity
- Play skills may be delayed.
- Academic skills usually are below the child's chronological age.

Leisure
The child may have few leisure interests.

TREATMENT/MANAGEMENT
Models of treatment vary.

Motor
- Increase or improve the child's gross motor skills.
- Increase or improve fine motor skills.
- Increase or improve coordination (eye-hand, eye-foot, two sides of the body).
- Improve balance reactions.

Sensory
- Increase or improve visual motor skills (scanning, tracking).
- Increase or improve visual perception skills.
- Normalize response to tactile and vestibular stimuli. (See sections on tactile defensiveness and gravitational insecurity if needed.)

Cognitive
- Teach the child to pay attention to and follow directions.
- Plan and perform a series of steps leading to task completion.
- Practice problem-solving techniques, including alternate solutions to problems.
- Have the child practice critiquing (evaluating) his or her own work, including positive and negative aspects.
- Help the child learn time orientation (past, present and future) by reviewing a sequence of activities during a day, week, month, and year.
- Help the child plan and review daily routines.

Intrapersonal
- Increase the child's self-mastery and sense of competence by completing tasks.
- Have the child accept responsibility for his or her own actions by acknowledging his or her behavior and accepting the consequences.
- Help the child develop internal control by expressing feelings in words rather than actions.
- Practice channeling anger and aggression into socially acceptable activities.
- Demonstrate goal-directed behavior by stating or writing a goal, methods for achieving the goal, progress in achieving the goal, and the reward for completing the goal.
- Have the child practice changing behavior based on suggestions from adults or peers.

Interpersonal
- Teach the child to respect the rights of others by sharing space and materials.
- Have the child practice expressing ideas and feelings in a group situation.
- Practice praising others for expressing good ideas, controlling behavior, or performing good work.
- Practice new roles and increasing responsibility within old roles.
- Practice following the rules of a game, driving a vehicle, and observing safety.

Self-Care
Perform activities of daily living without reminders.

Productivity
- Practice working in groups of increasing size.
- Practice taking directions, suggestions, and corrections from a supervisor.

Leisure

Explore the child's interests and provide opportunities for participation.

Treatment Approaches Used by
Occupational Therapists with Emotionally Disturbed Children

- Sensory Integration Techniques (King, Ayres)
- Play Behavior (Reilly)
- Human Occupation (Kielhofner & Burke)
- Structured Activities (Nelson)
- Developmental Tasks (Llorens)
- Task Oriented Groups (G.S. Fidler. 1969. Task-oriented group as a context for treatment. *American Journal of Occupational Therapy* 23:43–8.)
- Activity Therapy (A. Mosey. 1973. New York, Raven Press.)

PRECAUTIONS

- Watch for signs of side effects of medication.
- Be aware of changes in the environment that may alter the child's behavior.

PROGNOSIS AND OUTCOME

- The child demonstrates increased ability to concentrate on a task.
- The child demonstrates problem-solving skills.
- The child is able to remember and follow directions.
- The child demonstrates improved and positive self-concept.
- The child demonstrates judgment regarding safety of self and others.
- The child is able to participate in a group setting.
- The child is able to perform self-care activities.
- The child is able to learn academic skills in a classroom setting.
- The child demonstrates improved play skills.
- The child demonstrates leisure interests and skills

REFERENCES

Adelstein, L.A., M.A. Barnes, F.M. Jensen, et al. 1989. A broadening frontier: Occupational therapy in mental health programs for children and adolescents. *Mental Health Special Interest Section Newsletter* 12(1):2–4.

Agrin, A.R. 1987. Occupational therapy with emotionally disturbed children in a public elementary school. *Occupational Therapy in Mental Health* 7(2):105–14.

Baker, R., S. Gaffney, and L. Trocchi. 1989. Dyadic treatment. *Mental Health Special Interest Section Newsletter* 12(1):4–6.

Baron, K.B. 1987. The model of human occupation: A newspaper treatment group for adolescents with a diagnosis of conduct disorder. *Occupational Therapy in Mental Health* 7(2):89–104.

Baron, K.B. 1989. Occupational therapy: A program for child psychiatry. *Mental Health Special Interest Section Newsletter* 12(1):6–7.

Burnell, D.P. 1985. Children with severe emotional or behavioral disorders. In *Occupational therapy for children*, ed. P.N. Clark and A.S. Allen, 456–70. St. Louis: C.V. Mosby.

Cronin, A.F. 1989. Children with emotional or behavioral disorders. In *Occupational therapy for children*, 2d ed., ed. P.N. Pratt and A.S. Allen, 563–79. St Louis: C.V. Mosby.

Davidson, D.A., M.A. Short, and D.L. Nelson. 1984. The measurement of empathic ability in normal and atypical five and six year old boys. *Occupational Therapy in Mental Health* 4(4):13–24.

Fraenkel, L., and B. Tallant. 1987. "Mostly me": A treatment approach for emotionally disturbed children. *Canadian Journal of Occupational Therapy* 54(2):59–64.

Goldstein, P.K. 1983. Sensory integration groups: An effective treatment modality in child psychiatry. *Sensory Integration Special Interest Section Newsletter* 6(1):1–2.

Madison, Y. 1984. Activities of daily living program for emotionally disturbed adolescents in a residential treatment setting. *Mental Health Special Interest Section Newsletter* 7(3):1,3.

McKie, S., and J. Mathai. 1987. Combined treatment approach in the management of a 12-year-old boy presenting with disturbance of emotions. *British Journal of Occupational Therapy* 50(3):98–100.

Melia, M.A., and K. Weikert. 1987. Evaluation and treatment of adolescents on a short-term unit. *Occupational Therapy in Mental Health* 7(2):51–66.

Nelson, R.R., and J.L. Condrin. 1987. Vocational readiness and independent living skills program for psychiatrically impaired adolescents. *Occupational Therapy in Mental Health* 7(2):23–38.

Ottenbacher, K.J. 1982. Vestibular processing dysfunction in children with severe emotional and behavior disorders: A review. *Physical and Occupational Therapy in Pediatrics* 2(1):3–12.

Sholle-Martin, S. 1987. Application of the model of human occupation: Assessment in child and adolescent psychiatry. *Occupational Therapy in Mental Health* 7(2):3–22.

Sholle-Martin, S., and N.E. Alessi. 1988. Adaptive functioning in children hospitalized for psychiatric disturbance. *Journal of the American Academy of Child and Adolescent Psychiatry* 27(5):636–41.

Sholle-Martin, S., and N.E. Alessi. 1990. Formulating a role for occupational therapy in child psychiatry: A clinical application. *American Journal of Occupational Therapy* 44(10):871–82.

Wright, M. 1981. Incest: A historical and behavioural perspective in family life. *Canadian Journal of Occupational Therapy* 48(3):121–4.

Forensic Psychiatry

DESCRIPTION

Forensic psychiatry includes a group of disorders that have as their common denominator a person who has entered the criminal justice system due to aggressive, dangerous, or socially unacceptable behavior. Among the typical diagnoses are personality disorders, such as antisocial personalities, major psychiatric disorders, such as schizophrenia, and compulsive behavior.

CAUSE

The causes include a variety of etiological factors, such as inherited disorders, congenital disorders, family interaction disturbances, and social deprivation.

ASSESSMENT

Areas
- time management
- activities of daily living

- productivity, including history, skills, aptitudes, and interests
- leisure activities, including skills and interests

Instruments
- occupational history (See L. Moorhead. 1969. The occupational history. *American Journal of Occupational Therapy* 23:329–34.)
- Singer Vocational Evaluation System, Rochester, NY: Singer Educational Division
- Valpar Component Work Sample, Tucson, AZ: Valpar Corporation
- leisure checklist

PROBLEMS

Motor
There may be no major problems in the person's motor system.

Sensory
There may be no major problems in the person's sensory system.

Cognitive
- The person may lack decision-making and problem-solving skills.
- The person may have learning disorder patterns, such as dyslexia, poor bilateral integration, or hyperactivity.
- The person may lack basic education skills, such as reading, arithmetic, and writing.
- The person may lack time-management skills.

Intrapersonal
- The person may be unable to manage affect in a socially acceptable manner.
- The person may have feelings of inadequacy and inferiority (a poor self-concept).
- The person usually lacks coping skills or adaptive behavior.

Interpersonal
- The person may lack the social skills necessary to carry on a social conversation.
- The person may lack interpersonal skills related to caring and sharing.
- The person usually lacks role skills.

Self-Care
- The person may be unable to perform functional skills, such as meal preparation and paying bills.
- The person may lack community skills, such as how to shop or read a bus schedule.

Productivity
- The person may lack job-seeking skills.
- The person may lack the knowledge or skill necessary to keep a job.
- The person may lack home-management skills.

Leisure
The person may lack leisure interests and skills.

TREATMENT/MANAGEMENT
Major program models are based on increasing the sense of competency (Reilly) and human occupation (Kielhofner).

Motor
No specific programs are suggested beyond maintaining general physical fitness.

Sensory
Sensory integration programs may be helpful to those identified as having problems in bilateral integration, dyspraxia, or gravitational security.

Cognitive
• Teach the person to recognize and break into the cycle of criminal behavior pattern.
• Teach the person alternate behaviors to suppress, control, manage, or stop the criminal behavior pattern.
• Provide situations for individual and group decision making and problem solving through the use of craft projects, games, or task groups.
• Provide tasks and activities that require basic reading, arithmetic, and writing, such as reading the directions to assemble a project, adding up the costs of groceries, or writing a letter.
• Teach time management through a daily schedule, organizing the steps in a project, or discussions about the health and social values of balancing work, rest, and play.

Intrapersonal
• Encourage the person to accept responsibility for his or her own behavior and an internal locus of control.
• Encourage the person to express feelings related to acts of criminal behavior.
• Improve the person's self-concept through completion of tasks, such as craft projects, playing board games, musical activities, or drama.
• Provide instruction in relaxation training to manage stress.
• Provide insight-oriented groups through the use of psychodrama, simulated games, or goal-oriented group tasks.

Interpersonal
• Assist the person to experience positive interpersonal relationships that are satisfying, pleasurable, and nonthreatening through the use of sports or musical activities or discussion groups based on viewing films or television programs.
• Provide group situations through discussion, role playing, and task groups to explore different role behaviors, such as leader, follower, supervisor, employee, parent, or child.

Self-Care
Provide group instruction in cooking and nutrition, budgeting, shopping, and finding living accommodations.

Productivity
- Provide work-skills training, including work readiness, work habits, and job practice.
- Provide job survival skills, including human relations skills, worker characteristics, resume writing, practicing employment interviews, and completing job applications.
- Provide vocational information and discussion related to employment resources, assessing the job market, contacting prospective employers, and coping with stress on the job.

Leisure
Provide group sessions to explore and develop leisure interests.

PRECAUTIONS
The therapist must understand the basics of the legal system to understand the rules of sentencing and the rights of prisoners.

PROGNOSIS AND OUTCOME
- The person can demonstrate skills in behavioral control.
- The person can demonstrate skills in self-care.
- The person can demonstrate skills in locating and maintaining employment.
- The person can demonstrate leisure skills.

REFERENCES

Farnworth, L., S. Morgan, and B. Fernando. 1987. Prison-based occupational therapy. *Australian Occupational Therapy Journal* 34(2):47–52.

Lederer, J.M., G. Kielhofner, and J.H. Watts. 1985. Values, personal causation and skills of delinquents and nondelinquents. *Occupational Therapy in Mental Health* 5(2):59–77.

Lloyd, C. 1986. Vocational evaluation in a forensic psychiatry setting. *Canadian Journal of Occupational Therapy* 53(1):31–5.

Lloyd, C. 1987. The role of occupational therapy in the treatment of the forensic psychiatric patient. *Australian Occupational Therapy Journal* 34(1):20–25.

Lloyd, C. 1987. Working with the female offender: A case study. *British Journal of Occupational Therapy* 50(2):44–6.

Lloyd, C. 1987. Sex offender program: Is there a role for occupational therapy? *Occupational Therapy in Mental Health* 7(3):55–67.

Lloyd, C., and F. Guerra. 1988. A vocational rehabilitation programme in forensic psychiatry. *British Journal of Occupational Therapy* 51(4):123–6.

Personality Disorders

DESCRIPTION
Personality disorders are stylized reactions to stress that represent the individual's way of dealing with other people and external events regardless of existing realities.

CAUSE
The cause is unknown but associated with early childhood experiences. The disorders are more common in men than women. Individuals rarely seek help; they are usually referred by

family members or social agencies because of the difficulties their maladaptive behavior causes others.

ASSESSMENT

Seven behavioral or mental coping mechanisms are observed in personality disorders:

1. *dissociation* (neurotic denial)—a temporary but significant change of personality or sense of personal identity, including fugues, hysterical conversion reactions, short-term denial of responsibility for one's actions or feelings, trance states, chance taking, and intoxication
2. *projection*—allows one to attribute one's own unacknowledged feelings to others
3. *schizoid fantasy*—the tendency to use imaginary relationships and private belief systems for the purpose of conflict resolution and relief from loneliness
4. *hypochondriasis*—transforms internal feelings into social complaints
5. *turning against the self*—transforms aggression toward others into agression toward self
6. *acting out*—expression of internal conflict that is not acknowledged (unconscious) to avoid being conscious of the feelings involved
7. *splitting*—allows the person to divide personalities in his or her life into all good and all bad by displacing part of the feelings to another personality, thus avoiding the discomfort of living and being angry at one personality

PROBLEMS

Motor
There are no specific motor problems associated with the disorders. Any motor problems may occur as part of a secondary diagnosis.

Sensory
There are no specific sensory problems associated with the disorders. Any sensory problems may occur as part of a secondary diagnosis.

Cognitive
- The person may have a short attention span and poor concentration of attention.
- The person may have poor comprehension or understanding of situations and the possible consequences of personal actions.
- The person may have difficulty integrating learned skills into useful patterns of behavior.
- The person usually has difficulty with problem-solving and decision-making tasks. He or she tends to select from a very narrow list of possible choices.
- The person's judgment may be impaired relative to his or her personal safety.
- Memory skills may be underdeveloped.
- Time-management skills usually are poor.

Intrapersonal
- The person may have a poor self-concept, including a poor sense of mastery.
- The person usually lacks a sense of responsibility for individual actions.

- The person may have difficulty distinguishing self needs from others' needs.
- Coping skills are limited.The person does not tolerate frustration or anxiety, has poor impulse control, and does not sublimate his or her drives into socially acceptable channels.
- The person usually has low motivation to change behavior.
- The person may have suicidal ideation.

Interpersonal
- The person may have a charming personality in casual relations but lacks ability to engage in sustained interdependent relationships.
- The person may have difficulty relating to authority figures.
- The person may have difficulty cooperating with a group to perform tasks unless the task is performed according to personal specifications.
- The person may have difficulty maintaining relationships within the family.

Self-Care
The ability to perform activities of daily living is not a problem but motivation may be.

Productivity
- The person may experience conflict with supervisors leading to a poor work history.
- The person may lack motivation to assist with home-management tasks.
- The person usually has poorly defined vocational goals.

Leisure
- The person usually has limited leisure interests.
- The person may experience difficulty engaging in group leisure activities, such as sports, due to low tolerance for frustration and the need to maintain control.

TREATMENT/MANAGEMENT

No specific treatment has been suggested by occupational therapists. The suggestions below are general, based on borderline and multiple personality disorders which follow.

Motor
No specific treatment or management techniques are suggested unless a secondary diagnosis exists.

Sensory
No specific treatment or management techniques are suggested unless a secondary diagnosis exists.

Cognitive
- Provide activities to improve reality testing and the person's understanding of the consequences of his or her actions.
- Provide graded tasks requiring few decisions or choices to many possibilities in order to improve the person's ability to solve problems and make decisions.
- Assist the person to develop time-management skills by requiring the person to organize and follow a schedule.

Intrapersonal

- Maintain or improve the person's self-concept through the use of craft or game activities.
- Assist the person to rechannel his or her behavior into more socially accepted activities.

Interpersonal

Use group activities as a base for providing instruction and giving feedback on communication skills and for confronting the person on the effects of his or her social behavior on others.

Self-Care

Praise the person for completing self-care activities or performing other activities of daily living which the individual has tended not to perform.

Productivity

- Assist the person to explore vocational interests, including simulated or temporary job responsibilities.
- Assist the person to learn and perform life-management and home-management skills.

Leisure

Assist the person to explore leisure interests and learn about community resources.

PRECAUTIONS

- A person with a personality disorder often tries to bend or break the rules. The management team must agree on the rules and consistently follow through on carrying out the rules and their assigned consequences. Otherwise, the person may spend most of his or her time looking for ways to divide the staff or undermine authority and will spend little time on learning better self-management behaviors.
- A person with a personality disorder may be skilled in playing uproar games or "let's you and him fight." These games also serve to distract attention from the self to avoid efforts at changing behavior patterns.

PROGNOSIS AND OUTCOME

The prognosis is guarded. People with personality disorders usually require long-term therapy.

- The person demonstrates the ability to manage time for self-care, productive, and leisure activities.
- The person demonstrates knowledge of daily life-management and home-management tasks.
- The person demonstrates socially approved behaviors in social group situations.
- The person demonstrates improved work skills, work tolerance, work habits, and work attitudes.
- The person is able to maintain a productive role or situation.

REFERENCES

Berkow, R. ed. 1987. *The Merck manual*. Rahway, NJ: Merck, Sharpe and Dohme Research Laboratories, 1471–76.

Personality Disorders— Borderline Personality

DESCRIPTION

Borderline personality disorder is characterized by a pervasive pattern of instability of self-image, interpersonal relationships, mood, and behavior.

CAUSE

The exact etiology is unclear, but the disorder probably begins in early childhood with a failure of the mother-child interaction during the time the child should develop a sense of self. Usually the disorder is not diagnosed until early adulthood. It is more common in females.

ASSESSMENT

Areas
- level of arousal or awareness
- orientation to person, place, and time
- recognition
- attending behavior
- attention span
- memory
- concept formation
- comprehension
- generalization and integration of learning
- problem-solving and decision-making skills
- judgment of safety
- time management
- self-concept and self-esteem
- self-identity or role identity
- coping skills
- self-control
- social skills or conduct
- language and communication skills

- group interaction skills
- social support
- daily living skills
- productivity history, skills, and interests
- leisure skills and interests

Instruments

No specific instruments developed for this disorder by occupational therapists were identified in the literature. The following types of instruments may be useful:

- activities of daily living scale
- occupational and role history
- leisure checklist

PROBLEMS

Motor

The person may complain of vague somatic symptoms.

Sensory

Brief episodes of delusions or hallucinatory experiences may occur.

Cognitive

- The person has difficulty planning long-term goals and tends to go with the moment.
- The person tends to take extreme views: The world is either black or white.
- Problem-solving skills are limited.

Intrapersonal

- The person exhibits impulsive behavior that is potentially self-damaging.
- Affective mood shifts among depression, irritability, or anxiety may occur.
- The person lacks control of anger and may display a temper or get into physical fights.
- The person makes recurrent suicidal threats or gestures or exhibits self-mutilating behavior.
- The person's self-image is unstable and may vacillate between dependency and self-assertion.
- The person has chronic feelings of emptiness or boredom.
- The person may be unsure about his or her sexual orientation.
- The person is uncertain about which values to adopt.
- The person may have unrealistic expectations for perfection.
- A splitting of feelings into good and bad with no integration may have led to identity diffusion.

Interpersonal

- The person has a pattern of unstable interpersonal relationships characterized by alternating between extremes of overidealization and devaluation.
- The person tries to avoid real or imagined abandonment and hates to be alone.

- The person has difficulty deciding what type of friends to have and maintaining friendships.
- The person may manipulate others through self-destructive behavior.

Self-Care
The person does not have suitable clothes for productive role.

Productivity
- The person tends to be unclear about career choices.
- The person may have a poor work history and a marginal school record.
- Supervision in work recreates the dependency/independency problem.
- The person usually states a dissatisfaction with work situations and sees work activities as meaningless.
- The person may have poor work habits accompanied by avoidance and procrastination.

Leisure
- Leisure interests are poorly defined.
- Leisure activities are not viewed as satisfying experiences, especially those involving non-human objects.

TREATMENT/MANAGEMENT
Models of treatment include cognitive, psychosocial, developmental and human occupation (Kielhofner).

Cognitive
Provide opportunities for problem solving and decision making within strict limits initially, and gradually broadening the person's choices and options.

Intrapersonal
- Provide an outlet for mixed feelings through the use of creative media.
- Provide opportunities for the person to select an activity, choosing what to do, to encourage self-awareness.
- Encourage mastery of the task activities to reinforce the concepts of rewarding, pleasurable, self-actualizing experiences with objects in the environment.
- Permit the objects created to be used as projections for the person's vacillating feeling states.

Interpersonal
- Confront the defensive behavior expressed in group situations.
- Provide opportunities for cooperative behavior in a group setting by using tasks that require two or more persons to get the job done within the time frame.
- Contracting (behavior therapy) may be useful to encourage the person to demonstrate responsible behavior, control actions, and make decisions.

Self-Care
Increase skills in self-care and daily living, such as cooking, meal planning, shopping, and

personal finance. The person may need assistance in shopping for suitable clothes for productive role.

Productivity

- Supervised work activities will be useful in assisting the person to learn to continue performing while experiencing conflicting feelings.
- The work setting should provide a consistent set of demands within a given time period to permit the development of work cycles that can be discussed later in a group or individual session.
- The work activities should permit exploration and curiosity about how the work is done, such as how leather is carved or how clay becomes a solid object.
- Encourage the person to sort out productive from unproductive work habits.
- Assist the person to explore vocational interests and identify career goals.
- Increase the person's skills in home management.

Leisure

- Assist the individual to select leisure activities that will provide a creative outlet for feelings.
- Encourage exploration of activities that are fun to do and support the person's recognition of having fun.

PROGNOSIS AND OUTCOME

- The person demonstrates the ability to plan a daily calendar of activities and follow the schedule as planned.
- The person is able to participate in group activities and settings.
- The person is able to perform daily living activities independently.
- The person demonstrates improved performance of work skills, work tolerance, and work habits.
- The person is able to select and perform productive activities.
- The person is able to perform leisure activities.

REFERENCES

Calabretta-Caprini, T. 1989. Contracting with patients diagnosed with borderline personality disorder. *Canadian Journal of Occupational Therapy* 56(4):179–84.

Goodman, G.B. 1983. Occupational therapy treatment: Interventions with borderline patients. *Occupational Therapy in Mental Health* 3(3):19–31.

Kaplan, C.A. 1983. Inpatient management of the borderline patient. *Occupational Therapy in Mental Health* 3(3):47–65.

Kernberg, P.F. 1983. Update of borderline disorders in children. *Occupational Therapy in Mental Health* 3(3):83–91.

Lewin, J.V., and R.A. Lewin. 1987. On treatment integration: Psychotherapy and work therapy. *Occupational Therapy in Mental Health* 7(3):21–36.

Lewis, J.M. 1983. Early treatment planning for hospitalized severe borderline patients. *Occupational Therapy in Mental Health* 3(3):67–81.

Peters, C.P. 1983. An historical review of the borderline concept. *Occupational Therapy in Mental Health* 3(3):1–18.

Salz, C. 1983. A theoretical approach to the treatment of work difficulties in borderline personality. *Occupational Therapy in Mental Health* 3(3):33–46.

Personality Disorders— Multiple Personalities

DESCRIPTION
The criteria for the diagnosis of multiple personality disorder (MPD) are (1) the existence within the individual of two or more distinct personalities, each of which is dominant at a particular time, (2) the personality that is dominant at any particular time determines the individual's behavior, and (3) each individual personality is complex and integrated with its own unique behavior patterns and social relationships.

CAUSE
The causative factors are assumed to be related to extreme psychosocial stress, shock, or trauma, or physical, emotional, or sexual abuse occurring early in childhood. The reaction is dissociation or splitting, an intrapsychic defense process in which one or more mental processes separates from the normal consciousness and functions as a whole within itself.

ASSESSMENT

Definitions
- personality: an entity with a firm persistent sense of self having a range of functions, emotions, and history
- birth personality: personality or identity developed just after birth which at some point splits off the first new personality in order to help the body to survive severe stress
- presenting personality: the personality seeking treatment
- host personality: the personality that maintains executive control of the body
- anesthetic personality: the personality that is impervious to pain; it is developed to endure abuse
- alter: a generic term used to denote a fragment or personality
- fragment: an entity with limited function, emotion, and history
- splitting: creating a new personality
- switching: changing from one personality to another
- fusion/integration: the unification of personalities into one functional individual

Areas
Note: Different alters usually have different abilities and skills. These abilities and skills may or may not be transferred to the fused or integrated personality. Some abilities and skills that are performed well by one or more alters may have to be learned as new skills by the fused or integrated personality.

- memory
- problem-solving skills
- generalization of learning
- integration of learning

- synthesis of learning
- self-concept
- coping skills
- goals and values
- social skills
- communication skills
- daily living skills
- productive history, skills, and interests
- leisure interests and skills

Instruments
- Allen Cognitive Level Test by C.K. Allen, in *Occupational therapy for psychiatric diseases: Measurement and management of cognitive disabilities*, Boston: Little, Brown & Co., 1985, pp. 108–13
- Comprehensive Occupational Therapy Evaluation by S.J. Brayman and T. Kirby, in *The evaluative process in psychiatric occupational therapy*, ed. B. Hemphill, Thorofare, NJ: Slack, Inc., 1982

Greaves Suggestive Signs of MPD

- Person reports time loss or time distortion.
- Observers report changes in behavior.
- Person reports being told of disremembered behavior.
- Personalities can be elicited by hypnosis.
- Person uses "we" when referring to self.
- Person discovers objects in his or her possession that he or she cannot explain.
- Person reports severe headaches.
- Person reports hearing internal voices that are separate from the self.

Source: Based on Greaves, G. 1980. Multiple personality: 165 years after Mary Reynolds. *Journal of Nervous and Mental Disorders* 168:577–96.

PROBLEMS

Motor
The person has unexplained headaches.

Sensory
The auditory sense is most commonly involved because the personalities talk to or about the other personalities at various times.

Cognitive
- The person is unable to account for certain time periods.

- Certain times and events are distorted by the person.
- The person cannot explain the discovery of some objects in his or her possession.

Intrapersonal
- The person tends to use the pronoun "we" when referring to him- or herself.
- The person reports hearing voices that are separate from the self.
- In stressful situations, various personalities come out to deal with the situation and then retreat.
- The person may be suicidal or homicidal in an attempt to solve the original trigger event.

Interpersonal
The person has been told that his or her personality sometimes changes dramatically.

Self-Care
The degree to which activities of daily living are performed may depend on which personality is in charge at a particular time.

Productivity
The degree to which the person can perform work tasks may depend on a personality being in charge when the self is at the work setting or getting ready to report to work.

Leisure
The personalities may have different leisure interests.

TREATMENT/MANAGEMENT
Models of treatment are based on functional performance, (Fidler), human occupation (Kielhofner), and cognitive disabilities (Allen).

Cognitive
- All of the personalities are encouraged to learn about multiple personality disorder and how the disorder works.
- Set limits or rules that the therapeutic community will support because the person will try to break as many rules as possible.
- Provide learning situations that emphasize the importance of consistent behavior in a normal group situation.
- Provide an opportunity to plan and carry out goal-directed activities independently and in groups.
- Provide time-management training.

Intrapersonal
- The person must learn normal coping skills instead of splitting, especially in handling anger and rage. Opportunities to practice handling emotions need to be provided.
- Task-oriented activities provide different levels of structure and organization to which different personalities can be assigned and be encouraged to achieve a higher level of organization.

Interpersonal
- Task-oriented activities may permit other personalities to emerge that should be observed, evaluated, and reported to the case manager. In particular, nonverbal personalities may present since the occupational therapy clinic may provide more opportunities for nonverbal behavior, such as drawing and painting.
- Different personalities may be assigned to different social group situations to encourage further development of social and communication skills.

Self-Care
- Include self-care activities in the time-management program.
- Provide instruction in activities of daily living that may not have been learned.

Productivity
- Explore work interests and work capacities.
- Provide basic work skill training if needed.

Leisure
Explore leisure interests and provide opportunities for tryout.

PRECAUTIONS
- Therapists who themselves were abused as children should consider professional care if they choose to work with persons with MPD.
- Therapists may experience secondary post-traumatic stress syndrome as a result of working with persons with MPD.

PROGNOSIS AND OUTCOME
- The person is able to function as an integrated whole without splitting or switching.
- The person demonstrates normal coping skills.
- The person performs daily living activities independently.
- The person performs productive activities on a regular basis.
- The person performs leisure activities.

REFERENCES

Angel, S.L. 1990. Toward becoming one self. *American Journal of Occupational Therapy* 44(11):1037–43 (case report).

Baldwin, L.C. 1990. Child abuse as an antecedent of multiple personality disorder. *American Journal of Occupational Therapy* 44(11):978–83.

Braun, B.G. 1990. Multiple personality disorder: An overview. *American Journal of Occupational Therapy* 44(11):971–6.

Dawson, P.L. 1985. The value of occupational therapy in the treatment of multiple personality disorder. In *Dissociative disorders: 1985. Proceedings of the Second International Conference on Multiple Personality/Dissociate States*, ed. B.G. Braun, 66. Chicago: Rush-Presbyterian-St. Luke's Medical Center.

Dawson, P.L. 1985. An interdependence activity scale designed for MPD patients. In *Dissociate disorders: 1985. Proceedings of the Second International Conference on Multiple Personality/Dissociate States*, ed. B.G. Braun, 117. Chicago: Rush-Presbyterian-St. Luke's Medical Center.

Dawson, P.L. 1990. Understanding and cooperation among alter and host personalities. *American Journal of Occupational Therapy* 44(11):994–97.

Dawson P.L. 1990. Understanding skepticism toward multiple personality disorder. *American Journal of Occupational Therapy* 44(11):1048–50.

Fike, M.L. 1990. Childhood sexual abuse and multiple personality disorder: Emotional sequelae of caretakers. *American Journal of Occupational Therapy* 44(11):967–9.

Fike, M.L 1990. Clinical manifestations in persons with multiple personality disorder. *American Journal of Occupational Therapy* 44(11):984–90.

Fike, M.F. 1990. Considerations and techniques in the treatment of persons with multiple personality disorder. *American Journal of Occupational Therapy* 44(11):999–1007.

Frye, B. 1990. Art and multiple personality disorder: An expressive framework for occupational therapy. *American Journal of Occupational Therapy* 44(11):1013–22.

Frye, B., and L. Gannon. 1990. The use, misuse, and abuse of art with dissociative/multiple personality disorders. *Occupational Therapy Forum* 5(24):1,3-5,8.

Higdon, J.F. 1990. Expressive therapy in conjunction with psychotherapy in the treatment of persons with multiple personality disorder. *American Journal of Occupational Therapy* 44(11):991–3.

Sachs, R.G. 1990. The sand tray technique in the treatment of patients with dissociative disorder: Recommendations for occupational therapists. *American Journal of Occupational Therapy* 44(11):1045–7.

Sepiol, J.M., and J. Froehlich. 1990. Use of the Role Checklist with the patient with multiple personality disorder. *American Journal of Occupational Therapy* 44(11):1008–12.

Skinner, S.T. 1985. MPD: Occupational therapy strategies in assessment/treatment planning/implementation on an acute psychiatric unit. In *Dissociative disorders: 1985. Proceedings of the Second International Conference on Multiple Personality/Dissociate States*, ed. B.G. Braun, 64. Chicago: Rush-Presbyterian-St. Luke's Medical Center.

Skinner, S.T. 1987. Multiple personality disorder: Occupational therapy intervention in acute care psychiatry. *Occupational Therapy in Mental Health* 7(3):93–108.

Skinner, S.T. 1990. Occupational therapy with patients with multiple personality disorder: Personal reflections. *American Journal of Occupational Therapy* 44(11):1024–7.

Schizophrenia

DESCRIPTION

Schizophrenic disorders are a group of mental disorders that tend to be chronic and impair functioning. They are characterized by psychotic symptoms involving disturbances of thinking, feeling, and behavior. Specific criteria for the diagnosis are (1) psychotic symptoms, such as delusions, hallucinations, and thought disorders; (2) deterioration from a previous level of functioning; (3) continuous signs of illness for at least six months; (4) tendency towards onset before age 45; (5) dysfunction not due to mood disorders; and (6) dysfunction not due to organic mental disorders or mental retardation.

CAUSE

The cause is unknown. Current thinking suggests that the disorder is caused by a complex interaction of inherited and environmental factors.

ASSESSMENT

Areas
- postural control and balance
- gross movement patterns

- stereotypical behaviors
- sensory awareness and discrimination
- judgment of personal safety
- problem-solving and decision-making skills
- reality testing
- orientation
- self-concept
- coping skills
- social skills
- daily living skills
- productivity history, skills, interests, and values
- leisure interests and skills

Instruments
- Kohlman Evaluation of Living Skills (KELS) by L.K. McCourty, Seattle, WA: KELS Research, 1979
- Bay Area Functional Performance Evaluation (BAFPE), 2d ed., by S.L. Williams and J.S. Bloomer, Palo Alto, CA: Consulting Psychologists Press, 1987
- Allen Cognitive Level Test by C.K. Allen, in *Occupational therapy for psychiatric diseases: Measurement and management of cognitive disabilities,* Boston: Little, Brown & Co., 1985, pp. 108–113
- Meaningfulness of Activity Scale by M. Gregory, in Occupational behavior and life satisfaction among retirees. *American Journal of Occupational Therapy* 37(8):548–53, 1983 (See correction in 37(12):860, 1983.)
- Motor-free Visual Perception Test by R.P. Colarusso and D.D. Hamill, Novato, CA: Academic Therapy Publications, 1972 (not occupational therapists)

PROBLEMS

Motor
- The person may exhibit catatonia, stupor or immobility.
- The person may exhibit repetitive movement patterns, such as rocking or pacing.

Sensory
Auditory hallucinations are most common but visual, tactile, gustatory, or olfactory hallucinations may also occur.

Cognitive
The person may have difficulty in organizing thoughts in a goal-directed manner.

Intrapersonal
- The person may have blunted or flat affect.
- The person's emotions may alternate from depression to excitement, anxiety, elation, or sadness.
- Delusions of persecution or religious ideas are common but other themes also occur.

Interpersonal
- The person usually has difficulty maintaining social relations.
- The person may become aggressive toward others.

Self-Care
The person may be indifferent to performing activities of daily living.

Productivity
The person may be unable to perform job tasks consistently.

Leisure
The person usually has few leisure interests.

TREATMENT/MANAGEMENT

Motor
- Increase the person's gross motor coordination.
- Increase motor planning ability.
- Decrease body rigidity.

Sensory
- Increase the person's balance and equilibrium.
- Increase body awareness.
- Provide sensory stimulation.

Cognitive
- Increase the person's mental alertness.
- Teach appropriate coping mechanisms.
- Increase problem-solving ability.
- Encourage independent decision making.
- Increase knowledge of community resources.
- Provide opportunity to practice time-management skills.

Intrapersonal
- Decrease the person's depressed behavior.
- Decrease inappropriate expressions of anger.
- Provide reality orientation training.
- Provide values clarification exercises.
- Increase self-esteem and positive self-image through individual accomplishment.

Interpersonal
- Provide opportunities for graded, structured verbalization.
- Provide opportunities for working cooperatively in a group setting.
- Provide opportunities for practicing appropriate behavior in the community.

Outline of Cognitive Levels According to Allen

Level 1:   Automatic actions. Person is conscious but can perform only reflexive behaviors, such as yawning, sneezing, and withdrawing from painful stimuli, or automatic behaviors, such as sitting, walking, chewing, and swallowing. Arousal and attention can be obtained only for short periods of time. Usually the person stares into space. The person is not aware of cause and effect. The person requires constant nursing care. Diagnoses at this level include advanced dementia, recent head trauma, including recent cerebrovascular accident or head injury, and severe toxicity, such as drug overdose. Psychiatric diagnoses occasionally may fit this level.

Level 2:   Postural actions. Person spontaneously changes position in response to proprioceptive cues. Behavior appears to be related to feelings of comfort or discomfort in relation to an activity which the caregiver is performing such as dressing, grooming, or bathing. Behaviors may include moving an arm or leg, shifting body weight or actively resisting the caregiver's help. Other behavior may include aimless wandering or pacing and inappropriate use of objects. The person is disoriented and requires constant observation. Diagnoses include dementia, head trauma, toxicity, and severe psychotic disorders.

Level 3:   Manual actions. The person spontaneously performs activities requiring tactile or touch cues. Behavior is usually related to familiar objects that attract the person's attention or interest, such as seeing a pencil and paper, which may lead to picking up the pencil and trying to write. The action may be repeated many times without apparent purpose for up to 30 minutes. The person can perform self-care activities independently but needs reminders to do so. The person continues to be easily disoriented to time and place and becomes confused as to what action to do next. Persons discharged at Level 3 need supervision or an adult day-care program. Diagnoses include dementia, head trauma, toxicity, acute mania, and acute schizophrenia.

Level 4:   Goal-directed actions. The person is able to perform steps to achieve a specific goal but does not learn to generalize to similar situations. Attention span may be as long as one hour. The person can understand and follow simple instructions if visual cues are present. The person is not able to understand situations that may be dangerous and may refuse assistance when it is offered for protection. The person may not understand why medication is necessary and may refuse or forget to take it. The person can function in a supervised environment but cannot live independently.

Level 5:   Exploratory actions. The person is able to initiate action to explore the environment, is able to learn new information if the learning task is demonstrated, is able to use concrete relations and cues to solve

continues

Cognitive Levels (continued)

problems, is able to evaluate the effects of motor action based on trial and error problem solving, and is able to remember doing a task at a previous session. The person is not able to think before acting and is unable to reflect on possible consequences of an action before the action occurs, tends to have poor judgment of social and safety situations, is unable to use abstract reasoning, is unable to follow verbal directions unless a demonstration is used, tends to use rigid social behavior, and may be impulsive. The person can live independently but needs assistance with unusual situations or dramatic changes in the environment.

Level 6: Planned actions. The person is able to use symbolic cues, imagination, and abstract reasoning in planning ahead and determining the consequences of his or her actions. The person is able to think and question before acting. The person is able to learn from verbal instructions as well as demonstration. The person is able to think independently and to individualize a task or use original approaches to perform a task. The person is able to make contingency plans for unexpected situations and develop alternate strategies if routine plans cannot be used. Level 6 behaviors tend to be associated with a higher educational and occupational background that has included practice in performing such behaviors and tasks. The person can live independently.

Source: Based on Allen, C.K. 1985. *Occupational therapy for psychiatric diseases: Measurement and management of cognitive disabilities*, 31–62. Boston: Little, Brown & Co.

Self-Care
- Encourage attention to personal hygiene, including bathing, grooming, and dressing.
- A reward system, such as verbal praise, for improving and maintaining personal appearance has been used successfully.

Productivity
- Improve the person's work habits and work skills.
- Provide opportunities to try out different jobs.

Leisure
- Provide leisure counseling.
- Provide opportunities to practice recreational pursuits.

PRECAUTIONS
- The variety of symptoms and levels of function or dysfunction in schizophrenia suggest that any single treatment approach will not be successful for all cases. Multiple approaches may be needed for different clients and for any one client at a particular point in the course of the disorder.
- Schizophrenia is a life-long process. Relapses occur frequently in some cases.

PROGNOSIS AND OUTCOMES

- The person is able to take responsibility for and control of his or her life.
- The person is able to interpret his or her environment correctly and react appropriately.
- The person is able to solve problems independently.
- The person is able to make decisions independently.
- The person can perform self-care skills and function independently in the community.
- The person can express emotions in socially approved ways.
- The person can plan and follow a time schedule.
- The person is oriented to reality.

REFERENCES

Barris, R. 1986. Review of current research on schizophrenia. *Mental Health Special Interest Section Newsletter* 8(2):1–2.

Blakeney, A.B., L.R. Strickland, and J.H. Wilkinson. 1983. Exploring sensory integrative dysfunction in process schizophrenia. *American Journal of Occupational Therapy* 37(6):399–406.

Boronow, J.J. 1986. Rehabilitation of chronic schizophrenic patients in a long-term private inpatient setting. *Occupational Therapy in Mental Health* 6(2):1–19.

Brouet, V.M. 1986. Individual behavioural programme planning with long-stay schizophrenic patients. *British Journal of Occupational Therapy* 49(7):227–32.

Chamove, A.S. 1986. Positive short-term effects of activity on behaviour of chronic schizophrenic patients. *British Journal of Clinical Psychology* 25(Pt. 2):125–33.

Chamove, A.S. 1986. Exercise improves behaviour: A rationale for occupational therapy. *British Journal of Occupational Therapy* 49(3):83–6.

Chun, K.A., and H.A. Davidson. 1987. Examining the affect of chronic schizophrenic male patients towards three occupational therapy activities. *Occupational Therapy in Mental Health* 7(4):81–97.

Crist, P.H., P.P. Thomas, and B.L. Stone. 1984. Pre-vocational and sensorimotor training in chronic schizophrenia. *Occupational Therapy in Mental Health* 4(2):23–37.

Eimon, M.C., P.L. Eimon, and S.A. Sermak. 1983. Performance of schizophrenic patients on a motor-free visual perception test. *American Journal of Occupational Therapy* 37(5):327–32.

Gopinath, P.S., S.K. Chaturvedi, T. Murali, et al. 1985. Work performance of schizophrenic day boards in an occupational therapy centre. *Indian Journal of Psychiatry* 27(3):207–12.

Hayes, R. 1989. Occupational therapy in the treatment of schizophrenia. *Occupational Therapy in Mental Health* 9(3):51–68.

Hixson, V.J., and A.W. Mathews. 1984. Sensory integration and chronic schizophrenia: Past, present and future. *Canadian Journal of Occupational Therapy* 51(1):19–24.

Hunter, L. 1987. Computers: Keyboard rehabilitation. *Nursing Times* 83(32, Aug 12):45–7.

Johnston, F., and G. Spratt. 1987. Planning ability in schizophrenia: A comparative study. *British Journal of Occupational Therapy* 50(9):309–13.

Johnston, M.T. 1987. Occupational therapists and the teaching of cognitive behavioral skills. *Occupational Therapy in Mental Health* 7(3):69–81.

King, L.J. 1984. Current schizophrenia research: Implications for occupational therapy practice. *Mental Health Special Interest Section Newsletter* 7(4):1–2,4.

Klasson, E.M. 1989. A model of the occupational therapist as case manager: Two case studies of chronic schizophrenic patients living in the community. *Occupational Therapy in Mental Health* 9(1):63–90.

Klasson, E.M., and A. MacRae. 1985. A university based occupational therapy clinic for chronic schizophrenics. *Occupational Therapy in Mental Health* 5(2):1–11.

Klyczek, J.P., and W.C. Mann. 1986. Therapeutic modality comparisons in day treatment. *American Journal of Occupational Therapy* 40(9):606–11.

Krupa, T., et al. 1985. Occupational therapy issues in the treatment of long-term mentally ill. *Canadian Journal of Occupational Therapy* 52(3):107–11.

Krupa, T., and J. Thornton. 1986. The pleasure deficit in schizophrenia. *Occupational Therapy in Mental Health* 6(2):65–78.

Mauer, T.L., D.A. Smith, and C.L. Armetta. 1989. Single purpose vs. added purpose activity: Performance comparisons with chronic schizophrenics. *Occupational Therapy in Mental Health* 9(3):9–20.

Neville, A., A. Kreisberg, and G.. Kielhofner. 1985. Temporal dysfunction in schizophrenia. *American Journal of Occupational Therapy* 5(1):1–19.

Pettit, K.A. 1987. Sensory integration and ego development in a schizophrenic adolescent male. *Occupational Therapy in Health Care* 4(2):87–100.

Stein, F., and S. Nikolic. 1989. Teaching stress management techniques to a schizophrenic patient. *American Journal of Occupational Therapy* 43(3):162–9.

Turvey, A.A., C.J. Main, and A. McCartney. 1985. Social activity groups with chronic schizophrenics: The influence of the therapist's behaviour. *British Journal of Occupational Therapy* 48(10):302–4.

Weeder, T.C. 1986. Comparison of temporal patterns and meaningfulness of the daily activities of schizophrenic and normal adults. *Occupational Therapy in Mental Health* 6(4):27–48.

Self-Injurious and Stereotyped Behavior

DESCRIPTION

Self-injurious behavior results in physical injury to the individual. Stereotyped behavior may result in self-injury or interfere with more purposeful behavior.

CAUSE

Self-injurious behavior occurs frequently in persons with mental retardation and mental disorders. It is more common in females than males at a ratio of about 3 to 1. The suggested causes are (1) learned behavior that is reinforced by caretakers who provide attention when stopping the behavior, (2) learned avoidance behavior to escape aversive stimulus, (3) self-stimulation to provide additional somatosensory input, (4) organic deficits or abnormal physiologic response systems, and (5) psychodynamic attempts to establish ego boundaries and body reality.

ASSESSMENT

Areas

- gross motor skills
- fine motor skills
- mobility skills
- hand functions
- sensory registration—hypo- or hyperresponsiveness to tactile, auditory, and visual stimuli in particular
- sensory processing—discrimination
- attending behavior
- communication skills
- interaction skills
- daily living skills
- play skills
- stereotypical behaviors

Instruments
- The Tactile-Vestibular Behavioral Checklist by J. Brocklehurst-Woods, *American Journal of Occupational Therapy* 44(6):538, 1990
- developmental profiles
- frequency counts of stereotyped behavior per minute, hour, or day

PROBLEMS
The division of problems into motor and sensory categories is arbitrary.

Motor
- rocking—When sitting, the person usually sways the body in a back and forth repetitive pattern, but when standing, the movement is more often side to side as weight is transferred from one foot to the other.
- head banging or hitting—The person repeatedly bangs or hits his or her head on some hard surface, such as a wall or the back of a chair.
- rotating the head clockwise or counterclockwise
- pinching or squeezing a body part between the thumb and fingers
- scratching the skin with the fingernails
- pulling a body part away from the body, usually with the hands
- sucking a body part with the tongue, mouth, and lips, causing inflammation and swelling

Sensory
- eye rubbing—The person repeatedly rubs his or her eyes.
- eye poking or hitting—The person repeatedly pokes or hits his or her eye.
- waving a hand or moving fingers through the visual field
- patting or touching the face on the checks with the fingers
- hitting the chin or forehead with a closed fist
- putting one or more fingers in the mouth

Cognitive
These behaviors do not appear to require cognitive thinking, memory, or problem solving.

Intrapersonal
The person does not exercise judgment for personal safety.

Interpersonal
Some behaviors may have a communication or attention-getting objective.

Self-Care
The person smears saliva, food, or excrement on his or her face, hands, or other parts of the body.

Productivity
Behaviors do not have a productive objective, goal, or purpose, and they frequently interfere with such activities.

Leisure

The person usually has few, if any, leisure interests.

TREATMENT/MANAGEMENT

Treatment techniques are based primarily on sensory integration (Ayres) and general techniques of inhibition and relaxation based on the concept that slow repetitive activity sends inhibitory impulses to the bulbar section of the brain (reticular area), which results in total body inhibition.

Motor

Motor skills are not used in treatment, although the person may be permitted to play with toys or other objects between sessions of sensory stimulation.

Sensory

- vestibular stimulation (linear)—Use slow, repetitive rocking in a net hammock or a rocking chair on a rocker board, on a platform swing, or in the inverted position over a large therapy ball. Movements may be anterior-posterior, lateral, or up and down. Positions may include prone, supine, or sitting. A rate of 40 rocking movements per minute has been used, but maximally effective rates have not been established (see Bonnadonna, 1981, in the reference section). A metronome may be helpful to maintain the rate of movement. Length of stimulation using one-minute to 15-minute intervals has been successful, but maximally effective lengths of stimulation have not been established (see Bonnadonna, 1981; Bright et al, 1981). A total length of treatment session of 20 to 50 minutes has been used, but maximally effective lengths of treatment have not been established.
- vestibular stimulation (angular)—Use slow, repetitive turning or spinning in a hammock, or a wheelchair or other surface that can be turned.
- firm, deep, tactile stimulation—Stimulation is supplied through vibration. Vibration is supplied by a cylindrical, battery-operated vibrator, hands-on massage applied to hands, neck, arms, shoulders or temples, rolling a large bolster over legs, back, and shoulder, rolling up in a blanket, or using two mats to form a sandwich through which pressure may be applied.
- other tactile stimulation—The person locates objects in a medium such as plastic foam beads, or receives tactile stimuli from a feather duster, lotion, powder, a clothes brush, a dish mop, a terry-cloth towel, and a vegetable brush.
- slow continuous stroking—The person is placed in a prone position without clothing on his or her back so that the skin is exposed. The therapist places the index and middle fingers on either side of the spinal column on the posterior primary rami, starting at the neck and stroking slowing to the coccyx. As one hand reaches the coccyx, the other hand begins at the neck so as to provide continual stimulation. Three-minute lengths have been used successfully.
- other inhibitory (dampening) stimuli, including dimmed lighting and soft music

Cognitive

The person may be encouraged to make choices in the specific sensory activity.

Intrapersonal
Intrapersonal skills are not used.

Interpersonal
- The therapist or other staff member or caregiver may hold a child in the lap while rocking in a rocking chair.
- Two people can share a platform swing, push a ball back and forth, or push and pull on each other's arms while seated on a mat.

Self-Care
Self-care activities are not used.

Productivity
Productivity activities are not used.

Leisure
Leisure activities are not used.

PRECAUTIONS
- Vestibular stimulation may be contraindicated for some persons with seizure disorders, especially if the person is photosensitive. Sources of light may need to be blocked or dimmed.
- Do not use slow continuous stroking on persons with hair growth on the back that forms swirls or irregular patterns because the stroking will stimulate rather than inhibit behavior.

PROGNOSIS AND OUTCOME
- The person has decreased self-injury or self-stimulatory activity.
- The person has increased attention span to external sources of stimuli.

REFERENCES

Bonnadonna, P. 1981. Effects of a vestibular stimulation program on stereotypic rocking behavior. *American Journal of Occupational Therapy* 35(12):775–81.

Bracklehurst-Woods, J. 1990. The use of tactile and vestibular stimulation to reduce stereotypic behaviors in two adults with mental retardation. *American Journal of Occupational Therapy* 44(6):536–41.

Bright, T., K. Bittick, and B. Fleeman. 1981. Reduction of SIB using sensory integrative techniques. *American Journal of Occupational Therapy* 35(3):167–72.

Dura, J.R., J.A. Mulick, and D. Hammer. 1988. Rapid clinical evaluation of sensory therapy for self-injurious behavior. *Mental Retardation* 26(2):83–7.

Hirama, H. 1989. *Self-injurious behavior: A somatosensory treatment approach*. Baltimore, MD: Chess Publications.

Iwasaki, K., and M.B. Holm. 1989. Sensory treatment for the reduction of stereotypic behaviors in persons with severe multiple disabilities. *Occupational Therapy Journal of Research* 9(3):170–83.

Wells, M.E., and D.W. Smith. 1983. Reduction of self-injurious behavior of mentally retarded persons using sensory-integrative techniques. *American Journal of Mental Deficiency* 87(6):664–6.

Substance Abuse/Dependence— Alcohol

DESCRIPTION

Alcoholism is defined as the development of characteristic deviant behaviors associated with prolonged consumption of excessive amounts of alcohol. Alcoholism is a chronic illness. Associated behaviors include (1) frequent intoxication that interferes with the individual's ability to socialize and to work, (2) drunkenness that leads to marriage failure and absenteeism from work, (3) cumulative problems at work that lead to being fired or let go, (4) being ar-rested for driving under the influence, (5) being arrested for public drunkenness, (6) being hospitalized for delirium tremens or cirrhosis of the liver, and (7) seeking medical treatment for injury or illness related or unrelated to drinking.

CAUSE

The cause is unknown. Frequent personality traits include (1) schizoid qualities (isolation, loneliness, shyness) (2) depression, (3) dependency, (4) hostile and self-destructive impulsivity, and (5) sexual immaturity. A family history of drinking increases the risk. The ratio of men to women is 4:1. About one in 10 persons experiences some problem with alcoholism.

ASSESSMENT

Areas
- physical tolerance and endurance
- fine motor coordination, manipulation, dexterity
- sensory registration and processing
- attending behavior, concentration
- orientation
- ability to follow instructions
- problem solving and decision making
- learning skills
- self-concept
- self-control
- social skills
- daily living skills
- productivity history, values, skills, and interests
- leisure values, skills, and interests

Instruments
- Comprehensive Occupational Therapy Evaluation (COTE) by S.J Brayman and T. Kirby. 1982. In *The evaluative process in psychiatric occupational therapy*, ed. B.J. Hemphill, 211–226, 381–388. Thorofare, NJ: Slack, Inc.

- Activity Laboratory Questionnaire by G. Fidler. 1982. In *The evaluative process in psychiatric occupational therapy*, ed. B.J. Hemphill, 195–208, 379–380. Thorofare, NJ: Slack, Inc.
- Activities Clock by S. Cynkin. 1979. In *Toward health through activities*, 19–29. Boston: Little, Brown & Co.
- Initial Evaluation Interview by F. Ehrenberg. 1982. In *The evaluative process in psychiatric occupational therapy*, ed. B.J. Hemphill, 155–168, 363–364. Thorofare, NJ: Slack, Inc.
- Assessment of Occupational Functioning (See J.H. Watts, et al. 1986. The assessment of occupational functioning: A screening tool for use in long-term care. *American Journal of Occupational Therapy* 40(4):231–40, and The Assessment of Occupational Functioning: The second revision. *Occupational Therapy in Mental Health* 8(4):61–88.)

PROBLEMS

Motor
- The person may have decreased physical tolerance and endurance.
- The person may have a peripheral neuropathy.

Sensory
The person may have sensory changes associated with peripheral neuropathy.

Cognitive
- The person may have cognitive disorders associated with brain damage.
- The person frequently may have poor time-management skills leading to an imbalance between self-care, productivity, and leisure activities.

Intrapersonal
- The person may have a poor self-concept and low self-esteem.
- The person may be depressed.
- Values and beliefs may be poorly defined.
- Goals may be poorly defined and goal-oriented behavior lacking.
- The person may tend to be a perfectionist.

Interpersonal
The person may have immature or impaired social skills.

Self-Care
The person may neglect activities of daily living.

Productivity
- The person usually has a poor job history.
- The person may have unrealistic expectations of his or her job skills.
- Poor time management may result in the person being late for work.
- The person may have difficulty organizing and performing job duties.

Leisure
The person may have few leisure interests.

TREATMENT/MANAGEMENT
Models of treatment include occupational behavior (Reilly), human occupation (Kielhofner), the psychoeducational approach, and others. For an overview of the use of models in occupational therapy see Moyers, 1988, in the reference section.

Motor
- Improve fine motor coordination, manipulation, and dexterity through the use of craft projects requiring fine motor skills.
- Encourage regular participation in recreational activities and exercise to increase physical fitness.

Cognitive
- Increase the person's awareness of his or her strengths and weaknesses through participation in arts and crafts activities, creative writing, psychodrama, and group discussion.
- Help the person sort out priorities through group discussion.
- Provide instruction in organizing an activity schedule and learning time-management skills that include planning for leisure time.
- Increase problem-solving and decision-making skills through arts and crafts activities and group projects.
- Increase the person's ability to concentrate and his or her attention span through the use of arts and crafts projects.

Intrapersonal
- Increase the person's ability to tolerate frustration through stress-management techniques.
- Help the person learn new behavior patterns through the performance of a variety of activities.
- Increase the person's self-esteem and sense of mastery by using short-term projects in which success is relatively assured.
- Increase the person's ability to channel anger and aggression into acceptable activities, such as crafts that include destruction (sawing wood), hammering, and drilling.
- Increase the person's self-confidence through experience in dealing with problems arising in completing craft or other activity tasks.
- Increase the person's sense of autonomy and independence by learning to perform activities without direct supervision.
- Encourage the person to set goals and plan a course of action to met those goals.
- Encourage the person to control impulsive behavior through practice in handling frustration and anger.

Interpersonal
- Encourage the person to share feelings and experiences in group discussion, role playing, or psychodrama.
- Increase social relationships, including group cooperation.

- Encourage socially acceptable behavior by rewarding such behavior and using the topic in group discussion.
- Encourage the person to participate in a self-help group in the community, such as Alcoholics Anonymous (AA).

Self-Care
Increase the person's skills in organizing and managing daily life tasks, including grooming, using public transportation, managing money, and arranging living accommodations.

Productivity
- Increase the person's skills in organizing and completing work tasks, such as organizing a workspace, pacing the work activities, trying new ideas, making decisions, and organizing a project into manageable steps.
- Increase the person's ability to follow verbal and written directions.
- Increase the person's skills in managing and organizing the home and preparing meals.
- If needed, assist the person to explore career options, apply for a job, and maintain a job.

Leisure
Assist the person to explore and develop a variety of leisure activities and skills.

PRECAUTIONS
Observe for relapses in drinking behavior.

PROGNOSIS AND OUTCOME
- The person demonstrates self-control.
- The person is able to initiate a goal and follow through to completion.
- The person participates in social activities.
- The person performs self-care and daily living activities regularly.
- The person has improved work skills.
- The person performs productive activities on a regular schedule.
- The person performs leisure activities on a regular schedule.

REFERENCES

Cassidy, C.L. 1988. Occupational therapy intervention in the treatment of alcoholics. *Occupational Therapy in Mental Health* 8(2):17–26.

Klein, J.M. 1988. Abstinence-oriented inpatient treatment of the substance abuser. *Occupational Therapy in Mental Health* 8(2):47–59.

Lange, B.K. 1988. Ethnographic interview: An occupational therapy needs assessment tool for American Indian and Alaska Native alcoholics. *Occupational Therapy in Mental Health* 8(2):61–80.

Lindsay, W.P. 1983. The role of the occupational therapist in treatment of alcoholism. *American Journal of Occupational Therapy* 37(1):36–43.

Malorana, R. 1984. Early recognition and management of alcohol problems: Occupational therapy treatment. *Mental Health Special Interest Section Newsletter* 7(2):1–2.

Moyers, P.A. 1988. An organizational framework for occupational therapy in the treatment of alcoholism. *Occupational Therapy in Mental Health* 8(2):27–46.

Moyers, P.A., and C.E. Barrett. 1990. Treating the alcoholic's family. *Mental Health Special Interest Section Newsletter* 13(3):2–4.

Nixon, J. 1988. The role of the occupational therapist in the field of alcohol abuse. *British Journal of Occupational Therapy* 51(10):359–63.

Raymond, M. 1990. Life skills and substance abuse. *Mental Health Special Interest Section Newsletter* 13(3):1–2.

Rotert, D.A. 1989. Occupational therapy in alcoholism. *Occupational Medicine: State of the Art Reviews* 4(2):327–37.

Rotert, D.A., and F.E. Gainer. 1986. The chemically dependent adolescent. In *The certified occupational therapy assistant*, ed. S.E. Ryan, 183–88. Thorofare, NJ: Slack, Inc.

Searth, P.P. 1990. Services for chemically dependent adolescents. *Mental Health Special Interest Section Newsletter* 13(3):7–8.

Smith, T.M., and C.S. Gilckstein. 1980–81. Art as a therapeutic modality for individuals with alcohol-related problems in a milieu setting. *Occupational Therapy in Mental Health* 1:33–43.

Stensrud, M.K., and R.S. Lushbough. 1988. The implementation of an occupational therapy program in an alcohol and drug dependency treatment center. *Occupational Therapy in Mental Health* 8(2):1–15.

Stone, N. 1985. Occupational therapy involvement in assessment and primary individual work with alcohol dependent patients. *British Journal of Occupational Therapy* 48(9):263–5.

Van Deusen, J. 1989. Alcohol abuse and perceptual-motor dysfunction: The occupational therapist's role. *American Journal of Occupational Therapy* 43(6):384–90.

Viik, M.K., J.H. Watts, M.J. Madigan, and D. Bauer. 1990. Preliminary validation of the assessment of occupational functioning with an alcoholic population. *Occupational Therapy in Mental Health* 10(2):19–33.

Substance Abuse/Dependence—Drugs

DESCRIPTION

The drug-dependent person must, or feels he must, use (drink, snort, shoot into veins) chemical substances for psychological or physiological reasons or both to continue functioning. Addiction refers to drug dependence and style of living, which involve primarily the psychological craving and compulsive use of a drug even though physical harm may result if the use continues indiscriminately. Drug abuse is defined in relation to disapproval by society. There are three behavioral types: (1) experimental and recreational use of drugs, (2) use of psychoactive drugs to relieve personal problems or symptoms, and (3) initial use of drugs in categories one or two but later resulting in dependence.

CAUSE

The causes are not well understood but three factors must exist: (1) an addictive drug, (2) a predisposing condition, and (3) the personality or disposition of the user. General factors are related to the culture, socioeconomic class, and psychology of the individual and the availability of the drug. Specific factors include peer or group pressure, emotional distress, and perception of the ability to change the situation.

ASSESSMENT

Definitions
- psychological dependence—feelings of satisfaction and a desire to repeat the administration of the drug to produce pleasure or avoid discomfort
- physical dependence—physiological adaptation to a drug accompanied by development of tolerance and manifested by a withdrawal or abstinence syndrome
- tolerance—the need to increase the dose progressively in order to produce the effect originally achieved by smaller amounts
- withdrawal syndrome—characterized by physiological changes that occur when the drug is discontinued or when its effect is counteracted by a specific antagonist

Areas
- physical appearance
- attending behavior and concentration
- ability to follow instruction
- organization skills
- problem solving and decision making
- time-management skills
- mood or affect
- judgment and safety awareness
- self-concept
- self-control
- social interaction skills
- communication skills
- role behavior
- daily living skills
- productivity history, interests, skills, and values
- leisure interests and skills

Instruments
- Jamestown Occupational Therapy Assessment (See M.L. Gangl. 1987. The effectiveness of an occupational therapy program for chemically dependent adolescents. *Occupational Therapy in Mental Health* 7(2):67–88.)
- Allen Cognitive Level Test (In *Occupational therapy for psychiatric diseases: Measurement and management of cognitive disabilities,* ed. C.K. Allen, 1985, 108–113. Boston: Little, Brown & Co.)

PROBLEMS

Motor
- The person may have reduced range of motion, especially in the upper extremities.
- The person may have low physical endurance or poor physical fitness.
- The person may have impairments in balance and posture.
- The person may have poor muscle tone due to inactivity.
- The person may have impaired coordination and dexterity.

Sensory
- The person may have slower than normal reaction time.
- The person may have pain, especially in the lower back.

Cognitive
- The person may have impaired judgment.
- The person may have difficulty following instructions.

Intrapersonal
- The person may have low self-concept (self-esteem or self-confidence).
- The person may show signs of immaturity.
- The person usually shows signs of depression.
- The person may show hostility or self-destructive impulsivity.
- The person may be suicidal.

Interpersonal
- The person may have schizoid qualities (isolation, loneliness, shyness).
- The person may be dependent on others.
- The person may be withdrawn.

Self-Care
- The person may neglect to perform certain activities of daily living.
- The person may lack skills in money management.

Productivity
- The person may have a history of irregular work performance.
- The person may have a history of irregular school attendance.

Leisure
The person may have few, if any, leisure interests except drugs.

TREATMENT/MANAGEMENT
Models of treatment include human occupation (Kielhofner) and the psychoeducational approach.

Motor
- Increase range of motion through performance of tasks in the environment and selected exercises.
- Participation in a group exercise program to increase physical tolerance, endurance, fitness, and muscle tone may include stretching, bending, twisting, jogging in place, and jumping jacks.
- Increase standing balance and postural reactions.
- Improve coordination and dexterity through activities requiring imitation of simple and complex movements, including crossing the midline.

Cognitive

- Provide opportunities to learn to follow verbal and written instructions through the use of leisure or work activities.
- Provide opportunities to practice problem-solving and decision-making skills through the use of leisure or work activities.
- Provide question and answer sessions on the effects of drug withdrawal on physical and psychological health including how to cope with the craving.
- Provide time-management training and daily scheduling to organize a drug-free lifestyle.
- Teach the person about community resources.
- Provide opportunities in setting short- and long-term goals and identifying the steps needed to achieve the goals.
- Provide opportunities to practice money-management skills, including planning a budget, opening and managing a checking account, and controlling spending habits.

Intrapersonal

- Provide the opportunity to learn to deal with frustration and develop frustration tolerance and coping skills using actual or real learning situations.
- Increase self-esteem and self-concept through the use of creative activities, such as art, crafts, drama, music, or dance.
- Increase the person's ability to set obtainable goals and work toward meeting the goals using behavior-modification techniques.
- Provide instruction in relaxation training as a stress-management technique.

Interpersonal

- Provide group-oriented tasks that can be used as a basis for group discussion regarding attitudes, feelings, emotions, and reactions, especially regarding authority figures.
- The use of drama therapy and role playing may be helpful in providing opportunities for the person to try out different roles and alternative behaviors to situations. Sessions may be videotaped to assist in analysis.
- Encourage the person to participate in support or self-help groups.
- Special groups may be organized to concentrate on specific problems, such as women's issues or marital issues.
- Increase the person's social interaction skills, such as meeting new people, expressing ideas, maintaining relationships, and the role of physical appearance in social relationships.

Self-Care

Provide instruction and practice in daily living activities, such as shopping, meal planning, using public transportation, and budgeting and money management.

Productivity

- Improve work habits and work skills through structured work programs.
- Increase the person's knowledge and skills in applying for jobs, such as preparing a resume, completing an application form, and interviewing.
- Provide opportunities to practice home-management techniques, such as cleaning, washing clothes, and preparing meals.

- Encourage the person to explore volunteer work, continuing education courses, or study groups.

Leisure
- Provide opportunities to develop and explore leisure interests that can be done individually or in groups.
- Provide opportunities to locate and participate in socially or community organized leisure and recreational activities.

PRECAUTIONS
- Note shortness of breath, increased sweating, or dizziness, especially during exercises, which may indicate a need for referral to a physician for further analysis of health status.
- Program modifications may be necessary if the person has a history of hypertension, seizures, back pain, or other physical injury.

PROGNOSIS AND OUTCOME
- The person demonstrates the ability to organize and follow a drug-free lifestyle.
- The person is able to solve problems and make decisions without the use of drugs or other unacceptable social behavior.
- The person is able to set goals and plan and execute a program to meet goals without the use of drugs.
- The person is able to participate in group activities without the use of drugs.
- The person performs activities of daily living independently.
- The person is able to plan a budget and manage money using checking, savings, or credit accounts.
- The person is able to obtain and hold a job.
- The person is able to manage a home independently or in cooperation with others.
- The person has identified leisure interests in which the person participates on a regular basis.
- The person is knowledgeable about community resources, such as self-help groups.

REFERENCES

Allen, C.K. 1985. Phencyclidine-hydrochloride abuse. In *Occupational therapy for psychiatric diseases: Measurement and management of cognitive disabilities,* ed. C.K. Allen, 173–7. Boston: Little, Brown & Co.

Busuttil, J. 1989. Setting up an occupational therapy programme for drug addicts. *British Journal of Occupational Therapy* 52(12):476–9.

Gangl, M.L. 1987. The effectiveness of an occupational therapy program for chemically dependent adolescents. *Occupational Therapy in Mental Health* 7(2):67–88.

Kunz, K. 1988. A certified occupational therapy assistant's contribution to a substance abuse treatment program. *Occupational Therapy in Health Care* 5(2/3):119–25.

Lowe, L., and A. Brodrick. 1986. Activities of daily living in psychiatry: Develop an approach to drug dependence. *British Journal of Occupational Therapy* 49(5):154–6.

O'Rourke, G.C. 1990. The HIV-positive intravenous drug abuser—Case report. *American Journal of Occupational Therapy* 44(3):280–3.

Raymond M. 1990. Life skills and substance abuse. *Mental Health Special Interest Section Newsletter* 13(3):1–2.

Scarth, P.P. 1990. Services for chemically dependent adolescents. *Mental Health Special Interest Section Newsletter* 13(3):7–8.

Stevens, S. 1984. A multidisciplinary day unit for the treatment of substance abuse. *British Journal of Occupational Therapy* 47(4):117–20.

Stopforth, B. 1986. Outpatient benzodiazepine withdrawal and the occupational therapist. *British Journal of Occupational Therapy* 49(10):318–23.

Evaluating Hand Injuries

DEGREE OF NERVE INJURY

First Degree

Axonal conduction is interrupted, but all structures remain intact. Loss of nerve function is temporary, and proceeding from the largest to smallest fiber diameter: motor, proprioception and vibration, touch, and pain. Recovery is spontaneous and complete.

Second Degree

Axons are interrupted but not the endoneurium, perineurium, or epineurium. Wallerian degeneration occurs, but recovery is spontaneous because the tube or shaft remains intact.

Third Degree

Axons and endoneurial tube are interrupted. Recovery occurs but may not be complete because of scarring or failure of the axons to reenter their original tubes.

Fourth Degree

Axons, endoneurial tube, and perineurium are interrupted. Scarring and internal disorganization (axons entering the wrong tubes or failing to find a tube) are greater and the integrity of the fiber bundles is lost. Some spontaneous recovery may occur but frequently is not functional. Surgical excision and repair usually are required to achieve maximum functional return, but some residual deficits will occur.

Fifth Degree

Entire nerve (axon, endoneurial tube, perineurium, and epineurium) is interrupted. Surgical repair is essential to achieve any functional recovery, but motor and sensory deficits will persist.

Source: Based on Callahan, A. 1984. Nerve injuries in the upper extremity. In *Manual on management of specific hand problems,* ed. M.H. Malick and M.C. Kasch, 17–18. Pittsburgh: American Rehabilitation Educational Network (AREN).

ORDER OF RECOVERY OF SENSATION

1. protective sensation (response to deep pressure and pinprick)
2. moving touch or tactile sensation
3. static light touch
4. discriminative touch

Source: Based on Dellon, A.L.. 1981. *Evaluation of sensibility and re-education of the sensation in the hand*, 115–22. Baltimore, MD: Williams & Wilkins.

TESTING FOR STATIC TWO-POINT DISCRIMINATION

Use a blunt instrument with two points, which is applied on a longitudinal axis of the digit. The pressure applied should not blanch the skin. Support the person's hand on a table surface and occlude his or her vision. Seven out of 10 correct responses are required for each zone of the hand tested. Begin testing at 5 mm distance between the two points. Randomly touch with one or two points. The person states whether one or two points is felt on the skin. Discontinue test if the person cannot discriminate at 15 mm between the stimulus points.

Ratings
1. normal—less than 6 mm
2. fair—6 to 10 mm
3. poor—11 to 15 mm
4. protective—one point perceived
5. anesthetic—no point perceived

Source: Based on American Society for Surgery of the Hand. 1990. *The hand: Examination and diagnosis*, 3d ed., 121. Edinburgh, Scotland: Churchill Livingstone.

TESTING FOR MOVING TWO-POINT DISCRIMINATION

Use a blunt instrument with two points, which is applied in a proximal to distal direction. Support the person's hand on a table surface and occlude his or her vision. Begin testing at 8 mm distance between the two points. Seven out of 10 responses must be accurate for scoring. Stop testing at 2 mm, which represents normal moving two-point discrimination.

Source: Based on Callahan, A. 1984. Nerve injuries in the upper extremity. In *Manual on management of specific hand problems*, ed. M.H. Malick and M.C. Kasch, 24. Pittsburgh: American Rehabilitation Educational Network.

TESTING FOR LIGHT TOUCH AND DEEP PRESSURE
(SEMMES-WEINSTEIN PRESSURE AESTHESIOMETER)

Testing begins with the monofilament marked 2.83, which is applied perpendicularly to the skin in the center of a selected zone of the hand until the monofilament bows (bends). Vision is occluded. Each monofilament is applied for 1 to 1.5 seconds. Filaments marked 1.65 through 4.08 are applied three times. A positive response (person perceives the stimulus) must be recorded two out of three times to record a positive result in that zone of the hand. If the person cannot detect the stimulus in the range 1.65 to 4.08, continue with filaments marked 4.17 to 6.65 but apply only once. Stop when the person is able to detect the pressure.

Interpretation of Monofilaments

Green	Normal light touch	2.36–2.83
Blue	Diminished light touch	3.22–3.61
Purple	Diminished protective sensation	3.84–4.31
Red	Loss of protective sensation	4.56–6.65

Source: Based on Callahan, A. 1984. Nerve injuries in the upper extremity. In *Manual on management of specific hand problems*, ed. M.H. Malick and M.C. Kasch, 23. Pittsburgh: American Rehabilitation Educational Network.

TESTING FOR LOCALIZATION OF STIMULUS

Use the monofilament from the Semmes-Weinstein series that could be detected in all zones of the hand. Apply the stimulus perpendicular to the skin in the center of a selected zone of the hand until the monofilament bows (bends). Vision is occluded. Then ask the person to open his or her eyes and point to the exact spot touched by the monofilament stimulus. Use a grid worksheet marked with zones and subdivided into approximately equal square areas. If the person responds correctly, circle the dot; if the answer is incorrect, draw an arrow from the dot in the zone stimulated to the point the person indicated was touched.

Source: Based on Callahan, A. 1984. Nerve injuries in the upper extremities. In *Manual on management of specific hand problems*, ed. M.H. Malick and M.C. Kasch, 25. Pittsburgh: American Rehabilitation Educational Network.

MOBERG PICK-UP TEST

Small common objects are placed on a table surface (car key, 1" paper clip, 1" safety pin, 1" screw, 3/8" diameter wing nut, 3/8" hexagon nut, a nickel, a dime). Examiner notes the time required and the type of prehension. With vision occluded, the person will tend not to use sensory surfaces with poor sensibility.

Subtest 1—Person picks up objects with the involved hand, eyes opened, and places them in a box.

Subtest 2—Person picks up objects with the noninvolved hand, eyes opened, and places them in a box.

Subtest 3—Person picks up objects with the involved hand, eyes closed, and places them in a box.

Subtest 4—Person picks up objects with the noninvolved hand, eyes closed, and places them in a box.

Source: Based on Callahan, A. 1984. Nerve injuries in the upper extremities. In *Manual on management of specific hand problems*, ed. M.H. Malick and M.C. Kasch, 25. Pittsburgh: American Rehabilitation Educational Network.

Technique Summaries

ENERGY CONSERVATION AND WORK SIMPLIFICATION

- Use good body mechanics and muscles that use the least energy.
  a. Use both hands and arms whenever possible (symmetrical vs. asymmetrical).
  b. Use hip and shoulder muscles for lifting tasks (weight-bearing muscles).
- Sit rather than stand whenever possible or alternate sitting and standing.
- Keep frequently used items within easy reach to avoid stretching and straining, including bending, reaching, stooping, and twisting.
- Let your fingers do the walking: shop by telephone if possible.
- Tell them to deliver: let the postal or other delivery service bring items to the house.
- Let the laws of physics (gravity and momentum) help reduce the work load.
  a. Slide rather than lift or carry objects.
  b. Toss instead of placing unbreakable items; toss item into wastebasket rather than putting the item into the wastebasket.
- Use proper work heights according to the job task and the individual. Jobs requiring hand activity require a taller work surface than those requiring arm motion.
- Plan ahead to eliminate wasted motion and time.
  a. Plan activities and assemble needed items before starting. Use a cart, wagon, or basket to keep items assembled.
  b. Reschedule tasks so they can be done less frequently, such as shopping for groceries less often and at times that are less busy at the store.
- Avoid doing unnecessary tasks.
  a. Delegate some tasks to other family members.
  b. Let the grocery clerks carry the bags.
- Schedule rest breaks as well as activities.
- Let power tools do the work when possible, such as electric can openers.

REFERENCES

Furst, G., L.H. Berber, and C. Smith. 1985. *Rehabilitation through learning: Energy conservation and joint protection: Workbook for person with rheumatoid arthritis.* Washington, DC: U.S. Government Printing Office. Stock No. 017-045-00-04-7.

Gerber, L., et al. 1987. Patient education program to teach energy conservation behaviors to patients with rheumatoid arthritis: A pilot study. *Archives of Physical Medicine and Rehabilitation* 68(7):442–5.

Gilbert, D.W. 1965. Energy expenditures for the disabled homemaker: Review of studies. *American Journal of Occupational Therapy* 19:321–28 (classic article).

Hopkins, H.L., and H.A. Smith, eds. 1988. *Willard and Spackman's occupational therapy*, 7th ed., 264. Philadelphia: J.B. Lippincott.

Trombly, C.A., ed. 1990. *Occupational therapy for physical dysfunction*, 3d ed., 411–12. Baltimore, MD: Williams & Wilkins.

Vulpe, S., and B.K. Yoshioka-Maxwell. 1989. Energy conservation as a frame of reference for serving families of the disabled. *Developmental Disabilities Special Interest Section Newsletter* 12(2):6–8.

INHIBITION AND FACILITATION TECHNIQUES

I. Categories of Inhibition Techniques

General characteristics of inhibiting or damping techniques to the central nervous system are slow and repetitive movements and activities that send inhibitory impulses to the bulbar section of the brain in the reticular formation. Some techniques can be used in combination with others.

- *Inversion*—By turning the person upside down so that the head is lower than the rest of body, the carotid sinus produces a calming and inhibiting effect on all the stretch reflexes except those facilitated by the labyrinthine reflex. Do not invert person with shunts and use caution with persons who have tracheostomies to be sure the airway is clear and with persons with abdominal feeding tubes to be sure the tube does not cause discomfort.
- *Joint Compression*—The therapist uses one hand to stabilize the shoulder while the other hand is placed on the flexed elbow. Force is applied up through the humerus into the shoulder. Gradually and slowly the therapist rotates the elbow in large radius circles increasing the amount of flexion and abduction. Joint compression that is less than the person's body weight is inhibitory to all muscles around the joint being compressed.
- *Mobilization of Proximal Joints*—Mobilization of the shoulder girdle and pelvis assists in reducing abnormal muscle tone. Techniques include separation of movement of the upper and lower trunk, elongating the trunk musculature, increasing movement of the shoulder, and increasing anterior pelvic tilt.
- *Neutral Warmth*—Wrap the person's total body in a cotton blanket for 10 to 20 minutes. Avoid extremes of temperature, which may relax initially but may result in rebound later, causing the person to tighten up or experience pain.
- *Pressure on the Insertion of a Muscle*—To relax a tight muscle group, apply pressure on the insertion of the muscle. In the hand, wrist flexors can be relaxed by placing a hand cone in the hand.
- *Reciprocal Inhibition*—Contraction of the agonist muscle causes the motor neurons that supply the antagonist to be inhibited. For example, contraction of the triceps causes the motor neurons in the biceps to be inhibited and thus more relaxed.
- *Reflex-Inhibiting Postures*—Reflex-inhibiting postures are movement patterns that inhibit abnormal postural reactions and thus facilitate voluntary movements. Generally a reflex-inhibiting posture is based on the use of one or more key points of control, which are the neck, shoulder, and pelvic girdle. Key points of control usually are proximal body units that tend to influence the rest of the particular posture. For example, to inhibit or

counteract an abnormal flexion pattern of the upper extremity, the neck and spine are extended, the shoulder is externally rotated, the elbow is extended, the forearm is supinated, and the thumb is abducted.

- *Selected Sensory Stimuli*—Auditory stimuli that have a regular rhythm less than the heart rate are inhibitory. Dimmed lights or natural indirect light tends to be inhibiting. Perfume or pleasant odors tend to have a calming effect. Warm fluids inhibit hyperactive swallowing.
- *Slow Rocking*—Rhythmic slow rocking in a rocking chair or over a large diameter ball in a forward and backward position is inhibitory. If a ball is used, the therapists should stabilize the person at the pelvis to reduce any fear of falling.
- *Slow Rolling*—The therapist places one hand on the person's shoulder and the other hand on the person's pelvis. The person is slowing rolled from supine to side-lying and back to supine for several minutes.
- *Slow Stroking*—Slow stroking is done to the posterior primary rami located on either side of the spinal cord. When the person is prone, the therapist places the index finger on one side and the middle finger on the other side of the spinal cord starting at the neck or occiput. Applying light but firm touch, the fingers are slowly moved through the coccyx. Before the first hand is lifted, the second hand begins at the neck and slowly moves down the back. Slow stroking should be applied directly to the skin, not through clothing. Slow stroking should not be used on any person with swirls or irregular hair patterns on the back because the movement of the hairs will stimulate rather than calm the person.
- *Weight Bearing and Cocontraction*—Weight bearing through the lower extremities and pelvis can reduce spasticity. In the upper extremities, cocontraction can assist in restoring the normal agonist and antagonist relationship and muscle tone.

II. Facilitating Techniques

General characteristics of facilitating techniques are rapid, irregular rhythms in a movement or activity.

- *Brushing* is accomplished by using a rotary mixer to which a soft camel hair brush has been inserted. The brushing is applied to the dermatomal representation of the muscle to be facilitated, which usually is the skin area over the muscle belly. The stimulus is applied 10 to 15 seconds per area. It is assumed that the exteroceptors, probably C fibers, are stimulated.
- *Icing* is accomplished by using an ice cube wrapped in a towel or cloth that is rubbed with pressure over the belly muscle to be facilitated. Usually three quick swipes are applied in a distal to proximal direction and then the skin is dried. Chewing ice is useful for facilitating swallowing and tongue movement. Do not ice the forehead, anterior midline of the trunk, or posterior trunk because blood pressure may be increased.
- *Pressure* (tapping, rubbing, quick stretching) applied to the muscle belly as a quick stretch facilitates the movement produced by the muscle being stretched. Do not apply pressure or quick stretch to a spastic muscle.
- *Joint Approximation or Compression* (pressing the joint together) applied with more than body weight facilitates extensor patterns and cocontraction patterns. Do not use if the person has a fracture of any bones whose joints are being compressed.
- *Joint Traction* (pulling the joint apart) facilitates flexor patterns. Do not use if the person has a fracture of any bones involved with the joints to which traction is being applied.

- *Resistance* is most effective when applied in a pattern of apply, hold, release, apply, hold, release, rather than in a steady pull. The apply, hold, release pattern permits the muscle fibers to adjust rather than fatiguing under the steady pull. The amount of resistance applied must be adjusted according to the person (adult or child), particular pattern (static or movement), or position (finger flexion or elbow flexion). Application of strong, steady, static resistance will result in cocontraction. Less resistance is needed for movement patterns.
- *Postural Change* (changes in posture) can be used to increase or decrease muscle tone through the response to gravity. Generally, positions that cause the person to work against gravity increase muscle tone.
- *Sensory Stimuli* (fast, loud, irregular rhythms) are stimulating; bright colors (red, yellow, orange) are stimulating; salty and oily fluids, thin mucus that facilitates swallowing, and noxious odors have a stimulating effect.
- *Successive Induction* is based on the concept that a muscle will contract more strongly if its contraction is preceded by a contraction of the antagonist. In other words, alternate contraction of agonist and antagonist. For example, if the wrist flexors are weak, first give maximum resistance to the wrist extensory then give resistance to wrist flexors.
- *Vestibular Stimulation* (fast rolling, spinning, tilting, and swinging) can be used to increase muscle tone. Always watch the person for emotional reactions and sympathetic nervous system response. If the person becomes fearful or becomes pale or flushed, reduce the rate of stimulation. Generally, spinning should not be used with persons who are prone to seizures or who have seizure disorders.
- *Vibration* is applied through a battery-operated vibrator. The reaction is immediate but wears off in about three minutes. Vibration is assumed to stimulate proprioceptors and arouse the reticular system which activates the cortex. Vibration should not be used with persons prone to seizures or who have seizure disorders.

REFERENCES

Kovich, K., and D. Bermann. 1988. Handling and facilitation of functional movement. In *Head injury: A guide to functional outcomes in occupational therapy*, ed. K.M. Kovich and D.E. Bermann, 69–106. Gaithersburg, MD: Aspen Publishers, Inc.

Neufeld, P.S. 1981. Neurobehavioral evaluation and management. In *Physical disabilities manual*, ed. B.C. Abreu, 117–40. New York: Raven Press.

JOINT PROTECTION

- Maintain joint in correct position and avoid positions of deformity.
- Maintain body in correct posture and avoid positions that lead to injury.
- Use stronger, larger joints and the biggest muscles to lift and carry. Use shoulders instead of hands. Use palms of hands instead of fingers.
- Use each joint in the most stable anatomic and functional position. Stand with both feet on the floor in flat shoes with toes pointed ahead. Bend hips and knees, but keep back straight when picking up objects.
- Distribute load over two or more joints. Lift small objects, such as a bowl or pan, with two hands.

- Avoid sustaining the same position for long periods of time, such as holding a pencil. Use a built-up or enlarged diameter pencil.
- Avoid static positions for long periods of time, such as standing or sitting.
- Plan alternate periods of activities and rest.
- Stop before becoming fatigued. Bad habits creep in more easily when a person is tired and not concentrating.
- Divide work into light and heavy tasks. Alternate and take frequent rest breaks.
- Reduce effort needed to do the job.
- Avoid tight grasp.
- Avoid pressure against the radial side of each finger (thumb side).
- Avoid strong and constant pressure against the pad of the thumb.

REFERENCES

Melvin, J.L., 1989. Joint-protection and energy-conservation instruction. In *Rheumatic disease in the adult and child: Occupational therapy and rehabilitation*, 3d ed., ed. J.L. Melvin, 419–37. Philadelphia: F.A. Davis.
Pedretti, L.W., J.H. Hittle, and M.C. Kasch. 1990. Rheumatoid arthritis. In *Occupational therapy: Practice skills for physical dysfunction*, 3d ed., ed. L.W. Pedretti and B. Zoltan, 458–73. St. Louis: C.V. Mosby.
Trombly, C.A. 1990. Arthritis. In *Occupational therapy for physical dysfunction*, 3d ed., ed. C.A. Trombly, 543–54. Baltimore, MD: Williams & Wilkins.
For additional resources, see the resource bibliography on Media, Modalities, and Techniques in Appendix D.

MUSCLE TONE

Hypotonia
The person has diminished or lost deep tendon reflexes, has less than normal resilience or resistance to movement (limbs feel heavy when moved), has muscles that feel flabby and soft when palpated, and may have instability or laxity of joints and weakened or lost reflexive or voluntary motion.

Severe Hypotonia
The person exhibits an inability to resist gravity, lack of cocontraction at proximal joints for stability, weakness, limited voluntary movements. For passive movement, there is joint hyperextensibility, no resistance to movement imposed by examiner, full or excessive passive range of motion.

Moderate Hypotonia
There is a decreased tone primarily in axial muscles and proximal muscles of the extremities, which interferes with the rate of development and length of time a posture can be sustained. For passive movement, there is mild resistance to movement when imposed by an examiner in distal parts of extremities only, and joint hyperextensibility at elbows and knees.

Mild Hypotonia
A decreased tone interferes with axial muscle cocontraction, and delays initiation of movement against gravity and speed of adjustment to postural change. For passive movement, there is mild resistance in proximal as well as distal segments, and a full passive range of motion.

Normal Tone

There is quick and immediate postural adjustment during movement. The ability to use muscles in synergistic and reciprocal patterns for stability and mobility depends on task of the movement. For passive movement, body parts resist displacement, momentarily maintain new posture when placed in space, and can rapidly follow changing movements improved by examiner.

Hypertonicity

The person has hyperactive deep tendon reflexes; has resistance to passive motion or quick stretch of a joint when motion is against the involved muscle's action; has movements that are linked into total body patterns that prevent isolated joint motion, reduce the variability of active joint motion, and decrease relative consistency of strength and joint range; has isolated joint motions that are slow, weak, inefficient, and uncoordinated, especially in reciprocal movements; has inability to produce stabilizing and mobilizing components for skilled motor performance, and when conscious effort is used, the effort reinforces hypertonus and abnormal movement patterns.

Mild Hypertonus

The increased tone causes delay in postural adjustment, poor coordination, and slowness of movement. For passive movement, there is resistance to change of posture in part or throughout the range, and poor ability to accommodate to passive movements.

Moderate Hypertonus

An increased tone limits speed, coordination, a variety of movement patterns, and active range of motion. For passive movement, there is resistance to change of posture throughout the range, and limited passive range of motion at some joints.

Severe Hypertonus

A severe stiffness of muscles in stereotyped patterns limits the active range of motion. There is little or no ability to move against gravity, and very limited patterns of movement. The passive range of motion is limited. The person is unable to overcome resistance of muscle to complete the full range of motion.

Intermittent Tone

The person exhibits an occasional and unpredictable resistance to postural changes alternating with normal adjustment and may have difficulty initiating active movement or sustaining posture. For passive movement, there is an unpredictable resistance to imposed movements alternating with a complete absence of resistance.

Source: Adapted from Wilson, J.M. 1984. Cerebral palsy. In *Pediatric neurologic physical therapy*, ed. S.K. Campbell, 363. New York: Churchill Livingstone (Clinics in Physical Therapy, v.5); and Neufeld, P.S. 1981. Neurobehavioral evaluation and management. In *Physical disabilities manual*, ed. B. Abreu, 135–6. New York: Raven Press.

CATEGORIES OF REFLEXES

Primitive or Primary Reflexes

These reflexes are involuntary responses, usually present at birth, that affect posture and movement. Generally these reflexes are gradually suppressed or they integrate as higher control centers mature. All are assumed to be mediated at the brainstem level. The most commonly discussed reflexes are:

1. Moro Response or Reflex
   a. This response is elicited by extending the infant's head backwards, which results in an extension of the head, neck, and arms followed by a flexion or "embrace" posture.
   b. The Moro should integrate between three to five months of age.
   c. If the Moro remains active, it decreases sitting balance since the neck extension is transferred to the spine, resulting in the person slipping forward out of a chair.
   d. The Moro can be inhibited by keeping the head and neck in neutral or slight anterior flexion and keeping the hips and legs flexed.

2. Asymmetrical Tonic Neck Reflex (ATNR)
   a. The ATNR is elicited by turning the head to one side. The face limb is extended while the skull limb is flexed in the so-called "fencer's position." The lower limbs may follow a similar pattern.
   b. The ATNR should integrate between three to five months, except when the infant is asleep.
   c. Initially, the ATNR is useful in helping the infant look at his or her hand and experience eye-hand coordination, but if the ATNR remains active, it interferes with bringing the hands together at the midline of the body for such activities as eating or using both hands. Also structural changes may occur, such as scoliosis and hip subluxation due to the asymmetrical posture.
   d. The ATNR may be inhibited by positioning the person with the head in the midline in any of the following positions: sidelying, supine with legs flexed at about 100 degrees over a bolster, prone with arms extended over a bolster, sitting with legs extended at 160 to 180 degrees in front of the body.

3. Tonic Labyrinthine Reflex, Supine (TLR, supine)
   a. The TLR, supine, is elicited when the labyrinth (and head) are in the supine position, which results in extension of the neck and legs, retraction of the shoulders, and variable positions of the arms.
   b. The TLR, supine, usually integrates between one to three months, permitting lifting of the head or head righting.
   c. If the TLR, supine, remains active it is difficult for the person to lift his or her head from the supporting surface.
   d. The TLR, supine, can be inhibited by flexing the head, neck, and legs. Generally it is best to avoid this position when possible by using the sidelying position.

4. Tonic Labyrinthine Reflex, Prone (TLR, prone)
   a. The TLR, prone, is elicited when the labyrinth (and head) is in the prone position, which results in flexion of the neck, arms, and legs.
   b. The TLR, prone, usually integrates between one to three months, permitting lifting of the head or head righting.
   c. If the TLR, prone, remains active, it is difficult for the person to lift his or her head from the supporting surface.

d. The TLR, prone, can be inhibited by placing a bolster under the shoulder and a pillow or small wedge under the legs or by placing under the person a wedge long enough to accommodate the length of the body from the shoulders to the thighs. The shoulders should be positioned at the high end of the bolster and the arms permitted to extend to the floor. A wedge may be placed between the legs to keep them in abduction.

5. Symmetrical Tonic Neck Reflex, Extension (STNR, extension)
   a. The STNR, extension, is elicited when the head and neck are extended in the horizontal plane (all fours position), which results in extension of the arms and flexion of the legs.
   b. The STNR, extension, usually integrates between the fourth and sixth month.
   c. If the response is obligatory, it will interfere with creeping on all fours, kneeling, and half-kneeling needed to get to standing.
   d. The STNR, extension, can be inhibited by keeping the head in a neutral position when the person is on all fours, kneeling, or half-kneeling.

6. Symmetrical Tonic Neck Reflex, Flexion (STNR, flexion)
   a. STNR, flexion, is elicited when the head and neck are flexed in the horizontal plane (all fours position), which results in flexion of the arms and extension of the legs.
   b. The STNR, flexion, usually integrates between the fourth and sixth month.
   c. If the response is obligatory, it will interfere with creeping on all fours, kneeling, and half-kneeling needed to get to a standing position.
   d. The STNR, flexion, can be inhibited by keeping the head in a neutral position when the person is on all fours, kneeling, or half-kneeling.

7. Positive Supporting Reflex
   a. The reflex is elicited by touching the soles of the feet to a hard surface, which results in extension of the legs so they straighten out to support the body's weight.
   b. The positive supporting reflex usually integrates between six to nine months.
   c. Abnormally strong influences of the reflex will result in crossing or scissoring of the legs. If the reflex remains, walking will not be possible.
   d. The positive supporting reflex can be inhibited by placing body weight or greater on the heels of the foot before touching the soles.

Automatic Reflexes
These reflexes are not present at birth but evolve during the first two years of life and remain active throughout the lifespan in the normal individual.

1. Righting Reflexes
These reflexes assist in maintaining the position of the head, trunk, arms, and legs in proper relationship to one another and to gravity by supplying information regarding the position of the body in relationship to the up/down, right/left, straight/rotated position of the body parts. These reflexes are assumed to be mediated at the midbrain level.
   a. Labyrinthine Head-Righting Reflex
      • This reflex is responsible for keeping the head in an upright or vertical posture regardless of the position of the rest of the body.

- The reflex begins to develop at about four to six weeks and matures through the third month.
- This reflex facilitates head control as the person's body moves in space and permits the person to lift the head from prone and supine positions.
- The reflex can be stimulated by occluding the person's vision and holding the person in space in various positions. Usually this reflex is not treated directly because people do not like their vision occluded. Since the optical righting reflex usually develops at the same time, therapy is directed toward promoting the optical righting reflex and indirectly promoting the head-righting reflex.
  b. Optical Righting Reflex
     - The optical righting reflex uses vision to right the head.
     - The reflex develops between four and six weeks and matures throughout the third month.
     - It assists in orienting the head to the vertical position by righting the head and body in relation to space.
  c. Body Righting Acting on the Head
     - This reflex acts to right the head in relation to the body.
     - The reflex develops during the first two months and matures by eight months.
     - It facilitates head control in relation to the body in all positions of the body—supine, prone, sitting, on hands and knees, and standing.
  d. Neck Righting Acting on the Body (derotation righting)
     - This reflex acts to turn the body in the direction the head is turning, starting with the rotation of the shoulders, then the trunk, and then the pelvis.
     - The reflex develops between four and six months. It can be inhibited by age five.
     - It facilitates rolling from supine to prone and prone to supine.
  e. Body Righting Acting on the Body (derotation righting)
     - If the head and neck are rotated to one side, the shoulder, thorax, abdomen, hips, and legs will tend to rotate in the same direction in sequential order. The sequence may be started from the legs and hips and move up toward the neck and head.
     - The reflex starts about four to six months and becomes mature at eight to 10 months. It can be inhibited by the age of five.
     - It facilitates attainment of the sitting position, getting to the all fours position, and attaining the standing position.

2. Protective or Propping Reflexes/Reactions/Responses
  a. These reflexes are activated by rapid changes in body position to break a fall.
  b. The subtypes and age of onset are
     - Downward (sometimes called Parachute)—occurs at about four months.
     - Posterior (also called Backward)—occurs at about 10 months.
     - Lateral (also called Sideward)—occurs at about eight months.
     - Forward (sometimes called Parachute)—occurs at about seven to nine months.
  c. The reflexes are needed to protect the person in upright positions, including when sitting, kneeling, and standing.
     - Downward—The legs and arms externally rotate and abduct. The feet dorsiflex in preparation for landing. If the hips internally rotate and adduct, and the feet planter flex, the person has increased muscle tone, which is abnormal. Also if the response is asymmetrical, brain injury may have occurred on one side of the brain, or there

may be muscle weakness or peripheral nerve injury.

- Posterior—The arms extend backward at the shoulder, elbow, and wrist and the fingers are extended and abducted to break the fall. An alternate response may be one arm extended with trunk rotation. If the response is asymmetrical, brain injury may have occurred on one side of the brain, or there may be muscle weakness or peripheral nerve injury.
- Lateral—The person abducts an arm on the side opposite from the force, with abduction at the shoulder, extension of the elbow and wrist, and abduction and extension of the fingers to break the fall. Asymmetrical response may indicate brain injury, muscle weakness, or peripheral nerve injury.
- Forward—The person flexes and abducts his or her shoulder, extends elbow and wrist, and extends and abducts fingers to break the fall. Asymmetrical response may indicate brain injury, muscle weakness, or peripheral nerve injury.

d. Protective reflexes can be facilitated by pushing the person off balance in the sitting, kneeling, or standing positions in any of the four directions: downward, posterior, lateral, or forward. Note: The therapist should be prepared to catch the person if the reflex does not function or should create an environment in which it is safe to fall, such as with the use of mats.

3. Equilibrium or Tilting Reflexes/Reactions/Responses

These reflexes are activated when there is a mild change in the position of the body. Equilibrium reflexes differ from protective reflexes in that they develop in all body positions, including prone, supine, sitting, and standing positions. The proficiency increases from initial appearance at about four months in the prone position, eight months in the sitting position, and one year in the standing position. These reflexes are assumed to be mediated at the cortex level.

a. Equilibrium reflexes are activated by subtle or slow changes in the posture or position of the body.
b. The types and age of development are
- Prone—onset about six months and persists throughout life
- Supine—onset about seven to eight months and persists throughout life
- Sitting—onset about seven to eight months and persists throughout life
- All Fours—onset about nine to 12 months and persists throughout life
- Standing—onset about 12 to 21 months and persists throughout life
c. Equilibrium reflexes modify the righting (labyrinthine) reflexes. Asymmetrical responses suggest unilateral brain injury or muscle weakness.
- Prone—The person's trunk is curved away from the tilt, with the concavity of the spine upward toward the tilt; the upper arm and leg may be slightly abducted.
- Supine—The person's trunk is curved away from the tilt, with the concavity of the spine upward toward the tilt; the upper arm and leg may be slightly abducted.
- Sitting, Lateral Tilt—The body remains in an upright position flexed against the tilt, with the concavity of the spine upward, neck flexed laterally, and the head slightly rotated with the face toward the upper side. The arm and leg on the upper side are abducted while those on the lower side are adducted and extended.
- Sitting, Forward (anterior) Tilt—The body remains in an upright position with the spine extended and the limbs retracted.

- Sitting, Backward (posterior) Tilt—The body remains in an upright position with the spine flexed and the limbs slightly extended and abducted.
- All Fours, Lateral Tilt—The body is flexed against the tilt with the concavity of the spine upward. The head is slightly rotated so that the face is turned toward the upper side. The arm and leg on the upper side flex while the arm and leg on the lower side extend and abduct.
- All Fours, Anterior Tilt—The body remains in an upright position with the trunk moving posterior while the head and arms extend and the legs flex.
- All Fours, Posterior Tilt—The body remains in an upright position with the trunk moving anterior, head and elbows flex, and the shoulders and hips extend.
- Standing, Lateral Tilt—The body is flexed against the tilt with the concavity of the spine upward. The upper arm is abducted while the upper leg is flexed. The lower leg is extended to act as a strong brace.
- Standing, Anterior Tilt—The body remains in an upright position with the spine extended, displacing the body backward; the arms are extended at the shoulder but flexed at the elbows.
- Standing, Posterior Tilt—The body remains in an upright position with the spine flexed, displacing the trunk forward; the arms are flexed at the shoulders but extended at the elbows while the legs are extended.

d. Facilitation of the equilibrium reflexes can be done using a tilt board, large ball, rolls, bolsters, or t-stool (sitting surface is mounted on one peg in the center.) The person should be slowly tilted in the direction desired. The therapist should be prepared to catch the person if the reflex does not function.

Source: Based on Johnston, R.B. 1976. Motor function: normal development and cerebral palsy. In *Developmental disorders: Assessment, treatment, education*, ed. R.B. Johnston and P.R. Magrab, 15–55. Baltimore, MD: University Park Press.

FUNCTIONAL SIGNIFICANCE OF POSTURAL REFLEXES

Activity (reflex, reaction)	Assist	Interfere
Early Prone Head up	Head righting	Tonic labyrinthine, supine, and prone Asymmetrical tonic neck Symmetrical tonic neck
Early Supine Head lift	Head righting	Tonic labyrinthine, supine, and prone Asymmetrical tonic neck
Reach		Tonic labyrinthine, supine, and prone Asymmetrical tonic neck
Rolling Over	Head righting Derotation	Tonic labyrinthine, supine, and prone Asymmetrical tonic neck
Sitting Come to sit	Head righting Derotation	Asymmetrical tonic neck Tonic labyrinthine, supine, and prone

Stable sitting	Protective Equilibrium	Asymmetrical tonic neck Symmetrical tonic neck, flexed and extended Tonic labyrinthine, supine and prone Moro
Crawling		
Reciprocal crawl	Equilibrium	Symmetrical tonic neck, flexed and extended Tonic labyrinthine, supine and prone Positive supporting
Standing		
Pull to stand	Positive support	Positive supporting Asymmetrical tonic neck
Stable stand	Positive support Protective Equilibrium	Positive supporting Tonic labyrinthine, supine and prone
Ambulating		
Cruise	Equilibrium	Positive supporting
Walk	Protective Equilibrium	Positive supporting Tonic labyrinthine, supine and prone Asymmetrical tonic neck Moro
Crossing		
Midline		Tonic labyrinthine, supine and prone Asymmetrical tonic neck Symmetrical tonic neck, flexed and extended
Derotation		Tonic labyrinthine, supine and prone Asymmetrical tonic neck Neonatal neck righting (log rolling)

Source: Based on Johnston, R.B., and P.R. Magrab. 1976. *Developmental disorders: Assessment, treatment, education*. Baltimore, MD: University Park Press.

RELAXATION

Simple Techniques
1. *Deep Breathing*. Deep breath is taken through the nose or mouth, held briefly, released slowly and then another breath is taken. Counting the number of breaths taken focuses attention on breathing.
2. *Fist Tightening*. A deep breath is taken while clenching the fists, position is held for a count of three, breath is released, and fists are unclenched. Action is repeated.
3. *Stretching*. Person stands on toes, raises arms overhead (reaches for the sky or ceiling) and takes a deep breath. Position is held and then person goes limp while exhaling. Action is repeated. Technique can be done while sitting by having person extend legs and point toes. Arm position is the same.
4. *Shoulder Shrug*. Shoulders are lifted toward the ears, held for five seconds, slowly brought down, held in position, and relaxed.

Progressive Relaxation

Beginning with either the top or bottom of the body, a group of muscles is tightened while taking a deep breath and then relaxed while breath is released. The routine may be altered to begin with a group of muscles that are causing discomfort. In either case the routine progresses through groups of muscles until attention has been paid to all parts of the body. The procedure is called a "script" and may be done while sitting, standing, or lying down. The person may memorize the script, have it tape recorded, or have it read. Total length of time may be a few minutes to half an hour.

Imagery

The person begins by visualizing a peaceful scene or fantasizing being in a peaceful setting. Some people may need to write their script while others may prefer to tape record it. Eventually the script is memorized. For persons who need ideas to get started, some examples may be useful, such as lying on the sand at a favorite beach, floating like a balloon looking down at the earth, sitting by a brook in the woods, listening to the birds sing on an early spring morning, resting on a soft cloud gazing at the blue sky, or fishing in a lake on a lazy afternoon. The procedure then follows a theme from progressive relaxation.

Visualization

The person focuses on getting rid of or plucking the tension or pain from a tense or painful part of the body and sending it away. Technique is similar to imagery except for the localization of the problem. For example, the person might visualize plucking the pain from a knee joint, putting it in a brook, and watching it bubble away or take the tension from a headache, put it on a balloon, and watch it sail away.

Meditation

The person selects a word, object, or body part on which to focus or center. The person then centers or concentrates on the selected target while sitting and breathes deeply and regularly. A quiet environment is usually helpful when learning the technique.

Self-Hypnosis

To prepare for self-hypnosis, the person is told by the therapist to concentrate on an object or on breathing. When a state of hypnosis has been achieved, a suggestion is given to the person, such as "Picture yourself floating on a soft cloud and begin to relax...." After practicing several times, the person will be able to self-recall the image and begin relaxing without help from another person.

Biofeedback

The person practices a relaxation technique as described above but is observing the relaxation response in muscles through an audiovisual response from the biofeedback machine. Usually, training begins in a clinic by a trained therapist, but after the person has learned the technique, the training may be used at home. The therapist then monitors the person's progress in using the technique.

REFERENCES

Hansen, M., and G. Ritter. 1989. *Understanding stress: strategies for a healthier mind and body*. Rockville, MD: American Occupational Therapy Association.

Lysaght, R., and E. Bodenhamer. 1990. The use of relaxation training to enhance function outcomes in adults with traumatic head injuries. *American Journal of Occupational Therapy* 44(9):797–802.

McCormack, G. 1988. Pain management by occupational therapists. *American Journal of Occupational Therapy* 42(9):582–90.

(See also Resource Bibliography—Media, Modalities, and Techniques on Relaxation and Stress Management in Appendix D.)

SELF-CARE TECHNIQUES

Bathing and Toileting

- Use long-handled sponge or brush to soap body (range of motion).
- Use reacher to hold toilet paper for wiping (range of motion).
- Use a tub or shower bench or webbed plastic lawn chair to permit sitting in tub or shower (energy conservation).
- Put nonskid safety strips or rubber bathmat on tub or shower floor to avoid slipping (safety).
- Consider installing grab bars to assist in climbing in and out of the tub or shower (safety).
- Use a long shower spray hose to make rinsing easier (range of motion).
- Use a terry cloth robe to soak up water on body; pat the body dry (energy conservation).
- Install a grab bar on the wall or floor next to the toilet to assist in sitting and standing (safety).
- Use electric toothbrushes or Water-Piks instead of manual toothbrushes (energy conservation).
- Use a device that holds the dental floss rather than using fingers (fine motor).
- Use the heel of hand to squeeze the toothpaste tube instead of fingers (fine motor).

REFERENCES

Malick, M.H. 1988. Activities of daily living and homemaking. In *Willard and Spackman's occupational therapy*, 7th ed., ed. H.L. Hopkins and H.A. Smith, 258-71. Philadelphia: J.B. Lippincott.

Pedretti, L.W. 1990. Activities of daily living. In *Occupational therapy: Practice skills for physical dysfunction*, 3d ed., ed. L.W. Pedretti and B. Zoltan, 230-71. St. Louis: C.V. Mosby.

Ritt, B.J., and J.J. McColey. 1981. Functional living skills. In *Comprehensive rehabilitation nursing*, ed. N. Martin, N.B. Holt, and D. Hicks, 299–357. New York: McGraw-Hill.

Shah, M., R. Avidan, and R.D. Sine. 1988. Self-care training: Hemiplegia, lateralized stroke program, parkinsonism, arthritis, and spinal cord dysfunction. In *Basic rehabilitation techniques: A self-instructional guide*, ed. R.D. Sine, et al., 153–89. Gaithersburg, MD: Aspen Publishers, Inc.

Trombly, C.A., and L.A. Quintana. 1990. Activities of daily living. In *Occupational therapy for physical dysfunction*, 3d. ed., ed. C.A. Trombly, 386–410. Baltimore, MD: Williams & Wilkins.

Cooking/Meal Preparation

- Microwave ovens save time and energy, can be placed at a convenient height, and are safer to use because the food heats rather than the container (energy conservation, range of motion, safety).

- Avoid lifting heavy pans of food and water. Either remove the food first by ladling the contents out or use a fry basket inside the pot so the food is separate from the water (energy conservation, safety).
- Use lightweight cooking utensils, bowls, and dishes. Avoid cast-iron skillets and heavy ceramic bowls (joint protection).
- Use a jar opener that grips the lid, permitting the person to use both hands to turn the jar itself (joint protection).
- Use an electric can opener to open cans rather than a manual one (energy conservation, one handed).
- Select appliances with controls that are easy to operate; that is, their location is easy to reach and the action is easy to engage or stop (safety, range of motion, energy conservation).
- Organize canned goods within easy reach and place labels so they can be easily read (range of motion, energy conservation).
- Plan meals that are easy to fix and easy to clean up. Consider frozen meals, one pot meals, ready mixes, and convenience foods (energy conservation).
- Serve foods in the same containers in which they were prepared (energy conservation).
- Use throwaway utensils, paper plates, and cups to reduce dishwashing (energy conservation).
- Use a dishwasher that is easy to load rather than manually washing dishes (energy conservation).
- Cook a double portion and freeze the extra portion for easier preparation of a meal on a day that will be busier than most (energy conservation).
- Use pans with nonstick surfaces or spray with nonstick product to reduce clean-up time (energy conservation).
- Line containers with aluminum foil or put aluminum foil on a cookie sheet to prevent sticking to the surface to reduce clean-up time (energy conservation).
- Use a hook (cup holder hook on the end of a dowel or bent coat hanger) to pull out a hot oven shelf (safety).
- Use mitt pot holders so palms can be used to lift pans and bowls instead of fingers (joint protection).
- Place heavy containers, such as flour and sugar, where they do not need to be lifted to get small quantities, or buy smaller quantities (joint protection).
- Place bowls on a nonskid surface (wet washrag, wet terry cloth towel, certain types of plastic mats) so that both hands can be used to stir (joint protection).
- Use a food processor for recipes that require foods to be chopped, sliced, or grated.
- Use a spray to rinse dishes and pour water into cooking pans immediately after use to avoid food drying to the surface before cleaning (energy conservation).

REFERENCE

Pedretti, L.W. 1990. Activities of daily living. In *Occupational therapy: Practice skills for physical dysfunction.* 3d ed., ed. L.W. Pedretti and B. Zoltan, 230–71. St. Louis: C.V. Mosby.

Dressing: Clothing, Shoes
- Sew Velcro on clothing to replace small buttons. Sew the button on the top side (fine motor manipulation).

- Sew elasticized thread on button cuffs to provide give for fingers to slide through (fine motor).
- Buy clothes that are easy to put on (range of motion). Get front fasteners and elastic bands that slip over hips.
- Buy clothes that are easy to care for (energy conservation).
- Lower the rod in the closet for easier reach (range of motion).
- Use long-handled shoe horn to assist in putting on shoes (range of motion).
- Use elastic shoe laces that can remain tied (fine motor).
- Place large rings, thread, or leather loops on zipper tabs to facilitate zipping (fine motor).
- Fasten bra in front and then turn it around and pull in place or get front closure bras (range of motion).
- Use reacher or dressing stick to assist with pulling up pants, straightening skirts, or getting clothes slightly out of reach (range of motion).
- Use powder on legs before putting on pantyhose to reduce friction (fine motor).
- Buy low heels—no higher than 1-inch shoes (safety).
- Cushion plantar surface with shoe inserts (safety).
- Look for shoes with soft upper material that gives or stretches to relieve pressure (safety).

REFERENCES

Malick, M.H. 1988. Activities of daily living and homemaking. In *Willard and Spackman's occupational therapy*, 7th ed., ed. H.L. Hopkins and H.A. Smith, 258–71. Philadelphia: J.B. Lippincott.
Pedretti, L.W. 1990. Activities of daily living. In *Occupational therapy: Practice skills for physical dysfunction*, 3d ed., ed. L.W. Pedretti and B. Zoltan, 230–71. St. Louis: C.V. Mosby.
Ritt, B.J., and J.J. McColey. 1981. Functional living skills. In *Comprehensive rehabilitation nursing*, ed. N. Martin, N.B. Holt, and D. Hicks, 299–357. New York: McGraw-Hill.
Shah, M., R. Avidan, and R.D. Sine. 1988. Self-care training: Hemiplegia, lateralized stroke program, parkinsonism, arthritis, and spinal cord dysfunction. In *Basic rehabilitation techniques: A self-instructional guide*, 3d ed., ed. R.D. Sine, et al. 153–89. Gaithersburg, MD: Aspen Publishers, Inc.
Trombly, C.A., and L.A. Quintana. 1990. Activities of daily living. In *Occupational therapy for physical dysfunction*, 3d ed., ed. C.A. Trombly, 386–410. Baltimore, MD: Williams & Wilkins.
(See also Resource Bibliography—Media, Modalities, and Techniques on Clothing Adaptations and Dressing Techniques in Appendix D.)

Driving

- If possible, buy or lease a car with doors that are easy to open and close, seats that are adjustable, and storage space that is easy to reach (fine motor, grasp manipulation, and range of motion).
- Reduce low back strain by using a cushion designed to fit the curve of the back (joint protection).
- Attach loops to inside door handles so that forearm can be used to assist door closing instead of hand (joint protection).
- Attach auxiliary or wide-angle mirrors to allow for increased visibility when neck motion is limited (range of motion).
- Get a handicapped sticker to permit parking closer to stores (energy conservation).
- Drive and shop when energy level is highest, such as when medication effect is at a peak (energy conservation).
- Shop with family or friends who can carry items (joint protection).

- Avoid peak shopping and traffic hours that will lengthen time standing in line or moving through traffic (energy conservation).
- Shop by telephone or mail when possible (energy conservation).
- Keep shopping trips short by planning what and where to buy. Call ahead to make sure items are available, if unsure (energy conservation).
- If tired after shopping for groceries, bring perishable items in first. Other items can wait until later after a nap (energy conservation).

REFERENCES

Pedretti, L.W., and B. Zoltan, eds. 1990. *Occupational therapy: Practice skills for physical dysfunction*, 3d. ed. St. Louis: C.V. Mosby.

Trombly, C.A., ed. 1990. *Occupational therapy for physical dysfunction*, 3d ed. Baltimore, MD: Williams & Wilkins.

Eating/Feeding

- Enlarge or build up handles for easier grasp (fine motor, grasp manipulation). Foam curlers, washrags secured with tape, or commercial designs may be used. Applies to forks, knives, spoons, spatulas, or any device with a handle.
- Extend or lengthen the handle for restricted range of motion (range of motion).
- Rocker knife or spooks (spoon and fork combined) may be used for persons with only one functioning hand (one handed).
- Small diameter glasses, such as juice glasses, may be useful for persons with limited grasp (fine motor, grasp manipulation).
- Use nonbreakable items (safety).
- Use a friction or nonskid surface (Dycem, suction cup or wet washrag) for persons using one hand or who have uncontrolled movements (one handed; tremor, spastic or athetoid movements).
- Use cups with handles large enough to insert fingers for persons with poor grasp (fine motor, grasp manipulation).
- Use a plate guard for persons using one hand or who have uncontrolled movements to keep food on plate and aid in getting food on eating utensil (one handed; tremor, spastic or athetoid movements).
- Use long straw for persons with limited range of motion (range of motion).
- Use sandwich holders for persons with uncontrolled movements or high level paralysis (tremor, spastic, or athetoid movement; paralyzed).
- Use a utensil cuff for person with limited or no grasp (fine motor, grasp manipulation).
- Use swivel utensils that stay level regardless of the position of the hand, wrist, or forearm for persons with restricted motions (range of motion).
- Use bent handles for persons with limited motion patterns (range of motion). May be combined with extended and enlarged handles.

REFERENCES

Malick, M.H. 1988. Activities of daily living and homemaking. In *Willard and Spackman's occupational therapy*, 7th ed., ed. H.L. Hopkins and H.A. Smith, 258–71. Philadelphia: J.B. Lippincott.

Pedretti, L.W. 1990. Activities of daily living. In *Occupational therapy: Practice skills for physical dysfunction*, 3d ed., ed. L.W. Pedretti and B. Zoltan, 230–71. St. Louis: C.V. Mosby.

Ritt, B.J., and J.J. McColey. 1981. Functional living skills. In *Comprehensive rehabilitation nursing*, ed. N. Martin, N.B. Holt, and D. Hicks, 299–357. New York: McGraw-Hill.

Shah, M., R. Avidan, and R.D. Sine. 1988. Self-care training: Hemiplegia, lateralized stroke program, parkinsonism, arthritis, and spinal cord dysfunction. In *Basic rehabilitation techniques: A self-instructional guide*, 3d ed., ed. R.D. Sine, et al., 153–89. Gaithersburg, MD: Aspen Publishers, Inc.

Trombly, C.A., and L.A. Quintana. 1990. Activities of daily living. In *Occupational therapy for physical dysfunction*, 3d ed., ed. C.A. Trombly, 386–410. Baltimore, MD: Williams & Wilkins.

Grooming

- Sit on a stool to apply makeup or shave. Prop elbows on the counter top, if possible (energy conservation).
- Allow enough time to groom "in phases" to permit short rest breaks (energy conservation).
- Use long-handled attachments to combs or brushes to reduce need to reach arms over shoulder height (range of motion, energy conservation).
- Enlarge handles on makeup items, combs, brushes, toothbrush with foam curlers to make grasp easier (fine motor, grasp manipulation).
- Squeeze toothpaste using the palm of the hand on a flat surface rather than with fingers (fine motor, grasp manipulation).
- Take short showers or baths using warm, not hot water when getting ready to go out. Save longer showers or baths for bedtime (energy conservation).

REFERENCES

Malick, M.H. 1990. Activities of daily living and homemaking. In *Willard and Spackman's occupational therapy*, 7th ed., ed. H.L. Hopkins and H.A. Smith, 358–71. Philadelphia: J.B. Lippincott.

Pedretti, L.W. 1990. Activities of daily living. In *Occupational therapy: Practice skills for physical dysfunction*, 3d ed., ed. L.W. Pedretti and B. Zoltan, 230–71. St. Louis: C.V. Mosby.

Ritt, B.J., and J.J. McColey. 1981. Functional living skills. In *Comprehensive rehabilitation nursing*, ed. N. Martin, N.B. Holt, and D. Hicks, 299–357. New York: McGraw-Hill.

Shah, M., R. Avidan, and R.D. Sine. 1988. Self-care training: Hemiplegia, lateralized stroke program, parkinsonism, arthritis, and spinal cord dysfunction. In *Basic rehabilitation techniques: A self-instructional guide*, 3d ed., ed. R.D. Sine, et al., 153–89. Gaithersburg, MD: Aspen Publishers, Inc.

Trombly, C.A., and L.A. Quintana. 1990. Activities of daily living. In *Occupational therapy for physical dysfunction*, 3d ed., ed. C.A. Trombly, 386–410. Baltimore, MD: Williams & Wilkins.

Housekeeping

- Keep cleaning supplies in each area where they will be needed to reduce walking with loads or put cleaning supplies in easy to reach containers and place on a movable cart that can be wheeled about the house (energy conservation).
- Use a short stool to sit on to clean low-level surfaces, such as the tub, toilet bowl, or floor (energy conservation).
- Use long-handled or create extended handles for sponges, dustpans, mops, or small brooms to reduce the need for stretching and bending (energy conservation, range of motion).
- Use an ironing board that can be adjusted to permit sitting while ironing (energy conservation). Better yet, buy clothes that require little, if any, ironing.

- Use a front loading washing machine, if possible. Clothes can be dumped out when wet and heavy rather than lifted (joint protection).
- Arrange to shop for groceries with someone who can carry the groceries from the car into the house or check to see if delivery service is available and affordable. Volunteers may be available to shop (energy conservation, joint protection).
- For light switches on lamps, buy enlarged knobs or a device that allows lamps to be turned on and off by touching them (fine motor, grasp manipulation).
- Casters on furniture make moving the furniture easier when vacuuming (joint protection).

REFERENCES

Malick, M.H. 1988. Activities of daily living and homemaking. In *Willard and Spackman's occupational therapy*, 7th ed., ed. H.L. Hopkins and H.A. Smith, 258–71. Philadelphia: J.B. Lippincott.

Pedretti, L.W. 1990. Activities of daily living. In *Occupational therapy: Practice skills for physical dysfunction*, 3d ed., ed. L.W. Pedretti and B. Zoltan, 230–71. St. Louis: C.V. Mosby.

Trombly, C.A. 1990. Homemaking and child care. In *Occupational therapy for physical dysfunction*, 3d ed., ed. C.A. Trombly, 411–21. Baltimore, MD: Williams & Wilkins.

References for Occupational Therapy Tests

TESTS FOR THE AGED

Activities of Daily Living (ADL) Situation Test

Skurl, E., J.C. Rogers, and T. Sunderland. 1988. Direct assessment of activities of daily living in Alzheimer's disease: A controlled study. *Journal of the American Geriatrics Society* 36(2):97–103.

Activity Assessment

Crepeau, E.L.B. 1989. The process of activity assessment in geriatrics. *Topics in Geriatric Rehabilitation* 4(4):31–44.

Boston Diagnostic Aphasia Examination

Farver, P.F., and T.B. Farver. 1982. Performance of normal older adults on tests designed to measure parietal lobe functions. *American Journal of Occupational Therapy* 36(7):444–9.
Goodglass, H., and E. Kaplan. 1972. *Assessment of aphasia and related disorders*. Philadelphia: Lea and Febiger.

Clinical Dementia Rating Scale (CDR)

Hughes, C.P., L. Berg, W.L. Danziger, et al. 1982. A new clinical scale for the staging of dementia. *British Journal of Psychiatry* 140:566–572.
Skurl, E., J.C. Rogers, and T. Sunderland. 1988. Direct assessment of activities of daily living in Alzheimer's disease: A controlled study. *Journal of the American Geriatrics Society* 36(2):97–103.

Functional Assessment Scale

Breines, E. 1988. The Functional Assessment Scale as an instrument for measuring changes in levels of function of nursing home residents following occupational therapy. *Canadian Journal of Occupational Therapy* 55(3):135–40.
Breines, E. 1983. *Functional Assessment Scale*. Lebanon, NJ: Geri-Rehab, Inc.

Hooper Visual Organization Test

Farver, P.F., and T.B. Farver. 1982. Performance of normal older adults on tests designed to measure parietal lobe functions. *American Journal of Occupational Therapy* 36(7):444–9.
Hooper, H.E. 1958. *The Hooper Visual Organization Test.* Los Angeles: Western Psychological Services.

Household Management Screening Assessment

Olin, D.W. 1984. Assessing and assisting the persons with dementia: An occupational behavior perspective. *Physical and Occupational Therapy in Geriatrics* 3(4):25–32.

Interest Checklist

Katz, N. 1988. Interest checklist: A factor analytical study. *Occupational Therapy in Mental Health* 8(1):45–55.
Kelley, F.A. 1986. The occupational therapist's role in geropsychiatry interdisciplinary team evaluation. *Physical and Occupational Therapy in Geriatrics* 4(3):81–94.
Olin, D.W. 1984. Assessing and assisting the persons with dementia: An occupational behavior perspective. *Physical and Occupational Therapy in Geriatrics* 3(4):25–32.
Rogers, J.C. 1986. The NPI Interest Checklist. In *Mental health assessment in occupational therapy*, ed. B.J. Hemphill, 93–114. Thorofare, NJ: Slack, Inc.

Leng Rating Scale

Leng, N.R.C., S.R. Tylor, and O. Hanely. 1988. A rating scale for assessing elderly patients. *British Journal of Occupational Therapy* 51(2):160–2.

Life Satisfaction Index (LSI)

Maguire, G.H. 1983. An exploratory study of the relationship of valued activities to the life satisfaction of elderly person. *Occupational Therapy Journal of Research* 3(3):164–72.
Wood, V., M.L. Wylie, and B. Sheafer. 1969. Analysis of a short self-report measure of life satisfaction. Correlation with rater judgment. *Journal of Gerontology* 24:405–09.

Meaningfulness of Activity Scale

Gregory, M. 1983. Occupational behavior and life satisfaction among retirees. *American Journal of Occupational Therapy* 37:548–53.
Weeder, T.C. 1986. Comparison of temporal patterns and meaningfulness of the daily activities of schizophrenic and normal adults. *Occupational Therapy in Mental Health* 6(4):27–48.

Modified Needs Satisfaction Schedule

Tickle, L.S., and E.J. Yerxa. 1981. Need satisfaction of older persons living in the community and in institutions, Part 1. The environment. *American Journal of Occupational Therapy* 35(10):644–9.

Need Satisfaction of Activity Interview

Tickle, L.S., and E.J. Yerxa. 1981. Need satisfaction of older persons living in the community and in institutions, Part 2. Role of activity. *American Journal of Occupational Therapy* 35(10):650–5.

Occupational Therapy Assessment of Older Adults with Depression

Rogers, J.C. 1986. Occupational therapy assessment for older adults with depression: Asking the right questions. *Physical and Occupational Therapy in Geriatrics* 5(1):13–33.

Parachek Geriatric (Behavior) Rating Scale

Miller, E.R., and J.F. Parachek. 1974. Validation and standardization of a goal-oriented, quick screening geriatric scale. *Journal of the American Geriatrics Society* 22(6):278–83.

Parachek, J.F., and L.J. King. 1986. *Parachek geriatric rating scale and treatment manual*, 3d rev. Phoenix, AZ: Center for Neuro-developmental Studies, 8434 North 39th Ave.

Rogers, J.C., C.I. Marcus, and T.L. Snow. 1987. Case report—Maude: A case of sensory deprivation. *American Journal of Occupational Therapy* 41(10):673–77.

Philadelphia Geriatric Center Morale Scale

Lawton, M.P. 1975. The Philadelphia Geriatric Morale Scale. A revision. *Journal of Gerontology* 30:85–9.

Ray, R.O., M.L. Gissal, and E.L. Smith. 1982. The effect of exercise on morale of older adults. *Physical and Occupational Therapy in Geriatrics* 2(2):53–62.

Poppelreuter Superimposed Figures Test

Farver, P.F., and T.B. Farver. 1982. Performance of normal older adults on test designed to measure parietal lobe functions. *American Journal of Occupational Therapy* 36(7):444–9.

Teuber, H.L. 1950. Neuropsychology. In *Recent advances in diagnostic psychological testing*, ed. R.A. Harris, 30–52. Springfield, IL: Charles C Thomas.

Riverdale Hospital's Home and Community Skills Assessment

Brown, H. 1988. The standardization of the Riverdale Hospital's Home and Community Skills Assessment. *Canadian Journal of Occupational Therapy* 55(1):9–14.

Rivermead Perceptual Assessment Battery

Cockburn, J., G. Bhavnani, S.E. Whiting, et al. 1982. Normal performance on some tests of perception in adults. *British Journal of Occupational Therapy* 45(2):67–8.

Cramond, H.J., M.S. Clark, and D.S. Smith. 1989. The effect of using the dominant or nondominant hand on performance of the Rivermead Perceptual Assessment Battery. *Clinical Rehabilitation* 3(3):215–21.

Edmans, J.A. 1987. The frequency of perceptual deficits after stroke. *Clinical Rehabilitation* 1:273–81.

Edmans, J.A., and N.B. Lincoln. 1989. Treatment of visual perceptual deficit after stroke: Four single case studies. *International Disabilities Studies* 11:25–33.

Lincoln, N.B., and D. Clarke. 1987. The performance of normal elderly people on the Rivermead Perceptual Assessment Battery. *British Journal of Occupational Therapy* 50(5):156–7.

Lincoln, N.B., et al. 1987. An evaluation of perceptual retraining. *International Rehabilitation Medicine* 7:273–81.

Lincoln, N.B., and J.A. Edmans. 1989. A shortened version of the Rivermead Perceptual Assessment Battery. *Clinical Rehabilitation* 3:199–204.

Whiting, S.E., et al. 1985. *The Rivermead Perceptual Assessment Battery*. Windsor, England: NFER Nelson, 1985.

Role Change Assessment

Jackoway, I.S., J.C. Rogers, and T.L. Snow. 1987. The Role Change Assessment: An interview tool for evaluating older adults. *Occupational Therapy in Mental Health* 7(1):17–37.

Satisfaction with Performance Scaled Questionnaire (SPSQ)

Yerxa, E.J., et al. 1988. Development of the Satisfaction with Performance Scaled Questionnaire (SPSQ). *American Journal of Occupational Therapy* 42(4):215–21.

Screening for Physical and Occupational Therapy Referral (SPOTR)

Woosley, T., D.E. Sands, and W. Dunlap. 1987. An instrument to screen sensory impaired persons for referral to physical and occupational therapy. *Journal of Rehabilitation* 53(4):66–9.

Short Portable Mental Status Questionnaire (SPMSQ)

Pfeiffer, E.A. 1975. A short portable mental status questionnaire for the assessment of organic brain deficit in elderly patients. *Journal of the American Geriatrics Society* 23:433–41.

Skurl, E., J.C. Rogers, and T. Sunderland. 1988. Direct assessment of activities of daily living in Alzheimer's disease: A controlled study. *Journal of the American Geriatrics Society* 36(2):97–103.

Stanford Health Assessment Questionnaire

Baron, M., et al. 1987. Hand function in the elderly: Relation to osteoarthritis. *Journal of Rheumatology* 14(4):815–9.

Fries, J.F., P. Spitz, and P.G. Kraines. 1980. Measurement of patient outcome in arthritis. *Arthritis and Rheumatology* 23:137–45.

Wolfe, F., et al. 1988. The clinical value of the Stanford Health Assessment Questionnaire Functional Disabilities Index in patients with rheumatoid arthritis. *Journal of Rheumatology* 15(10):1480–88.

PEDIATRIC TESTS

Activity Cards Gross Motor Scale

Kramer, L.A., T.K. Crowe, J.C. Deitz. 1988. Effect of activity level on Southern California Postrotary Nystagmus Test scores. *Occupational Therapy Journal of Research* 8(6): 345–55.

Amiel-Tison Neurologic Evaluation

Amiel-Tison, C. 1986. *Neurological assessment during the first year of life.* New York: Oxford University Press.

Amiel-Tison, C. 1983. *Neurological evaluation of the newborn and the infant.* New York: Masson Publishing Co.

McCarraher-Wetzel, A.P., and R.C. Wetzel. 1984. A review of the Amiel-Tison Neurologic Evaluation of the Newborn and Infant. *American Journal of Occupational Therapy* 38(9): 585–93.

ATNR Rating Scale

Parmenter, C.L. 1983. An asymmetrical tonic neck reflex rating scale. *American Journal of Occupational Therapy* 37(7):462–5.

Zemke, R. 1985. Application of an ATNR rating scale to normal preschool children. *American Journal of Occupational Therapy* 39(3):178–80.

Assessment of Preterm Infant's Behavior

Als, H. 1986. A synactive model of neonatal behavioral organization: Framework for the assessment of neurobehavioral development in the premature infant and for support of infants and parents in the neonatal intensive care environment. *Physical and Occupational Therapy in Pediatrics* 6(3/4):3–53.

Assessment of Sensorimotor Integration in Preschool Children (ASIPC) See Test of Sensory Integration

Harris, S.R. 1984. The relationship between tests of sensorimotor integration, tactile sensitivity and gross motor skills in normal and developmentally delayed preschool children. *Physical and Occupational Therapy in Pediatrics* 4(2):5–18.

Bayley Scales of Infant Development

Anzalone, M. 1988. Neonatal outcome: From clinical result to research. *Developmental Disabilities Special Interest Section Newsletter* 11(3):1–3.

Bayley, N. 1969. *Bayley Scales of Infant Development.* New York: Psychological Corporation.

Crowe, T.K., J.C. Deitz, and F.C. Bennett. 1987. The relationship between the Bayley Scales of Infant Development and preschool gross motor and cognitive performance. *American Journal of Occupational Therapy* 41(6):374–8.

Schnider, J.W., and E.A. Brannen. 1984. A comparison of two developmental evaluation tools used to assess children with Down's syndrome. *Physical and Occupational Therapy in Pediatrics* 4(4):19–29.

Valvano, J., and G.A. DeGangi. 1986. Atypical posture and movement findings in high risk pre-term infants. *Physical and Occupational Therapy in Pediatrics* 6(2):71–81.

Behavioral Assessment Scale of Oral Functions

Ottenbacher, K., et al. 1985. Reliability of the Behavioral Assessment Scale of Oral Functions in feeding. *American Journal of Occupational Therapy* 39(7):434–40.

Stratton, M. 1981. Behavioral Assessment Scale of Oral Functions in feeding. *American Journal of Occupational Therapy* 35:719–21.

Bender Visual Motor Gestalt Test

Bender, L. 1939. *Bender Visual Motor Gestalt Test*. New York : American Orthopsychiatric Association.

Watson, P.J., et al. 1982. Visual motor difficulties in emotionally disturbed children with hyporesponsive nystagmus. *Physical and Occupational Therapy in Pediatrics* 2(2/3): 67–72.

Brazelton Neonatal Behavioral Assessment Scale

Brazelton, T.B. 1973. *Neonatal Behavioral Assessment Scale*. Clinics in Developmental Medicine no. 50. Philadelphia: J.B. Lippincott.

Brazelton, T.B. 1984. *Neonatal Behavioral Assessment Scale*, 2d ed. Clinics in Developmental Medicine no. 88. Philadelphia: J.B. Lippincott.

Clopton, N., and A.S. Martin. 1984. A criticism of interrater reliability procedure for the Brazelton Neonatal Behavioral Assessment Scale. *Physical and Occupational Therapy in Pediatrics* 4(4):55–65.

DeGangi, G.A. 1982. The relationship of vestibular responses and developmental functions in high risk infants. *Physical and Occupational Therapy in Pediatrics* 2(2/3):35–49.

Lydic, J.S., and J.K. Nugent. 1982. Theoretical background for and uses of the Brazelton Neonatal Behavioral Assessment Scale. *Physical and Occupational Therapy in Pediatrics* 2(2/3):117–31.

Bruininks-Oseretsky Test of Motor Proficiency

Bruininks, R. 1978. *Bruininks-Oseretsky Test of Motor Proficiency*. Circle Pines, MN: American Guidance Service

Palisano, R.J. 1989. Comparison of two methods of service delivery for students with learning disabilities. *Physical and Occupational Therapy in Pediatrics* 9(3):79–100.

Stewart, K.B., and J.C. Deitz. 1986. Motor development in children with Sotos' cerebral gigantism. *Physical and Occupational Therapy in Pediatrics* 6(1):41–53.

Ziviani, J., A. Poulsen, and A. O'Brien. 1982. Correlation of the Bruininks-Oseretsky Test of Motor Proficiency with the Southern California Sensory Integration Tests. *American Journal of Occupational Therapy* 36(8):519–23.

DeGangi-Berk Test of Sensory Integration

DeGangi, G.A., and R.A. Berk. 1983. Psychometric analysis of the Test of Sensory Integration. *Physical and Occupational Therapy in Pediatrics* 3(2):43–60.

DeGangi, G.A., and R.A. Berk. 1983. *DeGangi-Berk Test of Sensory Integration.* San Antonio, TX: Psychological Corporation.

Royeen, C.B. 1988. Review of the DeGangi-Berk test of sensory integration. *Physical and Occupational Therapy in Pediatrics* 8(2/3):71–5.

Denver Developmental Screening Test (DDST)

Campbell, S.K., and L.J. Wilhelm. 1982. Development of infants at risk for central nervous system dysfunction. *Physical and Occupational Therapy in Pediatrics* 2(1):61–62.

Diamond, K.E., and W.G. Le Furgy. 1988. Screening for developmental handicaps: outcomes from an early childhood screening program. *Physical and Occupational Therapy in Pediatrics* 8(1):43–59.

Frankenburg, W.F., J. Dodds, and A. Fandal. 1975. *Denver Developmental Screening Test Revised.* Denver, CO: Ladoca Publishing Foundation.

Niparko, N. 1982. The effect of prematurity on performance on the Denver Developmental Screening Test. *Physical and Occupational Therapy in Pediatrics* 2(1):29–50.

Slavik, B.A. 1982. Vestibular function in children with nonparalytic strabismus. *Occupational Therapy Journal of Research* 3(4):220–33.

Developmental Indicators for the Assessment of Learning—Revised

Mardell-Czudnowski, C., and D. Goldenberg. 1983. *Developmental Indicators for the Assessment of Learning—Revised.* Edison, NJ: Childcraft.

Miller, L.J., and T.A. Srong. 1987. A comparison of the Miller Assessment for Preschoolers and Developmental Indicators for the Assessment of Learning—Revised. *Physical and Occupational Therapy in Pediatrics* 7(1):57–69.

Developmental Test of Visual-Motor Integration (VMI)

Beery, K.E., and N.A. Bukenica. 1982. *Developmental Test of Visual-Motor Integration.* Cleveland, OH: Modern Curriculum Press.

Lederer, J.M., G. Kielhofner, and J.H. Watts. 1985. Values, personal causation and skills of delinquents and nondelinquents. *Occupational Therapy in Mental Health* 5(2):59–77.

Oliver, C.E. 1990. A sensorimotor program for improving writing readiness skills in elementary-age children. *American Journal of Occupational Therapy* 44(2):111–6.

Watson, P.J., et al. 1982. Visual motor difficulties in emotionally disturbed children with hyporesponsive nystagmus. *Physical and Occupational Therapy in Pediatrics* 2(2/3): 67–72.

Diagnosis and Remediation of Handwriting Problems

Daniels, L.E. 1988. The Diagnosis and Remediation of Handwriting Problems: An analysis. *Physical and Occupational Therapy in Pediatrics* 8(1):61–7.

Stott, D.H., F.A. Moyes, and S.E. Henderson. 1985. *Diagnosis and Remediation of Handwriting Problems*. Guelph, Ontario, Canada: Brook Educational Publishing Ltd., P.O. Box 1171.

Erhardt Developmental Prehension Assessment (EDPA)

Dunn, W. 1983. Critique of the Erhardt Developmental Prehension Assessment (EDPA). *Physical and Occupational Therapy in Pediatrics* 3(4):59–68.
Erhardt, R. 1984. *Erhardt Developmental Prehension Assessment*. Phoenix, AZ: Therapy Skill Builders.

Feeding Interaction Report—Scale and Treatment (FIRST)

Sparling, J.W., and J.C. Rogers. 1985. Feeding assessment: Development of a biopsychosocial instrument. *Occupational Therapy Journal of Research* 5(1):3–23.

Frostig Developmental Test of Visual Perception (FDTVP)

Frostig, M., P. Maslow, D.W. Lefever, and J.R.B. Whittlesey. 1966. *Frostig Developmental Test of Visual Perception*. Palo Alto, CA: Consulting Psychology Press.
Kelly, G. 1983. The Frostig Test: A review. *British Journal of Occupational Therapy* 46(9): 252–4.
Mitcham, M. 1982. Visual perception and its relationship to an activity of daily living. *Occupational Therapy Journal of Research* 2(4):245–6.

Gesell Developmental Schedules—Revised

Knoblock, H. 1980. *Manual of developmental diagnosis: The administration and interpretation of the revised Gesell and Amatruda Developmental and Neurologic Examination*. New York: Harper & Row.
Schneider, J.W., and E.A. Brannen. 1984. A comparison of two developmental evaluation tools used to assess children with Down's syndrome. *Physical and Occupational Therapy in Pediatrics* 4(4):19–29.

Goodenough-Harris Draw-A-Person Test

Goodenough, F., and D.B. Harris. 1963. *Goodenough-Harris Drawing Test*. San Antonio, TX: Psychological Corporation.
Slansky, L., and M.A. Short-DeGraff. 1989. Validity and reliability issues with human figure drawing assessment. *Physical and Occupational Therapy in Pediatrics* 9(3):127–42.

Griffiths Mental Developmental Scales

Griffiths, R. 1954. *The abilities of babies*. New York: McGraw-Hill.
Harris, S.R. 1983. Comparative performance levels of female and male infants with Down's syndrome. *Physical and Occupational Therapy in Pediatrics* 3(2):15–21.

Home Observation for Measurement of Environment (HOME)

Caldwell, B.M., R.H. Bradley, et al. 1984. *Home Observation for Measurement of*

Environment (HOME). College of Education, University of Arkansas at Little Rock: Center for Child Development and Education.

Huber, C.J. 1982. Critique of the screening test HOME (Home Observation for Measurement of Environment). *Physical and Occupational Therapy in Pediatrics* 2(1):63–74.

Illinois Test of Psycholinguistic Abilities

Clark, F.A. 1982. The Illinois Test of Psycholinguistic Abilities: Considerations of its use in occupational and physical therapy practice. *Physical and Occupational Therapy in Pediatrics* 2(4):29–39.

Kirk, S.A., J.J. McCarthy, and W.D. Kirk. 1968. *Illinois Test of Psycholinguistic Abilities (ITPA).* Champaign, IL: University of Illinois Press.

Interpersonal Awareness Test

Davidson, D.A., M.A. Short, and D.L. Nelson. 1984. The measurement of empathic ability in normal and atypical five and six year old boys. *Occupational Therapy in Mental Health* 4(4):13–24.

KIDS + 3 Chart (Kansas Infant Development Screen)

Holmes, G.E., and R.S. Hassanein. 1987. The KIDS + 3 chart: Development screen for two to five-year-old children: A preliminary study. *Physical and Occupational Therapy in Pediatrics* 7(4):19–38.

Knickerbocker Sensorimotor History Questionnaire

Carrasco, R.C. 1990. Reliability of the Knickerbocker Sensorimotor History Questionnaire. *Occupational Therapy Journal of Research* 10(5):280–2.

Knickerbocker, B.M. 1980. The Sensorimotor History. In *A Holistic Approach to the Treatment of Learning Disorders,* ed. B.M. Knickerbocker, 349–60. Thorofare, NJ: Charles B. Slack.

Milani-Comparetti Motor Development Screening Test

Ellison, P., et al. 1983. Development of a scoring system for the Milani-Comparetti and Gidoni method of assessing neurologic abnormality in infancy. *Physical Therapy* 63(9): 1414–23.

Kliewer, D., et al. 1977. *The Milani-Comparetti Motor Development Screening Test.* Omaha, NE: Meyer Children's Rehabilitation Institute.

VanderLinden, D. 1985. Ability of the Milani-Comparetti developmental examination to predict motor outcome. *Physical and Occupational Therapy in Pediatrics* 5(1):27–38.

Miller Assessment for Preschoolers (MAP)

Banus, B.J. 1983. The Miller Assessment for Preschoolers (MAP): An introduction and review. *American Journal of Occupational Therapy* 37(5):333–40.

Bracken, B.A. 1987. Limitations of preschool instruments and standards for minimal levels of technical adequacy. *Journal of Psychoeducational Assessment* 5(4):313–26.

Daniels, L.E., and S. Bressler. 1990. The Miller Assessment for Preschoolers: Clinical use with children with developmental delays. *American Journal of Occupational Therapy* 44(1):48–53.

Daniels, L. 1990. The Miller Assessment for Preschoolers: Analysis of score patterns for children with developmental delays. *Canadian Journal of Occupational Therapy* 57(4):205–10.

DeGangi, G.A. 1983. A critique of the standardization of the Miller Assessment for Preschoolers. *American Journal of Occupational Therapy* 37(6):407–11.

Denning, J., and W. Mayberry. 1987. Vestibular dysfunction in preschool children with a history of otitis media. *Occupational Therapy Journal of Research* 7(6):335–48.

Miller, L.J. 1982. *Miller Assessment for Preschoolers*. Littleton, CO: The Foundation for Knowledge in Development.

Miller, L.J., and P.A. Lemerand. 1986. Neuromaturational variables with the Miller Assessment for Preschoolers. *Occupational Therapy Journal of Research* 6(2):123–5.

Miller, L.J., and T.A. Sprong. 1986. Psychometric and qualitative comparison of four preschool screening instruments. *Journal of Learning Disabilities* 19(8):480–4.

Miller, L.J. 1987. Response to "A critique of the standardization of the Miller Assessment for Preschoolers" (letter) *American Journal of Occupational Therapy* 41(8):537–8.

Miller, L.J., and T.A. Sprong. 1987. A comparison of the Miller Assessment for Preschoolers and Developmental Indicators for the Assessment of Learning—Revised. *Physical and Occupational Therapy in Pediatrics* 7(1):57–69.

Miller, L.J., P.A. Lemerand, and S.H. Cohn. 1987. A summary of three predictive studies with the MAP. *Occupational Therapy Journal of Research* 7(6):378–81.

Miller, L.J. 1987. Longitudinal validity of the Miller Assessment for Preschoolers: I. *Perceptual and Motor Skills* 65(1):211–7.

Miller, L.J. 1988. Longitudinal validity of the Miller Assessment for Preschoolers: Study II. *Perceptual and Motor Skills* 66(3):811–4.

Miller, L.J., and P.G. Schouten. 1988. Age-related effects on the predictive validity of the Miller Assessment for Preschoolers. *Journal of Psychoeducational Assessment* 6(2):99–106.

Miller, L.J. 1988. Differentiating children with school-related problems after four years using the Miller Assessment for Preschoolers. *Psychology in the Schools* 25(1):10–5.

Provost, B., et al. 1988. A comparison of scores on two preschool assessment tools: Implications for theory and practice. *Physical and Occupational Therapy in Pediatrics* 8(4):35–51.

Slaton, D.S. 1985. The Miller Assessment for Preschoolers: A clinician's perspective. *Physical and Occupational Therapy in Pediatrics* 5(1):65–70.

Widerstrom, A.H., L.J. Miller, and R.J. Marzano. 1986. Sex and race differences in the identification of communicative disorders in preschool children as measured by the Miller Assessment for Preschoolers. *Journal of Communication Disorders* 19(3):219–26.

Motor Development Checklist

Doudlah, A. 1976. *A motor development checklist*. Madison, WI: Central Wisconsin Center for the Developmentally Disabled, 317 Knutson Drive.

Gevelinger, M., K.J. Ottenbacher, and T. Tiffany. 1988. The reliability of the Motor Development Checklist. *American Journal of Occupational Therapy* 42(2):81–6.

Motor-Free Visual Perception Test

Bouska, M.J. 1985. Application of the motor-free visual perception test. *Physical Disabilities Special Interest Section Newsletter* 8(1):6–7.

Bouska, M.J., and E. Kwatny. 1980. *Manual for application of the motor-free visual perception test to the adult population.* PO Box 12246, Philadelphia, PA: Authors.

Calarusso, R.P., and D.D. Hammill. 1972. *The Motor-Free Visual Perception Test (MVPT),* San Rafael, CA: Academic Therapy Publications.

Eimon, M.C., P.L. Eimon, and S.A. Cermak. 1983. Performance of schizophrenic patients on a motor-free visual perception test. *American Journal of Occupational Therapy* 37(5):327–32.

Reid, D., and S. Drake. 1990. A comparative study of visual perceptual skills in normal children and children with diplegic cerebral palsy. *Canadian Journal of Occupational Therapy* 57(3):141–6.

Movement Assessment of Infants (MAI)

Campbell, S.K. 1982. Movement Assessment of Infants: An evaluation. *Physical and Occupational Therapy in Pediatrics* 1(4):53–7.

Chandler, L.S., M.S. Andres, and M.W. Swanson. 1980. *Movement Assessment of Infants: A manual.* Rolling Bay, WA: Infant Movement Research.

Deitz, J.C., T.K. Crowe, and S.R. Harris. 1987. Relationship between infant neuromotor assessment and preschool motor measures. *Physical Therapy* 67(1):14–7.

Haley, S.M., et al. 1986. Item reliability of the Movement Assessment of Infants. *Physical and Occupational Therapy in Pediatrics* 6(1):21–39.

Harris, S.R., et al. 1984. Predictive validity of the Movement Assessment of Infants. *Journal of Developmental and Behavioral Pediatrics* 5:337–42.

Lydic, J.S., M.A. Short, and D.L. Nelson. 1983. Comparison of two scales for assessing motor development in infants with Down's syndrome. *Occupational Therapy Journal of Research* 3(4):213–221.

Lydic, J.S., et al. 1985. Effects of controlled rotary vestibular stimulation on the motor performance of infants with Down syndrome. *Physical and Occupational Therapy in Pediatrics* 5(2/3).

Neonatal Oral Motor Assessment Scale (NOMAS)

Braun, M.A., and M.M. Palmer. 1986. A pilot study of oral-motor dysfunction in "at-risk" infants. *Physical and Occupational Therapy in Pediatrics* 5(4):13–25.

Case-Smith, J., P. Cooper, and V. Scala. 1989. Feeding efficiency of premature neonates. *American Journal of Occupational Therapy* 43(4):245–50.

Neurological Assessment of the Preterm and Full-Term Infant

Dubowitz, L., and V. Dubowitz. 1981. *The Neurological Assessment of the Preterm and Full-term Newborn Infant.* Clinics in Developmental Medicine. No. 79, Philadelphia: J.B. Lippincott.

Dubowitz, L., V. Dubowitz, P.G. Palmer, et al. 1984. Correlation of neurologic assessment in the preterm newborn infant with outcome at 1 year. *Journal of Pediatrics* 105:452–6.

Pelletier, J., and J.S. Lydic. 1986. Neurological assessment of the preterm and full-term newborn infant: An analysis. *Physical and Occupational Therapy in Pediatrics* 6(1): 93–104.

Sweeney, J.K. 1986. Physiological adaptation of neonates to neurological assessment. *Physical and Occupational Therapy in Pediatrics* 6(3/4):155–69.

Neuromotor Evaluation

Laegreid, J.M., C.D. Lew, and J.M. Walker. 1988. Neuromotor behavior and cardio-respiratory responses of premature infants with bronchopulmonary dysplasia. *Physical and Occupational Therapy in Pediatrics* 8(1):15–42.

Oral Speech Mechanism Screening Examination

Knobeloch, C. 1982. Critique of the Oral Speech Mechanism Screening Examination. *Physical and Occupational Therapy in Pediatrics* 2(4):43–51.

Oromotor Feeding Assessment

Johnson, L.M. 1986. Development of an oromotor feeding assessment. *Occupational Therapy Journal of Research* 6(6):377–9.

Peabody Developmental Motor Scales

Crowe, T.K., J.C. Deitz, F.C. Bennett, et al. 1988. Preschool motor skills of children born prematurely and diagnosed as having cerebral palsy. *Journal of Developmental and Behavioral Pediatrics* 9(4):189–93.

Deitz, J.C., and T.K. Crowe. 1985. Developmental status of children exhibiting postrotary nystagmus durations of zero seconds. *Physical and Occupational Therapy in Pediatrics* 5(2–3):69–79.

Folio, R., and R.R. Fewell. 1983. *Peabody Developmental Motor Scales.* Allen, TX: DLM Teaching Resources.

Harris, S.R. 1984. The relationship between tests of sensorimotor integration, tactile sensitivity and gross motor skills in normal and developmentally delayed preschool children. *Physical and Occupational Therapy in Pediatrics* 4(2):5–18.

Jenkins, J.R., et al. 1982. Effects of developmental therapy on motor impaired children. *Physical and Occupational Therapy in Pediatrics* 2(4):19–28.

Kramer, L.A., T.K. Crowe, and J.C. Deitz. 1988. Effect of activity level on Southern California Postrotary Nystagmus Test scores. *Occupational Therapy Journal of Research* 8(6):345–55.

Kramer, L.A., J.C. Deitz, and T.K. Crowe. 1988. A comparison of motor performance of preschoolers enrolled in mental health programs and non-mental health programs. *American Journal of Occupational Therapy* 42(8):520–5.

Lydic, J.S., M.A. Short, and D.L. Nelson. 1983. Comparison of two scales for assessing motor development in infants with Down's syndrome. *Occupational Therapy Journal of Research* 3(4):213–221.

Lydic, J.S., M.M. Windsor, M.A. Short, et al. 1985. Effects of controlled rotary vestibular stimulation on the motor performance of infants with Down syndrome. *Physical and Occupational Therapy in Pediatrics* 5(2–3):93–118.

Palisano, R.J., and J.S. Lydic. 1984. The Peabody Developmental Motor Scales: An analysis. *Physical and Occupational Therapy in Pediatrics* 4(1):69–75.

Palisano, R.J., M.A. Short, and D.L. Nelson. 1985. Chronological vs. adjusted age in assessing motor development of healthy twelve-month-old premature and fullterm infants. *Physical and Occupational Therapy in Pediatrics* 5(1):1–16.

Provost B., et al. 1988. A comparison of scores on two preschool assessment tools: Implication for theory and practice. *Physical and Occupational Therapy in Pediatrics* 8(4):35–51.

Stokes, N.A., J.L. Deitz, and T.K. Crowe. 1990. The Peabody Developmental Fine Motor Scale: An interrater reliability study. *American Journal of Occupational Therapy* 44(4):334–40.

Peabody Individual Achievement Test

Dunn, L.M., and F.C. Markwardt. 1970. *Peabody Individual Achievement Test*. Circle Pines, MN: American Guidance Service.

Polatajko, H.J. 1987. Visual-ocular control of normal and learning-disabled children. *Developmental Medicine and Child Neurology* 29:477–85.

Peabody Picture Vocabulary Test

Davidson, D.A., M.A. Short, and D.L. Nelson. 1984. The measurement of empathic ability in normal and atypical five and six year old boys. *Occupational Therapy in Mental Health* 4(4):13–24.

Dunn, L.M., and L.M. Dunn. 1981. *Peabody Picture Voabulary Test—Revised (PPVT-R)*. Circle Pines, MN: American Guidance Services.

Piers-Harris Children's Self-Concept Scale

Piers, E.V., and D.B. Harris. 1984. *Piers-Harris Children's Self-Concept Scale*. Los Angeles: Western Psychological Services.

Zemke, R., S. Knuth, and J. Chase. 1984. Change in self-concepts of children with learning difficulties during a residential camp experience. *Occupational Therapy in Mental Health* 4(4):1–12.

Play History

Behnke, C.J., and M.M. Fetkovich. 1984. Examining the reliability and validity of the Play History. *American Journal of Occupational Therapy* 38(2):94–100.

Takata, N. 1974. Play as a prescription. In *Play as exploratory learning*, ed. M. Reilly, 209–46. Beverly Hills, CA: Sage Publishing Co.

Play Scale

Bledsoe, N.P., and J.T. Shepherd. 1982. A study of reliability and validity of a preschool play scale. *American Journal of Occupational Therapy* 36(12):783–8.

Knox, S. 1974. A play scale. In *Play as exploratory learning*, ed. M. Reilly, 247–66. Los Angeles: Sage Publishing Co.

Posture and Fine Motor Assessment of Infants

Case-Smith, J. 1989. Reliability and validity of the posture and fine motor assessment of infants. *Occupational Therapy Journal of Research* 9(5):259–72.

Preschool Language Scale (PLS)

Short, M.A., and G.N. Fincher. 1983. Intercorrelations among three preschool screening instruments. *Occupational Therapy Journal of Research* 3(3):180–2.

Purdue Perceptual-Motor Survey

Roach, E.G., and N.C. Kephart. 1966. *Purdue Perceptual-Motor Survey*. Columbus, OH: Merrill.

Zemke, R., S. Knuth, and J. Chase. 1984. Change in self-concepts of children with learning difficulties during a residential camp experience. *Occupational Therapy in Mental Health* 4(4):1–12.

Quick Neurological Screening Test

Ingolia, P., S.A. Cermak, and D. Nelson. 1982. The effect of choreoathetoid movements on the Quick Neurological Screening Test. *American Journal of Occupational Therapy* 35(12):801–7.

Mutti, M., H.M. Sterling, and N.V. Spalding. 1978. *QNST: Quick Neurological Screening Test manual* (rev. ed.). Novato, CA: Academic Therapy Publishing Co.

Screening for Physical and Occupational Therapy Referral (SPOTR)

Woosley, T., D.E. Sands, and W. Dunlap. 1987. An instrument to screen sensory impaired persons for referral to physical and occupational therapy. *Journal of Rehabilitation* 53(4): 66–9.

Sensorimotor Integration Test Battery

Jongbloed, L.E., J.B. Collins, and W. Jones. 1986. A Sensorimotor Integration Test Battery for CVA clients: Preliminary evidence of reliability and validity. *Occupational Therapy Journal of Research* 6(3):157–70.

Ottenbacher, K.J., and D. Goar. 1986. Commentary: "A Sensorimotor Integration Test Battery for CVA clients: Preliminary evidence of reliability and validity." *Occupational Therapy Journal of Research* 6(3):151–6.

Sensory Developmental Expectation Questionnaire

Parush, G., and F. Clark. 1988. The reliability and validity of a sensory developmental expectation questionnaire for mothers of newborns. *American Journal of Occupational Therapy* 42(1):11–6.

Sensory Integration and Praxis Tests

Ayres, A.J. 1989. *Sensory Integration and Praxis Tests*. Los Angeles: Western Psychological Services.

Cermak, S.A., M.L. Morris, and J. Koomar. 1990. Praxis on verbal command and imitation. *American Journal of Occupational Therapy* 44(7):641–5.

Fanchiang, S., C. Snyder, J. Zobel-Lackiusa, et al. 1990. Sensory integrative processing in delinquent-prone and non-delinquent-prone adolescents. *American Journal of Occupational Therapy* 44(7):630–9.

Kimball, J.G. 1990. Using the Sensory Integration and Praxis Tests to measure change: A pilot study. *American Journal of Occupational Therapy* 44(7):603–8.

Mailloux, Z. 1990. An overview of the sensory integration and praxis tests. *American Journal of Occupational Therapy* 44(7):589–94.

McAtee, S., and W. Mack. 1990. Relations between design copying and other tests of sensory integrative dysfunction: A pilot study. *American Journal of Occupational Therapy* 44(7):596–601.

Murray, E.A., S.A. Cermak, and V. O'Brien. 1990. The relationship between form and space perception, constructional abilities, and clumsiness in children. *American Journal of Occupational Therapy* 44(7):623–8.

Stallings-Sahler, S. 1990. Report of an occupational therapy evaluation of sensory integration and praxis. *American Journal of Occupational Therapy* 44(7):650–3.

Stallings-Sahler, S. 1990. Certification in administration and interpretation of the Sensory Integration and Praxis Tests. *American Journal of Occupational Therapy* 44(7):655–7.

Tupper, L.C. 1990. Report of an occupational therapy evaluation using the Sensory Integration and Praxis Tests. *American Journal of Occupational Therapy* 44(7):647–9.

Sensory-Motor Appraisal

DeGangi, G.A. 1987. Critique of a sensory-motor appraisal. *Physical and Occupational Therapy in Pediatrics* 7(1):71–80.

Walingford, H. 1984. *A sensory-motor appraisal.* Centre for Sensory Motor Maximization, Suite 12, Box 33, S.S. No. 1, Sudbury, Ontario, Canada P3E 4S8.

Walingford, H., and C. Topo. 1983. *A sensory-motor appraisal: Assessment birth to 2 years.* Centre for Sensory Motor Maximization, Site 12, Box 33, S.S. No. 1, Sudbury, Ontario, Canada P3E 4S8.

Slosson Intelligence Test (SIT)

Polatajko, H.J. 1987. Visual-ocular control of normal and learning-disabled children. *Developmental Medicine and Child Neurology* 29:477–85.

Short, M.A., and G.N. Fincher. 1983. Intercorrelations among three preschool screening instruments. *Occupational Therapy Journal of Research* 3(3):180–2.

Slosson, R.L. 1983. *Slosson Intelligence Test.* East Aurora, NY. Slosson Educational Publishers.

Southern California Figure-Ground Visual Perception Test

Bieleauskas, L.A., and B.H. Newberry. 1988. Young adult norms for the Southern California Figure-Ground Visual Perception Test. *Clinical Neuropsychologist* 2(3):239–45.

Petersen, P., D. Goar, and J. Van Deusen. 1985. Performance of female adults on the Southern California Visual Figure-Ground Perception Test. *American Journal of Occupational Therapy* 39(8):525–30.

Petersen, P., and R.L. Wikoff. 1983. The performance of adult males on the Southern California Figure-Ground Visual Perception Test. *American Journal of Occupational Therapy* 37(8):554–60.

Southern California Postrotary Nystagmus Test

Ayres, A.J. 1975. *Southern California Postrotary Nystagmus Test.* Los Angeles: Western Psychological Services.

Becker, M.S. 1982. Level of sensory integrative functioning in children of Vietnam veterans exposed to Agent Orange. *Occupational Therapy Journal of Research* 2(4):234–44.

Clayton, K., et al. 1986. The effects of rotary movement on nystagmus in normal 4 year olds. *Occupational Therapy Journal of Research* 6(1):47–8.

Clyse, S.J., and M.A. Short. 1983. The relationship between dynamic balance and postrotary nystagmus in learning disabled children. *Physical and Occupational Therapy in Pediatrics* 3(3):25–32.

Cohen, H. 1989. Testing vestibular function: Problems with the Southern California Postrotary Nystagmus Test. *American Journal of Occupational Therapy* 43(7):475–7.

Crowe, T.K., J.C. Deitz, and C.G. Siegner. 1984. Postrotary nystagmus response of normal four-year-old children. *Physical and Occupational Therapy in Pediatrics* 4(2):19–28.

DeGangi, G.A. 1982. The relationship of vestibular responses and developmental functions in high risk infants. *Physical and Occupational Therapy in Pediatrics* 2(2/3):35–49.

Deitz, J.C., and T.K. Crowe. 1985. Developmental status of children exhibiting postrotary nystagmus durations of zero seconds. *Physical and Occupational Therapy in Pediatrics* 5(2/3):69–79.

Dutton, R.E. 1985. Reliability and clinical significance of the Southern California Postrotary Nystagmus Test. *Physical and Occupational Therapy in Pediatrics* 5(2/3):57–67.

Kennedy, K.S. 1983. The Southern California Postrotary Nystagmus Test: Development of a revised procedure for use with preschool children. *Occupational Therapy Journal of Research* 3(2):93–103.

Kramer, L.A., T.K. Crowe, and J.C. Deitz. 1988. Effect of activity level on Southern California Postrotary Nystagmus Test scores. *Occupational Therapy Journal of Research* 8(6):345–55.

Montgomery, P.C., and D.M. Rodel. 1982. Effect of state on nystagmus duration on the Southern California Postrotary Nystagmus Test. *American Journal of Occupational Therapy* 36(3):177–82.

Morrison, D., and J. Sublett. 1983. Reliability of the Southern California Postrotary Nystagmus Test with learning-disabled children. *American Journal of Occupational Therapy* 37(10):694–8.

Nelson, D.L., et al. 1984. The Southern California Postrotary Nystagmus Test and electronystagmography under different conditions of visual input. *American Journal of Occupational Therapy* 38(8):535–40.

Ottenbacher, K. 1982. Patterns of postrotary nystagmus in three learning-disabled children. *American Journal of Occupational Therapy* 36(10):657–63.

Pettit, K.A. 1984. The Southern California Postrotary Nystagmus Test: Test-retest reliability for a chronic, psychiatric patient population. *Sensory Integration Special Interest Section Newsletter* 7(2):1,4.

Polatajko, H.J. 1983. The Southern California Postrotary Nystagmus Test: A validity study. *Canadian Journal of Occupational Therapy* 50(4):119–23.

Punwar, A. 1982. Expanded normative data: Southern California Postrotary Nystagmus Test. *American Journal of Occupational Therapy* 36(3):183–7.

Royeen, C.B. 1984. Incidence of hypoactive nystagmus among behaviorally disordered children. *Occupational Therapy Journal of Research* 4(31):237–40.

Short, M.A., et al. 1983. Vestibular-proprioceptive functions in 4 year olds: Normative and regression analyses. *American Journal of Occupational Therapy* 37(2):102–9.

Siegner, D.B., T.K. Crowe, and J.D. Deitz. 1982. Interrater reliability of the Southern California Postrotary Nystagmus Test. *Physical and Occupational Therapy in Pediatrics* 2(2/3):83–91.

Utley, E., K. Pettit, and D. Robertson. 1983. Southern California Postrotary Nystagmus test: Adult normative data. *Occupational Therapy in Mental Health* 3(4):29–34.

Watson, P.J., et al. 1982. Visual motor difficulties in emotionally disturbed children with hyporesponsive nystagmus. *Physical and Occupational Therapy in Pediatrics* 2(2/3):67–72.

Weiss-Lambrou, R., S. Messier, and U. Maag. 1988. Montreal normative data for the Southern California Postrotary Nystagmus Test. *Canadian Journal of Occupational Therapy* 55(4):200–5.

Wiss, T., and F. Clark. 1990. Validity of the Southern California Postrotary Nystagmus Test: Misconceptions lead to incorrect conclusions. *American Journal of Occupational Therapy* 44(7):658–60.

Zee-Chen, E.L., and M.L. Hardman. 1983. Postrotary nystagmus response in children with Down's syndrome. *American Journal of Occupational Therapy* 37(4):260–5.

Southern California Sensory Integration Tests (SCSIT)

Ayres, A.J. 1972. *Southern California Sensory Integration Tests, Revised.* Los Angeles: Western Psychological Services.

Becker, M.S. 1982. Level of sensory integrative functioning in children of Vietnam veterans exposed to Agent Orange. *Occupational Therapy Journal of Research* 2(4):234–44.

Cermak, S.A., and A.J. Ayres. 1984. Crossing the body midline in learning-disabled and normal children. *American Journal of Occupational Therapy* 38(1):35–9.

Falk-Kessler, J., M.S. Quittman, and R. Moore. 1988. The SCSIT: A potential tool for assessing neurological impairment in adult psychiatric outpatients. *Occupational Therapy Journal of Research* 8(3):131–46.

Gliner, J.A., and C.G. Davis. 1982. The effects of movement speed and initial position on movement reproduction accuracy. *Occupational Therapy Journal of Research* 4(3): 181–92.

Saeki, K., F.A. Clark, and S.P. Azen. 1985. Performance of Japanese and Japanese-American children on the Motor Accuracy-Revised and Design Copying Tests of the Southern California Sensory Integration Tests. *American Journal of Occupational Therapy* 39(2):103–9.

Schwartz, R.K. 1984. Commentary: "The effects of movement speed and initial position on movement reproduction accuracy." *Occupational Therapy Journal of Research* 4(3): 193–7.

Smith, S.M. 1983. Performance difference between hands in children on the motor accuracy test-revised. *American Journal of Occupational Therapy* 37(2):96–101.

Stilwell, J.M. 1987. The development of manual midline crossing in 2- to 6-year-old children. *American Journal of Occupational Therapy* 41(12):783–9.

Su, R.V., and E.J. Yerxa. 1984. Comparison of the motor tests of the SCSIT and the L-NNBC. *Occupational Therapy Journal of Research* 4(2):96–108.

Yerxa, E.J. 1982. A response to testing and measurement in occupational therapy: A review of current practice with special emphasis on the Southern California Sensory Integration Tests. *American Journal of Occupational Therapy* 36(6):399–404.

Zemke, R., S. Knuth, and J. Chase. 1984. Change in self-concept of children with learning difficulties during a residential camp experience. *Occupational Therapy in Mental Health* 4(4):1–12.

Ziviani, J., A. Poulsen, and A. O'Brien. 1982. Correlation of the Bruininks-Oseretsky Test of Motor Proficiency with the Southern California Sensory Integration Tests. *American Journal of Occupational Therapy* 36(8):519–23.

Special Services Screening Tool (SSST)

Short, M.A., G.N. Fincher. 1983. Intercorrelations among three preschool screening instruments. *Occupational Therapy Journal of Research* 3(3):180–2.

Steps Up Developmental Screening Program

Carr, D., et al. 1981. *Steps Up Developmental Screening Program*. El Paso, TX: El Paso Rehabilitation Center.

Tactile Sensitivity Checklist (TSC)

Bauer, B.A. 1977. Tactile sensitivity: Development of a behavioral responses checklist. *American Journal of Occupational Therapy* 31:357–61.

Harris, S.R. 1984. The relationship between tests of sensorimotor integration, tactile sensitivity and gross motor skills in normal and developmentally delayed preschool children. *Physical and Occupational Therapy in Pediatrics* 4(2):5–18.

Test of In-Hand Manipulation Skills

Exner, C.E. 1990. The zone of proximal development in in-hand manipulation skill of nondysfunctional 3- and 4-year-old children. *American Journal of Occupational Therapy* 44(10):884–91.

Test of Motor Impairment

Slaton, D.S., and P.J. Nichols. 1987. Test of motor impairment: An overview. *Physical and Occupational Therapy in Pediatrics* 7(4):91–100.

Stott, D.H., F.A. Moyes, and S.E. Henderson. 1966. *Test of Motor Impairment*. Guelph, Ontario: Brook Educational Publishing, Ltd.

Stott, D.H., F.A. Moyes, and S.E. Henderson. 1984. *Test of Motor Impairment-Henderson Revision (TOMI)*. San Antonio, TX: Psychological Corporation.

Test of Motor and Neurological Functions

Connolly, B.H. 1986. Atypical posture and movement findings in high risk pre-term infants: Commentary. *Physical and Occupational Therapy in Pediatrics* 6(2):82–4.

DeGangi, G.A., R.A. Berk, and J. Valvano. 1983. Test of motor and neurological functions in high-risk infants: Preliminary findings. *Developmental and Behavioral Pediatrics* 4(3):182–9.

Valvano, J., and G.A. DeGangi. 1986. Atypical posture and movement findings in high risk pre-term infants. *Physical and Occupational Therapy in Pediatrics* 6(2):71–81.

Valvano, J., and G.A. DeGangi. 1986. Atypical posture and movment findings in high risk pre-term infants: Reply. *Physical and Occupational Therapy in Pediatrics* 6(2):84–5.

Test of Sensory Functions in Infants

DeGangi, G.A., R.A. Berk, and S.E. Greenspan. 1988. The clinical measurement of sensory functioning in infants: A preliminary study. *Physical and Occupational Therapy* 8(2/3): 1–23.

DeGangi, G.A. 1988. *Test of Sensory Functions in Infants.* Los Angeles: Western Psychological Services.

DeGangi, G.A., and S.I. Greenspan. 1988. The development of sensory functions in infants. *Physical and Occupational Therapy in Pediatrics* 8(4):21–33.

Test of Visual-Motor Skills

Gardner, M.F. 1986. *TVMS: Test of Visual-Motor Skills-Manual.* San Francisco: Children's Hospital of San Francisco.

Palisano, R.J. 1989. Comparison of two methods of service delivery for students with learning disabilities. *Physical and Occupational Therapy in Pediatrics* 9(3):79–100.

Test of Visual-Perceptual Skills

Gardner, M.F. 1982. *Test of Visual-Perceptual Skills (Non-Motor), Manual.* San Francisco: Children's Hospital of San Francisco.

Hung, S.S., A.G. Fisher, and S.A. Cermak. 1987. The performance of learning-disabled and normal young men on the test of visual-perceptual skills. *American Journal of Occupational Therapy* 41(12):790–7.

Palisano, R.J. 1989. Comparison of two methods of service delivery for students with learning disabilities. *Physical and Occupational Therapy in Pediatrics* 9(3):79–100.

Reid, D., and S. Drake. 1990. A comparative study of visual perceptual skills in normal children and children with diplegic cerebral palsy. *Canadian Journal of Occupational Therapy* 57(3):141–6.

TIP—Touch Inventory for Preschoolers

Royeen, C.B. 1987. TIP—Touch Inventory for Preschoolers: A pilot study. *Physical and Occupational Therapy in Pediatrics* 7(1):29–40.

Touch Scale

Royeen, C.B. 1986. The development of a touch scale for measuring tactile defensiveness in children. *American Journal of Occupational Therapy* 40(6):414–9.

Royeen, C.B. 1987. Test-retest reliability of a touch scale for tactile defensiveness. *Physical and Occupational Therapy in Pediatrics* 7(3):45–52.

Wechsler Preschool and Primary Scale of Intelligence (WPPSI)

Deitz, J.C., and T.K. Crowe. 1985. Developmental status of children exhibiting postrotary nystagmus durations of zero seconds. *Physical and Occupational Therapy in Pediatrics* 5(2/3):69–79.

Wechsler, D. 1967. *Wechsler Preschool and Primary Scale of Intelligence.* San Antonio, TX: The Psychological Corporation.

TESTS FOR PHYSICAL DISABILITIES

Adult Skills Evaluation Survey (ASES)

Herrick, J.T., and H.E. Lowe. 1984. Adult Skills Evaluation Survey (ASES) for persons with mental retardation. *Occupational Therapy in Health Care* 1(2):71–7.

"Apfel Hand Function Test" (no proper name)

Apfel, E. 1990. Preliminary development of a standarized hand function test. *Journal of Hand Therapy* 3(4):191–4.

Barthel Self-Care Index

Davies P., J. Bamford, and C. Warlow. 1989. Remedial therapy and functional recovery in a total population of first-stroke patients. *International Disabilities Studies* 11:40–4.

Mahoney, R.I., and D.W. Barthel. 1965. Functional evaluation: The Barthel Index. *Maryland State Medical Journal* 14:61–5.

Olin, D.W. 1984. Assessing and assisting the persons with dementia: An occupational behavior perspective. *Physical and Occupational Therapy in Geriatrics* 3(4):25–32.

Ostrow, P., et al. 1989. Functional outcomes and rehabilitation: An acute care field study. *Journal of Rehabilitation Research and Development* 26(3):17–26.

Shah, S., F. Vanclay, and B. Cooper. 1989. Predicting discharge status at commencement of stroke rehabilitation. *Stroke* 20(6):766–9.

Shah, S., F. Vanclay, and B. Cooper. 1989. Improving the sensitivity of the Barthel Index for stroke rehabilitation. *Journal of Clinical Epidemiology* 42(8):703–9.

Borg Scale of Perceived Exertion

Bloch, M.W., D.A. Smith, and D.L. Nelson. 1989. Heart rate, activity, duration, and affect in added-purpose versus single-purpose jumping activities. *American Journal of Occupational Therapy* 43(1):25–30.

Box and Block Test

Goodkin, D.W., D. Hertsgaard, and J. Seminary. 1988. Upper extremity function in multiple sclerosis: Improving assessment sensitivity with box-and-block and nine-hole peg tests. *Archives of Physical Medicine and Rehabilitation* 69(10):850–4.

Mathiowetz, V., et al. 1985. Adult norms for the Box and Block Test of manual dexterity. *American Journal of Occupational Therapy* 39(6):386–91.

Mathiowetz, V., S. Federman, and D. Wiemer. 1985. Box and block test of manual dexterity: Norms for 6–19 year olds. *Canadian Journal of Occupational Therapy* 52(5):247–9.

Brief Activities of Daily Living

Turner, A., and G.M. Humphris. 1989. A Brief Activities of Daily Living (BADL) measure to assess dependency of psychogeriatric patients with change of location. *British Journal of Occupational Therapy* 52(9):339–41.

Brunnstrom Recovery Scale

Brunnstrom, B. 1966. Motor testing procedures in hemiplegia: Based on sequential recovery stages. *Journal of the American Physical Therapy Association* 46(4):357–75.

Shah, S.K. 1984. Reliability of the original Brunnstrom recovery scale following hemiplegia. *Australian Occupational Therapy Journal* 31(4):144–51.

Cambridge Apraxia Battery

Fraser, C., and A. Turton. 1986. The development of the Cambridge Apraxia Battery. *British Journal of Occupational Therapy* 49(9):248–52.

Environmental Assessment Scale

Kannegieter, R.B. 1986. The development of the Environmental Assessment Scale. *Occupational Therapy in Mental Health* 6(3):67–83.

Extended Activities of Daily Living Scale

Nouri, R.M., and N.B. Lincoln. 1987. An extended activities of daily living scale for stroke patients. *Clinical Rehabilitation* 1:301–5.

Fitts' Tapping Test

Turton, A., and C. Fraser. 1987. The use of simple aiming task to measure recovery following stroke. *Physiotherapy* 3:117–25.

Functional Meal Preparation Scale (FMPS)

Sarno, M.R., and A. Buonaguro. 1983. Factors associated with independent meal preparation of aphasic females: A pilot study. *Occupational Therapy Journal of Research* 3(1):23–34.

Function Test

Wilson, D.J. 1984. Assessment of the hemiparetic upper extremity: A functional test. *Occupational Therapy in Health Care* 1(2):63–9.

Hand Sensitivity Test

Yerxa, E.J., et al. 1983. Development of a hand sensitivity test for the hypersensitive hand. *American Journal of Occupational Therapy* 37(3):176–81.

Jebsen Hand Function Test

Agnew, P.J., and F. Maas. 1982. Hand function related to age and sex. *Archives of Physical Medicine and Rehabilitation* 63(6):269–71.

Carlson, J.D., and C.A. Trombly. 1983. The effect of wrist immobilization on performance of the Jebsen Hand Function Test. *American Journal of Occupational Therapy* 37(3): 167–75.

Jebsen, R., N. Taylor, et al. 1969. An objective and standardized test of hand function. *Archives of Physical Medicine and Rehabilitation* 50:311–9.

Lynch, K.B., and M.J. Bridle. 1989. Validity of the Jebsen-Taylor Hand Function Test in predicting activities of daily living. *Occupational Therapy Journal of Research* 9(5): 316–8.

Rider, B., and C. Linden. 1988. Comparison of standardized and non-standardized administration of the Jebsen Hand Function Test. *Journal of Hand Therapy* 1(3):121–3.

Kenny Self-Care Evaluation

Gresham, G.E., et al. 1987. The Quadriplegia Index of Function (QIF): Sensitivity and reliability demonstrated in a study of thirty quadriplegic patients. *Paraplegia* 24:38–44.

Klein-Bell ADL Scale

Klein, R.M., and B.J. Bell. 1982. Self-care skills: Behavioral measurement with the Klein-Bell ADL scale. *Archives of Physical Medicine and Rehabilitation* 63(7)335–8.

Klein, R.M., and B. Bell. 1979. The Klein-Bell ADL Scale manual. Seattle, WA: University of Washington Medical School, Health Sciences Resource Center/SB–56.

Law, M., and R. Usher. 1988. Validation of the Klein-Bell Activities of Daily Living Scale for children. *Canadian Journal of Occupational Therapy* 55(2):63–8.

Lynch, K.B., and M.J. Bridle. 1989. Validity of the Jebsen-Taylor Hand Function Test in predicting activities of daily living. *Occupational Therapy Journal of Research* 9(5): 316–8.

Smith, R.O., M.E. Morrow, J.K. Heitman, et al. 1986. The effects of introducing the Klein-Bell ADL Scale in a rehabilitation service. *American Journal of Occupational Therapy* 40(6):420–4.

Loewenstein Occupational Therapy Cognitive Assessment (LOTCA)

Natz, N., et al. 1989. Loewenstein Occupational Therapy Cognitive Assessment (LOTCA) battery for brain-injured patients: Reliability and validity. *American Journal of Occupational Therapy* 43(3):184–92.

Verbuch, S., and N. Katz. 1988. Assessment of perceptual cognitive performance: Comparison of psychiatric and brain injured adult patients. *Occupational Therapy in Mental Health* 8(1):57–71.

Luria-Nebraska Neuropsychological Battery

Barrett, C.E. 1986. In search of brain-behavior relationships in dementia and the Luria-Nebraska Neuropsychological Battery. *Physical and Occupational Therapy in Geriatrics* 4(3):113–39.

Falk-Kessler, J., M.S. Quittman, and R. Moore. 1988. The SCSIT: A potential tool for assessing neurological impairment in adult psychiatric outpatients. *Occupational Therapy Journal of Research* 8(3):131–54.

Golden, C.J., A.D. Purisch, and T.A. Hammeke. 1979. *The Luria-Nebraska Neuropsychological Battery: A manual for clinical and experimental users.* Lincoln, NE: University of Nebraska Press.

Su, R.V., and E.J. Yerxa. 1984. Comparison of the motor tests of the SCSIT and the L-NNBC. *Occupational Therapy Journal of Research* 4(2):96–108.

Nine-Hole Peg Test

Goodkin, D.W., D. Hertsgaard, and J. Seminary. 1988. Upper extremity function in multiple sclerosis: Improving assessment sensitivity with box-and-block and nine-hole peg tests. *Archives of Physical Medicine and Rehabilitation* 69(10):850–4.

Mathiowetz, V., et al. 1985. Adult norms for the Nine Hole Peg Test of finger dexterity. *Occupational Therapy Journal of Research* 5(1):24–38.

Northwick Park ADL Index

Benjamin, J. 1976. The Northwick Park ADL Index. *British Journal of Occupational Therapy* 39(12):301–6.

Sheikh, K., D.S. Smith, T.W. Meade, et al. 1979. Repeatability and validity of a modified ADL index in studies of chronic disability. *International Rehabilitation Medicine* 60: 145–54.

Spencer, C., M. Clark, and D.S. Smith. 1986. A modification of the Northwick Park ADL Index (the Australian ADL Index). *British Journal of Occupational Therapy* 49(11): 350–3.

Occupational and Leisure Assessment for Adults with Epilepsy (OLAAE)

Day, S. 1984. Occupational therapy assessment and treatment in a hospital setting for patients with epilepsy. *Occupational Therapy in Health Care* 1(2):53–62.

Odstock Hand Assessment

Roberts, C. 1989. The Odstock Hand Assessment. *British Journal of Occupational Therapy* 52(7):256–61.

OSOT Perceptual Evaluation (Ontario Society of Occupational Therapists)

Boys, M., et al. 1988. The OSOT Perceptual Evaluation: A research perspective. *American Journal of Occupational Therapy* 42(2):92–8.

Parietal Lobe Battery

Sarno, M.R., and A. Buonaguro. 1983. Factors associated with independent meal preparation of aphasic females: A pilot study. *Occupational Therapy Journal of Research* 3(1):23–34.

Physiological Monitored Evaluation (PME)

Shanfield, K.C. 1984. Physiological monitoring: Assessment of energy cost. *Occupational Therapy in Health Care* 1(2):87–97.

Purdue Pegboard Test

Gardner, R.A., and M. Broman. 1979. The Purdue Pegboard: Normative data on 1334 school children. *Journal of Clinical Child Psychology* 7:156–62.

Mathiowetz, V., et al. 1986. The Purdue Pegboard: Norms for 14- to 19-year-olds. *American Journal of Occupational Therapy* 40(3):174–9.

Neeman, M. 1986. The Purdue Pegboard: Its predictive validity for work potential for persons with mental retardation (letter). *American Journal of Occupational Therapy* 40(6):433–4.

Tiffin, J. 1947, 1968. *Purdue Pegboard Test.* Chicago, IL: Science Research Associates.

Quadriplegia Index of Function (QIF)

Gresham, G.E., et al. 1987. The Quadriplegia Index of Function (QIF): Sensitivity and reliability demonstrated in a study of thirty quadriplegic patients. *Paraplegia* 24:38–44.

"Recovery of Voluntary Movement Control" (No exact title)

Turton, A.M., and C.M. Fraser. 1988. A test battery to measure the recovery of voluntary movement control following stroke. *British Journal of Occupational Therapy* 51(1):11–4.

Ritchie Articular Index

Bohannon, R.W., and A.W. Andrews. 1990. Shoulder subluxation and pain in stroke patients. *American Journal of Occupational Therapy* 44(6):507–9.

Riverdale Hospital's Home and Community Skills Assessment

Brown, H. 1988. The standardization of the Riverdale Hospital's Home and Community Skills Assessment. *Canadian Journal of Occupational Therapy* 55(1):9–14.

Rivermead Perceptual Assessment Battery

Cockburn, J., G. Bhaynani, S.E. Whiting, et al. 1982. Normal performance on some tests of perception in adults. *British Journal of Occupational Therapy* 45(2):67–8.

Cramond, H.J., M.S. Clark, and D.S. Smith. 1989. The effect of using the dominant or nondominant hand on performance of the Rivermead Perceptual Assessment Battery. *Clinical Rehabilitation* 3:215–21.

Edmans, J.A. 1987. The frequency of perceptual deficits after stroke. *Clinical Rehabilitation,* 1:273–81.

Edmans, J.A., and N.B. Lincoln. 1989. Treatment of visual perceptual deficit after stroke: Four single case studies. *International Disabilities Studies* 11:25–33.

Lincoln, N.B., and D. Clarke. 1987. The performance of normal elderly people on the Rivermead Perceptual Assessment Battery. *British Journal of Occupational Therapy* 50(5):156–7.

Lincoln, N.B., et al. 1987. An evaluation of perceptual retraining. *International Rehabilitation Medicine* 7:273–81.

Lincoln, N.B., and J.A. Edmans. 1989. A shortened version of the Rivermead Perceptual Assessment Battery. *Clinical Rehabilitation* 3:199–204.

Whiting, S.E., et al. 1985. *The Rivermead Perceptual Assessment Battery*. Windsor, England: NFER Nelson.

Robinson Bashal Functional Assessment

McCloy, L., and L. Jongbloed. 1987. Robinson Bashall functional assessment for arthritis patients: Reliability and validity. *Archives of Physical Medicine and Rehabilitation* 68(8):486–9.

Robinson, H.S., and D.A. Bashall. 1962. Functional assessment in rheumatoid arthritis. *Canadian Journal of Occupational Therapy* 29:123–138.

Rosenbusch Test of Finger Dexterity

Stein, C., and E.J. Yerxa. 1990. A test of fine finger dexterity. *American Journal of Occupational Therapy* 44(6):499–504.

St. Marys CVA Evaluation

Fox, J.V., and D. Harlowe. 1984. Construct validation of occupational therapy measures used in CVA evaluation: A beginning. *American Journal of Occupational Therapy* 38(2):101–6.

Harlowe, D., and J. Van Deusen. 1984. Construct validation of the St. Marys CVA evaluation: Perceptual measures. *American Journal of Occupational Therapy* 38(3): 184–6.

Van Deusen, J., and D. Harlowe. 1986. Continued construct validation of the St. Marys CVA evaluation: Brunnstrom arm and hand stage ratings. *American Journal of Occupational Therapy* 40(8):561–3.

Van Deusen, J., and D. Harlowe. 1987. Continued construct validation of the St. Marys CVA Evaluation: Bilateral Awareness Scale. *American Journal of Occupational Therapy* 41(4):242–5. Published erratum appears in *Am J Occup Ther* 41(10):637, 1987.

Van Deusen, J., L. Shalik, and D. Harlowe. 1990. Construct validation of an acute care occupational therapy cerebral vascular accident assessment tool. *Canadian Journal of Occupational Therapy* 57(3):155–9.

Schultz Structured Interview

Schultz, K.S. 1984. The Schultz Structured Interview for assessing upper extremity pain. *Occupational Therapy in Health Care* 1(3):69–82.

"Screening Tool for Cumulative Trauma Disorder"

Muffly-Elsey, D., and S. Flinn-Wagner. 1987. Proposed screening tool for the detection of cumulative trauma disorders of the upper extremity. *Journal of Hand Surgery* 12A(5 pt2):931–5.

Sensorimotor Intergration Test Battery

Jongbloed, L.E., J.B. Collins, and W. Jones. 1986. A Sensorimotor Integration Test Battery for CVA clients: Preliminary evidence of reliability and validity. *Occupational Therapy Journal of Research* 6(3):157–70.
Ottenbacher, K.J., and D. Goar. 1986. Commentary: "A Sensorimotor Integration Test Battery for CVA clients: Preliminary evidence of reliability and validity." *Occupational Therapy Journal of Research* 6(3):151–6.

Smith Hand Function Test

Baron, M., et al. 1987. Hand function in the elderly: Relation to osteoarthritis. *Journal of Rheumatology* 14(4):815–9.
Smith, H. 1973. Smith Hand Function Test. *American Journal of Occupational Therapy* 27:244–51.

Smith Physical Capacities Evaluation

Smith, S.L., S. Cunningham, and R. Weinberg. 1983. Predicting reemployment of the physically disabled worker. *Occupational Therapy Journal of Research* 3(3):178–9.
Smith, S.L., S. Cunningham, and R. Weinberg. 1986. The predictive validity of the functional capacities evaluation. *American Journal of Occupational Therapy* 40(8):564–7.

Stanford Health Assessment Questionnaire

Baron, M., et al. 1987. Hand function in the elderly: Relation to osteoarthritis. *Journal of Rheumatology* 14(4):815–9.
Fries, J.F., P. Spitz, and P.G. Kraines. 1980. Measurement of pattern outcomes in arthritis. *Arthritis and Rheumatology* 23:137–45.
Wolfe, F., et al. 1988. The clinical value of the Stanford Health Assessment Questionnaire Function Disabilities Index in patients with rheumatoid arthritis. *Journal of Rheumatology* 15(10):1480–88.

Stanford Health Assessment Disability Index (HAQ)

Cathey, M.A., F. Wolfe, and S.M. Kleinheksel. 1988. Functional ability and work status in patients with fibromyalgia. *Arthritis Care and Research* 1(2):85–98.

Third Party Assessment of Work Capabilities

Griffiths, R.D.P. 1973. A standardized assessment of the work behavior of psychiatric patients. *British Journal of Psychiatry* 113:841–6.
McPhee, S.D. 1989. A third party assessment of work capabilities. *Military Medicine* 154(2):76–80.

PSYCHIATRY/MENTAL HEALTH

Activity Configuration

Weeder, T.C. 1986. Comparison of temporal patterns and meaningfulness of the daily activities of schizophrenic and normal adults. *Occupational Therapy in Mental Health* 6(4):27–48.

Activity Pattern Indicator

Fordyce, W.E. 1978. Activity Pattern Indicator. Department of Rehabilitation Medicine, RJ–30, University of Washington School of Medicine, Seattle, WA 98195.

Larson, K.B. 1990. Activity patterns and life changes in people with depression. *American Journal of Occupational Therapy* 44(10):902–6.

Affective Self-Report Checklist

Boyer, J., et al. 1989. Affective responses to activities: A comparative study. *American Journal of Occupational Therapy* 43(2):81–8.

Allen Cognitive Level Test

David, S.K., and W.T. Riley. 1990. The relationship of the Allen Cognitive Level Test to cognitive abilities and psychopathology. *American Journal of Occupational Therapy* 44(6):493–7.

Assessment of Occupational Functioning

Brollier, C., et al. 1988. A content validity study of the assessment of occupational functioning. *Occupational Therapy in Mental Health* 8(4):29–47.

Brollier, C., et al. 1988. A concurrent validity study of two occupational therapy evaluation instruments: The AOF and OCAIRS. *Occupational Therapy in Mental Health* 8(4):49–60.

Watts, J.H., et al. 1986. The assessment of occupational functioning: A screening tool for use in long-term care. *American Journal of Occupational Therapy* 40(4):231–40.

Watts, J.H., et al. 1988. A comparison of two evaluation instruments used with psychiatric patients in occupational therapy. *Occupational Therapy in Mental Health* 8(4):7–27.

Watts, J.H., et al. 1988. The assessment of occupational functioning: The second revision. *Occupational Therapy in Mental Health* 8(4):61–88.

Barth Time Construction

Barth, T. 1986. A new variation on an old theme: The Barth Time Construction. *Mental Health Special Interest Section Newsletter* 9(1):4–5.

Barth, T. 1986. Barth Time Construction. In *Mental health assessment in occupational therapy*, ed. B.J. Hemphill, 115–29. Thorofare, NJ: Slack, Inc.

Barth, T. 1985. *Barth Time Construction*. New York: Health Related Consulting Services.

Bay Area Functional Performance Evaluation (BAFPE)

Brockett, M.M. 1987. Cultural variations in Bay Area Functional Performance evaluation scores—considerations for occupational therapy. *Canadian Journal of Occupational Therapy* 54(4):201–3.

Houston, D., and S. Williams. 1986. Use of the Bay Area Functional Performance Evaluation (BAFPE) with the depressed patient: A preliminary impression. In *Depression: Assessment & treatment update: Proceedings*. 22–35. Rockville, MD: American Occupational Therapy Association.

Houston, D., et al. 1989. The Bay Area Functional Performance Evaluation: Development and standardization. *American Journal of Occupational Therapy* 43(3):170–83.

Klyczek, J.P., and W.C. Mann. 1990. Concurrent validity of the Task-Oriented Assessment component of the Bay Area Functional Performance Evaluation with the American Association on Mental Deficiency Adaptive Behavior Scale. *American Journal of Occupational Therapy* 44(10):907–12.

Mann, W.C., J.P. Klyczek, and R.C. Fiedler. 1989. Bay Area Functional Performance Evaluation (BAFPE): Standard scores. *Occupational Therapy in Mental Health* 9(3):1–8.

Thibeault, R., and E. Blackmer. 1987. Validating a test of functional performance with psychiatric patients. *American Journal of Occupational Therapy* 41(8):515–21.

Williams, S.L., and J.S. Bloomer. 1987. *Bay Area Functional Performance Evaluation*, 2d ed. Palo Alto: Consulting Psychological Press.

Clinical Dementia Rating Scale (CDR)

Hughes, C.P., L. Berg, W.L. Danziger, et al. 1982. A new clinical scale for the staging of dementia. *British Journal of Psychiatry* 140:566–72.

Skurl, E., J.C. Rogers, and T. Sunderland. 1988. Direct assessment of activities of daily living in Alzheimer's disease: A controlled study. *Journal of the American Geriatrics Society* 36(2):97–103.

Edwards Personal Preference Schedule (EPPS)

Baldwin, L.C., and C.H. Christiansen. 1985. Self as known and self as knower: Testing an insight/empathy hypothesis. *Occupational Therapy Journal of Research* 5(2):125–8.

Edwards, A.L. 1959. *Edwards Personal Preference Schedule*. San Antonio, TX: Psychological Corp.

Environmental Assessment Scale

Kannegieter, R.B. 1986. The development of the Environmental Assessment Scale. *Occupational Therapy in Mental Health* 6(3):67–83.

House-Tree-Person Test

Buck, J.N. 1981. *House-Tree-Person (H-T-P) projective technique: A revised manual.* Los Angeles: Western Psychological Services.

Polatajko, H., and E. Kaiserman. 1986. House-Tree-Person projective technique: A validation of its use in occupational therapy. *Canadian Journal of Occupational Therapy* 53(4):197–207.

Interest Checklist

Katz, N. 1988. Interest checklist: A factor analytical study. *Occupational Therapy in Mental Health* 8(1):45–55.

Kelley, F.A. 1986. The occupational therapist's role in geropsychiatry interdisciplinary team evaluation. *Physical and Occupational Therapy in Geriatrics* 4(3):81–94.

Olin, D.W. 1984. Assessing and assisting the persons with dementia: An occupational behavior perspective. *Physical and Occupational Therapy in Geriatrics* 3(4):25–32.

Rogers, J.C. 1986. The NPI Interest Checklist. In *Mental health assessment in occupational therapy*, ed. B.J. Hemphill, 93–114. Thorofare, NJ: Slack, Inc.

Interpersonal Awareness Test

Davidson, D.A., M.A. Short, and D.L. Nelson. 1984. The measurement of empathic ability in normal and atypical five and six year old boys. *Occupational Therapy in Mental Health* 4(4):13–24.

Kohlman Evaluation of Living Skills

McGourty, L.K. 1986. Kohlman Evaluation of Living Skills (KELS). In *Mental health assessment in occupational therapy*, ed. B.J. Hemphill, 131–46. Thorofare, NJ: Slack, Inc.

McGourty, L.K. 1979. *Kohlman Evaluation of Living Skills*. Seattle, WA: KELS Research, Box 33201.

Radonsky, V.E., et al. 1986. Step ahead—occupational therapy in the community. *Occupational Therapy in Mental Health* 6(2):79–87.

Meaningfulness of Activity Scale

Gregory, M. 1983. Occupational behavior and life satisfaction among retirees. *American Journal of Occupational Therapy* 37:548–53.

Weeder, T.C. 1986. Comparison of temporal patterns and meaningfulness of the daily activities of schizophrenic and normal adults. *Occupational Therapy in Mental Health* 6(4):27–48.

Magazine Picture Collage

Stugess, J. 1983. The magazine picture collage: A suitable basis for a pre-fieldwork teaching clinic. *Occupational Therapy in Mental Health* 3(1):43–53.

Milwaukee Evaluation of Daily Living Skills

Leonardelli, C.A. 1986. The process of developing a quantifiable evaluation of daily living skills in psychiatry. *Occupational Therapy in Mental Health* 6(4):17–26.

Leonardelli, C.A. 1986. The Milwaukee Evaluation of Daily Living Skills (MEDLS). In *Mental health assessment in occupational therapy*, ed. B.J. Hemphill, 149–62. Thorofare, NJ: Slack, Inc.

Leonardelli, C.A. 1988. *The Milwaukee Evaluation of Daily Living Skills: Evaluation in long-term psychiatric care*. Thorofare, NJ: Slack, Inc.

Motor-Free Visual Perception Test

Bouska, M.J. 1985. Application of the motor-free visual perception test. *Physical Disabilities Special Interest Section Newsletter* 8(1):6–7.

Bouska, M.J., and E. Kwatny. 1980. *Manual for application of the motor free visual perception test to the adult population.* PO Box 12246, Philadelphia, PA: Authors.

Calarusso, R.P., and D.D. Hammill. 1972. *The Motor-Free Visual Perception Test (MVPT).* San Rafael, CA: Academic Therapy Publications.

Eimon, M.C., P.L. Eimon, and S.A. Cermak. 1983. Performance of schizophrenic patients on a motor-free visual perception test. *American Journal of Occupational Therapy* 37(5): 327–32.

Nurses' Observation Scale for Inpatient Evaluation

Chamove, A.S. 1986. Exercise improves behaviour: A rationale for occupational therapy. *British Journal of Occupational Therapy* 49(3):83–6.

Honigfeld, G., and C.J. Klett. 1965. Nurses Observation Scale for Inpatient Evaluation: A new scale for measuring improvement in chronic schizophrenia. *Journal of Clinical Psychology* 21:65–71.

Occupational Case Analysis Interview and Rating Scale

Brollier, C., et al. 1988. A concurrent validity study of two occupational therapy evaluation instruments: The AOF and OCAIRS. *Occupational Therapy in Mental Health* 8(4):49–60.

Kaplan, K.L., and G. Kielhofner. 1989. *Occupational Case Analysis Interview and Rating Scale.* Thorofare, NJ: Slack, Inc.

Watts, J.H., et al. 1988. A comparison of two evaluation instruments used with psychiatric patients in occupational therapy. *Occupational Therapy in Mental Health* 8(4):7–27.

Occupational History Questionnaire

Katz, N., N. Giladei, and C. Peretz. 1988. Cross-cultural application of occupational therapy assessments: Human occupation with psychiatric inpatients and controls in Israel. *Occupational Therapy in Mental Health* 8(1):7–30.

Occupational Performance History Interview

Kielhofner, G., and A. Henry. 1986. Use of the Occupational History Interview in occupational therapy. In *Mental health assessment in occupational therapy*, ed. B.J. Hemphill, 59–71. Thorofare, NJ: Slack, Inc.

Kielhofner, G., and A.D. Henry. 1988. Development and investigation of the occupational performance history interview. *American Journal of Occupational Therapy* 42(8):489–98.

Kielhofner, G., A.D. Henry, and D. Walens. 1989. *A user's guide to the Occupational Performance History Interview.* Rockville, MD: American Occupational Therapy Association.

Occupational Role History

Florey, L.L., and S.M. Michelman. 1982. Occupational Role History: A screening tool for psychiatric occupational therapy. *American Journal of Occupational Therapy* 36(5):301–8.

Moorhead, L. 1969. The occupational history. *American Journal of Occupational Therapy* 23:329–34.

Profile of Mood States

Lorr, M., and D. McNair. 1982. *Profile of mood states, bi-polar form (POMS-BI)*. San Diego, CA: Educational & Industrial Testing Service.

McNair, D.M., M. Loor, and L.F. Droppleman. 1971. *ETIS manual for the profile of mood states*. San Diego, CA: Educational & Industrial Testing Service.

Shih, L.S., D.L. Nelson, and L.W. Duncombe. 1984. Mood and affect following success and failure in two cultural groups. *Occupational Therapy Journal of Research* 4(3):213–30.

Riverdale Hospital's Home and Community Skills Assessment

Brown, H. 1988. The standardization of the Riverdale Hospital's Home and Community Skills Assessment. *Canadian Journal of Occupational Therapy* 55(1):9–14.

Rivermead Perceptual Assessment Battery

Cockburn, J., G. Bhaynani, S.E. Whiting, et al. 1982. Normal performance on some tests of perception in adults. *British Journal of Occupational Therapy* 45(2):67–8.

Cramond, H.J., M.S. Clark, and D.S. Smith. 1989. The effect of using the dominant or nondominant hand on performance of the Rivermead Perceptual Assessment Battery. *Clinical Rehabilitation* 3(2):15–21.

Edmans, J.A. 1987. The frequency of perceptual deficits after stroke. *Clinical Rehabilitation* 1:273–81.

Edmans, J.A., and N.B. Lincoln. 1989.Treatment of visual perceptual deficit after stroke: Four single case studies. *International Disabilities Studies* 11:25–33.

Lincoln, N.B., and D. Clarke. 1987. The performance of normal elderly people on the Rivermead Perceptual Assessment Battery. *British Journal of Occupational Therapy* 50(5):156–7.

Lincoln, N.B., et al. 1987. An evaluation of perceptual retraining. *International Rehabilitation Medicine* 7:273–81.

Lincoln, N.B., and J.A. Edmans. 1989. A shortened version of the Rivermead Perceptual Assessment Battery. *Clinical Rehabilitation* 3:199–204.

Whiting, S.E, et al. 1985. *The Rivermead Perceptual Assessment Battery*. Windsor, England: NFER Nelson.

Role Activity Performance Scale

Good-Ellis, M.A., et al. 1987. Developing a Role Activity Performance Scale. *American Journal of Occupational Therapy* 41(4):232–41.

Good-Ellis, M.A. 1986. Quantitative role performance assessment: Implications and application to treatment of depression. In *Depression: Assessment and treatment update: Proceedings*, 36–48. Rockville, MD: American Occupational Therapy Association.

Role Checklist

Barris, R., F. Oakley, and G. Kielhofner. 1986. The role checklist. In *Mental health assessment in occupational therapy*, ed. B.J. Hemphill, 73–91. Thorofare, NJ: Slack, Inc.

Oakley, F., et al. 1986. The Role Checklist: Development and empirical assessment of reliability. *Occupational Therapy Journal of Research* 6(3):157–70.

Oakley, F., G. Kielhofner, and R. Barris. 1985. An occupational therapy approach to assessing psychiatric patients' adaptive functioning. *American Journal of Occupational Therapy* 39(3):147–54.

Rokeach Values Survey

Bailey, D.M. 1988. Occupational therapy administrators and clinicians: Differences in demographics and values. *Occupational Therapy Journal of Research* 8(5):299–315.
Barris, R., G. Kielhofner, and D. Bauer. 1985. Educational experience and changes in learning and value preferences. *Occupational Therapy Journal of Research* 5(4):243–56.
Rokeach, M. 1973. *The nature of human values.* New York: Free Press.

Routine Task Inventory

Heimann, N.E., C.K. Allen, and E.J. Yerxa. 1989. The Routine Task Inventory: A tool for describing the functional behavior of the cognitively disabled. *Occupational Therapy Practice* 1(1):67–74.
Routine Task Inventory. 1985. In *Occupational therapy for psychiatric diseases: Measurement and management of cognitive disabilities*, ed. C.K. Allen, 63–77. Boston: Little, Brown & Co.

Satisfaction with Performance Scaled Questionnaire (SPSQ)

Yerxa, E.J., et al. 1988. Development of the Satisfaction with Performance Scaled Questionnaire (SPSQ). *American Journal of Occupational Therapy* 42(4):215–21.

Schedule of Recent Experiences

Homes, T.H. 1981. *Schedule of Recent Experiences.* Seattle, WA: University of Washington Press. Available from the Department of Psychiatry and Behavioral Science, University of Washington School of Medicine, Seattle, WA 98195.
Larson, K.B. 1990. Activity patterns and life changes in people with depression. *American Journal of Occupational Therapy* 44(10):902–6.

Schroeder-Block-Campbell Adult Psychiatric Sensory Integration Evaluation

Hamada, R.S., and C. Van Schroeder. 1988. Schroeder-Block-Campbell Adult Psychiatric Sensory Integration Evaluation: Concurrent validity and clinical utility. *Occupational Therapy Journal of Research* 8(2):75–88.
Schroeder, C.V., M.P. Bolci, E.C. Trottier, et al. 1983. *SBC Adult Psychiatric Sensory Integration Evaluation*, 3d ed. Kailua, HI: Schroeder.

Screening for Physical and Occupational Therapy Referral (SPOTR)

Woosley, T., D.E. Sands, and W. Dunlap. 1987. An instrument to screen sensory impaired persons for referral to physical and occupational therapy. *Journal of Rehabilitation* 53(4):66–9.

Shipley Institute of Living Scale

David, S.K., and W.T. Riley. 1990. The relationship of the Allen Cognitive Level Test to cognitive abilities and psychopathology. *American Journal of Occupational Therapy* 44(6):493–7.

Zachary, R.A. 1986. *Shipley Institute of Living Scale: Revised manual.* Los Angeles: Western Psychological Services.

Short Portable Mental Status Questionnaire (SPMSQ)

Pfeiffer, E.A. 1975. A short portable mental status questionnaire for the assessment of organic brain deficit in elderly patients. *Journal of the American Geriatrics Society* 23:433–41.

Skurl, E., J.C. Rogers, and T. Sunderland. 1988. Direct assessment of activities of daily living in Alzheimer's disease: A controlled study. *Journal of the American Geriatrics Society* 36(2):97–103.

Sixteen Personality Factor Questionnaire (16PF)

Bailey, D.M. 1988. Occupational therapy administrators and clinicians: Differences in demographics and values. *Occupational Therapy Journal of Research* 8(5):299–315.

Cattell, R.B. 1979. *Sixteen Personality Factor Questionnaire,* 2d ed. Champaign, IL: Institute for Personality and Ability Testing.

Symbol-Digit Modalities Test

David, S.K., and W.T. Riley. 1990. The relationship of the Allen Cognitive Level Test to cognitive abilities and psychopathology. *American Journal of Occupational Therapy* 44(6):493–7.

Smith, A. 1982. *Symbol-Digit Modalities Test manual.* Los Angeles: Western Psychological Services.

Wheel Diagram

Bell, C.H. 1986. A strategy for assessing occupational behavior: II. An inter-rater reliability study. *Occupational Therapy in Mental Health* 6(3):1–17.

Appendix D

Suggested Reading

ALLEN'S THEORY OF COGNITIVE DISABILITIES

Allen, C.K. 1982. Independence through activity: The practice of occupational therapy. *American Journal of Occupational Therapy* 36:731–9.

Allen, C.K. 1985. *Occupational therapy for psychiatric diseases: Measurement and management of cognitive disabilities.* Boston: Little, Brown & Co.

Allen, C.K. 1987. Activity: Occupational therapy's treatment method. *American Journal of Occupational Therapy* 41:563–75.

Allen, C.K., and R.E. Allen. 1987. Cognitive disabilities: Measuring the social consequences of mental disorders. *Journal of Clinical Psychiatry* 48(5):185–90.

Allen, C.K. 1988. Occupational therapy: Functional assessment of the severity of mental disorders. *Hospital and Community Psychiatry* 39(2):140–2.

Allen, C.K. 1988. Cognitive disabilities. In *Mental health focus skills for assessment and treatment*, ed. S.E. Robertson, 3–32. Rockville, MD: American Occupational Therapy Association.

David, S.K., and W.T. Riley. 1990. The relationship of the Allen Cognitive Level Test to cognitive ability and psychopathology. *American Journal of Occupational Therapy* 44(6):493–98.

Kiernan, K., and A. Stoudemire. 1989. Occupational therapy program development for medical-psychiatry units: A cognitive model. *General Hospital Psychiatry* 11:109–18.

Levy, L.L. 1986. Coping with confusion: The cognitive disability perspective. *Gerontology Special Interest Section Newsletter* 9(3):1–3.

Levy, L.L. 1986. A practical guide to the care of the Alzheimer's disease victim: The cognitive disability perspective. *Topics in Geriatric Rehabilitation* 1(2):16–26.

Levy, L.L. 1989. Activity adaptation in rehabilitation of the physically and cognitively disabled aged. *Topics in Geriatric Rehabilitation* 4(4):53–66.

Mayer, M.A. 1988. Analysis of information processing and cognitive disability therapy. *American Journal of Occupational Therapy* 42(3):176–83.

AYRES' THEORY OF SENSORY INTEGRATION

Ayres, A.J. 1955. Proprioceptive facilitation elicited through the upper extremities. Part I: Background. *American Journal of Occupational Therapy* 9(1):1–9,50.

Ayres, A.J. 1955. Proprioceptive facilitation elicited through the upper extremities. Part II: Application. *American Journal of Occupational Therapy* 9(2):57–8,76–7.

Ayres, A.J. 1955. Proprioceptive facilitation elicited through the upper extremities. Part III: Specific application of occupational therapy. *American Journal of Occupational Therapy* 9(3):121–6,143.

Ayres, A.J. 1958. The visual-motor function. *American Journal of Occupational Therapy* 12(3):130–8,155–6.

Ayres, A.J. 1961. Development of the body scheme in children. *American Journal of Occupational Therapy* 15(3):99–102,128.

Ayres, A.J. 1962. Methods of evaluating perceptual-motor dysfunction. In *Proceedings of the World Federation of Occupational Therapy*, 113–7. Philadelphia: University of Pennsylvania.

Ayres, A.J. 1962. Perception of space of adult hemiplegic patients. *Archives of Physical Medicine and Rehabilitation* 43:552–5.

Ayres, A.J. 1963. Occupational therapy directed toward neuromuscular integration. In *Occupational therapy*, 3d ed., ed. H.S. Willard and C.S. Spackman. Philadelphia: J.B. Lippincott.

Ayres, A.J. 1963. The development of perceptual-motor abilities: A theoretical basis for treatment of dysfunction. *American Journal of Occupational Therapy* 17(6):221–5.

Ayres, A.J. 1963. Perceptual-motor training for children. In *Approaches to the treatment of patients with neuromuscular dysfunction, study course VI*, ed. C. Sattely, 17–22. Third International Congress of the World Federation of Occupational Therapy. Dubuque, IA: William C. Brown.

Ayres, A.J. 1963. Integration of information. In *Approaches to the treatment of patients with neuromuscular dysfunction, study course VI*, ed. C. Sattely, 49–57. Third International Congress of the World Federation of Occupational Therapy. Dubuque, IA: William C. Brown.

Ayres, A.J. 1964. *Perceptual-motor dysfunction in children*. Goodwill Industries, Cincinnati, OH: Greater Cincinnati District of the Ohio Occupational Therapy Association.

Ayres, A.J. 1964. Tactile functions: Their relation to hyperactive and perceptual motor behavior. *American Journal of Occupational Therapy* 18(1):6–11.

Ayres, A.J. 1964. Perspectives on neurological bases of reading. *Claremont Reading Conference* 28:113–8.

Ayres, A.J. 1965. A factor analytic study. *Perceptual and Motor Skills* 20:335–68.

Ayres, A.J. 1965. A method of measurement of degree of sensorimotor integration. *Archives of Physical Medicine and Rehabilitation* 46:433–5.

Ayres, A.J. 1966. Interrelations among perceptual-motor abilities in a group of normal children. *American Journal of Occupational Therapy* 20:288–92.

Ayres, A.J. 1966. Interrelationships among perceptual-motor functions in children. *American Journal of Occupational Therapy* 20:68–71.

Ayres, A.J., and W. Reid. 1966. The self-drawing as an expression of perceptual-motor dysfunction. *Cortex* 2:254–65.

Ayres, A.J. 1966. Interrelation of perceptual function and treatment. *Physical Therapy* 46(7):741–4.

Ayres, A.J. 1968. Sensory integrative processes and neuropsychological learning disabilities. In *Learning disabilities*, v.III. Seattle, WA: Special Child Publication.

Ayres, A.J. 1968. *Effect of sensorimotor activity on perception and learning in the neurologically handicapped child (Project No. H-126)*. Los Angeles: University of Southern California (ERIC Document No. ED033757).

Ayres, A.J. 1968. Reading—a product of sensory integrative process. In *Perception and reading*, ed. H.K. Smith, 77–82. Newark, DE: International Reading Association.

Ayres, A.J. 1969. Relation between Gesell developmental quotients and later perceptual-motor performance. *American Journal of Occupational Therapy* 23:11–7.

Ayres, A.J. 1969. Deficits in sensory integration in educationally handicapped children. *Journal of Learning Disabilities* 2:160–8.

Ayres, A.J. 1971. Characteristics of types of sensory integrative dysfunction. *American Journal of Occupational Therapy* 25(7):329–34.

Ayres, A.J. 1972. Improving academic scores through sensory integration. *Journal of Learning Disabilities* 5:338–43.

Ayres, A.J. 1972. *Sensory integration and learning disorders*. Los Angeles: Western Psychological Services.

Ayres, A.J. 1972. Types of sensory integrative dysfunction among disabled learners. *American Journal of Occupational Therapy* 26(1):13–8.

Ayres, A.J. 1972. Sensory integrative processes: Implications for the deaf-blind from research with learning disabled children. In *Proceedings of the National Symposium for Deaf-Blind*, ed. W.A. Blea, 81–9. Asilomar, Pacific Grove, CA.

Ayres, A.J. 1973. The influence of the vestibular system on the auditory and visual systems. In *New techniques for work with deaf-blind children,* ed. J.L. Horsley and W.J. Smith, 1–13. Denver CO: Mountain Plains Regional Center.

Ayres, A.J. 1973. An interpretation of the role of the brain stem in intersensory integration. In *The body senses and perceptual deficit*, ed. A. Henderson and J. Coryell, 81–9. Rockville, MD: U.S. Department of Health, Education and Welfare.

Ayres, A.J. 1975. Sensorimotor foundations of academic ability. In *Perceptual and learning disabilities in children*, vol. 2, *Research and theory*, ed. W.M. Cruickshank and D.P. Hallahan, 301–58. Syracuse, NY: Syracuse University Press.

Ayres, A.J. 1976. *The effect of sensory integrative therapy on learning disabled children*. Los Angeles: University of Southern California. Available from Sensory Integration International.

Ayres, A.J. 1977. Cluster analyses of measures of sensory integration. *American Journal of Occupational Therapy* 31(6):362–6.

Ayres, A.J. 1977. Dichotic listening performance in learning disabled children. *American Journal of Occupational Therapy* 31(7):441–6.

Ayres, A.J. 1977. Effects of sensory integrative therapy on the coordination of children with choreoathetoid movements. *American Journal of Occupational Therapy* 31(5):291–3.

Ayres, A.J. 1978. Learning disabilities and the vestibular system. *Journal of Learning Disabilities* 11:18–29.

Ayres, A.J. 1980. *Sensory integration and the child*. Los Angeles: Western Psychological Services.

Ayres, A.J. 1985. *Developmental dyspraxia and adult-onset apraxia*. Torrance, CA: Sensory Integration International.

Ayres, A.J., and Z. K. Mailloux. 1981. Influence of sensory integration procedures on language development. *American Journal of Occupational Therapy* 35(6):383–90.

Ayres, A.J., and Z.K. Mailloux. 1983. Possible pubertal effect on therapeutic gains in an autistic girl. *American Journal of Occupational Therapy* 37(8):535–40.

Ayres, A.J., and L.S. Tickle. 1980. Hyper-responsivity to touch and vestibular stimuli as a predictor of positive response to sensory integration procedures by autistic children. *American Journal of Occupational Therapy* 34(6):375–81.

SENSORY INTEGRATION

Arendt, R.E., W.E. MacLean, Jr., and A.A. Baumeister. 1988. Critique of sensory integration therapy and its application in mental retardation. *American Journal of Mental Retardation* 92(5):401–9.

Atwood, R.M., and S.A. Cermak. 1986. Crossing the midline as a function of distance from midline. *American Journal of Occupational Therapy* 40(10):685–90.

Babayov, D., H. Omer, and J. Menczel. 1985. Sensorimotor integration therapy for hip fracture and CVA patients. *Canadian Journal of Occupational Therapy* 52(3):133–7.

Bocher, S. 1980. Sensory integration therapy and learning disabilities: A critique. *Australian Occupational Therapy Journal* 27:125–38.

Bright, T., K. Bittick, and B. Fleeman. 1981. Reduction of SIB using sensory integrative techniques. *American Journal of Occupational Therapy* 35:167–72.

Carte, E., D. Morrison, J. Sublett, et al. 1984. Sensory integration theory: A trial of a specific neurodevelopmental therapy for the remediation of learning disabilities. *Journal of Developmental and Behavioral Pediatrics* 5(4):189–94.

Cermak, S.A., E.A. Ward, and L.M. Ward. 1986. The relationship between articulation disorders and motor coordination in children. *American Journal of Occupational Therapy* 40(8):546–50.

Chappiro, C. 1985. Australian Association of Occupational Therapists position paper on sensory integration. *Australian Occupational Therapy Journal* 32:23–6.

Chee, F.K.W., J.R. Kreutzberg, and D.L. Clark. 1978. Semicircular canal stimulation in cerebral palsied children. *Physical Therapy* 58:1071–5.

Densem, J.F., et al. 1989. Effectiveness of a sensory integrative therapy program for children with perceptual-motor deficits. *Journal of Learning Disabilities* 22(4):221–9.

Dilts, C.V., C.A. Morris, and C.O. Leonard. 1990. Hypothesis for development of a behavioral phenotype in Williams Syndrome. *American Journal of Medical Genetics Supplement* 6:126–31.

Doyle, B.A., and D.C. Higginson. 1984. Relationships among self-concept and school achievement, maternal self-esteem and sensory integration abilities for learning disabled children, ages 7 to 12 years. *Perceptual and Motor Skills* 58(1):177–8.

Dura, J.R., J.A. Mulick, and D. Hammer. 1988. Rapid clinical evaluation of sensory therapy for self-injurious behavior. *Mental Retardation* 26(2):83–7.

Harten, G., U. Stephani, G. Henze, et al. 1984. Slight impairment of psychomotor skills in children after treatment of acute lymphoblastic leukemia. *European Journal of Pediatrics* 142(3):189–97.

Hixson, V.J., and A.W. Mathews. 1984. Sensory integration and chronic schizophrenia: Past, present and future. *Canadian Journal of Occupational Therapy* 51(1):19–24.

James, M.R. 1984. Sensory integration: A theory for therapy and research. *Journal of Music Therapy* 21(2):79–88.

Jaroma, M., P. Danner, and E. Koiveuniemi. 1984. Sensory integrative therapy and speech therapy for improving the perceptual motor skills and speech articulation of a dyspractic boy. *Folia Phoniatrica* 36(6):261–6.

Jenkins, J.R., R. Fewell, and S.R. Harris. 1983. Comparison of sensory integrative therapy and motor programming. *American Journal of Mental Deficiency* 88(2):221–4.

Kantner, R., et al. 1976. Effects of vestibular stimulation on nystagmus response and motor performance in the developmentally delayed infant. *Physical Therapy* 56:414–21.

Kimball, J.G. 1986. Prediction of methylphenidate (Ritalin) responsiveness through sensory integrative testing. *American Journal of Occupational Therapy* 40(4):241–8.

Kimball, J.G. 1988. Hypothesis for prediction of stimulant drug effectiveness utilizing sensory integrative diagnostic methods. *Journal of the American Osteopathic Association* 88(6):757–62.

Kuharski, T., et al. 1985. Effects of vestibular stimulation on sitting behaviours among pre-schoolers with service handicaps. *Journal of the Association of Persons with Severe Handicaps* 10:137–45.

Montgomery, P., and E. Richter. 1977. Effect of sensory integrative therapy on the neuromotor development of retarded children. *Physical Therapy* 57:799–806.

Morrison, D., and J. Sublett. 1986. The effects of sensory integration therapy on nystagmus duration equilibrium reactions and visual-motor integration in reading retarded children. *Child: Care, Health and Development* 12(2):99–110.

Ottenbacher, K., M.A. Short, and P.J. Watson. 1981. The effects of a classically applied program of vestibular stimulation on the neuromotor performance of children with severe developmental disability. *Physical and Occupational Therapy in Pediatrics* 1:1–11.

Ottenbacher, K. 1982. Patterns of postrotary nystagmus in three learning-disabled children. *American Journal of Occupational Therapy* 36(10):657–63.

Ottenbacher, K.J., and P. Petersen. 1983. The efficacy of vestibular stimulation as a form of specific sensory enrichment. *Clinical Pediatrics* 23(8):428–33.

Ottenbacher, K. 1983. Developmental implications of clinically applied vestibular stimulation. *Physical Therapy* 63(3):338–42.

Ottenbacher, K.J., and P. Pederson. 1985. A meta-analysis of applied vestibular stimulation research. *Physical and Occupational Therapy in Pediatrics* 5:119–34.

Ottenbacher, K.J., et al. 1987. The effectiveness of tactile stimulation as a form of early in-tervention: A quantitative evaluation. *Journal of Developmental and Behavioral Pediat-rics* 8(2):68–76.

Parmenter, C.L. 1983. An asymmetrical tonic neck reflex rating scale. *American Journal of Occupational Therapy* 37(7):462–5.

Parush, S., and F. Clark. 1988. The reliability and validity of a sensory developmental expectation questionnaire for mothers of newborns. *American Journal of Occupational Therapy* 42(1):11–6.

Peterson, P., and R.L. Wikoff. 1983. The performance of adult males on the Southern California Figure-Ground Visual Perception Test. *American Journal of Occupational Therapy* 37(8):554–60.

Polatajko, H.J. 1985. A critical look at vestibular dysfunction in learning-disabled children. *Developmental Medicine & Child Neurology* 27:283–92.

Pothier, P.C., and K. Cheek. 1984. Current practices in sensory motor programming with developmentally delayed infants and young children. *Child: Care, Health and Develop-ment* 10:341–8.

Potter, C.N., and L.N. Silverman. 1984. Characteristics of vestibular function and static balance skills in deaf children. *Physical Therapy* 64(7):1071–5.

Saeki, K., F.A. Clark, and S.P. Azen. 1985. Performance of Japanese and Japanese-American children on the Motor Accuracy-Revised and Design Copying Tests of the Southern California Sensory Integration Tests. *American Journal of Occupational Therapy* 39(2):103–9.

Sellick, K.J., and T. Over. 1980. Effects of vestibular stimulation on motor development of cerebral palsied children. *Developmental Medicine and Child Neurology* 22:476–83.

Shaffer, R. 1984. Sensory integration therapy with learning disabled children: A critical review. *Canadian Journal of Occupational Therapy* 51(2):73–7.

Shaffer, R. 1990. Play behavior and occupational therapy. *American Journal of Occupational Therapy* 44(1):68–75.

Short, M.A., P.J. Watson, K. Ottenbacher, et al. 1983. Vestibular-proprioceptive functions in 4 year olds: Normative and regressive analyses. *American Journal of Occupational Therapy* 37(2):102–9.

Smith, C.M., S.A. Cermak, and D.L. Nelson. 1984. Sequential versus simultaneous graphesthesia tasks in 6- and 10-year-old children. *American Journal of Occupational Therapy* 38(6):377–81.

Stepp-Gilbert, E. 1988. Sensory integration dysfunction. *Issues in Comprehensive Pediatric Nursing* 11(5–6):313–8.

Stepp-Gilbert, E. 1988. Sensory integration: A reason for infant enrichment. *Issues in Comprehensive Pediatric Nursing* 11(5–6):319–31.

Storey, K., et al. 1984. Reducing the self-stimulatory behavior of a profoundly retarded female through sensory awareness training. *American Journal of Occupational Therapy* 38:510–16.

Tickle-Degnen, L. 1988. Perspectives on the status of sensory integration theory. *American Journal of Occupational Therapy* 42(7):427–33.

Werry, J.S., R. Scaletti, and F. Mills. 1990. Sensory integration and teacher-judged learning problems: A controlled intervention trial. *Journal of Paediatrics and Child Health* 26(1):31–5.

White, M. 1979. A first-grade intervention program for children at risk for reading failure. *Journal of Learning Disabilities* 12(4):231–7.

Wilson, B.N., and C.A. Trombly. 1984. Proximal and distal function in children with and without sensory integrative dysfunction: An E.M.G. study. *Canadian Journal of Occupational Therapy* 51(1):11–7.

Yack, E. 1989. Sensory integration: A survey of its use in the clinical setting. *Canadian Journal of Occupational Therapy* 56(5):229–35.

Ziviani, J., A. Poulsen, and A. O'Brien. 1982. Correlation of the Bruninks-Oseretsky Test of Motor Proficiency with the Southern California Sensory Integration Tests. *American Journal of Occupational Therapy* 36(8):519–23.

See all articles in the *American Journal of Occupational Therapy* 44(7):610–57, 1990.

BRUNNSTROM'S THEORY OF RECOVERY FROM HEMIPLEGIA

Brunnstrom, S. 1956. Associated reactions of the upper extremity in adult patients with hemiplegia. *Physical Therapy Review* 36:225–36.

Brunnstrom, S. 1961. Motor behavior in adult hemiplegic patients. *American Journal of Occupational Therapy* 15:6–12.

Brunnstrom, S. 1964. Recording gait patterns of adult hemiplegic patients. *Journal of the American Physical Therapy Association (JAPTA)* 44(1):11–8.

Brunnstrom, S. 1964. Training the adult hemiplegic patient: Orientation of techniques to patient's motor behavior. In *Approach to the treatment of patients with neuromuscular dysfunction*, ed. C. Sattely, 44–48. Dubuque, IA: Wm. C. Brown Book Co.

Brunnstrom, S. 1965. Walking preparation for adult patients with hemiplegia. *Journal of the American Physical Therapy Association (JAPTA)* 45(1):17–29.

Brunnstrom, S. 1966. Motor testing procedures in hemiplegia based on recovery stages. *Journal of the American Physical Therapy Association (JAPTA)* 46(4):357–75.

Brunnstrom, S. 1970. *Movement therapy in hemiplegia*. New York: Harper & Row.

Hughes, E. 1972. Bobath and Brunnstrom: Comparison of two methods of treatment of a left hemiplegia. *Physiotherapy Canada* 24(5):262–66.

Pedretti, L.W. 1990. Movement therapy: The Brunnstrom approach to treatment of hemiplegia. In *Occupational therapy: Practice skills in physical dysfunction*, 3d ed., ed. L.W. Pedretti and B. Zoltan, 334–50. St. Louis: C.V. Mosby.

Perry, C. 1967. Principles and techniques of the Brunnstrom approach to the treatment of hemiplegia. *American Journal of Physical Medicine* 46:789–97.

Reynolds, G.G., K.C. Archibald, S. Brunnstrom, et al. 1958. Preliminary report on neuromuscular function testing of the upper extremity in adult hemiplegic patients. *Archives of Physical Medicine and Rehabilitation* 39(5):303–10.

Shah, S.K. 1984. Reliability of the original Brunnstrom recovery scale following hemiplegia. *Australian Occupational Therapy Journal* 31(4):144–51.

Shah, S.K. 1986. Stroke rehabilitation outcome based on Brunnstrom recovery stages. *Occupational Therapy Journal of Research* 6:365–76.

BOBATH'S THEORY OF NEURODEVELOPMENT THERAPY

Bobath, B. 1948. For the physiotherapist: A new treatment of lesions of the upper motor neurone. *British Journal of Physical Medicine* 11:26–9.

Bobath, B. 1948. The importance of the reduction of muscle tone and the control of mass reflex action in the treatment of spasticity. *Occupational Therapy and Rehabilitation* 27:371–83.

Bobath, K., and B. Bobath. 1950. Spastic paralysis: Treatment of by the use of reflex inhibition. *British Journal of Physical Medicine* 13(6):121–7.

Bobath, K., and B. Bobath. 1952. A treatment of cerebral palsy: Based on the analysis of the patient's motor behaviour. *British Journal of Physical Medicine* 15:107–17.

Bobath, B. 1953. Control of postures and movements in the treatment of cerebral palsy. *Physiotherapy* 39:99–104.

Bobath, B. 1954. A study of abnormal postural reflex activity in patients with lesions of the central nervous system—I. *Physiotherapy* 40(9):259–67; 40(10):295–300; 40(11):326; 40(12):295–300; 40(12):368; 41(1):146.

Bobath, K., and B. Bobath. 1954. Treatment of cerebral palsy by the inhibition of abnormal reflex action. *British Orthoptic Journal* 11:88–98.

Bobath, B. 1955. The treatment of motor disorders of pyramidal and extra-pyramidal origin by reflex inhibition and by facilitation of movements. *Physiotherapy* 41(5):146–53.

Bobath, K., and B. Bobath. 1955. Tonic reflexes and righting reflexes in the diagnosis and assessment of cerebral palsy. *Cerebral Palsy Review* 16(5):4–10.

Bobath, K., and B. Bobath. 1956. The diagnosis of cerebral palsy in infancy. *Archives of Diseases and Childhood* 31:408–14.

Bobath, K., and B. Bobath. 1956. Control of motor function in the treatment of cerebral palsy. *Australian Journal of Physiotherapy* 2(2):75–85.

Bobath, K., and B. Bobath. 1957. Control of motor function in the treatment of cerebral palsy. *Physiotherapy* 43(10):295–303.

Bobath, B., and N. Finnie. 1958. Re-education of movement patterns for everyday life in the treatment of cerebral palsy. *Occupational Therapy* 21(6):23–30.

Bobath, K. 1959. The neuropathology of cerebral palsy and its importance in treatment and diagnosis. *Cerebral Palsy Bulletin* 1(8):13–33.

Bobath, K. 1959. The effect of treatment by reflex-inhibition and facilitation of movement in cerebral palsy. *Folia Psychiatric Neurologica et Neurochirurgica Neelandica* 62(5): 448–57.

Bobath, B. 1959. Observations on adult hemiplegia and suggestions for treatment. *Physiotherapy* 45(12):279–89.

Bobath, B. 1960. Observations on adult hemiplegia and suggestions for treatment. *Physiotherapy* 46(1):5–15.

Bobath, K. 1960. The nature of the paresis in cerebral palsy. In *Child neurology and cerebral palsy, 88–93.* Oxford, England: Spastic Society Study Group.

Bobath, K. 1962. The prevention of mental retardation in patients with cerebral palsy. *Acta Paedopsychiatrica* 30:141–54.

Bobath, K., and B. Bobath. 1962. An analysis of the development of standing and walking patterns in patients with cerebral palsy. *Physiotherapy* 48(6):144–53.

Bobath, B. 1963. Treatment principles and planning in cerebral palsy. *Physiotherapy* 49(4):122–4.

Bobath, B. 1963. A neuro-developmental treatment of cerebral palsy. *Physiotherapy* 49(8):242–4.

Bobath, K., and B. Bobath. 1964. The facilitation of normal postural reactions and movements in the treatment of cerebral palsy. *Physiotherapy* 50(8):246–62.

Bobath, B., and E. Cotton. 1965. A patient with residual hemiplegia: And his response to treatment. *Journal of the American Physical Therapy Association* 45:849–64.

Bobath, K. 1966. *The motor deficits in patients with cerebral palsy.* Clinics in Developmental Medicine, no. 23. London, England: Heinemann Medical Books.

Bobath, B. 1967. The very early treatment of cerebral palsy. *Developmental Medicine and Child Neurology* 9(4):373–90.

Bobath, B. 1967. The neuro-developmental treatment of cerebral palsy. *Journal of the American Physical Therapy Association* 47(11):1039–41.

Bobath, B. 1969. The treatment of neuromuscular disorders by improving patterns of coordination. *Physiotherapy* 55(1):18–22.

Bobath, K. 1969. *The motor deficit in patients with cerebral palsy.* Clinics in Development Medicine No. 23. London, England: The Spastic Society and William Heinemann Medical Books.

Bobath, B. 1970. *Adult hemiplegia: Evaluation and treatment.* London, England: William Heinemann Medical Books.

Bobath, K. 1971. The problem of spasticity in the treatment of patients with lesions of the upper motor neuron. In *Proceedings of the Sixth International Congress of the World Federation for Physical Therapists*, 456–64. Amsterdam: Assen van Gorcus.

Bobath, K. 1971. The normal postural reflex mechanism and its deviation in children with cerebral palsy. *Physiotherapy* 57:515–25.

Bobath, B. 1971. *Abnormal postural reflex activity caused by brain lesion*, 2d ed. London, England: William Heinemann Medical Books.

Bobath, K., and B. Bobath. 1972. Diagnosis and assessment of cerebral palsy—Part 1. In *Physical therapy services in the developmental disabilities*, ed. P. Pearson and C. Williams, 31–113. Springfield, IL: Charles C. Thomas.

Bobath, K., and B. Bobath. 1972. The neurodevelopmental approach to treatment—Part 2. In *Physical therapy services in the developmental disabilities*, ed. P. Pearson and C. Williams, 114–185. Springfield, IL: Charles C Thomas.

Bobath, K., and B. Bobath. 1974. The importance of memory traces of motor efferent discharges for learning skilled movement. *Developmental Medicine and Child Neurology* 16:837–8.

Bobath, B., and K. Bobath. 1975. *Motor development in the different types of cerebral palsy*. London, England: William Heinemann Medical Books.

Bobath, B. 1977. Treatment of adult hemiplegia. *Physiotherapy* 63:310–13.

Bobath, B. 1978. *Adult hemiplegia: Evaluation and treatment*, 2d ed. London, England: Heinemann Medical Books. 3d ed. 1990.

Bobath, K. 1980. *A neurophysiological basis for the treatment of cerebral palsy*. Clinics in Development Medicine No. 75. London, England: The Spastic Society and William Heinemann Medical Books.

Bobath, B., and K. Bobath. 1984. The neurodevelopmental treatment. In *Management of the motor disorders of children with cerebral palsy*, ed. D. Scrutton, 6–18. Philadelphia: J.B. Lippincott Co.

Bobath, B. 1985. *Abnormal postural reflex activity caused by brain lesions*, 3d ed. Gaithersburg, MD: Aspen Publishers, Inc.

NEURODEVELOPMENTAL THERAPY

Adler, L.J. 1983. Neurodevelopmental treatment perspective of disorders in sensory integration. *Sensory Integration Special Interest Section Newsletter* 6(4):1–3.

Arsenault, A.B. 1988. An evaluation of the hemiplegic subject based on the Bobath approach: A validation study, part 3. *Scandinavian Journal of Rehabilitation Medicine* 20(1):13–6.

Basmajian, J.V., et al. 1987. Stroke treatment: Comparison of integrated behavioral-physical therapy vs traditional physical therapy programs. *Archives of Physical Medicine and Rehabilitation* 68(5 Pt 1):267–72.

Bertoti, D.B. 1986. Effect of short leg casting on ambulation in children with cerebral palsy. *Physical Therapy* 66(1):1522–9.

Boehme, R. 1983. Self care assessment and treatment from an NDT perspective. *Developmental Disabilities Special Interest Section Newsletter* 6(4):1,3.

Campbell, P.H., and B. Steart. 1986. Measuring changes in movement skills with infants and young children with handicaps. *Journal of the Association of Severely Handicapped* 11(3):153–61.

Carlson, P. 1975. Comparison of two occupational therapy approaches for treating the young cerebral palsied child. *American Journal of Occupational Therapy* 29:267–71.

Corriveau, H., et al. 1988. An evaluation of the hemiplegic subject based on the Bobath approach: The evaluation protocol, part 2. *Scandinavian Journal of Rehabilitation Medicine*

20(1):5–11.

Davis, J.Z. 1990. Neurodevelopmental treatment. In *Occupational therapy: Practice skills in physical dysfunction*, 3d ed., ed. L.W. Pedretti and B. Zoltan, 351–62. St. Louis: C.V. Mosby.

DeGanti, G.A., L. Hurley, and T.R. Linscheid. 1983. Toward a methodology of the short-term effects of neurodevelopmental treatment. *American Journal of Occupational Therapy* 37(7):479–84.

Dickstein, R., et al. 1986. Stroke rehabilitation. Three exercise therapy approaches. *Physical Therapy* 66(8):1233–8.

Goodman, M. 1985. Effect of early neurodevelopmental therapy in normal and at-risk survivors of neonatal intensive care. *Lancet* 2(8468):1327–30.

Guarna, R. 1988. An evaluation of the hemiplegic subject based on the Bobath approach: The model, part 1. *Scandinavian Journal of Rehabilitation Medicine* 20(1):1–4.

Harris, S.R. 1981. Effects of neurodevelopmental therapy on motor performance of infants with Down's syndrome. *Developmental Medicine and Child Neurology* 23:477–83.

Herndon, W.A., et al. 1987. Effects of neurodevelopmental treatment on movement patterns of children with cerebral palsy. *Journal of Pediatric Orthopedics* 7(4):395–400.

Kong, E. 1966. Very early treatment of cerebral palsy. *Developmental Medicine and Child Neurology* 8:198–202.

Laskas, C.A., S.L. Mullen, D.L. Nelson, et al. 1985. Enhancement of two motor functions of the lower extremity in a child with spastic quadriplegia. *Physical Therapy* 65(1):11–6.

Logigian, M.K., M.A. Samuels, J. Falconer, et al. 1983. Clinical exercise trial for stroke patients. *Archives of Physical Medicine and Rehabilitation* 64(8):364–7.

Morrison, D., and J. Sublett. 1986. The effects of sensory integration therapy on nystagmus duration, equilibrium reactions and visual-motor integration in reading retarded children. *Child: Care, Health and Development* 12(2):99–110.

Mulder, T., W. Hulstign, and J. van der Meer. 1986. EMG feedback and the restoration of motor control. A controlled group study of 12 hemiparetic patients. *American Journal of Physical Medicine* 65(4):173–88.

Ottenbacher, K.J. 1986. Quantitative analysis of the effectiveness of pediatric therapy. Emphasis on the neurodevelopmental treatment approach. *Physical Therapy* 66(7):1095–101.

Parette, H.P., Jr., L.F. Holder, and J.D. Sears. 1984. Correlates of therapeutic progress by infants with cerebral palsy and motor delay. *Perceptual and Motor Skills* 58(11):159–63.

Piper, M.C., et al. 1986. Early physical therapy effects on the high-risk infants: A randomized controlled trial. *Pediatrics* 78:216–224.

Scherzer, A., V. Mike, and J. Ilson. 1976. Physical therapy as a determinant of change in the cerebral palsied infant. *Pediatrics* 58:47–52.

Smith, M.M. 1983. Applying the neurodevelopmental treatment approach to OT. *Developmental Disabilities Special Interest Section Newsletter* 6(4):1–2.

Sussman, M.D. 1983. Casting as an adjunct to neurodevelopmental therapy for cerebral palsy. *Developmental Medicine and Child Neurology* 25(6):804–5.

Watt, J., et al. 1986. A prospective study of inhibitive casting as an adjunct to physiotherapy for cerebral-palsied children. *Developmental Medicine and Child Neurology* 28(4):480–8.

Wright, T., and J. Nicholson. 1973. Physiotherapy for the spastic child: An evaluation. *Developmental Medicine and Child Neurology*, 15:146–63.

KIELHOFNER'S THEORY OF HUMAN OCCUPATION

Barris, R., and G. Kielhofner. 1985. Generating and using knowledge in occupational therapy: Implication for professional education. *Occupational Therapy Journal of Research* 5(2):113–24.

Barris, R., and G. Kielhofner. 1986. Beliefs, perspectives, and activities of psychosocial occupational therapy educators. *American Journal of Occupational Therapy* 40(8):535–41.

Barris, R., G. Kielhofner, and D. Bauer. 1985. Educational experience and changes in learning and value preferences. *Occupational Therapy Journal of Research* 5(4):243–56.

Barris, R., G. Kielhofner, and D. Bauer. 1985. Learning preferences, values and student satisfaction...Occupational therapy students and physical therapy students. *Journal of Allied Health* 14(1):13–23.

Barris, R., G. Kielhofner, R.B. Martin, et al. 1986. Occupational function and dysfunction in three groups of adolescents. *Occupational Therapy Journal of Research* 6(5):301–17.

Duellman, M.K., R. Barris, and G. Kielhofner. 1986. Organized activity and the adaptive status of nursing home residents. *American Journal of Occupational Therapy* 40(9):618–22.

Fisher, A.G., G. Kielhofner, and C. Davis. 1989. Research values of occupational and physical therapists. *Journal of Allied Health* 18(2):143–55.

Harrison, H., and G. Kielhofner. 1986. Examining reliability and validity of the Preschool Play Scale with handicapped children. *American Journal of Occupational Therapy* 40(3):167–73.

Kielhofner, G. 1977. Temporal adaptation: A conceptual framework for occupational therapy. *American Journal of Occupational Therapy* 31(4):235–42.

Kielhofner, G. 1978. General systems theory. *American Journal of Occupational Therapy* 32(10):637–45.

Kielhofner, G. 1979. The temporal dimension in the lives of retarded adults: A problem of interaction and intervention. *American Journal of Occupational Therapy* 33(3):161–8.

Kielhofner, G. 1980. A model of human occupation, Part 2. Ontogenesis from the perspective of temporal adaptation. *American Journal of Occupational Therapy* 34(10):657–63.

Kielhofner, G. 1980. A model of human occupation, Part 3. Benign and vicious cycles. *American Journal of Occupational Therapy* 34(11):731–7.

Kielhofner, G. 1982. A heritage of activity: Development of theory. *American Journal of Occupational Therapy* 35(11):723–12.

Kielhofner, G., ed. 1983. *Health through occupation: Theory and practice in occupational therapy*. Philadelphia: F.A. Davis.

Kielhofner, G. 1984. An overview of research on the model of human occupation. *Canadian Journal of Occupational Therapy* 51(2):59–67.

Kielhofner, G., ed. 1985. *A model of human occupation: Theory and application*. Baltimore, MD: Williams & Wilkins.

Kielhofner, G. 1985. The demise of diffidence: An agenda for occupational therapy. *Canadian Journal of Occupational Therapy* 52(4):165–71.

Kielhofner, G. 1986. A review of research on the model of human occupation. Part 1. *Canadian Journal of Occupational Therapy* 53(2):69–74.

Kielhofner, G. 1986. A review of research on the model of human occupation. Part 2. *Canadian Journal of Occupational Therapy* 53(3):129–34.

Kielhofner, G., and R. Barris. 1984. Collecting data on play: A critique of available methods. *Occupational Therapy Journal of Research* 4(3):150–80.

Kielhofner, G., and R. Barris. 1984. Mental health occupational therapy: Trends in literature and practice. *Occupational Therapy in Mental Health* 4(4):35–50.

Kielhofner, G., and R. Barris. 1986. Organization of knowledge in occupational therapy: A proposal and a survey of the literature. *Occupational Therapy Journal of Research* 6(2):67–84.

Kielhofner, G., R. Barris, D. Bauer, et al. 1983. A comparison of play behavior in nonhospitalized and hospitalized children. *American Journal of Occupational Therapy* 37(5):304–12.

Kielhofner, G., R. Barris, and J.H. Watts. 1982. Habits and habit dysfunction: A clinical perspective for psychosocial occupational therapy. *Occupational Therapy in Mental Health* 2(1):1–21.

Kielhofner, G., and M. Brinson. 1989. Development and evaluation of an aftercare program for young chronic psychiatrically disabled adults. *Occupational Therapy in Mental Health* 9(2):1–25.

Kielhofner, G., and J.P. Burke. 1977. Occupational therapy after 60 years: An account of changing identity and knowledge. *American Journal of Occupational Therapy* 31(10): 676–89.

Kielhofner, G., and J.P. Burke. 1980. A model of human occupation, Part 1. Conceptual framework and content. *American Journal of Occupational Therapy* 34(9):572–81.

Kielhofner, G., J.P. Burke, and C.H. Igi. 1980. A model of human occupation, Part 4. Assessment and intervention. *American Journal of Occupational Therapy* 34(12):777–88.

Kielhofner, G., B. Harlan, D. Bauer, et al. 1986. The reliability of a historical interview with physically disabled respondents. *American Journal of Occupational Therapy* 40(8):551–6.

Kielhofner, G., and A.D. Henry. 1988. Development and investigation of the Occupational Performance History Interview. *American Journal of Occupational Therapy* 42(8): 489–98.

Kielhofner, G., and S. Miyake. 1981. The therapeutic use of games with mentally retarded adults. *American Journal of Occupational Therapy* 35(6):375–82.

Kielhofner, G., and G. Nelson. 1983. A study of patient motivation and cooperation/participation in occupational therapy. *Occupational Therapy Journal of Research* 3(1):35–46.

Kielhofner, G., and M. Nicol. 1989. The model of human occupation: A developing conceptual tool for clinicians. *British Journal of Occupational Therapy* 52(6):210–4.

Kielhofner, G., and N. Takata. 1980. A study of mentally retarded persons: Applied research in occupational therapy. *American Journal of Occupational Therapy* 34(4):252–8.

Lederer, J.M., G. Kielhofner, and J.H. Watts. 1985. Values, personal causation and skills of delinquents and nondelinquents. *Occupational Therapy in Mental Health* 5(2):59–77.

Neville, A., A. Kreisberg, and G. Kielhofner. 1985. Temporal dysfunction in schizophrenia. *Occupational Therapy in Mental Health* 5(1):1–19.

Oakley, F., G. Kielhofner, and R. Barris. 1985. An occupational therapy approach to assessing psychiatric patients' adaptive functioning. *American Journal of Occupational Therapy* 39(3):147–54.

Oakley, F., G. Kielhofner, R. Barris, et al. 1986. The Role Checklist: Development and empirical assessment of reliability. *Occupational Therapy Journal of Research* 6(3):157–70.

Smith, N.R., G. Kielhofner, and J.H. Watts. 1986. The relationships between volition, activity pattern, and life satisfaction in the elderly. *American Journal of Occupational Therapy* 40(4):278–83.

Smyntek, L., R. Barris, and G. Kielhofner. 1985. The model of human occupation applied to psychosocially functional and dysfunctional adolescents. *Occupational Therapy in Mental Health* 5(1):21–39.

Watts, J.H., G. Kielhofner, D.F. Bauer, et al. 1986. The assessment of occupational functioning: A screening tool for use in long-term care. *American Journal of Occupational Therapy* 40(4):231–40.

HUMAN OCCUPATION

Baron, K.B. 1987. The model of human occupation: A newspaper treatment group for adolescents with a diagnosis of conduct disorder. *Occupational Therapy in Mental Health* 7(2):89–104.

Barris, R. 1986. Occupational dysfunction and eating disorders: Theory and approach to treatment. *Occupational Therapy in Mental Health* 6(1):27–45.

Barris, R., V. Dickie, and K.B. Baron. 1988. A comparison of psychiatric patients and normal subjects based on the model of human occupation. *Occupational Therapy Journal of Research* 8(1):3–23.

Burrows, E. 1989. Clinical practice: An approach to the assessment of clinical competencies. *British Journal of Occupational Therapy* 52(6):222–6.

Burton, J.E. 1989. The model of human occupation and occupational therapy practice with elderly patients: I. Characteristics of ageing. *British Journal of Occupational Therapy* 52(6):215–8.

Burton, J.E. 1989. The model of human occupation and occupational therapy practice with elderly patients: II. Application. *British Journal of Occupational Therapy* 52(6):219–21.

Cubie, S.H., and K. Kaplan. 1982. A case analysis for the model of human occupation. *American Journal of Occupational Therapy* 36(10):645–56.

Ebb, E.W., W. Coster, and L. Duncombe. 1989. Comparison of normal and psychosocially dysfunctional male adolescents. *Occupational Therapy in Mental Health* 9(2):53–74.

Elliott, M.S., and R. Barris. 1987. Occupational role performance and life satisfaction in elderly persons. *Occupational Therapy Journal of Research* 7(4):215–24.

Gusich, R.L. 1984. Occupational therapy for chronic pain: A clinical application of the model of human occupation. *Occupational Therapy in Mental Health* 4(3):59–73.

Kaplan, K.L. 1986. The directive group: Short-term treatment for psychiatric patients with a minimal level of functioning. *American Journal of Occupational Therapy* 40(7):474–81.

Kaplan, K. 1984. Short-term assessment: The need and a response. *Occupational Therapy in Mental Health* 4(3):29–45.

Katz, N., N. Giladei, and C. Peretz. 1988. Cross-cultural application of occupational therapy assessment: Human occupation with psychiatric inpatients and controls in Israel. *Occupational Therapy in Mental Health* 8(1):7–30.

Katz, N., N. Josman, and N. Steinmetz. 1988. Relationship between cognitive disability theory and the model of human occupation in the assessment of psychiatric and nonpsychiatric adolescents. *Occupational Therapy in Mental Health* 8(1):31–43.

Khoo, S.W., and R.M. Renwick. 1989. A model of human occupational perspective on the mental health of immigrant women in Canada. *Occupational Therapy in Mental Health* 9(3):31–49.

Levine, R.E. 1984. The cultural aspects of home care delivery. *American Journal of Occupational Therapy* 38(11):734–8.

Morgan, D., and L. Jongbloed. 1990. Factors influencing leisure activities following a stroke: An exploratory study. *Canadian Journal of Occupational Therapy* 57(4):223–9.

Oakley, F. 1987. Clinical application of the model of human occupation in dementia of the Alzheimer's type. *Occupational Therapy in Mental Health* 7(4):37–50.

Olin, D.W. 1984. Assessing and assisting the persons with dementia: An occupational behavior perspective. *Physical and Occupational Therapy in Geriatrics* 3(4):25–32.

Pizzi, M. 1990. The model of human occupation and adults with HIV infection and AIDS. *American Journal of Occupational Therapy* 44(3):257–64.

Rust, K., R. Barris, and F.H. Hooper. 1987. Use of the model of human occupation to predict women's exercise behavior. *Occupational Therapy Journal of Research* 7(1):23–35.

Salz, C. 1983. A theoretical approach to the treatment of work difficulties in borderline personalities. *Occupational Therapy in Mental Health* 3(3):33–46.

Sholle-Martin, S. 1987. Application of the model of human occupation: Assessment in child and adolescent psychiatry. *Occupational Therapy in Mental Health* 7(2):3–22.

Wieringa, N., and M. McColl. 1987. Implications of the model of human occupation for the intervention with Native Canadians. *Occupational Therapy in Health Care* 4(1):73–91.

RESOURCE BIBLIOGRAPHY

EVALUATION PROCEDURES

Coordination

Zoltan, B., and L.W. Pedretti. 1990. Evaluation of muscle tone and coordination—coordination. In *Occupational therapy: Practice skills for physical dysfunction*, 3d ed., ed. L.W. Pedretti and B. Zoltan, 137–40. St. Louis: C.V. Mosby.

Endurance

Trombly, C.A., and A.D. Scott. 1989. Evaluation-endurance. In *Occupational therapy for physical dysfunction*, 3d ed., ed. C.A. Trombly, 284–5. Baltimore, MD: Williams & Wilkins.

Equilibrium

Fisher, A.G., J. Mixon, and R. Herman. 1986. Validity of the clinical diagnosis of vestibular dysfunction. *Occupational Therapy Journal of Research* 6:3–20.

Fisher, A.G., S.E. Wietlishach, and J.L. Wilbarger. 1988. Adult performance on three tests of equilibrium. *American Journal of Occupational Therapy* 42(1):30–5.

Fisher, A.G. 1989. Objective assessment of the quality of response during two equilibrium tasks. *Physical and Occupational Therapy in Pediatrics* 9(3):57–78.

Izraelevitz, T.A., A.G. Fisher, and A.C. Bundy. 1985. Equilibrium reactions in preschoolers. *Occupational Therapy Journal of Research* 5:154–69.

Force Gauge—Muscle Tone

McPherson J.J., et al. 1985. Muscle tone: Objective evaluation of static components at the wrist. *Archives of Physical Medicine and Rehabilitation* 66(10):170–4.

Grip Strength

Ager, C.L., B.L. Olivett, and C.L. Johnson. 1984. Grasp and pinch strength in children 5 to 12 years old. *American Journal of Occupational Therapy* 38(2):107–13.

Apfel, E. 1985. The effect of thumb interphalangeal joint position on strength of key pinch. *Journal of Hand Surgery* 11A:47–51.

Bowman, O.J., and B. Katz. 1984. Hand strength and prone extension in right-dominant, 6 to 9 year olds. *American Journal of Occupational Therapy* 38(6):367–76.

Fess, E.E. 1987. A method for checking Jamar dynamometer calibration. *Journal of Hand Therapy* 1(1):28–32.

Fike, M.L., and E. Rosseau. 1982. Measurement of adult hand strength: A comparison of two instruments. *Occupational Therapy Journal of Research* 2(1):43–5.

Flood-Joy, M., and V. Mathiowetz. 1987. Grip-strength measurement: A comparison of three Jamar dynamometers. *Occupational Therapy Journal of Research* 7(4):235–43.

Hinson, M., and B.E. Gench. 1989. The curvilinear relationship of grip strength to age. *Occupational Therapy Journal of Research* 9(1):53–60.

King, J.W. 1988. A comparison of two static grip testing methods and its clinical application: A preliminary study. *Journal of Hand Therapy* 1(5):204–8.

Mathiowetz, V., K. Weber, G. Volland, et al. 1984. Reliability and validity of hand strength evaluations. *Journal of Hand Surgery* 9A:222–6.

Mathiowetz, V., N. Kashman, G. Volland, et al. 1985. Grip and pinch strength: Normative data for adults. *Archives of Physical Medicine and Rehabilitation* 66:69–72.

Mathiowetz, V., C. Rennells, and L. Donahoe. 1985. Effect of elbow position on grip and key pinch strength. *Journal of Hand Surgery* 10A:694–7.

Mathiowetz, V., D.M. Wiemer, and S.M. Federman. 1986. Grip and pinch strength: Norms for 6- to 19-year-olds. *American Journal of Occupational Therapy* 40(10):705–11.

Mathiowetz, V. 1990. Grip and pinch strength measurements. In *Muscle strength testing: Instrumented and non-instrumented systems*, ed. L.R. Amundsen, 163–77. New York: Churchill Livingstone.

Mathiowetz, V. 1990. Effects of three trials on grip and pinch strength measurements. *Journal of Hand Therapy* 3(4):195–8.

Petersen, P., et al. 1989. Grip strength and hand dominance: Challenging the 10% rule. *American Journal of Occupational Therapy* 43(7):444–7.

Robertson, A., and J. Deitz. 1988. A description of grip strength in preschool children. *American Journal of Occupational Therapy* 42(10):647–52.

Trossman, P.B., and P.W. Li. 1989. The effect of the duration of intertrial rest periods on isometric grip strength performance in young adults. *Occupational Therapy Journal of Research* 9(6):362–78.

Woody, R., and V. Mathiowetz. 1988. Effect of forearm position on pinch strength measurements. *Journal of Hand Surgery* 1(3):123–6.

Young, V.L., et al. 1989. Fluctuation in grip and pinch strength among normal subjects. *Journal of Hand Surgery* 14A:124–9.

Muscle Strength

Clarkson, H.M., and G.B. Gilewich. 1989. *Musculoskeletal assessment: Joint range of motion and manual muscle strength*. Baltimore, MD: Williams & Wilkins.

Kendal F.P., and E.K. McCreary. 1983. *Muscles: Testing and function*, 3d ed. Baltimore, MD: Williams & Wilkins (not occupational therapists).

Pedretti, L.W. 1990. Evaluation of muscle strength. In *Occupational therapy: Practice skills for physical dysfunction*, 3d ed., ed. L.W. Pedretti and B. Zoltan, 89–130. St. Louis: C.V. Mosby.

Trombly, C.A., and A.D. Scott. 1989. Evaluation of motor control—muscle strength. In *Occupational therapy for physical dysfunction*, 3d ed., ed. C.A. Trombly, 231–81 Baltimore, MD: Williams & Wilkins.

Muscle Tone

Trombly, C.A., and A.D. Scott. 1989. Evaluation of motor control—muscle tone. In *Occupational therapy for physical dysfunction*, 3d ed., ed. C.A. Trombly, 56–9. Baltimore, MD: Williams & Wilkins.

Zoltan, B., and L.W. Pedretti. 1990. Evaluation of muscle tone and coordination—muscle tone. In *Occupational therapy: Practice skills for physical dysfunction*, 3d ed., ed. L.W. Pedretti and B. Zoltan, 131–37. St. Louis: C.V. Mosby.

Range of Motion

American Academy of Orthopaedic Surgeons. 1965. *Joint motion: Method of measuring and recording*. Chicago, IL: The Academy.

Clarkson, H.M., and G.B. Gilewich. 1989. *Musculoskeletal assessment: Joint range of motion and manual muscle strength*. Baltimore, MD: Williams & Wilkins.

Horger, M.M. 1990. The reliability of goniometric measurements of active and passive wrist motions. *American Journal of Occupational Therapy* 44(4):342–8.

Pedretti, L.W. 1990. Evaluation of joint range of motion. In *Occupational therapy: Practice skills for physical dysfunction*, 3d ed., ed. L.W. Pedretti and B. Zoltan, 61–88. St. Louis: C.V. Mosby.

Sullivan, J., and S. Poole. 1981. Range of motion. In *Physical disabilities manual*, ed. B.C. Abreu, 9–21. New York: Raven Press.

Trombly, C.A., and A.D. Scott. 1989. Evaluation. In *Occupational therapy for physical dysfunction*, 3d ed., ed. C.A. Trombly, 184–230. Baltimore, MD: Williams & Wilkins.

Reflexes and Reactions

Fiorentino, M.R. 1973. *Reflex testing methods for evaluating CNS development*. Springfield, IL: Charles C Thomas.

Henderson, A. 1980. Problems in the assessment of change in abnormal reflex behavior. In *Intervention with at-risk and handicapped infants: From research to application*, ed. D.D. Bricker, 129–38. Baltimore, MD: University Park Press.

Lawler, J. 1981. Testing reflexes. In *Physical disabilities manual*, ed. B.C. Abreu, 99–116. New York: Raven Press.

Stilwell, J.M. 1981. Relationship between development of the body-righting reaction and manual midline crossing behavior in the learning disabled. *American Journal of Occupational Therapy* 35(6):391–8.

Trombly, C.A., and A.D. Scott. 1989. Evaluation of motor control—evaluation of reflex integration. In *Occupational therapy for physical dysfunction*, 3d ed., ed. C.A. Trombly, 59–64. Baltimore, MD: Williams & Wilkins.

Zoltan, B. 1990. Evaluation of reflexes and reactions. In *Occupational therapy: Practice skills in physical dysfunction*, 3d ed., ed. L.W. Pedretti and B. Zoltan, 141–5. St. Louis: C.V. Mosby.

Semmes-Weinstein Monofilaments (Light Touch-Deep Pressure)

Bell-Krotoski, J., and E. Tomancik. 1987. The repeatability of testing with Semmes-Weinstein monofilaments. *Journal of Hand Surgery* 12A(1):155–61.

Bell, J.A. 1984. Light touch-deep pressure testing using Semmes-Weinstein monofilaments. In *Rehabilitation of the hand*, 2d ed., ed. J.M. Hunter, et al., 399–406. St. Louis: C.V. Mosby. 3d ed., 1990, 585–93.

Szabo, R.M., R.H. Gelberman, R.V. Williamson, et al. 1984. Vibratory sensory testing in acute peripheral nerve compression. *Journal of Hand Surgery* 9A:104–9.

Sensation

Callahan, A.D. 1984. Sensibility testing: Clinical methods. In *Rehabilitation of the hand*, 2d ed., ed. J.M. Hunter, et al., 407–31. St. Louis: C.V. Mosby. 3d ed., 1990, 594–610.

Pedretti, L.W. 1990. Evaluation of sensation and treatment of sensory dysfunction. In *Occupational therapy: Practice skills in physical dysfunction,* 3d ed., ed. L.W. Pedretti and B. Zoltan, 177–93. St. Louis: C.V. Mosby.

Trombly, C.A., and A.D. Scott. 1989. Evaluation and treatment of somatosensory sensation. In *Occupational therapy for physical dysfunction*, 3d ed., ed. C.A. Trombly, 41–54. Baltimore, MD: Williams & Wilkins.

Torque Strength

Wolf, L.D., L. Klein, and E. Cauldwell-Klein. 1987. Comparison of torque strength measurements on two evaluation devices. *Journal of Hand Therapy* 1(1):24–7.

Two-Point Discrimination Testing

Crosby, P.M., and A.L. Dellon. 1989. Comparison of two-point discrimination testing devices. *Microsurgery* 10:134–7.

Dellon, A.L., S.E. Mackinnon, and P.M. Crosby. 1987. Reliability of two-point discrimination measurement. *Journal of Hand Surgery* 12A(5, pt.1):693–6.

Levin, L.S., et al. 1989. Variations in two-point discrimination as a function of terminal probes. *Microsurgery* 10:236–41.

Vibration

Szabo, R.M., R.H. Gelberman, R.V. Williamson, et al. 1984. Vibratory sensory testing in acute peripheral nerve compression. *Journal of Hand Surgery* 9A:104–9.

Volumetry

Schultz-Johnson, K. 1988. *Volumetry: A literature review*. Santa Monica, CA: Upper Extremity Technology, 2210 Santa Monica Blvd., Suite A. (Available from Smith and Nephew.)

RESOURCE BIBLIOGRAPHY
MEDIA, MODALITIES, AND TECHNIQUES

Accessibility—Barrier-Free Design

Aino, E.A., and R.D. Loversidge. 1977. *Access for all: An illustrated handbook of barrier free design*. Columbus, OH: Special Press (not occupational therapists).

Bruck, L. 1978. *Access: The guide to a better life for disabled Americans*. New York: Random House (not an occupational therapist).

Cary, J.R. 1978. *How to create interiors for the disabled: A guidebook for family and friends.* New York: Pantheon Books (not an occupational therapist).

Hughes, D. 1988. Housing modifications. In *Rehabilitation of the physically disabled adult,* ed. C.J. Goodwill and M.A. Chamberlain, 637–47. London, England: Croom Helm (not an occupational therapist).

Martin, L.M. 1987. Wheelchair accessibility of public buildings in Utica, New York. *American Journal of Occupational Therapy* 41(4):217–21.

Somervile, N.J., and H.M. Pendleton. 1985. Evaluating and solving home access problems. *Clinics in Physical Therapy* v.6, 243–65. Edinburgh, Scotland: Churchill Livingstone.

Activity Programs

Crepeau, E.L. 1986. *Activity programming for the elderly.* Boston: Little, Brown and Company.

Curley, J.S. 1983. An activities program in a long term care facility: Development of a documentation system that focuses on problems and goals. *Quarterly Review Bulletin,* republished in *Activities, Adaptation & Aging* 3:9–19.

Deichman, E.S., and C.P. O'Kane. 1980. *Working with the elderly,* rev. ed. Buffalo, NY: Potentials Development, Inc.

Judd, M.W. 1983. *Keep in touch.* Winnipeg, Canada: Winnipeg Municipal Hospital.

Lang, E., and M. Mattson. 1985. The multidisciplinary treatment plan: A format for enhancing activity therapy department involvement. *Hospital and Community Psychiatry* 36(1):62–8.

Art and Crafts

Bessell, J.C., and Z. Mailloux. 1981. The use of crafts in occupational therapy for the physically disabled. *American Journal of Occupational Therapy* 35(6):369–74.

Conroy, R.M., M. McDonnel, and J. Swinney. 1986. Process-centred art therapy in anorexia nervosa. *British Journal of Occupational Therapy* 49(10):322–3.

Dioda, A., and K. Hunter. 1990. Woodcarving and ceramics as therapeutic activities. In *Rehabilitation of the hand,* 3d ed., ed. J.M. Hunter, et al., 1165–74. St. Louis: C.V. Mosby (not occupational therapists).

Fidler, G.S. 1981. From crafts to competence. *American Journal of Occupational Therapy* 35(9):567–73.

Kelly, G. 1984. Children's drawings as a means of nonverbal communication: An introduction. *British Journal of Occupational Therapy* 47(8):244–6.

King, P., et al. 1987. Using pottery with elderly people. *British Journal of Occupational Therapy* 50(11):384.

Williams, D. et al. 1987. Crafts: A criminal offence? *British Journal of Occupational Therapy* 50(1):12–5.

Biofeedback

Abildness, A.H. 1982. *Biofeedback strategies.* Rockville, MD: American Occupational Therapy Association.

Abildness, A. 1988. Biofeedback. In *Willard and Spackman's occupational therapy,* 7th ed., ed. H.L. Hopkins and H.D. Smith, 346–53. Philadelphia: J.B. Lippincott.

Blackmore, S.M., and D.A. Williams. 1990. The use of biofeedback in hand rehabilitation. In *Rehabilitation of the hand,* 3d ed., ed. J.M. Hunter, et al., 979–93. St. Louis: C.V. Mosby.

Brown, D.M., and F. Nahai. 1989. Biofeedback strategies of the occupational therapist in total hand rehabilitation. In *Biofeedback: Principles and practice for clinicians*, 3d ed., ed. J.V. Basmajian, 123–40. Baltimore, MD: Williams & Wilkins.

Brown, D.M. 1984. Current concepts and capabilities of electromyographic and electrokinesiologic feedback in the total management of traumatic hand injuries. In *Rehabilitation of the hand*, 2d ed., ed. J.M. Hunter, et al., 729–46. St. Louis: C.V. Mosby.

Crofts, F., and J. Crofts. 1988. Biofeedback and the computer...use of the Myolink with orthopaedic patients. *British Journal of Occupational Therapy* 51(2):60–2.

Harburn, K., and S. Spaulding. 1987. Use of a biofeedback device to promote appropriate muscle involvement during prescribed activities. *Canadian Journal of Occupational Therapy* 54(2):79–80.

Lee, W.A. 1989. A control systems framework for understanding normal and abnormal posture. *American Journal of Occupational Therapy* 43(5):291–301.

Shumway-Cook, A., D. Anson, and S. Haller. 1988. Postural sway biofeedback: Its effect on reestablishing stance stability in hemiplegic patients. *Archives of Physical Medicine and Rehabilitation* 69(6):395–400.

Trombly, C.A. 1989. Biofeedback as an adjunct to therapy. In *Occupational therapy for physical dysfunction*, 3d ed., ed. C.A. Trombly, 316–28. Baltimore, MD: Williams & Wilkins.

Clothing Adaptations
Dallas, M.J., and L.W. White. 1982. Clothing fasteners for women with arthritis. *American Journal of Occupational Therapy* 36(8):515–8.

Goldsworthy, M. 1981. *Clothes for disabled people*. London, England: B.T. Batsford Ltd. (not an occupational therapist).

Hoffman, A.M. 1979. *Clothing for the handicapped, the aged, and other people with special needs*. Springfield, IL: Charles C Thomas (not an occupational therapist).

Kernaleguen, A. 1978. *Clothing designs for the handicapped*. Edmonton, Alberta, Canada: The University of Alberta Press (not an occupational therapist).

Morrison, S. 1986. Clothing adaptations for the disabled. *Journal of Practical Nursing* 36(1):46–7.

Cognitive Retraining
Dougherty, P.M., and M.V. Radmonski. 1987. *The cognitive rehabilitation workbook: A systematic approach to improving independent living skills in brain-injured adults*. Gaithersburg, MD: Aspen Publishers, Inc.

Holloran, S.M. 1983. *Cognitive reorganization: A stimulus handbook*. Tigard, OR: C.C. Publishing (not an occupational therapist).

Parker, V.S., and N.L. TenBroek. 1987. *Problem solving, planning and organizational tasks: Strategies for retraining*. Tucson, AZ: Communication Skill Builders.

Communication Aids
Brandenburg, S.A., and G.C. Vanderheiden, eds. 1987. *Communication, control, and computer access for disabled and elderly individuals*, 3 vols. Boston: College-Hill (not occupational therapists).

Lossing, C.A. 1984. Occupational therapists' role in a Morse-code-based communication system. *Developmental Disabilities Special Interest Section Newsletter* 7(1):3.

Quanbery, A., and K. Spuling. 1985. Electronic aids for the physically handicapped. In *Atlas of orthotics*, 2d ed., American Academy of Orthopaedic Surgeons, 513–25. St. Louis: C.V. Mosby.

Richardson, N.K. 1959. *Type with one hand*, 2d ed. Cincinnati, OH: Southwestern Publishing Co. (not an occupational therapist).

Smith, R.O., et al. 1989. Effectiveness of a writing system using a Computerized Long-range Optical Pointer and 10-Branch Abbreviation Expansion. *Journal of Rehabilitation Research and Development* 26(1):51–62.

Trefler, E., and D. Crislip. 1985. No aid, an Etran, a Minspeak: A comparison of efficiency and effectiveness during structured use. *Augmentative and Alternative Communication* 1(4):151–5.

Workman, D., C. Geggie, and G. Creasey. 1988. The microcomputer as an aid to written communication. *British Journal of Occupational Therapy* 51(6):188–90.

Computers

Armstrong, J., and J. Rennie. 1986. We can use computers too. The setting up of a project for mentally handicapped residents. *British Journal of Occupational Therapy* 49(9):297–300.

Bischof, J., and G. Hedmann. 1990. Computer access. *Physical and Occupational Therapy in Pediatrics* 10(2):93–121.

Clark, E.N., ed. 1986. *Microcomputers: Clinical applications*. Thorofare, NJ: Slack Inc.

Clark, Y.U. 1984. The microcomputer: Managerial aid and therapy tool for the profession. *British Journal of Occupational Therapy* 47(9):274–7.

Cromwell, F.C., ed. 1986. *Computer applications in occupational therapy*. New York: Haworth Press.

Frank, B. 1987. Accessible computing: An overview. *Developmental Disabilities Special Interest Section Newsletter* 10(3):1,4–5.

Hume, C. 1984. Microcomputers in occupational therapy departments: The therapeutic application. *British Journal of Occupational Therapy* 47(6):175–77.

Kirsch, N.L. 1987. Focus on clinical research: The microcomputer as an "orthotic" device for patients with cognitive deficits. *Journal of Head Trauma Rehabilitation* 2(4):77–86.

Okoye, R. 1985. Computer games and cognitive rehabilitation. *Physical Disabilities Special Interest Section Newsletter* 8(1):5–6.

Okoye, R.L. 1988. Computer technology in occupational therapy. In *Willard and Spackman's occupational therapy*, 7th ed., ed. H.L. Hopkins and H.D. Smith, 330–5. Philadelphia: J.B. Lippincott.

Reid, J. 1990. Computers and occupational therapy. In *Occupational therapy and mental health: Principles, skills and practice*, ed. J. Creek, 267–88. Edinburgh, Scotland: Churchill Livingstone.

Roberts, D. 1986. The use of computers in occupational therapy at the rehabilitation unit, Odstock Hospital: A review. *British Journal of Occupational Therapy* 49(5):157–60.

Smart, S., and D. Richards. 1986. The use of touch sensitive screens in rehabilitation therapy. *British Journal of Occupational Therapy* 49(10):335–8.

Smart, S. 1988. Computers as treatment: The use of the computer as an occupational therapy medium. *Clinical Rehabilitation* 2:61–9.

Spicer, M.M., and S.L. McMillan. 1987. Computers and occupational therapy. *American Journal of Occupational Therapy* 41(11):726–32.

Tan, J.C. 1990. Computerizing your private practice. *Occupational Therapy Forum* 5(43): 7–11.

Treviranus, J., and R. Tannock. 1987. A scanning computer access system for children with severe physical disabilities. *American Journal of Occupational Therapy* 41(11):733–8.

Wall, N. 1984. Microcomputer activities and occupational therapy. *Developmental Disabilities Special Interest Section Newsletter* 7(1):1–2.

Weber, M.P., ed. 1984. Microcomputers in occupational therapy. *Physical Disabilities Special Interest Section Newsletter* 7(2):1–4.

Winter, J., A.F. Newell, and J.L. Arnott. 1985. The therapeutic applications of computerised games. *International Journal of Bio-Medical Computing* 17:185–93.

Workman, D., C. Geggie, and G. Creasey. 1988. The microcomputer as an aid to written communication. *British Journal of Occupational Therapy* 51(6):188–90.

Wright, C., and M. Nomura. 1985. *From toys to computers: Access for the physically disabled child.* P.O. Box 700242, San Jose, CA 95170: author. Revised, 1987. Revised, 1988. (Available from Fred Sammons.)

Continuous Passive Motion (CPM)

Covey, M. 1988. Application of CPM devices with burn patients. *Journal of Burn Care & Rehabilitation* 9(5):496–7.

Covey, M., K.D. Dutcher, J.A. Marvin, et al. 1988. Efficacy of continuous passive motion (CPM) devices with hand burns. *Journal of Burn Care & Rehabilitation* 9(4):397–400.

Dimick, M.P. 1990. Continuous passive motion for the upper extremity. In *Rehabilitation of the hand*, 3d ed., ed. J.M. Hunter, et al., 1140–6. St. Louis: C.V. Mosby.

Giudice, M.L. 1990. Effects of continuous passive motion and elevation on hand edema. *American Journal of Occupational Therapy* 44(10):914–20.

McGough, C.E. 1988. Introduction to CPM (continuous passive motion). *Journal of Burn Care & Rehabilitation* 9(5):494–5.

Cooking

Bachner, S. 1984. *Picture this—an illustrated guide to complete dinners.* Greenwich, CT: Special Additions, Inc.

Bingham, B. 1985. *Cooking with fragile hands.* Naples, FL: Creative Cuisine, Inc.

Mealtime manual for people with disabilities and the aging. 1978. Camden, NJ: Campbell Soup Co.

McLean, V., and T. Mcnamara. 1987. Cooking program: A pilot study. *Occupational Therapy Journal of Research* 7(1):57–60.

Whiteman, E. 1989. Microwave cookers: Their value for people with disabilities. *British Journal of Occupational Therapy* 52(2):55–8.

Dance

Evans, S. 1984. Social dance in an occupational therapy programme. *Australian Occupational Therapy Journal* 31(1):28–31.

Van Deusen, J., and D. Harlowe. 1987. A comparison of the ROM dance home exercise/rest program with traditional routines. *Occupational Therapy Journal of Research* 7(6): 349–61.

Van Deusen, J., and D. Harlowe. 1987. Efficacy of the ROM dance program for adults with rheumatoid arthritis. *American Journal of Occupational Therapy* 41(2):90–95.

Developmental Therapy

Boehme, R. 1988. *Improving upper body control: An approach to assessment and treatment of tonal dysfunction.* Tucson, AZ: Therapy Skill Builders.

Campbell, P.H. 1989. Posture and movement. In *Implementing early intervention*, ed. C. Tingey, 189–208. Baltimore, MD: Paul H. Brookes Publishing.

Click, M., and J. Davis. 1982. *Moving right along: Developmental goals for physically disabled children.* Phoenix, AZ: EdCorp.

Siegling, L.S., and M. Click. 1984. *At arm's length: Goals for arm and hand function.* Phoenix, AZ: EdCorp.

Drama/Psychodrama

Beagan, D. 1985. Spontaneity and creativity in the NHS: Starting a new group—psychodrama with adult day patients. *British Journal of Occupational Therapy* 48(12):370–4.

Brown, T. 1990. Drama and occupational therapy. In *Occupational therapy in mental health: Principles, skills and practice*, ed. J. Creek, 211–27. Edinburgh, Scotland: Churchill Livingstone.

Trafford, G., and A. Perks. 1987. Drama therapy in a child and family psychiatry unit. *British Journal of Occupational Therapy* 50(3):94–6.

Dressing Techniques

Davies, A.D.M., C. Smith, P. Gargaro, et al. 1990. A method for assessing dressing skills in elderly patients. *British Journal of Occupational Therapy* 53(7):272–74.

Dunn, M.L. 1983. *Pre-dressing skills: Skill starters for self-help development.* Tucson, AZ: Communication Skill Builders.

Farmer, A.R. 1986. Dressing. In *Spinal cord injuries: A guide to functional outcomes in occupational therapy*, ed. J. Hill, 125–44. Gaithersburg, MD: Aspen Publishers, Inc.

Hofmeister, A.M., and J. Hofmeister. 1977. *Training for independence: A program for teaching independent dressing skills.* Niles, IL: Developmental Learning Materials (not occupational therapists).

Hofmeister, A.M., and J. Hofmeister. 1977. *Training for independence: A program for teaching the independent use of zippers, buttons, shoes, and socks.* Niles, IL: Developmental Learning Materials (not occupational therapists).

Driver Training

Bowker, J.H., C. Edwards, and J.C. Smiltzer. 1985. Orthotic and adaptive devices for recreation and driving. In *Atlas of orthotics*, 2d ed., American Academy of Orthopaedic Surgeons, 487–512. St. Louis: C.V. Mosby.

Caust, S. 1988. Occupational Therapy Driver Assessment Course: A report by a course participant. *Australian Occupational Therapy Journal* 35(4):181–5.

Croft, D., and R.D. Jones. 1987. The value of off-road tests in the assessment of driving potential of unlicensed disabled people. *British Journal of Occupational Therapy* 50(10):357–61.

Galski, T., H.T. Ehle, and R.L. Bruno. 1990. An assessment of measures to predict the outcome of driving evaluations in patients with cerebral damage. *American Journal of Occupational Therapy* 44(10):709–13.

Gouvier, W.D., et al. 1989. Psychometric prediction of driving performance among the disabled. *Archives of Physical Medicine and Rehabilitation* 70(10):745–50.

Jones, R., H. Giddens, and D. Croft. 1983. Assessment and training of brain-damaged drivers. *American Journal of Occupational Therapy* 37(11):754–60.

Quigley, F.L., and J.A. DeLisa. 1983. Assessing the driving potential of cerebral vascular accident patients. *American Journal of Occupational Therapy* 37(7):474–8.

Shimeld, A. 1983. A clinical demonstration program in quality assurance. *American Journal of Occupational Therapy* 37(1):32–5.

Strano, C.M., ed. 1987. Special issue on driver evaluation. *Physical Disabilities Special Interest Section Newsletter* 10(4):1–8.

Strano, C.M. 1989. Effects of visual deficits on ability to drive in traumatically brain-injured population. *Journal of Head Trauma Rehabilitation* 4(2):35–43.

Early Intervention

Dunn, W., et al. 1989. *Guidelines for occupational therapy services in early intervention and preschool services.* Rockville, MD: American Occupational Therapy Association.

Dunn, W. 1989. Occupational therapy in early intervention: New perspectives create greater possibilities. *American Journal of Occupational Therapy* 43(11):717–21.

Hanft, B.E. 1989. *Family-centered care: An early intervention resource manual.* Rockville, MD: American Occupational Therapy Association.

Environment Control Technology

Bischof, J. 1988. Technical aids. In *Head injury: A guide to functional outcomes in occupational therapy*, ed. K.M. Kovich and D.E. Bermann, 173–90. Gaithersburg, MD: Aspen Publishers, Inc.

Dickey, R. 1988. High technology at home. *Physical Medicine and Rehabilitation: State of the Art Reviews* 2(3):415–44.

Ergonomics

Dahl, R.T. 1988. Occupational therapy, the underutilized resource for human factors research and design. *Work Programs Special Interest Section Newsletter* 2(2):3–4.

Edwards, C.H. 1990. Applied ergonomics. *Work: A Journal of Prevention, Assessment and Rehabilitation* 1(1):27–38.

Feeding/Swallowing Problems and Oral Motor Development—Child

American Occupational Therapy Association. 1987. *Problems with eating: Interventions for children and adults with developmental disabilities.* Rockville, MD: The Association.

Bazyk, S. 1990. Factors associated with the transition to oral feeding in infants fed by nasogastic tubes. *American Journal of Occupational Therapy* 44(12):1070–78.

Blackman, J.A., and C.L.A. Nelson. 1985. Reinstituting oral feeding in children fed by gastrostomy tube. *Clinical Pediatrics* 24(8):434–8.

Blackman, J.A., and C.L.A. Nelson. 1987. Rapid introduction of oral feedings to tube-fed patients. *Journal of Developmental and Behavioral Pediatrics* 8(2):63–67.

Candlish, E. 1984. A feeding workshop for the mentally handicapped. *British Journal of Occupational Therapy* 47(3):79–80.

Morris, S.E. 1977. *Program guidelines for children with feeding problems.* Edison, NJ: Childcraft Education Corp. (not an occupational therapist).

Morris, S.E., and M.D. Klein. 1987. *Pre-feeding skills: A comprehensive resource for feeding development.* Tucson, AZ: Therapy Skill Builders.

Nelson, C.L.A., and R.A. Hallgren. 1989. Gastrostomies: Indications, management, and weaning. *Infants and Young Children* 2(1):66–74.

Occupational therapy and eating dysfunction (position paper). 1989. *American Journal of Occupational Therapy* 43(12):805.

Petersen, P., and K. Ottenbacher. 1986. Use of applied behavior techniques and an adaptive device to teach lip closure to severely handicapped children. *American Journal of Mental Retardation* 90:535–9.

Petersen, P., et al. 1987. Reducing abnormal drinking patterns in the severely disabled: A multiple baseline study. *Clinical Rehabilitation* 1:119–25.

Pipes, P.L. 1989. *Nutrition in infancy and childhood*, 4th ed. St. Louis: Times Mirror/Mosby.

Richter, E.W., F. Rosen, and C.G. Warner. 1986. *PRESPOT: A curriculum guide using a sensorimotor approach to oral motor development.* Hugo, MN: PDP Press.

Shaw, G., and C. Wright. 1982. A two-handle spoon: An aid for independent eating. *American Journal of Occupational Therapy* 36(1):45–6.

Wiemann, G. 1977. *Feeding the multihandicapped.* Cambridge, MN: C.A.D.R.E. Center.

Wyckoff, E., and M. Mitani. 1982. The spoon plate: A self-feeding device. *American Journal of Occupational Therapy* 36(5):333–5.

Games—Indoors

Burton, C. 1985. The use of games in occupational therapy. *British Journal of Occupational Therapy* 48(5):135–6.

Kielhofner, G., and S. Miyake. 1981. The therapeutic use of games with mentally retarded adults. *American Occupational Therapy Association* 35(6):375–82.

Mercer, F. 1981. *Handbook of indoor social activities.* Becester, England: Winslow Press.

O'Donnell, R., et al. *Occupational therapy activities for the severely neurologically and cognitively impaired patient group.* St. Cloud, MN: Veterans Administration Medical Center.

Toglia, J.P. 1985. Use of games in cognitive retraining. *Physical Disabilities Special Interest Section Newsletter* 8(1):3,8.

van Straten, O. 1986. The use of games in occupational therapy of hand burns. *Burns* 12(7):521–5.

Winter, J., A.F. Newell, and J.L. Arnott. 1985. The therapeutic applications of computerised games. *International Journal of Bio-Medical Computing* 17:285–93.

Group Techniques

Crouch, R.B. 1987. A study of the effectiveness of certain occupational therapy group techniques in the assessment of the acutely disturbed adult psychiatric patient. *British Journal of Occupational Therapy* 50(3):86–90.

Howe, M.C., and S.L. Schwartzberg. 1986. *A functional approach to group work in occupational therapy.* Philadelphia: J.B. Lippincott Company.

Kaplan, K.L. 1988. *Directive group therapy: Innovative mental health treatment.* Thorofare, NJ: Slack Inc.

Posthuma, B.W. 1989. *Small groups in therapy settings: Process and leadership.* Boston: College-Hill.

Spall, R., A. Hills, and M. Whitworth. 1988. Evaluation of a small group on a psychogeriatric ward and the implications for nursing staff and occupational therapy staff. *Psychological Reports* 62:283–9.

Vezzetti, D. 1988. Therapeutic use of groups. In *Head injury: A guide to functional outcomes in occupational therapy*, ed. K.M. Kovich and D.E. Bermann, 197–204. Gaithersburg, MD: Aspen Publishers, Inc.

Hand Functions—Child
Hirschel, A., C. Pehoski, and J. Coryell. 1990. Environmental support and the development of grasp in infants. *American Journal of Occupational Therapy* 44(8):721–7.
Hohlstein, R.R. 1982. The development of prehension in normal infants. *American Journal of Occupational Therapy* 36(3):170–6.
McBryde, C., and J. Ziviani. 1990. Proximal and distal upper limb motor development in 24 week old infants. *Canadian Journal of Occupational Therapy* 57(3):147–54.
Schneck, C.M., and A. Henderson. 1990. Descriptive analysis of the developmental progression of grip position for pencil and crayon control in nondysfunctional children. *American Journal of Occupational Therapy* 44(10):893–900.

Hand Functions—Adult
Bergmann, K.P. 1990. Incidence of atypical pencil grasps among nondysfunctional adults. *American Journal of Occupational Therapy* 44(8):736–40.

Handwriting
Harries, R., and H. Yost. 1981. *Elements of handwriting: A teacher's guide.* Navato, CA: Academic Therapy Publishing.
Klein, M.D. 1982. *Pre-writing skills: Skill starters for motor development.* Tucson, AZ: Communication Skill Builders.
Maddox, V. 1986. Postural preparation for writing. *Developmental Disabilities Special Interest Section Newsletter* 9(3):3,6–7.
Miller, S., and S. Engelmann. 1980. *Cursive writing program.* Tigard, OR: C.C. Publications.
Price, A. 1986. Applying sensory integration to handwriting problems. *Developmental Disabilities Special Interest Section Newsletter* 9(3):4–5.
Rioux, J.E., and J.R. Kagan. 1989. Evaluation and treatment of adult graphomotor deficiencies. *Physical Disabilities Special Interest Section Newsletter* 11(4):1–3.
Wesier, D. 1986. Handwriting: Assessment and remediation. *Developmental Disabilities Special Interest Section Newsletter* 9(3):1–3.
Ziviani, J. 1982. Children's prehension while writing: A pilot investigation. *British Journal of Occupational Therapy* 45:306–7.
Ziviani, J. 1983. Qualitative changes in dynamic tripod grip between seven and 14 years of age. *Developmental Medicine & Child Neurology* 25:778–82.
Ziviani, J. 1984. An evaluation of handwriting performance. *Educational Review* 36:249–62.
Ziviani, J., and J. Elkins. 1986. Effect of pencil grip on handwriting speed and legibility. *Educational Review* 38(3):247–57.

Handwriting—Left
Gardner, W.H. 1958. *Left handed writing: Instruction manual.* Danville, IL: The Interstate (not an occupational therapist).
Harvey, G., and T. Simard. 1984. Functional reeducation and electromyographic evaluation of left handwriting in right hemiplegic patients: A pilot study. *Canadian Journal of Occupational Therapy* 51(5):225–30.

Plunkett, M.B. 1954, 1967. *A writing manual for teaching the left-handed.* Cambridge, MA: Educators Publishing Service, Inc. (not an occupational therapist).

Plunkett, M.B. 1954. *Writing exercises for the left-handed.* Cambridge, MA: Educators Publishing Service, Inc. (not an occupational therapist).

Homemaking and Child Care

Anderson, H. 1981. *The disabled homemaker.* Springfield, IL: Charles C Thomas.

Malick, M.H., and B.S. Almasy. 1988. Activities of daily living. In *Willard and Spackman's occupational therapy*, ed. H.L. Hopkins and H.D. Smith, 246–71. Philadelphia: J.B. Lippincott.

Trombly, C.A. 1989. Homemaking and child care. In *Occupational therapy for physical dysfunction*, 3d ed., ed. C.A. Trombly, 411–21. Baltimore, MD: Williams & Wilkins.

Home Management

Jones, R. 1986. Home management. In *Spinal cord injuries: A guide to functional outcomes in occupational therapy*, ed. J. Hill, 185–92. Gaithersburg, MD: Aspen Publishers, Inc.

Pongrac, M. 1986. Evaluating a home management program. *Canadian Journal of Occupational Therapy* 53(1):5–11.

Home Safety and Accident Prevention

Buchanan, A.J. 1986. A home safety awareness program for the well aged: A preventive approach. *Gerontology Special Interest Section Newsletter* 9(2):2,4.

Deily, J. 1989. Home safety program for older adults. *Occupational Therapy in Health Care* 6(1):113–24.

Kern, T. 1986. Safety first: Modifying and adapting the environment for the patient with Alzheimer's disease. *Gerontology Special Interest Section Newsletter* 9(3):4–5.

Horticulture/Gardening

Dennis, L., H. Mogford, and A.C. Harper. 1980. Evaluation of Horticulture-As-Therapy Workshop. *Canadian Journal of Occupational Therapy* 47(4):155–8.

Goodban, A., and D. Goodban. 1990. Horticultural therapy: A growing concern, Part 1. *British Journal of Occupational Therapy* 53(10):425–29.

Hagedorn, R. 1988. Environment and opportunity: The potential of horticulture for enriching the life of disabled people. *Clinical Rehabilitation* 2:239–51.

Hagedorn, R. 1987. *Therapeutic horticulture.* Bicester, England: Winslow Press.

Hughes, E.F., and M.C. Bryden. 1983. The development of an occupational therapy program in a solarium area. *Canadian Journal of Occupational Therapy* 50(1):15–9.

McBey, M.A. 1985. The therapeutic aspects of gardens and gardening: An aspect of total patient care. *Journal of Advanced Nursing* 10:591–5.

Imagery

Riccio, C.M., D.L. Nelson, and M.A. Bush. 1990. Adding purpose to the repetitive exercise of elderly women through imagery. *American Journal of Occupational Therapy* 44(8):714–9.

Independent Living

Bachelder, J. 1985. Independent living programs: Bridges from hospital to community. *Occupational Therapy in Health Care* 2(1):99–107.

Fine, S.B., and P. Schwimmer. 1986. The effects of occupational therapy on independent living skills. *Mental Health Special Interest Section Newsletter* 9(4):2–3.

Hale, G. 1979. *The source book for the disabled.* New York: Paddington Press (not an occupational therapist).

Holzhauser, G.K. 1986. *Making the best of it: How to cope with being handicapped.* New York: Ballantine (not an occupational therapist).

Johnson, J. 1986. Centers for independent living: A new concept in promoting independence. *Physical Disabilities Special Interest Section Newsletter* 9(3):4–5.

Lifchez, R., and B. Winslow. 1979. *Design for independent living.* Berkeley, CA: University of California Press (not occupational therapists).

Occupational therapy's role in independent living situations (position paper). 1981. *American Journal of Occupational Therapy* 35(12):812–4.

Peterson, R.L. 1988. The home evaluation. *Physical Medicine and Rehabilitation: State of the Art Reviews* 2(3):341–52.

Raschko, B.B. 1982. *Housing interiors for the disabled and elderly.* New York: Van Nostrand Reinhold (not an occupational therapist).

Industrial Safety and Accident Prevention

Blair, S.J., J. Bear-Lehman, and E. McCormick. 1990. Industrial hand injuries: Prevention and rehabilitation. In *Rehabilitation of the hand*, 3d ed., ed. J.M. Hunter, et al., 1218–22. St. Louis: C.V. Mosby.

Carlton, R.S. 1987. The effects of body mechanics instruction on work performance. *American Journal of Occupational Therapy* 41(1):16–20.

Holman, C., and V. Becker. 1989. The role of occupational therapy in injury prevention at the workplace. *Work Programs Special Interest Section Newsletter* 1(1):2–3.

Schwartz, R.K. 1989. Occupational therapy in industrial accident and injury prevention. *Work Programs Special Interest Section Newsletter* 3(1):2–6.

Schwartz, R.K. 1989. Cognition and learning in industrial accident injury prevention: An occupational therapy perspective. *Occupational Therapy in Health Care* 6(1):67–85.

Job Modification

MacFarlane, B. 1989. Job modification. *Work Programs Special Interest Section Newsletter* 2(1):1–2.

Niemeyer, L.O. 1989. Job modification for injured workers in sedentary jobs. *Work Programs Special Interest Section Newsletter* 2(2):1–4.

Joint Protection

Brattstrom, M. 1987. *Joint protection and rehabilitation in chronic rheumatic disorders.* Gaithersburg, MD: Aspen Publishers, Inc. (not an occupational therapist).

Haviland, H., L. Kamil-Miller, and J. Sliwa. 1978. *A workbook for consumers with rheumatoid arthritis: Joint protection principles for rheumatoid arthritis.* Rockville, MD: American Occupational Therapy Association.

Kwasniewski, C.T., and E.G. Rossky. 1988. Joint protection and occupational therapy. In *Diagnosis and management of rheumatic diseases*, 2d ed., ed. W.A. Katz, 872–7. Philadelphia: J.B. Lippincott.

Leonard, J. 1990. Joint protection for inflammatory disorders. In *Rehabilitation of the hand*, 3d ed., ed. J.M. Hunter, et al., 908–11. St. Louis: C.V. Mosby.

Post, D. 1986. Joint protection in rheumatic disease. In *Advances in upper extremity surgery and rehabilitation*, ed. J.A. Boswick, 289–93. Gaithersburg, MD: Aspen Publishers, Inc.

Leisure/Recreation Skills

Beck-Ford, V., and R.I. Brown. 1984. *Leisure training and rehabilitation: A program manual.* Springfield, IL: Charles C Thomas (not occupational therapists).

Freedman, J. 1987. *Traveling—like everybody else: A practical guide for disabled travelers.* New York: Adama Books (not an occupational therapist).

Hurd, K. 1986. Leisure skills. In *Spinal cord injuries: A guide to functional outcomes in occupational therapy,* ed. J. Hill, 177–83. Gaithersburg, MD: Aspen Publishers, Inc.

Speidel, L.K. 1984. Air transportation and the disabled: Current and future trends. *Occupational Therapy and Health Care* 1(4):55–67.

Trombly, C.A. 1989. Leisure time activities for the physically disabled. In *Occupational therapy for physical dysfunction,* 3d ed., ed. C.A. Trombly, 422–6. Baltimore, MD: Williams & Wilkins.

Wilson, M. 1984. Leisure. In *Occupational therapy in short-term psychiatry,* ed. M. Wilson, 219–39. Edinburgh, Scotland: Churchill Livingstone.

Life Skills

Bell, C., and J. Quintal. 1985. A life skills program for physically disabled adolescents. *Canadian Journal of Occupational Therapy* 52(5):235–9.

Carruthers, C. 1987. *A life skills manual: Personal care.* Tucson, AZ: Therapy Skill Builders.

Hughes, P.L., and L. Mullins. 1981. *Acute psychiatric care: An occupational therapy guide to exercises in daily living skills.* Thorofare, NJ: Charles B. Slack, Inc.

Wilkinson, J., and S. Canter. 1982. *Social skills training manual: Assessment, programme design, and management of training.* Chichester, NY: John Wiley & Sons.

Microswitches, Automated Learning Devices

Cicharz, M.K., and L. Scherfenberg. 1986. Automated learning devices for the person with a severe/profound handicap. *Developmental Disabilities Special Interest Section Newsletter* 9(2):1,7.

Einis, L.P., and D.M. Bailey. 1990. The use of powered leisure and communication devices in a switch training program. *American Journal of Occupational Therapy* 44(10):931–4.

Shein, G.F., and A.R. Mandel. 1982. Large area flap switch to control battery operated toys. *American Journal of Occupational Therapy* 36(2):107–10.

Mobile Arm Supports (Ball-Bearing Forearm Orthoses or Balanced Forearm Orthoses)

Drew, W.E., and P.H. Stern. 1979. Modular adjustment mechanisms for the balanced forearm orthosis. *Archives of Physical Medicine and Rehabilitation* 60(2):81.

Haworth, R., S. Dunscombe, and P.J.R. Nichols. 1978. Mobile arm supports: An evaluation. *Rheumatology and Rehabilitation* 17:240–4.

Pedretti, L.W. 1985. Mobile arm support and suspension slings. In *Occupational therapy: Practice skills for physical dysfunction,* 2d ed., ed. L.W. Pedretti and B. Zoltan, 250–3. St. Louis: C.V. Mosby.

Thenn, J.E. 1975. *Mobile arm support: Installation and use.* San Jose, CA: author (Distributed by Fred Sammons Inc., Box 32, Brookfield, IL. 60513.

Trombly, C.A. 1989. Mobile arm supports (MAS). In *Occupational therapy for physical dysfunction,* 3d ed., ed. C.A. Trombly, 344–51. Baltimore, MD: Williams & Wilkins.

Wilson, D.J., M.W. McKenzie, and L.M. Barber. 1984. *Spinal cord injuries: A treatment guide for occupational therapists,* rev. ed., 62–82. Thorofare, NJ: Slack, Inc.

Yasuda, Y.L., K. Bowman, and J. Hsu. 1986. Mobile arm supports: Criteria for successful use in muscle disease patients. *Archives of Physical Medicine and Rehabilitation* 67(4):253–6.

Movement Therapy
Burr, L.A., ed. 1986. *Therapy through movement.* West Bridgford, England: Nottingham Rehab Limited.
Couper, J.L. 1981. Dance therapy: Effects on motor performance of children with learning disabilities. *Physical Therapy* 61(1):23–6.
Feldenkrais, M. 1972. *Awareness through movement.* New York: Harper & Row (not an occupational therapist).
Fowler, R.F., and L.J. King. 1984. The use of dance in therapy. *Sensory Integration Special Interest Section Newsletter* 7(2):2–3.
Garnet, E.D. 1982. *Movement is life: A holistic approach to exercise for older adults.* Princeton, NJ: Princeton Book Co. (not an occupational therapist).
Miller, K.J. 1983. Music for movement. *Mental Health Special Interest Section Newsletter* 6(1):1–2.

Music Activities
Nelson, D.L., V.G. Anderson, and A.D. Gonzales. 1984. Music activities as therapy for children with autism and other pervasive developmental disorders. *Journal of Music Therapy* 21(3):100–16.

Orthoses (Other Than Splints)
Baumgarten, J.M. 1985. Upper extremity adaptations for the person with quadriplegia. *Clinics in physical therapy* v.6., 219–42. Edinburgh, Scotland: Churchill Livingstone.
Braile, L.E. 1981. Support for the drooping head. *American Journal of Occupational Therapy* 35(10):661–2.
Collins, K., P. Oswald, G. Burger, et al. 1985. Customized adjustable orthoses: Their use in spasticity. *Archives of Physical Medicine and Rehabilitation* 66(6):397–8.
Friedman, R., and M. Cohen. 1985. A modified cervical collar for the immediate postoperative care of the burned neck. *Annals of Plastic Surgery* 14(6):548–9.
Garcia, S., and J. Greenfield. 1981. Dynamic protractible mouthstick. *American Journal of Occupational Therapy* 35(8):529.
Hedman, G.E., and A.M. Yasukawa. 1986. An adjustable writing device for use with a definitive wrist hand orthosis. *Orthotics and Prosthetics* 39(4):40–3.
Kohler, K.C., N.E. Brennan, and J. Glancy. 1987. The Indiana University clubfoot orthosis. *Orthotics and Prosthetics* 41(2):18–22.
Krusen, N.E., and L.C. Harris. 1985. Soft contact lens remover for persons with impaired hand function. *Journal of Rehabilitation* 51(1):67–8.
Nolinske, T., ed. 1986. Special issue on orthotics. *Physical Disabilities Special Interest Section Newsletter* 9(2):1–8.
Spector, P., and J. Davis. 1982. Hip-abduction, knee-extension orthosis. *American Journal of Occupational Therapy* 36(7):461–2.
Trombly, C.A. 1989. Orthoses: Purposes and types. In *Occupational therapy for physical dysfunction*, 3d ed., ed. C.A. Trombly, 329–55. Baltimore, MD: Williams & Wilkins.

Pet Therapy

Cusask, O., and E. Smith. 1984. *Pets and the elderly: The therapeutic bond.* New York, NY: Haworth Press (not occupational therapists).

McQuillen, D. 1984. Pet therapy: Initiating a program. *Canadian Journal of Occupational Therapy* 52(2):73–6.

Physical Fitness and Exercise

Berland, T. 1986. *Fitness for life: Exercises for people over 50.* Glenview, IL: Scott, Foresman (not an occupational therapist).

Bracegirdle, H. 1990. Developing physical fitness to promote mental health. In *Occupational therapy and mental health: Principles, skills and practice,* ed. J. Creek, 143–59. Edinburgh, Scotland: Churchill Livingstone.

Chamove, A.S. 1986. Exercise improves behaviour: A rationale for occupational therapy. *British Journal of Occupational Therapy* 49(3):83–6.

Fletcher, B.J., J.D. Cantwell, and G.F. Fletcher. 1985. *Exercise for heart and health.* Atlanta, GA: Pritchett & Hull Association (not occupational therapists).

Mullins, C.S., D.L. Nelson, and D.A. Smith. 1987. Exercise through dual-purpose activity in the institutionalized elderly. *Physical and Occupational Therapy in Geriatrics* 5(3):29–39.

Short, L., and C.A. Leonardelli. 1987. The effects of exercise on the elderly and implications for therapy. *Physical and Occupational Therapy in Geriatrics* 5(3):65–73.

Play

American Occupational Therapy Association. 1986. *Play: A skill for life.* Rockville, MD: The American Occupational Therapy Association.

Baker, B.L., A.J. Brightman, and J.B. Blacher. 1983. *Play skills.* Champaign, IL: Research Press.

Fewell, R.R., and P.F. Vadasy. 1983. *Learning through play: A resource manual for teachers and parents: Birth to three years.* Hingham, MA: Teaching Resources Corporation.

Jeffrey, L.I. 1984. Developmental play therapy: An assessment and therapeutic techniques in child psychiatry. *British Journal of Occupational Therapy* 47(3):70–4.

Jeffrey, L.K. 1990. Play therapy. In *Occupational therapy and mental health: Principles, skills and practice,* ed. J. Creek, 247–66. Edinburgh, Scotland: Churchill Livingstone.

Miller, K.S. 1984. Aspects of play schemas in young children with developmental disabilities. *Developmental Disabilities Special Interest Section Newsletter* 7(3):1,3.

Rast, M.M. 1984. The use of play activities in therapy. *Developmental Disabilities Special Interest Section Newsletter* 7(3):1,4.

Sparling, J.W., D.F. Walker, and J. Singdahlsen. 1984. Play techniques with neurologically impaired preschoolers. *American Journal of Occupational Therapy* 38(9):603–612.

Positioning/Seating—Child

Bellefeuille-Reid, D., and S. Jakubek. 1989. Adaptive positioning intervention for premature infants: Issues for paediatric occupational therapy practice. *British Journal of Occupational Therapy* 52(3):93–5.

Bergen, A.F., and C. Colangelo. 1985. *Positioning the client with central nervous system deficits,* 2d ed. Valhalla, NY: Valhalla Rehabilitation Pub. Ltd.

Butt, D.S., and G. Truett. 1988. Seating children with special needs: Construction of a seat insert. *Developmental Disabilities Special Interest Section Newsletter* 11(4):1–4.

Gaines, B.J. 1986. Molded foam posture supports. *Developmental Disabilities Special Interest Section Newsletter* 9(3):5,7.

Inge, K.J., and M.E. Snell. 1985. Teaching positioning and handling techniques to public school through inservice training. *Journal of the Association of Severely Handicapped* 10(2):105–10.

Mulcahy, C.M., et al. 1988. Adaptive seating for the motor handicapped: Problems, a solution, assessment and prescription. *Physiotherapy* 74(10):531–6.

Mulcahy, C.M., and T.E. Pountney. 1987. Ramped cushion. *British Journal of Occupational Therapy* 50:97.

Mulcahy, C.M., and T.E. Pountney. 1986. The sacral pad. *Physiotherapy* 72:473–4.

Mulcahy, C.M. 1986. An approach to the assessment of sitting ability for the prescription of seating. *British Journal of Occupational Therapy* 49:367–8.

Nelham, R.L., C.M. Mulcahy, T.E. Pountney, et al. 1988. Clinical aspects of the Chailey adaptaseat. *Journal of Biomedical Engineering* 10:175–8.

Presperin, J. 1990. Seating systems: The therapist and rehabilitation engineering team. *Physical and Occupational Therapy in Pediatrics* 10(2):11–45.

Rockey, J., and R.L. Helham. 1983. Seating for the chairbound child. In *Physically handicapped child*, ed. G.T. McCarthy, 155–73. London, England: Faber & Faber.

Trefler, E., ed. 1984. *Seating for children with cerebral palsy: A resource manual.* Memphis, TN: University of Tennessee Center for the Health Sciences, Rehabilitation Engineering Program.

Trefler, E. 1988. Positioning: Concepts and technology. *Exceptional Parent* 18(5):28–33.

Trefler, E. 1982. Arm restraints during functional activities. *American Journal of Occupational Therapy* 36(9):599–600.

Ward, D.E. 1984. *Positioning the handicapped child for function*, 2d ed. rev. St. Louis: Phoenix Press, Inc.

Wright, C., and M. Nomura. 1984. Positioning and motor control. *Exceptional Parent* 15(4):40–4.

Positioning—Adult

Jay, P. 1988. Seating and support systems. In *Rehabilitation of the physically disabled adult*, ed. C.J. Goodwill and M.A. Chamberlain, 687–700. London, England: Croom Helm.

Presperin, J. 1988. Positioning: An adjunct to therapy. In *Head injury: A guide to functional outcomes in occupational therapy*, ed. K.M. Kovich and D.E. Bermann, 125–39. Gaithersburg, MD: Aspen Publishers, Inc.

Shaw, R. 1986. Persistent vegetative state: Principles and techniques for seating and positioning. *Head Trauma Rehabilitation* 1(1):31–7.

Powered Mobility

Chase, J., and D.M. Bailey. 1990. Evaluating the potential for powered mobility. *American Journal of Occupational Therapy* 44(12):1125–9.

Jones, C.K. 1990. In search of power for the pediatric client. *Physical and Occupational Therapy in Pediatrics* 10(2):47–68.

Kittle, K.S. 1987. Assessment for the use of powered mobility devices. *Developmental Disabilities Special Interest Section Newsletter* 10(3):2–3.

Schiaffino, S., and J. Laux. 1986. Prerequisite skills for the psychosocial impact of powered wheelchair mobility on young children with severe handicaps. *Developmental Disabilities Special Interest Section Newsletter* 9(2):1,3,8.

Trefler, E. 1986. Powered vehicles for the very young. *Rx Home Care* 8(2):55–6.

Trefler, E., K. Kozole, and E. Snell, eds. 1986. *Selected readings on powered mobility for children and adults with severe physical disabilities*. Washington, DC: RESNA: Association for the Advancement of Rehabilitation Technology.

Trefler, E., and S.J. Taylor. 1987. Powered mobility for severely physically disabled children: Evaluation and provision practices. In *Childhood powered mobility: Developmental, technical and clinical perspectives*, ed. K.M. Jaffe, 117–26. Washington, DC: RESNA: Association for the Advancement of Rehabilitation Technology.

Zazula, J.L., and R.A. Foulds. 1983. Mobility device for a child with phocomelia. *Archives of Physical Medicine and Rehabilitation* 64(3):137–9.

Reality Orientation

Bailey, E.A., et al. 1986. Twenty-four hour reality orientation: Change for staff and patients. *Journal of Advanced Nursing* 11:145–51.

Cerny, J., and R. McNeny. 1983. Reality orientation therapy. In *Rehabilitation of the head injured adult*, ed. M. Rosenthal, et al., 345–54. Philadelphia: F.A. Davis.

Corrigan J.D., J.A. Arnett, L.J. Houck, et al. 1985. Reality orientation for brain injured patients: Group treatment and monitoring of recovery. *Archives of Physical Medicine and Rehabilitation* 66(9):626–30.

Holden, U.P. 1988. *Reality orientation: Psychological approaches to the 'confused' elderly*, 2d ed. Edinburgh, Scotland: Churchill Livingstone.

Jennison, M. 1988. Reality orientation groups. *British Journal of Occupational Therapy* 51(2):56.

Kohut, S., J.J. Kohut, and J.J. Fleishman. 1987. *Reality orientation for the elderly*, 3d ed. Oradell, NJ: Medical Economics Books.

McNeny, R., and J. Dise. 1990. Reality orientation therapy. In *Rehabilitation of the adult and child with traumatic brain injury*, ed. M. Rosenthal, et al., 366–73. Philadelphia: F.A. Davis.

Rimmer, L. 1982. *Reality orientation: Principles and practice*. Winslow, England: Photographic Teaching Materials.

Relaxation Techniques

Davis, M., E.R. Eshelmann, and M. McKay. 1988. *The relaxation and stress reduction workbook*, 3d ed. Oakland, CA: New Harbinger Publications (not occupational therapists).

Keable, D. 1985. Relaxation training techniques: A review: I. What is relaxation? *British Journal of Occupational Therapy* 48(5):132–4.

Keable, D. 1985. Relaxation training techniques: A review: II. How effective is relaxation training? *British Journal of Occupational Therapy* 48(7):301–4.

Lichstein, K.L. 1988. *Clinical relaxation strategies*. New York: John Wiley & Sons (not an occupational therapist).

Van Deusen, J., and J. Keirnat. 1985–86. An exploration of the rocking chair as a means of relaxation. *Physical and Occupational Therapy in Geriatrics* 4(2):31–38.

Westland, G. 1988. Relaxing in primary health care…project to introduce relaxation groups. *British Journal of Occupational Therapy* 51(3):84–8.

Zahourek, R.P., ed. 1988. *Relaxation and imagery: Tools for therapeutic communication and intervention*. Philadelphia: W.B. Saunders (not an occupational therapist).

Reminiscence

Bennett, S.L., and F. Maas. 1988. The effect of music-based life review on the life satisfaction and ego integrity of elderly people. *British Journal of Occupational Therapy* 51(12):433–6.

Buechel, H. 1986. Reminiscence: A review and prospectus. *Physical and Occupational Therapy in Geriatrics* 5(2):25–37.

Friedlob, S.A., and J.J. Kelly. 1984. Reminiscing groups in board and care homes. In *Working with the elderly: Group process and techniques*, ed. I. Burnside, 308–27. Monterey, CA: Wadsworth Health Sciences Division.

Harwood, K.J. 1989. The effects of an occupational therapy reminiscence group: A single case study. *Physical and Occupational Therapy in Geriatrics* 7(4):43–57.

Hoff, S. 1988. A thousand small deliberations. *Physical and Occupational Therapy in Geriatrics* 6(2):75–7.

Jones, C.M., and P. Clark. 1984. The use of memory "recall" on a psychogeriatric ward. *British Journal of Occupational Therapy* 47(10):315–6.

Kiernat, J.M. 1983. Retrospection as a life span concept. *Physical and Occupational Therapy in Geriatrics* 3(2):35–48.

Kiernat, J.M. 1984. The use of life review activity. In *Working with the elderly: Group process and techniques*, ed. I. Burnside, 298–307. Monterey, CA: Wadsworth Health Sciences Division.

Sable, L.M. 1984. Life review therapy: An occupational therapy treatment technique with geriatric clients. *Physical and Occupational Therapy in Geriatrics* 3(4):3–10.

Sullivan, C.A. 1982. Life review: A functional view of reminiscence. *Physical and Occupational Therapy in Geriatrics* 2(1):39–52.

Self-Help Devices

Arthritis Foundation. 1980. *Self-help manual for patients with arthritis*, 2d ed. Atlanta, GA: The Arthritis Foundation.

Breuer, J.M. 1982. A handbook of assistive devices for the handicapped elderly: New help for independent living. *Physical and Occupational Therapy in Geriatrics* 1(2):all.

Christiansen, C.H., R.K. Schwartz, and K.J. Barnes. 1988. Self-care: Evaluation and management. In *Rehabilitation medicine: Principles and practice*, ed. J.A. DeLisa, 95–115. Philadelphia: J.B. Lippincott.

Directory of living aids for the handicapped: A guide to products and devices for the handicapped. Santa Monica, CA: Ready Reference Press, 1984.

Freed, M.M., J.L. Klinger, and L. Squires. 1988. Help for the single-handed. *Patient Care* 22(June, 15):211–16,221–24,227,230–31,235.

Itoh, M., M. Lee, and J. Shapiro. 1984. Self-help devices for the elderly population living in the community. In *Rehabilitation in the aging*, ed. T.F. Williams, 345–58. New York: Raven Press.

Kreisler, N., and J. Kreisler. 1982. *Catalog of aids for the disabled*. New York: McGraw-Hill Book Company (not occupational therapists).

Lunt, S. 1982. *A handbook for the disabled: Ideas and inventions for easier living*. New York: Charles Scribner's Sons (not an occupational therapist).

Paul, S.M., and T.L. Baron. 1988. Toileting device for patients with decreased hand function. *Archives of Physical Medicine and Rehabilitation* 69:142–3.

Rockey, J. 1983. Aids to daily living. In *The physically handicapped child*, ed. G.T. Mc-Carthy, 350–61. London, England: Faber & Faber.

Sargent, J.V. 1981. *An easier way: Handbook for the elderly and handicapped*. Ames, Iowa: Iowa State University Press.

Schweidler, H. 1984. Assistive devices, aids to daily living. In *Rheumatic diseases: Rehabilitation and management*, ed. G.K. Riggs and E.P. Gall, 263–76. Boston: Butterworth Publication.

Takai, V. 1988. Self-help devices. *Physical Medicine and Rehabilitation: State of the Art Review* 2(3):353–76.

Warren, C.G., and A. Enders. 1986. Introduction to systems and devices for the disabled. In *Orthotics etcetera*, 3d ed., ed. J.B. Redford, 708–38. Baltimore, MD: Williams & Wilkins.

Wright, C., and G. Shaw. 1982. A two-handle spoon. An aid for independent eating. *American Journal of Occupational Therapy* 36(1):45–6.

Wyckoff, E., and M. Mitani. 1982. The spoon plate: A self-feeding device. *American Journal of Occupational Therapy* 36(5):333–5.

Sensory Integration
Bissell, J., et al. 1988. *Sensory motor handbook: A guide for implementing and modifying activities in the classroom*. Torrance, CA: Sensory Integration International.

Bonder, B.R., and A.G. Fisher. 1989. Sensory integration and treatment of the elderly. *Gerontology Special Interest Section Newsletter* 12(1):2–4.

Henry, D.A. 1990. Hydrotherapy: A sensory integration treatment modality. *Sensory Integration Special Interest Section Newsletter* 13(2):1–2.

Komich, P. 1983. Sensorimotor integration in children. In *Detection of developmental problems in children*, 2d ed., ed. M.J. Krajicek and A.I.T. Tomlinson, 123–38. Baltimore, MD: University Park Press.

McCallion, S. 1990. Sensory integration. In *Occupational therapy and mental health: Principles, skills and practice,* ed. J. Creek, 161–78. Edinburgh, Scotland: Churchill Livingstone.

Montogomery, P., and E. Richter. 1977. *Sensorimotor integration for developmentally disabled children: A handbook*. Los Angeles: Western Psychological Services.

Roest, L.L., and S.T. Clements. 1983. *Sensory integration: Rationale and treatment activities for groups*. Grand Rapids, MI: South Kent Mental Health Services, Inc.

Ross, M., and D. Burdick. 1981. *Sensory integration: A training manual for therapists and teachers for regressed, psychiatric and geriatric patient groups*. Thorofare, NJ: Slack, Inc.

Urbanik, C. 1986. Sensory integrative treatment for people with developmental disabilities. *Developmental Disabilities Special Interest Section Newsletter* 9(1):1–2.

Serial and Plaster Casting
Bell-Krotoski, J.A. 1990. Plaster cylinder casting for contractures of the interphalangeal joints. In *Rehabilitation of the hand*, 3d ed., ed. J.M. Hunter, et al., 1128–33. St. Louis: C.V. Mosby.

Fess, E.E., and C.A. Philips. 1987. Plaster casting for the remodeling of soft tissue. In *Hand splinting: Principles and methods*, 2d ed., ed. E.E. Fess and C.A. Philips, 449–66. St. Louis: C.V. Mosby.

Hill, J. 1988. Management of abnormal tone through casting and orthotics. In *Head injury: A guide to functional outcomes in occupational therapy*, ed. K.M. Kovich and D.E. Bermann, 107–24. Gaithersburg, MD: Aspen Publishers, Inc.

King, T.I. 1982. Plaster splinting as a means of reducing elbow flexor spasticity: A case study. *American Journal of Occupational Therapy* 36(10):671–3.

Tribuzi, S.M. 1990. Serial plaster splinting. In *Rehabilitation of the hand*, 3d ed., ed. J.M. Hunter, et al., 1120–7. St. Louis: C.V. Mosby.

Yasukawa, A. 1990. Upper extremity casting: Adjunct treatment for a child with cerebral palsy hemiplegia. *American Journal of Occupational Therapy* 44(9):840–6.

Zablotny, C., M.F. Andric, and C. Gowland. 1987. Serial casting: Clinical applications for the adult head-injured patient. *Journal of Head Trauma Rehabilitation* 2(2):46–52.

Sexuality for Persons with Handicaps/Disabilities

Conine, T.A., and L.N. Quastel. 1983. Occupational therapists' roles and attitudes toward sexual habilitation of chronically ill and disabled children. *Canadian Journal of Occupational Therapy* 50(3):81–6.

Evans, J. 1987. Sexual consequences of disability: Activity analysis and performance adaptation. *Occupational Therapy in Health Care* 4(1):149–54.

Kennedy, M. 1987. Occupational therapists as sexual rehabilitation professionals using the rehabilitation frame of reference. *Canadian Journal of Occupational Therapy* 54(4): 189–93.

Miller, W.T. 1984. An occupational therapist as a sexual health clinician in the management of spinal cord injuries. *Canadian Journal of Occupational Therapy* 51(4):172–5.

Slings

Boyd, E., and A. Gaylard. 1986. Shoulder supports with stroke patients: A Canadian survey. *Canadian Journal of Occupational Therapy* 53(2):61–8.

Rajaram, V., and M. Holtz. 1985. Shoulder forearm support for the subluxed shoulder. *Archives of Physical Medicine and Rehabilitation* 55(3):191–2.

Smith, R.O., and G.A. Okamoto. 1981. Checklist for the prescription of slings for the hemiplegic patient. *American Journal of Occupational Therapy* 35(2):91–5.

Walker, J. 1983. Modified strapping of roll sling. *American Journal of Occupational Therapy* 37(2):110–1.

Social Skills Training

Franklin, L. 1990. Social skills training. In *Occupational therapy and mental health: Principles, skills and practice*, ed. J. Creek, 229–46. Edinburgh, Scotland: Churchill Livingstone.

Wilson, M. 1984. Training in social skills. In *Occupational therapy in short-term psychiatry*, ed. M. Wilson, 131–56. Edinburgh, Scotland: Churchill Livingstone.

Splints, Splintmaking

Anderson, L.J., and J.M. Anderson. 1988. Hand splinting for infants in the intensive care and special care nurseries. *American Journal of Occupational Therapy* 42(4):222–6.

Balkeney, A.B., H.T. Bergtholdt, and H.W. Ramsammy. 1984. Static splinting and temperature assessment of the injured insensitive hand. In *Rehabilitation of the hand*, 2d ed., ed. J.M. Hunter, et al., 881–8. St. Louis: C.V. Mosby.

Barber, L.M., and W.L. Hill. 1987. *Guidelines for use of LMB orthoses*, 2d ed. P.O. Box 1181, San Luis Obispo, CA 93406: LMB Hand Rehab Products.

Barr, N.R., and D. Swan. 1988. *The hand: Principles and techniques of splintmaking*, 2d ed. London, England: Butterworths.

Beribak, L., et al. 1984. Trauma splinting. In *Current concepts in orthotics: A diagnosis-related approach to splinting,* ed. E.M. Ziegler, 123–65. Menomonee Falls, WI: Roylan Medical Products.

Bielawski, T., and J. Bear-Lehman. 1986. A gauntlet work splint. *American Journal of Occupational Therapy* 40(3):199–201.

Byron, P.M. 1990. Splinting the hand of a child. In *Rehabilitation of the hand,* 3d ed., ed. J.M. Hunter, et al., 1147–53. St. Louis: C.V. Mosby.

Callahan, A.D., and P. McEntee. 1986. Splinting proximal interphalangeal joint flexion contractures: A new design. *American Journal of Occupational Therapy* 40(6):408–13.

Cannon, N.M., et al. 1985. *Manual of hand splinting.* New York: Churchill Livingstone.

Colditz, J.C. 1983. Low profile dynamic splinting of the injured hand. *American Journal of Occupational Therapy* 37(3):182–8.

Colditz, J.C. 1984. Dynamic splinting of the stiff hand. In *Rehabilitation of the hand,* 2d ed., ed. J.M. Hunter, et al., 231–40. St. Louis: C.V. Mosby.

Colditz, J.C. 1984. Spring-wire splinting of the proximal interphalangeal joint. In *Rehabilitation of the hand,* 2d ed., ed. J.M. Hunter, et al., 875–80. St. Louis: C.V. Mosby. Revised in 3d ed., 1990, 1109–19.

Colello-Abrahan, K. 1990. Dynamic pronation-supination splint. In *Rehabilitation of the hand,* 3d ed., ed. J.M. Hunter, et al., 1134–9. St. Louis: C.V. Mosby.

English, C.B., R.A. Rehm, and R.L. Petzoldt. 1982. Blocking splints to assist finger exercise. *American Journal of Occupational Therapy* 36(4):259–62.

Feinberg, J., and K.D. Brandt. 1981. Use of resting splints by patients with rheumatoid arthritis. *American Journal of Occupational Therapy* 35(3):173–8.

Fess, E.E. 1984. Splinting for mobilization of the thumb. In *Rehabilitation of the hand* 2d ed., ed. J.M. Hunter, et al., 241–5. St. Louis: C.V. Mosby.

Fess, E.E., and C.A. Philips. 1987. *Hand splinting: Principles and methods,* 2d ed. St. Louis: C.V. Mosby.

Fess, E.E. 1984. Principles and methods of splinting for mobilization of joints. In *Rehabilitation of the hand,* 2d ed., ed. J.M. Hunter, et al., 853–61. St. Louis: C.V. Mosby. Revised in 3d ed., 1990, 1101–08.

Fora, F.W., et al. 1989. A flexible wrist splint. *Journal of Hand Surgery* 14A:574–5.

Hooper, R.M., and E.R. North. 1982. Dynamic interphalangeal extension splint design. *American Journal of Occupational Therapy* 36(4):257–8.

Johnson, B.M., M.J.G. Flynn, and R.D. Benkenbaugh. 1981. A dynamic splint for use after total wrist arthroplasty. *American Journal of Occupational Therapy* 35(3):179–84.

Kiel, J.H. 1983. *Basic handsplinting: A pattern-designing approach.* Boston: Little, Brown and Company.

Kobe, C.T. 1981. Shunt splint for adult renal patients. *American Journal of Occupational Therapy* 35(3):195–6.

Lucas, B.B. 1988. Roll splints: An option in low-profile dynamic splinting. *American Journal of Occupational Therapy* 42(1):49–52.

Malick, M.H. 1982. *Manual on dynamic hand splinting with thermoplastic materials: Low temperature materials and techniques,* 3d ed. Pittsburgh: American Rehabilitation Education Network.

Malick, M.H. 1988. Upper extremity orthotics. In *Willard and Spackman's occupational therapy,* 7th ed., ed. H.L. Hopkins and H.D. Smith, 308–15. Philadelphia: J.B. Lippincott.

Mildenberger, L.A., P.C. Amadio, and K. An. 1986. Dynamic splinting: A systematic approach to the selection of elastic traction. *Archives of Physical Medicine and Rehabilitation* 67(4):241–44.

Murphy, M.S. 1990. An adjustable splint for forearm supination. *American Journal of Occupational Therapy* 44(10):936–9.

Neuhaus, B.E., E.R. Ascher, B.A. Coullon, et al. 1981. Survey of rationales for and against hand splinting in hemiplegia. *American Journal of Occupational Therapy* 35(2):83–90.

Pearson, S.O. 1984. Splinting the nerve-injured hand. In *Rehabilitation of the hand* 2d ed., ed. J.M. Hunter, et al., 452–6. St. Louis: C.V. Mosby.

Pedretti, L. 1990. Hand splinting. In *Occupational therapy: Practice skills in physical dysfunction*, 3d ed., ed. L.W. Pedretti and B. Zoltan, 401–18. St. Louis: C.V. Mosby.

Poole, J.L., S.L. Whitney, N. Hangeland, et al. 1990. The effectiveness of inflatable pressure splints on motor function in stroke patients. *Physical and Occupational Therapy in Pediatrics* 10(6):360–6.

Pullium, G.F. 1984. Splinting and positioning. In *Comprehensive rehabilitation of burns*, ed. S.V. Fisher and P.A. Helm, 64–95. Baltimore, MD: Williams & Wilkins.

Rossi, J. 1987. Concepts and current trends in hand splinting. *Occupational Therapy in Health Care* 4(3/4)53–68.

Shimeld, A., G. Campbell, and M. Ernest. 1984. Clinical results of a comparative evaluation of splinting materials. *Canadian Journal of Occupational Therapy* 51(2):81–91.

Smith, S.A. 1990. Splinting the severely involved hand. *Occupational Therapy Forum* 5(49):9–11.

Walters, C. 1987. *Splinting the burn patient.* Laurel, MD: RAMSCO Publishing.

Ziegler, E.M., ed. 1984. *Current concepts in orthotics: A diagnosis-related approach to splinting.* Menomonee Falls, WI: Roylan Medical Products.

Sports

Adams, R.C., et al. 1982. *Games, sports, and exercises for the physically handicapped*, 3d ed. Philadelphia: Lea & Febiger (not occupational therapists).

Bowker, A.M. 1988. Water sports. *Physical Disabilities Special Interest Section Newsletter* 11(1):1–2.

Bowker, J.H., et al. 1985. Orthotic and adaptive devices for recreation and driving. In *Atlas of orthotics: Biomechanical principles and mechanics,* 2d ed., American Academy of Orthopaedic Surgeons, 487–512. St. Louis: C.V. Mosby.

Crase, N. 1988. Track and road racing. *Physical Disabilities Special Interest Section Newsletter* 11(1):4.

Engel, B.T. 1985. Competitive sports for the disabled athlete: A challenge to excellence. *Occupational Therapy in Health Care* 2(1):145–51.

Hopper, R. 1988. Wheelchair court sports. *Physical Disabilities Special Interest Section Newsletter* 11(1):2–4.

Stress Management

Cherry, D.B. 1989. Stress and coping in families with ill or disabled children: Application of a model to pediatric therapy. *Physical and Occupational Therapy in Pediatrics* 9(2): 11–32.

Gier, M.D., M.D. Levick, and P.J. Blazina. 1988. Stress reduction with heart transplant patients and their families: A multidisciplinary approach. *Journal of Heart Transplantation* 7(5):342–7.

Mueller, S., and M. Suto. 1983. Starting a stress management programme. *Mental Health Special Interest Section Newsletter* 6(2):1–3.

Neistadt, M.E. 1988. Stress management. In *Willard and Spackman's occupational therapy*, 7th ed., ed. H.L. Hopkins and H.D. Smith, 321–9. Philadelphia: J.B. Lippincott.

Stein, F., and J. Smith. 1989. Short-term stress management programme with acutely depressed in-patients. *Canadian Journal of Occupational Therapy* 54(4):185–92.

Stein, F., and S. Nikolic. 1989. Teaching stress management techniques to a schizophrenic patient. *American Journal of Occupational Therapy* 43:162–9.

Therapeutic Horse Riding (Hippotherapy)

Bertoti, D.B. 1988. Effect of therapeutic horseback riding on posture in children with cerebral palsy. *Physical Therapy* 68(10):1505–12 (not an occupational therapist).

Biery, M.J. 1985. Riding and the handicapped. *Veterinary Clinics of North America: Small Animal Practice* 15(2):345–54 (not an occupational therapist).

Brock, B.J. 1988. Effect of therapeutic horseback riding on physically disabled adults. *Therapeutic Recreation Journal* 22(3):34–43 (not an occupational therapist).

DePauw, K.P. 1984. Therapeutic horseback riding in Europe and North America. In *The pet connection: Its influence on our health and quality of life*, ed. R.K. Anderson, B.L. Hart, and L.A. Hart, 141–53. Minneapolis, MN: University of Minnesota (not an occupational therapist).

DePauw, K.P. 1986. Horseback riding for individuals with disabilities: Programs, philosophy, and research. *Adapted Physical Activity Quarterly* 3:217–26 (not an occupational therapist).

Dismuke, R.P. 1984. Rehabilitative horseback riding for children with language disorders. In *The pet connection: Its influence on our health and quality of life*, ed. R.K. Anderson, B.L. Hart, and L.A. Hart, 131–40. Minneapolis, MN: University of Minnesota (not an occupational therapist).

Engel, B.T. 1984. The horse as a modality for occupational therapy. *Occupational Therapy in Health Care* 1(1):41–8.

Fox, V.M., V.A. Locricchio-Lawlor, and M.W. Luttges. 1983. Functional assessment: Evaluation of a therapeutic riding program. *6th Annual Conference on Rehabilitation Engineering*, 304–6. San Diego, CA: RESNA (not occupational therapists).

Fox, V.M., V.A. Lawlor, and M.W. Luttges. 1984. Pilot study of novel test instrumentation to evaluate therapeutic horseback riding. *Adapted Physical Activity Quarterly* 1(1):30–6 (not occupational therapists).

Freeman, G. 1984. Hippotherapy/therapeutic horseback riding. *Clinical Management* 4(3):20–5 (not an occupational therapist).

Gentry, L. 1986. "My therapist weighs 900 lbs." *Children Today* 15(1):30–3 (not an occupational therapist).

Horse therapy: A special treat for children in psychiatric hospital. 1984. *Review-Federation of American Hospitals* 17(5):57–9 (not occupational therapists).

Lawton-Shirley, N. 1990. The sensory integrative value of horseback riding therapy. *Sensory Integration Special Interest Section Newsletter* 13(2):3–4.

Saywell, S.Y. 1988. The history and development of riding for disabled persons. *Physiotherapy Practice* 4:146–54 (not an occupational therapist).

Wingate, L. 1982. Feasibility of horseback riding as a therapeutic and integrative program for handicapped children. *Physical Therapy* 62(2):184–6 (not an occupational therapist).

Toys

Goldberg, S. 1981. *Teaching with toys: Making your own educational toys.* Ann Arbor, MI: The University of Michigan Press (not an occupational therapist).

Langley, M.B. 1990. A developmental approach to the use of toys for facilitation of environmental control. *Physical and Occupational Therapy in Pediatrics* 10(2):69–91.

Lederman, E. 1986. *Developmental toys and equipment: A practical guide to selection and utilization.* Springfield, IL: Charles C Thomas.

Shein, G.F., and A.R. Mandel. 1982. Large area flap switch to control battery-operated toys. *American Journal of Occupational Therapy* 36(2)107–10.

Sinker, S. 1983. *The Lekotek guide to good toys.* Evanston, IL: Lekotek (not an occupational therapist).

Wright, C., and M. Nomura. 1985. *From toys to computers: Access for the physically disabled child.* P.O. Box 700242, San Jose, CA: Author. Revised 1987.

Wright, C., and M. Monura. 1988. Toy ideas for children with special needs. *Exceptional Parent* 18(5):58–60.

Transcutaneous Electrical Nerve Stimulation and Other Electrical Currents

Apfel, L.M., et al. 1987. Functional electrical stimulation in intrinsic/extrinsic imbalanced burned hands. *Journal of Burn Care & Rehabilitation* 8(2):97–102.

Cannon, N.M., and P.T. Mullins. 1984. Modalities in upper extremity rehabilitation: Use of electrical currents for therapeutic purposes. In *Manual on management of specific hand problems*, ed. M.H. Malick and M.C. Kasch, 71–86. Pittsburgh: AREN.

Lee, V.H., and C.C. Reynolds. 1984. Clinical application of the transcutaneous electrical nerve stimulator in patients with upper extremity pain. In *Rehabilitation of the hand*, 2d ed., ed. J.M. Hunter, et al., 538–46. St. Louis: C.V. Mosby.

Transfer Techniques

Pelosi, T., and M. Gleeson. 1988. *Illustrated transfer techniques for disabled people.* Melbourne, Australia: Churchill Livingstone.

Tarling, C., and J. Stowe. 1988. Patient transfers: Hoists and stairlifts. In *Rehabilitation of the physically disabled adult*, ed. C.J. Goodwill and M.A. Chamberlain, 724–40. London, England: Croom Helm.

Wellness Programs

Clark, C.C. 1981. *Enhancing wellness: A guide for self-care.* New York: Springer Publishing Co. (not an occupational therapist).

Johnson, J.A. 1985. Wellness: Its myths, realities and potential for occupational therapy. *Occupational Therapy in Health Care* 2(2):117–38.

Johnson, J.A. 1986. *New dimensions in wellness: A context for living.* Thorofare, NJ: Slack, Inc.

Maurer, K.E., and Y.R. Teske. 1989. Barriers to occupational therapy practice in wellness. *Occupational Therapy in Health Care* 5(4):57–67.

Ryan, R.S., and J.W. Travis. 1981. *Wellness workbook.* Berkeley, CA: Ten Speed Press. 2d ed., 1988 (not an occupational therapist).

Wheelchairs and Accessories

Bradey, E., et al. 1986. A validity study of guidelines for wheelchair selection. *Canadian Journal of Occupational Therapy* 53(1):19–24.

Brammell, C.A., and F.P. Maloney. 1981. Wheelchair prescriptions. In *Interdisciplinary rehabilitation of multiple sclerosis and neuromuscular disorders*, ed. F.P. Maloney, J.S. Burks, and S.P. Ringel, 364–91. Philadelphia: J.B. Lippincott.

Cardi, M.D. 1988. Guidelines for selecting wheelchair cushions. *Physical Disabilities Special Interest Section Newsletter* 11(2):3–4.

Epstein, C.F. 1980. Wheelchair management: Developing a system for long-term care facilities. *Journal of Long Term Care Administration* 8(2):1–11.

Epstein, C.F. 1981. *Wheelchair management guidelines*. Somerville, NJ: Occupational Therapy Consultants.

Garber, S.L., and T.A. Kroushop. 1984. Wheelchair cushion modification and its effect on pressure. *Archives of Physical Medicine and Rehabilitation* 65(10):579–83.

Garber, S.L. 1985. Wheelchair cushion: A historical review. *American Journal of Occupational Therapy* 39:453–9.

Garber, S.L. 1985. Wheelchair cushions for spinal cord-injured individual. *American Journal of Occupational Therapy* 39:722–5.

Kozole, K.P., and G.E. Hedman. 1985. Modular hand tiller system for joystick operation of powered wheelchairs. *Archives of Physical Medicine and Rehabilitation* 66(3):193–4.

Krouskop, T.A., P.C. Noble, S.L. Garber, and W.A. Spencer. 1983. The effectiveness of preventative management in reducing the occurrence of pressure sores. *Journal of Rehabilitation Research and Development* 20(1):74–83.

Krouskop, T.A., R. Williams, M. Krebs, et al. 1985. Effectiveness of mattress overlays in reducing interface pressures during recumbency. *Journal of Rehabilitation Research and Development* 22(3):7–10.

Krouskop, T.A., R. Williams, M. Krebs, et al. 1985. Evaluating the effectiveness of mattress overlaps. *Rx Home Care* 7(12):97–103.

Mayall, J.K., G. Desharnais. 1990. *Positioning in a wheelchair: A guide for professional caregivers of the disabled adult.* Thorofare, NJ: Slack.

Pedretti, L., and G. Stone. 1990. Wheelchairs and wheelchair transfers. In *Occupational therapy: Practice skills in physical dysfunction*, 3d ed., ed. L.W. Pedretti and B. Zoltan, 380–96. St. Louis: C.V. Mosby.

Pezenik, D., M. Itoh, and M. Lee. 1984. Wheelchair prescription. In *Current therapy in physiatry: Physical medicine and rehabilitation,* ed. A.S. Ruskin, 475–98. Philadelphia: W.B. Saunders.

Scott, K.W. 1986. Establishing a wheelchair review clinic. *Developmental Disabilities Special Interest Section Newsletter* 9(2):2,7.

Taylor, S.J. 1987. Evaluating the client with physical disabilities for wheelchair seating. *American Journal of Occupational Therapy* 41(11):711–6.

Trombly, C.A., and A.D. Scott. 1989. Wheelchair measurement and prescription. In *Occupational therapy for physical dysfunction*, 3d ed., ed. C.A. Trombly, 369–74. Baltimore, MD: Williams & Wilkins.

Wilson, A.B. 1986. *Wheelchairs: A prescription guide*. Charlottesville, VA: Rehabilitation Press.

Wilson, G.B., and V.L. Kerr. 1988. Wheelchairs: Selection, uses, adaptations, and maintenance. In *Basic rehabilitation techniques: A self-instructional guide,* 3d. ed., ed.

R.D. Sine, S.E. Liss, R.E. Roush, et al., 190–201. Gaithersburg, MD: Aspen Publishers, Inc.

Zacharkow, D. 1984. *Wheelchair posture and pressure sores.* Springfield, IL: Charles C Thomas.

Work Hardening

Chairsell, A., B.L. Elmore, and T. Jones. 1989. Work hardening: No gamble in Las Vegas. *Work Programs Special Interest Section Newsletter* 2(1):3–4.

Curry, R.T. 1989. Understanding patients with chronic pain in work hardening programs. *Work Programs Special Interest Section Newsletter* 3(3):1–2.

Doherty, C. 1989. Beyond work hardening 101. In *Work injury management: Advances in evaluation treatment and prevention of injuries in industry: Proceedings*, 84–91. Eugene, OR: Center for the Advancement of Industrial Rehabilitation and Evaluation. Also in *Work: A Journal of Prevention, Assessment & Rehabilitation* 1(1):62–8,1990.

Edgcomb, J. 1987. Practitioner's point of view: Work hardening guidelines 1984: As proposed by California V.E.W.A.A. *Vocational Evaluation and Work Adjustment Bulletin* 20:133–4.

Ellexson, M.T. 1990. The impact of CARF standards on the practice of work hardening. *Work: A Journal of Prevention, Assessment & Rehabilitation* 1(1):69–72.

Kornblau, B.L. 1989. Work hardening. In *Interdisciplinary rehabilitation of low back pain*, ed. C.D. Tollison and M.L. Kriegel, 277–290. Baltimore, MD: Williams & Wilkins.

Lett, C.F., N.E. McCabe. 1988. Work hardening. In *Work injuries: Management and prevention*, ed. S.J. Isernhagen, 195–229. Gaithersburg, MD: Aspen Publishers, Inc.

Matheson, L.N. 1990. Work hardening in the new age: Health care enters the industrial revolution. *Work Program Special Interest Section Newsletter* 4(4):2–3.

Matheson, L.N., et al. 1985. Work hardening: Occupational therapy in industrial rehabilitation. *American Journal of Occupational Therapy* 39(5):314–21.

May, V.R. 1988. Work hardening and work capacity evaluation: Definition and process. *Vocational Evaluation and Work Adjustment Bulletin* 21(2):61–6.

Ogden-Niemeyer, L., and K. Jacobs. 1989. *Work hardening: State of the art.* Thorofare, NJ: Slack, Inc.

Tamayo, R. 1990. Work hardening: A different treatment approach. *Occupational Therapy Forum* 5(48):10–1.

Work-Related Programs

Ballard, M., et al. 1986. Work therapy and return to work. *Hand Clinics* 2(1):247–58.

Baxter, P.L., and S.L. Fried. 1984. The work tolerance program of the Hand Rehabilitation Center in Philadelphia. In *Rehabilitation of the hand,* 2d ed., ed J.M. Hunter, et al., 889–99. St. Louis: C.V. Mosby. Revised in 3d ed., 1990, 1155–64.

Baxter, P.L., and P.M. McEntee. 1984. Physical capacity evaluation. In *Rehabilitation of the hand*, 2d ed., ed. J.M. Hunter, et al., 909–18. St. Louis: C.V. Mosby.

Baxter, P.L. 1986. Physical capacity evaluation and work therapy for industrial hand injuries. In *Hand rehabilitation*, ed. C.A. Moran, 137–46. New York: Churchill Livingstone.

Baxter-Petralia, P., and D. Beaulieu. 1986. Therapeutic activity in treatment of industrial injuries. *Physical Disabilities Special Interest Section Newsletter* 9(4):3,6.

Benner, C.L., A.D. Schilling, and L. Klein. 1987. Coordinated teamwork in California industrial rehabilitation. *Journal of Hand Surgery* 12A(5 pt. 2):936–9.

Blair, S.J., J. Bear-Lehman, and E. McCormick. 1984. Industrial hand injuries: Prevention and rehabilitation. In *Rehabilitation of the hand*, 2d ed., ed. J.M. Hunter, et al., 919–26. St. Louis: C.V. Mosby.

Carlson, L., and P.M. Wilson. 1990. Hands at work. *Work: A Journal of Prevention, Assessment & Rehabilitation* 1(1):57–61.

Creighton, D. 1985. Three frames of reference in work-related occupational therapy programs. *American Journal of Occupational Therapy* 39(5):327–30.

Curtis, R.M., G.L. Clark, and R.A. Synder. 1984. The work simulator. In *Rehabilitation of the hand*, 2d ed., ed. J.M. Hunter, et al., 905–8. St. Louis: C.V. Mosby.

Heck, C. 1987. Job-site analysis for work capacity programming. *Physical Disabilities Special Interest Section Newsletter* 10(2):2–3.

Herbin, M.L. 1987. Work capacity evaluation for occupational hand injuries. *Journal of Hand Surgery* 12A(5 pt.2):958–61.

Hertfelder, S., and C. Gwin, eds. 1989. *Work in progress: Occupational therapy in work programs*. Rockville, MD: American Occupational Therapy Association.

Holmes, D. 1985. The role of the occupational therapist-work evaluator. *American Journal of Occupational Therapy* 39(5):308–13.

Jacobs, K. 1985. *Occupational therapy: Work-related programs and assessments*. Boston: Little, Brown & Co.

Jacobs, K., and S. Taylor. 1988. Occupational therapy for the workplace. In *Willard & Spackman's occupational therapy*, 7th ed., ed. H.L. Hopkins and H.D. Smith, 272–307. Philadelphia: J.B. Lippincott.

Krefting, L.M., and A. Bremner. 1985. Work evaluation: Choosing a commercial system. *Canadian Journal of Occupational Therapy* 52(1):20–4.

Matheson, L.N., and L.D. Ogden. 1983. *Work tolerance screening*. Trabuco Canyon, CA: Rehabilitation Institute of Southern California.

Matheson, L.N., and L. Ogden-Niemeyer. 1986. *Work capacity evaluation: Systematic approach to industrial rehabilitation*. Trabuco Canyon, CA: Employment and Rehabilitation Institute of California.

Melnik, M.S. 1990. Enlisting participation in an injury prevention and management program. *Work: A Journal of Prevention, Assessment & Rehabilitation* 1(1):39–48.

Ogden, L.D., and M.C. Wright. 1985. Work related programs in occupational therapy: A ren-aissance. *Occupational Therapy in Health Care* 2(1):109–26.

Olsen, P.J. 1990. What motivates the injured worker? *Occupational Therapy Forum* 5(48): 7–9.

Pietruski, W., et al. 1982. *Vocational training and curriculum for multihandicapped youth with cerebral palsy*. Richmond, VA: Virginia Commonwealth University School of Education.

Rhomberg, S., and N.N. Bernstein. 1990. Employment screening: Legal and clinical considerations. *Work: A Journal of Prevention, Assessment & Rehabilitation* 1(1):49–56.

Schultz-Johnson, K. 1987. Assessment of upper extremity-injured persons' return to work potential. *Journal of Hand Surgery* 12A(5 pt.2):950–7.

Schwartz, R.K. 1989. Cognition and learning in industrial accident/injury prevention: An occupational therapy perspective. *Occupational Therapy in Health Care* 5(2):67–85.

Schwartz, R.K. 1989. Occupational therapy in industrial accident and injury prevention. *Work Programs Special Interest Section Newsletter* 3(1):2–7.

Schwartz, R.K. 1990. Preventing the incurable: Proactive risk management. *Work: A Journal of Prevention, Assessment & Rehabilitation* 1(1):12–26.

Smith, B.L. 1987. An inside look: Hand injury-prevention program. *Journal of Hand Surgery* 12A(5 pt.2):940–3.

Index

C